BTEC NATIONAL Early Years

Sandy Green

Nelson Thornes

a W

Published in 2006 by:
Nelson Thornes Ltd
Delta Place
27 Bath Road
CHELTENHAM
GL53 7TH
United Kingdom

06 07 08 09 10 / 10 9 8 7 6 5 4 3 2 1

A catalogue record for this book is available from the British Library

ISBN 0 7487 9718 1

Cover photograph by © Whiskey Tango/Corbis
Illustrations by Jane Bottomley, Angela Lumley and Pantek Arts Ltd.
Page make-up by Pantek Arts Ltd, Maidstone, Kent

Printed and bound in Slovenia by Korotan-Ljubljana

Contents

Introduction

Early years professionals work predominantly with children from 0 to 8 years. They work in a variety of settings such as schools, nurseries, pre-schools, crèches and hospitals, and within their own or other people's homes as either a nanny or a childminder. More and more multi-agency centres are also being created supported by central government investment, providing a range of exciting new posts.

Working within the early years field is both rewarding and exhilarating. The opportunity to share in and help shape and encourage the development of young children is a huge privilege. If you enjoy being with this wonderful age group, and have commitment and enthusiasm, then the BTEC National course will provide you with a nationally recognised qualification that will prepare you well for a role as an early years practitioner and a rewarding career. There will be plenty of opportunities for career progression and for further study too.

How do you use this book?

BTEC National Early Years provides you with comprehensive coverage of all 10 Core units, giving you an in-depth knowledge of the key areas of study for BTEC National Certificate or Diploma in Early Years.

Simple to use and understand, this book is designed to provide you with the skills and knowledge for you to gain your qualification. We guide you through your qualification through a range of features:

- Each Unit is mapped to the 2006 specification so you can easily work your way through the qualification.
- You will find plenty of **Activities** and **Case Studies** that will help you understand the topics and offer you an insight into working practice.
- **Links** direct you to other parts of the book that relate to the topic currently being covered and show you how the units are linked together.
- **Information points** give you suggestions for further reading or web based research.
- At the end of each unit you will find **Progress Checks**, quick questions, designed to test you knowledge and ensure you have understood the important aspects of the unit.

We hope you enjoy your BTEC course – Good Luck!

Acknowledgements

I would like to express thanks to my husband John and all my family for their ongoing support. This has been so important to me during my recent encounter with cancer, as keeping up with the writing has been quite a challenge.

Thanks are also due to the editorial and production staff at Nelson Thornes for their patience and understanding. I know they wanted to get this book out much earlier than this, but their faith in me and willingness to work with my difficult time schedule has meant a lot to me. To their credit and professionalism, no one has ever hassled me, although they must have wanted to on many occasions.

Finally, a huge thank you to Jeanne Smith, who added in the final material for me, when I ran out of time and had to go in for surgery. Her input meant that I could concentrate on recovering without worrying about getting back to work.

Sandy Green

The author and publishers would like to thank the following for permission to reproduce photographs and other material:

Andersen Press, Hodder and Stoughton Ltd., Milet Publishing, Office for National Statistics, Open University Press, Scholastic Publications.

Crown copyright material is reproduced with the permission of the Controller of HMSO and the Queen's Printer for Scotland. Licence number: C2006009492.

Photo credits:
Billy Ridgers/Team Video, p.30; Medipics, p.76; Digital Vision (NT), p.158; ASCO Educational Supplies Ltd., p.248; Ryan McVay/Photodisc 76 (NT), p.408; Bananastock LT (NT), p.408; Bob Watkins/Photovision, p.426.

Every effort has been made to contact copyright holders and we apologise if any have been overlooked.

UNIT 1

Equality, Diversity and Rights in Early Years Work

This unit covers the following objectives:

■ Show an understanding of the meaning of diversity in today's society

■ Investigate the importance of understanding equality, recognising diversity and rights in early years services

■ Explore the ways in which early years services recognise and promote equality, diversity and rights, making reference to related policies

■ Examine the ways in which the individual worker can promote equality, diversity and rights in their own practice.

Good practice in early years work addresses all issues of prejudice, racism and discrimination. This unit explores the principle of equity and considers how early years settings can promote equality and rights. It begins by describing some of the cultural and other differences in people that contribute to the diversity of British society and then looks at why it is important that the individual early years worker is aware that prejudice and inequality can adversely affect children's opportunities for development before examining the ways in which legislation, policies and settings promote diversity and equality and protect the rights of children and their families.

You will be encouraged to explore your personal values, your own practice and the practice of others. Reviewing your own practice and identifying how you can promote equality of opportunity and diversity will help you develop professionally and will have a positive effect on much of your work during your course of study.

Diversity in today's society

In contemporary society, we need to consider diversity within each of the following areas.

Figure 1.1

Diversity in society

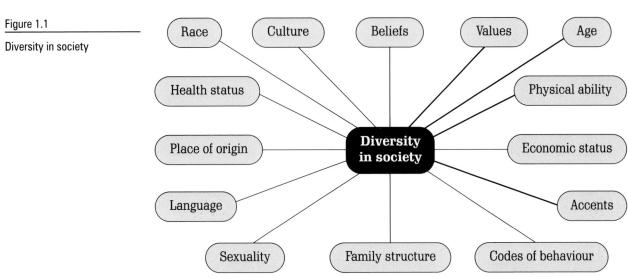

1

Having looked at the spidergram above, consider how each aspect of diversity can be supported within early years. The following examples will get you started:

1 Physical ability: this can involve the variety of skill levels reached by children within any given age range and applies to children with and without a specific need. It also applies to adults: staff, parents and other carers. The layout of the environment may need adjusting to enable access for some individuals. Specific equipment may help others to achieve greater independence. What examples can you find in your placement?

2 Language diversity: this includes children and adults for whom English is not their first language, children with identified speech difficulties, and children with delayed speech, including those with hearing loss. Consideration of language diversity will be needed in relation to notices, letters and general information, books, posters, and methods of personal address. Where have you identified the support of language diversity within your placement?

Importance of understanding equality, recognising diversity and promoting rights in early years services

Equity

The terms **equity**, **equality**, **diversity** and **rights** are used often, but what do the terms actually mean?

The dictionary definitions of these terms are:

- equity – an impartial or fair act, decision etc.

- equality – the state of being equal

- diversity – the state or quality of being different or varied

- rights – any claim … that is morally just or legally granted as allowable or due to a person (*Collins Dictionary*, 1991).

But what do these definitions mean in practice?

Equity is about giving individuals an equal chance, valuing and acknowledging the difficulties they face and allowing for those difficulties in your planning for, dealing with, and tolerance of, each individual.

This would sometimes be referred to as the concept of tolerance.

Equality is about what is fair and what is not. It means that an individual's family or cultural background, the way they live, or the individual's past or current state of health should not prevent that person from receiving the same opportunities as anyone else in society. Intervention is needed to ensure that all children have an equal chance to achieve, to learn, to join in activities, to be parented appropriately and to live according to the cultural practices chosen by their families.

Diversity refers to the range of different levels of ability within any group of individuals, to the variety of **cultures** and religions, each with its own experiences, which make up a group or society, and to the age range of any group.

Rights are the entitlements of each individual to receive the same opportunities as others. Many rights are linked to standards of service and are protected by legislation (laws).

A **cycle of disadvantage** can occur. Children can be disadvantaged whatever their ethnic background, religion, language, social class or gender; however, when children are members of social or cultural groups which are already **marginalised** by society it is harder to break out of this cycle. As children move through life, they experience the consequences of their family's lifestyle, type of housing and employment opportunities. Some will, of course, adopt different lifestyles as they grow older, but others will not and the situation may well be perpetuated for their own children.

Figure 1.2

The cycle of disadvantage

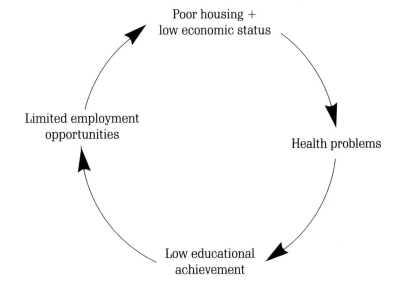

case study

1.1

Traveller families

A travelling group of five families was heading for an authorised traveller site near a maternity unit as two of the women were due to give birth. On arrival, they found that the site was completely full and so they moved on to an unauthorised site at which they had stopped in the past. Whilst the first woman was giving birth in hospital that night, the five men were arrested and charged with unauthorised occupation and ordered to move on and not return to the authority. They waited until the second woman had given birth two days later; she returned to her trailer almost immediately. When the community midwife went to visit the next day, both women and all the families had gone.

activity

1   What inequalities can you identify here?
2   In what ways were these families facing disadvantage?
3   Do you consider these families to be a marginalised group?
4   What rights do you think these families were entitled to?
5   What might be the long-term health issues for these new babies?
6   What are the implications for the education of children who are moved on like this?

In the case study above, there were examples of:

■   inequality

■   marginalisation

■   disempowerment

■   vulnerability

■   potential economic disadvantage

■   educational disadvantage.

The families were being denied equal access to services, because of the likely imprisonment of the men if the group did not move on.

Other marginalised or vulnerable groups include:

■ older people

■ disabled people

■ people from any **minority ethnic group**

■ economically disadvantaged people

■ educationally disadvantaged people.

activity
1.2

With a partner, explore why each of these groups might be vulnerable. Include health, education and social issues such as housing, employment and leisure facilities in your discussion.

The value base of the early years care sector

The overriding values in early years support the all-round welfare of a child, in partnership with the child's family.

Figure 1.3

The welfare of a child

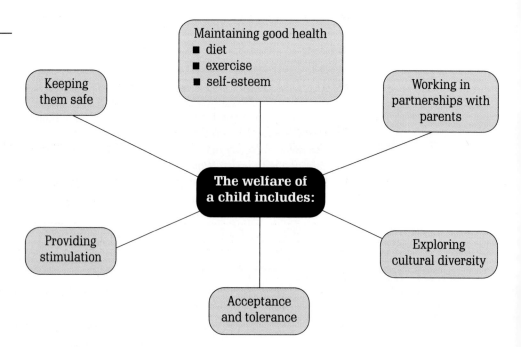

Keeping them safe

Maintaining good health
■ diet
■ exercise
■ self-esteem

Working in partnerships with parents

The welfare of a child includes:

Providing stimulation

Exploring cultural diversity

Acceptance and tolerance

Inequality within society

Inequality within any society can result in some individuals or groups being less able to take advantage of the benefits available in their society or feeling less valued than others. This can lead to a feeling of isolation, exclusion from mainstream society and can affect self-esteem and confidence.

For a fuller discussion of equal opportunities in society in general, look at the 'Equal Opportunities' chapter in Stephen Moore's *Social Welfare Alive* (3rd edition).

Within our society, some children and their families may be subject to certain types of inequality that may affect their health, development and well-being on a short-term or permanent basis. It is important that early years workers are aware of these differences so that children and families in need can be identified and interventions planned.

Figure 1.4

Inequality within society

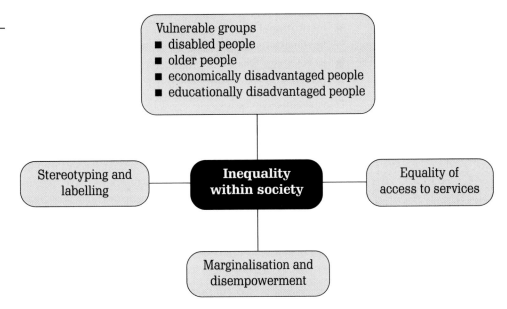

The effects of inequality on people
- Certain groups may be regarded as less able or less valued than others, owing to ethnic origin, gender, age, ability, income, social class, etc.
- Members of these groups may find it harder to obtain the benefits of a society that the majority enjoy.
- This can lead to short- or long-term effects on health, education and employment, as well as affecting emotional and social well-being.

Stereotyping and labelling
- Belonging to a group that is seen as 'different' or experiences unequal treatment can lead to **stereotyping** or labelling.
- Stereotypical judgements are frequently both inappropriate and incorrect.
- Upholding stereotypes takes away people's individuality or personal identity.

You will find more about stereotyping on page 18.

Marginalisation and disempowerment
- Certain groups may find themselves at the edges of society owing to oppression, **discrimination** or inequalities.
- This can then lead to members of that group being excluded from mainstream society, feeling isolated and less able to participate in the activities of daily life.
- Someone belonging to a marginalised group may be denied opportunities to take control of their lives and make choices.

Vulnerable groups and equality of access to services
- Certain groups may be more vulnerable to inequality than others owing to disability, poor health, age, gender, poverty, nationality, religious beliefs or lack of educational opportunities.
- Being treated less fairly because of vulnerability may result in individuals becoming trapped in 'cycles of disadvantage' from which it may be difficult to break free.
- Disadvantaged and vulnerable groups may then find that they are less able to obtain or gain access to services that may help and support them – this is known as the 'inverse care law'.

Discrimination and prejudice
To discriminate means to give favourable or unfavourable treatment to someone or something because of a specific factor. Discrimination can be:

- **institutional discrimination**, where the policies or practices of a workplace result in treating certain groups of people differently;
- or individual, where the **prejudice** (an opinion formed in advance) is the personal bias of one person.

Discrimination can be:

- direct, by telling people that they are not allowed to do something because of their race, sex, situation or disability;
- indirect, by excluding individuals who are unable to take part in or do something because of their race, sex, situation or disability. For example, a school which refuses to allow hats or headgear to be worn will be indirectly discriminating against those who traditionally wear them as part of their cultural dress. This would include Jewish boys who wear a yarmulke, Sikh boys who wear a turban, and Pakistani girls who wear a hijaab.

Groups of individuals can become marginalised by society through prejudice and discrimination, making them feel unable to initiate change or make their voices heard. This is disempowerment and it can have far-reaching effects. People who are disempowered see themselves as being 'less than equal' in society.

activity 1.3

Consider the practice in any early years settings that you are familiar with. Can you identify any element of practice that could be classed as prejudiced or discriminatory?

remember

Prejudice + Power = Discrimination (a pre-formed opinion) + (the practice of the setting) = (certain individuals may not receive equal opportunities)

There are a number of groups who face discrimination in society. These include people who are the victims of prejudice on the grounds of their:

- age
- class
- disability and differing abilities
- race, culture and religion
- sexual orientation
- gender
- marital status.

activity 1.4

1 Think of ways in which each group listed above faces discrimination.
2 Explain how any of these apply to early years settings. Remember to consider issues of staffing, access, communication, economics, clothing, cultural rituals and diet.

Examples of discrimination in early years settings include:

- age – teenage parents/older parents
- class – 'wrong' class from the wrong area/not good enough/too 'posh' for 'us'
- disability, differing abilities – inaccessibility/not asked to help out/avoided/limited
- race, culture, religion – only one culture catered for/devaluing or non-recognition of other cultures and religious festivals
- sexual orientation – homophobia (a dislike of homosexual people)/suspicions
- gender – fathers not encouraged/stereotyping of 'help' (men to fix toys, women to cook)
- marital status – values attached to marital status/meetings not accessible to single parents.

What else have you included?

Refer to page 14, where the importance of policies and the contents of a policy are discussed.

Effects of prejudice and discrimination

Being the target of prejudice and discrimination causes a multitude of negative feelings in an individual, including hurt, devaluing of self, confusion, disempowerment and uncertainty. It is an intolerable situation which must be addressed. As an early years professional, you have an obligation to protect the rights of the children in your care, by speaking up for them when they are unable to do so for themselves, and to support their value as a person.

You need to consider how you will address negativity when you come across it, because, if you fail to speak out when you hear or see an act of prejudice or discrimination, you will be failing the children or families you are supposed to be supporting. To ignore an offensive comment made to one child by another will be to passively condone the comment. This passivity will compound the hurt for the child receiving the comment (as you will not have stepped in to correct the 'wrong' and to give support) and will fail to help develop more positive values in the child making the comment (sometimes children simply need guidance in how to speak and act). It is pointless having a 'correct' range of resources available to explore and promote culture and disability if negative incidents are ignored.

At times, you may feel you need support in redressing prejudice and/or discrimination. Your supervisor or tutor will be able to advise you. Alternatively, there are a variety of organisations, written materials and on-line sources that may help you.

Sources of help

Help and advice about prejudice or discrimination can be found through the:

■ Race Relations Act 1976 as amended by the Race Relations (Amendment) Act 2000 – these Acts make it unlawful to discriminate against anyone on the grounds of race, colour, nationality (including citizenship) or ethnic or national origin. The newest legislation also gives public bodies and authorities the power to promote racial equality

■ Commission for Racial Equality (CRE) – monitors the way in which race relations legislation is working; gives advice to those who think they have been discriminated against and aims to promote equality of opportunity and promote good relations between people from different racial and ethnic backgrounds (www.cre.gov.uk)

■ Sex Discrimination Act 1985 – makes sex discrimination against men or women illegal and is monitored by the Equal Opportunities Commission

■ Commission for Equal Opportunities – deals with sex discrimination and inequality issues related to gender (www.eoc.org.uk)

■ Disability Rights Commission – an independent body that aims to stop discrimination and promote equality of opportunity for disabled people (www.drc-gb.org).

activity
1.5

What is wrong with the following statement: 'We do not have **racism** here. All the children are treated exactly the same.'?

Discuss this statement with others in your group.

The origins of discriminatory practices

So where does discrimination stem from?

Much discriminatory practice comes from ignorance and lack of understanding; it is sometimes accidental but often intentional. As a professional in the early years sector, you need to become informed in order to avoid the accidental, and to address any personal prejudices in order to remove the intentional.

Refer to page 17 for an activity to help you reflect on how and when you developed your personal values.

Historical perspective of racial prejudice and discrimination

The UK has been a diverse society throughout history, beginning with the Bronze Age and the Neolithic migrants who settled in northern Europe 5000 years ago. There have been invasions by the Romans, Saxons, Vikings and Normans, and many refugees have come to the UK, for example from France, Ireland, Russia, Uganda and Eastern Europe, fleeing war, persecution or famine in their own countries.

Significant groups of immigrants include the following:

- Jews, who first came at the invitation of William I (William the Conqueror) in the eleventh century. They were the founders of banking and financial services in the UK. Throughout history they have been persecuted, discriminated against and even expelled from the country at times.

- From the fourteenth century, Flemish and French weavers, German mining engineers and Dutch canal builders came, bringing with them new skills.

- In the sixteenth and seventeen centuries, Protestant refugees (Huguenots) came from France; they played a major role in British society.

- African slaves brought to the UK by the slave trade to work as servants (the slave trade was abolished in 1807 and slavery in 1838).

- Irish refugees, fleeing poverty and famine in the 1830s–1850s, worked in the new industries, in the mines, docks, canals and railways.

Other significant groups of immigrants have come from Italy, China and the Indian sub-continent. In fact, according to the Commission for Racial Equality, most people in the UK today have origins somewhere else and can probably trace the immigrants in their family histories. Only about 7 per cent of the British population were not born in the UK, but immigrants have been met with hostility and resentment.

Black people, in particular, have suffered prejudice and discrimination in the UK. They were expelled by Queen Elizabeth I in 1601 and attempts were made to return them to their country of birth at various times during that century. As recently as 1925, laws were passed which prevented black people from working on British ships, and anti-black riots were seen in areas of the UK in 1919 and 1948.

When the UK suffered a serious shortage of labour after the Second World War, the British government encouraged immigration, first from European refugees, then from Ireland and the Commonwealth. In 1948, the first of these immigrant recruits arrived, being employed to do the low-paid, unskilled jobs that British workers had not been able to fill. However, tension arose between the ethnic minority groups and the white population, resulting in race riots. Some people claimed that the large numbers of immigrants that had relocated to the UK were causing greater economic problems for the country. In 1962, the Commonwealth Immigrants Act was introduced, with entry into the UK allowed only if certain criteria were met: for example, if the applicant had a job arranged.

Since this time the UK has continued to see large numbers of black and Asian workers employed in lower-paid and unskilled jobs, which has continued to reinforce the message of lower values for these groups of people. There are, however, greater numbers of people from ethnic minority groups than ever before achieving positions of management and power in the UK, indicating that acceptance and equality is developing. As an early years professional, you will need to uphold and promote this thinking too.

In what ways has reading the historical perspective helped you understand issues of discrimination?

An ideal source of information about the historical perspective of racial discrimination and prejudice is *Sociology: Themes and Perspectives*, by Haralambos and Holborn (2000).

Advantages of diversity

The UK is a pluralist society (one which consists of groups of people of distinctive ethnic origins, cultures or religions) which offers us the opportunity to explore a range of customs and distinctive elements of other ways of life. Its diversity also enables us to work and socialise with people with disabilities through the increased (although still inadequate) accessibility of places of recreation, and through the greater recognition rightly given to disabled people in the workplace. There are more opportunities to interact with older people because the population is living longer, and our personal understanding is further enhanced by recognising that minority and vulnerable groups face hurdles not experienced by the rest of us and by our working to address them.

A diverse culture enriches our lives by opening up new experiences to us. It helps us to learn about the wider world and to explore and appreciate the distinctions and similarities between cultures, races and religions.

Figure 1.5

Advantages of diversity in the UK

- Diversity of family make-up helps us to understand the particular importance of the extended family in some cultures
- Opportunities for new knowledge and experiences of the rest of the world
- Opportunities to learn a variety of languages
- Increased knowledge of religious etiquette and relevant rituals helps us understand the needs of people who follow that religion
- Social, moral and ethical understanding is enhanced by witnessing perseverance
- **Advantages of diversity in the UK**
- Opportunities to learn about other religions help us identify the similarities and appreciate the differences between religions
- Patience shown by people facing restrictions gives a positive role model
- Festivals and celebrations throughout the year offer enrichment and opportunities for shared cross-cultural experiences
- Diverse lifestyles demonstrate how different cultures can live successfully within a joint society
- Clothing and costumes from various cultures adds a richness to life
- Foods from around the world are explored and enjoyed by many different cultures

activity 1.7

What else would you add to the spidergram, based on your personal experiences?

Professional Practice

■ It is of even greater importance to introduce diversity into early years settings where few cultures are represented. This will extend children's knowledge and understanding of alternative languages, religions and ways of life. This preparation will help children form values, and help them deal with any discrimination and prejudice that they may encounter later in life.

An excellent resource for understanding discrimination and legislation in particular, is *The Equal Opportunities Handbook*, 3rd edition, by Clements and Spinks (2000).

Link

Refer to pages 11–13 for information on both human rights and specifically the rights of children.

remember

As individuals we each have rights.

Good practice ensures that the best quality of care is provided and supports the directive of the Children Act 1989, that local authorities provide day-care provision that is staffed appropriately.

> People working with young children should value and respect the different racial origins, religions, cultures and languages in a multi-racial society so that each child is valued as an individual without racial or gender stereotyping. Children from a very young age learn about different races and cultures including religion and languages and will be capable of assigning different values to them. The same applies to gender and making distinctions between male and female roles. It is important that people working with young children are aware of this, so that their practice enables the children to develop positive attitudes to differences of race, culture and language and differences of gender.
> (Children Act 1989, Guidance and Regulations, Volume 2, Section 6.10)

Working to the principles of the Children Act will ensure that your professional practice is consistently good, rather than consistently adequate, and that the children you care for benefit holistically.

In *Supporting Identity, Diversity and Language in the Early Years*, Siraj-Blatchford and Clarke state that the first two foundations of learning are:
■ 'The child needs to be in a state of emotional well-being and secure'.
■ 'The child needs a positive self-identity and self-esteem' (Siraj-Blatchford and Clarke, 2000).

The aim of all early years staff should be to build up a child's self-identity and self-esteem by providing them with **positive images** of people, their lives and job roles with which they can identify. If you do not acknowledge and place value on the diversity within your working environment, you will not be fulfilling your professional role adequately and the children's sense of identity will be less positively reinforced.

Link

Refer to Unit 7 for information on self-identity and emotional development.

Professional Practice

■ It is important to remember that acknowledging difference is not the same as being prejudiced. It is the value that you place on difference that indicates whether prejudice exists or not.

How early years services recognise and promote equality, diversity and rights

Settings should recognise and promote equality, diversity and rights.

The promotion of equality and rights by any organisation can be considered in terms of:

- legislation
- individuals' rights
- policies and practice.

Legislation

Legislation involves a range of charters and Acts of Parliament which control and monitor the treatment of individuals. These acts form the basis for many of the policies and procedures on which early years practice is based.

Examples include:

- Children Act 1989
- Human Rights Act 1998
- **UN Convention on the Rights of the Child** 1989
- Disability Discrimination Act 1995 and 1997.
- Special Education Needs and Disability Act 2001.
- Code of Practice for Special Educational Needs 2001.

This is the legislation most relevant to your role as an early years professional.

More about legislation can be found below.

Other legislation which it would be useful to know about includes:

- Race Relations Act 1976
- Race Relations (Amendment) Act 2000.
- Sex Discrimination Act 1975, 1976
- Criminal Justice Act 1994
- Mental Health Act 1993
- Equal Pay Act 1970
- Equal Pay Act (Amendment) 1983
- Citizen's Charter
- Patient's Charter.

activity 1.8

Find out what you can about each of these to build up an overall picture of the legislative rights of all people in society.

Copies of all government legislation are available from HMSO bookshops and on UK government websites.

Formal policies on equality and rights

The legislation most directly relevant to early years professionals is described below. This legislation may affect the children in your care either directly, regarding their own rights or needs, or indirectly, through the rights or needs of their families.

Children Act 1989

The principles of the Children Act 1989 include the following points:

- The welfare of the child is paramount and should be safeguarded and promoted at all times by those providing services.

- Children with disabilities are children first with the same rights to services as all children.

- Parents and families are important in children's lives. Local authorities should support them in carrying out their responsibilities.

- Parents should be valued as partners with local authorities and other agencies such as health and education services.

- Children have a right to be consulted and listened to when decisions about them are being made. Their views and the views of their parents must always be taken into account.

- Health, education and social services for children with disabilities should be co-coordinated (Dare and O'Donovan, 1997).

Volume 2 of the Children Act specifically covers day care, and states that parents have a right to influence the quality of education that their child receives, which involves the need to make enquiries about what is available and to be able to understand the information they receive. Parents with limited use of English are disadvantaged in this and may need the help of an advocate or interpreter.

Professional Practice

- Early years settings can help parents by presenting information in languages other than English whenever possible. Visual information will help to some extent. Involving an advocate or interpreter will show that you value the family's heritage language and their need for information.

Refer to Unit 2, page 64.

Section 22(5)(c) of the Children Act states that local authorities must give consideration to the religious persuasion, racial origin, cultural and linguistic background of any child within their care. Any provider of care for children can be deregistered if these needs and rights are not properly cared for, as they would not be considered to be a 'fit' person to care for children, under the Act.

Gillick Competence (now known as the Fraser Ruling)

Although it does not form a part of the Children Act, children's rights are sometimes considered under the principle of **Gillick Competence**. This is based on a child's ability to make their own decisions and give informed consent. This principle was first drawn up in connection with the question of providing medical treatment (contraception) without the agreement of parents. It is a principle that is not applied at any one particular age, as each 'child' and the relevant situation is considered individually, to ascertain whether the child is considered to be 'Gillick Competent'. The principle of Gillick Competence has been used in connection with Section 8 of the Children Act (particularly the prohibited steps order) in which a child may challenge the directive of the courts: for example, in the contact the child is allowed to have with a parent. A child does not have an automatic right to appeal under Section 8, and Gillick Competence is determined by health professionals, together with others relevant to the case, such as a child psychologist, to decide whether a child has sufficient understanding of all the relevant circumstances. The term 'Gillick Competent' has now been replaced by the term 'the Fraser Ruling'.

Human Rights Act 1998

The Human Rights Act focuses on the individual's right to a life free from torture, loss of liberty, unfair punishment or discrimination. It also refers to respect for private and family life (Article 8), freedom of thought, conscience and religion (Article 9) and the freedom of expression (Article 10). The Act is linked to the drawing-up of no-smacking policies and is also relevant to female circumcision.

Refer to Unit 3, page 85, for discussion of these issues.

UN Convention on the Rights of the Child 1989

This is an international agreement on human rights which has been ratified by 191 countries. It consists of 54 articles (statements) and its four main principles are:

- Non-discrimination – all children have the same rights and are entitled to the same treatment.
- Children's best interests – the best interests of the child should be placed as highest priority when making decisions about the child's future.
- Survival and development of children – children have the right to survive and the right to be able to develop to their full potential.
- Rights to participation – the views of children should be taken seriously and they should be able to take part in what is going on around them.

The Convention is important because it brings together in one document all the rights of children, and adults are asked to view children as individuals with all human rights being applied to children everywhere (based on a paper by Save the Children, 2000).

Examples of articles set out within the Convention have been unofficially summarised by Flekkøy and Kaufman (1997) as follows:

- Article 2 – All rights apply to all children without exception, and the state is obliged to protect children from any form of discrimination. The state must not violate any right and must take positive action to promote them all.
- Article 22 – Special protection to be granted to children who are refugees or seeking refugee status, and the state's obligation to co-operate with competent organisations providing such protection and assistance.
- Article 23 – The right of handicapped children to special care, education and training designed to help them achieve greatest possible self-reliance and to lead a full and active life in society.
- Article 30 – The right of children of minority communities and indigenous populations to practise their own culture, their own religion and language.

Disability Discrimination Act 1995, 1997

This Act is directly relevant to early years in that it supports the **ethos** of the Education Act 1993 which underlines the need to provide all children who have a special need with an appropriate education at a suitable school. All settings should have a Special Educational Needs Co-coordinator (SENCO) who is responsible for ensuring that the special needs of children are met. In schools, this would be a member of the teaching staff who liaises with parents and other staff and keeps records of the special educational needs within the school.

The Special Educational Needs and Disability Act 2001 and revised Regulations (SENDA)

This Act and its associated Regulations came into force in January 2002 and clarified the duties of local education authorities (LEAs) and early years settings with regards to the needs of children with additional needs. Part II of SENDA emphasised the additional duty of LEAs and settings to ensure that children with special or additional needs are not discriminated against and are treated as favourably as those children who are not disabled.

The Special Educational Needs Code of Practice

The Special Educational Needs Code of Practice also came into force in January 2002, replacing the 1994 Code. It contains detailed guidance for early years practitioners in order to ensure that children with additional or special needs are supported to reach their potential.

Further discussion of legislation and special educational needs policies and the role of the SENCO are set out in *Good Practice in Caring for Young Children with Special Needs* by Dare and O'Donovan, 2nd edition (2002).

Policies and practice

An equal opportunities policy is a plan of how a setting will put its legal responsibilities for promoting equal opportunities into action. The policy should give clear guidelines to follow should an incident or concern arise. All staff at the setting should comply with the policy.

All early years settings must have an equal opportunities policy and many will also have statements linked to anti-racism, gender and the code of practice for special needs. These should be drawn up and agreed by all members of staff. When staff have been involved in drawing up a policy they are more likely to feel 'ownership' of it, understanding it fully and supporting it openly. Copies of the policy should be given to parents when they first take up a place for their child at the setting. A written policy that has been agreed by parents and staff provides a point of referral, if challenging a breach of the setting's policy seems difficult to face.

Figure 1.6

Equal opportunities policies

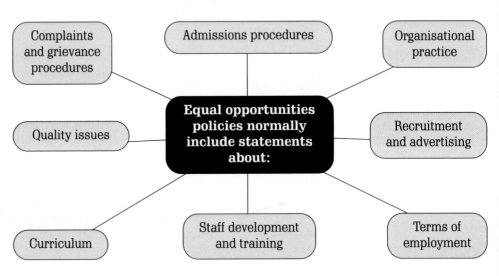

Complaints and grievance procedures

Admissions procedures

Organisational practice

Equal opportunities policies normally include statements about:

Quality issues

Recruitment and advertising

Curriculum

Staff development and training

Terms of employment

Implementing the policy

Training is important, to ensure that the policy is fully understood. It will need to be monitored and reviewed to ensure that it meets the needs of the setting. A named person should take overall responsibility for its implementation.

---

activity

1.9

1   Ask your placement supervisor and your college's day-care setting (if there is one) for a copy of their equal opportunities policy and any accompanying statements or separate policies for anti-racism, special educational needs or sex discrimination.
2   Make a comparison of the two settings' policies, noting the similarities and differences.
3   Does either policy, or set of policies, seem more comprehensive than the other? If so, why is this, do you think?
4   Do the policies include all the statements listed in the diagram above? What else is included?

For policies and equal rights legislation, refer to *Good Practice in Nursery Management* by Sadek and Sadek (1996).

---

remember

A policy should set out clearly the grievance and complaints procedures step-by-step. The process should be available to all, and people should feel able to raise a complaint or concern without anxiety or risk of harassment. The procedures should help to raise and maintain quality of provision and should be viewed as a positive aspect of the overall framework of the setting.

Overriding individual rights

Promoting the rights of the individual is one of the core principles of the Care Value Base and early years workers have a moral and legal responsibility to protect and promote children's rights. Children's rights are protected by:

- Legislation such as the Children Act 1989, the Children Act 2004 and the Human Rights Act 1998
- Guidance and recommendations such as the United Nations Convention on the Rights of the Child
- Government interventions such as Commissioners for Children's Rights
- Voluntary bodies such as the Alliance for Children's Rights.

activity

1.10

Look up the Convention on the Rights of the Child and, in groups, discuss which rights are most important to the children you care for.

However, there are certain circumstances in which the rights of a child or parent may need to be overridden in their own best interests. The factors that lead to an individual's rights needing to be overridden are often complex and intervention must be sensitive to the feelings of those involved and the consequences, as well as the legal implications.

Figure 1.7

Overriding individual rights

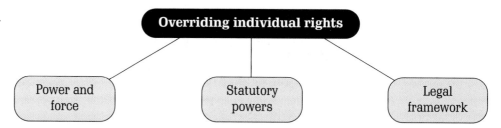

Children's or parents' rights may need to be overridden:

- in cases of actual or suspected abuse – this is one instance when issues of confidentiality or parental rights must be overridden in order to safeguard a child's health, development and well-being
- when a child's behaviour threatens their own safety or well-being, or that of others
- when custody or access issues fail to acknowledge a child's best interests or wishes
- when a child's or parent's mental health problems leads to them being a danger to themselves or others
- when a child's offending behaviour makes the child liable to statutory powers of redress, such as ASBOs (Antisocial Behaviour Orders) or secure accommodation.

Power and force

- Early years workers need to be aware of the power that adults have over vulnerable children and ensure that their work with children respects children's autonomy and individuality, whilst acknowledging their right to protection.
- Children need to feel that their wants and wishes are respected and that they are actively consulted and involved in choices and decisions that concern them.
- Children should never be subjected to force although the boundaries of safe practice may sometimes curtail some elements of choice or behaviour.

Statutory powers

- Legislation protects an individual's rights but may also be used to override those rights in certain circumstances.

- Children's rights are not always promoted or respected by adults, and legislation and guidance can enforce these rights on their behalf.
- Statutory powers can be used to protect children from harm and from adults who are not acting in the child's best interests.

Legislation

- The Mental Health Act 1983 can be used to detain an individual against their will when their mental health poses a threat to themselves or others.
- The Children Act 1989 covers many aspects of best practice for children, but it enshrines their right to grow and develop in a safe environment where their best interests are paramount.
- Children's rights are often interpreted and mediated by the adults that care for them, and so early years workers need to be aware of the appropriate legislation and of an individual child's ability to make informed decisions and choices.

Staff actively promote equality and individual rights

Staff working with children and families have a professional duty to ensure actively that their practice is guided by the promotion of equality and individual rights. They can do this by underpinning their practice with the guiding principles of the Care Value Base and by ensuring that they are fully conversant with the appropriate legislation and guidance. This will mean much more than just treating people equally, and aspects of a setting where equality and rights are promoted will feature:

- good practice in data protection and confidentiality
- acknowledgement of the inherent tensions to be found in challenging discrimination and promoting equality of rights
- creating an inclusive and anti-oppressive environment that acknowledges the rights of the individual and which has a clear and accessible complaints procedure
- fair employment and recruitment practices that promote equality and diversity
- regular opportunities for staff to undertake development and training in equality, diversity and rights.

Communication

Equality is needed in communicating too. At times it may be necessary to involve an interpreter or translator. Some parents will benefit from the support of an advocate.

For information on improving communication and avoiding the potential for barriers to clear communicating forming, refer to Unit 2, page 39.

Professional Practice

- Signing can be a useful and important skill in early years work.

Refer to Unit 2, page 60 for more information.

Partnership with parents

activity
1.11

Imagine you are a parent, leaving your child at a day-care setting for the first time. What forms of interaction would you hope to have with the staff? Make a note of your hopes and expectations.

You may well have included some of the following:

- having opportunities for regular discussion and feedback on your child
- feeling welcomed by the staff
- feeling that your role as parent to your child is valued and respected
- feeling that your requests / suggestions / ideas are valued
- feeling that your cultural practices and beliefs are respected and upheld with regard to your child's care
- having opportunities to be involved with the setting and your child's care.

There are many ways each of the above expectations can be supported. For example:

- through initial printed material and visits
- via a home-setting diary
- through notices to parents
- within the curriculum activities
- through the setting's key worker system.

How the individual worker can promote equality, diversity and rights in their own practice

Personal awareness

Personal awareness involves identifying one's own beliefs and prejudices and avoiding stereotyping and labelling.

Children learn values and attitudes at a very young age from those of us who are their role models. When they are unsure about a new person or a new experience, children look to their role models for guidance, approval or encouragement, and therefore absorb their attitudes. These role models include their families (part of their primary socialisation) and their friends, both adults and peers, early years staff, teachers and health professionals (secondary socialisation). This also includes you!

As an early years student, you will work with a diverse range of children and families. It is therefore important that you understand discrimination, stereotyping and prejudice, and are clear in your mind as to what is good practice. You might find it helpful to explore how you initially formed your own views, and who or what influenced them.

---

activity
1.12

To explore how your own views were shaped, you will need to think back to your childhood. Consider the following questions.

1. Who had most influence over you? This almost certainly included your parents, teachers and any nursery or pre-school workers.
2. Who else would you include?
3. How did each of them influence you?
4. Were the influences on you positive or negative?
5. What made them so?
6. Have you ever challenged a negative comment or action?
7. Have you ever felt you wanted to but not done so?
8. When was this and what stopped you?

Developing personal values is just the first step. Upholding them when others have different views is often hard to do, and sometimes it can seem easier to keep your views quiet and go along with the practice of others. You need to be aware that this could mean that you are not working to good practice and are compromising your own values.

- If you find that your views are not free from prejudice, how might you deal with this?
- If your views have been influenced by your parents, you could find yourself confronting the values of your family. This can be difficult.
- Exploring your thinking, obtaining information and becoming better informed about the effects of prejudice and discrimination will help you.

Stereotyping

Stereotyping means prejudging a group of people on the basis of one individual, or labelling an individual because they are part of a particular group. Stereotyped judgements are frequently both inappropriate and incorrect. Upholding stereotypes takes away people's individuality or personal identity.

Stereotypical images can be positive or negative and, although they are sometimes built up by personal experience, they are more often due to the influences of others, including the media.

An example of a stereotyped idea might be that 'all students are nightclubbers'. While many students do, of course, enjoy nightclub life, many do not, but students in general are a good example of a social group who are 'lumped together' for many stereotyped assumptions.

activity 1.13

What other examples of stereotyping can you think of? Make a list.

Changing one's own beliefs and prejudices

It is unlikely that individuals would change their beliefs simply because they were told to. They need to experience first hand the alternatives and identify for themselves what the advantages of the alternative is likely to be, and who would benefit from it.

For most of us, it is only by exploring the impact of words or actions and how they affect others that we can begin to see fully the power of those words and actions.

activity 1.14

1 Can you think of an occasion where words or actions have caused pain or distress to someone?
   a) In what way was the recipient affected?
   b) How could the distress have been avoided?
   c) If you were the cause, how do you feel about that now?
2 Can you think of an example of how your thinking has changed?
   a) In what way has it changed?
   b) What was it that influenced you?
   c) How do you feel now that your thinking has changed?

Challenging oppressive and discriminatory behaviour

- By exploring issues of prejudice, you come to understand the effects it can have, helping you to consider your personal values further.
- Changing your viewpoint is not easy. It will only change by exploring alternative views and ideas and re-evaluating your own thoughts and feelings based on new information and understanding.
- You cannot force your views on anyone, and similarly the views of others cannot be forced upon you.

In a small group, explore at least one of the following case studies. Consider the concept of tolerance in the context of values promoted by the early years sector.

case study 1.2 — Ross

Ross is an extremely active five-year-old whose behaviour is often challenged by Miss Fergus, his Reception class teacher, and Mrs Stains, the classroom assistant. Mrs Stains spends a great deal of her time focusing on Ross to keep him 'on task'. At break times Ross is disruptive in the playground, and he has recently been kept inside for much of the dinner break each day.

This morning, Ross's mother came into school and informed staff that Ross is to be given Ritalin, a (sometimes controversial) stimulant medication used in treating Attention Deficit Hyperactivity Disorder (ADHD). After Ross's mother had gone, Miss Fergus turned to Mrs. Stains and said, 'Thank goodness for that. At least the medication might start to do what his mother has so far failed to do, control him. What the boy really needs is a man around to instil some discipline in him.'

activity

1 What do you think of Miss Fergus's comment?
2 How should Mrs Stains respond?
3 What does this tell you about Miss Fergus's views generally?
4 What forms of prejudice were being displayed here?
5 What impact do you think Miss Fergus's views might have had on Ross in the past?
6 How would you have expected Miss Fergus to have responded?

case study 1.3 — Job and Charlie

Job and Charlie have both just turned three and have temporarily joined the pre-school where you are on placement, having moved into the area with the Gregory Brothers Touring Fair. Neither boy has been to an early years setting before, but they are very confident children who are full of life and rush around excitedly, exploring all the resources. They are particularly intrigued by water, favouring the water tray and anything 'messy' that will give them the opportunity to wash their hands in the bathroom.

A parent helper, Mrs Brownlow, comments that, 'It is just as well they like washing their hands, as they are probably in need of a good wash, and we don't want their germs.'

activity

1 What do you think of this comment?
2 How do you think the other pre-school staff should respond?
3 What does this tell you about Mrs Brownlow's views generally?
4 What forms of prejudice were being displayed here?
5 Why might the boys have been so fascinated by water?

Professional Practice

■ Unacceptable personal views have been expressed in both of these case studies. Think about how you would want to respond if you are ever present during a similar incident.

Links between discrimination and behaviour

Discrimination can be directly linked to behaviour through children 'living up to the adult expectation' of them. For example:

Figure 1.8

Expectation/Achievement Cycle

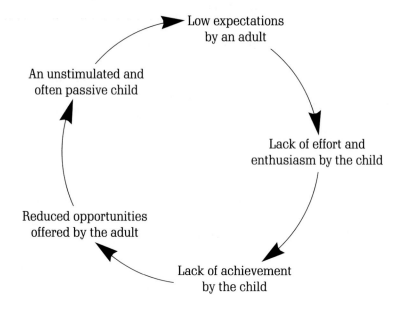

Add into this equation a prejudiced belief – e.g. 'girls are no good at playing football' or 'boys never read' – and it is easy to see how such negativity can have an impact on both learning and behaviour.

Appropriate use of language

In an early years setting, it is important not only to provide appropriate resources and opportunities but also to use appropriate terminology. The use of such statements as 'big strong boy' and 'quiet little girls' is outdated, stereotypical and wrong. Most importantly, such statements give confused messages to children about what is expected of them. It is also important to address a family's ethnicity correctly. If you are unsure about any terms, ask. Most people would rather you asked, and addressed them correctly, than continue to address them inappropriately.

Role modelling

As an early years student you need to consider:

- what you do; your actions, gestures and behaviour
- what you say; the terminology you use and its suitability for the situation of the person you are talking to
- how you communicate; your attitude, gestures, eye contact, tone and language level.

remember

Children are learning from you all the time. Make sure they learn positively, never negatively.

Application of the early years Care Value Base

Ensuring that you demonstrate respect for individual differences, identity and the dignity of children and families requires you to work to the overriding values of early years care. You need to:

1 Keep children safe at all times.
2 Help children maintain good health through
   - diet
   - exercise
   - self-esteem.
3 Work in partnership with parents.
4 Provide a stimulating learning environment.
5 Model acceptance and tolerance.
6 Promote and provide experiences of cultural diversity.

Hopefully, reading this unit will help you understand how to achieve much of this.

You will also find it useful to refer to Unit 5 for information on safety, to Units 5 and 10 for information on children's health, and to Unit 5 for ideas on suitable play provision.

Inclusive practice

Inclusive practice applies to:

- the environment
- the equipment and materials
- care routines
- play and curricular activities.

The following section provides you with examples to think about.

Staff, children and parents should promote and encourage the ethos that all children should experience all activities. At times, parents will be uncertain about their child enjoying particular activities, and sensitivity and encouragement will be needed. A common example is parents' concern over their son ironing in the role-play area or dressing up in a nurse's uniform. It should be sufficient to explain to the anxious parent that many men share the household task of cleaning and hopefully Jeremy will too. However, where possible, obtain dressing-up clothes for both genders when these usually differ, as in nursing. This will establish the correct dress code while still promoting the role of male nurses.

Carrying out an audit of a setting

A useful way of exploring how successfully your setting is meeting its commitment to equality is to carry out an **audit** (a type of inspection) of the various activities that are offered, looking at how many depict positive messages supporting a positive self-image, how many are simply neutral, neither particularly promoting diversity nor causing offence or confusion, and most importantly, considering if any depict negative messages through the images portrayed or the resources provided. If **negative images** are found, they should be brought to the setting manager's notice.

activity
1.15

In a small group, draw up a checklist of points to use when carrying out an audit of an early years setting. Think about:

- policies
- staffing
- equipment
- resources
- accessibility.

When you have drawn up your checklist, discuss it with your tutor and then arrange to carry out an audit of a setting. Remember to ask permission of the setting supervisor first.

Does your setting convey positive messages?

Tokenism

You will need to be aware of **tokenism**, which is a pretence at being committed to diversity and equality. Settings which have only a tokenistic approach may have a few items depicting positive messages in prominent places but, when you explore the resources further, a less positive picture of equality emerges.

The tourist approach

The **tourist approach** is said to be taken by settings that focus on the diversity of other cultures and festivals as a 'tourist experience' but do not have equality fully embedded in their practice. It can be a wonderful experience for children to explore the Diwali festival of light in late autumn, but the dietary and belief requirements of families who celebrate Diwali also need to be valued and supported throughout the year, together with any communication needs of those learning English as an additional language.

Figure 1.9

Does your setting convey positive messages?

> Professional Practice

- Having the right resources does not in itself ensure that equality and diversity is being promoted. It needs positive language and attitudes on the part of staff to place the correct values on the resources and activities that are provided.

Books and stories

To truly represent society, positive messages within books should include:

- boys in caring roles or carrying out household tasks

- girls involved in activities or occupations involving strength or occupations of power and management

- minority ethnic groups depicted in both traditional cultural situations and occupations of power and management

- illustrations showing mixed cultural activities or the sharing of each other's festivals by a group of children or adults

- disabled people carrying out the same tasks as everyone else, and joining in activities alongside able-bodied people

- different family groupings – nuclear, extended, stepfamilies, mixed race families.

> **remember**
>
> Books and stories should give positive messages about equality and diversity.

It is important to have some dual-language books. These will help to involve parents who speak the languages portrayed, and give all children an opportunity to see the written word in an alternative script.

Figure 1.10

Cover images of dual language books

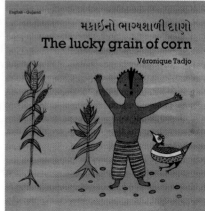

Figure 1.11

Books conveying a positive message

activity
1.16

1   From either your current placement, or from your college library's children's section if you have one, select three books which you feel give a positive message, and share the reasons for your choice within a small group.
2   Have you found any that give a negative message?
3   Have you reported this to anyone?

case study
1.4

Katya

Katya is in her first term of her nursery nursing course and is currently on placement in the Reception class of the local primary school. She is enthusiastic and keen to be involved and asks the teacher, Mrs Davis, if she can read to the class on her placement day next week. Mrs Davis agrees and suggests that she reads a book that she is very familiar with. Katya says she will bring a book that she reads regularly when she is baby-sitting. The following week Katya settles down to read a home-time story to the children, while Mrs Davis sorts out the paintings. Mrs Davis is horrified when she realises that Katya is reading a story about a naughty black golliwog. She lets Katya finish the story as she is unsure what to do. The children then go home.

activity

1   What are the problems here?
2   Should Mrs Davis have checked what Katya was going to read?
3   What form of discrimination is depicted here?
4   How should Mrs Davis broach the 'error' with Katya?
5   What would you do tomorrow, if you were Mrs Davis?

Professional Practice

■   It is important that negative incidents are dealt with promptly. Mrs Davis needed to talk to both Katya and the children.

Negative messages within books include:

■   boys as always physically stronger than girls, in 'macho' roles or positions of power

■   girls as cute, pretty and clean, only as carers, in supportive occupations

- minority ethnic groups inappropriately or negatively characterised, depicted in manual occupations or only in traditional cultural situations
- disabled people only as wheelchair-bound, seated to the side of activities, on a different level to others in the illustration
- family groupings always of the nuclear type (two parents and two children).

Figure 1.12

Encourage all children to enjoy all the resources

Professional Practice	- It is acceptable for there to be a range of images, some neutral and some positive, as long as there is an overall emphasis on the positive. - It is never acceptable for a setting to continue to include negative images within its resources. - The examples of positive and negative images set out for books and stories apply to all resources and activities that involve illustrations.

Role play

In the role-play corner, issues of gender are mostly found in the use of the resources rather than the resources themselves. A way to address gender stereotyping here is to encourage all the children to enjoy all the resources, taking different roles within their play. An array of artefacts, clothes and foods from a range of cultures will enhance the learning of all children and positively promote the self-image of children from those cultures.

Which cultures are portrayed by the dolls in your placement? If they are all pink skinned, blonde haired and stereotypically English, they are likely to support a racist message of who is important and needs caring for.

Figure 1.13

What message do the dolls in your placement give?

case study 1.5 · Children playing 'at home'

A group of children are playing 'at home' when you overhear the following:

'Get the baby, mummy, she's crying.'

'You get it.'

'No! I'm reading the paper and I've had a hard day at work.'

'I'm cooking tea.'

'So what!'

activity

1 Would you interrupt the play?
2 Is discrimination taking place here?
3 What can be the issue with 'correcting' what some children think of as normal, as they see and hear it at home each day?

Figure 1.14

A range of resources is available to depict other cultures through role play

remember
Parents of children from different cultures will usually be pleased to help with improving the resources of the setting.

The illustration above shows a readily available range of resources for depicting other cultures through role play. How well resourced is your placement? Where finances are limited, many cultural costumes can easily be made – dyeing and printing materials appropriately – and foods can be made from salt dough, copying real items or pictures.

Construction materials

Children often consider construction kits to be boys' toys. Encouraging both boys and girls to use construction materials will help dissipate stereotypical views, but be aware of who dominates the construction area. At times, it can be appropriate to encourage girls to use construction materials without the 'help' of the boys. This will ensure that girls have the opportunity to plan, predict, experiment and achieve on their own.

 Link

Refer to Unit 7, page 315 and carry out the gender activity recommended there. What results did you get when you carried out the activity in your placement?

Professional Practice

■ How gender specific are pictures on the boxes of the construction kits in your placement? This is an easy aspect to change. Simply remove the construction material from its original box and place in a more suitable container.

Figure 1.15

Encourage both boys and girls to use construction materials to help dissipate stereotypical views

Creativity

This is an area where children can experiment and be involved in a non-competitive way, as you cannot paint a 'wrong' picture. Opportunities for creative expression involve the use of a range of media and a range of utensils.

Brushes or alternatives need to be suitable for all hands. A child with limited manipulative dexterity will benefit from chunky brush handles (light-weight wallpaper brushes can be useful), and all children will enjoy the experience of painting with (thoroughly cleaned) roll-on deodorant containers (plastic) or large sponge rollers.

When children have skin problems such as eczema, the irritation can be exacerbated if they have direct contact with paint and other 'messy' media. Supervised activities such as finger painting under a length of clingfilm can keep them involved without risking infection or further discomfort. Using large bubble-wrap as an alternative can add to the sensory experience. Disposable gloves can be a useful resource here too.

The range of festivals throughout the year, representative of many different cultures, offer enormous scope for creative activity. Examples include:

■ Diwali, the Hindu festival of light
  ▪ Rangoli patterns – a decoration laid at the entrance to the home to welcome the Goddess of fortune, Lakshi
  ▪ Diwali cards – a popular design would be to use a hand shape and decorate it in the traditional Mehndi patterns.

Figure 1.16

A Mehndi hand pattern

- Chinese New Year, the first day of the lunar calendar each year
  - Teng Chieh, the lantern festival, denotes the end of the new-year celebrations
  - decorated sheets of paper are cut and made into lanterns
  - money envelopes (lai see); it is traditional for children to receive money in red envelopes decorated with gold writing
  - dragons, one of the twelve animals in the Chinese animal years; making a huge dragon can be a super whole-group activity, culminating in the 'dance of the dragon'. Activities such as this allow every child to contribute, working together towards a joint goal.

Figure 1.17

Lanterns used in the celebration of the Chinese New Year

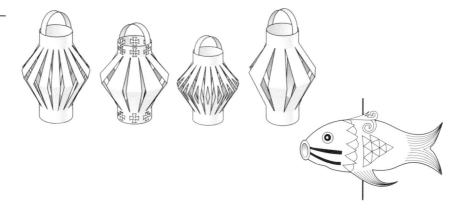

Professional Practice

- A range of skin-tone colours in both paints and crayons will enable all children to represent themselves and their families accurately in their pictures.

> **remember**
>
> Just because a child needs large pieces to meet their physical need does not necessarily mean that they cannot enjoy a challenging picture. Physical and cognitive needs are not always parallel with each other.

Puzzles

Puzzles can be for table or floor use, and can have both large and small pieces. Consider differentiation of manipulative control: the use of large pieces will help the less-able child, as will puzzles with sturdy knobs that make it easy to lift and replace pieces. Issues of positive images apply in the same way as with books and stories.

Music, movement and singing

It is very easy to include diversity in this area of the curriculum. There is an abundance of musical instruments available from a vast array of cultures and to suit most physical needs. A musical instrument box should not simply hold tambourines, drums and cymbals as this is limiting for expression and restricts opportunities to explore the multitude of other options available.

Figure 1.18

It is very easy to include diversity in music activites

Tapes and CDs of world music can be borrowed from music libraries. Children can enjoy a range of songs from around the globe, enjoying learning to sing in different languages, placing emphasis on rhythm and dance, linked to appropriate cultures.

Dance is also an important part of many cultures. It can encourage children to explore and communicate through a range of expressions and movements. It can be combined with the use of instruments, encouraging children to accompany each other, building up co-operation and appreciation of each other as equal partners in a joint activity.

Electronic musical activities, and those involving vibration, are particularly useful for children with severe hearing loss, as they offer a multiple-sensory experience.

activity 1.17

What songs and music have you heard in your placement? Are any from cultures other than British? Make a list.

Examples might include: 'Kookaburra sits in an old gum tree' (Australia) and 'Frère Jacques' (France).

What other examples can you think of?

Professional Practice

■ It is important to look at the content of traditional nursery rhymes and songs too. For example, 'Taffy was a Welshman, Taffy was a thief' is not a good example for promoting cultures and raising self-esteem.

■ Inviting musicians into the setting allows children to hear a variety of instruments for real. Musicians from various cultures can explain how the instruments link with festivals and special occasions.

■ Hand and body signs for musical notes can be used with older children. The Addison body notation and Curwen hand signs are two examples. Curwen hand signs are similar to Addison body notation but do not involve the whole body (as their name suggests).

Figure 1.19

Addison body notation

| Doh | Ray | Me | Fah |
| Soh | Lah | Te | Doh |

Cooking activities

What food-related activities have you seen, and what are planned for the future at your placement? Ask your supervisor to let you see the plans for the full academic year, as this will enable you to gain a more accurate picture.

The customs and diets of all children need to be taken into account when planning activities with food, including practical, medical and cultural needs. There are dietary considerations for children with medical conditions, such as:

- diabetes
- coeliac disease
- cystic fibrosis
- food allergies, particularly those who have an anaphylactic response.

Refer to Unit 10, page 431, Common childhood illnesses for more information.

Some children have ethical and/or cultural dietary needs; such children might be:

- vegetarian
- from cultures where certain foods, or combinations of foods, are not allowed.

Refer to Unit 5, page 186, for a table setting out the cultural requirements for diet.

Festivals lend themselves to a range of cooking activities, for example:

- Baisakhi – the Sikh festival to celebrate the start of Guru Nanak's travels; people provide vegetarian foods, such as dahl and chapattis, both of which can be made with children
- Lent – the Christian period of 40 days leading up to Easter which Christ spent in the Wilderness; pancakes are traditionally made on Shrove Tuesday, the day before the start of Lent
- Raksha Bandhan – the Hindu festival of protection and care between siblings and close friends; a traditional offering is coconut barfi, similar to coconut ice, which needs no actual cooking so is an ideal cookery activity.

activity
1.18

What other festivals can you think of that would provide opportunities for cooking activities? Make a list.

case study
1.6

Pete and Sammy

Pete is making pancakes with small groups, as part of the exploration of the Christian festivals of Lent and Easter. The children join him eagerly and clamour to be next. Pete chooses his next helpers, and turns to Sammy, saying, 'You can make them, Sammy, but you won't be able to eat them, as they have wheat in them'. Sammy, who has coeliac disease, looks disappointed but joins in anyway.

activity

1 How would you deal with this situation?
2 What form of discrimination is described here?
3 Are there any problems with Sammy cooking with a wheat-based flour?
4 What could Pete have done to enable Sammy to be fully involved in the activity?

■ Parents are the ideal people to involve in cooking recipes from their own cultures.

Persona dolls

Promoting a child's self-esteem is an important way of making them feel valued. **Persona dolls** can be used to help to promote self-esteem. The dolls represent children from various cultures and with a range of disabilities. A persona doll can be provided for any individual need and can be an ideal way of encouraging children to accept difference and pave the way for a child to settle and integrate easily into the group or class.

When using a persona doll, the adult explains the doll's background and tells a special story which can lead to a discussion with the children, exploring difficulties that can be faced by an individual, bias that can be experienced and the hurt that can be felt.

Figure 1.20

Persona dolls

 For information on using persona dolls, refer to *Persona Dolls in Action* by Brown (2001).

Self-esteem can also be promoted during circle time, which gives each child an opportunity to speak and be listened to.

 See *Quality Circle Time in the Primary Classroom: Your Essential Guide to Enhancing Self-esteem, Self-discipline and Positive Relationships*, by Mosely (1998).

Improving your own practice

To improve your understanding of equality and therefore your professional practice, it can be helpful to explore a range of scenarios. This last section is designed to help you think and reflect on your ability to work to good practice. Try the following activities.

activity 1.19

1 a) What would concern you about the following statements?
    i) Nursery nurse: 'We can't ask Mrs. Jones to help because she's got five kids.'
    ii) Nursery nurse: 'Mr. Daniels will be useful to have around as there'll be plenty of heavy lifting.'
    iii) Nursery manager: 'I've put Darren on bathroom duty, but always with another member of staff.'
    iv) Parent: 'Is it true you've accepted a child with HIV? If it is, I'll take my Michael away, you know.'
    v) Parent: 'I don't want my Jess to have Darren as a key worker. He's a man; it's not natural.'
    vi) Child: 'My dad says I can't play with Ephram anymore. He's black.'
    vii) Child: 'I don't want Jenny to help me, her arm's all funny.'
  b) What assumptions are being made?
  c) What forms of discrimination are seen here?
  d) How would you challenge each of these statements?
  e) What do the children's comments tell you?
  f) Will you follow up any of these comments?
  g) How will an equal opportunities policy help you?
  h) Share your answers with a partner. Were you both in agreement?

2 a) Which of the comments below (or similar) have you heard being used?
    i) 'The girls are sitting lovely and quiet as always!'
    ii) 'Would a strong lad come and help me with the construction box, please?'
    iii) 'Which of you girls will look after the new children?'
    iv) 'Whose dad has got an electric drill?'
    v) 'Can you all ask your mummies if they would have time to help us sew the costumes for the play, please?'
  b) What stereotypes were being reinforced here?
  c) Rephrase each comment more appropriately.

3 a) Which of the following statements will be more likely to ensure equality of opportunity in an early years setting?
    i) All staff are entitled to staff development training.
    ii) All staff are entitled to equal amounts of staff development training.
  b) Explain the reason for your answer.
  c) What might be the implications in the long term of each statement?

Professional Practice

■ As an early years professional, you will at times have access to information that should be kept confidential. You will need to take this responsibility seriously. Confidentiality is linked directly to rights.

 Link

Refer to Unit 3, pages 90 and 106, for information on record-keeping and confidentiality.

Professional Practice

■ Working positively will encourage the promotion of equality in others: colleagues, parents and children.

■ Being a role model for children is a privilege and should be taken seriously.

■ You should always remember that your actions and words could have a lasting impact on the development of the values and self-esteem of the children in your care.

The practice implication of confidentiality

Maintaining confidentiality is one of the cornerstones of good practice and the Care Value Base, and so it is important that early years workers recognise the professional aspects of confidentiality and how it relates to practice. However, some practitioners may be uncertain as to which aspects of information about children and families should be kept confidential and which information can be shared. Knowing the difference between the two can be a key to good practice and can be the foundation for trusting relationships with parents and carers.

Figure 1.21

Confidentiality

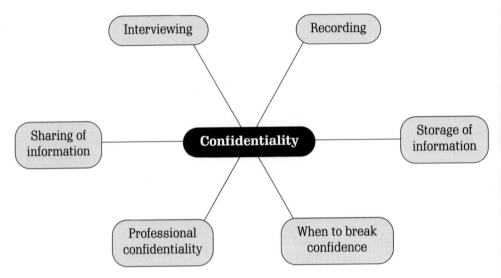

Interviewing

Early years workers gather and record data about children and families all the time and information is often collected during interviews when a child enters a setting or when circumstances warrant discussions between the staff and the parent or carer. Practitioners should regularly review the categories of information that they request at interview and consider the relevance of the data and the issues of confidentiality that may be important.

Recording and storing confidential information

All information that is held on children and families should be recorded accurately and stored securely, in accordance with the requirements of the Data Protection Act 1998. Senior staff may be aware of individual circumstances which dictate that even 'basic' information such as a child's address is held securely and not made public – for example, in the case of domestic violence. This may mean that some information is withheld from support staff, students or volunteers, whereas other agencies involved with the child or family may have access to confidential information. Written information that is sensitive or confidential needs to be kept in a secure, locked facility that is only accessible to those staff with a 'need to know'.

Disclosing

If information is disclosed inappropriately, parents may lose trust in individual workers or the setting in general and this can be detrimental to the principle of working in partnership with parents. However, there will be circumstances when information has to be disclosed or shared in order to safeguard a child or to promote their health, development or well-being. Cases of actual or suspected child abuse come under this heading and those working with children have a professional duty to break confidentiality in these circumstances.

 For a clear discussion of practice issues in confidentiality, see *Good Practice in the Early Years*, 2nd edition, by Kay (2004)

The requirement to maintain confidentiality of information about the children and families in your care is also governed by legislation that is designed to uphold their rights to privacy.

Figure 1.22

Legislation that affects
confidentiality

Legislation that affects confidentiality

1 Data Protection Act 1998 – designed to protect the rights of an individual not to have confidential information about them passed on without their permission. Updates to this Act now cover any information held on paper or computer and passing on information about children or families without their permission would be in breach of the Act

2 Access to Personal Files Act 1987 – gives individuals rights to access computerised and paper-based files of personal information held on them. Rights to see this data comes from the Data Protection Act 1998 (DPA) and includes medical records, social work, housing, and school records.

3 Access to Medical Reports Act 1988 – individuals also have rights of access to records of their physical and mental health under data protection legislation. Records held by any registered health professional may be accessed and, in some cases, copies made.

Progress Check

1 Give an example of tokenism.

2 Define 'institutional discrimination'.

3 What is prejudice?

4 Why is it not enough just to have a range of resources giving positive messages?

5 Explain one way of helping a child with a medical dietary need to be involved in cooking.

6 Which religions celebrate Diwali?

7 How could a deaf child's enjoyment of music be enhanced?

8 What is a persona doll?

Communication and Interpersonal Skills in Early Years Work

This unit covers the following objectives:

- Explore interpersonal communication and the factors that affect communication
- Investigate how interpersonal and communication skills can contribute to the development and maintenance of relationships with children, families and others
- Understand how interpersonal skills contribute to the care of distressed individuals
- Reflect upon the effectiveness of their own interpersonal and communication skills.

Being able to communicate and get on with others is extremely important in most people's personal and professional lives. Communication and interpersonal interactions, both verbal and non-verbal, are the means of giving and receiving information, and letting others know how you are feeling.

This unit will introduce you to different types of communication and look at the different factors that affect communication. You will learn how to develop and maintain good relationships with people, how to overcome the barriers that make communication difficult and how to communicate with and support someone who is distressed.

You will also reflect on your own interpersonal and communication skills and identify areas for improvement.

Interpersonal communication and the factors that affect communication

Effective communication is central to the good working practice of all early years professionals, and relationships with children and families may be impaired without it, reducing the effectiveness of your working in partnership with parents. The way you communicate sends a message about you as a person – your attitude, the way you talk, how well you listen and your approach to various situations. Communication involves a successful exchange between two people. Sometimes, your work as an early years practitioner and team member will be judged on your ability to communicate appropriately. It is important to remember that individuals with good interpersonal skills identify when communication has not been effective, by noting the responses of others, and are both willing and able to adjust their approach accordingly. As you read through this unit, there will be opportunities for you to reflect on your personal ability to communicate and interact, enabling you to review your current practice and build on it for the future.

Refer to page 55 for an explanation of the communication process, known as the **communication cycle**.

Types of communication

Communication can be verbal, written, visual, textual or aural, involving the written word, music, drama or creativity. When you begin a communication you need to consider how the other individual involved communicates best and whether there are any barriers to their communicating successfully with you.

Figure 2.1

Early years workers need to be able to respond appropriately to children from a variety of backgrounds

You will work with children from a variety of family situations and structures, including children from:

- nuclear families
- extended families
- lone-parent families
- stepfamilies
- economically challenged families, and children with:
- gay and lesbian parents
- a range of cultural influences.

It is your responsibility as a professional early years worker to communicate with, and respond appropriately and equally to, all families. You should be aware of any personal bias or preconceived ideas that you may have about any social groups. Your responsibility is to welcome all families and respect their rights, ensuring that both your attitude and your language are appropriate.

 Link

Refer to Unit 1 for more on this.

Personal space

remember

A diverse community is a rich community, and the opportunities to share and explore elements of each other's lives will enhance the learning of all.

It is important to consider whether communication is taking place in a suitable environment. Each individual needs to feel comfortable within the personal space available to them. Ask yourself if the situation really is appropriate. Are all those involved likely to feel relaxed? Do they all appear to be relaxed? Can you hear each other OK? Background noise can be an important contributory factor to poor communication too.

Children are likely to communicate best in small groups, or one to one. If you want them to concentrate carefully on something, then an area with few distractions will be best. A parent who needs to convey information is likely to want to speak somewhere where they receive the full attention of the staff member. If a person is feeling anxious, it is likely that they will want space around them and not want to feel hemmed in.

These issues need to be taken seriously.

Written skills

In early years you will at some point need to write reports and observations, keep records, write letters of application and draw up a CV (curriculum vitae). You will also write short- and long-term plans.

Information on writing CVs can be found in *Human Resources* by Brumfitt et al. (2001).

Writing effectively involves taking the appropriate approach and using the correct level of language. You will need to pay attention to both your spelling and your use of grammar as your material will lack credibility if it is poorly written.

A written report may be required, for example, to record the progress of a child, to contribute to a child protection enquiry or to record an accident or an incident within the setting.

Records need to be kept of illness and the details of any medication administered.

Refer to Unit 5 page 221, for information about writing these types of report.

Checklist for writing reports

- Ensure that you cover all the required details.
- Make clear what are facts and what are opinions.
- Set your report out clearly, with an introduction, a middle and a conclusion.
- Avoid the use of abbreviations.
- If you are writing a report as a student, make sure it is countersigned by your placement supervisor.
- Ensure that black ink is used if your report is to be photocopied.
- Add recommendations if requested.
- Ensure that the level of English used is appropriate for the target 'audience'(readership).
- Where appropriate, send the report to a named person, not simply to an office.

Visual forms of presenting information

Working in partnership with parents is strongly emphasised by most providers of early years care and education, and it is important to keep parents well informed. You need to pass on information through media which parents can readily access, and more than one medium may be needed to meet everyone's needs. Options include:

Figure 2.2

Different ways of presenting information

Newsletters

Home/setting books

Noticeboards

Posters

Photographs

Displays of children's creativity

Newsletters

A regular newsletter, set out clearly, with an outline of what has been happening and plans for the future, is ideal. Where possible, translate it into the heritage languages of the families involved. Illustrations will help non-readers and non-English-speaking parents to understand. For example, a sketch of a coach and a lunchbox with dates alongside will help indicate a forthcoming trip.

Figure 2.3

A newsletter

HOPES & DREAMS NURSERY NEWSLETTER

June 2006

News

The final topic for this term is 'farms to coincide with our end-of-term trip. Any relevant items for display will be appreciated particularly photographs of real farms and farm animals

Diary Dates

The end of year photographs of those children moving on to school will be taken on 28 June at 11.30 a.m..

Coach leaves the nursery at 10.00 a.m.

Please bring lunch boxes

Home/setting books

This simple idea involves an exercise book, usually kept in a plastic wallet, in which staff and parents can exchange comments and information about the child. They are particularly useful for children who are escorted to and from the setting via local authority transport, where contact with parents is minimal.

Noticeboards and posters

Bright, visually striking posters will attract attention and can be a particularly important means of conveying health and safety guidelines, such as skin protection in the sun and the hazards of toxocaria in animal faeces. Their visual emphasis reduces the need to read the accompanying wording, extending accessibility.

Parents will be more likely to look at a noticeboard that is updated regularly than one which displays the same material for weeks on end.

Careful consideration should be given to what information is set out on a noticeboard. If it is vital that parents have certain information then relying on their voluntarily reading a notice or poster is inappropriate. An individually addressed note should be sent home with each child in these instances.

Photographs

A montage of photographs showing what the children have been doing recently is a lovely way of keeping parents informed of their child's activities, particularly those parents who work full-time and have not been able to attend picnics, sports days and similar events.

Displays of children's creativity

Regularly changing wall and table displays will encourage parents to look around more frequently and appreciate the creations of their own child and those of others. Labelling items with children's names and mounting displays tidily are an important indication that you value what the children have been doing.

remember

- It is important that all children are represented in displayed material.
- Parents should be actively encouraged to show interest in their child's activities.
- Photographs of children should not be displayed outside the setting without parents' permission.

Figure 2.4

Displaying work encourages
children's interests

 Link   Refer to Unit 3 page 114, Case Study 3.5: Abigail.

Non-visual forms of presenting information

Non-visual forms of presenting information include the use of tape recordings, the telephone and, perhaps most importantly, touch.

The telephone or tape recording

If opting to provide information via a pre-recorded tape, it will be imperative to ensure that the person receiving the tape has the means of listening to it. Similarly, giving information by telephone will only be of benefit if the recipient is able to take in all the details in this way. Ask yourself the following:

- Why am I using this method?
- How much information am I giving at any one time?
- Could the message be misinterpreted? How can this be avoided?

You may be choosing to use the telephone or a tape because a person does not read, or their reading in English is perhaps limited. You may need to supplement your verbal information with a visual image to add clarity.

Touch

Touch is an important form of communication with babies and young toddlers, prior to the development of verbal skills. It should be a far less automatic form of communication with older children and adults. Touch can feel soothing, welcoming and show understanding in some circumstances, but it can also feel threatening and an invasion of personal space in others. It is important to consider a situation carefully before initiating physical contact with another person. Consider:

- What does their **body language** tell you? E.g. closed, withdrawn.
- What does their facial expression tell you? E.g. anxious, wary.
- What level of relationship already exists between you and this individual? E.g. close, brief, none whatsoever.

Professional Practice

- Touch and direct eye contact are unacceptable in some cultures. If you are unsure whether these forms of communication are acceptable to the families and colleagues with whom you work, ensure that you check.

Barriers to effective communication

A barrier to effective communication can be anything that causes an obstruction or prevents progress. **Barriers to communication** can include any of the points in the diagram below.

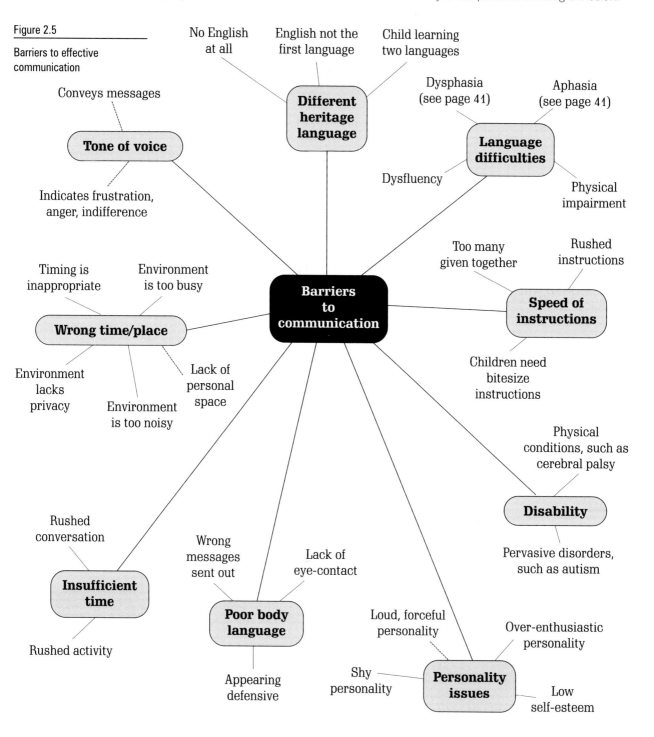

Figure 2.5

Barriers to effective communication

Let's look at some of these in more detail.

Tone of voice

The tone of your voice can convey many things. It can indicate frustration, anger and irritation as well as pleasure, encouragement and praise. We all respond better to positive tones and are hurt or confused by the negative. Young children may not always understand what is being said to them, but the tone of voice used conveys a message, which at times may be the wrong one. Also, the use of inappropriate language for the stage of development or depth of knowledge a child has can prevent communication taking place successfully.

For example, to ask a child 'What are you doing?' can be interpreted by a child as a negative question if the emphasis is placed wrongly: e.g. 'What *are* you doing?' This could convey frustration and annoyance to the child.

Link

Refer again to page 55 for the communication cycle diagram.

Language – different culture

The language usually spoken in the child's home is referred to as the first or heritage language, and it is passed on from generation to generation. An understanding of cultural practices, child-rearing, religious beliefs and elements of a child's heritage language will help you build appropriate communication pathways with the child and the family. It is important that you communicate within context (i.e. using words relevant to what is happening at a particular moment) and show that you value their heritage language by using it whenever you can, perhaps with a welcoming greeting at the door as a starting point.

Children will often quickly absorb a small amount of the main language used by children and staff in their school or nursery, but their parents may not as yet have done so. It is, therefore, important to explore other ways of communicating.

When asking non-English speaking children if they need to use the toilet, you will be more easily understood if you accompany them to the bathroom and use gesture, as well as vocabulary, emphasising the word 'toilet'. Similarly, if you need to find out whether a child has had chickenpox (if there is an outbreak in the nursery), it will be helpful to show non-English speaking parents a picture of the rash and give a questioning look. If a member of staff speaks a child's heritage language, it is usually sensible for that person to be the child's key worker. However, all staff should be encouraged to communicate with all families.

Language – speed of instructions

Giving instructions or guidance in bite-sized pieces and talking steadily is a more effective way of helping people who are struggling to understand an instruction than listing the process they need to follow and leaving them to it.

Professional Practice

■ Each of us has at some point been given instructions and left to get on with it. This neither fills us with confidence nor ensures that the task is achieved appropriately. Can you think of an example where you have been in this position? How did it make you feel?

---

case study 2.1   **Colleen**

Reception class teacher, Mrs Jackson, asks her nursery nursing student, Colleen, to organise the children for playtime. Colleen gets the children's attention and gives them the following instructions:

'It is playtime. Those of you who have finished your milk, get your coats on. Those of you who have not, please finish your milk, putting your straws and cartons in the bin and then get your coats.

'If you need the toilet, go now.

'If you have a hat or scarf, put them on please.'

---

activity

1 How did Colleen do?
2 How many different instructions were there?
3 Do you think all the children will have done all they needed to? If not, why not?
4 How could you have improved upon this?

Professional Practice

- Children will focus on whatever grabs their attention most – playtime! It is unlikely that they will have taken in all of the student's instructions. Colleen ought to have broken down her instructions and given them one at a time: 'Who has not yet finished their milk? Please finish it before doing anything else' and so on.

Figure 2.6

It is important to give clear, 'bite-size' instructions

Language – difficulties

Problems with speech can hold back the flow of communication and interaction. Such difficulties include:

- **aphasia** – aphasia refers to a child who is *unable* to express thought in words
- **dysphasia** – dysphasia refers to a child who has *difficulty in* expressing thoughts in words
- stammering (dysfluency)
- language impairment – which can be part of a condition, such as cerebral palsy, or an impairment in its own right.

Refer to Unit 7, page 329, where dysfluency is discussed.

remember

When talking to children, it is often the adult who initiates the development of conversation and, for some children, school or nursery is the only time of day when they have the full attention of an interested adult. It is particularly important for these children that you enrich their language as much as possible by extending and encouraging their use of new terms.

Personality issues

Sometimes people are loud and forceful in their approach to others, which can be off-putting to many individuals. This can be particularly so for young children.

activity 2.1

Imagine you are two years old and quietly sitting in your stroller, when suddenly a large face appears beaming at you, exclaiming loudly and poking at your cheeks.

1 How might you feel?
2 What response would you expect from a child in this situation?

Shyness

Sometimes both children and adults are simply too shy to communicate easily. These individuals need to feel comfortable and relaxed. They are likely to need encouraging smiles and gestures as well as the time to speak at their own pace. Trying to hurry them along, or pre-guess what they are going to say is not helpful.

Self-esteem

Self-esteem can be affected by poor communication skills.

For example, think how it might make you feel if you only had part of another person's attention when you were having a conversation. This situation is likely to affect how valued you feel by the person. Think about the impact of the tone of voice used, the other person's body language and whether **eye contact** is made with you (unless lack of eye contact is for cultural reasons).

Now consider this example. How might you feel if you were given a tatty piece of paper by your tutor with your assignment feedback scribbled on it hurriedly? Probably pretty annoyed that they hadn't taken more care when you had spent hours preparing the work for them. A sense of feeling valued can be impaired by the lack of time taken by others to prepare written material carefully. Think also how children might feel if the paper you give them for drawing is a piece torn roughly in half from a larger sheet.

activity
2.2

1 What examples can you think of where a lack of value and respect has been shown for another person. These could be in college, within your placement, or in your daily life.
2 How careful are you at getting this right?

Professional Practice

- When conversing with children or adults, always focus your attention on them fully unless the safety of other children could be compromised.

Think how you are communicating or presenting information to others. Would your own methods make you feel valued if you were the recipient?

remember

Good **interpersonal skills** enable you to support others. This may be by developing your listening skills, having good written skills and being able to present information clearly in a visual format. Support involves understanding the need for individuals to feel valued, building up their self-esteem, knowing when help is needed from additional sources and what form that help might take. As a good listener, you will develop a better understanding of the children in your care, and their families.

Refer to page 61 for guidance on developing listening skills.

Responding to different types of behaviour

You will no doubt have to use your interpersonal skills at some point to deal with confrontation. You may be faced with an angry parent or an awkward member of staff, and the approach you take will make a difference to whether you achieve a successful outcome. At times you will need to be **assertive**.

For some people, the word 'assertive' can sometimes be confused with '**aggressive**', so it is worth exploring the difference between them.

■ An assertive person is one who can remain calm during an incident of confrontation or disagreement, clearly outlining what they wish to say, and repeating the point if necessary without becoming over-excited or angry. Assertive people remain in control of themselves and stay within appropriate boundaries.

■ An aggressive person is one who often talks loudly and excitedly, displaying agitated and angry body language; such a person may make personal comments unrelated to the conflict or disagreement. Aggressive people are not, therefore, fully in control of themselves or the situation.

Assertive skills are useful when you need to stand up for something, for example, when:

■ justifying a course of action you have taken

■ challenging a request to take on a greater workload when you are already overstretched

■ declining to accept having to change your plans when you know that it will cause considerable stress at home for you to do so, and others are available

■ asking for an individual's views to be listened to by your headteacher or manager

■ requesting an increased level of support to enable you to achieve something specific.

Burnard (1992) describes three approaches to coping with confrontation, which are summarised below.

Three possible approaches to confrontation

■ **Submissive** approach (pussyfooting) – the person avoids conflict and confrontation by avoiding the topic in hand

■ Assertive approach – the person is clear, calm and prepared to repeat what they have to say

■ Aggressive approach (sledgehammering) – the person is heavy-handed and makes a personal attack of the issue

Burnard clarifies this further by describing the body language of each approach as follows:

■ Submissive approach

  - hunched or rounded shoulders

  - failure to face the other person directly

  - eye contact averted

  - nervous smile

  - fiddling with hands

  - nervous gestures

  - voice – low pitched and apologetic

■ Assertive approach

  - face to face with the other person

  - 'comfortable' eye contact

  - facial expression that is 'congruent' with what is being said

  - voice – clear and calm

■ Aggressive approach

  - hands on hips or arms folded

  - very direct eye contact

  - angry expression

  - loud voice

  - voice – threatening or angry

  - threatening or provocative hand gestures.

Professional Practice

In reflecting on your own practice, think about:

- where you see yourself in the above three descriptions;
- who you can identify as using each type of approach;
- what you are learning about your responsibilities as an early years professional;
- how well you are currently able to deal with aggression in a situation of conflict.

case study 2.2   Shabana

Shabana has just started work as a nursery nurse. Her working day is shared between two Reception classes of a primary school. She is unhappy with her list of duties for the coming term, as the majority of her time will be taken up with preparing materials for the class teachers and supervising domestic tasks, such as children undressing for PE, and toilet duties. Shabana understands that her role is as a support to the teaching staff, but feels that the knowledge, understanding and practical experience she has of young children, through her qualification and the two years of study taken to achieve it, is being underused and undervalued.

Shabana wishes to have her duties reviewed.

activity

1   How would you put your case across to the teaching staff if you were Shabana?
2   Share your ideas with another student.
3   Where would your planned approach fit in with the thinking of Burnard?
4   What changes would you need to consider?

Management of behaviour

Children need adult guidance and example to help them learn the social rules of the society into which they are born. In every family, the routines and boundaries vary but, whatever they may be, they are a crucial aspect of family life, enabling a household to run smoothly and the children to feel secure.

The boundaries set by parents need to be reasonable without being too rigid and, once agreed, it is important to keep to them, otherwise children will continually test them. Boundaries allow children to explore ever-increasing elements of their world, safe in the knowledge that the adults in their life are in overall control of the situation and are taking care of them.

The individual personality of each child will also have an impact on their behaviour.

 Link   Refer to Unit 7, page 308, for more about personality.

Setting boundaries
Setting boundaries involves making it clear to children which behaviours are acceptable and which are not.

case study 2.3 — Caleb

Mr Collins takes Caleb to the supermarket to do some shopping. He usually buys Caleb some sweets in the supermarket when they shop on Saturdays, but not when they shop midweek. It is Tuesday and Caleb decides he wants some sweets and he wants them now! He shouts and stamps his feet and Mr Collins is so embarrassed that he buys Caleb what he wants and quickly leaves the shop.

activity

1 What has Caleb learned?
2 What should Mr Collins have done (ideally)?
3 What might be the long-term implications of this incident?
4 What does this tell you about boundaries?

Professional Practice

■ Children need clear, consistent and fair boundaries.

Early years professionals need to set boundaries and make clear their expectations of children when they are in the school or pre-school setting, and these boundaries need to be reasonable, consistent and fair. This will contribute to the social and emotional stability of the children within the setting and to their development in general. Children need to learn the social rules of their own culture (their primary socialisation) in order to be fully accepted by others within that culture. Each culture places its own emphasis on certain social skills and children will be encouraged to comply with these, by noting the responses they receive.

 Link Refer to Unit 7, page 313, for information on social learning theory.

Reinforcement and learning by example

An approving look, a smile or a word of praise encourages a child to repeat an action, gesture or response, whereas a disapproving look or negative verbal comment is more likely to deter a child from repeating something. Parents and early years professionals should lead by example.

activity 2.3

Think of an incident where children were learning by example.

1 Was this important, do you think?
2 What might have been the outcome had there been no example for them to follow?

case study 2.4 Desmond

Desmond is six years old and is an only child, born to his mother, Denise, when she was just fourteen. Desmond and his mum lived with her parents for four years until she felt able to cope with him on her own. Desmond is a very lively little boy who is awake by 6.00 a.m. every morning and does not go to bed until Denise does – usually at around 11.30 p.m. Desmond's grandparents doted on him when he lived with them, giving him all that he asked for. They still come and see him most evenings, usually at around 9.00 p.m. This allows Denise time to tidy up a bit as she gets nothing done with Desmond there. In school, Desmond is difficult to manage, being irritable and unwilling to share. He clamours for the attention of the class teacher throughout the day.

activity

1 What is going wrong for Desmond?
2 What is Desmond learning from the adults around him?
3 What would be the first issue you would want to tackle for Desmond?
4 How could Denise help Desmond?
5 How could the grandparents help Desmond?
6 How could the class teacher help Desmond?

Sometimes we need to take a firm stand on issues for the long-term good of the child. Getting the balance right often comes with experience.

In setting boundaries for children, it is important to think them through carefully, considering how important each 'rule' or boundary actually is. In a busy early years setting, you do not want to be constantly reminding children of boundaries, as life will soon become very negative, if you are regularly repeating 'Don't do that please', 'Off there please', and so on.

Professional Practice

■ Children will test boundaries if the boundaries are not seen to be both clearly set and consistent, which is why a few really important boundaries are better than a whole range of desirable ones.

Newly qualified early years staff will benefit from observing the approaches taken by more experienced staff in setting and maintaining boundaries.

When **managing unacceptable behaviour**, it is important to make it clear that it is the behaviour that is unwanted and not the child.

activity 2.4

Think about the following statements and discuss them with a partner:

■ Children must say please and thank you before they get their snack.
■ Only the child holding the teddy at circle time is allowed to speak.
■ Children should never interrupt an adult.
■ Only three children are allowed in the sand tray at a time.
■ No more than five children are usually allowed in the play house.
■ No more than five children are allowed on the climbing frame.

1 How important do you consider each statement to be?
2 Which could be described as a clear and consistent boundary?
3 What makes them a clear boundary?

Figure 2.7

Only the child holding the teddy at circle time is allowed to speak

case study 2.5 Orange Blossom and Hillview Nurseries

Orange Blossom Nursery has recently opened, and can accommodate 24 children aged 2 to 5 years. They currently have 14 children each day, mostly aged 3. The managers of Orange Blossom have decided to run the nursery as a free-play nursery, and have interpreted this as allowing the children to play with whatever they like, whenever they want to, with no restrictions on how many children can play with any one resource.

You are visiting Orange Blossom as part of a professional practice studies task which asks you to make a comparison between different types of provision. You have already written notes on Hillview Nursery, which tries to ensure a balanced approach between free play and structured activities. At Hillview, the free-play activities are restricted to a range of resources predetermined by the staff and there are guidelines for the children as to how many children can play in any one place, whereas at Orange Blossom the children select or ask for whatever resources they want and play within small or large groups as they choose.

activity

1. What are your first thoughts about the ethos of Orange Blossom Nursery?
2. What are your first thoughts about the ethos of Hillview Nursery?
3. Draw up a list of benefits and drawbacks for each nursery.
4. How might the children's developing understanding of boundaries be affected at Orange Blossom?
5. How might this free-play approach affect the working practice of the staff?
6. What might the children miss out on at Orange Blossom?
7. Would you have any other concerns? What are they?

Professional Practice

- Children feel secure with boundaries, and their understanding of them is made clear when they are heard trying to enforce them on others in the setting: for example, 'You're not allowed to do that'.

- It helps children to understand the need for boundaries if you can give explanations to reinforce them whenever opportunities arise.

For example, following an incident on the climbing frame, the nursery manager of Hillview Nursery talked to the children, saying, 'Jenny has had a nasty fall from the climbing frame, which is a shame, but too many children were trying to use it at the same time and were not listening to Monica who was asking Jenny and Sarah to get off and wait their turn. Hopefully, everyone will remember this; it is why we only allow five children on the frame at the same time.'

This was a clear explanation that had meaning for the children. It is more likely to be remembered by them for the future.

Children can at times display a range of unacceptable behaviours, and responding to them in a positive and consistent manner will help them to learn what is and what is not acceptable. Certain behaviours may need to be eliminated because they:

- breach the boundaries of the setting
- affect the enjoyment and/or learning of others in the setting
- affect the enjoyment and/or learning of the child themselves
- are dangerous for the child or for others.

When challenging a child's behaviour, you need to be aware of what expectations there are of the child at home, and how your views of the child's behaviour will be interpreted. It is important that a child's home life is not seen to be criticised or devalued, but the boundaries of the setting should still be maintained.

It is common in many primary schools for each class to display a list of the school 'rules'. These include statements such as 'We will not run in school', 'We will be nice to everyone', and so on. These statements make it clear what is acceptable or not acceptable within the setting and make no judgements about any one child's upbringing.

For example, Kieron loves to jump on and off the tables. This is a game that he plays at home with his brothers who are both older than him. It will be far better for you to explain to Kieron that he cannot jump on and off the tables in nursery because he might hurt himself on the nursery floor, or that the younger children may try to copy him and hurt themselves, rather than simply telling him that it is wrong to jump off furniture. In Kieron's home, it may not be considered wrong and this could cause him confusion.

Similarly, it is better to explain to Maisie that shrieking at the top of her voice in the village hall (where she attends your pre-school group) cannot be allowed, as it echoes around and disturbs everyone, but is much more acceptable in the farmyard of the farm house where she lives, because it is an open space and the cows probably love to hear her coming to see them.

Professional Practice

- Children need to be given reasons and explanations which have meaning for them.
- On issues of health or safety, there is no room for negotiation. No must mean no.

---

activity

2.5

1   What forms of behaviour do you consider to be unacceptable, and why? Copy the table and try listing them under appropriate headings.

Breaching boundaries	Affects others	Affects the child themselves	Dangerous for child or others

2 Where would you place the following behaviours in the table?

tantrums
jealousy
withdrawn behaviour
extreme shyness
isolating behaviour
child without friends
repetitive crying
constantly seeking
   attention

telling tales
hitting
pushing over
bullying
taking somebody's toy
rudeness
refusing to share
group running away
   from another child

teasing
using aggression
defiance
disobedience
destruction of others'
   activities or drawings, etc.

3 What else can you add to the list?

Examples of strategies you could take in exploring and managing behaviour are set out below, based on some of the behaviours listed in the activity above.

The child without friends – Child A

1 Produce a sociogram of friendships within Child A's class or group.

   a) Who does Child A indicate as their friends?

   b) Which children indicate Child A as a friend?

Refer to Unit 8, page 355, for information on sociograms.

2 Consider the interests and personalities of the children identified in the observation above. Think about who most closely relates to the interests and personality of Child A.

3 Initiate activities to bring the children together (one or two at a time). It may be helpful to involve an adult working alongside them to start with.

4 Monitor the progress of the 'friendship' and, if it does not last, note what went wrong.

5 Use any information gained (from 4) to inform you in helping the child in developing another friendship.

Professional Practice

■ Sometimes, children need to be taught how to respond to others. A child with a naturally 'neutral' facial expression may need help in learning to make eye contact and give a welcoming look to others.

The destructive child – Child B

1 Make a note as to whose belongings the child destroys.

   a) Anybody's?

   b) Their own?

   c) The belongings of children of a particular social group or culture?

2 Does the child seem to want to 'get back at' anyone in particular? If so, monitor for antecedent behaviour.

See ABC strategy, page 52.

3 Does the child seem angry or frustrated? Offering opportunities for releasing anger and frustration may help.

4 Has the behaviour started suddenly? It may be appropriate to consider what is happening at home. Children may be taking out their confusion or unhappiness in the setting because they are unable to express it at home. Giving opportunities to be creative and making time to talk may help.

Professional Practice

- Whenever possible, ignore destructive behaviour (but comfort any child affected by the destruction), as sometimes the child's aim is to get your attention!
- Reward good behaviour with praise as this positively reinforces desirable behaviour.
- Whenever possible, work in partnership with parents to improve behaviour both at home and in the setting.

The withdrawn child – Child C

1 Make a note of how significant the problem is:
   a) How easy is it to involve the child in everyday activities?
      Easy? Sometimes difficult? Always difficult?
   b) How regularly does the child seem withdrawn?
      Occasionally? Regularly? All the time?
   c) How much do you consider the child's learning or activity to be affected?
      A little? Quite a lot? Almost totally?

2 It is important to establish whether the child is withdrawn in all situations, or just in the early years setting. If it is just in the setting, you will need to observe closely to identify where the problem lies. E.g:
   a) Is it linked to separation anxiety?
   b) Is the child being bullied?
   c) Is there a problem at home?
   d) Is the ABC strategy relevant?

See ABC strategy, page 52.

3 Use observation to guide you as to the best approach to take. Approaches might include:
   a) encouraging greater parental involvement to help the child feel more secure
   b) identifying children you need to keep separated from the withdrawn child, hoping to break the cycle and restore the child's confidence
   c) involving an adult in activities to help the child to develop 'joining in' skills.

Professional Practice

- Use your understanding of child development to help you approach the child concerned appropriately.

The attention-seeking child – Child D

1 Consider whether the attention-seeking behaviour is due to:
   a) not being accepted by others in the class or group.
   b) problems at home (feeling rejected, lack of interest shown in the child)
   c) anxiety in new situations
   d) the child being bored with the activities offered or the work set
   e) the child finding the activities or work too challenging, and therefore lacking a sense of achievement.

2 Use observation skills to identify when attention-seeking behaviour occurs.

3 Adult involvement in group situation may help alleviate any 'social' problems.

Professional Practice

- Giving plenty of praise and attention where appropriate can be beneficial. This will indicate to children that you are willing to give them your attention, but only at appropriate times.
- Providing more differentiation in the activities offered or the work set may help the child find the appropriate balance of stimulation and achievement.

Development and behaviour

The age or stage of development that a child has reached will of course have a bearing on the expectation of how a child behaves and how best to manage their behaviour if it becomes unacceptable.

activity 2.6

1 Think about how you would manage the following:
  (a) a five-year-old making a racist remark to another child
  (b) a two-year-old repeatedly undressing themselves on a very cold day
  (c) a seven-year-old actively encouraging his little sister to flick paint across the kitchen.
2 The ages of each child will influence how you respond to each incident. Now swap round the ages and think them through again. What difference would this make?

remember

What is acceptable at two is not always acceptable at four or older.

For example, a two-year-old who crayons on another child's drawing has not yet learned that this is not 'fun'. A four-year-old who does the same (usually) knows that it is not appropriate, but could be doing it for a number of reasons, such as:

- to try to gain your attention
- because they are jealous of the other child
- in retaliation for a previous act.

Before jumping to any conclusion, it is important to establish the facts, ensuring that the act itself is clearly acknowledged as unacceptable but exploring any other issues and helping the children to reach a resolution between themselves if one is required.

Professional Practice

- Explanations will only work if the child concerned has the ability to understand.
- Children's behaviour often regresses during illness or times of stress.

Refer to Unit 10, page 447, for further information about children who are ill. Refer also to the strategies below.

Behaviour policies

Any strategy used by early years staff will work best if supported by the parents and carers of the children who attend the setting. This is why having **behaviour policies** are important; they set out what is acceptable to the setting and how unacceptable behaviour will be handled.

activity 2.7

With a group of other students, collect a range of behaviour policies from a range of different settings. Having removed any form of identification of the settings from the policies, discuss the contents of each behaviour policy.

1 How do they compare?
2 Which policies do you think would be most useful to the staff in the setting?
3 Which would be least helpful? Why is this do you think?

For examples and discussion of behaviour (and other) policies, refer to *Good Practice in Nursery Management* by Sadek and Sadek (1996).

Coping with unacceptable behaviour

Strategies for coping with unacceptable behaviour include:

- the **ABC behaviour strategy**
- time out
- **containment**
- setting goals
- helping children cope with change.

ABC strategy

Behaviour, whether acceptable or not acceptable, follows the same process, that is, it is affected by the responses given to it whether they be positive or negative. A useful strategy is the ABC behaviour strategy. This is based on social learning theory.

Refer to Unit 7, page 313, for an explanation of social learning theory.

ABC stands for:

- **A**ntecedent – the antecedent is what occurs immediately before the behaviour
- **B**ehaviour – the incidence of behaviour being referred to, whether acceptable or not acceptable
- **C**onsequence – this is the outcome following the behaviour, which will be either positive or negative.

Think of it this way:

Positive antecedent + Positive behaviour = Positive consequence

Negative antecedent + Negative behaviour = Negative consequence.

---

case study   Cleo
2.6

Incident A: Cleo had been happily making a model using junk boxes for almost 20 minutes when Samuel came along and started telling her what to do next and interfering with her model. Cleo lost interest and went to play elsewhere.

Incident B: Cleo and Ginny were playing in the sand tray, driving cars through the sand. When Samuel joined them Cleo left immediately and went to play in the water.

Incident C: The whole group were playing circle games, and you became aware that Cleo was avoiding being next to Samuel, specifically changing places to avoid him. Clearly something is not right here.

activity

1 How do you think using observation skills will help you get to the bottom of this situation?

Professional Practice

- Noting and responding to antecedent behaviour is a good way of starting to manage children's behaviour.
- As an early years professional, your role would be to intervene in a situation before the antecedent behaviour has an effect.

Link Refer to Unit 8, pages 341 to 355, for information on useful observational techniques.

In the three incidents described in the case study, the antecedent was clearly Samuel, although he did not appear to be doing anything significant to upset Cleo (apart from some interference in incident A). Observation skills could be of importance here: observing Samuel, particularly when he is in close proximity to Cleo, could indicate why Cleo is anxious in his presence.

Professional Practice

- Sometimes a child can be anxious due to the larger size or louder personality of another child. The adult's role here would be to join in and help show the wary child that they can play or work on equal terms with the other child.

activity 2.8

With advice (and permission) from your placement supervisor, observe a child over a period of time and note any situations where the antecedent affects subsequent behaviour. If these were negative effects, think through what could be done by the adults responsible to alter the situation and avoid it being repeated.

Time-out

This is the term given to removing a child from a certain situation. It should be seen as a strategy rather than a punishment, allowing the child to calm down if distressed, and enabling others to continue with what they were doing. A child given time-out should still be within sight and hearing of the carer, and where the child is taken should be both safe and secure. Children should only be given time-out for very short periods of time. Many people use the estimate of 1 minute per year of age as a guide, but common sense should always prevail. Less will often be sufficient for most children.

Always explain to a child why they have been given time-out and make a point of giving the child your attention when there is no behaviour issue. This will reinforce the benefit of playing well and being rewarded with the adult's time, which is often the root of many unacceptable behaviour situations.

Containment

Sometimes children's frustration or anger overwhelms them and they are unable to deal with it themselves. At this point, a sensitive adult can step in and 'contain' their emotions for them, holding the child calmly and preventing the child losing control, gradually easing the child back into a relaxed state.

It is important for you as the adult to remain unflustered, offering children examples of how to behave another time by outlining alternative measures that they could have taken, where appropriate.

Professional Practice

- Different cultures place different values on possessions and this can at times be a cause of conflict.
- Clear explanations must always be given to children as to why their behaviour is not acceptable.
- Some children will benefit from taking 'time out' from the activity, to calm down, relax and compose themselves, once again.
- Sanctions should be used only as a last resort, and if sanctions are indicated to a child, they need to be carried through (part of setting boundaries for the setting).

Professional Practice

- Sometimes, children need opportunities to express anger. Providing them with clay, wood-working or a similar activity can be helpful.

- Distracting a child away from whatever is the problem can work well. This strategy can be particularly useful with younger children.

- If children continually have negative interactions with others, it may be helpful for an adult to join them in their work or play and help to direct their interactions, demonstrating a more positive way to play or work with others.

Helping children cope with planned and unplanned change

Behaviour can be affected by insecurity and anxiety about the unknown. When practitioners know that there is likely to be a new experience that could cause anxiety, such as going into hospital, moving home, etc., it can be helpful to read related stories with the children. Giving children the opportunity to discuss their feelings about past or forthcoming events can alleviate much of the issue for them.

The flexibility built into the daily routine of a school or day-care setting offers security for children, enabling them to face changes in other situations too whether planned or spontaneous. Sometimes the routine of a child's day in school or nursery is the only 'constant' in their lives. Occasional changes to that constancy help them realise that they can accept and cope with change. This is another good reason why the routine in any setting should never be too rigid.

Setting goals for behaviour

Self-esteem plays a large part in children's behaviour. If they are secure and feel confident, they are less likely to display unwanted behaviour. There are many ways of encouraging good behaviour and using reward stickers and star charts has become a popular approach. Some of these are aimed specifically at building self-esteem, for example:

- 'I have good thinking skills'
- 'I am a kind person'
- 'I have done really well today'.

Others will be direct rewards, such as:

- 'Good work'
- 'Well done'
- 'A kind act'.

Whole-class rewards are given in some schools by using Golden Time or something similar. Golden Time is often on a Friday afternoon, and children are given greater autonomy regarding what they do. In some schools, children can even change to another class for the Golden Time session.

remember

There is no substitute for praise given for effort and the giving of your time. These are usually the rewards a child wants most of all.

Setting targets for children can be successful, particularly if the children can see a tangible reward outcome. Many primary school classes use charts to indicate which books have been read, or how often good behaviour has been noted, and so on. These give **positive reinforcement** to the children and encouragement to continue.

Progress Check

1   What is a boundary?
2   Why do children need boundaries?
3   What effect can a lack of consistent boundaries have on children?
4   Why is structure and routine important in early years settings?
5   What is meant by positive reinforcement?
6   What does the ABC stand for in the ABC behaviour management strategy?
7   What is meant by containing a child's emotions?

Development and maintenance of relationships with children, families and others

For communication to be successful it needs to meet the needs of both speakers. Any breakdown in this will result in a lack of communication.

The communication cycle

The diagram below shows how communication can be explained as a cycle, in which we each in turn take the part of the 'encoder' (the person who sends the message) and the 'decoder' (the person who deciphers, and therefore understands, the message). During conversation, we continually swap roles from encoder to decoder and, as the diagram demonstrates, the common field of experience is where the message is initially decoded. Without a common field, the message is likely to get lost or distorted, and this can be likened to conversing with another person when there is no shared language between you.

Figure 2.8

The communication cycle

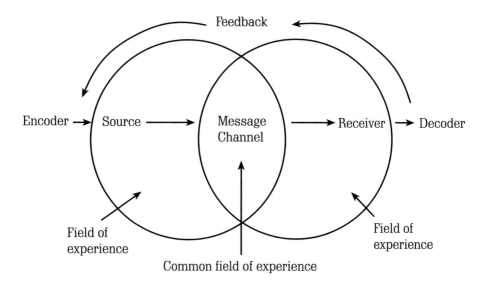

For communication to work successfully, the message channel needs to be a common field of experience for both the encoder (the speaker) and the decoder (the listener).

Communication can fail because of:

- lack of vocabulary
- inability to speak, see or hear
- lack of listening skills
- inability to concentrate
- lack of knowledge
- lack of interest
- misinterpretation
- wrong (or confusing) body language/facial expressions
- surrounding noises
- wrong timing/place/person.

Failing to communicate may make us feel:

- frustrated
- hurt
- angry
- misunderstood
- inadequate.

The importance of a common field of experience

A 'language' which is understood by both early years workers and parents is important to the building and maintaining of relationships. Without it, communication will break down quickly and hinder the sharing of information about the child's progress or needs and the setting's ability to work in partnership with parents.

Figure 2.9

A common field of experience is needed for successful communication

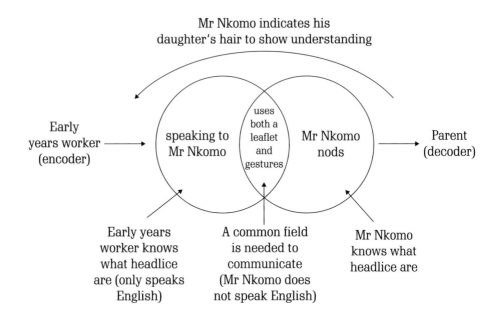

Mr Nkomo indicates his daughter's hair to show understanding

Early years worker (encoder)

speaking to Mr Nkomo

uses both a leaflet and gestures

Mr Nkomo nods

Parent (decoder)

Early years worker knows what headlice are (only speaks English)

A common field is needed to communicate (Mr Nkomo does not speak English)

Mr Nkomo knows what headlice are

---

case study

2.7

Henry

Henry's key worker, Sue, is talking to his mother when she comes to collect him. She asks her if she has noticed an increase in Henry's spatial awareness. Henry's mother looks slightly embarrassed and shrugs her shoulders. Sue goes on to say that there has been a great improvement noticed by the staff in the nursery and Henry is pleased with his newly acquired skills.

Sue was assuming Henry's mum's shared knowledge of the developmental term 'spatial awareness'. Henry's mum went away without understanding what skill he was developing.

activity

1   How else might Sue have phrased the question?
2   What affect might the embarrassment have had on Henry's mum?
3   Should Sue have noticed Henry's mother's discomfort?
4   What does this tell you about parent–staff relationships?

activity
2.9

It would have been far better for Sue to ask Henry's mum if she had noticed how Henry can now steer round obstacles or find a suitable space in which to carry out his roly-polies without knocking others over. This would have maintained a more positive form of communication, and Henry's mum would have understood what he had achieved.

Put this into a communication cycle like the one below.

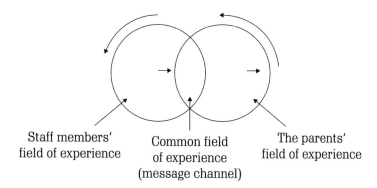

Staff members' field of experience | Common field of experience (message channel) | The parents' field of experience

Verbal and non-verbal behaviour
Verbal – open and closed questions

Conversation often involves asking questions. The way in which the questions are phrased makes a difference to the answers (feedback) you receive. Questions can be useful to clarify something you are unsure of and can indicate to the other person that you are interested in what they have to say, by extending the conversation further. **Open questions** offer the opportunity for a wide-ranging answer, whereas **closed questions** restrict the answer to one word, such as 'yes' or 'no', or a limited statement. You need to think carefully about the type of question you are asking and the message the question is giving.

Professional Practice

■ It is important to remember that many children do not have the opportunity for regular conversations with an adult who is interested in really listening to them. Your role as a professional is to listen to the children in your care and encourage them to converse, suggest, re-tell, estimate and evaluate, helping them build on their use of language and verbal skills.

For example, 'Did you enjoy your lunch?' is a closed question; 'Yes' or 'No' are the likely answers. Whereas 'What did you have for your lunch?' or 'What do you prefer to eat at lunch time?' offer the opportunity for a range of answers and therefore extend conversation.

activity
2.10

1   Decide whether the following questions are open or closed.
    a) Does Sangita have any allergies?
    b) Did you enjoy going on an aeroplane?
    c) Where did you go on your holiday?
    d) Do you enjoy listening to stories?
    e) Which is your favourite book?
    f) How did Mollie react to the new baby?
    g) What can you remember seeing when we went to the farm?
2   How could you alter the closed questions to make them more open?

Non-verbal communication

Non-verbal communication can tell us a great deal about how people are feeling. However, it is important to remember that different people have differing requirements regarding personal space, and different cultures have differing cultural practices. As an early years worker, you should, whenever possible, research the cultural customs and practices of the children in your care, recognising that a cultural 'norm' will not be followed by all families of that particular culture. This will help you to avoid causing offence or embarrassment.

Figure 2.10

Non-verbal communication

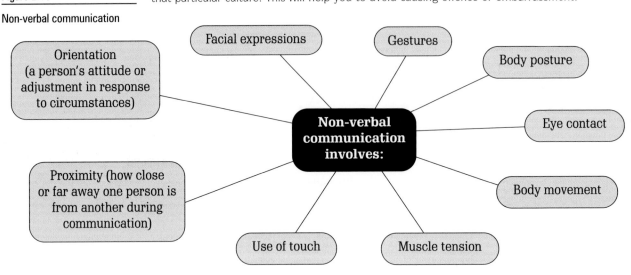

At times we need to interpret what children are trying to say to us through their actions and body language (their non-verbal communication), which can be displayed either consciously or subconsciously. This can be particularly important if they have been hurt or abused and the observation skills and level of understanding that you develop will enable you to be alert to such non-verbal signs.

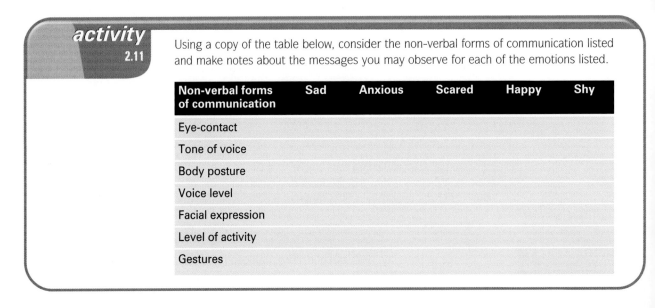

activity 2.11

Using a copy of the table below, consider the non-verbal forms of communication listed and make notes about the messages you may observe for each of the emotions listed.

Non-verbal forms of communication	Sad	Anxious	Scared	Happy	Shy
Eye-contact					
Tone of voice					
Body posture					
Voice level					
Facial expression					
Level of activity					
Gestures					

Link   Refer to Unit 3, pages 75 to 79, for indicators of abuse.

Professional Practice

■ A smile gives encouragement and a gesture can indicate how to approach an activity. To help to gain the confidence of a shy or anxious child, you can set up a favourite activity and take part in it alongside the child.

Touch

Each of us has contact with other people everyday; at times this contact may just be verbal, but at other times it is more tactile. You need to consider how closely others wish to be in contact with you and in what circumstances, asking yourself whether you ever 'invade the space' of anyone, and what signs they have given you to indicate this.

Earlier in the unit, the question of knowing when and when not to communicate through touch was mentioned and the importance of considering a person's facial expression and body language and noting the messages they give out.

activity 2.12

1   Think how you feel if another person sits or stands too close to you
    What message to indicate your discomfort do you give them?

2   Think about the contact you make with other people.
    a) Which circumstances involve physical contact?
    b) What determines whether you initiate touch?
    c) When do others initiate touch with you?
    d) Has physical contact ever felt inappropriate or unnecessary? If so, why was this?

Sometimes, as an early years worker, it is inadvisable to touch a child, especially if there is a danger of your touch being misinterpreted. You need to be aware of what forms of touch are appropriate and what are not. You also need to consider the issues of consent.

Link

Refer to Unit 5, page 174, for more about this important area of your professionalism.

Eye contact

Eye contact can be encouraging to a shy or nervous person, and can help keep a conversation going. When no eye contact is made, it is likely that the conversation will trail away. When individuals are feeling nervous, embarrassed, shy or guilty, it is a natural response to avoid eye contact.

Eye contact is a connection between the speaker and the listener. It makes them feel accepted by one another.

Body language

Your body language is part of your personality. Some people are more physically demonstrative than others. Gestures and positioning of the body can suggest a range of feelings, including submission, aggression, defensiveness and assertiveness. They can also demonstrate a welcome, humour, warmth and openness.

Link

Refer to pages 42–43 for information on assertiveness and aggression.

Other forms of communication

Signed languages

For children and adults with limited or no verbal skills, a variety of signed techniques can offer a helpful communication route.

- **signed language**
- Bliss symbols
- Makaton
- Braille
- cued speech.

They can each be used successfully and are favoured for different reasons.

Signing is used by deaf people, those with impaired hearing, people with certain forms of disability and by many people who communicate with them. Signed language does not only involve hand signs, but uses the whole face and body to communicate. Signed languages are languages in their own right; they are not simply a direct interpretation of a spoken language.

On page 152 of *Understanding Children's Language and Literacy*, Mukherji and O'Dea (2000)

Non-vocal communication can be defined as follows:

■ Signed language: 'The manual and gestural system of communication used by people who are deaf; the sign languages used in different countries are languages in their own right, and not manual means of communicating the spoken languages of those countries.'

Figure 2.11

The standard manual alphabet: each of the letters is represented by different hand positions

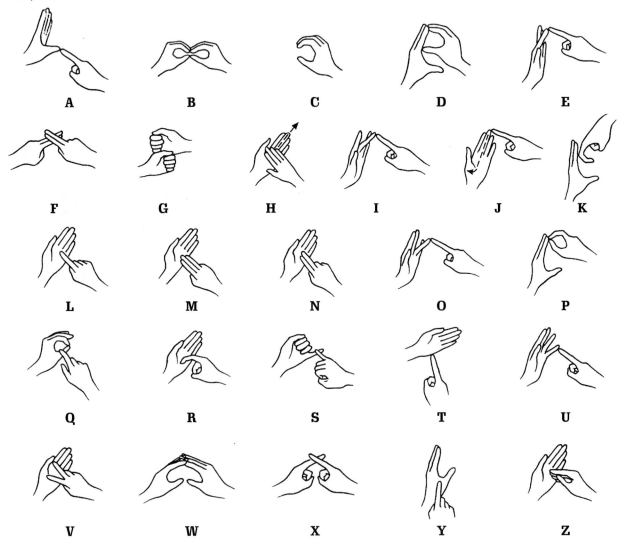

■ Bliss symbols: 'A universal language of pictographic symbols which is used by people with reading and writing disabilities.'

Figure 2.12

Bliss symbols: each child using this system has their own chart of the symbols they wish to use

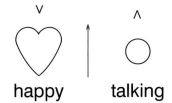

■ Makaton: 'A basic signing system using signs borrowed from British sign language, used by people who have severe learning difficulties.'

Figure 2.13

Makaton signs: a system used by many children and adults who have communication difficulties

boy
Brush right index pointing left across chin

rabbit
Palm forward 'N' hands, held at either side of head, bend several times to indicate ears

fish
Right flat hand waggles forward like a fish swimming

bird
Index finger and thumb open and close in front of mouth like a beak

■ Braille: 'A touch-based reading and writing system used by people who are blind.' Braille is a system of letters made from raised dots.

Figure 2.14

Braille is a system of letters made from raised dots

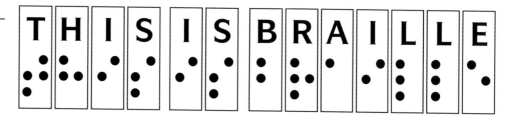

■ Cued speech: 'A system of eight handshapes made in four locations near the face to assist children (or adults) who are deaf, in lip-reading.'

Listening skills

Listening involves taking in a range of different sorts of information. It is not the same as hearing (as when listening to music), because you need to take in the information and often act upon it.

In an early years setting you will listen to:

■ children telling you their news

■ children asking for your help

■ children sharing their experiences of activities with you

■ children explaining their problems

■ parents giving you important information about feeds, diet, health, and so on

■ parents confiding in you about family issues that may affect their child

■ colleagues explaining changes to the daily routine

■ colleagues passing on useful hints and ideas

■ colleagues updating you through the cascading of information

■ outside professionals (for example, a Portage worker) giving you guidance.

Each of these speakers needs your attention to enable you to meet the needs of the children in your care adequately. Listening carefully is a skill which is well worth practising.

activity 2.13

1 Think about when you listen best and what affects your listening.
   Is it noise?
   Other people?
   The level of activity going on around you?

2 Do you consider that you always give people your full attention?

activity 2.14

1 Talk to a partner for three minutes on any subject you choose. When the time is up, your partner should repeat what you have said. What did your partner leave out? Change roles and repeat the exercise.
2 How hard was it to keep focused?
3 Which are you best at, speaking or listening? Why is this?
4 What did your partner's body language tell you? Did your partner appear interested in what you were saying? Or did your partner appear bored?
5 How did your partner's body language affect you?
6 Think about what effect a 'listener's' body language might have on a 'speaker'.

Professional Practice

■ It can be useful to study the communication processes in a range of early years settings, noting the effects of the staff's responses on the children.

case study 2.8   **Hopes and Dreams Day Nursery**

Hopes and Dreams Day Nursery is your new placement, and your supervisor has suggested that you take a couple of days to observe how the nursery day is structured and how the staff work with the children. You settle with a notebook and observe the following:

Observation 1

Tom is crying as someone has scribbled on his picture. Sarah (nursery nurse) stops what she is doing (clearing a table for snack time) and sits down with Tom to listen to what he is saying. At first he is very distressed but begins to calm down with her full attention and is able to explain to her what happened more clearly. Eventually, when he is completely calm and ready to go back to the activities, she finds a special piece of paper for him to draw another picture.

Observation 2

Sophie runs to Stella (nursery nurse) telling her that her model has been knocked down again by James. Stella is more focused on a conversation between two members of staff about the changes to the rota. Stella tells Sophie, 'Never mind; make another one.' Stella returns to the construction area and kicks the construction materials and then sits down in a corner and does nothing.

activity

1 What was the main difference between these two observations?
2 How should Stella have responded to Sophie?
3 What does this tell you about the importance of listening?

Consider what you find most difficult about listening:

- Think about when you have really listened to another person.
- Have you ever avoided listening to someone for any reason?
- Can you remember when someone has listened carefully to you?
- When have you not been listened to as carefully as you would have liked?
- How did you feel about each of these situations?

remember

It is important to:
- show that you are listening by focusing on the speaker;
- make eye contact and use encouraging smiles and gestures;
- try not to interrupt, let the other person's speech flow, particularly if they are upset or agitated.

Active listening

Active listening ensures that you are focused on what the speaker is saying; there are various ways of listening actively.

Paraphrasing

Paraphrasing involves summarising what has been said and is an easy means of checking that you have understood what you have heard. Your response would start with statements such as:

- 'So what you are telling me is …'
- 'Would I be right in thinking that …'.

This checks that you have understood what has been said to you and also shows other speakers that you value them and have been listening carefully to them.

Reflective listening

Reflective listening is more about showing that you understand what people are feeling, rather than the details of what they are saying. Your responses to them focus firstly on their feelings and emotions. These can be positive emotions, such as excitement or elation, or less positive emotions, such as anger, worry or sadness.

Figure 2.15

Reflective listening at any age involves understanding the feelings of others

activity 2.15

Use a copy of the following table and complete it to review your own performance in listening reflectively to children. An example has been included to get you started.

When	Where	Child's initials	Incident if known	Emotion being communicated	Response by you
Mon a.m.	Nursery	B H	Broken toy	Worry	Reassurance

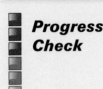

Progress Check

1   Explain the communication cycle.

2   Name three aspects of verbal communication.

3   What is the difference between an open and a closed question?

4   What examples can you give of non-verbal communication?

5   What does the term 'barrier to communication' mean? Give an example.

6   What is the difference between dysphasia and aphasia?

7   What is a heritage language?

8   How many alternative forms of communication can you name?

Communication differences

Overcoming barriers

Communication barriers that might affect conversation and the passing of information between setting and parent have already been covered. Overcoming barriers can, however, involve more than simply providing the right environment and using the appropriate skills. At times, other professionals will be needed too; such a person may be known as an advocate, an interpreter and/or a translator.

The support of advocates, interpreters and translators

Advocacy means speaking on behalf of another individual and representing that individual's interests, and the person taking on this role is referred to as an advocate.

Advocates are involved if parents are unable to gain access to the services they need because of a lack of sufficient spoken English, to ensure that the parents are understood, or to support them if they are unfamiliar with which services may be available to them and their children.

An advocate may also be brought in if parents feel that a child's needs are not being recognised by the professionals currently involved.

Whenever possible, children are encouraged to contribute to the decision made about their future. Advocates are often involved here too, particularly if a child is looked after by the local authority through one of its care systems.

The role of the advocate is to listen and interpret for the parent or child, following this with liaison and negotiation regarding the outcomes of any meeting or consultation. Advocates are usually known to the family through their role as health visitor, social worker or representative from an organisation to which they belong. They can be particularly useful to parents with a child who has a specific need, ensuring that the child's rights to suitable education provision are met.

It is likely to be less beneficial to use a non-specialist interpreter, as a family's needs will be best served by someone who can translate between the languages being used and also understands the education, health and support systems currently in place and is able to identify and advise parents accordingly.

Conflicting beliefs

Early years practitioners will not always agree with the actions and practices of parents, nor will they share their belief systems. However, practitioners should be working with parents to provide the best for the child concerned, within that family's cultural practices and belief system. Once again, this is where the quality of a practitioner's interpersonal skills will be revealed.

Progress Check

1   List at least five different sorts of information you will listen to as an early years worker.

2   What is paraphrasing?

3   Give an example of reflective listening.

4   When is visual information particularly important?

5   What does the role of an advocate involve?

Care of distressed individuals

This section looks at how communication and interpersonal skills can help to support others in a range of situations. Professionally, this can involve children, their parents and the colleagues you work with, but socially and at home the same skills apply. At times, we understand how others are feeling (we have empathy), perhaps due to previous experiences of our own, but at other times we cannot really imagine how an individual feels, or why they are so distressed about something. This is where your interpersonal skills will really help you to succeed. You will use these skills in respecting the views, feelings and needs of others and in finding an appropriate means of supporting them.

Distressed behaviour

Distressed behaviour can include:

- anger
- aggression
- being withdrawn.

Anger and aggression

Verbally, this can include shouting, swearing, pointed remarks and generalised unpleasant comments.

Non-verbal responses would include stamping, negative gestures, throwing objects, slamming doors and negative facial expressions.

Withdrawn behaviour

This is likely to be seen through a lack of eye contact, disinterest in what is going on around the individual, and limited verbal communication.

Reasons for distressed behaviour

The main reasons for distressed behaviour are shown in the diagram below.

Figure 2.16

Reasons for distressed behaviour

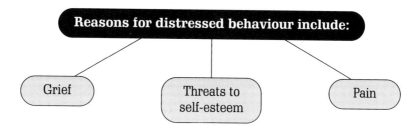

Reasons for distressed behaviour include:

Grief Threats to self-esteem Pain

Threats to self-esteem

This can be due to reduced confidence, following negative comments, or through bullying and abuse. Children need to be praised regularly to remind them that they are valued and appreciated. Bullying and any suspicion of abuse should be investigated.

Refer to Unit 3 page 79 for guidance.

Grief

Grief can be due to being parted from the main carer or the loss of a special object, as well as bereavement at the loss of a person or a loved pet. Understanding and your time will be helpful here.

Pain

Illness or injury can both result in pain. Adults and children have differing levels of pain tolerance and express feelings of pain in different ways. Young children can find it particularly difficult to explain pain to their carers. They often generalise their pain to a site that they can name or describe, for example, tummy ache.

Refer to Unit 5, page 212, for guidance on how to check for signs of injury, and Unit 10, page 431, for signs of childhood illness.

Communication difficulties

An inability to make oneself understood can cause practical difficulties as well as emotional frustration. Both can be equally distressing.

Refer back to the communication cycle on page 55.

Frustration

Being unable to achieve an objective can be hard to accept. This may lead to feelings of not being fully in control of a situation. Both adults and children can become frustrated.

Perceived loss of rights

Feeling disadvantaged by a lack of care or attention and missing out in some way can be seen by some as loss of rights. Equity of care should be considered and maintained at all times.

Any of these feelings of distress are difficult for an individual to cope with, but imagine how much harder it might be if you did not have the skills or the language to express yourself and ask for the help you need. Who would you turn to in these circumstances? It is worth exploring who you would turn to and why – what do you feel makes them approachable? Is it their calm nature, their practical approach, or what? How do you think you might feel if someone confided in you or sought your advice on a serious matter?

Skills for working with individuals

activity 2.16

1 What feelings do you think you (or others) might feel if a distressed person turned to you? Might you feel:
   - scared that you might 'get it wrong'?
   - pleased that they felt able to turn to you?
   - out of your depth?
   - unready for this level of responsibility?
2 What else?

Dealing with distress sometimes necessitates the helper (you) also being helped. This is the same for trained counsellors who are counselling clients regularly and have considerable experience. They have a mentor to whom they can turn when necessary, together with regular 'supervision' sessions, as taking on the stresses of another person can be stressful and, as the helper is bound by confidentiality much of the time, the lack of opportunity to 'off-load' stressful issues can be hard to cope with.

The following strategies for supporting distressed individuals are a useful starting point in considering how to prepare for any future situations you may find yourself in:

- Remain calm.
- Allow the distressed person time to sit quietly.
- Let the distressed person release their emotions through crying if that seems to be needed.
- Offer practical support; drink, tissues, and so on.
- Use reflective listening.
- Paraphrase when appropriate.
- Be aware that often you will only be able to start the helping process, not complete it.

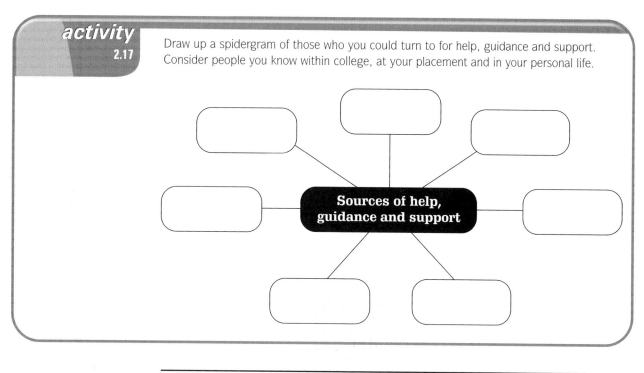

Refer to page 63 for reflective listening and how to paraphrase.

Professional Practice

■ It is important to remember that there are cultural differences in the mourning process following death; developing your knowledge of these differences will ensure that you respond appropriately to the families within your care.

■ Dealing with disclosure of abuse needs particularly careful handling.

Refer to Unit 3, page 89, for important guidelines on dealing with disclosure.

Figure 2.17

Your interpersonal skills will help you to support distressed individuals

Sources of support for carers and confidentiality

Sources of support

As an early years worker, once you have gained experience in day-care settings, and have been made a key worker or room supervisor, it is likely that parents will turn to you for advice. It can be helpful to have previously researched and drawn up a list of useful contact addresses that can be passed on if appropriate. These might include local support groups for people learning English as a second language, helplines such as Cry-sis for parents when an infant's crying becomes difficult to deal with, or Cruise, the bereavement support group. What others can you think of?

---

activity 2.18

With a partner, research a range of useful addresses, telephone numbers and websites and put them together in a pack or on an information sheet. Keep this in your professional practice portfolio for future reference.

Confidentiality

Confidentiality is directly linked to communication and will be a vital aspect of your professional role in the early years sector. Confidentiality can be particularly important if parents talk to you specifically about their child, and sometimes about matters that are worrying them. As your relationship builds up, you may be trusted with personal or family problems that are private to the individual or family. You should feel complimented that someone has trusted you sufficiently to speak to you in confidence, and that your ability to listen is clearly valued – that trust should never be abused.

At other times, you may have information passed on to you that is of concern to you. You will need to decide when it is appropriate to pass information on and when it is not.

Throughout this book you will find reference to the term 'need to know'. This means exactly what it says: the information that you are given only needs to be shared with those who need to know about it.

---

activity 2.19

In each of the following cases, who, if anyone, is the person who needs to know this information? How much do they need to be told?

1   David has a urine infection and needs to go to the toilet regularly (and urgently) throughout the day. He cannot 'hang on' for five minutes until breaktime.
2   Jessica's father has left the family home suddenly after a violent row with his wife. Jessica is very upset and unusually quiet.
3   Selina's mother is depressed and takes anti-depressants regularly.
4   Paula's mother leaves her alone for three hours each evening to work at the local store. There is a coal fire in the sitting room, which does not always have a fire-guard.
5   Jerome's dad (who helps out regularly in your pre-school) was placed on List 99 when he left his teaching post.
6   Earl's mother is a stripper in a night club and he is cared for by his older sister much of the time.

 Link   Refer to Unit 3, page 106, for an explanation of List 99.

Professional Practice

- Information should only be passed on to people to enable them to care for a child more appropriately or to maintain safety: of the child, or of the setting.
- Prejudging a situation based on 'hearsay' or 'gossip' can be dangerous.
- At times, you will have to break a confidence for the safety and well-being of a child. Whenever possible, the person who has initially given you information should be told if you have felt the need to pass it on. As a student always refer to and be guided by your tutor or placement supervisor.

 Link

Refer to Unit 3, page 90, for further discussion of confidentiality.

Confidentiality is protected through various Acts of Parliament, including:

- Data Protection Act (1998)
- Access to Personal Files Act (1987)
- Access to Health Records Act (1990)
- Access to Medical Reports Act (1988).

This legislation is important because it helps to ensure that personal details are recorded appropriately and that unauthorised access to them is prevented. It directs what may and what may not be kept on records and what information can be kept manually and through technological means. Legislation states the rights of individuals to see their personal records, although in certain cases there are exceptions to this, for example if having access to medical records would be detrimental to a person's well-being. Legislation sets out that each person should know who has access to their files and that records held in respect of any enquiry should hold only facts and not personal opinions.

It would be useful to familiarise yourself with each of the Acts listed above. They are available from HMSO publishers and are also on the Internet.

Own interpersonal and communication skills

Personal skills

If asked about good interpersonal communication, most people would give a positive response, explaining the importance of communicating well and taking the other person's needs into consideration, but how many of them would actually put this into action on a day-to-day basis? What about you? How well would you do?

activity
2.20

Think of the ways in which you communicate with others in a range of different settings, including college, home, your placement, social situations, in shops and so on.

1 How does your communication differ between the age groups you interact with and also the social groups you interact with? Include babies, young and older children, your peer group, your parents and your grandparents' generations in your thinking and consider how your communication differs when interacting with each of the groups you have identified.
2 Consider how you use your voice (verbal communication). Think about:
   - volume
   - tone
   - speed
   - the language used
   - the emphasis you place on words.

activity
continued

3   What about your body language (your non-verbal communication)? Consider:
- posture
- gestures
- eye contact
- physical contact
- spatial awareness.

4   Think of a conversation you have had where the communication felt unsuccessful to you? Why was this do you think? What could you have done to have improved it?

5   When has communication felt particularly successful? What made it so?

activity
2.21

1   Think about the range of communication and interpersonal interactions you have had during your placement experiences and which have been most successful. Which, on reflection, could have been improved upon?

2   Copy the table and add at least five examples from your practice. An example has been given to get you started.

Type of communication	With whom?	Any potential barriers identified in advance?	Evaluation of the success of the communication process
Informing parent about headlice in the nursery	Father of a child	Father speaks very little English	Information was successfully passed on through the use of a leaflet and gestures showing how headlice jump from head to head

Oral presentations

Communication skills are needed when presenting information orally to others. This may be required during your course of study, as you present a piece of research to a group or, once qualified, when giving a short presentation to groups of parents. Your tone of voice, use of body language and facial expression will again contribute to how well you keep the attention of those to whom you are speaking. Making eye contact will also be important, as this involves others in what you are saying and indicates that you are speaking to them personally. When you give a presentation, you may wish to use visual aids, such as overhead projector transparencies, video recordings or give your 'audience' a handout. These need to be prepared carefully, so that they add something to your presentation and do not detract from it.

Refer to Unit 9, page 400, for more on oral presentation skills.

A useful source with a section on preparing for an oral presentation is *Research Methods in Health, Social and Early Years Care* by Green (2000).

Identification of areas for development

Reflection

Reflection is another feature of professionalism. You will need to reflect regularly on each aspect of your work in early years.

Identify which aspects of communication you need to develop further by carrying out the following activity.

activity 2.22

Consider now how well you communicate with others. Copy and complete the table below (based on Burnard, 1992).

Person I am communicating with	How do I find communication with them?			
	Easy?	**Difficult?**	**Unsure?**	**OK?**
Child under 5				
Child 5–10				
Young person				
Teenagers				
Adults socially				
Adults in placement				
Parents in placement				
A complete stranger				
Non-English speakers				
Child with a special need				
Adult with a special need				

Having read the unit and reflected on your communication skills, use the findings of Activity 2.22 to help you place your skills into two categories: strengths, and areas for particular focus. Copy and use the table below to help you.

Current strengths	Areas for particular focus
1	1
2	2
3	3
4	4
5	5

Return to this table from time to time. Consider how your communication skills are developing. If there is no identifiable change, ask yourself why this might be. Consider what you need to do to help yourself build on your skills in this important area.

Professional Practice

■ Never be afraid to ask for help.

■ Your tutors and placement supervisors will be pleased to support you in building on (any) skills. They are likely to be able to suggest new strategies for you to try and to help you identify any specific problems you have in successfully carrying out appropriate communication.

Key skills

This unit of study will be of significance in the gathering of evidence for Key Skills, particularly in Communication, improving your own learning, problem solving and working with others. The ways in which you contribute to discussions, and invite the contributions of others in discussion and conversation, write reports, give oral presentations and interpret information will all be relevant. You should be able to draw on evidence from all aspects of your course: classroom discussion, placement experience and your professional practice portfolio.

UNIT 3

Protection of Children

This unit covers the following objectives:

■ Understand the signs and symptoms of child abuse

■ Explore the appropriate responses to signs and symptoms of child abuse within the current legal framework of child protection

■ Investigate a range of strategies and methods for supporting children and their families

■ Develop an awareness of the importance of multi-agency working with respect to protecting all children.

Child protection is one of the most difficult and sensitive areas of work for early years professionals, and responsibility for the protection of children is an essential requirement of anyone working in an early years setting. At some point in your career you are likely to be involved with a child who has been abused or is in danger of being abused, and it is, therefore, important that you have an understanding of child protection procedures and of different types of child abuse and that you learn how to support the children in your care.

This unit introduces and defines the term 'abuse' and discusses how those working with children should respond to incidents of abuse or suspected abuse. It also discusses the support available to parents and carers of abused or at-risk children, both within the local community and through the legal system. Issues of safety within individual childcare settings are explored and opportunities are given for evaluation.

Signs and symptoms of child abuse

Historically, children have suffered a great deal of abuse, partly due to a general lack of understanding and acceptance that children should have rights and protection as individuals. Social attitudes have thankfully moved on, although the process has been slow and haphazard, progressing from the seventeenth-century thinking that 'children's inherent [natural] badness needed disciplining' (Reder et al., 1993), moving through phases in which childhood was essentially denied and children were considered to be extensions of their parents rather than individuals in their own right, and leading eventually to the current **paramountcy principle** of the Children Act 1989.

The Children Act 1989 has encompassed the development of society's attitudes, together with a multitude of parliamentary Acts, producing one of the most important pieces of legislation ever for children in the UK.

The paramountcy principle gives priority to the welfare, safety and protection of children; any decision taken about children must be in their best interests. It demonstrates that children are at last being considered as people in their own right, who can contribute to decisions about their own futures.

 The Children Act 1989 will be referred to many times during this chapter. A copy of the Act, or volumes drawn from it, is usually available in college libraries; it is also available from Stationery Office bookshops.

Historical perspective on abuse

It is useful to adopt a **historical perspective**, looking at how what has happened in the past has implications for today.

The table below sets out the historical developments in the UK, outlining changes in thinking from medieval times through to the implementation of the Children Act 1989 in 1991.

Table 3.1 The evolution of 'child abuse' and child protection

Year/s	Transitional event	Prevalent social attitude	Professional involvement
Medieval	Poor Law Act	Childhood denied; caring problems caused by moral failings; communality of life	
17th century		Children's inherent badness needed disciplining	
18th century		Family life more private	
19th century		Influence of private philanthropists	Child maltreatment observed but denied
1833	Factory Act	Children's need for protection recognised	
1834	Poor Law Reform Act	Family's moral failings needed correction	
1872	Infant Life Protection Act	Children recognised as individuals	
1880	Education Act	Children's developmental needs recognised	
1889	Prevention of Cruelty to and Protection of Children Act	Child cruelty considered a crime	Emphasis on prosecution of perpetrators
1889	Poor Law (Children) Act		Poor Law Guardians for children introduced
1890			NSPCC established
1904	Prevention of Cruelty to Children Act		Local authority empowered to remove child from their family
1908	Children Act		Special courts for juveniles
1920s			Child's emotional life acknowledged; child guidance clinics established
1933	Children and Young Persons Act	Welfare of the child emphasised	Care proceedings introduced
1940s			Child abuse 'rediscovered'
1945	Denis O'Neill inquiry		
1948	Children Act	Children's best interest paramount	Attempts to keep families intact
1950s		Sanctity of the biological family	Attachment theory elaborated
1963	Guardianship of Infants Act		Local authorities to undertake preventative work to keep families intact
1969	Children and Young Persons Act		Local authorities given clear powers to remove children from their families
1970			At Risk Registers and Area Review Committees introduced
1974	Maria Colwell inquiry	Blood-tie re-evaluated; media interest in child abuse	
1975	Children Act		Permanency policy
1980s			Child sexual abuse 'rediscovered'
1985	Jasmine Beckford inquiry		
1987	Kimberley Carlile inquiry		
1988	Cleveland inquiry	Media interest in child sexual abuse	
1989	Children Act	Parental responsibility emphasised; ambivalence to family vs state	

Sadly, there have been many more cases like the ones shown in Table 3.1 since the implementation of the Children Act 1989, and in many instances failure of communication between the various agencies was condemned. However, the findings of the Laming Report into the death of Victoria Climbié in 2000 fed into the reorganisation of children's services in the government's 'Every Child Matters: Change for Children' agenda. This wholesale revision of services for children is underpinned by the legislation of the Children Act 2004 and aims to change and improve the quality, accessibility and coherence of children's services, whilst maximising opportunity and minimising risk.

---

activity 3.1

Having read the information in Table 3.1, you might find it useful to read further about past attitudes and legislation that you are not familiar with.

This will help you build a fuller understanding of the historical development of child protection.

Copies of government Acts and legislation are available through Stationery Office bookshops and many can be found on the Internet.

Alternatively:

■ Chapter 3 of Child Abuse by Carver (1980) is an accessible text about past legislation, although you should bear in mind that it was published before the Children Act came into being.

■ The Department of Health (1991a) publication Child Abuse: A Study of Inquiry Reports 1980–1989 provides a summary of some of the most high-profile cases during the 1980s.

Defining abuse

Across society (and indeed across the world), there are varying definitions of what constitutes discipline and what constitutes abuse. Some people consider that smacking a child is a harmless and effective form of managing unwanted behaviour, but others regard smacking as an offence. In most parts of the UK, however, parents are still able, by law, to smack their own child with a bare hand, but are not allowed to use any kind of implement. This continues to be a controversial issue. In Scotland, recent legislation has now declared it an offence to hit any child under the age of three and any child of any age around the head. This is seen by many childcare organisations as a starting point for greater legal protection of young children.

Professionals in early years consider smacking to be both unacceptable and ineffective, and early years trainers promote the use of a range of alternative strategies in the management of children's behaviour and promote the establishment of clear boundaries. In day-care settings, physical punishment of children is not allowed in any form, but controversially, the old National Standards for under-eights care for childminders (reference criteria 11.4–11.6) did allow children to be smacked by a childminder with the written agreement of parents. This has now been amended in the revised standards and Standard 11.4 and 11.5.

---

activity 3.2

The organisation **EPOCH** campaigns for changes to be made to the law regarding the physical punishment of children.

1 Find out what EPOCH stands for and what its aims are.
2 Do you agree with the ethos of EPOCH?
3 Were you smacked as a child?
4 If so, what do you remember about being smacked?
5 What is your view of smacking?

If asked to define the term 'abuse', you would most likely respond by referring to the four main categories: **physical abuse**, **neglect**, **sexual abuse** and **emotional abuse**. As a general summary, it can be said that abuse of a child occurs when any avoidable act, or avoidable failure to act, adversely affects the physical, mental or emotional well-being of a child.

You should be aware that abuse can be both deliberate and non-deliberate. The physical effects on the child are the same, but at times the intentions and understanding, or limitations in understanding, of the parent/abuser will be taken into account when a situation is investigated.

Cultural practices need to be understood and taken into consideration, particularly regarding the terminology used within some cultures.

Refer to page 85 for a discussion of cultural practices.

Kempe (1992) defined the four main categories of abuse. His definitions are useful, although each local authority will have its own definition set out in the literature given to each early years provider; you may also find it useful to refer to these. Kempe's definitions are:

- physical abuse

'Physical abuse implies physically harmful action directed against a child; it is usually defined by any inflicted injury such as bruises, burns, head injuries, fractures, abdominal injuries, or poisoning.'

- neglect

'Neglect can be a very insidious form of maltreatment, which can go on for a long time. It implies the failure of the parents to act properly in safe-guarding the health, safety and well-being of the child. It includes nutritional neglect, failure to provide care or to protect a child from physical and social danger.'

- sexual abuse

'Sexual abuse is defined as the involvement of dependent, developmentally immature children and adolescents in sexual activities they do not truly comprehend, to which they are unable to give informed consent, or that violate the social taboos of family roles.'

- emotional abuse

'Emotional abuse includes a child being continually terrorised, berated, or rejected.'

Professional Practice

- Researching the definitions drawn up by the authority in which you work or study will help you consolidate your understanding.

Indicators of abuse

This section sets out a range of **indicators of abuse**, that is, signs that could alert professionals that a child may be suffering abuse or may be at risk of being abused. It is important that the indicators are not used in isolation – they need to be noted carefully and any concerns considered, together with recent observations of the child and discussions with management or senior staff, with decisions for further investigation being made where applicable. Naturally, there can be times when one specific sign or injury is considered to be significant on its own, in which case immediate action will need to be taken.

Accidental injuries

It is important to remember that all children injure themselves from time to time, and it is common to see toddlers with blackened eyes or bruised foreheads as they tend to fall over or run into furniture such as coffee tables. Older children learn to ride bikes and climb trees and fences, tumbling in the process and scraping knees, grazing legs and arms, and on occasions suffering from more serious injuries, such as concussion and bone fractures. It is important that you consider the age and stage of development of the child concerned, when you make a judgement on whether an injury is considered to be of concern, and take into account the circumstances of the injury.

Although children regularly have physical marks following accidental falls, the site of the injury can be the easiest indicator of the need for concern.

Physical abuse

Possible indicators of physical abuse

- bruises on the soft areas of the body (inner arms, thighs, buttocks)
- bald patches
- unexplained injuries, including bruises, burns, bone fractures
- bite marks – remember that a dog bite will look very different from a human bite and that an adult's bite mark is considerably larger than a child's
- finger-tip bruising on the face – this could be caused by forced bottle feeding of a baby or young toddler
- unusually shaped bruises – consider how a child might show non-accidental bruising other than by being hit with an implement such as a stick or a lash

Figure 3.1

How do you think this bruise was caused?

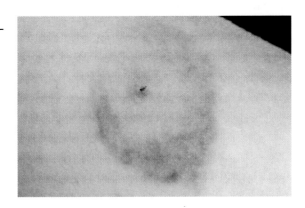

- thumb and finger-tip bruises each side of the torso, which can indicate that a child has been shaken or held forcefully
- pin-point haemorrhage in the ears, which can be caused by shaking
- scald and burn marks – an accidental scald (if, for example, a child pulls over a kettle of boiling water) will have different signs from a scald caused, say, by a cup of tea deliberately thrown. The photographs in Figure 3.2 show very severe scalding on the leg and foot of a baby, and a burn inflicted by a cigarette butt.

Figure 3.2

Severe scalding on a baby (l) and a cigarette burn (r)

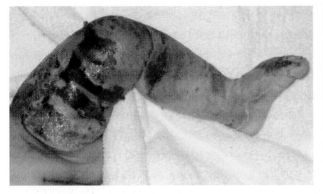
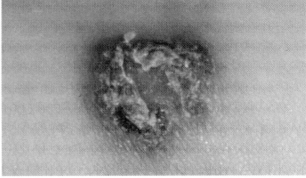

- evenly spaced scald marks which can indicate the deliberate placing of hands or feet in hot water – these will often have the appearance of socks or glove marks
- repeated black eyes or injuries which should start to raise alarm bells.

Professional Practice

- At times innocent injuries can be misinterpreted. Examples include:
  - the condition impetigo, which can be mistaken for cigarette burns
  - the 'hidden' condition osteogenesis imperfecta (brittle bone disease or Lobstein's syndrome), which can be mistaken for non-accidental fractures.

Behaviour

Physically abused children may display a change in behaviour, which can vary considerably from child to child. One child may become withdrawn and quiet, while another may become aggressive towards others. Children may show reluctance to go home, or be with particular adults, parents or carers. They may show physical signs of discomfort such as difficulty in movements when dressing, changing or during physical activity.

As children grow older, their bodies are less often seen by the adults who care for them. Be aware of a child who wishes to remain covered up or who always arrives at the setting in long-sleeved tops and long trousers, whatever the weather.

Bruises

Bruises are damaged blood vessels where the skin has not been broken. They develop through stages, initially appearing purple or blue shortly after the injury has occurred. Gradually they become yellow, and usually disappear within 10 to 12 days. Therefore, a yellowing bruise has not 'just appeared'. Similarly, a dark-blue bruise is unlikely to have been there for more than a couple of days.

remember

- The explanation of how and when a bruise occurred can at times be important.
- Bruises often appear darker on dark-skinned children.

Neglect

Possible indicators of neglect

Neglect can stem from ignorance and a lack of practical childcare skills, and is not always intentional. This does not, however, lessen the physical effects for a child. A neglected child may:

- be underweight, possibly emaciated
- be hungry, and may scavenge for food or wolf food down at mealtimes
- be dirty and unkempt, with poor personal hygiene
- suffer frequent minor injuries
- appear to have no regular bedtime pattern – the child may indicate that they watch late, and unsuitable, television programmes
- suffer from frequent minor infections, such as colds and coughs, due to inappropriate nutrition and subsequently become run-down
- have a lack of experience of common childhood activities such as looking at books and using creative materials
- be left unsupervised on a regular basis – the child may indicate this in conversation
- have parents who lack interest in the child's progress in school or at nursery
- display self-comforting behaviours, such as rocking and head banging.

Behaviour

Neglected children often seem constantly tired from going to bed when they choose, and not having a time set by their parent. They may display lack of concentration, and lack of attention (due to tiredness). Stealing of food is common (hunger), as is frequent and excessive masturbation (self-comfort). Neglected children frequently display low self-esteem and low self-confidence. They are likely to be fearful of new situations and can at times be over-friendly to any adult available, indicating their need for attention.

Sexual abuse

Possible indicators of sexual abuse

Sexual abuse often goes undetected and research has shown that two-thirds of all children who are sexually abused do not tell anyone about their experiences. These children may suffer long-term physical harm (depending on the nature of the abuse suffered, there may be medical effects in adulthood), as well as having the mental scars that abuse brings generally. The child's behaviour more often raises concerns than the actual physical signs.

Sexual abuse includes:

■ the use of pornographic material – showing it to children or involving children in the making of it

■ **incest** – an incestuous relationship is one which involves sexual activity between family members who are too closely related to be able to marry, for example between father and daughter or brother and sister.

Physical signs of sexual abuse

■ bruises on areas such as the inner thighs and genital areas

■ soreness in anal or vaginal areas, or in the throat

■ vaginal discharge in girls

■ swollen penis or discharge in boys

■ sexually transmitted diseases and urine infections, sometimes found if medical examination takes place

■ distress when having nappy changed (babies and toddlers)

■ difficulty or reluctance to pass urine or faeces, often resulting in constipation

■ difficulty in walking, and in standing up or sitting down

■ pain on movement generally

■ poor personal hygiene

■ obsession with sexual matters

■ having unexplained sums of money on a regular basis (older children).

Behaviour

A sexually abused child may cling on to a parent or trusted carer and may avoid individuals or show distress at being left with certain adults. The child's development may regress, for example, starting to bed wet again when previously dry at night. The child may become withdrawn and appear saddened, and concentration may suffer leading to poor progress at school.

Some children display sexually inappropriate behaviour towards adults. Their drawings may also include explicit body parts, for example, an erect penis, which does not fit in with the developmentally normal drawing process of 'a person'.

As children get older, they may want to talk about their 'friend's' problems and hint at secrets. Abused children regularly isolate themselves from their peers and do not form relationships which would involve inviting friends home. Eating disorders such as anorexia or bulimia are common, as is frequently running away from home. Poor hygiene and obsessive cleanliness can both be present.

Professional Practice

■ It is important to remember that not all cases of anorexia or bulimia are linked to abuse. Such cases do, however, need to be investigated and the appropriate support offered.

Emotional abuse

Possible indicators of emotional abuse

Emotional abuse accompanies all other experiences of abuse. Children quite understandably become bewildered and confused when a person they love or trust begins to abuse them. Emotional abuse is rarely cited as the main type of abuse in official reports, the term only being used if it is clearly defined as the only form of abuse suffered by the child concerned. This would perhaps occur if a child was cared for physically but was denied love and constantly rejected, or put down and ridiculed, by the abuser.

These children may:

■ have low self-esteem and lack confidence

■ have a poor concentration span

- show developmental delay
- be fearful of new situations
- be concerned about their parents being contacted
- respond inappropriately to situations
- have speech disorders
- find it hard to build social relationships with their peers
- use self-mutilating behaviours, such as head-banging and pulling out their hair.

Behaviour

Emotionally abused children learn from their abuser that they are not of value, and their feelings of self-worth can disappear. One child, Helen, described in Doyle (1990), felt that her mother only liked the children that she supported through her charity work, who were emaciated and deprived, and so Helen began to dress in her oldest clothes to become more desirable to her mother and gain her love.

Bullying

Bullying can take a number of forms but has a common factor in that it causes lasting harm to children and young people, leading to self-harm and suicide in some cases. Bullying encompasses a wide range of abusive behaviours such as physical and verbal hostility and aggression; extortion of goods or property; isolating or excluding a child from peer groups; discriminatory behaviours; and many other offensive verbal and physical acts. It is not possible to do justice to the seriousness of bullying in this brief overview and you are recommended to read the following.

See Chapter 11 of *Good Practice in Child Protection* by Hobart and Frankel (2005).

Behaviour that may indicate that a child is being bullied

- school or nursery refusal
- frequent complaints of general malaise early in the day
- returning home with clothes in disarray or torn; appearing to be hungry if food has been stolen
- showing signs of emotional distress
- disturbed sleep patterns
- starting to behave in an aggressive manner to others.

Predisposing factors to abuse

It is not easy to predict when a child may be at risk of abuse, but research has suggested that some factors may predispose individuals to abuse. These **predisposing factors** can be related to the past and current experiences of parents and to the child or children in a family unit.

Predisposing factors in relation to the parents

Such factors might include:

- parents who have not had good role models to follow themselves
  - this may affect their parenting practices and ability to manage their children's behaviour in a positive manner
  - they may have lowered self-esteem and a poor image of themselves
  - they may also have been abused themselves as a child
- very young or immature parents
  - they may not have as yet developed the skills to cope with difficult circumstances
  - they may have unrealistic expectations of their child's rate of development
- separation at birth through maternal illness, which can result in disruption of the bonding process

- lack of support
  - from a partner resulting in lone parenting
  - from extended family
  - through discord within a reconstituted family
- illness
  - of either parent or child
  - parental illness may result in inability to care for the child appropriately
  - illness in the child may cause resentment in the parent
- bereavement – any form of stress can lessen a person's ability to cope, particularly bereavement
- learning difficulties – parents whose understanding is limited may make inappropriate decisions and cause suffering unintentionally
- social problems – unemployment, poverty and housing problems can cause high levels of stress.

Predisposing factors in relation to the child

Such predisposing factors might include:

- prematurity
  - caring for such a vulnerable child increases a new parent's anxiety
  - premature and low birth weight babies are more difficult for parents to learn to care for
  - sometimes a child is born before the parents have fully prepared themselves
  - separation at birth may affect the bonding process
- disability
  - difficulty in feeding and general caring routines can cause resentment
  - at times, parents feel they have lost the child they thought they would have and need help in learning how to care for, and enjoy, their disabled child
  - children with communication difficulties are less likely to be able to seek help and can be more vulnerable.

Professional Practice

- It is important to note that the cycle of abuse is not automatic – many people who have been abused as children become caring and loving adults and parents.

The young abuser

From time to time, we hear reports in the media of abuse or murder which has been carried out on a child by another child, and this is met with shock and horror by society. A high proportion of these children have been abused themselves or have had 'less than ideal' parenting and need help in addressing their behaviour. Children abuse sexually, physically and by bullying. Many people find it hard to believe that sexual abuse can take place between children, but as with all other aspects of development, children learn by example.

Cases of children abusing and/or murdering other children include the Mary Bell case in Newcastle in 1968, and the Robert Thompson and Jon Venables case in Liverpool in the 1990s. Both cases are well documented and raise serious questions about how children are both supported and failed within society.

In *Cries Unheard: The Story of Mary Bell*, Sereny (1999) charts the 'terribly damaged life' of Mary Bell and follows her years of trial, detention and imprisonment. The book raises serious questions about the roles of some adults and of society in supporting children.

A more recent case occurred in 2005, when a 12-year-old girl was arrested by police on suspicion of trying to murder a 5-year-old boy. The boy was found alone and in a state of distress with ligature-type marks around his neck, leading police to suspect that some attempt to hang him had been made. Several other children were also arrested but released without charge.

Progress Check

1 What is your personal definition of abuse?
2 Explain the four main types of abuse.
3 What should indicators of abuse be considered in conjunction with?
4 Give at least five examples of indicators of physical abuse.
5 Give at least five examples of indicators of neglect.
6 Give at least five examples of indicators of sexual abuse.
7 Give at least five examples of indicators of emotional abuse.
8 What is meant by the term 'predisposing factor'?
9 What examples of predisposing factors can you think of relating to parents?
10 What examples of predisposing factors can you think of relating to a child?

Theories of abuse

The experience of one or both parents can influence the way in which their children are treated. The family's circumstances, both financial and environmental, and any medical complications can also have an effect.

The reasons why people abuse can be categorised according to four main models (or theories) of abuse:

- the **medical model**
- the **sociological model**
- the **psychological model**
- the **feminist model**.

The medical model of abuse

The medical model sees the abuse as an underlying physiological condition: that is, it is an illness which needs a cure. In some cases, poor attachments with the main carers in their lives are thought to have affected the abusive parents' own ability to parent appropriately, with the potential for an ongoing cycle. With regard to sexual abuse, there are medical treatments to reduce arousal, which are sometimes successful if used together with more generalised behavioural approaches.

The sociological model of abuse

The sociological model links abuse to the social environment, the support structures that are either available or absent and the family make-up (extended, reconstituted, and so on).

The psychological model of abuse

The psychological model links abuse to the abuser's previous experience. It includes the abuser's own upbringing, the role models the abuser had, the effects of the bonding process with both the abuser's parents and now with the abuser's children, and any problems regarding attachment to the abuser's main carer. It also involves the ability of the abuser to understand the care needs of an individual child.

The feminist model of abuse

The feminist model looks at the role of women and how they have always been perceived as carers and, in particular, as the main carer of the family. The model focuses on how women and children are offended against and ignores the offences that are perpetrated by some women, both alone and in conjunction with men. Many people find it inconceivable that a woman, for whom maternal instincts are seen as inherent, could harm a child but this is a dangerous misconception. As long as this view is held, society will continue to deny the full potential of women to injure, damage and exploit the children they give birth to or care for.

 Useful further sources of information on the models of abuse can be found in *Female Sexual Abuse of Children: The Ultimate Taboo* by Elliott (1993) and *Child Abuse and Child Abusers* edited by Waterhouse (1993).

Factitious illness (formerly known as Munchausen Syndrome by Proxy (MSBP))

Factitious illness is relatively uncommon but is an example of abuse that is mostly carried out by women. It is often referred to as 'factitious illness by proxy'. It involves parents (most often mothers) fabricating illness in their child and seeking repetitive medical investigations, often moving from doctor to doctor. This can result in children being subjected to unnecessary medical intervention and prolonged periods of monitoring and even hospitalisation. On rare occasions, children have been deliberately made ill (or more seriously ill) by a nurse on the ward in which they are already being treated.

The adult perpetrator of factitious illness abuse (usually a parent) tries to mirror in the child the symptoms of various conditions. The abuser often has a degree of knowledge of medical matters. Examples of falsely creating symptoms include:

- altering temperature charts or warming up thermometers
- giving a child laxatives to instigate diarrhoea
- adding blood (often their own) to a child's urine sample
- inducing vomiting by giving the child salt or an emetic (vomit-causing) drug
- simulating apnoea attacks (temporary inability to breathe) by partial suffocation.

The syndrome is a psychological condition in which adults seek attention themselves, or want to be seen as a good, caring parent. It can be very difficult to detect, and the child usually suffers for a considerable length of time before a diagnosis is reached. In many cases, other children in the family will have suffered abuse of some kind too.

 A graphic account of this condition can be found in the autobiography *Sickened* by Julie Gregory (2003).

activity
3.3

A well-documented case illustrating factitious illness by a medical professional is the investigation and subsequent conviction of Beverley Allitt, a nurse on a children's ward. Research the reports on this case. This will consolidate your understanding of how subtle the approach of such perpetrators can be.

Consequences of abuse

No child remains unscarred by the abuse they suffer, but some are able, or are enabled, to deal with some of what they experience and move on to lead fulfilling and positive lives. For those who are not so lucky, the future can be far bleaker.

The effects of childhood abuse can be both short-term and long-term, affecting the choices the children make as adults and the levels of achievement they reach, and limiting their feelings of self-worth.

The spidergrams below summarise the **short-term effects of abuse** and the **long-term effects of abuse**. Bear in mind that the effects on individual children will vary greatly and not all the effects will be experienced by all children.

Figure 3.3

Short-term effects of abuse

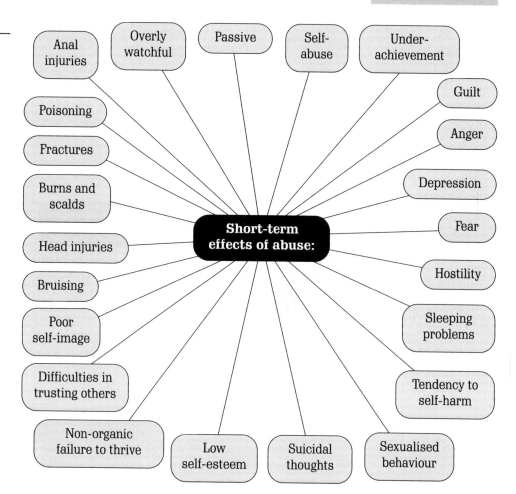

activity

3.4

Looking at the spidergram above, make a note of each 'consequence' under the following headings. You may wish to place some of them under more than one heading. Compare your answers with those of other students.

Emotional	Social	Physical

---

activity 3.5

Using the two spidergrams as a guide, discuss in a small group each effect. Consider:

1 the aspects of development affected, i.e. physical, emotional, social
2 the context in which the effects may be considered to be linked to abuse
3 the impact on families of children displaying these symptoms
4 the role of early years workers and other professionals (i.e. teachers, youth workers) in supporting the children
5 the role of early years and other professionals in supporting the children's families
6 how you could summarise the overall effects of abuse in your own words.

---

remember

Some of the behaviours and problems noted in the spidergrams can also be due to other reasons.

Variations in family functioning

Families are a central force in society and for most of us they are a positive influence on our lives. They provide much of our learning, emotional support and physical and health care needs. For some people, however, the family can be a source of violence, crime, neglect and abuse, and these are the families that are most often known to local authority social services departments.

Family types and partnership arrangements

Family structures include:

- the nuclear family – a heterosexual couple and their children
- the extended family – more than one generation of the nuclear family living together or very close by
- the lone-parent family – a lone parent (most often the mother), plus the children
- the reconstituted family – adults forming new relationships including their children from a previous relationship.

When parents live apart, there can be a range of often complex access agreements. At times, supervised access is the only situation in which a parent sees the child. This can be for a variety of reasons, often due to concern about the safety and well-being of the child.

The changing face of the family

As the structure of families continues to develop, with reconstituted families now being openly headed by heterosexual, lesbian or gay couples, the changing face of the family should be recognised. These 'new' families continue to fight prejudice in some areas of society to gain equal rights with 'traditional' families.

A useful discussion on the definition and diversity of the modern family can be found in *Social Policy and Welfare* by Walsh et al. (2000).

Professional Practice

■ Always remember that abuse occurs in all social classes, in all family structures and within all cultures.

Social disadvantage

The cycle of poverty increases the pressure on families and often lowers self-esteem as financial problems increase. This in turn can make it far harder for parents to focus on their child's needs, leading to emotional abuse and neglect, and to maintain self-control, leading to more physical forms of abuse.

Different concepts of discipline

Families and cultures have different ideas about what is a suitable form of discipline for their children, with some still leaving discipline to the father, seeing him as having the overall power within the family group.

activity 3.6

1. Where discipline is left to the father in a family, what message is this likely to give to the children?
2. How might this confuse a child?

Cultural practice

Terminology varies and what is meant by the word 'beat' in one culture is not the same as in another. Whatever your views on parents smacking their children, if a child told you that their father 'beat them last night' what would this conjure in your mind? In British culture, most people would immediately think of forceful, heavy-handed hitting of a child. In Caribbean culture, however, the term 'to beat a child' is to smack a child. The difference in understanding here could be crucial.

remember

It is important to consider cultural differences and practices before jumping to conclusions about a situation that raises concerns for you.

Some cultural practices, which are considered a normal part of life or a 'rite of passage' in some cultures, are considered to be acts of abuse in others. The most well-documented example is that of female circumcision, which is common in African cultures and is seen as a necessary act so as to present an 'unblemished' bride to her groom on their wedding day. Western societies consider it to be a barbaric act; it has been illegal in the UK since 1985, but it is suspected that the practice still continues, either covertly or by sending young girls on a 'cultural' visit back to their family's country of origin. The genital mutilation that the girls suffer frequently gives constant pain and causes problems with menstruation, urination and childbirth in later years. Anyone caught perpetrating female circumcision in the UK faces prosecution.

Pressures on some cultures regarding what is acceptable 'behaviour' prior to marriage can also have an impact on a child's or young adult's ability to disclose the abuse they have suffered.

case study

3.1

Sophie and Sungita

Sophie is 14 years old and has been sexually abused by her uncle since she was 9. She has recently disclosed the abuse to a trusted adult and is now being supported by her parents in bringing charges against her uncle.

Sungita is also 14 and has also been sexually abused by her uncle since she was 9. She is trying to raise the courage to disclose her abuse to her family. Sungita's family culture considers sexual contact before marriage for girls to be the ultimate disgrace for a family, and any girl known to have lost her virginity before marriage is disowned by both her family and the community.

Clearly the physical abuse and suffering has been similar for both Sophie and Sungita, but what extra pressure do you think Sungita faces as she considers disclosing?

For an in-depth look at the particular issues faced by children in minority cultures who are abused, refer to *Racism and Child Protection* by Jackson (1996).

Abuse within families

It should be remembered that in most cases the abuse of a child is by someone they know well, often a parent.

It is equally important to remember that abuse takes place across all cultures, at all levels within society and within all religions.

Responses to signs and symptoms of child abuse

The legal framework of child protection

The main aspects of law with an impact on child protection are those set out in the Children Act 1989. This Act has brought together all the legislation relevant to children and has been updated by the Children Act 2004.

Methods of supporting parents in their parenting

The implementation of the Children Act 1989 in October 1991 placed emphasis on parental responsibility, rather than parental rights. This responsibility for children refers to the 'collection of duties, rights and authority' which parents have regarding their child. Parental responsibility is automatically acquired by married couples and by unmarried mothers. Unmarried fathers can acquire it if they are made a legal guardian by the mother or by applying to the courts.

Where it is in the interests of a child, parental responsibility can be granted to other adults, such as grandparents, step-parents or the local authority when a **Care Order** or Emergency Order has been obtained. The responsibility would automatically end when an Emergency (or other) Order ends, or in the case of step-parents where responsibility is gained through a Residency Order, if that order ends.

The Children Act lays emphasis on parental responsibility continuing after the separation or divorce of the parents unless otherwise stated by a court of law.

The publication *Working Together under the Children Act 1989* (Department of Health, 1991b) sets out clearly the procedures, roles and responsibilities of all those who may become involved in child protection cases.

Police protection

A child may be taken into **police protection** for up to 72 hours, during which time the applicant can apply for an **Emergency Protection Order** (EPO) – see below.

Child Assessment Order

A **Child Assessment Order** can only be applied for through the courts by the local authority or the NSPCC. It is applied for when a child's parents are unlikely to give permission for an assessment of their child's state of health or level of development, when a concern is raised that a child is already suffering harm, or is likely to suffer significant harm. A Child Assessment Order can only last for seven days.

The *Framework for the Assessment of Children in Need and their Families* (DoH 2000) provides practice guidance for the assessment of children in need and recommends that all professionals working with the child are involved in the assessment process. It is also recommended that the assessment is made in collaboration with the child and family.

Emergency Protection Order (EPO)

An application for this short-term order can be made by anyone and, if the order is granted, the applicant subsequently takes on parental responsibility for the child for the duration of the order. The order is usually issued for eight days, with one extension opportunity of a further seven days. An applicant taking on parental responsibility 'must take (but may only take) action which is reasonably required to safeguard or promote the child's welfare' (Children Act 1989, Guidance and Regulations, Volume Two).

This might include an assessment of the child, or decisions about how much contact or who has contact with the child.

An Emergency Protection Order is always followed by an investigation by the local authority.

Recovery Order

A **Recovery Order** is designed to provide a legal basis for recovering a child who is the subject of an Emergency Protection Order, a Care Order or who is in police protection. It is used in situations where a child has been unlawfully taken away, or is being kept away from the person who has parental responsibility for the child. It also applies if the child runs away from the 'responsible' person or is considered to be missing.

The Recovery Order directs anyone who is in a position to do so to produce the child concerned, if asked to do so, or to give details of the child's whereabouts. The child will then be removed by the local authority. Police are authorised under the order to enter and search any premises as is necessary, using reasonable force.

Supervision Order

On occasions, a child is placed under the supervision of the local authority (for up to one year) if it is not felt that sufficient co-operation between the parents and the authority will ensure that the child is fully protected. Although the child continues to live at home, the local authority has a right of access to the child. **The Supervision Order** can be extended if deemed necessary.

Care Order

As with the Supervision Order, a child continues to live at home under a Care Order. The local authority has a shared responsibility for the protection of the child, and its decisions hold the greater balance of power in any disputes between the authority and the parents. At any time the authority can remove the child from the parents' home without the need to apply to the courts for any other order. The Care Order can last until the child reaches the age of majority (18 years old).

Area Child Protection Committees (ACPC)

Under the Children Act 1989, each area was required to have a joint forum for developing, monitoring and reviewing child protection policies. This is the responsibility of the **Area Child Protection Committee (ACPC)**.

ACPCs are made up of those persons who have contact with a child whose case comes before them, for example:

- social workers
- police officers
- medical practitioners
- community health team workers
- school teachers
- voluntary agencies.

An inter-agency approach to each case ensures that relevant information is passed on to all who need it. However, with the implementation of the recommendations of the Laming Report into the death of Victoria Climbié, the ACPCs are set to be replaced with Local Area Safeguarding Boards, although their primary purpose will remain largely the same.

Data Protection Act

The Data Protection Act 1998 covers the security and **confidentiality** of information held about individuals on paper and computer-held records. One of the perceived tenets of the Act is that security of information is sacrosanct and, in the case of the murder of Holly Wells and Jessica Chapman, police failure to share vital information about Ian Huntley was criticised. The Bichard Report (2004) confirmed that the Data Protection Act does not prevent information about a suspected sex offender being shared with the relevant authorities, but made recommendations about how information about is stored and shared.

Children's rights and parents' rights

Children have rights, and the United Nations Convention on the Rights of the Child, adopted by the United Nations in 1989, includes a range of rights directly relevant to child protection. For example:

- Article 3 – The best interests of the child should always be taken into account.
- Article 12 – The child's viewpoint should always be considered in conjunction with an assessment of the child's age and level of understanding.
- Article 16 – Children have the right to privacy.
- Article 19 – Children have a right to be looked after properly, and protected from violence and kept safe from harm.
- Article 37 – Children should not be punished cruelly.
- Article 39 – A child who has suffered ill treatment should be helped to recovery.

The Participation Rights of the Child by Flekkøy and Kaufman (1997) offers a useful discussion of children's rights; appendix 2 includes an 'unofficial' summary of the main provisions of the UN Convention on the Rights of the Child and is a helpful point of reference.

The Framework for the Assessment of Children in Need and their Families

This valuable document was published in 2000 as a partner to *Working Together to Safeguard Children* and recommended that child protection services would benefit from a wider perspective of what 'children in need' constituted. The Framework advocates:

- looking at children in need and their families from a viewpoint of their strengths as well as their weaknesses
- safeguarding children within a wider social framework that includes responding to their developmental needs
- a common assessment process shared by all professionals concerned with the child in need.

Figure 3.5

Assessment Framework
Triangle

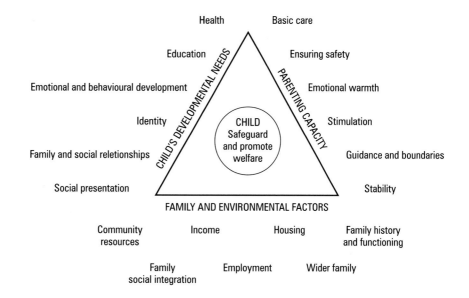

 Chapter 4 in *Protecting Children: Working Together to Keep Children Safe* by Flynn and Starns (2004) gives a clear and comprehensive overview of the Framework.

Every Child Matters

The Laming Report (2003) into the death of Victoria Climbié resulted in the publication of a Green Paper by the government entitled *Every Child Matters*. The circumstances involved in Victoria's death revealed a catalogue of missed opportunities on the part of social services, health services and the police to save her. The government response outlined in *Every Child Matters* was that the concept of safeguarding children needed to be embedded within a wider social context. Hobart and Frankel (2005) summarise the proposals as follows:

- statutory child-safeguarding boards to replace ACPCs
- a Children's Commissioner for England
- the establishment of 150 Children's Trusts by 2006
- the amalgamation of children's services such as education, health and social services.

Human Rights Act (1998)

 Look back at Unit 1 for discussion of the Human Rights Act 1998.

Disclosure

When a child discloses abuse to an adult, that is, tells an adult about it, the child is likely to have chosen that person for a reason and taken a great deal of both time and courage to speak out. It is therefore crucial that, when **disclosure** takes place, the child is given an appropriate response.

activity
3.7

Often, the disclosure comes 'out of the blue'. How do you think you or another adult might feel if a child discloses to you? Horrified? Shocked? Anger at the abuser? Scared about what to do? What other emotions do you think you might feel?

Listening and unconditional acceptance

It is important to explore these emotions in order to think through how you might deal with them if the need arises. The most important initial response to a child should be one of unconditional acceptance. By listening to children, showing them that you believe them and responding to them positively, you will have provided the first stage of help.

In responding to disclosure you need to:

- reassure the child that they have done the right thing by telling someone
- assure the child that you will help in whatever way you can
- explain that you understand how hard it is for the child to tell you this information
- find a more appropriate setting, or make arrangements to talk to the child somewhere else as soon as you can if you are not in a suitable place (for example, if it is very exposed to being overheard by others)
- do not ask leading questions; it is important that you do not influence the disclosure in any way
- remain calm
- keep your facial expressions and body language positive
- give the child time
- be a good listener
- be patient, the child will most likely need to stop to sort out their thoughts
- reassure the child that, whatever the situation, they are in no way to blame
- ensure that you do not make promises that you cannot keep; i.e. you cannot keep disclosed information a secret, and the child cannot come to your house to live
- explain that there are other people whom you may need to contact
- explain that these people will also want to help the child
- ask the child if they have told anyone else
- ask the child who else they think they could tell – a parent, aunt, etc. – it may be appropriate to offer to help the child tell that person
- maintain strict confidentiality, working on a 'need to know' basis
- follow the reporting guidelines for your setting
- write up a report of the disclosure immediately afterwards and date and sign it
- let the child know what will happen next
- keep the child informed until the situation is out of your hands.

Professional Practice

- It is important that you do not ask the child leading questions. They can invalidate a child's statement if there is a subsequent prosecution.

---

remember

If the abuse disclosed by another adult is current, consideration must be given to any children who may also be at risk.

Disclosure can also come from an adult who has grown to trust you. This may be a friend or a work colleague. The same approach is needed here as it would be for a child. The adult may have waited a long time to speak out and your response will be as important to the adult as it would be to a child. You may feel shocked, or even guilty that you had not been aware of what had been happening. These are natural responses, but you should remember that your level of understanding and awareness has developed further, and you were less equipped in the past to identify signs of abuse.

Boundaries of confidentiality

All information that you receive about children and their families, verbal or written, is confidential. You have been trusted to receive it and, as part of your professional role, you must respond to that trust. To break confidence may put a child at further risk. It could have an impact on an investigation, and it could place a slur on a person's character if the concern is subsequently unfounded. However, there is sometimes a fine line between maintaining confidentiality and failing to share vital information. In terms of safeguarding children, it is permissible to disclose confidential information if:

- the parent or child gives consent for information to be disclosed
- disclosure can also be made without consent if legislation requires it.

Professional Practice

- The primary duty of all those working with children is to always put the child's best interests first and to share information according to local policies and protocols.
- Confidentiality is always important, but within child protection it is essential.
- You should never discuss a parent with other parents.
- You should work with facts, not with gossip.
- Information should only be shared on a 'need to know' basis.

Unconditional acceptance for the child

Link Refer back to page 90.

The impact of abuse on families

Families are not always aware of what has been happening to a child even if the perpetrator lives within the same house. A significant percentage of abuse is carried out by close relatives or persons known to the child and the family. In some families, violence may be commonplace and adults dealing with their own suffering may not identify the suffering of their children, or may not have the physical or emotional energy to deal with it if they have.

As an early years worker, you will be dealing with the parents on a daily basis. If they are the subject of an enquiry instigated by the setting, you may have to face anger and hostility. If they had been unaware of the abuse and are in no way responsible, they are likely to feel distressed, guilty and saddened. They may wish to talk to staff, who know their child well, and require a greater level of feedback on their child's welfare and progress.

Parents who abuse are often in need of help and support themselves. This can be a difficult area to cope with. It is important that staff continue to interact with them positively, offering opportunities to talk where appropriate and being seen to be good role models with children.

case study 3.2 **Isobel**

Isobel, who has mild learning difficulties, is the single mother of James and was supported by staff at her local family centre in learning to look after James in his early weeks. They showed her how to prepare suitable foods for him when he was ready for solids and offered advice on developing a routine for him. Isobel has attended the family centre only occasionally since then as she often goes to stay with her mother, some distance away. In conversation with Isobel when she arrived today, it has become clear that she is very proud of the way she has managed to care for James, but you can see that she has not really moved James on very far in his development. James is now 11 months old and is still only being fed puréed foods, mostly from jars, with bottles of formula throughout the day. His playthings are still mostly rattles and soft toys, and he is a very passive baby, showing no real interest in moving. There does not seem to be any cause for concern regarding James's weight. As Isobel has been away a great deal, she has not had recent contact with her health visitor.

activity

1 What support and advice do you think Isobel needs first for James?
2 How could you help her develop more stimulating play for James?
3 What should be most important regarding your approach to Isobel?
4 What concern might there be for James' future if his mother did not have support offered to her?

Appropriate reporting procedures

Investigations into cases of abuse or suspected abuse, or where there is a concern that a child may be at risk, are carried out following a referral. Referrals can be made to the police, social services departments or to the NSPCC. Anyone can make a referral, and the impetus to do so may result from disclosure by a child to the individual making the referral, or the child's representative (early years settings and schools have a designated person who takes on this responsibility), or may result from the concern of an individual or a group of people represented by the individual. Referrals are also made by neighbours, family members and concerned members of the public. It is always preferred if individuals identify themselves when making a referral, but **referral procedures** allow for anonymous referrals to be accepted and investigated as necessary.

It is a misconception that following a referral the 'authority' goes immediately to the family and takes away the child. This only happens on rare occasions when there has been a clear case of abuse and the child faces imminent risk of further abuse. Most cases go through a set procedure to establish if the concern is justified, to explore the concerns raised with all those who are in contact with the child, or who might have relevant information, and to establish the level of risk to the child. A situation in which immediate action may be needed to remove the child to safety would be if physical violence is likely to increase following the referral being brought to the family's notice. If a child is not allowed to leave voluntarily, an Emergency Protection Order can be obtained.

Procedures

Although some procedures may vary slightly, all will be founded on the principles laid down by the Local Child Safeguarding Board and they are informed by *Every Child Matters* and *What to Do If You're Worried a Child Is Being Abused*. You must ensure that you are wholly familiar with the policy in your setting and that you know the appropriate lines of communication and reporting.

activity

3.8

Using your college resource centre, find the *What to Do If You're Worried a Child Is Being Abused* document online and print the flow charts that outline actions to be taken. Contact the appropriate address to request your own copy.

Communicating verbally or in writing

It is important that any signs of possible abuse are clearly noted in a signed and dated statement that outlines what has been noticed. This needs to be done within 24 hours of the observation being made. Hobart and Frankel (2005) advise that it may be good practice to discretely ask a senior colleague to confirm your findings before the report is made to the manager or designated person for child protection.

Sequence of events leading to registration on the Child Protection Register

The **Child Protection Register** is a list of children considered to be 'at risk' that is kept by the local authority.

Figure 3.6

The investigation procedure in cases of suspected child abuse

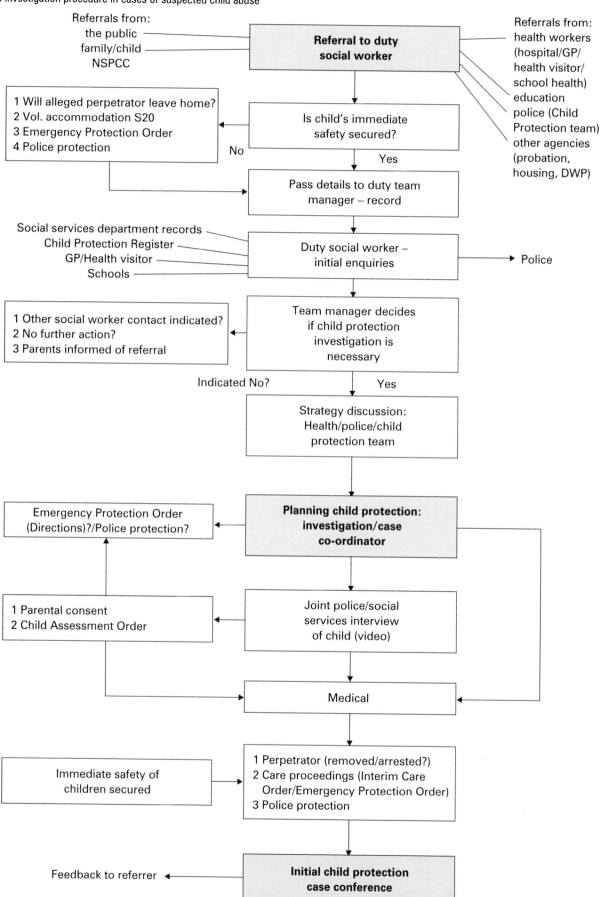

Referrals from:
the public
family/child
NSPCC

**Referral to duty
social worker**

Referrals from:
health workers
(hospital/GP/
health visitor/
school health)
education
police (Child
Protection team)
other agencies
(probation,
housing, DWP)

1 Will alleged perpetrator leave home?
2 Vol. accommodation S20
3 Emergency Protection Order
4 Police protection

Is child's immediate
safety secured?

No   Yes

Pass details to duty team
manager – record

Social services department records
Child Protection Register
GP/Health visitor
Schools

Duty social worker –
initial enquiries

Police

1 Other social worker contact indicated?
2 No further action?
3 Parents informed of referral

Team manager decides
if child protection
investigation is
necessary

Indicated No?   Yes

Strategy discussion:
Health/police/child
protection team

Emergency Protection Order
(Directions)?/Police protection?

**Planning child protection:
investigation/case
co-ordinator**

1 Parental consent
2 Child Assessment Order

Joint police/social
services interview
of child (video)

Medical

Immediate safety of
children secured

1 Perpetrator (removed/arrested?)
2 Care proceedings (Interim Care
Order/Emergency Protection Order)
3 Police protection

Feedback to referrer

**Initial child protection
case conference**

Think about how you might feel if you had concerns about a child. What range of emotions would you expect to feel regarding:

1   the child who you are concerned about?
2   the perpetrator of any abuse?
3   the prospect of making a referral?

Professional Practice

■ If, during your placement experience, you are concerned about a child for any reason, you should talk to your placement supervisor or, if you do not yet feel comfortable doing this, talk to your college tutor. Either will help you to explore your concerns further and take action appropriately.

■ It is never appropriate simply to talk to your friends about a concern, as confidentiality is of utmost importance in all cases, and information about any suspected case of abuse should only be discussed on a 'need to know' basis.

Child Protection Register

In the mid-1970s, Child Protection Registers were first set up within each local authority. A child's name is put on the register if there is concern about the safety of that child or their family. An unborn baby can be placed on the register, if there is a known abuser in the family.

The register contains relevant information (see below) about the child, so that the child's situation can be monitored and appropriate action taken when necessary. The child's case and inclusion on the register is reviewed regularly.

A senior professional with a concern about a child can ask for a check to be made of the register for the name of that particular child or the family. These registers are now computerised and held centrally, enabling checking to be done quickly. The information is not readily given out, and professionals wishing to consult the registers have their details and authority to apply to the register checked before information is released to them.

Deregistration can take place when a child's case is reviewed, if it is thought appropriate. Deregistration can occur if:

■ the original points that led to registration no longer apply

■ the child reaches the age of majority (18) and is no longer termed a 'child'

■ the child dies.

Contents of a register

The information held on a Child Protection Register includes:

■ the child's name (and any other names the child is known by)

■ the child's address, gender, date of birth, culture and any known religion

■ the name and contact details of the child's GP

■ the name and details of the main carer

■ details of any school or other setting the child is known to attend

■ if applicable, the name and details of any person who has parental responsibility for the child (if different from above)

■ outline details of any court orders

■ an outline of the alleged or confirmed abuse that has previously occurred

■ the date the child was placed on the register

■ the name and details of the professional responsible for the child's case (the child's key worker)

■ the date of the proposed review of the child's situation.

Progress Check

1   Briefly describe the four main models of abuse.
2   Name the main types of family structure.
3   What is meant by the 'changing face of the family'?
4   Why is it important to consider cultural practice in child protection?
5   How would you explain the difference between the short-term and long-term effects of abuse?
6   Who can apply for a Child Assessment Order?
7   How long can police protection last initially?
8   What is an Emergency Protection Order?
9   When might a Recovery Order be implemented?
10   What is the difference between a Supervision Order and a Care Order?
11   What is a Child Protection Register?
12   When might deregistration take place?

Security of records

In early years settings, clear record-keeping and report-writing help to provide all the details that may be asked of the setting in the event of an enquiry. Each setting should have an accident book, where all accidents and incidents are recorded, witnessed and signed by at least two members of staff. Many settings use 'body maps' to record marks and bruises that have been identified and date them. This can form a useful piece of supportive evidence in a case involving physical abuse. It is important that staff are able to identify signs and symptoms of abuse on different skin tones.

Figure 3.7

A bodymap

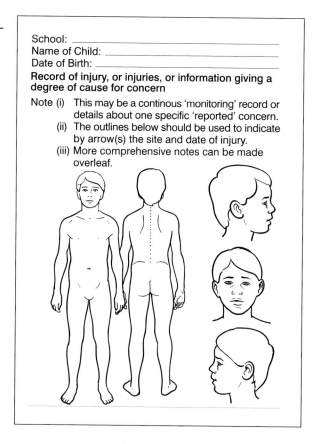

School: _____
Name of Child: _____
Date of Birth: _____
Record of injury, or injuries, or information giving a degree of cause for concern

Note (i)   This may be a continous 'monitoring' record or details about one specific 'reported' concern.
   (ii)   The outlines below should be used to indicate by arrow(s) the site and date of injury.
   (iii)   More comprehensive notes can be made overleaf.

case study

Kieron

3.3

Kieron arrives at nursery one morning with a bruise developing above his left eyebrow. Several staff members notice it, but no one mentions it to Kieron or his mother. At home time, Kieron's mother asks what has happened to Kieron for him to get such a nasty bruise. Staff are astounded at this, and protest that he arrived with it in the morning. His mother denies this emphatically and is angry with the staff, raising her voice and shouting her concerns about the quality of care and levels of safety in the nursery.

activity

1   How could this situation have been avoided?
2   What should happen now?
3   How differently might staff view Kieron's mother and her relationship with Kieron from now on?

Building up good relationships with parents is important in order to provide the best care possible for the child. If the setting has a policy on child protection which states what will happen in the event of any concerns, this lets parents know that you are making the welfare of their child of paramount importance, as set down by the Children Act 1989. This policy could include a clause stating that any child arriving in the setting with an injury will have it noted in the accident/incident book. This will offer added safety for the child and added safety for the staff, avoiding the situation described in the case study above.

Each setting should have a child protection procedure which follows the guidelines provided by the local authority.

activity

3.10

1   Ask to see a copy of the child protection guidelines and reporting procedures from both your local authority and from your work placement or place of employment.
2   If the guidelines are not clear, ask for an explanation.
3   Try explaining the guidelines and procedure to another person. If you can explain them clearly, it is likely that you understand them.

For further coverage of reporting procedures in child protection cases, it would be useful to refer to *Good Practice in Child Protection* by Hobart and Frankel (2005).

Role of the key worker

Security can be helped by consistency of staffing. A key-worker system where a staff member has responsibility for a set group of children will ensure that there is always one specific person keeping records and making observations on each child, and this close relationship will enhance that person's ability to pick up any changes in the child's behaviour or problems with their development. The key worker will also be more likely to build up a good relationship with the child's parents and be more likely to feel able to ask if there is anything troubling the child or to raise a concern with them. This will be less easy if no relationship has been established.

Key workers are also ideally placed to act as advocates for vulnerable children and their parents and, in terms of assessing children in need, they are also usually well informed of the family's circumstances and needs. More importantly, the key worker can represent a stable figure in the child's life during a period of stress, offering consistency of care and unconditional support. This can be of great value to a child when inconsistency of parental care can result in feelings of uncertainty, self-blame and anxiety.

activity

3.11

What might be the outcome for a troubled child where there is no consistency of care? Explore this both from the angle of the setting, and from the child's point of view.

Supporting children and families

Working in partnership with parents is an integral part of early years practice, and this holds true more than ever when issues of safeguarding children arise. The need to work closely with parents is established by:

- the Children Act 1989
- Working Together to Safeguard Children 1999
- the Framework for the Assessment of Children in Need and their Families 2000.

It is possible for early years workers to contribute to the safeguarding of children from abuse by enabling vulnerable parents to take adequate care of their children and by teaching and role modelling positive parenting skills. The central aim of working with parents of abused children is to ensure and promote the welfare of the child in need, and this is not always an easy process. Some parents will not be amenable to advice and support and may resent professional assessment of their child care and parenting abilities. However, this should not be allowed to compromise the care of the child and every effort should be made to work with parents in this situation, however difficult that might be.

Professional Practice

- Remember that the best interests and safety of the child must come first.

A term that is used from time to time is '**good-enough parenting**'. Few people would describe themselves, or be described by others, as 'perfect' parents, nor is perfection necessary for a positive parent–child relationship to develop, or for children to feel cared for and loved. Overall, it is consistency of care and being valued and supported by parents that counts, providing that it is 'good enough'.

---

activity
3.12

1. The term 'good-enough parenting' does not have a specific definition.
   a) What does the term mean to you?
   b) In a small group, discuss what factors you consider would be 'good-enough' aspects of parenting and what would not.
   c) Consider what you are basing your ideas on.
   d) How well did you agree within your group?
   e) Discuss the differences in your ideas and what may have influenced them.
2. Sometimes, parents need support to help them parent their children. Look at the spidergram below. In what ways do you think each form of support would help parents develop better parenting skills?

Providing feedback to parents about their parenting

Involving parents in the early years setting

Helping parents to relate to their children positively

Helping parents adapt as their child develops

Supporting children and parents

Helping parents to modify their children's behaviour

Offering ideas to parents for developing play and stimulation for their child

Offering general parenting skills training

Helping parents develop practical caring skills

Keeping parents informed about childcare and their child's development

activity

continued

As you consider each point, think:
a) about the impact on the child or children
b) how the parent might feel about themselves as a parent
c) how they might feel about themselves as a person
d) how early years settings can contribute.

Communication

Communication is an important aspect of supporting both children and their families. Good parent–staff relationships create a level of trust and respect that promotes honesty and openness and allows concerns to be raised more easily. An important aspect of this communication is to share information about the setting's child protection procedures with parents, so that in the event of an issue arising, it can be dealt with effectively.

Body language can also be part of an individual's personality.

Link   Refer back to Unit 2, pages 35 and 39, to refresh your understanding of communication and the barriers that can exist.

Professional Practice

- In cases of child abuse, you need to be aware that (non-abusing) parents can sometimes be embarrassed to talk to early years staff if they feel they have let their child down by not protecting them.
- You will at times need to continue to communicate with a known or suspected abuser. This will not always be easy. Personal feelings must never be allowed to affect your professionalism.
- You can help parents by being a good role model in how you interact with children.
- Keeping communication open between staff and parents is an important part of supporting both the child and their family.

Sources of advice and support

Help and advice can be given to parents by:

- known professionals, for example day-care providers, teachers, playgroup staff
- other professionals, for example health visitors, social workers, family support workers
- family members
- friends.

activity

3.13   What examples can you give of sources of help and advice for parents in your area?

The level of support available to parents can make a huge difference, tipping the balance between 'good-enough' parenting and the need for intervention. Many of the same agencies are able to offer support informally as well as through case involvement. An example of how these agencies are now working collaboratively to support children and parents is through Sure Start schemes.

Sure Start and Sure Start Programmes

Government funding has been provided to focus on areas that have been identified as having an unacceptable level of poverty and social deprivation. The initiative is called Sure Start. The Sure Start ethos is to work with local communities to improve and increase the range of support and provision for young children (under three) and their families. Information on projects incorporating Sure Start in your area is available from the local authority Family Information Service, which was set up by the Early Years Development and Childcare Partnership (EYDCP). Sure Start programmes and policies apply to England only as responsibility for early care and education in Scotland, Northern Ireland and Wales rests with the separate devolved administrations.

- Sure Start has created 45,000 affordable day-care places for children under 5 in the most deprived areas of Britain.
- Neighbourhood nursery projects have been developed in 142 local authorities in the 20% of the most deprived electoral wards in England.
- There are now 107 designated Early Excellence Centres which offer high quality integrated services from education, health and social services.
- The government is committed to providing a Sure Start Children's Centre in every neighbourhood by 2010 as part of its 10-year childcare strategy.

Family centres

A family centre is usually staffed by a multi-disciplinary team and offers a range of support. Centres can be used as access points for parents who have restricted or supervised access visits to their children. Many family centres receive funding through the Sure Start initiative. Some family centres run separate support sessions for fathers, with life skills, parenting skills, health, education and counselling being available to all family members. Families are mostly referred by health professionals, and there are strong links with the family support workers who are part of the social services children and families team.

Many family centres have now been amalgamated into Sure Start Children's centres or neighbourhood nurseries.

Encouraging the development of parenting skills

Early years workers can also support parents by trying to understand some of the problems that they face and initiate evidence-based strategies to develop their parenting. These may cover:

- developing a positive and realistic relationship with their children
- developing practical skills of child care and positive parenting
- sharing information about children's behaviour and development
- helping parents to enjoy playing with their children and to support their children's learning.

Positive relationships with children and practical skills

There is some evidence to suggest that parenting programmes based on the principles of 'positive parenting' and anger management have some success in helping parents to relate more positively. Staff may find it helpful to role model positive attitudes and ensure that parents have access to any supportive services and benefits they may need. Some parents may need more practical support as they may not possess the skills and knowledge needed to care for children effectively. Access to Basic Skills sessions may be offered, as well as the opportunity to learn more about child development and care.

Sharing information about children's behaviour and care

Parents may find it intimidating to have their care questioned by what they regard as 'authority' and it may take some time to gain their trust. It can be useful to discuss how children's behaviour is affected by tension or stress in the family, or to how to manage everyday behaviour problems. Parents in need of support often find that they harbour unrealistic expectations of children's development and behaviour, or that they do not know how to offer appropriate care. Working with them to increase their knowledge of nutrition and practical caring skills needs to be handled sensitively, and role modelling can be valuable. Supporting parents by helping them to respond positively to the changing demands of their developing child, or react with equanimity to a child's challenging behaviour, is an inherent part of working with children in need and their families. More specialist or intensive support may be needed for some parents whose tolerance levels are low or whose idea of appropriate discipline is skewed.

Helping parents to enjoy play and learning with their children

Some parents may not have had positive experiences of childhood themselves and may have little knowledge of how to play with their children or have fun. They may not have the income to support a wide range of play and learning activities, but they can be directed to resources such as toy libraries and Books for Babies schemes. Practical art and craft sessions may also be of use, as may 'coaching' in how to play and have fun.

Acknowledging cultural and social variations

Parenting support should not be undertaken without due regard to social and cultural variations. Patterns of behaviour and discipline will inevitably vary from family to family and some children may be confused when they experience different approaches in settings other than home. Staff need to be aware of the different cultural and child-rearing practices of the families they care for and use supportive services as needed. These may include the use of advocates, translators and interpreters.

Look back at Unit 2, page 64, for information on translators, interpreters and advocates.

Support for staff

Dealing with the feelings that arise when children are abused is never easy as it is often difficult to remain distanced from the experience. It is common to feel a wide range of emotions, ranging from anger and revulsion to sadness and disbelief, but objectivity is an essential component of a professional response. However, that is not to say that other feelings should be ignored or suppressed, merely that they should not hinder acting in the child's best interests.

Staff who are involved in the safeguarding of children may find it of great benefit to have regular supervision with a senior and experienced staff member, in order to maintain a professional response and discuss reactions and feelings. In some cases, referral to professional counselling services may be needed. Confidence in dealing with such situations and the feelings they engender will also be helped by professional development activities linked to safeguarding children and supporting parents.

Strategies and methods for supporting children and their families

Teaching children self-protection

Children can be taught **self-protection strategies**: the most important skill that we can teach children regarding their personal safety is to speak out when they need to. Activities which encourage children to take a lead, to demonstrate, illustrate or describe something will help them grow in confidence. Giving praise for effort rather than just for achievement will boost children's self-esteem, and giving them small responsibilities will make them feel valued and worthwhile as individuals.

Body awareness

Children need to learn that their bodies belong to them and that no one has the right to touch their body if they do not want them to. They need to know that this applies to all adults, but with exceptions for medical treatment, such as a doctor listening with a stethoscope or a nurse taking a blood sample or giving an injection. To a child, any of these procedures may be unwelcome.

Confidence building

Another aspect of learning self-protection is helping children to build their confidence and explore the issue of secrets with them. Parents and early years staff need to encourage children to be open and honest and to learn to say 'no' when they feel they want to, or their space is being intruded upon. Michele Elliott of the organisation Kidscape says that adults spend a great deal of time teaching children to obey adults, when really there is a need to encourage them to say 'no' when they are unhappy or uncomfortable with anything they are asked to do.

---

activity

3.14

Read the following statements that might be made to a young child and consider the questions that follow:

- You must always do what an adult tells you.
- Always go where an adult tells you to go.
- Never disobey an adult.
- If you get lost, ask an adult to help you.
- It is rude not to speak to someone, when they have spoken to you.

1 What problems could arise from each of the statements?
2 What alternative instructions to those given above would you give to young children?

Children can learn that the areas of their body covered by their bathing suit are private to them and should not be touched by anyone else. It would be inappropriate to state simply that these are areas that 'should not be touched' as this implies that the child also should refrain from the natural exploration of their own body.

Figure 3.8

Everywhere under your bathing suit is private

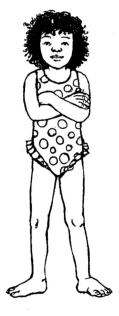

Secrets

Games can be played and activities developed to explore situations and problems that might be faced by children and to build children's self-esteem: for example, an activity about 'secrets'. Activities can be introduced within the general planning of the setting.

Secrets should be pleasurable and exciting, linked to birthdays, festivals and surprises, but for some children secrets mean abuse, with the abuser telling them, 'This is our little secret' or 'Make sure you don't tell anyone about this, because …'. You need to be able to help children understand the difference and to know when they should tell their parents about a secret they have been asked to keep.

---

activity

3.15

1 How could you introduce the concept of safe and unsafe secrets to a child?
2 What examples of safe and unsafe secrets would you give them?

The television characters Cosmo and Dibs are featured in a useful video addressing safety issues, including safe and unsafe secrets.

Treatment Strategies for Abused Children by Karp and Butler (1996), which was originally produced as a therapeutic aid for children who have been abused, includes a range of activities that can be used to help define boundaries for young children and to establish where they feel safe, for example:

- The Private Triangle
- Colour in the Personal Space
- People I Trust – the child draws a picture of someone they trust.

• Connect the dots and colour your picture.

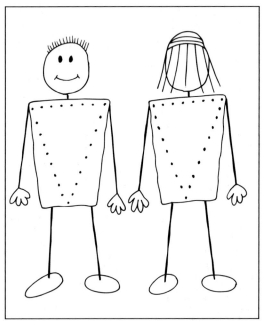

Figure 3.9

The private triangle – dot to dot

• Colour in the personal space.

Figure 3.10

Colour in the Personal Space

• Cut out the triangle and paste it on the picture, showing where the private triangle should go.

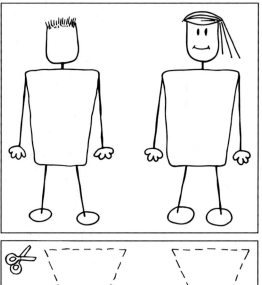

Figure 3.11

The private triangle – cut and paste

Empowering children

Working with abused and potentially vulnerable children can call on all of an early years worker's skills and knowledge, but one of the key aims should be to foster a sense of resilience and empowerment. Past experiences may have taught a child that adults are not to be trusted, or they may have made the child feel guilty or ashamed. All children have the right to enjoy their childhood without fear of harm and should be encouraged to be aware of their rights and be taught ways in which they can be treated with respect. This can be done by:

- teaching all children assertiveness skills and how to say 'no'
- encouraging their participation in decisions about their care and ensuring that the child's voice is heard
- helping them to identify what is acceptable behaviour and what behaviours are unwanted
- building trusting relationships with adults
- providing them with skills and strategies for personal safety.

Personal safety

Teaching children about personal safety can be one way of empowering them as long as they do not feel that they alone are responsible for keeping themselves safe. There are many areas of personal safety that are relevant for young children and these can be taught through age and developmentally appropriate activities. The children's organisation Kidscape provides excellent downloadable resources and ideas on its website. It is important that children are provided with effective strategies that will enable them to know that help is available to them.

Figure 3.12

Personal safety

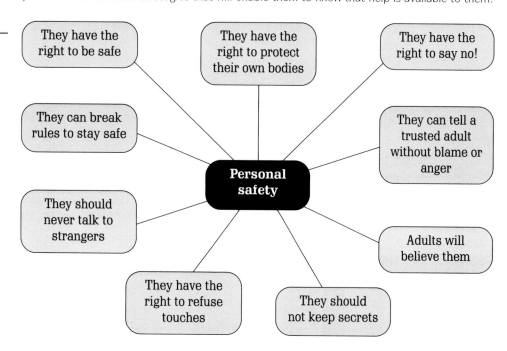

Paedophiles

The true definition of a **paedophile** is a person who is sexually attracted to children. However, the term is commonly used to describe adults who sexually abuse children. These abusers come from all walks of life and are often considered to be pillars of the community, holding posts of responsibility and trust and taking on roles that will bring them into regular contact with children, such as scout group leaders, sports coaches, youth workers and teachers.

Paedophiles spend a great deal of time and effort setting the scene for their abuse, often building up relationships with a child's parent or parents, increasing their level of trust in them. Children of single mothers can be particularly vulnerable as the mother may be pleased to encourage a male role model for her children, particularly if they do not see their father. This process is known as 'grooming'.

The Abel Study: 232 'First Time' Abusers

The 232 abusers who were involved in a research study by Gene Abel were 'first time' abusers who had no previous convictions for child sexual abuse. After serving their sentences, they were given immunity from further prosecutions and asked to relate the true number of children they had abused before they were caught and convicted.

This was done by asking them at what age they began abusing and approximately how many children they had abused per week (or month or year), so it is necessarily an estimate. On average:

- each abuser attempted 238 offences
- each abuser completed 166 offences
- each abuser molested 75 children.

If you add up the total number of offences and attempts by these 232 abusers, they:

- attempted 55,216 offences
- completed 39,512 offences
- molested 17,400 children.

This means that a small group of compulsive child abusers can create a huge number of victims and that the victims were either silent about what happened or were not believed if they told (Elliott, 1992).

As the paedophile gains the trust of the family, closer physical contact develops, gradually moving towards sexual contact or involvement in pornography. Intimidation, bribes and threats often follow, in return for promises that the activity is kept secret.

Professional Practice

- If an individual person begins to be closely involved with a child or family other than their own it may be appropriate to monitor the situation closely.
- Paedophiles are devious people and many operate for many years before being caught.

remember

Paedophiles are skilful in identifying vulnerable children, such as a child who:
- is a loner
- lacks confidence
- is very trusting of adults
- craves love and attention.

Motivation + Opportunity = Abuse
- Paedophiles have the motivation to abuse.
- They seek opportunities to abuse the children they have contact with.
- Early years staff can play a part in building up a barrier to their opportunities.

Megan's Law

In the state of New Jersey in the USA, a young girl named Megan was sexually abused and killed. Following her death, a campaign was successfully carried out to change the law regarding sex offenders. Courts in many states in the USA now have to inform local communities when a convicted sex offender moves into their area.

Many people have called for a similar law to be passed in the UK, claiming that it will improve the safety of all children. Others argue that it infringes the human rights of the offenders and will cause social unrest in communities, with the risk of vigilante-style ousting of the offenders and the wrong identification of innocent people as abusers of children.

In a group, debate the arguments for and against introducing Megan's Law in the UK. How does Megan's Law fit into the thinking on confidentiality? Do you still feel the same way about the situation there? If your views have changed, in what way have they changed, and why?

Refer to Unit 2 and the activity on confidentiality, page 68.

Formulating a child protection policy

Each setting needs:

- a copy of the local authority guidelines
- a person specifically responsible for child protection
- setting guidelines for all staff regarding behaviour, responsibilities and recording procedures
- police screening of all staff
- whenever possible, police screening of students.

Local authority guidelines

Most local authorities will have similar guidelines that will all centre on their duty to safeguard and promote the welfare of children in need within their designated area. Most will be developing a multi-agency response to safeguarding children following the recommendations of the Laming Report that children's services should be co-ordinated. Guidelines will also closely follow the guidance given in *What to Do if You're Worried a Child is Being Abused*. All staff should be aware of the guidelines that apply in their area and the content of their setting's policy and lines of reporting.

Guidelines for staff behaviour

It is a sad fact that abusive behaviour against children can sometimes happen in the settings that are mandated to care for and protect them. To ensure that this does not happen, staff should behave in appropriate and sensitive ways that demonstrate integrity and an awareness of their moral and professional duty.

Professional Practice

- Do not shout at children or talk in an aggressive tone of voice.
- Do not threaten them with frightening stories of what will happen to them if they don't behave.
- Do not use humiliating punishments for unwanted behaviour.
- Do not express any discriminatory or oppressive statements or opinions.
- Do not leave children inappropriately supervised or neglect routine aspects of care.
- Do make sure that the language you use is appropriate, anti-discriminatory and anti-oppressive.
- Do make sure that children are treated with unconditional, positive regard.
- Do use touch and affection appropriately and respect children's rights to refuse inappropriate touch.
- Do make sure that all aspects of care are delivered in a sensitive and respectful manner without any element of coercion or force.
- Do talk to somebody if you think that you might need support with any aspect of your practice.

Record-keeping

Any records made of children should be kept safely and only the appropriate member of staff (key worker, senior staff, manager, etc.) and parents should be allowed access to them. It is not usually appropriate for children's records to be shared with students, although in some settings this may be the case. As a student, you must be aware of the responsibility of being privy to this information and should ensure that you in no way pass any of it on.

In the case of a child protection concern, the records should make it clear what has been directly observed by staff and what information has been gathered from other sources. Records of any kind must always be dated and signed, and then witnessed by another person, usually a senior member of staff.

Accurate records

It is very important to keep **accurate records**. On occasions, 'hearsay' evidence may be accepted and included in a child's case. If a child has disclosed to you, it is important that you include the full details in your report. This must include any questions that you asked, the details of the disclosure and any non-verbal communication relevant to the disclosure, such as indicating a body part by pointing.

The facts will be the most important aspect of your report. However, for the future when you have more experience, a comment such as the example below may be appropriate if you are raising a concern following your own observations.

'In my professional judgement, following 18 years as a senior nursery worker working with children aged 0–5 years, I consider the overt sexual nature of Joseph's interactions with both staff and children to be beyond what would be expected of children of his age, taking into consideration the natural curiosity and exploration of the age group.'

In this example, the opinion of an experienced professional early years worker is based on developmental norms and what has been observed.

> **remember**
>
> - The safety of the child is paramount.
> - Early years settings have a duty to report any concerns about a child.
> - If you have a concern, discuss it with your line manager or designated member of staff.

Professional Practice

- The worst situation that can arise is that your concern is unfounded. You may be embarrassed, but you will know the child is safe. If you had not raised a concern and a child suffered further, how might you feel then?
- It takes courage to raise a concern, but it is part of your professional role as an early years worker.

activity 3.17

1   Why do you think it is important to date any comments recorded?
2   Why is it important to sign any comments you make?
3   Why should you get a witness to sign too?
4   Who is this protecting?

Allegations against staff

A vetting procedure will usually have been carried out prior to members of staff joining the setting; however, this only indicates when someone has been investigated and convicted. It does not tell you for certain that the new staff member is a 'safe' person. As was seen in the Abel Study on page 104, most convicted abusers have been offending for a long time prior to their conviction, and many of these individuals will have applied for posts working with children. Any teacher who is convicted of inappropriate conduct with children, or who is no longer considered safe to work with children, is placed on a list known as List 99. This list can be accessed by employers.

To prevent false allegations being made against innocent members of staff, early years settings need to look at ways in which staff can safeguard themselves. These safeguards should form part of the setting's child protection policy, for example:

■ Avoid unnecessary intimate care.

■ Record all accidents or incidents and have them witnessed by another member of staff.

■ If a child acts or talks in a sexually inappropriate way to you, record it and tell your manager.

■ Avoid spending time alone with individual children.

activity 3.18

What other guidelines could be included? Consider this in light of:

1 working with pre-school-age children
2 working in a primary school
3 working in residential care
4 being part of an organised trip.

Professional Practice

■ The same rules of confidentiality apply to staff facing an allegation as apply to parents.

■ Information will be given on a 'need to know' basis.

■ Speculation and gossip is never helpful.

■ Discussion with, or reassurance of, parents will be the responsibility of the manager of the setting or a designated senior member of staff.

■ You should pass any enquiries on, rather than deal with them yourself.

■ You should ask for guidance and support if you are unsure about your role or what action should be taken.

Police screening of staff

It is obligatory that all staff working with children in statutory or voluntary settings, or who are on premises where children are cared for, are screened for their suitability to work with children. The Protection of Children Act 1999 enabled the Criminal Records Bureau (CRB) to release data on those people who are identified as being unsuitable to work with children. CRB checks for students are likely to be standard checks whilst qualified staff will be required to undergo enhanced checks. However, nannies working in private homes are not screened so carefully.

Visiting and access rights

Some parents or family members may only have access to their children in a supervised setting such as a family centre or other designated centre. This is to ensure the child's continuing safety and is often also to comply with a court order. It is important that staff are aware of any children to whom these circumstances apply in order that inappropriate access is not granted. Such situations need to be treated with sensitivity in order for the child to be able to see that parent or family member in positive circumstances.

Building security and access

Security of early years settings has had to be reassessed in recent years after a number of incidents involving unauthorised entry into buildings, on occasions resulting in children being harmed or even killed (for example, at Dunblane Primary School in March 1996, when 16 children and their teacher died). Security is increasingly being made a high priority by local authorities and private owners, with staff teams having to consider how easy it might be to gain access to the premises and redefining who is allowed access.

Asking for proof of identity from visitors, such as course tutors or health visitors, should now be mandatory, and children should only be handed over to known adults or others by prior instructions from the usual parent collecting them. Most pre-school settings allow parents to stay for a short while to settle their child, but some degree of control of the numbers of visitors needs to be in place to ensure that setting staff can maintain a safe level of supervision at all times.

Visitors should never be allowed to take children anywhere on their own, and should not be involved in intimate care routines. Any child reluctant to work with a visitor should not have to do so, and staff need to monitor the effect that visitors have on the children in their care. If it is found that visitors disrupt the session to unacceptable levels or that children appear insecure, the frequency and level of involvement of visitors in the setting may need to be reassessed.

As an early years student, you too are a visitor, particularly in the early weeks of your placement. You will need to build up a rapport with the children and will not be involved in intimate care routines without supervision.

Outer doors should ideally be kept locked at all times, but if they need to be accessible by parents (for example, if a staff member leaving the room to answer the door would be the greater risk), they should be alarmed to indicate an arrival, and staff should ensure that they know who has arrived and where they have gone to. Any visitors who are staying for a specific length of time should be signed in and out of the setting and issued with a visitor badge, to be handed in as they leave.

A clear policy should be developed about not accepting visitors 'off the street'. All prospective visitors should make an appointment in advance, and anyone interested in the welfare and safety of children will not have a problem with this. Unexpected visitors can cause problems in maintaining staff:child ratios and can cause disruption to the planned structure of the session. They should be politely asked to return at a mutually convenient time unless the manager is supernumerary to numbers and it is practicable for the manager to accommodate unexpected visitors at that time.

case study 3.4   Sarah

Sarah is a BTEC National student, currently on placement at Greenwood Primary School. It is mostly an open-plan site, with the classrooms along three sides of a square and side areas for creativity, music and PE along the fourth. Sarah was preparing materials for a creative activity in one of the side areas when she was aware of a man walking slowly along the outside wall, looking through the windows. She watched him for a few minutes, but, as he did not seem to be making any attempt to get into the building, she did not do anything about it.

activity

1   What would you have done if you had been Sarah?
2   What might this tell you about the security of the school building?
3   What would you do if you were trying to get into a school on the first day of your placement, but were unable to find an open entrance?

It is always a good idea to report any suspicious individuals or occurrences and it is better to be proved wrong than to miss an opportunity to keep a child safe. In hindsight, the school perimeter should have been securely enclosed to deter intruders and to ensure that children were not able to be observed by inappropriate persons. Schools usually have a security code to enable access to entrances and, in the case of a student arriving but unable to gain entry, a prior phone call could have ensured that a member of staff was there to greet the student.

Carrying out a safety audit of the setting

Early years staff should, from time to time, reassess the safety of the setting, asking themselves:

■ What possibilities for abuse exist within the setting?

■ What risks can be identified and how can they be reduced?

■ How can the children be helped to lower the risk?

■ What can the staff do?

■ What external factors might have an impact on safety from abuse?

Support for children who disclose

Refer back to page 89 for guidance on how to respond to disclosure of abuse.

Children who have disclosed abuse are often in need of specialist support, as well as the continued support of early years workers who care for them. This may be in the form of supporting them through the process of giving evidence in court; acting as an advocate for a child in care proceedings; or supporting a child on supervised access visits. Children may be referred to counselling services or psychologists if needed, or they may self-refer to services such as Childline (now supported by the NSPCC).

Alleviating the effects of abuse

Children who have experienced abuse or trauma need opportunities to express themselves when they are ready to do so. Usually their self-esteem is low and the consequent feelings of worthlessness and lack of value can lead to a downward spiral if help and support is not available to them. Professional counselling is offered to some children, and early years staff can support children by giving them time, space and praise. Another approach to helping children is **play therapy**.

Play therapy

Play therapy shows children that they are valued and helps them to value themselves as they move through the healing process. Children have always re-enacted familiar situations through their play, exploring and making sense of roles and events so, on this basis, providing therapy through play makes good sense. The purpose of therapy following abuse is to help children move on from being victims to become survivors. It needs to be a non-threatening experience for the child, be relevant to their age and stage of development and be carried out by people who understand what they are doing and the limitations of the therapy that they are providing. It is not something that untrained individuals should attempt to involve themselves in, although early years settings are an excellent source of creative opportunities for children who can express themselves through paint, clay, role play, and so on.

The timing of structured play therapy sessions needs to be carefully considered. Sometimes, a child will have a greater need that must be fulfilled before successful therapy can begin. This might include establishing a more settled home life or setting up involvement with the child's family alongside the play therapy. Play therapists need to build up a trusting relationship with a child, and time for this will be incorporated into any programme that is devised. Trust is all important in helping children relax, feel safe and understand that they are able to express themselves in safety. Most often, sessions with a play therapist take place weekly for an hour at a time. Children are (within safety limits) able to direct the play, deciding what they will do and how they will go about it. Therapy sessions are the child's own special time and the therapist, while being present throughout, is often subsidiary to the play, remaining alert to what is happening and ready to respond where it is felt to be appropriate.

A useful definition of play therapy was drawn up by the British Association of Play Therapists:

> [Play therapy is] the dynamic process between child and therapist, in which the child explores, at their own pace and with their own agenda, those issues past and current, conscious and unconscious, that are affecting the child's life in the present. The child's inner resources are enabled by the therapeutic alliance to bring about growth and change. Play therapy is child-centred, in which play is the primary medium and speech the secondary medium.

> (*Association of Play Therapists Newsletter*, 1995)

This definition encompasses the main focus of play therapy, in that it is largely a non-verbal experience. Play is the most natural way in which children express themselves. Babies make sense of their world exploring through play, and a similar process occurs for traumatised children. Play therapy gives them the opportunity to express and make sense of what they have experienced, supported by the experience and understanding of a specialist adult.

Typical resources provided by play therapists

Some therapists will work from a specially set out room and will ensure that aspects of the room remain constant for the child to give added security. Others work peripatetically and may find themselves having to use a range of suitable (and barely suitable) places. Many of these therapists will establish a safe area for the child by using a rug or mat to define a special space, endeavouring to give some consistency to the sessions.

Puppets form an important part of most therapists' resources. They usually include puppets that represent dominant and passive individuals, puppets who might represent power, and also puppets of animals. These give opportunities for strength and power to be demonstrated (and overthrown) and to represent both victims and survivors. Animal puppets may offer a less personalised way for some children to symbolise their lives and experiences.

Dolls of different sizes, cultures, genders, and states of dress are also common, with or without dolls' houses and vehicles. These offer scope for children to illustrate their family members and the other significant adults in their lives within their play. Many children will have had a transient lifestyle and experienced multiple homes, therefore a considerable number of 'people' will allow for greater exploration for these children.

Monsters, bizarre creatures, snakes and worms are common items, allowing children to explore and deal with 'nasty', 'wicked' and 'evil' individuals.

Creative materials such as drawing, painting, collage, face painting and clay offer children the chance to immerse themselves in their chosen medium, and communicate some of their feelings, and sand play and water play are always therapeutic media through which children everywhere gain pleasure and express themselves. The trickling sensation of sand can be a very calming experience.

The following two titles give an interesting and accessible introduction to play therapy, offering examples drawn from experience: *Play Therapy with Abused Children* by Cattanach (1992); and *Introduction to Therapeutic Play* by Carroll (1998).

For general accounts of the work of therapists the following books are wonderful examples: *Poppies on the Rubbish Heap: Sexual Abuse – The Child's Voice* by Bray (1991); and *Dibs: In Search of Self* by Axline (1964). These two books are, however, quite explicit in content and you should be aware that they can at times be quite distressing.

Progress Check

1   List ten examples of how you should respond if a child discloses abuse to you.

2   What impact can a disclosure of abuse have on a family?

3   What is the purpose of play therapy?

4   How would you describe a play therapy session?

5   Give examples of typical play therapy resources.

Alternative forms of care

Alternative forms of care are considered when, even with the full support available within the community, a decision eventually has to be made to remove a child from the direct care of their parents. This decision is not taken lightly and the child's age and situation is always assessed before they are placed in an alternative form of care. Some children are better placed as the youngest or only child within a family, while others will benefit from having other children around. Whenever possible, and appropriate, siblings are placed together.

There is a range of care alternatives for children, which can be either temporary or permanent, depending on circumstances.

- Temporary care, for example foster care, applies when a child needs emergency or short-term care, for example as a result of a Care Order or the ill health of the main carer.
- Permanent care, for example adoption, is needed if a child is orphaned, where there is no alternative option available, or where parental responsibility is permanently removed by law for any reason.

Foster care

Foster carers undergo considerable assessment and in most areas receive training through the local authority. They need to have a high degree of emotional stamina, as many children they care for will have suffered trauma through abuse.

Respite care

Respite care is offered to parents when they need regular breaks from their children in order to cope with their parenting requirements. The parents may be struggling to cope generally, or the family may be facing specifically difficult circumstances. Respite care is also offered to families who care for a child with extreme physical needs or very challenging behaviour.

Adoption

Adoption is the permanent handing over of all responsibility for a child to permanent replacement parents. Adoptions can be either closed or open.

- A closed adoption is a total breaking of ties between parent and child, although children can apply for information to trace their parents when they reach 18 years of age.
- An **open adoption** means that limited contact is kept between the child and the birth family. They may exchange letters and cards, and even meet on occasions, although this does not alter the permanency of the adoption. The birth parents have no responsibility for the child and are not entitled to any say in their upbringing.

Residential care homes

It is now very unusual for young children to be placed in residential care; they are usually placed with foster families. Residential care no longer consists of dormitory-style wings in large centres, but is more likely to group children together in small family-sized units.

Family support workers

Wherever possible, children are supported within their own homes. This can be with the support of a family worker. These workers may spend time in the family home at times that are proving difficult for the parents to manage. For example, they may be present at meal times to establish good eating habits, or at bedtime to help bring about an accepted regular bedtime routine. The support worker may also be involved with the child and/or the family in day-care settings or family centres.

Multi-agency working with respect to protecting all children

Co-operation with other professionals

remember

Physical contact is permissible when a child needs comforting, during intimate care routines and at times when physical restraint might be required (such as when a child is about to run into a road).

Working in collaboration with other agencies and sharing information has been recommended by most of the reports into child abuse fatalities. It was legitimised in *Working Together to Safeguard Children*, the Children Act 1989 and 2004, and *Every Child Matters*. It cannot be stressed too highly that inter-agency working and the effective sharing of information is vital to the work of safeguarding children. The Laming Report into the death of Victoria Climbié noted that there were 12 occasions when she could have been saved if information had been shared and acted on.

Information concerning the safety of children who may be at risk of harm must be shared with the appropriate agencies. This would include social services, education and early year's services, police, health services, and any other agencies involved.

Boundaries of confidentiality

Look back to page 90 to remind yourself of the boundaries of confidentiality

Initiating and sustaining contact

The procedures for initiating and sustaining contact with the other agencies involved in safeguarding children will, to some extent, be governed by local guidelines and policies. Referrals about a child at risk may be made by practitioners in schools or nurseries; health care professionals; parents; other members of the extended family; or neighbours. In early years settings, it is customary for the referral to be made through the named person for child protection or the manager and they will make the initial contact with Social Services.

Professional Practice

- Respect the contribution and role of other professionals.
- Act within professional boundaries.
- Undertake regular professional training and updating – preferably multi-disciplinary.
- Communicate clearly, effectively and in a timely manner with members of other agencies.
- Share information about children who are, or who may be at risk of harm according to agreed policies and protocols.

Range of professionals and community support networks

The professionals and agencies that may become involved in a child protection case are set out in the diagram below, followed by a summary of each.

Figure 3.13

Professionals and agencies providing support in the community

Teachers/early years staff

- A designated person with responsibility for child protection issues should be named in each setting.
- Concerns should be taken to the designated person who will notify social services.
- Staff are trained in child development and are able to monitor signs of change or regression.
- Training in recognising and responding to signs of abuse should be undertaken.

School nurse

- School nurses have close and regular contact with children.
- They are particularly involved with children with special needs.
- They are aware of child development and the signs of abuse.
- Some, but not all, are trained children's nurses.

Health visitor

- Health visitors have ongoing contact with families, particularly those with very young children.
- They are specialists in child development and one of their main concerns is with the welfare of children and monitoring of their development.
- Most early years settings have an established health visitor link.
- Health visitors will refer suspected cases of abuse to the police or social services.

GP/paediatrician

- Children may be presented with injuries or health concerns either at their local GP surgery or at the casualty department.
- Community paediatricians may identify causes for concern during screening programmes for young children.
- Referrals will be made to police or social services.

Police officers

- Police officers uphold the law.
- Referrals can be made directly to the police.
- They have a duty to protect children and to follow up any referrals or concern brought to their notice.
- Police officers have responsibility for the safe keeping of any evidence in cases which may end in a prosecution.
- The police have emergency powers to remove a child to a place of safety.

NSPCC (RSSPCC in Scotland)

- Both organisations have qualified social workers who have powers to investigate cases of abuse.
- Referrals can be made directly to the NSPCC and to the RSSPCC.
- They can apply to remove a child to a place of safety, or start care proceedings.
- Both organisations have family support workers who work with families both during and after cases have been investigated.

Social services child protection worker/key worker

- The social services social worker who takes on the case will be the key worker for the child or family.
- Staff can apply to remove a child to a place of safety or start care proceedings.

Coroner

- The coroner is an independent law official who is involved in all cases of violent or unexplained death.
- Many coroners are also medical practitioners.
- They investigate a death to establish its cause.
- They are not involved in the prosecution of any perpetrator of abuse.

Guardian ad litem

- A guardian ad litem is an independent person who is appointed by the court.
- He or she speaks on behalf of children, ensuring that their welfare remains paramount.
- Where the child is sufficiently able, the guardian ad litem will help the child to understand the proceedings.

remember
Children deserve respect at all times, and should not, for example, be sat upon a potty in full view of a multitude of other people or asked to undress in front of a crowd.

remember
Children should not be photographed in early years settings partially clothed. Any photographs that are taken must be shown to parents before being displayed. This is particularly important if any materials are likely to be published in local newspapers.

Progress Check

1 What is the United Nations Convention on the Rights of the Child?
2 What is meant by the term 'good-enough parenting'?
3 How does the Children Act 1989 define parental responsibility?
4 Who is involved in an Area Child Protection Committee?
5 What is the role of the ACPC?
6 What support is available for parents in the community?
7 How will giving feedback to parents on their parenting help them develop their parenting skills?
8 What alternative forms of care are there for children?

Professional Practice

- To ensure good working practice with children means ensuring that physical care is always appropriate. Ask yourself:
  - How much can children do for themselves when dressing?
  - How much can children do for themselves in the bathroom?
  - How much privacy should I be giving them?
  - Is it appropriate for the children to kiss me goodbye?
  - Is it appropriate for the child to be having cuddles?
  - Is it appropriate for the child to be sitting on my lap?
  - Is the contact I have with the children fulfilling their need, or mine?

- You will probably find that your answers will partly depend on the age of the child and their stage of development. It will also be determined by the environment in which you are working, and the role you have in the children's lives, as a nanny, nursery manager, key worker, teacher, nursery nurse or student on placement.

case study 3.5   Abigail

Abigail is three and has recently joined the local pre-school group. Little Monkeys Pre-school is situated in a large village on the outskirts of a country town. It has recently had a very successful fundraising event and wishes to advertise this in the local press. A member of staff contacted the local newspaper who sent along a photographer. All the children lined up and had their photo taken, and it was subsequently printed in the local free newspaper. Abigail's mother was very upset when she found out about this. She had recently moved to the area, having been relocated to a safe house supported by the Women's Refuge Organisation as she had left a violent relationship with Abigail's father. She is very worried that he might see the photograph and trace them, as the paper is also distributed in the area in which he lives.

activity

1 What should have been the procedure here?
2 Were the pre-school staff wrong, do you think?
3 Should Abigail have been missed out of the photograph?
4 How could this have been resolved satisfactorily?

remember

Child protection, whilst being a difficult and sensitive area of the early years profession, is very rewarding. If, through your knowledge, understanding, observation or support, you are able to help lessen the trauma for just one child by your words or actions, it will have been an important element of your professional career.

Progress Check

1　How can access to early years settings be monitored safely?

2　In what way can the key-worker system contribute to the safety and welfare of children?

3　What examples can you give of teaching children self-protection strategies?

4　What should we teach children about secrets?

5　Why is confidentiality important?

6　Explain the importance of clear records in early years settings.

7　What should you consider when involved with a child's physical care?

8　Why is it important to gain permission from parents before taking and displaying photographs?

9　What is a paedophile?

10　Why is it important to understand how paedophiles operate?

11　What is Megan's Law?

Learning in the Early Years

This unit covers the following objectives:

- Understand the major theories of how children develop and learn
- Explore the work of early years educators and their influence on current principles and practice
- Investigate curriculum frameworks for children from 0 to 8 years of age
- Identify and promote learning opportunities for young children.

There are many different types of pre-school provision available. Any setting which receives funding from the nursery education grant needs to provide evidence of a high standard of care and a planned environment in which appropriate learning can take place. An understanding of how children learn is a mandatory requirement for all professionals working in the early years field.

This unit will describe a range of theories on the development of learning and will look at the work of several important early years educators, examining how their theories influence current thinking and practice.

Why, how and when to introduce new learning to children is also discussed, together with influences on the types of activities that can be offered and how they are presented. Advice is offered on how to extend and identify appropriate opportunities for learning within activities, enabling differentiation of need within any group of children.

Theories of how children develop and learn

Early years education has seen many changes in recent years as the learning needs of young children have gained greater status. The earlier stages of a child's learning are now recognised as important in their own right, rather than simply as a springboard for learning in later years.

Across the world, children's experiences of early learning vary considerably, and the starting age of formal education differs quite significantly between countries. Until recently, in the UK, learning opportunities across the range of settings offered have also varied a great deal. Government input, both educational and financial, has tried to address some of the imbalance between settings by introducing a comparable learning experience for all children of similar ages.

Development and learning

As with general development, a child's rate of learning is influenced by a range of factors. Development can be described as a progression or expansion of past achievements, building on previously set foundations, for example walking before running or sitting before standing, whereas learning is the process of acquiring new knowledge or a skill through a certain set of circumstances, for example being able to roll a ball and then learning to play the ball game, boules.

Children's development and learning is most usefully seen as a continuum, along which they progress according to the influences and opportunities available to them. Each stage of development is a defined part of the overall human life-span. It should not be seen as merely a prelude to the rest of life. The term 'life-long learning' is commonly used to describe how we all continue to develop our knowledge, understanding and skills throughout our lives, both formally and informally.

Both development and learning are influenced by:

- health
- genetics
- environment
- support levels
- timing.

The importance of neuroscience and brain studies
Recent neuroscientific research has highlighted the importance for brain development in the early years of the quality of the young child's environment and experiences. Consistent and loving care from responsive adults appears to be of vital importance, as does a stimulating and supportive environment.

These research studies also support the concepts of critical or sensitive periods for brain development during which particular skills or functions are being refined. The ability of the brains of infants and children to 'wire' themselves depends on optimal prenatal and postnatal environments, as well as the amount of stress that the individual is exposed to. It has also been noted that engaging children in formal learning at too early an age can lead to a child's disengagement and shutting off from the experience.

It is important to remember that not all the current findings about the links between brain and neurology, and infant and child development have been scientifically proven; therefore, if reference is made to findings, care needs to be taken that they are from reputable research studies and are not just media 'hype'.

activity
4.1

Using your college resource centre, research information about early brain and neuroscience studies. Discuss your findings as a class and identify the factors that may be relevant prenatally and after birth. Discuss the importance of these studies for the organisation and delivery of early years services.

For a clear explanation of the importance of neuroscience and brain studies, read pages 71–3 in *Essential Early Years* by Dryden et al. (2005), or 'Research into brain development' in *How Children Learn* by Pound (2005).

Factors that may influence development and affect learning
Babies and children will not be able to learn effectively unless their basic needs are met and certain conditions are favourable. This will include a variety of factors within the individual child, the family, and the wider social environment.

Refer to Unit 7, page 332, for the factors that affect development.

There are certain basic physiological needs that must be met in order to ensure healthy growth, development and learning. This will entail:

- unconditional love and affection
- consistent and appropriate care
- balanced and healthy nutrition
- being kept safe but allowed to explore and learn to take responsibility

- appropriate warmth, shelter and clothing
- protection from ill health and infection.

Link

Refer to Unit 5, page 157, for a description of children's basic needs.

In order to learn, children also need:

- a stimulating environment that is rich in play and learning opportunities
- opportunities to take part in care routines and activities that are designed to stimulate development
- knowledgeable early years practitioners who are aware of evidence-based practice and the frameworks and curricula that support care and education
- encouragement and support to play and learn from parents and carers
- timely interventions that are developmentally and culturally sensitive.

Health

The health of a child has an impact on both development and learning: a child who is unwell, undernourished or who has a chronic health problem is likely to be at a disadvantage because of repeated health-care needs. A hungry child will lack the energy levels usually associated with young children. Chronic health needs include asthma, diabetes, sickle cell anaemia or severe eczema. To be fully able to learn, a child needs to be physically and mentally alert. Therefore, children who are distracted by discomfort or pain will be less able to assimilate learning at the rate of their peers and will move more slowly along the development continuum.

case study   **Stewart**

4.1

Stewart is five and has chronic asthma. He tends to need to sit quietly and use his inhaler several times during an average school day.

activity

1 How might this affect Stewart in the classroom?
2 How might he be affected in the playground?
3 What impact might this have on Stewart's learning overall?

Link

Refer to Unit 10 for information on child health and to page 439 for information on asthma.

Genetics

Biological factors, such as chromosomal make-up (or our DNA) and dominant and recessive genes, determine the physical characteristics of each individual and have some influence on our achievements and the choices that we each make. However, the line between nature and nurture becomes blurred when factors present at birth are influenced by social factors, for example the effects of **foetal alcohol syndrome** (FAS) or of maternal drug use. Both of these can give rise to malformations, impaired **cognitive development** and either hyperactivity (associated with FAS) or lethargy (associated with drug use), and so both will have an impact on learning.

At times, adverse circumstances, either social or familial, do not have a negative affect on development, and, in some cases, the adverse effects that present in the early years can be reversed later on in life with relevant support.

Figure 4.1

DNA

 Refer to Unit 7, page 284, for information about genetic effects on development and page 283 about foetal alcohol syndrome.

Environment and support

Most modern-day theorists take a nature-plus-nurture approach to learning, considering that the genetic start we each have (nature) is enhanced by experience (nurture). Most agree that the environment in which children are brought up and educated has an effect on the rate at which they develop and learn and how well they achieve their potential. Factors such as a stable home life, the interest of parents in their children, the encouragement, provision of resources, opportunities for new experiences and emphasis on raising self-esteem are all seen as important.

Timing

Offering children opportunities at appropriate times ensures the best learning experiences. Some theorists in the past believed that children have 'critical' or 'sensitive' times for learning and that learning can be missed altogether if it does not occur at a certain point in a child's life. Modern theorists do not generally agree with this, but consider that most children are able to catch up on lost time once they have learned a new skill or been introduced to a new experience. However, these children may lack confidence and self-esteem owing to being slightly 'behind' their peers. Children who have been pushed on too fast at too early an age (**hot-housing**) are at risk of losing interest in learning (**burn-out**). The most successful approach to providing positive learning experiences for children is to direct the learning to each child's individual stage of development.

> **Professional Practice**
>
> ■ A child who is tired will gain less from a new experience than a child who is fresh and alert. The end of the day is not a suitable time to introduce an exciting new activity as children may be starting to go home, leaving some frustrated at missing out, whereas others may be too tired to appreciate the potential of the activity.

Major theories

Nature/nurture debate

Genetic inheritance and how it influences children's learning has been much debated, with the nature theorists (**nativists**) proposing that genetic factors influence behaviour and learning, that is, we are born ready primed for what we will achieve. The nurture theorists (**empiricists**), however, claim that environmental factors are the main influences on learning, that is, the circumstances we are born into and raised within will determine our achievements. This is the **nature/nurture debate**.

Models of learning – an overview

There are three main models of learning:

- the **transmission model**
- the **laissez-faire model**
- the **social constructivist model**.

Table 4.1 Advantages/disadvantages of models of learning

Model	Advantages	Disadvantages
Transmission - Learning takes place without inherent abilities (nurture)	- Behaviour can be modified - Learning comes from experience - Child may learn though imitation and observing others	- Oversimplifies children's learning - Inhibits exploration - Not child centred - Child takes a passive role in learning
Laissez-faire - Environment does not affect learning (nature)	- Child centred - Makes use of developmental scales - Identifies favourable periods for learning - Encourages a well-resourced environment	- Normative benchmarks may label child if not achieving - Disregards cultural influences on development - Children are passive learners - Opportunities for learning may be missed due to limited adult support
Social constructivist - Development and learning are linked (nature *and* nurture)	- Child centred and child is seen as active learner - Sees play as important part of learning - Adult support extends opportunities for learning - Recognises importance of family, community and cultural links to learning	- Expensive operating costs due to resources needed and high levels of adult support

Transmission model of learning

The seventeenth-century philosopher John Locke, an empiricist, considered that children were a blank page to be written on by adults. His view was that children were born with differing potentials for intelligence and temperament, but they had no facilities for innate learning. Therefore, Locke believed solely in the influences of nurturing. **Classical conditioning** (the process whereby learning results from the association of a neutral stimulus with a reflex response) and **operant conditioning** (the process of learning voluntary behaviour by association with reinforcement or punishment) reflect this philosophy.

The transmission model of learning is one in which adults keep control of the situation. Adults determine what learning will take place by their own direct involvement, controlling the learning process and suppressing the children's initiative. Children remain passive in these situations, and in the long term are less likely to try out new experiences because they are concerned about failing.

The main theorists linked to this model of learning are

- Ivan Pavlov – classical conditioning
- B. F. Skinner – operant conditioning.

Pavlov

Ivan Pavlov was most famous for an experiment he undertook with dogs in which he demonstrated that a neutral stimulus (a bell) elicited a conditional response (salivation) when it was paired with an unconditional stimulus (food). Put simply, he conditioned his dogs by stimulating them with a bell before they were fed. The dogs produced saliva when they saw the food, but, after a while, started to salivate when they heard the bell. Classical conditioning is one form of learning from experience, and you may be able to remember occasions when you learnt something significant from experience.

Skinner

B.F. Skinner developed Pavlov's **theories** and his work is based on a theory of learning known as behaviourism which was popular in the first half of the twentieth century. Skinner developed the Skinner box in which he trained rats to perform various tasks, such as negotiating a complex maze. When they were learning the route through the maze, the rats were rewarded with food when they took the right turns and received mild electric shocks when they made a mistake. Over time, the rats made fewer mistakes in order to gain the reward of the food. Skinner believed that we learn to behave in certain ways by being either punished or rewarded. According to this model of learning, adults can shape or modify children's learning by reinforcing wanted behaviours. You may observe some elements of this approach used in behaviour management in settings where rewards such as stickers or stars are used to reinforce wanted behaviours.

Refer to Unit 7, page 323, for more about operant conditioning.

Laissez-faire model of learning

The laissez-faire model of learning is based on the thinking of Jean Jacques Rousseau (a nativist) in the eighteenth century. He considered that children learn naturally, following pre-set biological processes, and that these biological processes would be best developed if supported by caring adults, who oversee what children are doing but do not intervene in the learning process.

The laissez-faire model of learning allows for exploration and choice. However, it lacks adult input which limits any extension of the learning by example, or by **scaffolding**. It is possible that with this approach children may not reach their potential because the adult hesitates to 'interfere' with the learning.

Refer to page 125 for more about scaffolding and Jerome Bruner.

The main theorists loosely linked to this model of learning are:

■ Noam Chomsky

■ Sigmund Freud.

Chomsky

Noam Chomsky is an American linguist who believes that children have a language acquisition device in their brain that enables them to acquire and decode language simply by hearing it spoken. He thinks that the decoder allows them to recognise and understand the complexities and grammatical constructions of language, no matter what language it is they are hearing. Other theorists have disagreed with Chomsky.

Refer to Unit 7, page 322, for further information on language development.

Freud

Sigmund Freud's theories, which are complex and have been fiercely debated, centre on psychoanalysis and personality development. He believed that the individual's unconscious mind is responsible for shaping his or her life, as are unresolved emotional conflicts with parents. Freud is only loosely linked to the laissez-faire model, but has inspired many modern developmental psychologists.

Social constructivist model of learning

According to this model, a child learns by interacting with the environment; children are thought to learn through practical experience. This model of learning is still in favour today and underpins many curricular developments. The social constructivist model has its roots in the work of Immanuel Kant (1724–1804) and combines elements of the transmission model which views the child as an empty vessel and the laissez-faire model which suggests that learning is pre-programmed to some extent. The social constructivist model of learning is the one that you are most likely to encounter in early years settings.

Theorists linked to the social constructivist model include:

- Jean Piaget
- Lev Vygotsky
- Jerome Bruner.

Piaget

Jean Piaget (1896–1980) was a Swiss psychologist who originally studied biology and became interested in knowledge and its origins, which he called the 'embryology of intelligence'. He was particularly interested in the way that children think, and concluded that their thinking was different from the thinking of adults. Piaget considered the interaction between the child and the environment to be the main factor in influencing cognitive development (the development of learning through thinking and problem-solving). According to Piaget the child is actively involved in their learning and through interaction with the environment acquires a series of **schemas** (principles). Piaget considered that these schemas changed and developed through the processes of **assimilation** and **accommodation**.

Refer to Unit 7, pages 348-349, for an explanation of assimilation and accommodation.

Piaget proposed four stages of cognitive development:

1. Sensorimotor stage (0–2 years)
2. Pre-operational stage, comprising the pre-conceptual (2–4 years) and the intuitive (4–7 years)
3. Concrete operations stage (7–11 years)
4. Formal operations stage (11 years onwards).

Professional Practice

- At what stage of Piaget's cognitive development are the children at your current placement?
- What examples could you give to evidence their stage of development?

case study   Donovan

4.2

Donovan is two years old. He is using clay and is trying to squeeze it in his hands. He says the word 'ball' twice. Eventually, Donovan leaves the clay and moves to play with the salt dough. Again, he tries to squeeze the material in his hands. He smiles as he is successful.

activity

1. Which of Piaget's stages of cognitive development would you place Donovan in?

Refer to Unit 7, page 317, for more about Piaget.

Figure 4.2

Piaget's first two stages of cognitive development

Source: p.24, Neaum and Tallack, 2000

Sensory motor stage, 0–2 years

Children gather information predominantly through their senses of sight and touch

Children process information imagistically

Sensory motor stage, 0–2 years

Children have a tendency to be egocentric, seeing the world from their own viewpoint

Children use trial and error as their main tool of discovery.

Children in this age range have a limited language ability, therefore senses other than hearing are predominant in gathering and processing information. Sight and touch are vital senses in enabling a child to gather the information in his or her environment. This information is then processed as images, similar to, but more sophisticated than, pictures or photographs. This processing system is inflexible and has limited use. For example, how would you store the concept of justice in this way? Children, therefore, need to acquire language. It thus becomes immediately obvious, even at this early stage, that there is an important link between language and intellectual development. It is an interdependent relationship.

Pre-operational stage, 2–7 years

Children continue to gather information predominantly through the senses of sight and touch but hearing becomes increasingly important

Initially children's information processing is predominantly imagistic. However, it gradually becomes mediated by thought processes as language develops. These are still basic and very dependent upon immediate perceptions of the environment

Children still have a tendency to be egocentric

Pre-conceptual stage, 2–4 years

Children begin to play symbolically, using one object to represent another, for example a bag as a hat, a doll as a baby

Children believe that everything has a consciousness, for example, teddies have feelings, chairs are naughty

Hearing gradually becomes an important sense for information gathering

Thought processes are increasingly mediated by language as it develops

Children are still dependent upon immediate perceptions of the environment and find abstract thought difficult

Intuitive stage, 5–7 years

Symbolic play continues

Children still have a tendency to be egocentric

As language develops children increasingly use this to gather and process information. Language is a complex system of representation and therefore enables a child to develop more complex ways of gathering and processing information. Again the link between language and intellectual development is shown to be vital in children's learning.

Vygotsky

Lev Vygotsky (1896–1935) also believed that children learn by active involvement. He saw the adult role as a crucial part of the learning experience, and central to his theory is the **zone of proximal development (ZPD)**, see the diagram below.

Figure 4.3

Vygotsky's zone of proximal development

Source: p.36, Neaum and Tallack, 2000

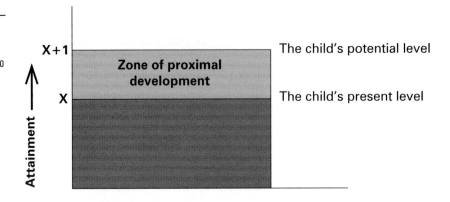

Vygotsky argued that children could often understand more than they demonstrated and that, while they were able to show understanding of some concepts through their play, they have the potential to develop further understanding, for example of more abstract concepts, if helped by an adult. Children can therefore achieve more than if there had been no adult involvement. This highlights the important role that a (more able) individual (usually an adult) can have in helping develop the learning of a (less able) individual (usually the child) by extending opportunities for experience.

case study 4.3 Yasmin and Thalia

Yasmin and Thalia were at the sand tray and were trying to make sand pies with a small bucket. The sand was very fine and dry, and they were not succeeding. Jenny, a member of staff, told them to add water to the sand. This they did, in large quantities, and saturated the sand tray. Yasmin and Thalia were still unable to make a sand pie as the sand had become too wet to turn out.

There was clearly an opportunity for Jenny to have extended the learning for Yasmin and Thalia here, but it did not happen.

activity

1   What went wrong?
2   How should Jenny have approached the situation?
3   How do you think Yasmin and Thalia might have felt?

Refer to Unit 7, page 321, for more about Vygotsky.

Bruner

Jerome Bruner (1915–) was influenced by Vygotsky's ideas, particularly the ZPD; he believes that scaffolding contributes to the child's learning. In scaffolding, the adult supports the learning experience of the child, enhancing the child's learning through the introduction of manageable levels of information, thus enabling the child to solve a problem or to achieve further.

Bruner felt that children move through three main stages of thinking:

1 **enactive thinking**, where information is recorded mentally and linked to physical activity; this is the stage of most infants under one year old

2 **iconic thinking**, where the mental images are linked to the senses; this stage is associated with children aged one to seven years

3 **symbolic thinking**, using a range of representative forms, such as language and number, to demonstrate their learning; this stage is seen mostly from seven years onwards.

Refer to Unit 7, page 321, for more about Bruner.

activity 4.2

Consider the three models of learning discussed on pages 120–125. Make a copy of the table below. Think of at least three statements to sum up each model and list them in the appropriate column. For example, under which heading would you place 'Believes that children achieve best if directed by an adult'? Compare your statements with those of another student.

Transmission model	Laissez-faire model	Social constructivist model

Professional Practice

■ When planning an activity for children, you need to consider the level of adult involvement required and include it in your planning.

Links to current research

activity 4.3

Using the academic and media resources available to you in your college resource centre, together with the Internet, explore current research linked to early years learning and find out about the perceived role of the adult in any proposed developments.

One useful source could be the journal *Early Childhood Practice: The Journal for Multi-Professional Partnerships*, edited by Professor Tina Bruce.

Professional Practice

- Early years education is affected by the ability of workers to understand the models of learning, the main theories of education, and how to implement them effectively.
- There are times when adult direction is needed in early years settings. Think of three examples.

Links to your own experience and practice

As a student, you will see many examples of good practice during your placement experience. This is an important learning opportunity for you. However, on occasions, less ideal practice may be evident, which is unfortunate but will add to your knowledge base as a professional early years worker, reminding you how not to approach certain situations.

activity
4.4

Think of situations in which you have identified particularly good examples of high-quality practice. What made it good practice, do you think?

Professional Practice

- With the regular inspections of settings and the quality assurance accreditation processes that are developing within early years, there should be fewer instances of below-standard practice. The quality assurance process is led by a government initiative that at least 40 per cent of all providers of early years care and education should be accredited with a nationally recognised quality assurance scheme 'kite mark' by 2004.

Progress Check

1   What is the difference between the transmission and the laissez-faire models of learning?
2   Name the three eminent theorists who support the philosophy of the social constructivist model of learning.

How children learn

Being active

Children learn by being actively involved in the exploration and discovery of their environment. Even the youngest infants are curious about their environment and make use of all of their sensory abilities to explore and learn. Children may need support, encouragement and opportunities to become competent and active learners, and adults need to make use of appropriate resources and frameworks to facilitate 'learning by doing'.

First-hand experiences

First-hand experiences are pivotal to learning and all children have a right to take an active role in a stimulating learning environment in which their competence is recognised and encouraged. Practitioners need to acknowledge the importance of play, developmentally appropriate care routines and experiential learning in order to provide a stimulating and dynamic learning environment. Children must also be given the freedom to learn in their own way and make mistakes without feeling under pressure.

Play

Children have a right to enjoy play opportunities from the earliest age and the adult needs to support this with encouragement and appropriate care and stimulation. Play is an essential part of children's lives and learning and it should not be seen as a passive activity that keeps children 'busy'. Children need play opportunities that are purposeful, innovative and worthwhile if learning is to take place.

Using language

Children will also learn from being in a language-rich environment from the earliest days. They will benefit from a wide variety of activities and resources that promote and celebrate spoken and written languages, but the importance of the role of the adult in speaking and listening to a child cannot be overemphasised. Routine care activities offer many opportunities for stimulating language, as do stories, nursery rhymes, music, poetry and singing. Babies and young children need the opportunity to hear and learn to use language and this demands a practitioner who is willing to talk and listen. They will also learn from non-verbal communication and this may involve the adult in helping the child to recognise facial expressions, gestures and signs.

Working with others

Children learn many useful skills from working with other children and with adults. They will learn how to co-operate and share, as well as how to take turns and wait. They benefit from the opportunity to share play and learning experiences with other children and may need adult support to help them negotiate social boundaries and behave in accepted ways.

Meaningful activities

Activities need to be meaningful in order that children are actively engaged and learning, rather than being passively amused or occupied. This means that the adult has the responsibility of providing high-quality activities and care that involve and engage the child. Activities need to be developmentally appropriate and culturally sensitive and should be centred on the needs of the individual child.

Feeling secure

It is impossible to flourish and learn in an atmosphere where a baby or child does not feel secure. Emotional security is pivotal to a positive learning experience and practitioners need to consider the 'emotional security' of the learning environment as carefully as health and safety considerations. Routine care and learning activities need to acknowledge a child's individual personality and changing needs and circumstances, as well as the more day-to-day events that affect children's emotional stability. Key worker systems are essential in providing consistency of care and responsiveness to children's changing needs.

Appropriate adult intervention

Adults rightly support children's care, play and learning, but there may be times when it is necessary to consider the nature and timing of adult intervention. This needs to be balanced between allowing the child the freedom to explore and experiment, and providing support to facilitate the next stage of learning.

Influences

Influences on the organisation of the early years environment

Children will learn well in many different environments and early years care and education takes place wherever children are to be found. The home is the traditional place where learning begins through appropriate care routines and play that stimulate all areas of development and learning. Current provision of early years environments outside of the family home is often influenced by external factors, such as:

- government legislation, policies, guidelines and recommendations – for example, the Birth to Three Matters framework and the **Foundation Stage Curriculum**

- provision linked to initiatives such as Sure Start programmes – for example, Children's Centres and Neighbourhood Nurseries

- the drive to integrate children's services in response to *Every Child Matters* and the National Service Framework

- organisational and cultural factors to be found in individual settings – for example, the underlying philosophy or approach that influences care and education. Examples of this would be the differences to be found in settings offering the Montessori approach as opposed to a Steiner or **High/Scope** setting.

Influences on the role of the adult and their interaction with children

The role of the adult may be interpreted differently in some settings and there may be both internal and external factors that influence this and the way in which adults interact with children. Examples of factors that may influence the role of the adult include:

- staff training and qualifications – it is generally accepted that effective learning environments require a high ratio of trained staff
- philosophy of the setting – for example, Montessori and Steiner settings will vary in how the role of the adult is perceived.

Early years educators

The work and influence of early educators

A number of early educators have had a significant influence on the practice of modern early years professionals, enabling a greater understanding of how children learn and what affects the learning process. This section summarises the contributions of some of the most influential early pioneers.

Friedrich Froebel (1782–1852)

Friedrich Froebel considered parents to be the main educators of their children. He founded the first kindergarten in 1840 and the children who attended were given the opportunity to learn through **exploratory play**, particularly with natural materials. He emphasised that children learn best when they are well motivated, and he focused on offering opportunities for a positive relationship between the child's home, school and the wider community. Froebel encouraged **symbolic play** and what is known today as free-flow play. He developed a set of learning materials which he called 'the gifts' and these materials went on to influence the work of Maria Montessori. Froebel's emphasis was always on the linking together of materials, and learning by their differences in a non-directed way.

Table 4.2 Froebel: key concepts

Key concepts	Types of play	The 'gifts'
Parents as the main educators of their children	Exploratory play	Materials and resources
Interaction between home, school and the community	Learning through nature	
Non-directed learning	Symbolic play	
Focus on the whole child		
No formal learning under seven		

Refer to page 139 for more about free-flow play and page 130 for Maria Montessori.

Rudolph Steiner (1861–1925)

Rudolph Steiner saw the child as having three developmental stages to pass through on the way to adulthood. He proposed that:

- up to seven years of age, the emphasis of learning should be on the will (the active stage)
- from 7 to 14 years old, the emphasis moves to the heart (the emphasis is now on feelings)
- from 14 years onwards, the head is of greatest importance (the cognitive stage).

Like Froebel, Steiner considered the child holistically (as a whole), maintaining that each stage of learning was fostered by the interaction of prior experience.

He firmly believed that formal reading and writing should not be introduced at an early age but should occur naturally at a child's own pace, fostered by opportunities for creativity. He also encouraged the use of natural materials and felt that learning should be initiated by the child – it should come from within. Steiner settings offer a carefully structured environment which particularly fosters non-pressurised personal and social learning. He promoted what was known as curative education for children with emotional, behavioural and learning difficulties. The use of textbooks was only seen as a support to the learning that was already developing; textbooks were not used to initiate it. The main emphasis of the Steiner approach is on learning from life's experiences.

Steiner Waldorf schools are run as private schools, but parents usually pay according to their means. Some (but not all) children are integrated back into the state sector when they reach the GCSE and post-GCSE stage of their education.

Table 4.3 Steiner: key concepts

Key concepts	Types of play	Materials and resources
Three stages of learning: ■ the will ■ the heart ■ the head Learning at own pace Focus on the whole child	Freeplay Exploratory play Learning through nature	Natural materials

The Steiner setting places a great emphasis on imaginative play and creativity. There are many opportunities for self-expression through music, dance, drama and art. A range of objects is provided to encourage imagination, and there is a marked lack of commercially produced artefacts.

The role of the adult is to guide and supply materials to enhance the child's creativity. Play is child-initiated and adults join them as appropriate.

Professional Practice

■ Although the **Steiner philosophy** attracts a significant following, there are limited opportunities for placement experience. If you are fortunate to gain a place in a Steiner setting, remember to share your experience with others, enhancing their learning too.

Figure 4.4

Children can often be seen concentrating hard on what they are doing

Maria Montessori (1870–1952)

Maria Montessori believed that, given the right stimuli, children are naturally self-motivating. She saw children as active learners in much the same way as Piaget did, but she did not value play in its free-flow sense, believing that children became independent learners if they are encouraged to work alone.

Montessori thought that children needed to work through the range of learning materials that she developed before they were ready to express their own ideas. This range of materials particularly encouraged dexterity, and as they worked with them children were guided from the simple to the more complex tasks. These included activities designed to enable children to learn particular skills. Montessori believed that each activity should only be used for the purpose for which it was designed and she did not value imaginative play.

She encouraged children to learn to form letters through sand and finger play, and no methods involving the formal learning of reading and writing were seen in a Montessori nursery, although great emphasis was placed on the richness of literature and use of language. Montessori encouraged independence and considered that children had reached the highest point of their learning when they were silently absorbed in their activity. She referred to this as the 'polarisation of the attention'.

Montessori believed that the adult's role is to 'follow the child'. She based her theories on extensive observation of children and today's acceptance that children are eager learners from birth is often attributed to her theories.

Table 4.4 Montessori: key concepts

Key concepts	Types of play	Materials and resources
Children are self-motivating	Free-flow play not valued	Developed own range of equipment
Independent learning was encouraged	Sensory learning	
Planned environment	Encouraged dexterous activity	
Adult should follow the child		

The **Montessori philosophy** initiated the need for child-sized equipment, including display tables and storage facilities, to allow children to select and return their chosen activities (this is similar to the High/Scope approach). Montessori settings also favour rugs, mats and cushions for the children to use at floor level, and children will often be seen selecting an activity, for example a grading board, and taking it to a mat (carpet square) to explore it. In line with Montessori thinking, each activity is to be used for its intended purpose, and imaginative play is not actively encouraged in most settings.

The adult role within a Montessori setting is to observe and guide; use your understanding of a child's needs to indicate when adult intervention is needed.

The materials that Montessori produced to encourage dexterity are still used in Montessori settings today, although the overall curriculum is generally more varied.

Margaret McMillan (1860–1931)

Margaret McMillan was influenced by Froebel and like him she was interested in allowing children to learn both freely and naturally. She considered that play helped children demonstrate their knowledge and understanding of materials and situations, and she emphasised manipulative dexterity, which was also later favoured by Montessori.

McMillan was the pioneer of nursery schools, school meals and medical services. She initiated the viewpoint that a hungry child or a sick child will be unlikely to reach their potential so feeding children and monitoring their health was crucial to the learning process.

She considered that children expressed what they had learned through their play and she was a pioneer of working in partnership with parents, encouraging them to learn alongside their children. McMillan's later work promoted the importance of the training of adults to enable them to work with young children in an informed manner.

Table 4.5 McMillan: key concepts

Key concepts	Types of play	Materials and resources
Emphasis on manipulative dexterity	Free-play	No special resources
Pioneer of nursery schools	Natural play	
Initiated school meals and health services	Exploratory play	
Partnership with parents		
No formal learning before seven		
Promoted training for adults		

Susan Isaacs (1885–1948)

Also influenced by the work of Froebel, Susan Isaacs believed that children should not enter formal learning situations before the age of seven. She considered that they should be allowed to learn through **free play** and individual experience, and she placed great emphasis on the need for movement in their play and learning. Isaacs also believed in the role of parents as the main educators of their children and, influenced by the work of Melanie Klein (a psychoanalyst), Isaacs was also interested in children's feelings and emotions. She believed that children were able to move in and out of reality during their play, learning to cope with their feelings, and that this was important to their emotional security.

Table 4.6 Isaacs: key concepts

Key concepts	Types of play	Materials and resources
Emphasis on need for movement	Free play	No special resources
Play fundamental to learning	Active play	
No formal learning before seven		
Parents as main educators		
Emotional regression common on entering school		

Isaacs recorded her observations of children before and after they had left the nursery. She noted that a marked regression in development was common when children entered formal schooling.

Professional Practice

■ Each of the five early educators has directly influenced some aspect of your professional practice experience. Think of an example relevant to each of them.

activity
4.5

Using outdoor play as the basis, plan activities for children in your current placement that could be directly relevant to the thinking of each of the five early educators.

1 How might the activities differ?
2 How might they be similar?

Progress Check

1   Which of the early educators supported learning through exploratory play?
2   Who initiated school meals and health services?
3   According to whose philosophy, should textbooks support, not initiate, learning?
4   According to Steiner, from which age do children learn particularly through feelings?

Approaches to practice

This section looks at curriculum models outside mainstream provision.

Although approaches to education outside the main curricula are more often found in privately funded settings, elements of these approaches may be incorporated into the curriculum and planning of maintained settings.

High/Scope

The High/Scope curricular model derives from work done in the USA and was originally intended to be used in areas of deprivation, in tandem with the Head Start schemes. Designed to meet perceived deficits in children's learning and life experiences, it was well resourced and involved parents. Parents were visited at home in order to ensure that the learning experiences in the High/Scope setting were consistent with those offered at home. Results from the USA appeared to show that there were reasonably good long-term benefits from this approach and children enrolled in these programmes appeared to have better long-term development and learning. Evidence from its use in the UK is less convincing.

The High/Scope curriculum encourages children to take responsibility for their own learning, making choices, planning their activities and reviewing them collectively at a set point. High/Scope is associated with the statement: '**plan, do and review**'.

Plan

Children decide, often with an adult, what they will do during the session. There are different ways in which children can relay their plans to others in the group; it could be through words, actions or simple gestures. The session often starts with a circle time, in which the whole group sits together, perhaps for weather-board or news time. The group then divides into smaller groups for planning. In many settings, you would, as a student, simply observe at this stage until the student supervisor is confident that you are able to support the planning process appropriately.

Do

Children select, use and put away their planned activities during the main 'work' time. The equipment is made easily accessible to the children with clear visual labels to enable them to identify and select for themselves. As independent learning is encouraged, the children develop responsibility and a sense of being part of the setting. Selecting and replacing resources becomes part of each day, adding to the child's social skills development.

The children make choices, exploring their environment freely and initiating ideas based on their interests and prior experiences. The adult role is to support those choices by providing an appropriate overall framework. As an adult working within this curriculum, you will encourage children to question and to find the answers for themselves wherever possible. The High/Scope curriculum requires a well-balanced level of child–adult interaction and many decisions are left to the child which you may at first find strange. Joint child–adult-led interaction, in which you join the child at their level, is an important aspect of the High/Scope philosophy. Use of observation skills will enable you to identify when it is appropriate to involve yourself in a child's activity, to extend their learning, and when to hold back.

Professional Practice

■   It is important that you ask for advice and guidance when you are unsure. You will not be expected to know everything and will be respected for your honesty.

Review

At the end of the High/Scope session, each child describes what they have been doing, often displaying the creative outcomes. This time of recall and reflection is led by an adult, usually in a small group setting.

The High/Scope curriculum promotes active learning, and adults assist and encourage the children but do not direct them. The adult responsible for a group of children (key worker) keeps a written record of each individual child's plans. This helps identify aspects of the setting that the child does not particularly enjoy and areas of special interest.

The plan, do, review approach is regularly incorporated into non-High/Scope schools and nurseries.

Reggio Emilia

Reggio Emilia is a region of Northern Italy where Loris Malaguzzi developed an innovative approach to early years care and education over 40 years ago. The Reggio approach differs greatly from the British system, as care and education are not considered to be separate concerns. However, it is not only this that makes the Reggio approach unique: care and education are woven together and offered in custom-built environments where the expressive arts are embedded into every aspect of the curriculum. It is loosely based on social constructivist theories of learning, drawing on the work of Vygotsky, Howard Gardner's Multiple Intelligences theory and Jerome Bruner. There is no set curriculum in these schools; instead, children are encouraged to undertake a variety of projects that will give them first-hand experiences and the opportunity to form hypotheses. All of the child's project work is fully recorded in writing and images, and all levels of work are valued.

Link to current practice and provision

The Reggio Emilia view of the child

According to this approach, the child is central to all that happens in a Reggio setting, and children are perceived as active contributors to their learning and not empty vessels waiting to be filled. The belief is that it is a child's fundamental right to realise and expand their potential and to be loved, valued and listened to. Children are considered to have immense potential, strength and competence and to learn best by being able to develop their own ideas and use adults to test these ideas out.

Materials

Children in Reggio settings are provided with a variety of expressive activities in the central 'atelier' space of the school, and there is a qualified 'atelierista' to facilitate. Resources that are likely to be found in a setting that uses the Reggio approach include:

- shells
- beads
- stones
- pulses
- clay and other materials for ceramics
- paper
- cardboard
- wood
- musical instruments
- paints, pastels, crayons, batik and other craft supplies
- cloth, wool and a variety of other materials
- open spaces
- different sensory resources – as well as more 'traditional' teaching and learning resources common to many settings.

Environment

The learning and care environment is of utmost importance in this approach and, although well known anecdotally, this is often misunderstood. The environment is not divided into separate spaces where discrete groups of children are taught in fixed groups; rather, the schools have a series of interconnected spaces that all open into a central space. Furniture and equipment is designed to be multi-functional and children are encouraged to move around freely. The environment in a Reggio Emilia setting is considered to be the 'third' teacher.

Role of the adult

The role of the adult is crucial to the Reggio approach as it is one of facilitation rather than transmission. It is not intended that the adult lets the child do completely as the child desires, but the child is free to explore and learn within an ordered and stimulating environment. Adults using this approach must be willing to let the child take measured risks and make mistakes in order to form hypotheses and learn from experimentation. The Reggio approach places great importance on the contribution that parents and grandparents have to make; this is valued by parents, children and staff and ensures that the whole community feels a sense of ownership of the learning that takes place.

Curriculum frameworks for children from 0 to 8 years of age

There are two main curricula and one framework that underpin the care and education of children from birth to eight years. These are:

- The Birth to Three Matters framework
- The Foundation Stage Curriculum
- The **National Curriculum**.

The introduction of the Birth to Three Matters framework was not an attempt to implement a curriculum for the under-3s, but it did represent an innovation in the care of the very youngest children. The framework links to other policy documents such as the Curriculum Guidance for the Foundation Stage, the National Standards for Day Care and the National Service Framework for Children, Young People and Maternity Services.

Formal learning begins with the Early Learning Goals (ELGs) in the Foundation Stage Curriculum (the Cwricwlwm Cymreig in Wales) when children reach their third birthday (see below). However, future initiatives being planned are the launch of a Birth to Five Framework which will provide a seamless link between Birth to Three and the Foundation Stage.

Current curriculum frameworks

Birth to Three Matters (DfES 2003)

The Birth to Three Matters framework is not intended to be a formal curriculum as such but was designed as a framework for effective practice that would inform work with the under-3s. There has long been an increasing awareness of the importance of the first three years of life for development and this has been supported by neurological research studies. The framework is designed to inform the practice of anyone working with the under-3s regardless of the nature of the setting and it has four main aspects:

- a strong child
- a skilful communicator
- a competent learner and
- a healthy child.

Each aspect is further broken down into key components that inform the delivery of care and early learning.

A strong child

- Me, Myself and I
- being acknowledged and affirmed
- developing self-assurance
- a sense of belonging.

A skilful communicator

- being together
- finding a voice
- listening and responding
- making meaning.

A competent learner

- making connections
- being imaginative
- being creative
- representing.

A healthy child

- emotional well-being
- growing and developing
- keeping safe
- healthy choices.

These aspects and components should be used to inform and structure innovative and imaginative care for the very youngest children. Babies are 'born to learn' and benefit from a rich, stimulating and emotionally supportive environment. Most provision for them is to be found within baby units or separate baby rooms. There is some evidence to suggest that they benefit from time spent with older babies and young children, but they also need a discrete and appropriate environment where there is a high ratio of qualified staff. The different aspects and components of the Birth to Three Matters framework can be used to inform daily care activities as well as more structured learning opportunities. It can be used equally by practitioners in day nurseries, family homes, children's centres and by childminders.

activity 4.6

Using your college resource centre, research the Birth to Three Matters framework and if possible, download the materials to be found on the website. Discuss how the activities and care routines that you have seen in practice fit with the four aspects and the different components.

The curriculum guidance for the Foundation Stage

The early year's curriculum is one part of a range of connected strategies for children's services and is based on six main areas of learning:

- personal, social and emotional development
- communication, language and literacy
- mathematical development
- knowledge and understanding of the world
- physical development
- creative development.

Environments that implement the Foundation Stage Curriculum successfully will centre their practice on play and the holistic development of the individual child. Each of the areas of learning has Early Learning Goals that are measurable, but it also values everything a child does in the setting as the curriculum includes 'everything children do, see, hear or feel in their setting, both planned and unplanned' (QCA, in Drake, 2000).

All settings offering the Foundation Stage Curriculum and achieving satisfactory inspection outcomes from Ofsted receive funding for their four-year-olds (and in some areas three-year-olds too) from the Nursery Education Grant.

Foundation Stage Curriculum

The Foundation Stage Curriculum is offered from the age of three, up until the child begins to follow the National Curriculum and its principles should be the basis of all future learning (QCA, 2000) by:

supporting, fostering, promoting and developing children's:

Personal, social and emotional well-being: in particular by supporting the transition to and between settings, promoting an inclusive ethos and providing opportunities for each child to become a valued member of that group and community so that a strong self-image and self-esteem are promoted;

Positive attitudes and dispositions towards their learning: in particular an enthusiasm for knowledge and learning and a confidence in their ability to be successful learners;

Social skills: in particular by providing opportunities that enable them to learn how to co-operate and work harmoniously alongside and with each other and to listen to each other;

Attention skills and persistence: in particular the capacity to concentrate on their own play or on group tasks;

Language and communication: with opportunities for all children to talk and communicate in a widening range of situations, to respond to adults and to each other, to practise and extend the range of vocabulary and communication skills they use and to listen carefully;

Reading and writing: with opportunities for all children to explore, enjoy, learn about and use words and text in a broad range of context and to experience a rich variety of books;

Mathematics: with opportunities for all children to develop their understanding of number, measurement, pattern, shape and space by providing a broad range of contexts in which they can explore, enjoy, learn, practise and talk about them;

Knowledge and understanding of the world: with opportunities for all children to solve problems, make decisions, experiment, predict, plan and question in a variety of contexts, and to explore and find out about their environment and people and places that have significance in their lives:

Physical development: with opportunities for all children to develop and practise their fine and gross motor skills and to increase their understanding of how the body works and what they need to do to be healthy and safe;

Creative development: with opportunities for all children to explore and share thoughts, ideas and feelings through a variety of art, design and technology, music, movement, dance and imaginative and role-play activities.

(QCA, 2000, pages 8–9)

There is a single assessment strategy for the Foundation Stage and it is known as the Foundation Stage Profile. Thirteen assessment scales are used to assess the six areas of learning. These are usually completed by the end of the Foundation Stage and observations of a child's progress will be made although the Early Learning Goals are not summatively assessed.

National Curriculum

The National Curriculum is intended to be a broad and balanced framework to meet the learning needs of children in Key Stages 1 and 2; its main principles are based on the Education Acts of 1988 and 1996. All state schools must offer the National Curriculum and although schools in the private sector can opt out, few do. It is considered to be a prescriptive curriculum in that it gives precise outcomes to be achieved at certain stages in a child's school career. Schools are also free to provide extra areas of learning in addition to the National Curriculum to reflect the particular needs and circumstances of the setting.

The National Curriculum is divided into key stages.

National Curriculum key stages

Table 4.7 Advantages/disadvantages of models of learning

Key stage	Age	Year groups
Key Stage 1 (KS1)	5–7 years	1–2
Key Stage 2 (KS2)	7–11 years	3–6
Key Stage 3 (KS3)	11–14 years	7–9
Key Stage 4 (KS4)	14–16 years	10–11

The key stage that follows on from the Foundation Stage is Key Stage 1. You will work with children who are following this stage during placement experience in a Year 1 or Year 2 class.

At the end of each key stage, there are a number of tests known as **Standard Attainment Tasks (SATs)**, which all children must complete. The purpose of SATs is to monitor each individual child's performance as they progress through school.

Key Stage 1
Key Stage 1 includes:

- English
- mathematics
- science
- technology (design and technology and information technology)
- history
- geography
- art
- music
- physical education.

The attainment targets at the end of Key Stage 1 are based around the following areas of learning:

- English
  - speaking and listening
  - reading
  - writing
- mathematics
  - using and applying mathematics
  - number and algebra
  - shape, space and measure
  - handling data

- science
  - experimental and investigative science
  - life processes and living things
  - materials and their properties
  - physical processes

- Design and technology
  - designing
  - making

- art
  - investigating and making
  - knowledge and understanding

- music
  - performing and composing
  - listening and appraising.

For each of the other subjects, teachers make a decision about the level attained, which is based on the range of descriptions set out for each key stage level.

Details of these can be found in DfEE (1995) *Key Stages 1 and 2 of the National Curriculum*.

case study 4.4 — Acorn Group

The Acorn group in Class 1 is growing beans in jars. Each child has their own bean.

activity

1 Which elements of the National Curriculum could you link to this activity?
2 How could the activity be extended further?

Professional Practice

- Most activities at both Foundation Stage and Key Stage 1 are cross-curricular, covering a range of learning intentions.

The role of play

Janet Moyles has written extensively on the importance of children's play. The following title may be of interest: *The Excellence of Play* excited by (Moyles 1994).

Moyles (1989) states that play should be 'viewed as a process'. She makes reference to Bruner who wrote: 'For the main characteristic of play – whether of child or adult – is not its content but its mode. Play is an approach to action, not a form of activity.'

Moyles introduced the idea of 'playing at our work' and 'working at our play'. If, as adults, we enjoy our work and it is stimulating, interactive and challenging, it is likely to be fulfilling the same desires and needs as our leisure activities, i.e. our play! Similarly, children can often be seen concentrating hard on what they are doing, with their tongue sticking out as they focus their attention. They are indeed 'working' at their play. When, as an adult, we buy a new 'toy', for example a camcorder or music system, we experiment with it, 'testing it out', seeing how it works and discovering its limitations. Basically, we are playing with it, learning about it in much the same way as children experiment and learn through their play.

The role of play in curricular frameworks

Play is an integral part of curricular planning, but becomes less evident as the child moves through to the National Curriculum stage. Play is highly valued in the Birth to Three Matters framework and the Foundation Stage Curriculum, but how does it fare within other approaches to learning?

- Montessori did not encourage free play, but expected the child to move through a series of graded activities with pre-selected materials. This may be interpreted more liberally in contemporary Montessori settings.

- Steiner promoted learning through the use of imaginative and creative play opportunities that took account of individual learning needs.

- High/Scope settings usually have a wide variety of resources and encourage children to take responsibility to plan, do and review.

- Reggio Emilia values play highly and provides a wealth of resources and an innovative environment to stimulate the child's sense of discovery.

Definitions of play

There are many different types of play. They can broadly be described as:

- free-flow play
- **structured play**
- **spontaneous play**.

Understanding what each type of play involves is important.

---

activity
4.7

1　What do the terms 'free-flow', 'structured' and 'spontaneous' mean to you? Think where else you have heard them. What do you associate them with?
2　What do you remember about play in your childhood?
　　a)　Did you explore outdoors? Or were you encouraged to stay near to home?
　　b)　Were you provided with lots of commercial resources, or did you make your own?
　　c)　Which aspects of play are most memorable for you? Why is this, do you think?
　　d)　When you have read the following summaries of the three main types of play consider which mostly applied to your childhood experiences.

Free-flow play

Free-flow play is described by Tina Bruce (1991) as the only true concept of play. It is often referred to as imaginative, pretend or ludic play – it allows children to learn by discovery.

'Games help children to understand external pressures and constraints; free-flow play helps children to see the function of rules for themselves' (Bruce, 1991).

Bruce illustrates her definition of free-flow play as follows:

$$\text{Free-flow play} \quad = \quad \begin{array}{c}\text{Wallowing in ideas,} \\ \text{feelings and} \\ \text{relationships}\end{array} \quad + \quad \begin{array}{c}\text{Application of competence} \\ \text{and technical prowess that} \\ \text{has already been developed}\end{array}$$

Bruce's 12 features of free-flow play are summarised as follows:

- It is an active process without a product.
- It is intrinsically motivated.

- There is no external pressure to conform.
- It is about lifting the 'players' to their highest levels of functioning, involving creativity and imagination.
- It involves reflection, the wallowing in ideas.
- It actively uses previous first-hand experiences.
- It is sustained and helps us to function ahead of our real-life ability levels.
- It allows control, using competence previously attained.
- It can be initiated by child or adult, but adults need to be aware of not imposing rules, or directing activity.
- It can be a solitary experience.
- It can be in partnership with others.
- It brings together what we learn, feel and understand (Bruce, 1991).

In *Time to Play in Early Childhood Education*, Bruce (1991) offers a detailed and fascinating explanation of play, bringing together the thinking of many theorists and educationists.

Professional Practice

- **Think where you have identified the greatest amount of free-flow play occurring. What was special about the play?**

Structured play

Structured play is planned and led by an adult, who may or may not work alongside the child during the activity. Most people agree that children benefit from a degree of structure, and every setting has its constraints regarding time, space and staffing which lead to the need to 'frame' the daily routine. This should not, however, result in lack of flexibility and lack of opportunity for play to flow. A balance has to be achieved with the structured introduction to a new experience leading the child to further (free-play) exploration of the material or subject.

Refer back to Unit 2, page 47.

Professional Practice

- Give an example of a structured play activity.

---

remember

If children are continually led by an adult, they are likely to be less involved in the process of their play, and some opportunities for learning will be missed.

Spontaneous play

Spontaneous play allows children to develop their play ideas for themselves, with the adult providing a range of resources and materials. Children learn successfully if they are allowed to 'seize the moment' and this is where adult flexibility is vital. The child who unexpectedly brings a jar of snails into the nursery offers the opportunity for an 'on the spot' discussion of minibeasts, life forms, houses, bodily needs (food, water, and so on). The interest of the children will be captured by the excitement of the snails' arrival, and therefore opportunities for learning are high. Similarly, the child who makes a pretend kite (perhaps triggered by observation of kites elsewhere) and runs around the garden trying to fly it will be learning the basis of aerodynamics, as well as having fun and fulfilling a spontaneous need to try something new.

Combining types of play

Janet Moyles developed the play spiral (see Figure 4.5). The spiral incorporates free play with directed (structured) play, showing how children move in and out of each mode as their learning develops, leading to the development (accretion) of knowledge, understanding and new skills. Once you have studied and understood the play spiral, try to think of a child in your placement whom you have specifically noticed developing in this way.

Figure 4.5
_____

Moyles' play spiral

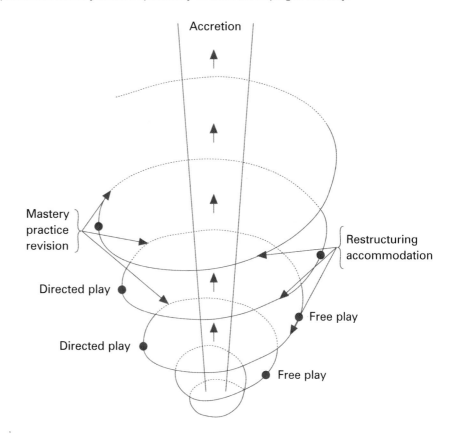

activity
4.8

Think back to Activity 4.7 on page 139.

1   Was your childhood play mostly free-flow play, structured play or spontaneous play?
2   What determined the mode of play you mostly experienced?

Professional Practice

■ Children learn through stimulus. They need a range of activities that will keep their interest and enhance their experience.

There is a fourth type of play – **therapeutic play** or play therapy – which helps children who are troubled in some way to begin to explore their troubles and work through them. It is also a medium of play used in preparing children for health care interventions and procedures, and with children who have a life-limiting illness who may need to act out negative emotions, fear or stress.

Refer to Unit 3, page 109, for information on play therapy.

Figure 4.6

Benefits of play

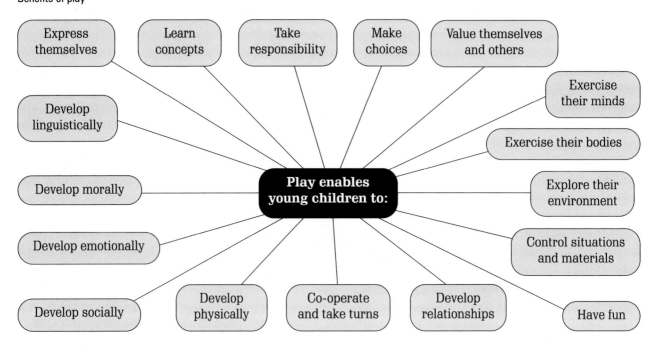

- Express themselves
- Learn concepts
- Take responsibility
- Make choices
- Value themselves and others
- Exercise their minds
- Develop linguistically
- Exercise their bodies
- Develop morally
- **Play enables young children to:**
- Explore their environment
- Develop emotionally
- Control situations and materials
- Develop socially
- Develop physically
- Co-operate and take turns
- Develop relationships
- Have fun

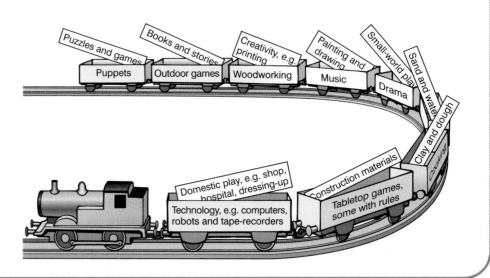

activity 4.9

Consider each of the three broad categories of play in conjunction with the range of practical activities listed below. How do they each link to the spidergram above? For example, which of the practical activities do you think would enable children to develop relationships? Learn concepts? Exercise their bodies, and so on?

Puzzles and games · Books and stories · Creativity, e.g. printing · Painting and drawing · Small-world play · Sand and water · Puppets · Outdoor games · Woodworking · Music · Drama · Clay and dough · Technology, e.g. computers, robots and tape-recorders · Domestic play, e.g. shop, hospital, dressing-up · Construction materials · Tabletop games, some with rules · Cooking

Stages of play development

Play is developmental, and the **stages of play** can be seen as children develop socially from **solitary play** (playing alone), to **parallel play** (alongside other children), to **associative play** (watching and copying other children) and finally to **co-operative play** (playing with other children).

Refer to Unit 7, page 344, where play development is discussed in detail as part of social development.

The role of the adult

Figure 4.7

Role of the adult in play

The spidergram below shows how adults support learning through play. You will find it helpful to refer back to this as you read through the section on planning activities to support early learning, page 147.

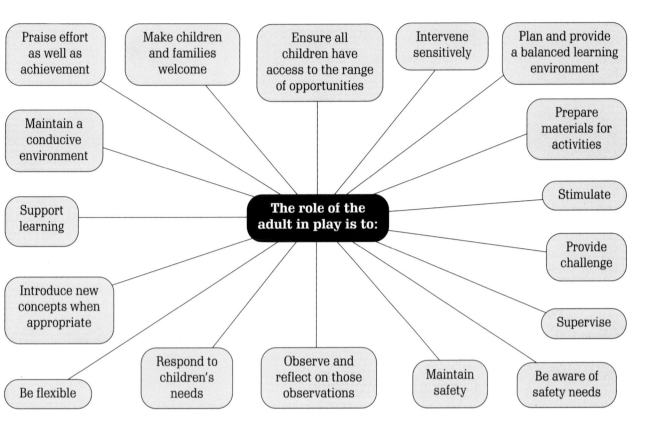

Professional Practice

- A planned setting is usually a successful setting in which the effective deployment of adults has a positive effect on the development of the children. Whatever the approach to play, directed or non-directed, there is always a need for careful adult supervision and childcare workers are responsible for the safety of all situations, including the range of equipment and resources.

remember

Safety awareness involves assessing the suitability of resources for the age groups present, removing small articles from the environment of the youngest children and giving guidance on safe use of utensils and materials to all children.

Adult–child relationships

The relationship between adult and child has an impact on the overall experience for the child. As you develop professionally, you need to consider how you build your relationships with the children in your care.

activity

4.10

The role of the adult is to facilitate learning. Consider the analogies (examples with similarities) of adult–child relationships in the table below.

Adult role	Child role
Conductor	Orchestra
Chef	Ingredients
Sales representative	Customer
Police officer	Citizen
Sergeant Major	Soldier
Gardener	Flower
Parent	Child
Potter	Clay
Teacher	Student
Performer	Audience

1   Which analogies represent the ideal relationships between early years worker and child?
2   Which represent relationships you have experienced in settings known to you?
3   Which link to the transmission, laissez-faire or social constructivist models?
4   Which most closely represent your own relationships?

Professional Practice

- What have you learned about yourself as a facilitator of children's learning from the activity above?
- How will what you have learned affect your future professional practice?

Curriculum provision

Room and area organisation

The environment for learning is just as important as the content of the curriculum and, although few children will enjoy the purpose-built Reggio environment, much can be done to enhance all areas for learning. Areas for learning need to be:

- safe – does the area conform to Health and Safety regulations? Are routines and care activities carried out safely? Is the relevant protective equipment used when needed? Are COSHH regulations complied with? Do staff and children know what to do in case of emergencies?

- organised – do children know what the expected pattern of the day is? Do they know where resources are to be found and stored? Do they know what they are supposed to do? Does the environment promote independence? Is it child friendly?

Choice and organisation of resources

It is important that children have access to a wide range of stimulating resources, but these need to be organised in such a way that children are able to select and use resources freely.

- Are resources clearly categorised and labelled? Can children understand the labelling system? Can they reach and access resources? What modifications have been made to support children with additional needs?

- Do children have access to a personal storage or display space that they can call their own? Are they consulted about the resources and activities?

- Is there sufficient space to enable large-group activities such as circle time or dance? Are activities and resources linked in themed areas? Do the children have easy access to creative spaces and activities? Can they easily gain access to outdoors activities and equipment?

- Do the resources and activities reflect diversity and inclusivity? Are there positive images of men/women/ability/ethnic origin? Are there quiet areas for rest and reading?

Storage of resources

Good storage methods enable easy access to resources and keep them in good condition. A separate area is needed for 'messy' resources, such as paint, glue, clay, collage items and junk modelling boxes. Clay should be kept slightly moist: otherwise small hands will not be able to manipulate it. Paint pots and spatulas should be washed regularly and brushes need thorough cleaning to keep the bristles soft and pliable. Glue lids need to be secured to prevent a skin forming. Ideally, surplus resources should be kept in a trolley or cupboard (most are now mobile). Items such as scissors are best kept in designated holders, and paper is ideally stored in a purposely designed storage unit. Keeping paper flat will keep it free of tears and easier to handle.

Figure 4.8

A pyramid for stroring paper

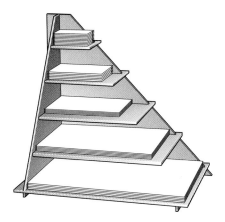

You need to consider how you will store paintings and models. An old clothes horse can be useful, but a special drying frame is even better, with a shelf or spare surface area for models.

Figure 4.9

A drying rack for paintings

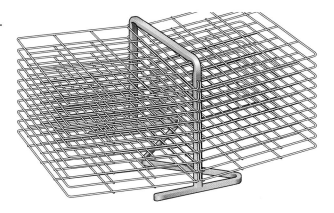

Storage boxes for items such as dressing-up clothes, construction kits and puppets can be purchased quite cheaply and will encourage children to take responsibility for clearing away.

A multitude of small items can be stored in trays and placed in cupboards and, again, specially designed tray-storage units can be purchased.

Organisation of resources

Organising where resources and activities are placed within the setting needs careful consideration, including:

- the amount of space needed for the activity
- the number of children likely to use the activity at any one time
- the importance of a quiet area for the activity
- whether hand-washing facilities are needed nearby
- the level of adult involvement needed (affecting deployment of staff)
- any level of interruption that could be posed to the activity by doorways, access points, etc.

Fountain Park Nursery

Fountain Park Nursery is shortly opening in its new premises. Each member of staff has been asked to plan where they would position the range of everyday activities. Everyone has been given a copy of a blank floor plan and the following list of what to include:

- water tray
- sand tray
- indoor slide
- mat for cars, farm, and so on
- area for puzzles, threading, and so on
- book corner
- painting easels

- a creative activity
- drawing and writing
- dough (or clay)
- role-play area with dressing-up clothes
- large-scale construction
- small-scale construction
- a topic table.

Not all the activities need to be available all of the time, but each are offered in some way every day.

activity

1   How would you set out the nursery if you were asked?
2   What would determine your decisions?
3   Which areas would you consider needed to be static, and why?
4   Which areas would you consider could be moved around?

Promoting independence

Promoting independence and mastery of skills is an important part of early year's play and learning. Even the youngest children can be encouraged to participate in their own care, even when this may only be holding a flannel to the face for a brief moment or helping to pull up a zip fastening. As children grow and mature, the development of the skills of independence and mastery become more important and the early years worker has an important role to play in this respect. Children should be encouraged to take supervised and acceptable risks and be allowed to make mistakes on the journey from relative dependence to independence. This will foster a sense of autonomy and competence that will increase learners' self-confidence.

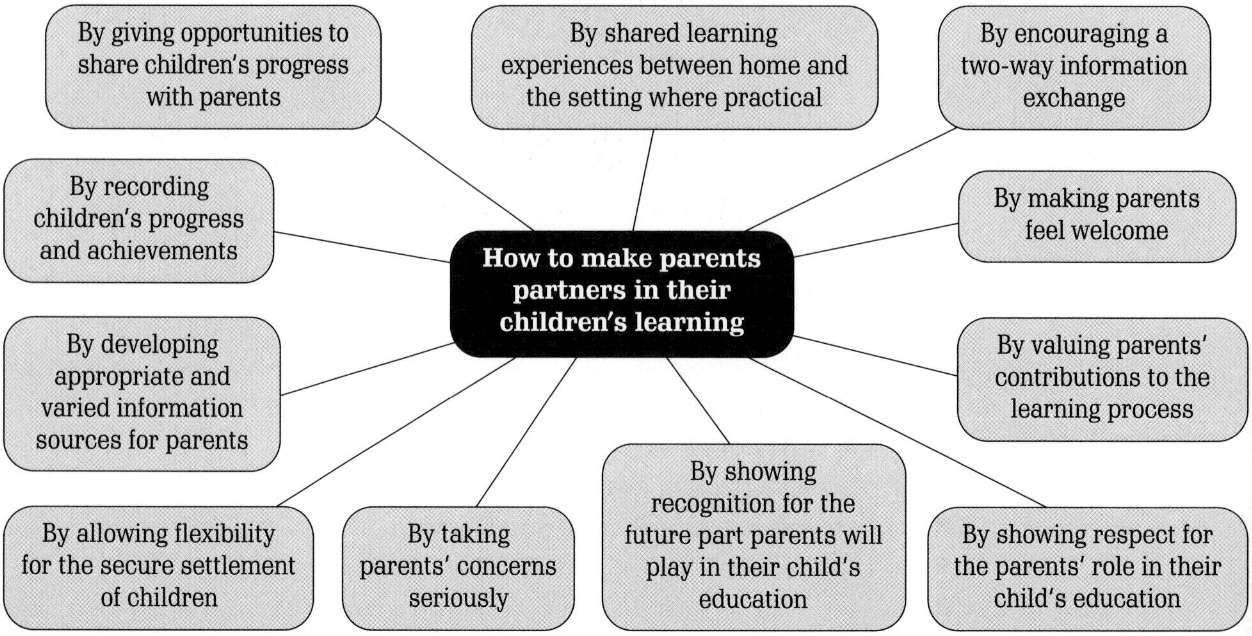

Figure 4.10

How to make parents partners in their children's learning

By giving opportunities to share children's progress with parents

By shared learning experiences between home and the setting where practical

By encouraging a two-way information exchange

By recording children's progress and achievements

By making parents feel welcome

How to make parents partners in their children's learning

By developing appropriate and varied information sources for parents

By valuing parents' contributions to the learning process

By allowing flexibility for the secure settlement of children

By taking parents' concerns seriously

By showing recognition for the future part parents will play in their child's education

By showing respect for the parents' role in their child's education

Learning opportunities for young children

Very young children need one key ingredient – a knowledgeable and enthusiastic practitioner who has a clear understanding of the child's holistic development needs. That practitioner will make sure that care and learning activities are offered in emotionally secure environments where key workers and the key-person concept ensure that individual needs are met. Older children will be more confident in their play and will, with appropriate support, make the most of learning opportunities. Environments for learning should be adequately resourced and staffed and underpinned by the required curricular frameworks.

Every adult is a potential human resource, extending learning and developing language by contributing to a child's play. Any curriculum for early years needs to be broad and balanced, involving a range of people, situations, values and resources. Learning takes place at all times, in all situations, and is enhanced by visits to places of interest and by the inclusion of visitors to the setting from the wider community.

Planning activities to support early learning

Practitioners will be keen to provide children with a wide range of activities to support their learning, and these are likely to be informed by curricular frameworks. Within the Foundation Stage Curriculum, the Early Learning Goals will inform planning; examples of the Foundation Stage Curriculum learning outcomes have already been given.

In *Curriculum Guidance for the Foundation Stage*, the QCA (2000) provides full details of the goals for each area of learning.

The Early Learning Goals are closely linked to the notion of Stepping Stones – the Stepping Stones lead a child up to the Early Learning Goals and are colour coded in order that a child's progression can be tracked.

The Early Learning Goals for personal, social and emotional development are as follows:

> By the end of the Foundation Stage, most children will:
> - continue to be interested, excited and motivated to learn;
> - be confident to try new activities, initiate ideas and speak in a familiar group;
> - maintain attention, concentrate, and sit quietly when appropriate;
> - have a developing awareness of their own needs, views and feelings and be sensitive to the needs, views and feelings of others;
> - have a developing respect for their own cultures and beliefs and those of other people;
> - respond to significant experiences, showing a range of feelings when appropriate;
> - form good relationships with adults and peers;
> - work as part of a group or class, taking turns and sharing fairly, understanding that there need to be agreed values and codes of behaviour for groups of people, including adults and children, to work together harmoniously;
> - understand what is right, what is wrong, and why;
> - dress and undress independently and manage their own personal hygiene;
> - select and use activities and resources independently;
> - consider the consequences of their words and actions for themselves and others;
> - understand that people have different needs, views, cultures and beliefs, which need to be treated with respect;
> - understand that they can expect others to treat their needs, views, cultures and beliefs with respect.
>
> (QCA (2000) *Curriculum Guidance for the Foundation Stage*.)

In order to help children meet the Early Learning Goals for Communication, Language and Literacy, practitioners need to:

- offer opportunities for children to take part in role play and other activities where they can practise speaking and listening
- ensure that the environment is language-rich
- support and encourage children to explore and enjoy books, stories, rhymes and poems
- support children in literacy activities and help them to delight in the written word and writing
- act as a positive role model by showing them how to listen, speak clearly and use language effectively
- provide a wide range of stimulating activities that provoke learning in communication, language and literacy.

For Mathematical Development, practitioners need to:

- provide children with a wide range of resources and activities that encourage numeracy and mathematical learning – this could include a wide range of materials and role play scenarios
- engage children in activities such as sorting, grading, weighing, and measuring, as these all underpin mathematical learning
- help them to see the 'pattern' of mathematics and number by the use of activities and games that encourage counting and number and shape recognition
- role model positive attitudes to numbers and maths and use mathematical language confidently
- support children to enable them to ask questions and form hypotheses by engaging in experiments.

For Knowledge and Understanding of the World, practitioners need to:

- ensure that children have access to real world experiences
- facilitate children's knowledge of their immediate environment and a wide variety of environments with which they are not familiar
- provide opportunities for visits to appropriate venues such as museums, places of historical and geographical interest
- introduce children to a wide range of artefacts and objects that represent an understanding of a diverse world.

For Physical Development, practitioners need to:

- make sure that all children have regular opportunities to practise and develop their fine and gross motor skills
- encourage and support them to master skills of independence in dressing, personal hygiene and feeding
- give children space, time and permission to experiment, take carefully supervised risks and make mistakes
- provide challenging yet safe indoors and outdoors environments in which to practise the skills for physical development
- make sure that all children have access to opportunities to maximise their personal potential for physical development, regardless of ability.

For Creative Development, practitioners need to

- provide a wide range of diverse, stimulating resources that encourage creativity
- allow children to enjoy the expressive arts in their own ways and not confine them to prescribed media
- ensure that the environment is arranged in such a way that there are provocations to creative learning and expression
- provide children with access to a range of experiences and people that represent the whole spectrum of expressive and creative arts.

In order to foster these goals, children need opportunities to work both alone and in groups of different sizes. They need to develop independence and be able both to lead and follow.

Identifying intended learning intentions

Providing appropriate resources to support the learning environment includes planning, storage and organisation of the resources, as well as the actual resources themselves. Each area of learning can be incorporated within most activities in some way or other. A range of these activities are explored here, linked to:

- personal, social and emotional development
- communication, language and literacy
- mathematical development
- knowledge and understanding of the world
- physical development
- creative development.

activity 4.11

1 Which areas of learning are supported by the activities listed in the table on page 150? Copy and complete the table.
2 In what way do the activities support a child's learning?
3 Return to this table once you have read the whole chapter and see what else you might add.

Linking activities and learning opportunities

This is an important part of the planning cycle and, once you have identified a child's learning needs, you can link the activity to learning outcomes. In the case of children in the Foundation Stage, activities will be linked to the Early Learning Goals. Most activities will cover several areas of learning at once, and you will be taught about this area of planning by your tutors and practitioners in settings. The following diagram will give you some idea of the areas of learning that an activity might cover. Please note that not all possible learning goals for each activity have been included.

Figure 4.11

Group cooking activity

Personal, Social and Emotional Development
- Be confident to try new activities, initiate ideas and speak in a group
- Maintain attention, concentrate and sit quietly when appropriate
- Work as part of a group or class, taking turns and sharing fairly
- Dress and undress independently and manage own personal hygiene
- Select and use activities and resources independently

Communication, Language and Literacy
- Use talk to organise, sequence and clarify thinking, ideas, feelings and events
- Interact with others, negotiate plans and activities and take turns in conversation
- Extend their vocabulary, exploring the meaning and sounds of new words

Mathematical Development
- Use language such as 'more' or 'less', 'greater' or 'smaller', 'heavier' or 'lighter' to compare two numbers or quantities
- Use language such as 'circle' or 'bigger' to describe the shape and size of solids and flat shapes

Group cooking activity

Creative Development
- Explore colour, texture, shape, form and space in two and three dimensions
- Respond in a variety of ways to what they see, hear, smell, touch and feel
- Express and communicate their ideas, thoughts and feelings by using a wide range of materials, suitable tools, imaginative play and role play, movement, designing and making a variety of songs and musical instruments

Physical Development
- Recognise the importance of keeping healthy and those things that contribute to this
- Handle tools, objects, construction and malleable materials safely and with increasing control

Knowledge and Understanding of the World
- Investigate objects and materials by using all of their senses as appropriate
- Select the tools and techniques they need to shape, join and assemble the materials they are using

Activity	Personal, social and emotional development	Communication, language and literacy	Mathematical development	Knowledge and understanding of the world	Physical development	Creative development
Settling into a group						
Sand and water play						
Shape sorting						
Puzzles						
Cooking						
Role play and dressing-up						
Small world play						
Woodwork						
Sorting and classifying						
Sequencing games						
Handwashing and toileting						
Interest tables						
Music and movement						
Book corner						
One-to-one stories						
Group storytime						
Drawing and colouring						
Clay and dough						
Climbing frames and large equipment						
Bikes and sit-ons						
Using scissors						
Helping to clear up						
Construction resources – small-scale						
Construction resources – large-scale						
Turn-taking games						
Board games						
Circle time						

NB: This is not an exhaustive list.

You may have thought that not all of each learning goal applies specifically to a given activity and, of course, you are right. However, it will be beneficial to you to write out the Early Learning Goals in full when you are planning activities for children in the Foundation Stage.

activity
4.12

Using the format above and a copy of the Early Learning Goals, work in small groups and try to identify the possible learning goals for:

1 a role play activity
2 a construction play activity.

case study
4.6

Maya

Maya brought a jar of caterpillars into the nursery. Her key worker, Savita, showed immediate interest and placed them on a table to display them. Maya and the other children went into the nursery garden to find 'treats' for them. They returned with some dandelions, daisies, grass and a few leaves. Savita helped them to open the jar and to gently add a selection from the garden. She talked to the children about the caterpillars, asking Maya where she had found them. As a group, they explored the book corner to find information on caterpillars, which they looked at together. Later in the day, Maya let the caterpillars go in the shrubbery. When she was collected, she gave an excited account to her mother of what she had done.

activity

1 Which Early Learning Goals for personal, social and emotional development were supported here?
2 How well do you think Savita responded to the arrival of the caterpillars?
3 Would you have done anything else?

case study
4.7

Fircone Class

Fircone Class are cooking with a parent, Kamala's mother, Mrs Behera. They are making chapattis and have each put on an apron and a cook's hat. Kamala's mother talks to the children about the process of kneading and flattening the dough and the importance of washing their hands. Kamala shows how she has brought chapattis in her lunch box, along with some dahl and fruit. Rajan says that he too brings chapattis for lunch. All the children are keen to try the chapattis when they are ready. They compare them to different types of bread (focaccia, rye bread, and so on), discussing the differences in texture and identifying the cultural origin of each food.

activity

1 Which Early Learning Goals for personal, social and emotional development are supported here?
2 What is the particular significance of Mrs Behera leading the cooking activity?
3 How can the activity be extended?

Professional Practice

■ Refer to a copy of the Early Learning Goals in your college library and identify which goals from the other areas of learning were also being supported in the case studies above.

The Early Learning Goals for mathematical development are as follows.

By the end of the foundation stage, most children will be able to:

- say and use number names in order in familiar contexts;
- count reliably up to 10 everyday objects;
- recognise numerals 1 to 9;
- use language such as 'more' or 'less, 'greater' or 'smaller', 'heavier' or 'lighter' to compare two numbers or quantities;
- in practical activities and discussion begin to use the vocabulary involved in adding and subtracting;
- find one more or one less than a number from 1 to 10;
- begin to relate addition to combining two groups of objects, and subtraction to 'taking away';
- talk about, recognise and recreate simple patterns;
- use language such as 'circle' or 'bigger' to describe the shape and size of solids and flat shapes;
- use everyday words to describe position;
- use developing mathematical ideas and methods to solve practical problems.

(QCA (2000) *Curriculum Guidance for the Foundation Stage.*)

case study 4.8 Sean and Callum

Sean and Callum are playing at the water tray with a range of graded containers. They are filling and pouring from one side of the tray to the other and are also filling up a large bucket.

activity

1 Which Early Learning Goals for mathematical development are supported here?
2 How can an adult enhance the learning still further?
3 What Early Learning Goals for personal, social and emotional development are also supported?

Professional Practice

- Refer to a copy of the Early Learning Goals in your college library and identify which goals from the other areas of learning were being supported in the case study above.

activity 4.13

Working with a partner, ask two different settings for samples of their curriculum plans. One should be a Reception class and the other a nursery. Study the plans and answer the following questions.

1 How easy is it to follow the plans?
2 Can you identify the curriculum areas to be covered in the plans?
3 How are the staff planning to identify the learning outcomes?
4 What key concepts can you identify?
5 Where is adult support intended?
6 How do the adults intend to support children's specific needs?
7 How are the content and style of the plans different?
8 How are the content and style of the plans similar?
9 Which style of planning do you feel works best for you?
10 Why is this, do you think?

activity
4.14

This activity should help you to start evaluating the clarity of written plans.

NB This is not an exhaustive list.

Learning Intention	Resources	Child's Activity	Adult's role	Language
Show a strong sense of self as a member of a setting or a family Differentiation Make connections between different parts of their life experiences Cross-curricula CLL1 P+S 3+4 K+U 4	Books *Just as well really* *Za-Za's Baby Brother* *The Nursery Collection* *A Quiet Night In* *John Joe and the Big Hen* *Will there be a lap for me?* *Billy & Belle* *My Mum is so Unusual* *Something Special*	<u>Listen to stories about different families</u> Listen to story and sit appropriately Begin to understand that everyone has different families Relate stories to their own family life and talk about it at end of story Talk in a small group – talking about family (relating to story) i.e. about new baby	To read story – stopping and asking questions to encourage children to use picture clues and relate story to life at home/feelings etc Lead discussion about family – relating to story in book	Listen Look Sit Family Names of family members Grandma Grandpa Granny Grampfer Nanny etc

Months
Heads Up, Lookers and Communicators
Sitters, Standers and Explorers
Movers, Shakers and Players
Walkers, Talkers and Pretenders

The plan shown above uses the Birth to Three Matters framework – working in small groups, devise appropriate care routines and learning experiences to match the four main areas of development. You will need to refer to a copy of the framework to complete this activity.

Planning, implementing and evaluating curriculum plans
Differentiation

Differentiation needs to be an integral part of curriculum planning in order that experiences and activities can meet the learning needs of individual children. Differentiation is part of short-term planning and provides the fine detail of how the activity may be altered or developed to meet the needs of specific individual children or groups. It will identify:

- activities
- experiences
- resources that may be needed
- teaching strategies that may be used
- support that may be needed.

An effectively planned educational provision will include:

- a high quality of staffing, planning and resources
- positive relationships between adults and children
- opportunities for children to build on what they already know
- equality of opportunity regarding ethnicity, culture, religion, disability and gender
- differentiated plans to incorporate all children's developmental levels
- a balance of adult- and child-initiated activities
- adults who are able to intervene in the learning process appropriately to help extend learning.

Children with special educational needs and disabilities

When a child has special needs, an individual education plan (IEP) needs to be drawn up and the focus placed on removing as many barriers as possible so that the child can have access to the mainstream curriculum. Early years settings will either have, or be linked to, a special needs co-ordinator (SENCO) who will oversee the IEPs and support children and their families and will usually also have a link with an educational psychologist and other members of the multi-disciplinary education and health care teams.

IEPs should:

- assess the level of a child's difficulty
- give an overview of what intervention is needed
- outline what SEN provision is required
- identify who is currently supporting the child
- suggest time scales and review dates.

There is a five-stage Code of Practice for special needs:

- Stage 1: a concern is expressed by parent, teacher or health professional
- Stage 2: involvement of a SENCO and the development of an IEP
- Stage 3: outside help from an educational psychologist is required
- Stage 4: a detailed assessment by the local authority in conjunction with parents and school
- Stage 5: a binding document (the statement) setting out the agreed provision for the child by the local authority.

Code of Practice on the Identification and Assessment of Special Educational Needs (DfEE, 1994) gives a clear and detailed explanation of the whole Code of Practice. It should be noted, however, that the Code is currently being reviewed and changes to the assessment process may be put into practice in the near future.

Children with English as an additional language

The curriculum of any setting will need to plan for supporting children in developing their English and, where possible, enabling children to use their home language too. This should help both languages to develop alongside each other.

Supporting Identity, Diversity and Language in Early Years by Siraj-Blatchford and Clarke (2000) is an excellent source of reference.

Professional Practice

- Remember that children learning a new language will usually understand a considerable amount of what they hear before they attempt to use the new language vocally. You will need to give continued emphasis to supporting spoken language, with visual cues such as pictures, signs and artefacts.

Figure 4.12

Learning English alongside a home language

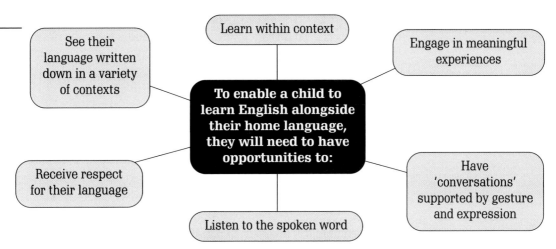

To enable a child to learn English alongside their home language, they will need to have opportunities to:

- Learn within context
- Engage in meaningful experiences
- See their language written down in a variety of contexts
- Have 'conversations' supported by gesture and expression
- Receive respect for their language
- Listen to the spoken word

Progress Check

1 Which curriculum model includes the plan, do and review process?

2 What is an IEP?

3 How would you describe free-flow play?

4 What does Moyles' play spiral illustrate?

5 In what ways can an adult have an impact on a child's learning?

6 What would you describe as being most important in the Reggio Emilia approach to learning?

7 Identify the three main types of planning.

8 What framework supports work with the under-3s?

9 What are the six main areas of learning in the Foundation curriculum?

10 What is meant by differentiation?

11 What are the four main aspects of the Birth to Three Matters framework?

12 How many components of each aspect can you name?

13 What are the six areas of learning in the Foundation Stage Curriculum?

14 Give examples of what is considered to be suitable storage for early year's resources.

15 What needs to be taken into account when organising the positioning of resources and activities?

16 Give at least three examples of activities to promote personal, social and emotional development.

17 Give at least three examples of activities to promote mathematical development.

18 What is important about written curriculum plans?

Assessment

Types of assessment

Assessment is carried out at regular intervals in order to estimate how successful learning has been for individual children and is usually undertaken in three main forms:

- baseline assessments
- formative assessments
- summative assessments.

Baseline

All state-maintained primary schools have to conduct a baseline assessment at the end of the Foundation Stage. Baseline assessments are important in identifying children's individual needs by providing a measure of a child's attainments.

Formative

Formative assessment of children's learning and progress takes place every day as children play, learn and interact together. It usually involves careful observation of children taking part in a range of activities. Parents can also be involved in the formative assessment process as they are not only the child's first educator, but may be able to put a child's behaviour or learning pattern in context.

Summative

Summative assessment is more structured and formal and is measured in graded scores. Judgements are met according to pre-set criteria which have been graded in numerical order in respect of levels of achievement. SATs are an example of summative assessment.

The assessment process

Assessment can be a complex process but careful attention to the following can help:

- Who will gather the evidence needed? Who will make the observations? If untrained staff members are making the observation, are they confident in what they are observing? Are they aware of key learning intentions, behaviour, vocabulary etc?

- Assessments will enable the observer to gather a wide range of information that will link to the planning of care and activities. Questions that can be asked include: if an observation is being made, does it have a clear aim? Does the observation cover all aspects of learning? What language does the child use? What skills and competencies have been identified? What strengths does the child show? What areas need to be developed?

- When assessing children's behaviour and learning, it is necessary to choose the method that is most suitable to meet the aim of the observation. What method is most suitable? Do staff have knowledge of a wide range of observation methods? Are there sufficient staff to enable time out for observations? Have staff accounted for potential bias? Has account been taken of the factors that influence observations?

Refer to Unit 8 for further information on observing children.

Links to planning

Planning and assessment are closely linked and depend on each other, although there is some debate as to which should come first in the cycle of planning, implementing and evaluating learning. As Gardner (1993) points out, children come into their learning settings with a very wide range of skills, attributes and competencies, and planning could start with the assessment of what children already know, using that as a baseline. Assessment informs all areas of planning, whether this is planning for a child's short-term or medium-term needs or longer-term curricular planning.

Progress Check

1   What are the three main areas of assessment?

2   When is baseline assessment undertaken?

3   What is meant by formative assessment?

4   What is meant by summative assessment?

5   When does the formal assessment of children begin?

Child Care Practice

This unit covers the following objectives:
- Show the knowledge and understanding required to care for babies and children aged 0–8 years
- Develop the skills required to care for babies and children aged 0–8 years
- Promote the maintenance of a healthy, safe and secure environment
- Carry out safety and emergency procedures.

The Child Care Practice unit forms the foundation of professional practice within the BTEC National courses. Children of different ages need differing types and degrees of care; this unit looks at the specific needs of babies and children and how routine plays a part in their development and considers the nutrition, environment, and stimulation necessary for them to develop fully.

Information on diet and nutrition is provided, enabling you to plan, prepare and support the feeding of babies and young children. This is an important aspect of children's overall development, physical and social.

All young children need careful supervision, but levels of independence should be encouraged at a level appropriate to both their age and stage of development. You will learn how to maintain a safe and secure environment and how to cope with emergencies.

Knowledge, understanding and skills required to care for babies and children aged 0–8 years

Human infants are totally dependent on their carers for all their health, care and developmental needs. Caring for babies takes a great deal of time, patience and energy. It is, however, extremely rewarding. Babies are usually very responsive to the adults who care for them, showing enjoyment of cuddles and close contact and rewarding the adult with smiles and by vocalising. The needs of young babies are simple: to be kept warm, clean, fed, happy and stimulated. Their care should be viewed holistically (looking at the baby as a whole person), rather than by compartmentalising their care into feeds, physical care and stimulation, as each of these areas is inter-related. Caring for babies includes caring for their environment, their diet, establishing a daily routine, providing stimulation and managing their times of distress. Caring for their physical needs includes their skin, hair and tooth care, bathing and nappy changing, rest, sleep and play **routines**.

Routines and care needs of babies and young children

Continuity of care is important as it is central to making babies feel secure. Care can involve a range of carers, but each must be familiar to the individual baby, and in a day-care setting it is particularly important that the baby has one main carer (their key worker). Assessing the needs of a baby involves knowledge of their stage of development, their current state of health, usual feeding patterns and any specific requirements or parental choices. Each baby should have a routine that suits them; they should not all be included in a routine care 'regime'.

Link

Refer to page 165 for discussion and activities on rest, sleep and play routines in day-care settings.

activity
5.1

During your placement with babies, ask to see the planning and assessment charts held by the staff. Ask yourself:

1   How clearly can the charts be followed?
2   What aspects of the charts are most significant, do you think?
3   Do the charts give you sufficient information for you to care for the relevant baby?
4   If not, what else would you like to see included?

Figure 5.1

Human infants are totally dependent on their carers for all their health, care and development needs

Care of the environment

Care of the environment involves consideration of the safety aspects of the setting. One of the first points that you will need to understand is how to prepare an environment suitable for a baby. Room temperature and levels of ventilation are important, and any room where a baby spends much of their time should be a constant 20°C (68°F), day and night. A room thermometer should be placed on the wall in the baby room of any early years setting and be checked regularly, and the heating should be adjusted accordingly when necessary. Overheating of babies is thought to be a contributory factor in Sudden Infant Death Syndrome (cot death), and recommendations are that babies should not be piled high with blankets – just a sheet and two layers of blankets are normally sufficient. Duvets and baby nests are no longer recommended, as they do not allow for temperature regulation. Cot bumpers are also advised against as these add extra warmth to a baby's cot, as well as having the potential for suffocation. Having a well-ventilated room will help to prevent **cross-infection** and make the working or living environment a more pleasant place to be, both for the babies and their carers.

remember

A blanket folded in half counts as two layers.

Professional Practice

■ You can check if a well baby is too warm or too cool by feeling their abdomen. If it feels warm and clammy, then they are hotter than necessary. A slightly cool-to-touch abdomen is usual. Removing a layer of clothing should be sufficient to keep the baby at a more comfortable temperature.

■ Cool hands and feet do not automatically indicate a 'cold' baby. Young babies are not able to regulate and control their temperature as well as adults and older children, and many babies have cool extremities, especially before they become mobile.

■ If you are concerned that a baby is unwell or has a raised temperature, always check, using a thermometer, and seek medical advice as necessary.

A high temperature (pyrexia)

Normal body temperature is between 36 and 37°C. A temperature above 37.5°C indicates **pyrexia** (fever). Young children's temperatures are often a sensitive indicator of the onset of illness and a raised temperature should never be ignored.

Professional Practice

■ Deal with overheating in the first instance by:
  ▪ removing clothing or a layer of bedding
  ▪ reducing the temperature of the room
  ▪ sponging the child with a cool flannel.

■ If fever is suspected:
  ▪ take the child's temperature and record the outcome
  ▪ remove clothing or a layer of bedding
  ▪ sponge with a cool flannel
  ▪ offer plenty of fluids
  ▪ use a fan to circulate cool air around the child
  ▪ observe the child carefully, particularly very young babies.

■ Febrile convulsions can occur in some children when their temperature rises, involving loss of consciousness, flickering of eyes and general jitteriness.
  ▪ A child who has one febrile convulsion is more likely to have another. It does not however mean that they have developed epilepsy.
  ▪ Medical advice should be sought if a febrile convulsion occurs.
  ▪ The child should be placed in the **recovery position** when the convulsion is over whilst medical advice is sought.
  ▪ The child needs reassurance and rest following a febrile convulsion.

 Refer to page 212, for information regarding emergency **first aid**.

activity 5.2

Ask your placement supervisor about the setting's policy on dealing with a child with a raised temperature.

Types of thermometers

Mercury thermometer

Mercury thermometers should never be used in childcare settings, but are sometimes still used in the family home. They are made of glass and should never be placed in the mouth: mercury is a poison and any breakage would mean a high risk of mercury poisoning. It takes a few minutes to get an accurate reading, which is not practical with very young children. This type of thermometer is normally placed under the armpit. It is less frequently used nowadays, being replaced by the digital thermometer.

Digital thermometer

A digital thermometer is a popular alternative to the mercury thermometer and gives a quick and accurate reading. It is usually placed in the armpit and offers no chemical risk. It should be cleaned after each use.

Temperature strip thermometer

The temperature strip thermometer is placed on the forehead. It is easy to use but less accurate than the digital or mercury thermometers.

Tympanic thermometer

The tympanic thermometer is favoured in hospitals. It is funnel shaped and is placed in the outer ear. It gives a quick and accurate reading. A disposable ear-piece is used each time and then discarded.

Figure 5.2

The four types of thermometer

Mercury thermometer

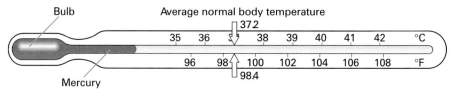

Digital thermometer

Temperature strip thermometer

A tympanic thermometer

Child Health: Care of the Child in Health and Illness by Keene (1999) is a useful source of further information on febrile convulsions and managing ill health in young children.

Caring for babies

Skin care

Skin care is important as it is one of the body's front-line defences against infection. Protecting the skin against damage has short-term benefits (from discomfort and infection) and long-term benefits (from sun damage and scarring). Babies have sensitive skin and many of our everyday products are far too harsh for them. It is therefore important to use specially prepared baby products suitable for sensitive skins during all care routines.

Skin types vary, as do cultural practices, and it is important that in any early years setting the preferences of parents are taken into account. For example, many parents of black babies prefer their baby to have cocoa butter rubbed into their skin after bathing, as black skin often has a tendency to be dry. Some babies will also require a daily massage with an oil to alleviate the dryness. Most day-care settings ask parents to provide their own products, which are clearly labelled and kept solely for the use of their baby.

Professional Practice

- Any oil used on babies and young children should be free of nut traces (almond oil used to be popular but is no longer used), as there is concern about links with the increase in nut allergies in young children.
- Many specialists recommend the use of organic sunflower oil.
- A common skin complaint in young children is eczema.

Link

Refer to Unit 10, page 437, for details of how to care for a child with eczema.

i

A range of other skin problems is described in *Child Health: Care of the Child in Health and Illness* by Keene (1999).

Care of hair

Hair care is necessary to prevent infestation from head lice and to encourage good grooming for the future. Cultural practices differ: for example, Muslim babies will have their heads shaved within 40 days of birth as part of the cultural tradition, and many Caribbean parents traditionally weave and plait their babies' hair at a very early age.

Washing babies' hair can at times be traumatic, as not all babies are happy to have water in their eyes. Hair rings are available; these prevent water from reaching the eyes and can make for a happier bathtime. Hair washing products should be 'non-stinging' for the eyes and specially formulated for babies.

Link

Refer to Bathing and nappy changing, page 163, for advice on how to wash a baby's hair.

Tooth care

Brushing of teeth should commence as soon as the first ones arrive and definitely when a baby has corresponding teeth top and bottom. Soft baby toothbrushes are specially designed for the delicate gums and first teeth, and their regular use will encourage the baby into a habit of good oral health care. In day-care settings, each baby should have their own toothbrush, which should be labelled and kept separately from others.

Figure 5.3

The usual order in which milk teeth appear

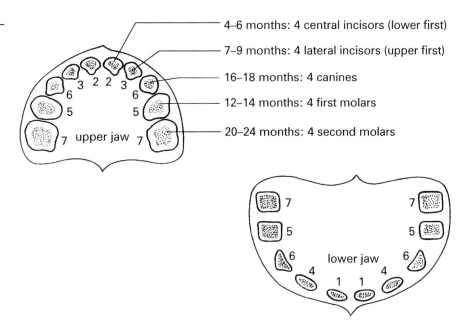

4–6 months: 4 central incisors (lower first)

7–9 months: 4 lateral incisors (upper first)

16–18 months: 4 canines

12–14 months: 4 first molars

20–24 months: 4 second molars

Bathing and nappy changing

Hygiene is top priority when dealing with body fluids of any kind, and in day-care settings the use of disposable gloves is now the norm. In the home, good personal hygiene practice should be sufficient.

Refer to page 192, for information on health, safety and personal hygiene practice.

Babies are usually topped and tailed in the mornings and bathed at night before being put to bed.

Topping and tailing

Topping and tailing involves washing the face and refreshing the top half of the body, and changing the nappy.

Preparation

Get everything ready in advance. You will need:

- towel
- changing mat
- bowl of **cooled boiled water**
- bowl of warm water
- cotton wool
- barrier cream (if using)
- clean nappy
- fresh set of clothes
- access to nappy bucket (for towelling nappies) or a nappy sack (if using disposables)
- access to laundry basket for clothes.

Method

1   Place baby on changing mat and undress to their vest and nappy.

2   Using the cooled boiled water and cotton wool, wipe each eye from the nose corner outwards, using each piece of cotton wool only once.

3   Repeat two or three times for each eye.

4   Dry gently with the corner of a clean towel.

5   Gently clean ears and around the face using moistened cotton wool, ensuring that you reach all the creases, particularly under the chin and behind the ears. Dry gently.

6   Using a larger piece of moistened cotton wool, freshen up the baby's armpits and hands, removing all fibres collected between the fingers. Dry gently.

7   For newborn babies, check that the umbilical stump is clean but do not clean unnecessarily. Whenever possible, the stump should be left alone. (It tends to shrivel up and drop off 7 to 10 days after birth.)

8   Remove soiled nappy and place in bucket or nappy sack.

9   Clean the nappy area thoroughly, with warm water (or baby wipes if used), ensuring that you clean all creases, wiping from the front to the back.

10   Put on clean nappy (applying barrier cream if used), dress and have a cuddle!

Bathing

Bathing babies can be carried out by the traditional method or the modern method. Early years professionals need to be proficient at both, to meet with parental preferences.

Prepare everything in advance, ensuring that the temperature of the room is suitable (at least 20°C/68°F) with no draughts, and that all windows and doors are closed. All that you will need must be to hand and the bath should be in a safe and secure place. A special bath stand or a firm surface is ideal, but many people choose to place the baby bath in their own bath or on the floor. Any of these options is acceptable.

remember

- When changing a baby girl's nappy, always wipe from the front to the back to avoid any infection from the bowels passing into the vaginal area.
- When changing a baby boy's nappy, do not pull back the foreskin. Excessive cleaning can cause irritation and infection, rather than prevent it.

You will need:

- bath, with water at 37°C – always check this (preferably with bath thermometer or use your elbow) before putting the baby in
- changing mat
- towels
- cotton wool
- bowl of cooled boiled water (for the eyes)
- baby shampoo (if using)
- soap
- barrier cream (if using)
- clean nappy
- fresh set of clothes
- access to nappy bucket (for towelling nappies) or a nappy sack (if using disposables)
- access to laundry basket for clothing.

Figure 5.4

Have everything prepared in advance

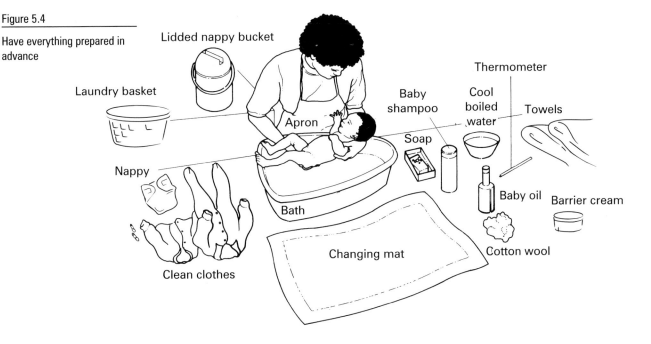

Traditional method

1 Undress baby to just the nappy and wrap in towel with the top corner folded away from you.

2 Wash the baby's eyes and face as in topping and tailing.

3 Hold baby (still wrapped in towel) under your arm with the head over the bath, resting on your hip.

4 Gently wet the hair all over.

5 Add shampoo or soap and rub in gently but firmly.

6 Rinse hair by leaning baby backwards over the bath. Towel dry the hair with the folded-over corner of the towel

7 Lay the baby across your lap and remove nappy, cleansing away excess faeces.

8 With your spare hand, gently wet and soap baby all over, turning them onto their tummy by pulling them over towards you, holding shoulder and thigh. When their back and bottom are also soaped, turn again in the same way (always towards you).

> **remember**
>
> Always keep hold of the baby, by firmly holding the arm and shoulder furthest away from you. Even very young babies can move suddenly.

9   Supporting baby's head and neck with one hand, and their bottom with the other, lower the baby into the bath.

10 Gently rinse the baby all over, continually supporting the head and neck, and holding their shoulder and arm.

11 When the baby is ready to be dried, lift the baby onto your lap, wrap in towel and cuddle dry!

12 Apply nappy and clothing as before.

13 Brush or groom hair as appropriate.

14 Trim nails as necessary using blunt baby scissors (with parents' permission).

Professional Practice

- Babies usually have a feed after a bath and are then put down to sleep.
- Only use talcum powder if parents insist. It has been suggested that its use may be linked to the development of asthma in early childhood.
- Cultural practice regarding hair care, use of oils and creams should be adhered to.
- Never poke cotton buds into ears, noses, and so on.
- Babies need total supervision by a responsible adult at all times when being bathed.

Figure 5.5

Support the baby's head and neck while holding their shoulders and arm

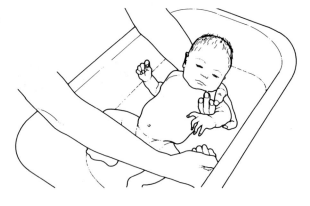

Modern method

1   Prepare bath water, clothing and so on in the same way as the traditional method.

2   Add a bathing preparation to the water.

3   Lower the baby into the water after the eyes and face have been washed.

4   Soap the baby using the 'bubble bath'.

5   Continue as in the traditional method.

Using a bathing preparation can make the water (and baby) quite slippery, so particular care is needed to hold the baby securely.

Bathing older babies

From seven or eight months onwards, babies can be bathed in the family bath, although some babies will prefer the security of the baby bath for far longer. Babies are usually much more active by this time and the additional room for splashing is appreciated. Babies are often able to sit alone quite well by this stage, but remember that the water will make them buoyant and you will need to be ready to support them if they slip.

> **remember**
>
> - If a bathing preparation causes irritation of the baby's skin, do not continue to use it.
> - Some preparations irritate a baby's skin in the early weeks but can be used later on.

The same precautions are needed regarding temperature, preparation and supervision as with younger babies.

■ Ensure that the baby cannot touch the hot tap, which remains hot for some time after use.

■ Do not have the water too deep, or the baby will 'float'.

■ Sitting on a rubber mat can help the baby feel more secure.

■ Provide a range of containers and bath toys for the baby to play with.

■ Many babies enjoy bathing with a parent.

■ Never leave a baby under the supervision of an older child.

■ No child under eight years of age should be left alone in the bathroom at any time.

Rest, sleep and play routines

Babies need a routine which is not rigid but which provides them with continuity and security – a secure baby is usually a settled baby. Babies have periods of wakefulness and periods of deep sleep. They can appear very alert and content at times and restless and irritable at others.

Figure 5.6

A baby's day

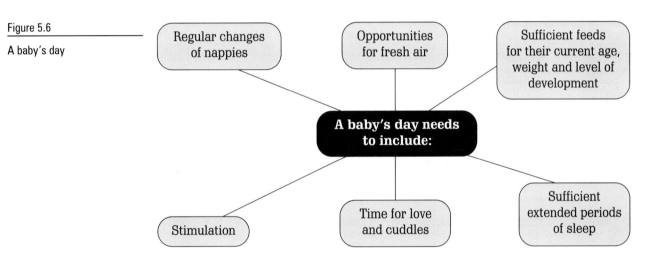

Regular changes of nappies

Opportunities for fresh air

Sufficient feeds for their current age, weight and level of development

A baby's day needs to include:

Stimulation

Time for love and cuddles

Sufficient extended periods of sleep

Planning, implementing and evaluating routines

Jefferson, Chloe and Ainsley

Jefferson is 6 weeks old, Chloe is 5 months old and Ainsley is 10 months old. Each of them is the first child. Imagine that they all have a non-working parent at home to look after them each day.

1 What similarities and differences will there be in their daily needs?

2 Plan a suitable day for each baby.

3 Imagine that all three babies now attend the Lilac Tree Nursery, where the following routine is set out for the baby room, and that Jefferson, Chloe and Ainsley are cared for each day in this baby room. How well do you think the routine will meet the needs of these children?

8.30 a.m.	Arrival, settling in and play with key worker
10.00 a.m.	Feed or snack; nappy change
10.30 a.m.	Walk around the nursery grounds in prams/buggies
11.15 a.m.	Play with key worker and other staff
12.15 p.m.	Feed and/or lunch; nappy change and sleep
1.45 p.m.	Play with key worker and other staff
3.00 p.m.	Feed or snack; nappy change
3.30 p.m.	Play or fresh air
4.00 p.m.	Play until collected

4   What might indicate to you that the needs of a baby are not being met by the routine?

5   What changes would you make if you could?

activity 5.3

Ask to see plans for different aged babies and children at your current setting. Evaluate the plans for three specific children, thinking carefully about:

1   The relevance of the plans to the age of the children concerned?

2   How well the plans actually meet the children's needs.

3   How much opportunity for flexibility there was in the planning?

Professional Practice

■   The planning of a suitable routine for a baby needs to be carefully thought through.

■   Practitioners should allow time for verbal interaction and play within care routines.

■   Practitioners should take their lead from the baby in their care as much as possible.

remember

A baby who is mostly content, feeds as usual, and settles to sleep without uncustomary distress is usually receiving a care routine suitable to their needs.

Feeding

Principles of nutritional requirements

The decision whether to breast- or bottle-feed is a personal one, and a mother's choice should be respected. However, all health professionals agree that the best start for any baby is to be breast-fed, as breast milk is the most natural and well-prepared food they can be given. For the first few months of life, most babies will need only milk feeds – either breast or bottle – to give them all the nutrients they need for their development.

Breast-feeding

Breast milk offers a degree of **natural immunity** to the infant through the mother's own immunity, and it is considered to be nature's 'designer food' because, as the infant grows, the mother's breast milk changes to meet her child's developing needs. The colostrum-rich early milk (a thick, yellowish substance with a high protein content, secreted prior to the mother's full milk production) offers some protection against common infections and is particularly important to newborn infants. Even when mothers are not intending to breast-feed long term, they are encouraged to do so for the first few days to allow their babies to benefit from this.

For breast-feeding to be successful, the mother needs to eat well and drink plenty of fluids. The more the baby feeds, the more milk is produced, on a supply-and-demand basis. Once the initial stages of breast-feeding are passed, and any soreness or discomfort has been overcome, breast-feeding is usually considered a pleasurable part of mothering.

Babies suckle for different lengths of time – some will take all they need in just a few minutes, while others will suck for far longer. Letting the baby decide the length of a feed maintains a balance and helps to prevent engorgement of the breasts. At each feed, the baby initially receives the 'fore' milk, which offers satisfaction in the short term, but the richer 'hind' milk which follows often gives satisfaction for a longer period. It is usual for babies to feed from alternate breasts at alternate feeds.

Figure 5.7

Breast milk offers the baby natural immunity

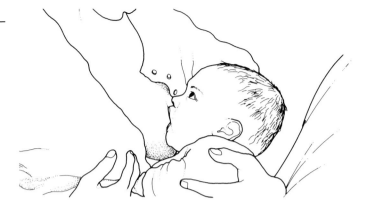

Expressing breast milk

Many mothers choose to express some of their breast milk, which can be given in a bottle or cup, and this can be a useful solution to the question of how to continue breast-feeding when returning to work. Breast pumps can be either manual or mechanical and they produce a vacuum which draws out the milk in much the same way as the baby's sucking. Battery or mains-operated pumps are far quicker to use than expressing by hand, and are suitable for expressing significant quantities.

Expressed milk can allow other family members to enjoy feeding the baby too. It can give the mother some time for herself and can alleviate any issues of embarrassment or cultural indiscretions regarding feeding in front of other people. Expressed milk needs to be kept in sterile containers and refrigerated until needed. Breast milk can be frozen (ice-cube trays are useful for this) and used in preparing solid food when the baby reaches the onset of mixed feeding. The usual sterilising procedures should be followed.

Refer to pages 168 to 171 for information on sterilising and making up a formula feed.

The diet of a breast-feeding mother

As well as eating well, a lactating mother needs to be aware that whatever she eats will be passed on to her child. This includes alcohol, spicy food, medication and the effects of smoking. Medication should never be taken without checking that it is safe for the breast-feeding child too. This applies to cough and cold remedies as well as prescribed items.

Breast-feeding mothers need plenty of support, especially in the early days and weeks. It can be very tiring as the mother is usually needed at each feed time and may have few uninterrupted rest periods. At times, breast-feeding can be hard to establish and the sensitive support and encouragement of health professionals and early years workers can be crucial to whether a mother feels able to continue. Support can be given in the form of:

- encouragement
- help with positioning of the infant
- advice on length of suckling
- advice regarding 'latching' the infant on to the breast
- advice regarding removing the infant from the breast.

Each of these is necessary to establish a feeding process which is free from soreness and discomfort.

Professional Practice

- Feeding on demand allows babies to satisfy their hunger.
- If a baby sleeps well between feeds, it usually means they are getting sufficient nutrients.
- Regular weighing of babies allows mothers to monitor the sufficiency of their milk production and gives them peace of mind.
- Green, slimy stools may indicate that a baby is not getting enough feeds – longer or more frequent feeds may need to be encouraged.
- The breast-feeding mother needs to sit comfortably, with her back supported. The baby sucks with lips curled back and takes the whole of the areola (the pigmented area around the nipple) into the mouth. Eye contact is made between mother and child and as the baby develops they pat the breast contentedly.

remember

Breast-feeding is *always* the best choice for a baby, although, as an early years professional, you should respect the choices made by others and offer support accordingly.

Formula feeding

Formula milk is an alternative to breast milk, but no artificial milk can be as ideal for a baby's stomach as breast milk. As the baby's nutritional needs change, parents need to decide when the next stage formula is required, whereas breast-feeding copes with changes naturally, linked to the growth rate of the baby and their levels of hunger.

In early years settings, babies' feeds will usually be supplied ready prepared by the parents and will need to be stored in a refrigerator until needed.

Figure 5.8

The baby should be held securely, with good eye contact

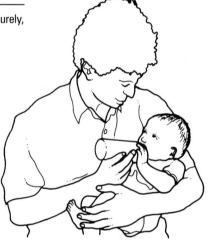

Professional Practice

- Each baby must have their feeds labelled clearly and stored separately to avoid confusion or cross-infection.

Making a formula feed

Preparation

You will need:

- formula feed
- bottle
- teats
- knife
- kettle of water, pre-boiled and allowed to cool
- sterilising equipment.

- Wash your hands thoroughly before you handle any feeding equipment.
- Prepare feeds on a cleaned surface.
- Have spare teats handy in case you drop one!

Method

1. Boil the kettle in advance and allow the water to cool.
2. Remove bottle from the steriliser unit and rinse with boiled water.
3. Pour sufficient cooled boiled water into the bottle for the feed required, following the manufacturer's guidelines.
4. Check the level is accurate.
5. Open the tin of formula.
6. Using the scoop enclosed in the tin, add the correct number of scoops to the bottle. Level each scoop off with a flat knife.
7. If using straight away, put on the teat, ring and lid, and shake the bottle gently to dissolve the formula.
8. The feed is ready for use after checking the temperature is OK.
9. If storing the feed for later, put a disc and ring on the bottle and shake gently to mix.
10. Remove disc and replace with upside-down teat (do not allow formula to touch the teat, as bacteria could begin to form).
11. Cover with disc and lid and refrigerate until needed.

remember
- It is important that the scoops of formula are level. Heaped scoops or packed-down scoops lead to over-feeding, and over-feeding can lead to excessive weight gain, high levels of salt intake and possible kidney strain. Using insufficient scoops of formula for the number of ounces of water leads to under-feeding, and under-feeding can lead to poor weight gain and a hungry baby.
- A baby needs 75 ml of formula per 500g of body weight ($2^{1}/_{2}$ fl oz per pound) in each 24-hour period.

- It is easier to make up enough feeds for the day in one go, if suitable refrigeration is available. This is particularly useful for families with twins or other multiples.

activity 5.4

Calculate the amount of formula needed in each bottle for the following babies:

1. Colin, who weighs 5.5 kg and is having seven feeds in each 24-hour period;
2. Alice, who weighs 8.0 kg and is having six feeds in each 24-hour period.

remember
Wash your hands thoroughly before feeding a baby or handling feeding equipment.

Giving a formula feed

It is important to be prepared in advance, with everything that you might need easily to hand. You should be seated comfortably and able to give the baby your full attention. Often a baby will be more comfortable having their nappy changed prior to feeding, but individual routines will vary.

1. Have all equipment together and suitably covered. The bottle can be kept warm in a jug of hot water whilst you settle with the baby.
2. Hold the baby close to you, offering a sense of security and pleasure.
3. Test the temperature of the formula against the inside of your wrist. It should feel warm, not hot.

4 Check that the milk is flowing at the appropriate rate for the baby you are feeding. Several drops per second is usual, but rates do vary from baby to baby.

5 Encourage the onset of feeding by touching the teat against the baby's lips before placing the teat into the mouth. The milk should always cover the whole teat to stop the baby taking in excess air and becoming frustrated at not receiving enough milk at a time. If the baby is reluctant to suck, pull the teat gently, as the tension will often give them the impetus to suck harder.

6 About half-way through the feed, stop and wind the baby (see below).

7 Wind again when the feed is over and settle the baby down. They may need another nappy change.

8 When a baby has finished feeding, discard any remaining formula and wash the bottle thoroughly before placing it in a steriliser.

Winding

Winding a baby is the process of helping them release any trapped air taken in during the feeding process. The baby is best held in an upright position to allow the air to rise. Useful positions for this include:

- sitting the baby forward, resting against your hand, which allows you to rub or gently pat their back with your other hand

- placing the baby on your shoulder and rubbing or gently patting their back

- resting the baby along your forearm (very young babies only) and rubbing their back

- with some babies, laying them prone across your lap and rubbing their back works well.

Professional Practice

- It is always useful to have a cloth handy as many babies posset (regurgitate) some milk during the winding process.

- Remember to keep the head and neck of young babies well supported.

activity 5.5

You have been asked to prepare a leaflet on feeding choices for your local antenatal class. This has to set out the advantages and disadvantages of both breast- and bottle-feeding and you should also include health, social, cultural and environmental factors in your information.

Sterilising techniques

Bottles and all other feeding utensils need sterilising to prevent illness occurring from the growth of bacteria. There are various **sterilising techniques** to choose from.

Cold-water sterilisers

This method of sterilising uses chemicals either in solution or tablet form. The steriliser needs to be filled to the required capacity and the solution added (or sterilising tablet allowed to dissolve) before adding bottles and other feeding equipment. Each bottle, teat or other item needs to be fully submerged, and held under water by a float. Sterilising takes 30 minutes from the time the last piece of equipment has been added. The solution needs to be replaced every 24 hours, and most tanks hold a large amount of feeding equipment.

Steam sterilisers

The steam-sterilising method is quick and efficient but is expensive and, once opened, the bottles need to be prepared within a short period of time, as opening the steriliser allows the potential growth of bacteria. There is a risk of scalding from the release of steam if the unit is opened whilst still very hot, so care must be taken. Steam sterilisers usually hold six or eight bottles at a time. They are ready for use within approximately 12–15 minutes from switching the unit on.

Figure 5.9

A microwave steriliser

Microwave sterilisers

This method works on the same principle as the steam steriliser. The units usually only hold four bottles, but the method is quick. Metal objects cannot be placed in the microwave steriliser.

Boiling method

Boiling an infant's feeding equipment is cheap but no longer a popular choice. It has considerable potential for accidents owing to the large quantities of boiling water used. It can, however, give reassurance that equipment is clean and free from germs if no other form of sterilising is available. This method only needs 10 minutes of boiling time to be ready. All equipment must be fully submerged, as with the cold water method.

case study 5.2 — Janice

Janice is shortly due to give birth to her first baby and is unsure which sterilising method to use. She is currently on maternity leave and is due to return to work when her baby is about three months old. Janice intends to breast-feed for the first few weeks, moving her baby onto formula feeds by about two months as she will be working full time and this will be a more practical option for her. Janice has asked for your advice.

activity

1 What advice would you give Janice?
2 What are the advantages and disadvantages of the various sterilising methods?

Weaning and feeding older babies

Weaning is the process of introducing a baby to 'solid' food alongside their usual milk feeds. The onset of this process should be led by the individual baby's hunger needs, and health professionals now recommend this to start when the baby is around six months old. It is a good indicator that the infant is ready to start to be weaned when they begin to seem less satisfied with just breast or formula milk and are ready for their next feed more quickly.

Another important factor is that breast and formula milk do not contain sufficient iron for continued healthy development, and prolonged (exclusive) milk feeding will not provide enough of this important mineral. Initially, an infant has sufficient stocks of iron taken from the mother during pregnancy, and much earlier the baby's digestive system is not usually mature enough to cope with the components of solid food.

Weaning should be a pleasurable experience for both carer and child, encouraging them to explore new tastes over a period of time. It should not be a situation of stress or tension. At times it can be difficult to get a baby interested in trying to take solids from a spoon, but it is important to keep on trying, without worrying about regular refusals. The baby will get there in time, and in the early stages of weaning the baby will still be having all of their milk feeds and so will not be losing out nutritionally.

Suitable foods for babies

Most babies start with baby rice, which is bland in taste and very smooth. They usually progress quite quickly to other puréed foods once they are used to taking food from a spoon. Whenever possible, freshly prepared foods should be given, rather than packets, jars or tins, as this will enable the carer (you) to control what the baby is eating more fully, particularly regarding additives such as sugar, salt, colourings and preservatives. Preparing fresh food helps to integrate the baby into family mealtimes. Convenience foods are ideal as emergency options or when travelling and many commercially prepared foods now have symbols showing whether they are sugar-free, salt-free, gluten-free, and so on.

Carers should avoid giving babies foods containing wheat or gluten (a protein found in wheat, barley and rye) up to eight months of age, with oats (which also contains the protein gluten)

Figure 5.10

Babies progress quickly onto
other foods once they are
used to taking food from a
spoon

only being allowed if there is no family history of coeliac disease – there is a suspected link
between early introduction of these products and the development of coeliac disease later on.
Nuts or products containing nuts should be avoided completely, as early introduction to these
has been linked to later development of nut allergy.

 Link   Refer to Unit 10, page 445, for an outline of coeliac disease.

> ### Professional Practice
>
> ■ Milk remains an important part of the baby's diet and will remain so until they are
>   at least a year old.
>
> ■ The aim of weaning is to introduce babies to a variety of textures, tastes and
>   experiences to integrate them fully into family mealtimes.
>
> ■ Do not introduce weaning (or a new food) when the baby is unwell or tired.
>
> ■ Offering half of the milk feed before the solids and half afterwards works well for
>   most babies, but each baby is different and they will soon indicate their preference!

As the level of solid food intake increases, the milk feeds will decrease until the baby is
having sufficient solid food at a mealtime to be satisfied with a drink of water to accompany
it. Weaning a baby is explored on page 173.

> ### Professional Practice
>
> ■ A Bristol University research project (The Children of the Nineties researching) into
>   children's development has shown that babies who are not introduced to mashed
>   (rather than puréed) food by 10 months of age are likely to be fussier eaters later
>   on in their life.

Planning to wean a young infant

The recent thinking by health professionals, based on research into children's development, recommends that babies are not introduced to solid foods until they are around six months old. Up until quite recently most infants were given their first food experiences at around four months.

One of the main aims of waiting until the child is six months, is to try and reduce the level of food allergies among young children which have increased considerably in recent years, e.g. Coeliac disease, nut allergy, lactose intolerance.

 Link

See Unit 10, page 445.

remember

There will of course always be some infants that will need to start the weaning process earlier than others. No infant should be kept hungry simply to fit in with new thinking. Health visitors are always happy to advise parents and carers, and anyone with concerns should not hesitate to ask for their advice. Avoiding foods containing gluten etc., is a sensible precaution for all infants under six months old.

activity 5.6

Research weaning plans through parenting and child health magazines and books, or through the internet.

1. Using the blank table below as a guide, plan a week's menu for a baby aged:
   - 6–7 months or
   - 8–9 months.
2. Compare your menu with another student.
3. How much of your menu could easily be prepared fresh?
4. How much of your menu could be taken from the family meals?

Table 5.1 Planning a menu

Age/months	6–7 months	8–9 months	10–11 months	12 months
On waking				
Breakfast				
Lunch				
Tea				
Late evening				

Communication with babies and children

Take time to observe an adult with a young baby; this will give you an example of pre-verbal communication, as the adult encourages the baby to take a share in the conversation, asking them questions and supplying them with answers or making reaffirming comments following their own vocalisations. Welcoming the vocal sounds of babies encourages them to vocalise further, and responding to babies and watching them respond to you will enhance their communication with you.

Figure 5.11

Methods of communication with babies

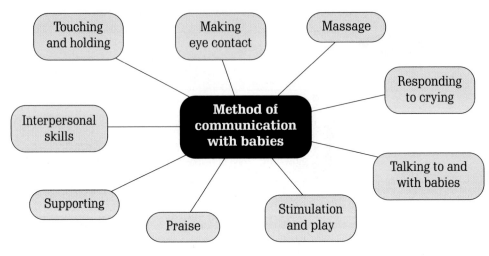

Adults communicate with babies in many ways. This can be through:

- eye contact during breast or formula feeds
- **turn-taking** vocally or visually
- initiating 'conversations' with babies as you play
- observing their needs through their body language or facial expression
- responding to their cries, for example, by giving them a cuddle
- encouraging them to vocalise, for example, by clapping and smiling
- showing appreciation of their vocalising, for example, by clapping and smiling
- giving praise, for example, by clapping and smiling
- calling to them when out of their visual range
- **aural stimulation**, for example singing to the baby
- **visual stimulation**, for example, holding a mirror in front of the baby.

---

activity 5.7

Take time to observe an early years worker in a baby room setting, working with young babies.

1 Which forms of communications listed above did you see?
2 Were there opportunities for any other form of communication to have taken place, do you think?
3 Do you think the adult you observed missed any opportunities for communication? If yes, what were they?
4 What might be the outcome for a baby who does not have opportunities for communication?

Baby massage

Baby massage can improve communication between a parent and their baby, as it enhances the parent's understanding of their baby's needs. Baby massage involves eye contact, touch, smiling and other pleasurable facial expressions and, as it involves such close contact, interaction between parent and baby is heightened. Baby massage is used by therapists to help mothers who are suffering from postnatal depression; it strengthens contact between the mother and her baby.

Figure 5.12

Baby massage can improve communication between a parent and their baby

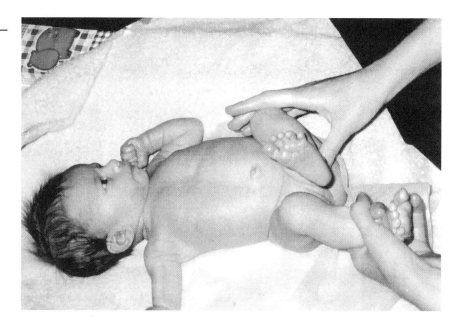

Figure 5.12

Baby massage can improve communication between a parent and their baby

Baby-signing

Baby-signing has been developed as a means of additional communication for hearing babies. The range of simple signs can be introduced very early on, and babies of just over a year old have been seen to communicate in this way, alleviating some of the frustration of not making their needs clear. This approach to communicating is not something that early years staff should introduce to the infants in their care unless parents express a wish for them to do so.

Sign With Your Baby by Garcia (2000) is a useful reference on baby-signing.

Refer to Unit 7, page 325, for a table showing how babies' language usually develops.

Stimulation and stimulating play

Stimulating play is an essential part of a child's daily experience and, as an early years professional, you will be responsible for providing the children in your care with a range of stimulating opportunities, both indoors and outside.

There are a number of excellent publications outlining ideas for providing stimulating play. See Bibliography and suggested further reading, page 463.

Stimulating play for very young babies

Very young babies initially obtain most of their stimulation from the interactions with their mother or main carers, through feeding, care routines, gentle rocking and soothing and the calming tone of their voice. By about six weeks, babies demonstrate that they have become much more visually alert and are usually smiling and focusing on the faces of their carers and familiar objects. By this time they will enjoy stimuli which hold their attention, such as mobiles, which should be brightly coloured and three-dimensional. Many mobiles have a musical element which adds to the stimulation.

Figure 5.13

By about six weeks, babies enjoy stimuli which hold their attention

From here, babies benefit from progressing to an activity frame or something similar which can be placed above them, encouraging them to focus visually and aurally on the items hanging in front of them and enjoying tactile experiences too as they come into contact with the items during their natural body movements. Eventually, these movements become more intentional, and repeated actions will be observed, often in response to the 'reward' of a noise or visual 'experience' (movement, reflection or fluttering of material). Bathtime and nappy changing offer opportunities to play when there is freedom from the restriction of clothes and full leg mobility is possible, and this play should be encouraged as often as possible.

Babies love music, and many will respond well to music familiar to them from the womb. They listen carefully to all that goes on around them and can often be seen to respond to gentle music (which has a soothing affect) and lively music (which can agitate or excite).

Babies also enjoy books and pictures from a very early age, and there is now a scheme specifically designed for them: Books for Babies (published by Friends of Libraries USA-FOLUSA) is a literacy programme that helps parents understand the importance of books in a baby's development.

Reading with a baby involves close and pleasurable contact. It also encourages an early interest in literature as a medium of pleasure.

Babies outside

Babies enjoy being outside, watching the leaves on trees flickering and taking in the sounds and smells of the garden. Fresh air is good for them, but they should never be left unsupervised and care should be taken to ensure that prams are not positioned in the sun, as a baby's delicate skin burns extremely quickly. Whenever possible, allow a baby to lie out of doors in warm weather without a nappy on, as exposure of the nappy area to fresh air is healthy and stimulating for their skin too.

Although most professionals agree that taking a baby out each day is a good idea, this does not apply if the weather is particularly cold or foggy.

remember

It is important to monitor the movement of the sun to ensure that a baby's pram has not moved from shade into sunlight.

Professional Practice

- Babies absorb information from all around them and benefit from as many experiences as it is possible to give them.

- It is, however, important not to over-stimulate them at any one time, as this can cause them to become tired and irritable.

Figure 5.14

An activity frame encourages babies to focus visually and aurally on the items in front of them

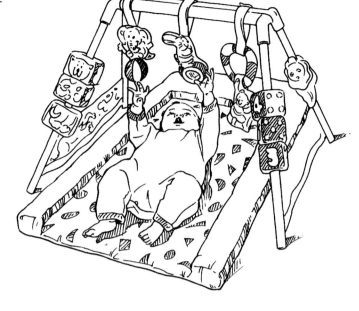

remember

The objects included in a treasure basket need to be kept very clean. They should not have sharp or rough edges or be at risk of coming apart, and none should be small enough to be swallowed or put up noses. The infant will need supervision whilst exploring their treasure basket – but not direct adult intervention.

Stimulating play for older babies

As they develop, older babies will be interested in a range of household articles. Sturdy boxes can be handled easily, being passed from hand to hand from about six months and knocked together as manipulative control is developed. Babies will also enjoy banging things in order to make a noise. A useful item for this is a wooden spoon on a saucepan lid or the tray of their high chair.

Treasure baskets

Babies enjoy activities which enable them to explore through all of their senses and an excellent resource for this is a treasure basket. A **treasure basket** includes a range of objects made of natural materials that can be easily handled by the infant. The items should be selected carefully to stimulate all the senses and should be completely safe. Nothing in a treasure basket should be made of plastic or any other man-made materials.

Infants of about six months will enjoy exploring a treasure basket. Ideally, they need to be able to sit up securely in order to benefit from the freedom to explore. They should be allowed to focus on the objects they are handling without distraction from the adult or older children.

Figure 5.15

From the age of about six months, a baby will enjoy exploring a treasure basket

case study Nasreen and Claire

5.3

Nasreen and Claire have been asked to prepare a treasure basket. They have selected the following items:

a silk hankie	a bag of lavender	a fir cone
a sheet of sandpaper	a wooden 'egg' permeated with lemon scent	
an orange	a wooden spoon	corrugated cardboard
a natural sponge	a large shell	a glass paper weight
a wooden clothes peg	a loofah	a large cork

activity

1   Are all the items suitable, do you think?
2   Would you remove any of the items? If yes, which ones and why?
3   What else would you add to the basket if you were preparing it?
4   Have Nasreen and Claire provided stimulation for all the senses?

Professional Practice

■ The adult's role is to provide, to oversee and to allow freedom of exploration.

■ Some older children with a special need may also benefit from exploring a resource prepared along the lines of a treasure basket.

 Link

For additional discussion of planning a suitable environment to stimulate a baby's all-round development refer to Unit 4, page 147.

remember

Babies sometimes want a drink in the same way as adults and older children do. Small amounts of cooled boiled water can be introduced to even very young babies, especially in hot weather.

Soothing a distressed baby

Babies become distressed for lots of reasons. It may be because they are tired, wet, hungry, uncomfortable, unwell, teething or simply bored. Working out the cause of their distress is not always easy and not all babies like to be comforted in the same way. It is important to respond to an infant's distress in a way that is best for them as an individual. This is why continuity of care through key worker systems is so important.

Professional Practice

■ Every baby is different and has their own individual personality.

■ Some babies cry much more than others.

■ It is possible to over-stimulate a baby, tiring them and causing irritability.

■ Illness must never be ruled out, but will usually be considered when other causes have been eliminated unless additional symptoms are present.

■ Offer support to the parents of a constantly crying baby as it can be very draining.

Link

For information on illness in babies (and children), refer to Unit 10, pages 431 to 445, Common childhood illnesses.

Figure 5.16

Why is the baby crying?

My tummy hurts
If a baby is distressed at the same time of day every day, it can often be attributed to **colic**. Colic is a painful condition, common in the first four months, in which the baby pulls up their legs indicating abdominal pain and is very difficult to console. There is no known cause for colic and it tends to disappear by itself by the time the baby reaches four months old. It is, however, distressing for both baby and carer and advice from a health visitor is advisable. The baby is usually thriving well in spite of the colic and no other symptoms are displayed.

I'm tired
Babies become over-tired if they do not have sufficient periods of restful sleep, and a baby who is constantly disturbed may become irritable. It is important to allow babies an extended period of sleep whenever possible.

I want my nappy changed
A wet or soiled nappy is uncomfortable, and most babies prefer to be clean and dry. Regular changing of babies helps prevent the development of nappy rash, as does allowing fresh air to their bottoms by leaving them to kick freely at some point each day.

I'm so bored
Sometimes, however, babies are simply bored, and so it is important to offer them stimulation. Mobiles over the cot or hanging from the ceiling are ideal visual stimulants and musical toys will stimulate them aurally. Babies also enjoy the company of their carers and will respond with pleasure and recognition from a very early age.

Please leave me alone
Sometimes babies become distressed when being handled, but this is usually a stage that passes quickly. Handling should be gentle and kept to a minimum until they find it more pleasurable.

Why is the baby crying?

I'm too hot
A baby who is too hot or too cool may also cry in discomfort. Adjusting the temperature of the room or their clothing will usually help.

My gums hurt
If a baby is unwell or teething, they may simply want to be cuddled. For a teething baby, a refrigerated teething ring will help cool down their gums and firm flexible teething toys will give them something appropriate to chew hard on. Preparations are available to rub onto the gums to alleviate discomfort of the gums and paediatric paracetamol can be given in times of extreme discomfort.

I want my bottle
A hungry or thirsty baby is often the easiest to identify as they tend to root for the breast or bottle when picked up or suck on whatever passes their mouth. In a day-care setting, making a note of the time and amount of feed taken by the baby helps you to anticipate their next feed time and is a general requirement of those caring for babies.

case study 5.4 Rosie

Rosie is seven months old and is teething. She has been unsettled for the past week during the day, and has hardly slept for the past two nights. Her mum is exhausted as she is a single parent with sole responsibility for Rosie and her three older brothers aged two to seven. You live next door to Rosie's family and want to help.

activity
1 What could you do to help?
2 What advice could you give Rosie's mum?
3 You have heard of a phone line called Cry-sis for parents with fretful babies. Where could you find out more about the help they offer?

Babies' clothing

Clothing for babies needs to:

- be easy to put on and take off
- allow room for the baby to grow
- allow unrestricted movement
- be suitable for the time of year and temperature of the environment they are in
- avoid cramping of toes (all-in-one suits)
- be free from long ties or ribbons (to avoid choking)
- be free from loose buttons or poppers (another choking hazard)
- be free from looped edgings on seams
- avoid lacy designs that may catch small fingers
- be easy to wash and dry
- be made of natural materials to allow skin to breathe
- not involve fluffy materials or wools such as mohair
- be of a suitable length – not long enough for dresses to get caught when toddling or crawling.

Figure 5.17

Babies' clothing should be suitable for the time of year and the environment they are in

Professional Practice

- It is better for babies to be dressed in several layers of clothes that can be removed or replaced according to temperature, rather than one warmer layer which offers no opportunity for adjustment, as babies are not able to control their body temperature and could therefore become overheated.

Care of babies' feet

Babies' feet are very delicate and their bones are still forming, therefore they should not be given shoes before they are able to walk, as this will hinder the natural growth of their feet, causing deformity. Socks, all-in-one suits and bootees should all have sufficient room for natural movement and growth.

Figure 5.18

Soft, roomy boottees are the ideal first footwear

Progress Check

1. At what temperature should a baby's room be?
2. Why are a baby's feet and hands sometimes cold even when their temperature is considered to be normal?
3. What body temperature indicates a potential fever?
4. What is a febrile convulsion?
5. Where is the temperature taken if using a tympanic thermometer?
6. What are the main benefits of breast-feeding?
7. Why is it important to add the correct ratio of formula to water when making a bottle feed?
8. What is meant by 'posseting'?
9. Name four methods of sterilising infant feeding equipment.
10. Why is six months the recommended age to introduce solid food to babies?
11. What type of skin has a particular tendency towards dryness?
12. List five points to remember about clothing for babies.
13. Why are nut oils not recommended for use in baby massage?
14. Why are mothers suffering from postnatal depression often encouraged to massage their babies?
15. What concern has been raised about the use of talcum powder on babies?
16. What temperature should a baby's bath water be?

Young children

Like babies, children require a suitable temperature in which to play, work and sleep and in an early years setting the room temperature should not drop below 18.5°C/65°F. A wall thermometer should be displayed and regularly monitored. Maintaining and promoting the healthy development of children includes consideration of their diet and daily routine, the development of self-esteem and independence appropriate to their age, and also ensuring that they are clothed appropriately for the time of year and the activities they are engaged in.

Link

A stimulating learning environment contributes to their all-round well-being, and a range of ideas for this are set out in Unit 4, page 147.

Feeding children – principles of diet and nutrition

A good balanced diet is one which includes all the nutritional requirements for the growth, maintenance and development of the body. The food we eat helps us maintain and repair our body tissues, keeping muscles and organs functioning. It also helps to prevent infection and supplies us with our energy needs. A balanced diet should abide by the **principles of diet and nutrition** and include elements from the four main food groups:

■ proteins, which help growth, development and tissue repair

■ carbohydrates, which provide energy

■ vitamins, minerals and fibre, for general good health and the prevention of illness

■ dairy products, which are high in calcium, enhancing and maintaining bones and teeth.

A fifth food group – fats and oils – are higher-level energy-giving foods which should be consumed sparingly by adults.

Many foods contribute to more than one food group, for example, meat is a good source of iron, and pulses are a good source of fibre, but the illustration below indicates where the main benefits of each food lie.

Figure 5.19

The food groups

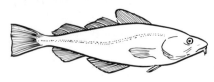

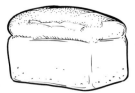

Proteins: meat, fish, poultry, offal, eggs, pulses, nuts (avoid giving to young children), textured vegetable protein (TVP, mostly made from soya)

Carbohydrates: cereals, breads, pasta, rice, starchy vegetables (e.g. potato, yam, plantain)

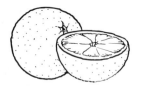

Vitamins, minerals and fibre: all vegetables, all fruits, fresh and dried

Fats and oils: butter, margarine, vegetable spreads, oils (cooking and dressing)

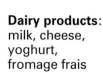

Dairy products: milk, cheese, yoghurt, fromage frais

The following tables show the benefits of a range of vitamins and minerals and the possible problems that can occur if there is a deficiency.

Table 5.2 The main vitamins

Vitamin	Food source	Function	Notes
A	Butter, cheese, eggs, carrots, tomatoes	Promotes healthy skin, good vision	Fat-soluble, can be stored in the liver; deficiency causes skin infections, problems with vision
B group	Liver, meat, fish, green vegetables, beans, eggs	Healthy working of muscles and nerves; forming haemoglobin	Water-soluble, not stored in the body, so regular supply needed; deficiency results in muscle wasting, anaemia
C	Fruits and fruit juices, especially orange, blackcurrant, pineapple; green vegetables	For healthy tissue, promotes healing	Water-soluble, daily supply needed; deficiency means less resistance to infection; extreme deficiency results in scurvy
D	Oily fish, cod liver oil, egg yolk; added to margarine, milk	Growth and maintenance of bones and teeth	Fat-soluble, can be stored by the body; can be produced by the body as a result of sunlight on the skin; deficiency results in bones failing to harden and dental decay
E	Vegetable oils, cereals, egg yolk	Protects cells from damage	Fat-soluble, can be stored by the body
K	Green vegetables, liver	Needed for normal blood clotting	Fat-soluble, can be stored in the body

Source: Beaver *et al.* (2001, p. 345)

Table 5.3 The main minerals

Mineral	Food source	Function	Notes
Calcium	Cheese, eggs, fish, milk, yoghurt	Essential for growth of bones and teeth	Works with vitamin D and phosphorus; deficiency means risk of bones failing to harden (rickets) and dental caries
Fluoride	Occurs naturally in water, or may be added artificially to water supply	Combines with calcium to make tooth enamel more resistant to decay	There are different points of view about adding fluoride to the water supply
Iodine	Water, sea foods, added to salt, vegetables	Needed for proper working of the thyroid gland	Deficiency results in enlarged thyroid gland in adults, cretinism in babies
Iron	Meat, green vegetables, eggs, liver, red meat	Needed for formation of haemoglobin in red blood cells	Deficiency means there is anaemia causing lack of energy, breathlessness; vitamin C helps the absorption of iron
Sodium chloride	Table salt, bread, meat, fish	Needed for formation of cell fluids, blood plasma, sweat, tears	Salt should not be added to any food prepared for babies: their kidneys cannot eliminate excess salt as adult kidneys do; excess salt is harmful in an infant diet

Other essential trace minerals include: potassium, phosphorus, magnesium, sulphur, manganese and zinc.

Source: Beaver *et al.* (2001, p. 246)

Figure 5.20

How a balanced diet promotes health and development

A healthy diet offers a range of foods from each food group, ensuring that the diet is well balanced, and is not deficient in any area. Encouraging children to try foods from a range of cultures and from amongst seasonal fruits and vegetables will promote a healthy and diverse approach to diet throughout life.

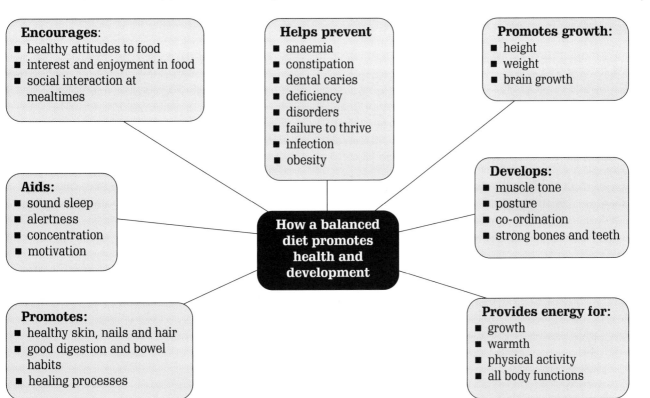

Encourages:
- healthy attitudes to food
- interest and enjoyment in food
- social interaction at mealtimes

Helps prevent
- anaemia
- constipation
- dental caries
- deficiency
- disorders
- failure to thrive
- infection
- obesity

Promotes growth:
- height
- weight
- brain growth

Aids:
- sound sleep
- alertness
- concentration
- motivation

How a balanced diet promotes health and development

Develops:
- muscle tone
- posture
- co-ordination
- strong bones and teeth

Promotes:
- healthy skin, nails and hair
- good digestion and bowel habits
- healing processes

Provides energy for:
- growth
- warmth
- physical activity
- all body functions

Planning a diet for children

- Children need a diet that is high in protein and carbohydrates to meet their high energy needs. The carbohydrates should ideally come from starchy foods such as potatoes, breads and cereals.

- Think about both colour and texture when planning meals, as an attractive meal will be more appealing, especially to a fussy or reluctant eater.

- Vary the meals that are offered to children, but do not offer more than one new food at a time.

- Large portions can be off-putting. It is better to have all of a small meal eaten, than half of a larger one, as it encourages good habits.

> **remember**
>
> Children have preferences too.

Daily portions for children

As a guideline for planning the dietary needs of young children, a good daily balance would include:

- five portions of fruit or vegetables

- two portions of protein foods

- two portions of dairy foods plus 1 pint of milk

- four portions of carbohydrates.

Snacks

Most children will also need to be offered snacks. It is important that these are mostly nutritional and healthy.

> **remember**
>
> Snacks need to be nutritional to be of benefit to a child; this should set them a healthy example for the future (see Table 5.4).

Snacks are an important part of a child's nutritional intake. Children use a lot of energy in their play and often need an energy boost in the middle of the morning or afternoon. This is particularly important if they are at a stage of developing particularly quickly physically, or becoming more active than usual.

---

case study 5.5 **Redhouse Nursery School**

Redhouse Nursery School has a fruit-only policy for snack time. Many children bring an apple or a carrot, but still seem to be flagging at the end of the morning.

activity

1   Why is this do you think?
2   What fruit would offer them a greater energy boost?
3   Is a fruit-only policy a good idea?
4   What other healthy options could be included?

activity 5.8

Plan a midday meal for a group of four-year-olds, ensuring that there are three colours and three textures within the meal. You can plan a meal from any culture you wish.

1   What have you included for colour?
2   What textures have you provided?
3   What food groups have you incorporated into your meal?
4   Are any food groups not represented? Is this a problem, do you think?

activity

5.9

Collect labels from a range of frequently used processed products that are enjoyed by children.

1 What proportions are the ingredients in?
2 How near to the top of the list are sugar or salt?
3 What does this tell you about processed foods?
4 What alternatives could you offer in their place?
5 Look at Table 5.5. How much of the Estimated Average Requirements (EARs) would the processed foods you looked at meet?

Professional Practice

■ There are many hidden extras in processed foods, particularly sugar and salt. Whenever possible, offer fresh foods to children and do not provide salt or sugar on the table for them to add to their foods.

Table 5.4 Ideas for healthy snacks

Good as regular snacks	Occasional snacks, not regular
Fresh fruit: banana, orange, pear kiwi, melon	Crisps Sweet biscuits Chocolate biscuits Chocolate and sweets Cakes
Raw vegetables (washed thoroughly): celery, carrot, tomato, cabbage leaves, Chinese leaves	
Dried fruits: raisins, sultanas, banana, dates and figs, apple rings, apricots Small cubes of cheese Sandwiches (savoury fillings) Pitta breads (savoury fillings)	

Healthy drinks	Less healthy drinks
Milk Water Milkshakes (fresh fruit) Fruit juices	Milkshakes (powdered) Squashes Carbonated drinks (Coke, Cola, etc.)

Table 5.5 Estimated average requirements (EARs) for energy in the UK (per day)

Age range	Males		Females	
	MJ	kcal	MJ	kcal
0–3 months (formula fed)	2.28	545	2.16	515
4–6 months	2.89	690	2.69	645
7–9 months	3.44	825	3.20	765
10–12 months	3.85	920	3.61	865
1–3 years	5.15	1230	4.86	1165
4–6 years	7.16	1715	6.46	1545
7–10 years	8.24	1970	7.28	1740

Source: Dare and O'Donovan (1996), p.7

Further information on nutritional sources can be found in *A Practical Guide to Child Nutrition* by Dare and O'Donovan (1996), *Feeding the Under-5s* by Dyson and Meredith (2006) or *Eating Well for the Under-5s in Child Care* by Walker (1998), which includes a CD-ROM, the CHOMP menu planner, to help with menu planning and nutritional advice for young children in all early years settings.

Using a chart like the one below, plan a range of meals and snacks for a group of similarly aged children in a day nursery. Take into account their age, level of activity and the appropriate guidelines regarding EARs. National guidelines state that children in full day care (over 8 hours) should be provided with 70 per cent of the EARs by the setting. Assume that all the children in your chosen group are in this category.

	Monday	Tuesday	Wednesday	Thursday	Friday
On arrival					
Morning snack					
Lunch					
Afternoon snack					
Tea					

Cultural and dietary needs

Children have their own preferences regarding food, which should be accommodated up to a point. A balance is needed between allowing a child to select what they eat or do not eat, and encouraging them to try a range of new and familiar foods. When preparing meals for children, dietary needs also need to be considered. This includes children with a food intolerance or allergy, family requirements such as vegetarian or vegan diets and cultural needs. Table 5.6 sets out the **food-related customs** of a range of cultures; 'some' means that some people within a religious group would find these foods acceptable.

Table 5.6 Food-related customs

	Jewish	Hindu[1]	Sikh[1]	Muslim	Buddhist	Rastafarian[2]
Eggs	No blood spots	Some	Yes	Yes	Some	Some
Milk/yoghurt	Not with meat	Yes	Yes	Yes	Yes	Some
Cheese	Not with meat	Some	Some	Possibly	Yes	Some
Chicken	Kosher	Some	Some	Halal	No	Some
Mutton/lamb	Kosher	Some	Yes	Halal	No	Some
Beef and beef products	Kosher	No	No	Halal	No	Some
Pork and pork products	No	No	Rarely	No	No	No
Fish	With fins and scales	With fins and scales	Some	Some	Some	Yes
Shellfish	No	Some	Some	Some	No	No
Butter/ghee	Kosher	Some	Some	Some	No	Some
Lard	No	No	No	No	No	No
Cereal foods	Yes	Yes	Yes	Yes	Yes	Yes
Nuts/pulses	Yes	Yes	Yes	Yes	Yes	Yes
Fruits/vegetables	Yes	Yes[3]	Yes	Yes	Yes	Yes
Fasting[4]	Yes	Yes	Yes	Yes	Yes	Yes

Source: Walker (1998), p. 68

'Some' means that some people within a religious group would find these foods acceptable.
1 Strict Hindus and Sikhs will not eat eggs, meat, fish, and some fats.
2 Some Rastafarians are vegan.
3 Jains have restrictions on some vegetable foods. Check with the individuals.
4 Fasting is unlikely to apply to young children.

activity
5.11

The menus for young children shown below do not take into account any special dietary requirements. You have been asked to suggest alternatives for Monday and Wednesday to accommodate a child with coeliac disease, and for Thursday and Friday to accommodate a child from a practising Buddhist family.

1 What will you change?
2 What difference will this make to the nutritional balance?
3 How will you ensure that the children are not made to feel different from anyone else?

Monday	On arrival	Diluted fruit juice, slice of bread with margarine, jam or marmite
	Morning snack	Milk or diluted juice and toast
	Lunch	Minced lamb, rice and peas
		Stewed apple and custard
		Water
	Afternoon snack	Bread with cheese spread
		Apple slices
		Milk or diluted juice
Tuesday	On arrival	Diluted fruit juice, slice of bread with margarine, jam or marmite
	Morning snack	Milk or diluted juice and oatcake
	Lunch	Pork hotpot, potatoes and carrots
		Custard tart
		Water
	Afternoon snack	Egg sandwiches
		Banana
		Milk or diluted juice
Wednesday	On arrival	Diluted fruit juice, slice of bread with margarine, jam or marmite
	Morning snack	Milk or diluted juice and toast
	Lunch	Bean and vegetable pastabake
		Milk pudding
		Water
	Afternoon snack	Toast and marmite
		Yoghurt
		Milk or diluted juice
Thursday	On arrival	Diluted fruit juice, slice of bread with margarine, jam or marmite
	Morning snack	Milk or diluted juice and rice cake
	Lunch	Pork curry and rice
		Fruit fool
		Water
	Afternoon snack	Fruitbread
		Apple slices
		Milk or diluted juice
Friday	On arrival	Diluted fruit juice, slice of bread with margarine, jam or marmite
	Morning snack	Milk or diluted juice and toast
	Lunch	Fish cakes, mashed potato and baked beans
		Cake and custard
		Water
	Afternoon snack	Bread with cheese spread
		Banana
		Milk or diluted juice

Link

Refer to Unit 10, page 445, for details of coeliac disease.

activity 5.12

With a partner, discuss the following statements made to children:

- 'No, you can't have pudding unless your dinner is eaten up.'
- 'Everybody is given the same amount, otherwise it is not fair.'
- 'Of course you like peas, everyone likes peas.
- 'You can have a drink after you have finished.'
- 'No, you're a coeliac, you can't have the pie.'

1   What would concern you if you heard these statements being made?
2   What messages are being given to the children?
3   How would you feel if the statements were made to you during your meal?

Professional Practice

- Mealtimes should be a time of pleasure and socialising.
- Forcing a child to eat more than they want to may make them resent food, or even vomit.
- The pudding should be an integral part of the meal, not a prize for those who eat their dinner.
- Some children have far greater appetites than others, so will need larger portions.
- Making meals exciting can entice children to eat foods they may usually refuse.

Ways of making foods more interesting
- Sandwiches can be cut into interesting shapes:
  - boats: an oblong with two triangle sails (from one round of sandwiches)
  - use large pastry cutters: trees, stars, moons, and so on.
- Arrange food on plates into pictures: faces, clowns, cat with whiskers.
- Give meals exciting names: magic mash, nursery noodles, rocket of rice, planet of pasta.

Figure 5.21

Fun foods for children

Skin and hair care
Skin and hair care applies to children in the same ways as it does to babies. It involves encouraging regular washing, bathing and teeth cleaning. Children may now, however, be able to tolerate some of the bath products that were unsuitable for the more sensitive skin of younger babies. Whenever a new product is used, it is sensible to watch for any reaction such as a slight rash or irritation. If a reaction occurs, refrain from using the product.

Skin care includes using sunblock whenever the child is exposed to the sun. Early years settings need a clear policy regarding outdoor activity and sun-screening, and parents should be responsible for putting sunblock on their child before leaving them at school or the day-care setting in hot weather. With parents' written permission, early years staff must take on this responsibility, following parents' instructions.

Figure 5.22

Children and babies should not be exposed to the sun for more than a short period of time

Professional Practice

■ Children who suffer any chronic skin problems, such as eczema, should not use perfumed bathtime products, unless sanctioned by their doctor, as these are likely to irritate the skin further.

■ Total sunblock should be used on babies and young children.

Dental care

All children should be encouraged to clean their teeth after each meal and before bedtime, to prevent a build up of tartar and tooth decay. Separate toothbrushes should be available for each child. These should never be shared.

Toilet training

By around 18 months, many toddlers are ready to start potty training, but others will not be ready to start until quite a few months later. Bladder and bowel control cannot be achieved until the nervous system is mature enough for the child to register that they want to use the potty and their muscles are able to control the process. Many people recommend having a potty around the house so that it becomes familiar to the child, which will eventually encourage them to sit on it. When doing so coincides with a successful 'outcome', much praise should be given (positive reinforcement).

The wishes of parents should be respected in early years settings regarding potty training, but this should in no way result in a child becoming anxious or upset about the process. A calm, patient approach is likely to be the most successful.

Clothing

Adults need to be responsible for what the children in their care wear, as young children are not able to make an informed choice but will state preferences with little regard to temperature, weather or planned activity.

Clothing for children needs to:

■ be easy to put on and take off, to encourage independence

■ allow for growth, as the growth rate of children is so rapid

■ allow unrestricted movement, particularly for outdoor and any physically active play

- be suitable for the time of year and temperature of the environment they are in
- be free from long or loose ties or ribbons that could get caught during play
- be kept in good repair and regularly washed, setting a good example regarding cleanliness
- be easy to wash and dry
- be made of natural materials to allow skin to breathe
- be of a suitable length to avoid the possibility of tripping
- be suitable for the activities being undertaken.

> **remember**
>
> Children's clothing should be suitable for the activities being undertaken.

Figure 5.23

Outdoor play

Foot-care

Children's feet develop quickly and it is not uncommon for a child to need four pairs of new shoes during the course of one year. Foot-care specialists recommend that children should have their feet measured every 12 weeks and sooner if there is any concern about cramping of toes or if soreness occurs.

> **Professional Practice**
>
> - Shoes made of leather allow children's feet to breathe, and it is therefore the ideal choice of material.
> - It is unhealthy for children to wear trainers or similar footwear for long periods of time.
> - Sock sizes should also be monitored – socks that are too tight can cause damage to the structure of a child's foot.
> - It is better for children to wear several layers of clothes that can be taken off or replaced according to temperature, rather that one warmer layer which offers no opportunity for adjustment.
> - Children should be able to play happily without worrying about getting their clothes messy.
> - Aprons for painting and water play are of course appropriate precautions to take in school or day care.

Progress Check

1   What are the main food groups?
2   What are the guidelines regarding daily portions for young children?
3   Why is it important to vary the colour and texture of meals for children?
4   Outline the food customs of one culture or religion.
5   List five points regarding clothing and shoes for young children.

Stimulation – stimulating play for toddlers

As they reach the toddler stage, children need opportunities to develop their large motor skills, particularly direction and spatial skills. Once they are walking, using push-a-long toys will help them become more stable and co-ordinated. Children at this stage need space, and careful positioning of unavoidable obstacles around the nursery room will help them develop spatial awareness and control.

The use of boxes and tables and chairs as places to hide is common and rewarding for children of this age, and opportunities to learn to climb skilfully will be beneficial. Indoor slides and mini climbing frames are ideal.

The interest in boxes and placing items in and taking them out is gradually replaced by the building of towers, and grading toys enhance both manipulative dexterity and early problem-solving.

Outside play

Wheeled toys are enjoyed, including ride-along toys and tricycles. Balls and beanbags, whilst possible to use indoors, are a real asset in the garden. Controlling large and small balls takes differing skills and paired games with an adult or an older child helps develop physical as well as social development.

Stimulation – stimulating play for older children

Activities should be planned to meet the needs of all children in the group or class, taking into account the differentiation of need. The stages of development set out in Unit 7, page 295, are only a guide. Many children will be ahead of the 'norms' and some will still be developing towards them. An environment in which there is too little stimulation will result in children who are bored and potentially disruptive to others in the group. An environment in which there is little opportunity to achieve will result in frustrated, disappointed children whose self-esteem could be negatively affected.

Outside play

Play out of doors needs careful supervision as it does with younger children because, as children become more independent, they sometimes take risks. Their interest and wish to climb higher, run faster and so on often outstrip their ability to carry the activity out safely. If climbing frames and other large items of play equipment are provided, they must be supported by safety surfaces.

 Link

Refer to page 205, for information on safe play surfaces.

Progress Check

1   What is a treasure basket?
2   At what age would you usually introduce treasure basket exploration?
3   Name five items that could be included in a treasure basket.
4   What is meant by a tactile experience?
5   Why do older children need careful supervision?

Healthy, safe and secure environment

Issues of safety and the security of early years environments are covered in this section, together with a discussion of personal hygiene, cross-infection, accident prevention and risk assessments (including health and safety legislation) both in early years settings and on outings. Reference is also made to the safe care of equipment and resources.

Hygiene

Hygiene includes personal care, together with the care and cleanliness of floors, feeding equipment, and food handling. There are a number of regulations and Acts that settings must abide by.

Food Safety Act 1990 and Food Safety (General Food Hygiene) Regulations 1995

This legislation includes guidelines on both personal and general kitchen hygiene. It can be summarised as follows.

Personal hygiene

This involves:

- regular hand washing throughout the day
- washing hands before all food preparation
- washing hands after any activity with the potential for bacteria:
  - nappy changing
  - using the toilet
  - coughing
  - sneezing
  - nose blowing
- use of antibacterial soaps
- nails kept clean and short
- cuts and sores covered
- use of disposable gloves. Also:
- Hair should be kept tied back to reduce the risk of infestation, cross-infection and general untidiness.
- Clean clothing and overalls should be worn at all times, changing as necessary for food preparation and cooking activities.
- Covering the nose and mouth when coughing and sneezing should be automatic and needs to be encouraged in all children too.

Kitchen hygiene

This involves:

- keeping surfaces cleaned and free from bacteria
- ensuring all surfaces used are unblemished and unchipped
- using separate boards for cooked and uncooked foods
- using separate knives for cooked and uncooked foods
- keeping floors cleaned thoroughly
- washing up as dirty utensils occur to eliminate additional bacteria growth (where possible use a dishwasher as this is the most effective method)
- wrapping all waste securely and emptying bins regularly
- regular cleaning and defrosting of refrigerators and freezers
- ensuring the temperature of a refrigerator is kept at 4–5°C (39–41°F)
- storing cooked foods at the top of the refrigerator, raw foods below

- minimal handling of all foods
- keeping food well covered
- ensuring use-by dates are adhered to
- serving any reheated food piping hot
- not keeping food warm for more than a few minutes.

activity
5.13

1   Check the temperature of the refrigerator at your home (if it has a thermometer).
2   Is the food in the refrigerator stored properly? Are all raw meats stored at the bottom?
3   Is there anything 'lurking' at the back? If yes, check its use-by date and discard if necessary.
4   Ask at your placement how often the refrigerator and freezer are defrosted and who is responsible. These procedures should be recorded.
5   How often is the temperature of the refrigerator at your placement checked and who checks it?
6   Is the food in the refrigerator at your placement stored properly? If not, talk to your supervisor about this.

Professional
Practice

- Some colleges include a certificated Food Hygiene course in their training for early years students.
- Taking the opportunity to obtain this additional certificate will enable you to consolidate and evidence your knowledge and understanding of food hygiene issues.
- Obtaining the certificate during your training may help you in gaining future employment.

Floors

Floors should be cleaned at the end of every session and at the end of the day, and regularly throughout the day to clear up spills, to control the spread of dust and dirt, and to control the development of general clutter. Cleaning would usually be through vacuuming, followed by washing thoroughly with soapy water. Any accidents involving body fluids should be immediately cleaned using an appropriate disinfectant, and all cloths disposed of safely.

Feeding equipment

Strict hygiene practices are paramount in the kitchen and appropriate sterilisation procedures should be carried out for all baby-feeding equipment.

   Link

Refer back to page 170 for details on a range of sterilisation techniques.

activity
5.14

Consider how you could encourage children to plan an activity that would show their awareness of the importance of personal hygiene.

1   What topics could they choose?
2   What activities could they include in their topics?
3   How might an activity differ for children aged four and children aged seven?
4   Compare your ideas with a partner.

Security

Maintaining a safe and secure environment

Each early years setting must be registered with its local authority and has to meet certain criteria in order to retain its registration. This involves adhering to a range of regulations, Acts, guidelines and care standards regarding the setting up and maintenance of safe and healthy practice in all provisions, including those in the diagram below. The regulations are overseen by statutory authorities such as Social Services Inspection and Registration Units (joined with Ofsted from September 2001), environmental health officers, local education authorities and the Health and Safety Executive.

Figure 5.24

Maintaining a safe and secure environment

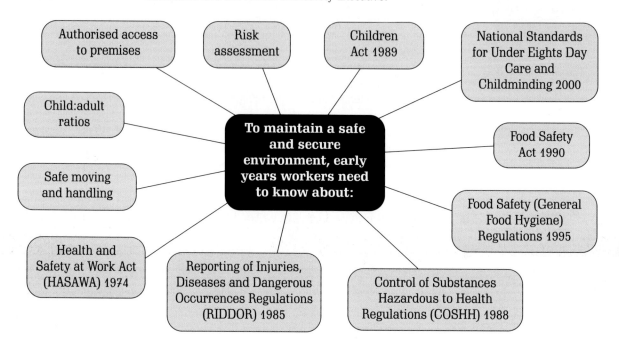

To maintain a safe and secure environment, early years workers need to know about:

- Authorised access to premises
- Risk assessment
- Children Act 1989
- National Standards for Under Eights Day Care and Childminding 2000
- Child:adult ratios
- Food Safety Act 1990
- Safe moving and handling
- Food Safety (General Food Hygiene) Regulations 1995
- Health and Safety at Work Act (HASAWA) 1974
- Reporting of Injuries, Diseases and Dangerous Occurrences Regulations (RIDDOR) 1985
- Control of Substances Hazardous to Health Regulations (COSHH) 1988

The Children Act 1989 includes statements on the safety of premises. To read these in detail, see Annex D of Volume 2, *Family Support, Day Care and Educational Provision for Young Children.*

The publication *Guidance to the National Standards for Under Eights Care* (2001, updated 2003, with addendum October 2005) also sets out guidelines for safety, including fire safety (reference criterion 6.9–6.11). The guidelines cover the following five types of setting and each can be downloaded from the Ofsted website (www.ofsted.gov.uk):

- full day care
- sessional day care
- childminding
- creches
- out of school care.

Settings should refer to the most appropriate Guidance document for the provision they are registered as. The main standards from the Guidance linked to safety are standards 4, 5, 6, 7 and 8. It will be useful to compare the difference between each type of provision. They each follow the same order for subject referencing.

Under the Fire Precautions Act 1971, some, but not all, premises require a fire certificate. This does not as yet automatically apply to day-care provision. However, advice from the fire services is available on request by a local authority or an individual provider, particularly when setting up a new facility, and fire safety information is usually available. In general, the main points of concern regarding fire safety in day-care settings, including childminders' homes, are:

- accessibilty of the register
- the presence of smoke alarms in suitable places
- the means of escape from the building
- the heating and any fire/heating guards used
- safety of electrical systems and electrical equipment
- storage of any flammable materials
- the means of preventing unsupervised access to the kitchen
- ensuring that fire exits remain unobstructed
- who is responsible for checking fire exits regularly.

Children Act 1989 and National Standards

Guidance and regulations under the Children Act and the National Standards also cover:

- adult:child ratios
- minimum space requirements
- maximum number of places in a setting
- toilets and handbasins.

Adult:child ratios

Table 5.7 Standard recommended staff:child ratios for the under-fives in day-care and education settings

Type of setting/Age range	Ratio	Comments
Under 5 years' full day care 0 to 2 years 2 to 3 years 3 to 5 years	 1:3 1:4 1:8	Because of management and administration duties, managers or officers-in-charge should not be included in these ratios where more than 20 children are being cared for
Nursery schools and nursery classes	2:20 (minimum)	One adult should be a qualified teacher and one a qualified nursery assistant
Reception classes in primary schools		Where 4-year-olds are attending Reception classes in primary schools, the staffing levels should be determined by the schools and local education authorities
Childminding Under 5 years 5 to 7 years Under 8 (no more than three being under 5) years	 1:3 1:6 1:6	All these ratios include the childminder's own children and apply to nannies employed by more than two sets of parents to look after their children
Day care services for school age children Where 5- and 7-year-olds are cared for on a daily or sessional basis (i.e. care at the end of the school day and full care in school holidays)	1:8	A higher ratio may be necessary if children with special needs are being cared for. A lower ratio may be appropriate for some short sessional facilities not lasting the full day
Where facilities are used by children aged over 8 years as well as under 8 years		Providers should ensure that there are sufficient staff in total to maintain the 1:8 ratio for the under eights.

Source: reproduced by kind permission of The Stationery Office, from © The Children Act 1989, *Guidance and Regulations Volume 2*, Seventh Impression, 1998

A higher ratio of staff to children will be required if staff are not all qualified or trained to the required level. The inclusion of children with a special need may also necessitate a higher staff ratio, depending on the children's level of individual need.

Minimum space requirements

Table 5.8 Minimum space requirements in an early years setting

Age of child	Square feet	Square metres
0–2 years	37.7	3.5
2 years	26.9	2.5
3–7 years	24.8	2.3

Maximum number of places

No setting is allowed to place more than 26 children in one room except for special occasions. This is regardless of the size of the room. A separate room is always needed for babies and toddlers, adjacent to changing and food preparation facilities.

Toilets and hand basins

- Hot and cold running water should be available.

- Water temperatures in children's hand basins should not exceed 39°C (102°F).

- There should be a minimum of one toilet and one hand basin for every 10 children in the setting.

- Staff should have separate toilet and hand-washing facilities.

Also refer to page 201, Physical environment, and page 202, Potential hazards.

Figure 5.25

Children's hand basins

Control of access

In any childcare setting, staff need to have a clear guidance on who can enter the setting, and when. Clear procedures should be in place and consideration should be given to the following;

Locks on doors

No child should be able to open doors and leave the setting. However, complex locks can hinder quick **evacuation procedures** and so simple child-proof locks should always be used. Some settings have coded entry and this works well, but it should be remembered that the code should be changed regularly and all appropriate staff notified. This will be of particular importance if there is any possibility of codes being used by unauthorised persons.

Control of visitors

Most early years settings have a variety of visitors, and these can enrich the learning of the children and are mostly to be welcomed. It is important, however, that visitors are restricted in their movements around the setting, are not privy to personal details of children and staff, and are not left alone with children or asked to be involved in the personal care of children, unless under the supervision of a member of staff.

Dealing with unwanted visitors

Most settings ask potential visitors to make an appointment in advance. This enables staff to ensure that the setting maintains a suitable adult:child ratio at all times. In settings with lower numbers of children at any one session where the supervisor is not supernumerary this is extremely important. Visitors should also be discouraged from arriving at inconvenient times, such as mealtimes or main rest times, although this will not always be possible.

Raising the alarm

In the event that the behaviour of any visitor causes concern to staff, there should be a clear procedure for them to raise the alarm with other staff, bringing in outside help if necessary. Staff should know what to do if they identify anyone loitering outside or peering through the windows. Ask your placement supervisor about the setting's procedure if it has not been explained to you.

Policy for child collection

A policy regarding how the collection of children is monitored should be held by all settings. It is likely to include the following or similar:

- A specific routine for handing over a child. This should be the same for all children to avoid confusion and maintain security for all. Many settings exchange a brief word with the parent/carer about the child at the time of the handover. Sufficient staff numbers would need to be maintained for this to take place safely and maintain legal ratios.

- A procedure where parents/carers sign their child out of the setting is quite common practice.

- A procedure for clarifying the named adult who should be collecting each child. This would usually be set out in the registration document for each child. Any permanent change to this would usually be required in writing.

- A procedure for checking validity if a different (planned) adult collects a child. This could involve the usual adult giving a clear description of the person who will collect their child on a certain day. Most nurseries ask for this in writing, in advance whenever possible.

- A procedure for checking validity if a different (un-planned) adult collects a child. This could occur for example, due to accident, delay or illness of the named adult. This would often involve a code word or phrase being used, in which case the code would then need to be changed for secure use another time. Alternatively, a clear description of the person would need to be given.

- A procedure for dealing with a parent unfit to take responsibility for a child due to alcohol, drug use etc. This would often involve social services, as the safety of the child must always come first.

Most settings will have included a statement in their registration document for each child regarding non-collection of, or regular late collection of, a child. The distress to the child will be pointed out, a fine may be issued by the setting, and parents may be warned that social services may be contacted if the child is not collected.

Legislation, policies and practices

Control of Substances Hazardous to Health Regulations (COSHH) 1998

Health problems such as skin irritation and asthma can occur owing to the presence of certain chemicals in some substances. The symbols drawn up by **COSHH** have been devised to warn people in advance of **potential hazards**. Most of the substances covered by the regulations will not be used in early years settings. However, bleach and some other common cleaning products are used and can cause irritation and respiratory reactions.

In schools, chemicals may be used within the context of design technology or art. Although many products are now 'safe', potentially harmful substances include some marbling inks and spirits for cleaning, and some spray paints and glues. These would usually only be handled by adults, but children may be present during their use.

Professional Practice

- Always read instructions for the use and dilution of any product, and the importance of ventilation when using them.
- A risk assessment is a systematic check of any potential 'risks' in a setting. An assessment should be carried out by all settings and any potentially hazardous products identified. Relevant information on storage, use and treatment following spills should be noted.
- Cleaning products should not at any time be left where they can be reached by children.

activity
5.15

1   Match each symbol above to the appropriate hazard that it is used for, from this list:
   a) corrosive
   b) explosive
   c) flammable
   d) harmful irritant
   e) oxidising
   f) toxic.
2   Ask permission to look around your current work placement to identify how many potentially hazardous substances there are. Make a note of what you find.
3   Were they all stored appropriately?
4   Were they all recorded on the register following the setting's risk assessment?
5   Have a look around your home. How many potentially hazardous substances can you find there?
6   Are they stored out of reach of children and pets?
7   How well do family members read instructions before use?
8   If you wanted to work as a childminder from your home, would you need to alter anything regarding the storage of these substances?

Reporting of Injuries, Diseases and Dangerous Occurrences Regulations (RIDDOR) 1985

The **RIDDOR** regulations require a setting to report by telephone to the local authority all deaths and any serious injuries that result in a child, a parent, a visitor or a member of staff being taken to hospital from the setting.

If a member of staff is injured (but not seriously) or becomes ill due to their work, the local authority should be informed in writing, using a specified form.

Professional Practice

■ All settings should have an accident book in which they report all accidents and incidents, both large and small.

Health and Safety at Work etc. Act (HASAWA) 1974 (1999)

This Act protects employees and anyone else who could be affected by the procedures of a setting. **HASAWA** requires settings to have a safety policy and to assess, and reduce accordingly, the risk of accident or injury.

There should be a written health and safety policy and a named person with responsibility for health and safety in any setting which employs more than five people. Local authorities can (under the Children Act 1989) ask early years settings to produce health and safety policies irrespective of how many people are employed by the setting.

---

activity 5.16

What would you include in a health and safety policy? Draw up a list of ideas.

Professional Practice

■ It is good practice to have a health and safety policy, whether or not it is required.

■ All staff and students should be asked to read the health and safety policy.

■ The policy should be available for parents to read if they so wish.

■ Ask to read the policy at your work placement if you have not seen it already.

■ Make a note of all areas of safety and health that it covers. How does it compare with your own ideas?

Examples of health and safety policies can be found in *Good Practice in Child Safety* by Dare and O'Donovan(2000) and in *Good Practice in Nursery Management* by Sadek and Sadek (1996).

Handling and disposing of body fluids and waste materials

Body fluids include urine, faeces, blood and vomit. To minimise the potential for cross-infection, staff should wear protective aprons and gloves when dealing with body fluids or waste materials.

Hands should be washed carefully and thoroughly, before and after dealing with personal care, and all parts of the hand, fingers and thumb should be well massaged with soap and hot water. Paper towels should be used for drying – never communal towels – or hot air dryers.

Clearing up body fluids

- All resources should be gathered before cleaning up begins.
- Protective apron and gloves to be worn.
- Absorb fluids with paper towels or kitchen paper.
- Use the towel to mop the main waste into a disposal bag.
- Clean the floor etc. with hot water and detergent. Disinfect if infection is suspected.
- Dispose of all waste, including apron and gloves.
- Always wash hands thoroughly.

Administering and recording of medication

Although children who are ill will not normally be attending school or an early years setting, there are occasions where a child has a chronic (ongoing) condition, which allows them to attend as usual but may need medication to be administered at certain times during the day. When this occurs, it is important that strict guidelines are adhered to.

Parents are responsible for keeping early years staff up to date with the health needs of their children. This includes any medication that needs to be administered during the child's time at the setting. They should provide all relevant details.

Guidelines for administering medication in early years settings

- Parents' consent to give the medication should be in writing, and signed by them.
- Parents should give exact doses, timings and any other information for administering the medication, again in writing.
- Any potential side effects of the medication should be noted.
- Any possible contraindications should be explained to staff by the parents.
- If more than one medication is to be given, check with a pharmacist that the proposed items are safe to be given together.
- A trained member of staff must take responsibility for administering the child's medication.
- A second member of staff should check that the dose given is correct and administered to the correct child.
- Medication should be administered quietly and without drawing undue attention to the child.
- Written records of when medication has been given must be kept by the setting.
- Parents should be informed of any reluctance or failure to administer the medication, and the incident should be recorded.

Healthcare plans

Each child with a specific health problem or care routine needs to have a regularly updated healthcare plan drawn up by the setting with input from all relevant parties: parents, staff, health visitor, GP, and/or any other health professional who supports the child.

Administering the medication

Each time medication is administered, staff should check details before hand and record the time and dose afterwards. As a child becomes able to administer their own medication, they should be supported to do this.

Storing medication

All medication should be clearly labelled with the child's name, the frequency with which the medication is to be given, and the correct dosage. Storage should be in a locked cabinet. Staff administering the medication should always check that the medication is within its use-by dates.

In case children may need quick access to an inhaler, these should be kept easily to hand and all staff should be able to gain access to them immediately. They should, however, be kept out of children's reach.

Professional Practice

- Medication can only be administered by staff with written parental consent.
- It is good practice for a member of staff to witness the administering of any medication by another member of staff.
- Children should never be given medication that is not their own.
- Hands should be thoroughly washed before handling medicines.
- An explanation should be given to the child as to what will take place, for example, that you will lay them back to administer eye drops, or lay them to one side to administer ear drops, and so on.
- Rewarding the child with a small treat if they have been reluctant or very 'brave' can be appropriate.
- The time and the dose or medication administered should be recorded immediately afterwards.
- Hands should be washed afterwards.
- Medicines should not be dissolved into food or drinks.

Disposing of medication

Parents are responsible for the safe disposal of their child's medication. Large quantities of medication should not be kept at the early years setting.

Physical environment

Ensuring that the physical environment of an early years setting is safe and secure includes giving consideration to the:

- layout of the setting
- space available
- furniture and fixtures and their positioning
- mobility of the children, taking into account any specific physical needs
- supervision levels
- safety of all toys, activities and equipment.

It also means considering the heating, lighting, ventilation and ease of cleaning of the equipment and the setting itself.

Refer back to page 196, for information about securing access to the premises.

Layout of the setting and space available

The design of every setting is different, determined by practicalities and the personal choice of the staff and management. The shape of rooms, levels of equipment and furnishings, and whether the setting has sole use of the building will all have an impact on how it is arranged and how flexible the arrangements can be.

The layout of the setting needs to allow sufficient space for:

- children to play in groups
- children to use the floor
- differentiated use of the rooms for quiet activities, messy activities, active play, and so on
- displaying children's creativity, both two-dimensional and three-dimensional
- storing equipment and activities, allowing access to some items by the children
- moving safely between activities
- safe evacuation of the building in an emergency
- rearranging activities and equipment without undue disruption to the setting
- staff to oversee activities in general whilst involved in other areas of the room.

Furniture and fixtures and their positioning

- All cupboards, shelving and any other permanent storage must be securely held in place, and any doors should close firmly and remain closed when not in use.
- Access to storage should not interrupt play or be hazardous to children playing.
- Mobile storage needs to be stocked carefully, avoiding overloading or the risk of items falling.
- Furniture should be child-sized.
- Ideally tables that can combine to extend or alter shape should be used.
- Furniture should be sturdy and be kept in good condition.
- Wooden chairs should be checked regularly for splinters and plastic moulded chairs examined for cracks.
- All surfaces used by the children should be hygienic and in good condition.

Adaptations needed for an inclusive environment

Mobility of children

- The layout of a setting needs to take into account the mobility needs of the children it caters for. For example, baby rooms will need a significant area of floor space to encourage mobility and floor play with staff.
- A child with a physical disability may benefit from a more spacious layout, enabling easier access between activities, particularly if they use a wheelchair or walking frame, or need support from an adult.
- The provision of ramps may be appropriate. This will increase a child's sense of independence and range of access. A lift would normally be installed if the setting is on more than one floor.
- If a setting is supporting a child who is blind or has significant vision impairment, keeping a familiar layout will allow the child a degree of autonomy and independence.
- The use of textured edges to specific play areas can help a visually impaired child to find their way around more easily, and provide warnings of a change to the floor surface.

Other considerations

When a child has a hearing impairment, an environment which is tactile and visually stimulating will help compensate for the sensory loss of their hearing. The use of vibration-based resources can be particularly helpful.

Keeping noise levels down throughout the setting will benefit a child with partial hearing loss as what they can hear will be less likely to become lost in the overall hubbub of the day. This can be helped enormously by careful use of carpets and table coverings.

Supervision levels

Not only must the correct adult:child ratios for the ages of the children within a setting always be maintained but the additional requirements of a child with a specific need must always also be taken into account. For example, some children will need one-to-one support at all times.

Consistency of care is important, both for the emotional security of children and for the smooth running of the day. However, at times staff may need to adjust their position within the setting in order to ensure that supervision levels remain safe and meet legal requirements.

Potential hazards

Hazards can occur through accidents and thoughtlessness, but also through poor planning. Early years staff need to consider a range of potential hazards, for example:

- the effect of a dirty environment
- safety of toys, resources and equipment
- the importance of checking for safety marks
- the impact of messy play
- safety of outdoor surfaces
- poor heating, lighting and ventilation.

Consideration needs to be given to:

- potential hazards in the home
- potential hazards in early years settings
- safety issues on outings.

The effect of a dirty environment

Cross-contamination and the spread of infection can easily occur within the close-contact environment of a classroom or early years setting. This leads to illness and poor attendance, which can in turn have an affect on a child's learning.

Refer to Unit 10, page 431, for a summary of common childhood illness and to page 208 for information on cross-infection.

Cleaning the environment

This includes both the setting itself and the equipment and furnishings within it.

- Cleaning should take place at the end of each session, or day, and as necessary throughout the day.
- Carpeted floor surfaces should be easily cleaned with a vacuum cleaner and washable non-slip surfaces with a mop (disinfected daily).
- Suitable anti-bacterial products should be used regularly to clean all surfaces.
- Toys and activities should be regularly cleaned with anti-bacterial products.

Professional Practice

- It is particularly important to clean surfaces before any food preparation, cooking activities and before snack time.
- If early years staff are responsible for the general cleaning of the setting, there should be a rota to ensure that it is kept clean and hygienic at all times.
- Staff should not carry out cleaning duties while still responsible for supervising children. They should be supernumerary to the adult:child ratio at this point.

Safety of toys, resources and equipment

All equipment used in early years settings should be made to a recognised safety standard. A range of safety marks are used by manufacturers as required by legislation and these are set out below. These are changed and updated from time to time, and it is worth checking for the most recent recommendations.

The impact of messy play

'Messy' play offers wonderful learning opportunities for young children. However, the fact that children are engaging with these materials at first hand means that they are potential routes of cross-contamination. The materials themselves can also cause accidents if not controlled and cleared up appropriately. For example:

- Sand should be sieved daily to remove any bits and cleaned regularly. Any sand that has been spilt on the floor should be sieved and cleaned before it is returned to the sand tray or be discarded.
- Outdoor sand pits should be kept securely covered when not in use to prevent fouling by animals and to prevent rubbish and garden debris settling there.
- Water should be replenished daily, and water trays cleaned and disinfected regularly.
- Any pets should be kept scrupulously clean, following normal pet-care routines.
- Dough should be renewed regularly and stored in a refrigerator.
- Dough should be discarded and replaced following any infectious illness in the setting to avoid cross-infection.

Table 5.9 Safety marks

Mark	Name	Meaning
	BSI Kitemark	Indicates a product has met a British safety standard and has been independently tested
	Lion Mark	Indicates adherence to the British Toy and Hobby Association Code of Practice and ensures a product is safe and conforms to all relevant safety information
	Age Warning	Indicates: 'Warning – do not give the toy to children less than 3 years, nor allow them to play with it' Details of the hazard, e.g. small parts, will be near the symbol or with the instructions
	BEAB Mark of the British Electrotechnical Approvals Board	Indicates that electrical appliances carrying this mark meet a national safety standard
	BSI Safety Mark on gas appliances, light fittings and power tools	Indicates the product has been made and tested to a specific safety standard in accordance with the British Standards Institute
	Safety Mark on upholstered furniture	Indicates upholstery materials and fillings have passed the furniture cigarette and match tests – a lighted cigarette or match applied to the material will not cause the article to burst into flames
	Low Flammability labels	Children's pyjamas, bathrobes made from 100% Terry towelling and clothes for babies up to 3 months old must carry a label showing whether or not the garment has passed the Low Flammability Test. Either of these two labels is acceptable. Always look for these labels when choosing such garments.
	Keep Away From Fire label	Indicates the garment is not slow burning and has probably not passed the Low Flammability Test. Great care must be taken anywhere near a fire or flame

Figure 5.26

Pets should be kept scrupulously clean

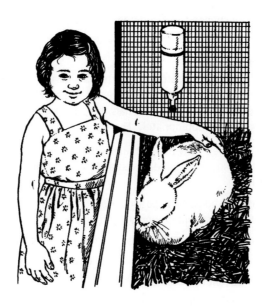

Safety of outdoor surfaces

In the outdoors environment, concrete, gravel and similar surfaces are not suitable for use in areas where young children play because they do not absorb impact. This can result in serious injury if a child should fall on them. A more suitable surface for general play is grass, but, in dry summer months, this will also become hard and unyielding.

It is particularly important that surfaces under and around play equipment from which a child may fall a distance of 60 cm (2 feet) or more should be able to absorb some of the impact of the fall, reducing the risk of serious injury.

Impact-absorbing playground surfaces (**IAPS**) include:

- loose-fill substances such as tree bark or sand (at least 30 cm (1 foot) deep)
- 'wet pour' rubber which sets to form a spongy surface
- thick rubber tiles.

Surfaces should meet the BSEN 1177 safety standard. They should be kept in good condition: any damage should be repaired and tree bark or sand raked regularly to remove debris and animal excrement.

Poor heating, lighting and ventilation

If the working or living environment is wrong, it can lead to poor health and lethargic individuals who are more prone to accidents and infection. The following guidelines should be considered:

Heating

- Room temperatures must be 18–20°C (65–68°F).
- A wall thermometer should be on display and checked regularly. The temperature of a room should be adjusted accordingly to reduce the risk of children overheating.
- Whenever possible, radiators should be controlled by individual thermostats.
- Fire guards or heater guards should be fitted where necessary.

Lighting

- Natural light is important to avoid headaches and eye strain.
- Lighting must be adequate for safe working practice.
- Accidents are more likely to occur in poorly lit settings.

Ventilation

- Children and staff work best within a well-ventilated environment.
- Good ventilation reduces the risk of cross-infection.
- Ventilation points need to be kept clean, as they can easily attract dirt and a build-up of bacteria.

Potential hazards are everywhere. There are many potential hazards for young children in the average home, with some also present in early years settings, and you will need to think about these carefully. As a student, you are likely to spend placement time in a family setting at some point and may go on to choose to work in the field of nannying or as a childminder when you have qualified.

Potential hazards in the home

Kitchens, bathrooms and gardens are the obvious places of concern when considering dangers, but think also about the hazards of glass front doors, sofas beneath windowsills (ideal for climbing on and reaching window catches), electric leads from televisions, DVD recorders and computers, and so on.

activity

5.17

1   Draw a diagram of a house and garden like the one below. List as many hazards as you can think of that could be present in each (average) room; then do the same for the garden, including the shed.
2   Compare your 'house of hazards' with a partner's.
3   What safety arrangement would need to be put in place if you wanted to care for children in that particular house?

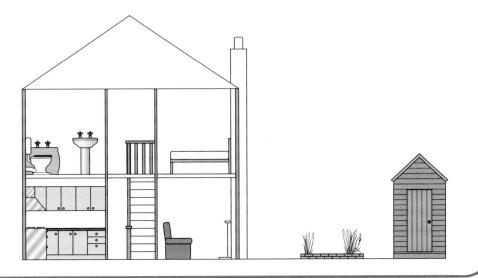

Potential hazards in early years settings

As in the home, kitchens and bathrooms are obvious places of potential hazard, but what else can you think of?

activity

5.18

Look at the picture below. How many good safety points can you identify here? What would you change if you were in a position to?

Professional Practice

- Children must be registered on arrival.
- Good adult supervision is needed at all times.
- Emergency evacuation procedures must be on display.
- Emergency exits should be clearly identified.
- Equipment must be stored safely.
- Safety glass should be used in any low level windows, dividing panels or glazed doors.
- Window locks must be fitted to any windows accessible to children.
- Fire or heating guards must be fitted.
- Electrical sockets must be covered, and ideally should not be within children's reach.
- Electrical appliances need to be checked regularly.
- Small parts should not be accessible to babies and toddlers.
- A safe area should be available for storing the personal belongings of staff, students and visitors.

activity 5.19

1 Empty out the contents of the bag you usually take to your placement.
2 How many potential hazards for a child have you found?

This activity should have highlighted why your personal belongings could be a hazard, if accessible to a young child, and why they should be stored safely away.

Safety issues on outings

Children gain a great deal from visiting other places, and for many of them it can be their only opportunity for such visits. There needs to be careful planning and a full check of details prior to the actual visit. The overall supervisor for the outing should:

- Ensure that the destination is suitable, for example, that there is no open water that will completely restrict the children's freedom.
- Ensure that appropriate adult:child ratios for outings are adhered to:
  0–2 years   1:1
  2–5 years   1:2
  5–8 years   1:5.
- Ensure that an accurate register is with them at all times.
- Ensure that the register is checked regularly throughout the day.
- Check that parental consent forms have been signed and returned before the outing takes place.
- Check that all adults know which children they are responsible for.
- Check that all adults understand their role and responsibilities for the day.
- Provide identification badges for children as a useful 'extra' precaution but ensure that these do not include their name or personal details, just the name of the school, nursery or group.
- Ensure that staff take a small emergency first aid kit with them.
- Identify in advance how they will call for emergency services if needed.
- Check that any transport used meets safety requirements regarding seat belts.

Figure 5.27

Transport used must meet safety requirements

Professional Practice

■ Always check that the coach meets the required safety standards.

Progress Check

1 In what year were the current National Standards for Under Eights Day Care and Childminding introduced?

2 What does COSHH stand for?

3 What does RIDDOR stand for?

4 What is the purpose of a risk assessment?

5 What are the required adult:child ratios for different types of provision?

6 What is the maximum number of children allowed in one room?

7 What is the maximum temperature for water that is accessible to children?

8 List as many points as you can about personal hygiene.

9 List as many points as you can about kitchen hygiene.

10 List at least 10 safety issues regarding the physical environment of a setting.

11 Why is concrete not a suitable surface under a climbing frame?

12 List at least five safety precautions that should be considered when taking children on an outing.

Cross-infection

Cross-infection is the passing of infection from one person to another. It can happen very quickly and can be an ongoing problem for early years settings, as parents do not always put their child's needs first due to pressures from work. Most settings and schools have experienced an obviously ill child arriving for the day with a parent who reassures the staff that the child is just 'a bit off-colour' but still wanted to come. Others will claim that their child was 'sick in the night, but fine now'. Clearly, this is unacceptable and is an example of how infections spread around the classroom or setting.

Policies to deal with this are necessary, and most settings refuse to take a child who has been sick or had diarrhoea, asking for them to be clear from their symptoms for 48 hours before attending again.

The most common infectious conditions that affect early years settings on a regular basis are:

- diarrhoea and/or vomiting – children should be kept away from the setting for at least 48 hours after suffering these symptoms;
- conjunctivitis – this condition is highly infectious and parents should be asked to get appropriate treatment and keep their child away until the infection has passed;
- threadworm, scabies and head lice.

Refer to page 423, for information about conjunctivitis, thread-worm, scabies and head lice.

Staff, students and parents should all be informed about the occurrence of these infections in the setting, so that they can be alert to signs or symptoms in themselves, their child or other children and get appropriate treatment. Most settings do not exclude children with these conditions.

Preventing cross-infection

In order to prevent cross-infection, every setting needs to plan how its staff should deal with any potentially infective material, including all body fluids (urine, faeces, blood and vomit) and associated waste materials. This is important when caring for children with any infectious condition, particularly HIV, AIDS or hepatitis.

Professional Practice

- You will not always know whether a child is potentially infectious, so sensible precautions at all times will protect both yourself and others.
- Having a standard policy for potential infection will prevent the labelling of any one child, where a known potential hazard such as HIV has been disclosed to the setting.

activity 5.20

Ask to see the policy for your setting if you have not already been shown it. If anything is unclear, ask for clarification.

General points for dealing with body fluids

- Disposable latex gloves and aprons should be worn during nappy changing and when clearing up any body fluids.
- Gloves and aprons should only ever be used once.
- For staff with an allergy to latex, alternative disposable gloves must be provided.
- After use, gloves and aprons should be placed in sealed disposal bags along with the disposable nappy or other waste material, and disposed of safely.
- Blood soaked items should be immersed in cold water to release the staining before washing in the normal way.
- Sluice facilities should be used to rinse off vomit, or solid matter from towelling nappies. These should be securely bagged (two layers) and labelled with the child's name if not being washed in the setting.
- Wet or soiled nappies should never be left around the setting.
- Following accidents or vomiting, the affected area should be cleaned thoroughly with disinfectant or bleach (diluted according to directions on container).
- Soft furnishings should be cleaned with hot soapy water (bleach will discolour them).

Sharing health and safety information with parents

Parents and staff need to work together to support the healthy and safe care of children. Consider the following:

case study 5.6 — Learn Through Play Nursery

When a parent takes up a place for their child at the Learn Through Play Nursery, they are given a contract setting out all the general aspects of nursery administration and nursery–parent agreements, together with a range of health and safety points. These points are as follows.

- An emergency telephone contact number is required for all parents.

- Parents have a responsibility to notify staff of alternative numbers in advance.

- A health record and details of GP are needed for each child.

- A list should be given to parents of exclusion periods following communicable or common illnesses.

- Details regarding the administering of medicines, including consent forms, are given.

- A statement regarding the handling of body fluids and washing responsibilities should be made.

- Notification of the whereabouts of evacuation procedure details and the assembly point should be given.

- Attention should be drawn to the nursery noticeboard where general health and safety information is placed.

activity

1 How comprehensive do you consider these points to be?
2 How else could the nursery keep parents up to date on relevant health issues?
3 Consider the following scenario: a child at the Learn Through Play Nursery has contracted meningitis; the nursery staff have been contacted and have informed all other parents in writing of the incident. What else could they do to dispel the fears of parents?

Professional Practice

- Staff need to deal with any incident calmly and in an informed manner.
- It is important to refer only to facts, and not to speculation or hearsay.
- At all times staff should ensure that a family's confidentiality is not breached.

Progress Check

1 Why is it important that all staff in a setting follow the same procedure when handling body fluids?
2 How does a setting's policy contribute to a child's right to confidentiality?
3 What is meant by cross-infection?
4 How can settings insist that children are kept away until clear of infectious symptoms?
5 What is needed before a setting can give medication to a child in its care?
6 What approach should you take before administering medication to a child?

Safety and emergency procedures

First aid procedures

Knowledge of first aid is essential in early years settings – the initial actions carried out following an accident or incident, before the arrival of the emergency services, can have a significant impact on the eventual outcome. First aid is about limiting the effects of an accident or incident and taking action to aid the recovery of the person concerned.

Every early years setting is required to have at least one person on duty at all times who is qualified in emergency first aid procedures. This person should be named and all staff should know who they are and where they can be found. All first aiders need to be regularly updated and assessed externally, and they are required to renew their qualification every three years to ensure that they remain up-to-date with current thinking and show that they can still remember and carry out basic procedures. Nannies and childminders need to take responsibility themselves for updating their first aid qualification.

Professional Practice

- Many people will (thankfully) never have to use most of the techniques they learned during their first aid training.
- Each college offering the BTEC National in Early Years will arrange first aid training for its students, but the timing of this will vary from college to college, as there is different thinking on where it is best placed within a programme of study.
- In some colleges, it will take place near to the beginning of the course, the thinking being to maximise your understanding of emergency procedures whilst you are on placement experience (although a student should never be considered to be the qualified first aider for the setting).
- In other colleges, it will be placed near to the end of the course, the thinking here being that you will have gained in confidence and that first aid training at this point will build on your all-round knowledge and understanding of children. It also enables you to qualify with three years of first aid 'currency' ahead of you.
- Some colleges will focus purely on first aid for young children, whereas others will incorporate the full first aid at work training into their programme, usually with a specific section on first aid for young children alongside it.
- As an early years worker, you will need to know how to:
  - check for signs and symptoms
  - prioritise treatment
  - deal with an unconscious casualty
  - use the ABC procedure
  - deal with allergies and anaphylaxis
  - treat minor and major injuries:
    - bleeding
    - fractures
    - poisoning
    - burns and scalds
    - choking and breathing difficulties
    - seizures.

Prioritising and checking for signs and symptoms

A potentially life-threatening injury must always take priority. Often (but not always), the silent unconscious casualty will be in greater need of immediate assistance than the casualty who is making a lot of noise, even though they may still have serious injuries. Training in first aid enables practitioners to make informed decisions in these situations based on the knowledge gained of assessing patients and checking for signs and symptoms of various injuries, and of prioritising the urgency of each injury.

In prioritising you need to:

- Keep calm and in control.
- Ensure other children are being cared for and kept away from any continuing danger.
- Ensure that the area is safe for you to be in (i.e. assess if you need to turn off the electricity); be vigilant, e.g. look out for broken glass etc.
- Check if the casualty is conscious and breathing. Start resuscitation if necessary. Call emergency services (if possible get someone else to do this for you), if the casualty is unconscious or has other obvious signs of serious injury.
- Assess the casualty's symptoms, e.g. bleeding, burns, breathing difficulties, temperature, changes to skin colour. Note any description of feelings vocalised by the casualty.
- Following initial first aid treatment, place casualty into the recovery position and stay with them until medical assistance arrives.

N.B. Young children are often unable to describe the symptoms (and often the site) of their injury accurately.

Training

To be both valid and relevant within the workplace, officially recognised programmes such as the level two paediatric first aid course, a vocationally recognised qualification on the National training framework, should be successfully completed.

First aid training is carried out by a number of recognised providers: e.g. St John Ambulance, St Andrews, the Red Cross, or independent fully qualified first aid trainers.

First aid manuals

Relevant training manuals are usually provided by the training provider. It is important that only current first aid manuals are referred to, as guidance on procedures change from time to time, based on new understanding. Outdated materials should always be discarded.

> **remember**
>
> First aid manuals, like all other written first aid instructions, should never be used as an alternative to attending a recognised training course in first aid.

The unconscious casualty

As children's bodies are still developing, to avoid injuring the child unnecessarily, it is not always appropriate to use the same techniques for emergency first aid as you would use on an adult. In some cases, techniques designed for adults can be extremely dangerous to a young child. For example, tilting the head of a young infant back too far may actually occlude (block) the airway, rather than open it. Similarly, if too much pressure is placed on the soft tissue under the jaw when opening the airway, this may block it.

Emergency procedures for babies and young children: a summary

Stage 1

- Review the situation, assessing as far as is possible what has happened.
- Decide your immediate priorities.
- Stay calm.
- Consider if there is anyone else who could help you.
- Professional help should be sought unless only a minor injury has occurred (if on your own, shout for help!).
- Whenever possible, any other children present should be reassured and led away.

> **remember**
>
> You should not put yourself in unnecessary danger too.

Stage 2

Remove any dangers. You will be of little use to the casualty if you become injured yourself. Ask yourself: Is it safe to proceed with first aid? For example:

- Is the fire out?
- Is the electricity turned off?

Stage 3

- Assess the casualty for any response. Remember that during the pre-verbal stage, the inability to speak will not automatically mean they are unconscious. Consider:
  - Is the child moving?
  - Have they opened their eyes?
  - Have they given a verbal response – a cry, moan or any other vocalisation?

- If no response is obtained, it is likely that they are unconscious.

- You will need to begin the **ABC procedure**.

The ABC of resuscitation

A stands for airway

The airway needs to be kept clear. If it becomes blocked, and the child stops breathing, they will soon become unconscious. This will eventually lead to the heart slowing down and stopping due to the lack of oxygen.

Remove any obvious obstructions from the child's mouth but be aware that a 'blind-sweep' may block the child's airway further!

Ask yourself:

- Is the child's chest rising and falling?
- Is the tongue well forward?
- Can you hear breathing sounds when your ear is close to the mouth?
- Can you feel the child's breath on your cheek?

If not you will need to open the airway for the child.

To open a baby's airway:

- Place the baby on their back tilting with the head back slightly.
- Use one finger under the chin to move it forwards (imagine the baby is sniffing a flower and position them accordingly).
- Look, listen and feel again for breathing.
- If there is no change, you will need to try **artificial ventilation** (see B below).

Figure 5.28

Opening a baby's airway

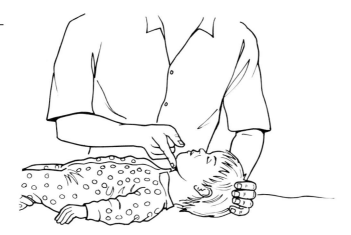

To open an older child's airway

- Place the child on their back.
- Place two fingers under the chin.
- Place a hand on the forehead and tilt the head backwards, again ensuring not to tip it too far!
- Look, listen and feel again for breathing.
- If there is no change, you will need to try artificial ventilation (see B below).

Figure 5.29

Opening a child's airway

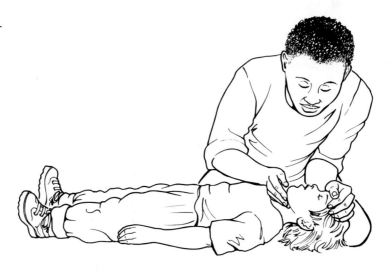

B stands for breathing

Have a look at the casualty's tummy. Can you see it moving? If breathing has stopped, you may need to do this for them. Whenever possible, send someone to call for an ambulance. If you are on your own, perform the following procedure for 1 minute and then go and call an ambulance yourself. If the casualty is a young baby, you may be able to take them with you and continue the breathing procedure for them.

To carry out artificial ventilation for a baby

- Open the airway as in A.
- Place your lips around the baby's mouth and nose.
- Give five 'rescue' breaths (breaths which are hard enough to make the chest move as though the casualty had taken a deep breath for themselves).
- Continue to blow, very gently at a rate of 20 breaths per minute.
- After each breath, remove your mouth and watch for the chest to fall as the air expires.
- If, after five rescue breaths, you have not been able to establish effective breathing, recheck their mouth and head position and try again.

Figure 5.30

Artificial ventilation for a baby

To carry out artificial ventilation for an older child

- Open the airway as in A.
- Pinch the child's nostrils together.
- Place your lips firmly over the child's mouth.
- As with a baby, give five rescue breaths, then …
- Blow gently in to the mouth at a rate of 20 breaths per minute.
- Again, as with a baby, remove your mouth after each breath and watch the chest fall as the air expires.

Figure 5.31

Artificial ventilation for a child

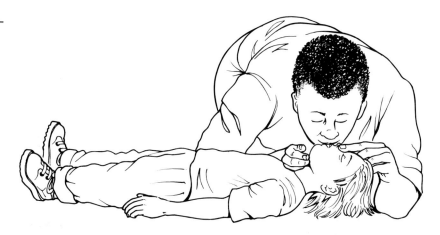

Professional Practice

- The updated UK Resuscitation Council guidelines state that only professionally trained health workers should check the pulse during resuscitation attempts.

C stands for circulation

The circulation is the beating of the heart which keeps the blood flowing through the body. The usual signs of circulation are breathing, coughing or movement. If you cannot see signs of circulation, you will need to start the procedure known as **chest compression**.

Chest compression for a baby

- Place the tips of your fingers one finger's width below the baby's nipple line.
- Press down sharply to between one-third and one-half of the depth of the chest.
- Give five compressions per one breath, 100 compressions per minute if working alone.

Figure 5.32

Chest compression for a baby

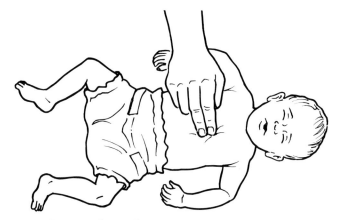

Press on lower breastbone with two fingers

Chest compression for a child

- Use the heel of your hand rather than your fingers.

- Press down sharply to between one third and one half of the depth of the child's chest.

- Work in cycles of 15 compressions per 2 breaths, 100 compressions per minute if working alone.

Figure 5.33

Chest compression for a child

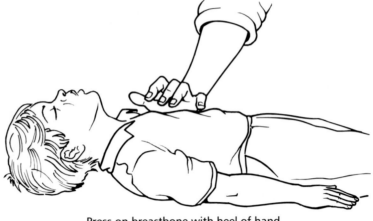

Press on breastbone with heel of hand

Professional Practice

- Remembering the ABC procedure will enable you to carry out procedures in the right order.

- The ABC procedure needs to be continued until either the child begins to recover or professional help arrives.

- It can be dangerous to continue with chest compressions once the casualty has started to recover.

The recovery position

Once a child has begun to breath for themselves, they need to be placed in the recovery position.

The recovery position for a baby

Hold the baby in your arms with their head tilted downwards to help keep the airway open.

Figure 5.34

The recovery position for a baby

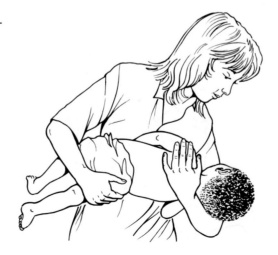

The recovery position for a child

1 Ensure that the airway is open.

2 Bend the arm nearest to you at a right angle. Bring the child's furthest arm across their chest and cushion their cheek with the back of their hand.

Figure 5.35

Recovery position Stage 1

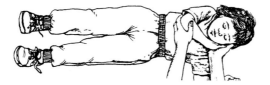

3 Roll the child towards you. Keep their hand pressed against their cheek. Bend their outside knee, grasp them under the thigh and, keeping their near leg straight, pull them towards you.

Figure 5.36

Recovery position Stage 2

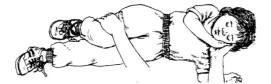

4 Bend the child's top leg at a right angle to their body to keep them on their side and to prevent them from rolling onto their front. Tilt their head back to ensure their airway remains open. Check their head is still cushioned by their hand.

Figure 5.37

Recovery position Stage 3

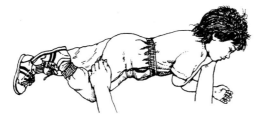

Once the child has been made comfortable in the recovery position, he should be closely monitored and reassured as necessary until professional help arrives.

Treatment of minor and major injuries

Bleeding

For cuts and grazes:

■ Sit the child down somewhere suitable.

■ Wash the cut with water and cotton wool or similar. Always wipe blood away from the open wound, not towards it.

■ Carefully remove any foreign bodies; gravel, dirt, grass etc.

■ If bleeding is continuous, apply pressure directly.

■ Cover cleaned area with a dressing (gauze or similar).

■ Inform parents of injury.

Fractures

When there is loss of the ability to walk, stand or use a limb, or there is tenderness, swelling and pain:

■ A qualified first aider should immobilise the affected limb.

■ Contact the child's parents.

■ If fracture is suspected the child needs to be taken to the accident and emergency department of the nearest hospital.

Poisoning

If, for example, the child swallows berries, fungi or leaves, bleach, alcohol or drugs:

- Reassure the child.
- Call emergency services.
- Do not try to make the child vomit.
- Do not give the child anything to eat or drink.
- If the child becomes unconscious, place them in the recovery position.
- Keep a sample of what has poisoned them if at all possible, to show medical staff.

Burns and scalds

If, for example, there is blistering, pain and reddened skin:

- Cool the affected area under cool running water for at least 10 minutes to help reduce pain.
- Do not remove anything stuck to the affected area.
- Remove any tight clothing as area is likely to swell.
- Cover affected area with a clean cloth (avoid the use of fuzzy or fluffy surfaces).
- Do not apply creams or lotions.
- Any affected area measuring more than the size of a 10-pence piece needs professional medical attention.

Choking and breathing difficulties

These may, for example, be caused by foreign bodies and 'cloying' foods:

- If you can see the obstruction, try and hook it out with your little finger, but DO NOT RISK pushing it down further.
- Lay a baby along your forearm, face downwards and give brisk slaps between their shoulder blades.
- Lean a child forward, and again, apply five brisk slaps between the shoulder blades.
- It is not appropriate to hold a child upside down. This can cause them further injury.
- Seek medical help if unsuccessful.

Seizures

Seizures (convulsions) can occur following a sudden surge of electrical activity in the brain. This can be due to high temperature, infection, injury or epilepsy. Seizures can vary in severity and may present as major or minor symptoms. In all cases, parents should be told and medical help sought in line with an agreed written plan for the child if they have a history of seizures. Always seek help if it is the first seizure a child has had.

Minor symptoms include:

- a blank expression or staring for a period of time
- seeming very vague and unfocused
- fluttering of eyelids or a slight twitching.

Major symptoms usually occur in stages, initially:

- a rapid rise in temperature
- pallor
- a sudden loss of consciousness
- blue lips
- involuntary urination.

This is likely to be followed by:

- body twitching, often involving the whole body.

The child then:

■ sleeps or is dazed;

■ often there is no memory of the seizure.

remember

■ Always sponge a child to cool them down if they show signs of a raised temperature.
■ Clear any obstructions away, to minimise the risk of a convulsing child hurting themself.
■ Supervise a child throughout a seizure.
■ Once the child is asleep, place the child in the recovery position.
■ Record the time, duration and any other relevant details of the seizure.
■ DO NOT EVER place anything between the child's teeth. This can cause further injury and choking.

Progress Check

1 How many qualified first aiders should be on duty in an early years setting?

2 How regularly should first aid training be updated and reassessed?

3 How many types of injury can you think of that you may need to deal with?

4 What does the A stand for in the ABC procedure?

5 What does the B stand for in the ABC procedure?

6 What does the C stand for in the ABC procedure?

7 How many compressions and ventilations should you give per minute?

8 To what depth should the chest be compressed?

9 Why is it important to put the injured person into the recovery position?

10 How does the recovery position differ between a young baby and a child?

11 What should be recorded following an accident?

12 At what point should parents be informed?

13 Why should a child be closely monitored following an accident?

First aid boxes

Every setting needs to have a first aid box. It is a legal requirement of all employers under the Health and Safety (First Aid) Regulations 1981.

The container should be both airtight and waterproof and it should be easily recognised – the most usual design is green with a white cross. The box should always include a guidance sheet on emergency first aid. Every setting will have different requirements according to the numbers and needs of its children and staff. The first aid box should be checked regularly and kept in good order by a specified person.

Contents of a first aid box

An employer with 10 or more staff is required by law to include the following in the first aid box:

■ 20 individually wrapped sterile adhesive dressings (various sizes)

■ 2 sterile pads

■ 4 triangular bandages (ideally sterile)

■ 6 safety pins

■ individually wrapped unmedicated wound dressings, six 12 × 12 cm; two 18 × 18 cm

■ 1 pair of disposable gloves

■ 1 first aid guidance leaflet

■ additional items.

Figure 5.38

Some of the contents of a first aid box

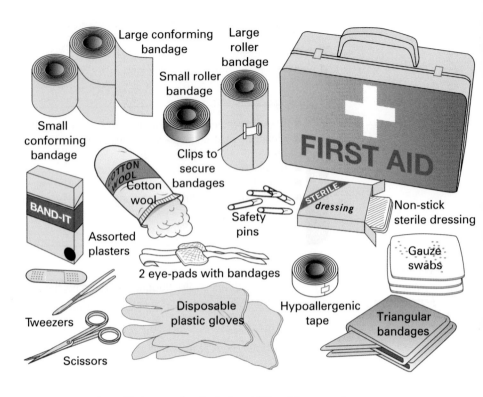

An early years setting will also need to include additional items such as:

- scissors (kept only for first aid use)
- tweezers
- several pairs of disposable gloves
- non-allergic tape
- non-allergic plasters (if used)
- bandages in various sizes
- sterile gauze
- digital thermometer (never a glass or mercury thermometer)
- a checklist of the contents.

Local policy

Some local authorities recommend settings not to use certain items, such as plasters and lotions, because of the risk of allergy in some children. Each setting needs to ensure that its first aid box is drawn up in accordance with local policy.

Parental consent forms

Written consent is needed regarding emergency treatment for a child. Some parents have cultural or religious beliefs that will mean they withhold permission for some forms of treatment.

Checking contents of first aid boxes

Professional Practice

- A specified person (or persons) should be responsible for checking and replenishing the first aid box regularly, and after every use.
- A checklist of the minimum requirements should be kept in the box.
- A form should be kept in the box, and be signed and dated after every check and each time the box has been cleaned.
- All staff should be aware of parents' wishes in the event of emergency treatment for their child.

Appropriate reporting procedures

Whenever possible, parents should be informed immediately that their child has had an accident, although in emergency situations you will dial 999 for an ambulance in the first instance. The parent consent form regarding emergency treatment should always go with the child to hospital to ensure that the wishes of the parents are acknowledged.

Every setting must have an accident book, in which the details of all accidents and incidents, however large or small, must be recorded. It is never sufficient simply to tell a parent or carer what has happened. A written account must be made, which must include:

- the child's name
- the date and time the accident occurred
- where the accident occurred
- a description of what happened
- any injuries sustained by the child (however slight)
- what first aid treatment was administered and by whom
- any further relevant information, for example:
    - Was it necessary to get outside help?
    - Were the child's parents contacted, and at what time?

Following a serious accident, a written account of what happened should be drawn up, giving as much detail as possible, as soon as is practicable. This should then be signed and then countersigned by another member of staff. Most settings give copies of accident records to the parent or carer of the child and keep a copy filed with the child's records.

Link

Refer to Unit 3, page 96, Case Study 3.3: Kieron, for an example of how the accident book can also help safeguard both children and staff in a setting.

Professional Practice

- Records are an important part of any setting.
- Sometimes a seemingly minor injury can result in complications.
- A child should be closely monitored by staff following an accident.
- Any change in a child's well-being should be assessed and treated accordingly.

Emergencies

There are many emergencies other than accidents that early years workers need to know how to react to, including fire, suspected or actual gas leaks, flooding and bomb scares. Each setting should have a clear procedure for evacuating the building, with all staff knowing who and what they are responsible for and where they are to congregate following the evacuation. An agreed procedure for ensuring that the emergency services have been called must be established. This is likely to be the responsibility of the manager, but settings need to consider what happens if it is the manager who has had the accident!

As a student you should not be given any responsibility for evacuating children from the setting during an emergency procedure, but it is important that you are fully aware of what the procedure involves and where you should go, and that you remain calm and help to reassure the children.

Emergency exits

Emergency exits should be signposted with appropriate symbols, like these below.

Figure 5.39

Emergency exit signs

Emergency exits should be kept clear at all times. Tables, cupboards, activities and temporary displays should not be placed as an obstruction. Each exit should be unlocked (though childproof) and be easily opened from inside.

Evacuation procedures

Clear instructions setting out the emergency evacuation procedure should be on display in the setting at all times. Copies should be placed near the main entrance and in all the rooms that are used. All staff, students and parents should be referred to these and asked to familiarise themselves with the instructions. Where more than one language is spoken in the setting, copies of the procedure should be translated accordingly.

activity
5.21

Find out the emergency procedures for your current work placement.

1   Ask to see the relevant policies.
2   Read the evacuation procedure carefully. It should be on display.
3   Note which members of staff have particular responsibilities during an emergency.
4   Look at where the assembly point is situated, and consider why this site has been chosen.
5   Following a practice evacuation, evaluate the success of the setting's procedure, considering timing, reactions of the children and staff, and the taking of the register at the assembly point.

Fire alarms and evacuation practice

An obvious fire alarm of some kind is needed, together with smoke detectors in suitable places. (The kitchen itself is not suitable, unless it is spacious, as steam from cooking may set the alarm off regularly, causing unnecessary anguish. By the kitchen doorway is more usual.) Alarms that automatically trigger lights when they are activated are ideal as they allow better vision in a smoky atmosphere.

Practising an evacuation (often called fire practice) should be a regular activity, and all new staff should be trained as to what their responsibility is to be. These practices should occasionally include having to take a different route, pretending that the straightforward route is unpassable. This will help staff think through the procedure more thoroughly.

Professional Practice

■   Times and days of practice evacuations should be varied so all children who attend the setting experience the procedure.

case study 5.7

Top of the World Nursery

Top of the World Nursery is based in the centre of a small town. Its sessions are held in the first-floor hall of a large community centre on a triangular 'island' of buildings. The emergency exit, which is approved by the registering authority for the nursery, involves taking the children down an outside staircase onto a narrow pavement below, which is the assembly point. The nursery staff are keen to have regular practices at evacuating the children, as some children are reluctant to walk down the outside staircase and staff worry about having to cajole them down it in a real emergency. The nursery currently has a fire practice every two weeks.

A new parent has questioned the wisdom of this, pointing out that the children are potentially in greater danger from being led onto a narrow pavement on such a regular basis. This has worried the staff further.

activity

1   What are the benefits of both arguments?
2   What are the drawbacks of both arguments?
3   How could the nursery reach a compromise on this, while still practising regularly?

Professional Practice

■ A member of staff should have responsibility for taking the register with them to the assembly site.

■ Children need to be taught to respond to emergencies, which is why practising is important.

■ Children need to be familiar with holding hands, grouping together and standing still when required (for a head count).

■ Early years staff need to promote the importance of fire practices without raising undue alarm in children.

case study 5.8

Safe as Houses Nursery

Safe as Houses Nursery looks after 20 children each day, predominantly for full day care, due to its proximity to a large local business.

Most of the children arrive between 8.00 and 8.30 a.m. each morning, with only three arriving later, usually just after 9.15. All the children gather together in one large group for news, weather and the register at 9.30, having played freely in the largest room until this point. The children then divide into their key-worker groups and move to pre-planned activity areas.

activity

1   Is there any problem with this practice, do you think?
2   Would you change anything, if you were able?
3   What might be the problem if a fire broke out at around 9.00 a.m?
4   How could Safe as Houses Nursery be made safer without altering its daily structure?

Rehearsing, reviewing and modifying procedures

It is important that practitioners continue to assess the effectiveness of the procedures they carry out. This applies particularly to all planned responses to emergency situations. Following any procedure, practitioners should be asking themselves:

■ Was the most effective procedure taken?

■ Was the procedure successful?

■ Was there any concern regarding the outcome of a procedure?

■ What could have been done to improve the situation and/or outcome?

Coping with children's emotional reactions

In an emergency, children may be scared to move or frightened by what they see. This is understandable as they will be feeling insecure. It is important that you:

■ remain calm

■ give them clear instructions

■ remove them from the scene if possible

■ comfort them and offer reassurance

■ be as honest with them as you can without adding to their fears.

After the event, children may refer back constantly to the incident. It is important to recognise that children sometimes need to talk about incidents in order to 'sort events out' in their minds. Reassuring books and stories, together with plenty of active play will eventually move most children on. On occasions, however, some children may need professional help to see them through the aftermath of a crisis or emergency.

Professional Practice

■ Early years staff need to consider the feelings and views of the parents as well as the children.

■ As an early years worker, you have responsibility for what a parent holds most dear to them – their child.

Information for parents following an emergency

If an early years setting has had to relocate mid-session due to an emergency, there needs to be clear, informative and reassuring information left for parents in a central and obvious place. To leave a message reading:

Figure 5.40

Inappropriate sign

will no doubt cause panic among parents and carers and much undue distress, thinking that children have been injured. Whereas to leave one reading:

Figure 5.41

Appropriate sign

will help to dispel any initial panic in parents and carers regarding their children's well-being.

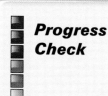

Progress Check

1 Why is it necessary to have a specific person responsible for the first aid box?
2 Give three important points regarding emergency exits.
3 Where should emergency evacuation procedures be displayed?
4 When should children's attendance be registered?
5 Why might children refuse to move or to co-operate in an emergency?

Risk assessment

There are four main stages in successful risk assessment procedures:

- identifying hazards
- assessing the level of risk
- implementing appropriate controls
- ongoing monitoring of procedures.

For example, in a babyroom you may:

1 Identify that individual infants' feeds are not always labelled clearly.
2 Assess that this could cause cross-infection between infants and also result in individual infants receiving the wrong amount and/or strength of feeds.
3 Ensure that appropriate labelling facilities are available and that all staff understand the importance of this being carried out rigorously.
4 Regularly check for correct labelling and set up a recording system for this purpose.

Whereas, in the nursery garden you may:

1 Identify a worn safety surface underneath the climbing frame.
2 Assess that children could incur serious injury if they fall, and that the setting could be liable for this as the surface is unlikely to meet safety standards.
3 Take the climbing frame out of use until the safety surface is replaced or repaired satisfactorily.
4 Monitor the wear and tear on all equipment as part of a regular recorded checking process.

activity
5.22

What other examples can you think of? Consider issues to do with:

1 Access, gate safety and fencing
2 Outdoor equipment and safety
3 Indoor equipment and fittings
4 Collection of children
5 Storage
6 Hygiene
7 Feeding
8 Medication.

Professional Practice

This unit covers the following objectives:

- Observe and identify the individual needs and skills of children
- Respond to children's need through care routines and procedures
- Provide a stimulating learning environment for children
- Understand working with codes of practice and policies
- Demonstrate workplace expectations of a professional carer and evaluation of own performance.

This unit is designed to help you achieve the core skills, attributes and competencies that are needed by everyone who works in an early years setting. You will learn to observe and identify the different stages and milestones of development and become aware of children's differing needs and how these are met within different types of setting.

The environment and activities that support learning and development are described and you will learn about the importance of health and safety and codes of practice.

The unit ends with a look at what is expected of a professional early years worker and you will be shown how to evaluate your own performance.

Individual needs and skills of children

Children develop at different rates within a professionally agreed set of developmental parameters, often referred to as the developmental 'norms'. In order to understand the current stage in development of any child, you need to understand these parameters and what influences them.

Refer to Unit 7 for discussion of how children develop and for charts setting out the average development of children at various stages. These charts cover:
- physical development
- social development
- emotional development
- language development
- cognitive development.

The underpinning knowledge and understanding set out in Unit 7 will enable you to focus on your current role as a student and how you can support the individual needs of a child or group of children appropriately in practical everyday situations.

The term **developmentally appropriate** is a significant one. It is rare to find a child who develops according to the norms in all developmental areas. It is therefore important to accommodate the advances and delays in individual children when you plan activities or give them instructions. Taking their developmental level into account in relation to the responses you expect from them is equally important.

It is important to remember that growth and development are very different.

- Growth refers to the measurable elements of how children change, for example their height and weight.
- Development refers to the stages of change in a child; although each stage may be reached at slightly different ages, they are usually reached in the same order. For example, the action of walking is mastered before the more complex actions of hopping, skipping and controlled running.

Observing and identifying ages/stages of the development of children

One of the primary methods of identifying the care and educational needs of babies and young children is **observation**, and, in order to understand the needs of the children in your care, you will use observation skills each and every day.

The acquisition of observational skills is an important aspect of your early years training. To complete BTEC National courses in early years successfully, you will need to provide evidence of your ability to monitor and plan for children's individual needs through the use of observation. There are many different ways of observing children, with some methods being more appropriate to certain situations than others. Your tutors will teach you about the practical aspects of how to go about observing children. You will also learn about how observations are written, interpreted and used, and how information is shared with parents and other **professionals**.

Observational methods

As a student you will be asked to carry out a range of appropriate observations, building up a portfolio throughout your programme of study which will be assessed by your tutors. This observation portfolio is likely to include some or all of the following observation methods:

- the written record
- target child
- baby study
- child study
- movement and flow chart
- time sampling
- checklist.

Refer to Unit 8, page 343, where methods for observing children are discussed and examples of each of the above methods are provided.

Children with particular needs

Identifying needs involves carefully considering each aspect of the child's current level of development. This may include identifying where they are placed on development charts, how they interact within the setting, how they manage to communicate or what limitations they currently face in everyday activities.

Once a child's particular needs have been identified, the appropriate professional intervention and support can be arranged. This may include:

- strategies for **behaviour management**
- encouragement of physical skills, either general or specific
- emotional support
- encouragement to socially interact
- supporting cultural differences.

There are also a number of government recommendations and frameworks that practitioners should use to consider children's holistic needs and to structure appropriate interventions. One key document is *Every Child Matters*.

Childcare settings

Day nurseries

Day nurseries provide full-time or sessional care and education for children between the ages of six weeks and five years of age. Day nurseries may be found in the statutory and the private sector and provision is usually linked to parental working hours. Statutory (provided by the state) day care is now to be found within Sure Start centres or Neighbourhood Nurseries, as well as within Children's Centres. Not all nurseries care for babies. Children are offered age-appropriate care and learning that is informed by the Birth to Three Matters framework and the Foundation Stage Curriculum, and regular inspections will be carried out by Ofsted.

Nursery schools and nursery classes

These provide childcare and early education for children from three to five years of age. Nursery schools are free if they are part of the state education system, but fees are payable if the class or school is part of private provision. Children are offered play and learning opportunities that are suitable for their age and development, and the staff team will include a qualified early years teacher. The Birth to Three Matters framework and the Foundation Stage Curriculum will **underpin** care and learning, and settings will be regularly inspected by Ofsted.

Pre-schools or playgroups

Pre-schools or playgroups usually offer sessional care and provide early education for the three to fives. They are usually organised by the community or by private individuals on a not-for-profit basis and often use the help of parents/volunteers. Sessions are often restricted to term times and may be run every day or on certain days of the week. Children will be offered age-appropriate learning and development activities based on the Birth to Three Matters framework and the Foundation Stage Curriculum. These settings are also regularly inspected by Ofsted.

Crèche

A crèche offers short, sessional care and tends to be used on an occasional basis. Crèches offer care and play facilities for children under eight and may be found in sports centres, shopping complexes and in conference and exhibition halls. A crèche needs to be registered if it runs for more than two hours each day. Crèches are unlikely to be suitable for Diploma-level placement experience, owing to their limited hours.

Children's Centres

Children's centres are usually, but not always, part of a Sure Start scheme. They provide full day care and education for children under five. Children's Centres offer integrated services across early years care and education, health and social services and provide family support and outreach work. Most are open for 10 hours each day and for a minimum of 48 weeks a year. All centres are inspected regularly by Ofsted and may have developed from previous local Sure Start programmes.

Paediatric Hospital Unit

Many general or specialist hospitals will have a paediatric unit that offers a range of children's services that may include inpatient care; outpatient care; a neonatal and baby unit; intensive care; developmental assessment centres; paediatric physical, occupational and speech therapy; play room and therapeutic play facilities; and a hospital school service. It may be possible to undertake placements in some of these, but priority may be given to nurses in training.

Childminding

Registered childminders look after small groups of children, usually in the childminder's home. They may care for up to six children under the age of eight years including their own, but only three may be under-fives. Hours offered depend on the childminder, and hours, terms and conditions are negotiated with the parent. Not all childminders will have childcare qualifications, although they will be registered with Ofsted and have received a police check, as will all adults over the age of 16 years living in the home.

Nannies

Nannies and other home-based carers are employed by parents and usually care for children in the family home. Hours, terms and conditions are negotiated to suit individual circumstances, and work may be full time, part time or shared with another nanny. Duties may include living in the family home, and some positions may also include light household duties as well as childcare. Many nannies will hold a recognised childcare qualification, although this is not compulsory.

Care routines and procedures

Health and safety issues

Health and safety awareness is crucial in all settings and, in order to comply with standard requirements, it is important that all those involved are clear as to what is meant by the term 'health and safety'. Each adult working in the field of early years care and education has a responsibility to ensure that children are protected from hazards and infection whilst in their care. This applies to daily activities, visits outside of the setting, and whilst travelling with children. Every setting must have a qualified first aider present, and colleges offering BTEC Nationals in Early Years include a first aid qualification as part of the course.

 Refer to Unit 5 for further discussion of health and safety issues.

Without the security of knowing that their child will be safe, most parents would not leave the child in the care of your setting. Issues of health and safety in early years settings can be divided into four main areas:

- supervision
- **policies** and practices
- safe use of equipment
- hygiene.

Figure 6.1

Every adult working in early years care has a responsibility for the children in their care

activity
6.1

1 What aspects of health and safety are relevant to your current setting?
2 Compare your setting with the settings of other members of your group. How do they differ?
3 What are the common factors between them all?
4 Copy the table below and place each health and safety issue discussed by your group into the appropriate column or columns (some may need to go in more than one).

Supervision	Policies and practice	Safe use of equipment and hygience

Consider the following questions about each health and safety area:

■ Supervision

- Who is responsible for watching or observing children at rest or during an activity?

■ Policies and practices

- Who writes them? What do they cover?

- Who has access to them?

- Who has 'ownership' of them?

- Where are they kept?

- How often are they updated?

- How often are they referred to?

■ Safe use of equipment

- Who carries out safety checks?

- How often does this take place?

- Who sets out the equipment on a day-to-day basis?

- What negotiation is there regarding positioning and use of equipment?

- Are staff and students trained in the operation of specialist equipment?

■ Hygiene

- What policies does the setting have that cover hygiene?

- Who has the primary responsibility for ensuring high standards of hygiene overall are maintained?

- Who is responsible for the hygiene and cleaning of each room?

- Are gloves and disposable aprons readily available?

- What policies does the setting have on the handling and disposal of waste and body fluids?

- What policies does the setting have on the control and prevention of infection?

Professional Practice

■ Your table for Activity 6.1, once checked and agreed with your tutor or placement supervisor, will serve as a useful reference for the future.

case study

6.1

Donna and Marlene

Donna and Marlene are planning a display about 'Autumn' with a group of Reception class children. They have selected a range of books and posters and have collected a variety of cones, leaves, berries and plants. Their aim is for the children to go to the park to enjoy a walk, collecting more autumn objects, and make bark rubbings from the trees to add further interest to their display.

activity

1 What arrangements do they need to make in advance?
2 What health and safety issues can you think of related to these ideas?
3 What else could they include to extend the topic further?

Figure 6.2

What health and safety issues need to be considered when taking children outside the setting?

---

remember

Remember to keep in mind the four main areas of health and safety.

The contribution of safety and security in the well-being of children

For children to reach their developmental potential, they need opportunities. Much of this will involve activities that need boundaries. For example, learning to climb needs an adult on hand to give guidance on limitations, and learning to cook needs adult guidance and support regarding the use of sharp implements and heat. When setting boundaries, it is important to take into account the developmental stage of the child or children concerned; appropriate boundaries make a vital contribution to their overall safety and security, whilst enhancing their development.

Care routines – general

Role of early years workers

Working with children involves being in constant close contact with others, both adults and children. Personal hygiene is therefore extremely important. Attention to personal hygiene procedures gives a positive role model for children to learn from, and ensures that staff smell fresh and pleasant as they carry out personal care routines where these are appropriate.

The sterilisation of equipment for babies may also be your responsibility. It is crucial to ensure the control of potential bacterial infection, and all equipment needs to be washed regularly to prevent cross-infection. All childcare workers need to be aware of the signs of infestations, for example head lice and threadworms. Observation and identification of potential problems are a vital part of the role.

Link

Refer to Unit 5 for a discussion of the main issues of health, safety and hygiene, and to Unit 10 for the identification of signs and symptoms of illness and infestation.

Professional Practice

■ In each placement, it is important that you know the answers to the following questions. This is part of taking responsibility for your **personal safety**.

- What are the fire drill procedures for the setting?
- What is the health and safety policy?
- Who are the first aiders?
- Where is the accident book kept? Who writes in it?
- What is in the first aid box? Where is it? Who is allowed access to it?
- What is the procedure if a child becomes ill?
- When and how should equipment and furniture be cleaned? By whom?
- What happens if unplanned visitors arrive?
- If you are not yet confident that you have this information in your current placement, it is important that you ask your placement supervisor.

remember

Settings should have procedures for recording when and how cleaning processes have taken place, and who was responsible for checking them. Ask to see an example of this at your placement.

Care routines – for children

Care routines include the physical and personal care of children. It is important that you understand your role in these care routines and also your limitations. As a student, you will not be allowed to change babies and toddlers unsupervised. This is part of the child protection strategy for the setting. It is in no way a reflection of how staff view you as a person or as a child carer. It is simply putting the safety of the children first.

Figure 6.3

Care routines

Feeding and mealtimes

remember

The role of the early years worker is to meet the needs of the individual child and provide personalised care that is developmentally and culturally sensitive.

You will gain experience of preparing food and drinks for babies and children and so will be able to participate in helping to provide a balanced and healthy diet. You will learn about the importance of meeting the individual child's nutritional needs and the significance of meal times as developmental and learning opportunities. You will also learn about specific dietary needs and conditions, safety and hygiene in food preparation and storage, and the influence of cultural and social customs.

Look back at Chapter 5, page 181, for more information on nutrition and diet.

Bathing

It is unlikely that you will have the opportunity to participate in bathing children in many settings, but you should still be aware of the principles of good practice and acquire the necessary skills. You will be able to undertake practical skills sessions in your college course, and it may be possible for you, with supervision, to undertake this aspect of care in a childminding or family setting. You will also acquire knowledge about safety issues when bathing children and how bath time can be used to **stimulate** all aspects of development.

Look back at Chapter 5, page 162, for more information on bathing routines.

Changing

You will be able to practice the skills required for changing routines in college, and may be able to assist in changing routines in the setting with supervision. You will learn about how changing time needs to be synchronised with a child's individual needs and why changes in skin and other conditions need to be reported. Changing routines also incorporate the principles of compliance with cultural and parental practice and present opportunities for stimulating development.

Look back at Chapter 5, pages 160 and 162, for more information about changing routines and skin care.

Dressing

You will be able to participate in some aspects of helping to dress children, and most settings will supervise this aspect of your care of children. You will also be able to support children in gaining mastery over the skills involved in learning to dress themselves and selecting appropriate clothing and footwear.

Look back at Chapter 5, page 180, for more information on dressing, clothing and footwear.

Rest and sleep

To be appropriate, sleep and rest routines should be in tune with the individual child's needs, and you will be able to participate in supporting these needs. You will learn about the benefits of sleep, rest and quiet times and about the need for safety and supervision during these periods.

Look back at Chapter 5, page 165, for more information on rest and sleep.

Toileting and other hygiene routines

You will be able to participate, with supervision, in assisting children with their elimination and hygiene needs. Certain aspects of this care may be carried out by a baby's or child's key worker, and you should not feel excluded when this happens. These routines also provide the opportunity to support older babies and young children with mastery of the skills needed for independence.

Look back at Chapter 5, page 189, for more information about toileting and other hygiene routines.

Professional Practice

- BTEC students will need to write up four different routines in each placement for inclusion in their professional practice log.

A stimulating learning environment

Children learn through stimulus. The verb 'to stimulate' means to encourage, to inspire or to act as an incentive. This refers not only to the provision of activities, but to the ways in which you interact with children, the use of body language, making eye contact, and the giving of encouraging looks and smiles. Early years professionals need to understand the importance of ensuring that all children have an appropriate share of their time and responses. You need to recognise that some children are more demanding than others, but that the less demanding child should not lose out because of this. You need to deal with a demanding child by positively reinforcing acceptable behaviour, making it clear what your expectations are and setting clear, consistent boundaries.

Refer back to Unit 2, page 44, for setting goals and boundaries in early years settings.

The setting

It is important that children are grouped appropriately; usually babies are either separate from the other children or are with the youngest age range of toddlers. Typically, nurseries group children in the following way:

- baby room: babies from 6 weeks can be found here, along with crawlers and standers, and the youngest of the walkers;
- toddler room – toddlers approximately between 1½ years and 2½ years are likely to be found here;
- pre-school room – all children working towards the early learning goals in the Foundation Stage Curriculum will be in this group, plus a few of the rising-threes;
- and in school, where Reception children will either be in a specific reception age group, or combined with the youngest of the children from Year 1.

Aims

The aims of every setting should be clear. These are written down, are given to parents when they take up a place for their child at the setting, and will be available for inspection and **reflection**. Written plans should be in place for all age groups, linked to curriculum or guidance strategies as appropriate.

Refer to Unit 4, page 134, for information on the Birth to Three Matters strategy, the Foundation Stage Curriculum and the National Curriculum.

Staffing and structure

Staff will hold a range of qualifications. Schools will, of course, be staffed by qualified primary teachers, usually supported by nursery nurses or classroom assistants who will often hold a level-three qualification in early years.

In day-care settings – nurseries, crèches, pre-schools, and play groups – staff are qualified to either level two or level three, as are childminders and nannies. Those staff holding supervisory posts will be qualified to at least level three.

The numbers of children in any group or room will usually determine the numbers and qualification levels of staff. More senior or experienced staff will often be key workers too, liaising with a specified group of the parents of the children for whom they have greater responsibility.

Each early years setting has its own aims, practice and structure. Most settings for three- to-five-year-olds will follow the Early Learning Goals set out in the Foundation Stage Curriculum, while others will incorporate their own educational school of thought, for example, High/Scope, Montessori and Steiner, each of which, despite their differences, places an emphasis on play and experiential learning.

Link   Refer to Unit 4, pages 128 to 133, for more about High/Scope, Montessori and Steiner philosophies.

Professional Practice

■ If you are fortunate enough to have a placement in a setting using the High/Scope, Montessori or Steiner educational methods, take the opportunity to learn as much as possible about it, using this knowledge to compare and contrast differing schools of thought.

■ This can be invaluable experience for assignment work on educational theory, and will help you to contribute usefully to classroom discussion and inform other students too.

As already set out on page 228, there are a variety of differing types of provision, all with the general aim of providing a safe and stimulating environment for the children in their care.

The staff of each provision need to be aware of the routines and procedures for the setting in which they work. These will vary according to the type of provision and the ages of the children with whom they are working. Changes to routines and procedures need to be agreed in advance, and all staff, students and any parent-helpers should be kept informed. Although routine is necessary in order to provide security for the children and to avoid chaos or confusion, it should not be so rigid that it cannot embrace the flexibility needed for staff and children to enjoy spontaneous experiences or opportunities. There has to be a balance.

activity 6.2

1 Think about the routine in your current setting. How rigid or flexible is it? How well do you think it meets the needs of the children and the requirements of the curriculum? Does the balance need adjusting?
2 Make a note of the main elements of the daily/weekly routine in your placement. How does this compare to the routine of a similar setting? Discuss this with another member of your group.
3 What changes would you make if you had the opportunity?
4 How would you justify the changes you suggest?

The type of setting, and the ages of the children catered for, as well as the curriculum followed, will by necessity have an impact on the structure of the day and the scope for activity planning.

Professional Practice

■ Consider, for example, a hospital ward, with a peripatetic teacher and play worker staff.

• Think about how the staff would differ in their approach to activity provision compared to staff in a nursery class or primary school. Consider, also, a childminder, who may well provide a different, and possibly more limited, range of activities than a pre-school.

• Why is this do you think, and what might the differences be?

activity 6.3

1 In each placement you attend, note in your professional practice log the activities that are available on a daily basis.
2 Which activities can children help themselves to?
3 Which are only provided on occasions?
4 What has influenced these decisions, do you think?
5 Would you make changes if you were in a position to?
6 How would the changes you would make enhance the opportunities for the children in the setting?

Provision

Resources

Resources available in early years settings can be described as either **human resources** or **physical resources**. It is important that consideration is given to what resources are available within the setting itself and what is available in the wider community. This will ensure that the talents and experience of the staff are fully utilised, and that the children are able to benefit from the facilities and other individuals that are available locally too.

Human resources

The human resources within the setting itself consist of the staff, students and, possibly, parent-helpers. Jointly, they are likely to have an array of experience and talent. Good **teamwork** will enable this talent and experience to benefit the children, encourage individuals to share their expertise and further individual staff members' development.

From the wider community, human resources will include such visitors as dental hygienists, police officers, and road safety officers. Visits to shops or to a local farm, for example, will enable children to interact with a range of adults in their natural working environments and learn about their roles in context.

activity 6.4

1   What specific talent, skill or experience do you consider you bring to your current setting?
2   Do you have 'hidden talents'?
3   In what ways have you shared your skills with others?
4   Has anyone shared a new skill with you?
5   How might this be encouraged?
6   What wider community involvement have you experienced?

Physical resources

The physical resources within the setting comprise the activities and equipment that are available, together with the space used for play, both indoors and outdoors. In a school, there are likely to be additional spaces that can be utilised, such as a hall, library or technology room.

In the wider community, there is a vast array of physical resources available to early years staff. As already mentioned, you could visit a shop or a farm, or you could simply go to the park, on a nature ramble, or a 'listening' walk. Each of these will open up additional avenues for exploration, discussion and learning.

Outings

A trip out, even if simply a local walk, will offer many opportunities for young children to build on their knowledge and understanding.

Link

Refer to Unit 5, page 207, for guidance on planning a safe outing.

Professional Practice

1   How well is the physical environment in your current setting being used?
2   Are areas being under-used, or not being used in the most logical way?
3   What would you change if you had the opportunity?
4   With whom would you need to discuss this?
5   Make notes of any ideas you have for using physical resources in the wider community.

activity
6.5

Drawing a plan of your current setting, and adding your comments and suggestions for change could form part of your professional practice log, evidencing your understanding of how to respond to the needs of children and contribute to the provision of a stimulating environment.

Any planning should take into consideration the impact on all concerned: for example, in terms of safety, staffing and policies on permission.

Figure 6.4

Children's play provides opportunities for them to develop and explore their understanding of the world

> **remember**
>
> A range of activities is needed to keep a child's interest and enhance their experience through the introduction of new ideas, by giving them the incentive to try something new and through the consolidation and extension of the familiar.

Curriculum activities

As the main focus is on learning through play, each setting has to offer an extensive range of resources and materials, including equipment and replica objects and creative resources derived from natural and household waste materials. Much of this will be bought by the settings, but some will be acquired from factories and offices in the community and possibly from the organisation 'Scrapstore', if there is one locally.

Parents can of course also be a valuable source of interesting objects and artefacts, particularly for inclusion in the role-play area, or to develop interest tables or themed interest boxes.

Responding appropriately

Part of the role of a professional early years worker is to respond to children in an appropriate manner. This includes providing appropriately stimulating activities in socially appropriate circumstances. The use of positive body language, voice intonation and eye contact is essential, to ensure that each child feels focused upon and valued.

In supporting the provision of a setting when on placement, you will be expected to plan and implement a range of stimulating activities appropriate to the needs of the children. When working with older, pre-school-age groups, plans will need to be linked to the Foundation Stage Curriculum, set up by the Department of Education and Skills' Qualifications and Curriculum Authority (QCA) in 2000. This curriculum is divided into six areas of learning.

In primary schools, plans will need to work within the framework of both the Foundation Stage Curriculum, for children in Reception classes, and the National Curriculum for children in Years 1 and 2. The six main areas of learning that make up the Foundation Stage Curriculum (Early Learning Goals) are:

- personal, social and emotional development
- communication, language and literacy
- mathematical development
- knowledge and understanding of the world
- creative development
- physical development.

---

activity
6.6

The Department of Education and Skills has published its aims for the Foundation Stage, and these are set out below. You will need to become familiar with them.

As you read the aims, make notes on how you could best support the children within your current setting, including both activities and general approaches. Use the subheadings in bold type as your prompts.

When you have completed the task, discuss your notes within your group and add to your notes as necessary.

The Department of Education and Skills' aims for the Foundation Stage

The curriculum for the foundation stage should underpin all future learning by supporting, fostering, promoting and developing children's:

Personal, social and emotional well-being: in particular by supporting the transition to and between settings, promoting an inclusive ethos and providing opportunities for each child to become a valued member of that group and community so that a strong self-image and self-esteem are promoted;

Positive attitudes and dispositions towards their learning: in particular an enthusiasm for knowledge and learning and a confidence in their ability to be successful learners;

Social skills: in particular by providing opportunities that enable them to learn how to cooperate and work harmoniously alongside and with each other and to listen to each other;

Language and communication: with opportunities for all children to talk and communicate in a widening range of situations, to respond to adults and to each other, to practise and extend the range of vocabulary and communication skills they use and to listen carefully;

Reading and writing: with opportunities for all children to explore, enjoy, learn about and use words and text in a broad range of contexts and to experience a rich variety of books;

Mathematics: with opportunities for all children to develop their understanding of number, measurement, pattern, shape and space by providing a broad range of contexts in which they can explore, enjoy, learn, practise and talk about them;

Knowledge and understanding of the world: with opportunities for all children to solve problems, make decisions, experiment, predict, plan and question in a variety of contexts, and to explore and find out about their environment and people and places that have significance in their lives;

Physical development: with opportunities for all children to develop and practise their fine and gross motor skills and to increase their understanding of how their bodies work and what they need to do to be healthy and safe;

Creative development: with opportunities for all children to explore and share their thoughts, ideas and feelings through a variety of art, design and technology, music, movement, dance and imaginative and role play activities.

(Qualifications and Curriculum Authority, 2000).

■ Activity 6.6 should have produced a considerable list of activities and situations. To consolidate your knowledge and understanding of development still further, discuss your findings in the context of SIMPLE (Social development, Intellectual development, Moral development, Physical development, Language development and Emotional development).

■ How do your outcomes compare with the outlines of the developmental areas as described in Unit 4, page 147?

■ You will need to provide **evidence** of your understanding of what you consider to be stimulating activities. This evidence should be applied to a range of ages and stages of development during your various placement experiences. Your ability to provide stimulating activities will be evidenced through your professional practice log and also by the practical assessments you undertake in the workplace, set by either your placement supervisor or a tutor.

Figure 6.5

Providing stimulating activities

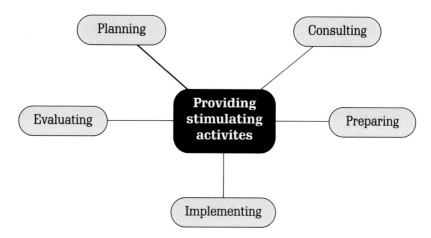

Planning
Planning care routines, play or learning activities is at the heart of good quality and effective provision. Whether the plan is being made for care, play or learning needs, it needs to be structured; and informed by appropriate frameworks such as the Birth to Three Matters framework or the Foundation Stage Curriculum. It also needs to be flexible, inclusive and responsive to the needs of the individual.

Consulting
Consultation with parents and other members of staff may be instrumental in planning effective care and, most importantly, children should also be consulted. Consultation is important in identifying additional needs as well as in planning culturally and developmentally sensitive care.

Preparing
Preparation should be linked to careful planning in order that care and activities can be successfully implemented. This means not only preparation of the items and resources needed for the activity or care routine, but also preparation of the environment.

Implementing
This is the pivotal phase of the planning, when the care routine or activity is put into action with the identified individual or group. Implementation may involve some element of instruction, demonstration and questioning as well as observation and assessment of how children react to the care or activity.

Evaluating
Planning care, play and learning activities has to be followed by careful evaluation of how successful these have been in meeting the needs of babies and children. Observation and assessment are also involved in the evaluation process, and evaluation is also an integral part

of reflective practice. Evaluation includes asking questions of children, other staff and self. These may include such questions as:

- Did all of the children enjoy and benefit from this activity and if not, why?
- Did the activity meet the set learning objectives?
- Was care effective in meeting children's needs? If not, what modifications need to be made?
- Was the preparation for this care or activity effective and were all the health and safety aspects considered?
- How could this be developed further?

Play activities

It is useful to consider everyday activities, evaluating how they enhance each aspect of children's development. If you initially consider the basic opportunities that each activity provides, you will move on to develop an understanding of how to extend activities further as you progress through your course of study. The following section outlines just a few of the many play activities you will enjoy with children during your training and career.

---

activity 6.7

Think about play activities, copying the following table and placing the activities under the headings you consider to be appropriate: i.e. indicating the developmental areas you consider they would be likely to enhance. NB Some will come under several (or all) of the headings.

Activities:

role play corner/imaginative play
games involving more than one child
sand, water, clay, wood (natural materials)
dough
group story times
group discussion times
lotto games
circle time
activities to encourage responsibility and
    taking turns
drama
music and movement
setting out the weather chart

books and stories
puzzles
construction activities
interest tables
farms, car mats, dolls houses and so on
    (small world play)
balls, hoops, beanbags, and so on
bikes
climbing frames
threading toys
pencil skill activities
painting easel
gardening

Social development	Intellectual development	Moral development	Physical development	Language development	Emotional development

---

Professional Practice

- Most of the above activities can be both child-led and adult-led. Whenever possible let children initiate the use of materials. They will learn through planning, consulting, experimentation and reflection.

Examples of play activities
Painting

Figure 6.6

Painting

Painting is a very popular medium for self-expression and communication and is usually a popular activity with children of all ages. Paints can also be used with other media – for example, wax crayons or candle wax can be used to make wax-resist painting. Children can be encouraged to experiment with different painting styles and techniques, as well as styles and techniques from other cultures.

Setting up
- Set up painting activities in a clearly defined space.
- Set up on an easily cleaned surface or floor.
- Ensure provision has been made for drying wet paintings.
- Make sure child wears protective overall.
- Provide a wide variety of paint, brushes, string, wax crayons, sponges etc.
- Ensure all materials are non-toxic and that children are supervised.

Benefits for physical development
- Painting encourages manipulative skills and some fine motor skills.
- It aids development of dexterity as the child uses and explores different materials and tools and learns how to control the brush.

Benefits for intellectual development
- Painting helps children to recognise concepts such as size, shape and colour.
- It encourages experimentation when mixing and creating new colours.
- It teaches that properties and textures of liquids and objects change.
- It helps children to gain confidence in choosing – colours, subject of painting, etc.
- It encourages language skills when textures and colours are being discussed.
- Painting supports the child in identifying and talking about ideas and intentions, and the finished product.

Benefits for emotional and social development
- Children can share their ideas with others although many children choose to work independently.
- Painting is satisfying and non-competitive, allowing the child free expression of their ideas and feelings.
- It can encourage an apprehensive child to join in messy activities as there is no 'right' or 'wrong'.
- Self-esteem and confidence can be boosted if the child sees that their work is valued.

Water

Figure 6.7

Water play

Water is an essential element of children's lives and water play is a popular activity that offers many valuable and pleasurable learning possibilities. Although it is a fun activity, safety and supervision must be a priority as accidental drowning can occur easily when adult vigilance is relaxed.

Setting up
- Make sure that the container used for water play is easy to fill and empty.
- The number of children using the water play area may be limited for safety and to ensure adequate supervision.
- Spillages must be wiped up immediately.
- Children should wear protective overalls.
- Provide a wide range of containers, scoops, funnels and other equipment, as well as items that will float and sink.
- Remember to change the water after each session and remind children to wash their hands and behave safely.

Benefits for physical development
- Children will be able to develop their hand–eye co-ordination when pouring water into a container or from one container to another.
- Water play offers opportunities to increase manipulative skills and control over body movements.

Benefits for intellectual development
- It offers valuable learning opportunities as children experiment with texture, feeling and properties.
- It enables development of concepts such as volume, capacity, sinking, floating, full, empty.
- It encourages experimentation and discussion of ideas.
- Language development can be stimulated by asking children questions and encouraging description.
- It may encourage the use of imagination.

Benefits for emotional and social development
- Water play can be therapeutic and relaxing and can encourage enjoyment although the play tends to be solitary or parallel.
- Self-esteem and confidence can be boosted as there is no right or wrong way to play with water (as long as play is safe!).
- It facilitates the expression of pleasure and excitement.

Sand

Figure 6.8

Sand play

Sand play, like water play, is a popular activity in most settings and is an absorbing and pleasurable play medium for children and adults alike. Whether it is used indoors or outdoors, children can involve themselves in sand play at whatever level they like, as there is no right or wrong way to play with sand.

Setting up

- Provide plenty of props to use with the sand: for example, different-sized cups and containers, spades, spoons, ladles, scoops, moulds, plastic biscuit cutters, toy people, toy cars, toy animals, shells, pebbles, colander, rakes, funnels, sieves, measuring cups and spoons, scales, magnifying glass.
- Store props where children can have easy access to them.
- Put sand play area near other active areas.
- Outside sand trays must be carefully checked for contamination from animal faeces.
- Ensure that the correct type of sand is used and change it regularly.
- Give close supervision and limit the number of children in the area at any one time.
- Provide protective covering – some settings provide head covering as well as overalls.
- Make sure children do not throw sand and make sure that spilt sand is swept up promptly in order to prevent falls.

Benefits for physical development

- Playing with sand improves fine motor and manipulative skills.
- It helps with hand–eye co-ordination.

Benefits for intellectual development

- It encourages sensory experiences as children explore the properties of wet or dry sand.
- It increases vocabulary as children use words like wet/dry/mould/sift/pour/trickle.
- It encourages children to talk to other children and adults as they play and experiment.
- It allows children to explore and experiment with concepts such as volume, capacity, and cause and effect, as children pour into and empty sand out of containers.

Benefits for emotional and social development

- The activity is usually soothing and may be used therapeutically for some children.
- Children's confidence can be built through co-operation and interaction with others.

Role play

Figure 6.9

Role play

Most children enjoy the role-play area of the setting; it may be referred to as the home corner. Regardless of the name, it must be an area that reflects the home life, experiences and abilities of *all* children and should contain culturally diverse equipment and props. The role-play area will benefit from regular changes of layout and emphasis and a wide range of resources will support creativity and lessen the chance of repetitious play.

Setting up
- The area should be set up with sufficient space and resources for several children to play at the same time.
- Resources should be checked for safety, suitability and ability to stimulate play and development.
- Children may need adult support to explore new concepts and topic areas.
- Dressing-up clothes should be easy to use and should represent a wide variety of cultures.
- Clothes should be washed regularly and some limitations may need to be imposed with role-play clothes and hats if children have contagious skin conditions or head lice.

Benefits for physical development
- Manipulative skills can be promoted when using the dressing-up clothes – dexterity and control will develop as children fasten buttons, manipulate zip fasteners and use equipment and props.

Benefits for intellectual development
- Depending on the 'role' that this area is being used for, children will be able to understand and explore different roles and processes – for example, going to the garage and writing a bill for repairs.
- Concepts such as numbers and money may be explored through pretend shopping.
- It provides opportunities for sorting, grouping, matching and pairing, for example, cups and saucers, knives and forks.
- It stimulates language through conversations and use of role-specific language.
- There are opportunities for writing skills when, for example, children write menus for the café, bills for the garage or tickets for the bus.

Benefits for emotional and social development

- There is no right or wrong way to undertake role play, so it provides children with the ability to use their imagination and understand other's roles.

- Role play helps children learn to share and co-operate with others whilst planning roles and exchanging ideas.

- It encourages expression of social greetings and conventions, such as hello, please, thank you.

- It promotes confidence in interacting with others.

- Children are helped to understand unfamiliar situations, such as going to the doctor or hospital, or having a new baby.

- The role-play and home-corner play can also be used therapeutically with a vulnerable child in order to explore feelings and anxieties.

Construction

Figure 6.10

Construction

Children find construction play to be stimulating and satisfying, and it helps them to experience the excitement of building something from assorted components. Many different types of construction toys are available, varying in the materials used and orientation. For example, settings may have wooden train sets, plastic interlocking bricks, puzzles, all of which could be called construction toys.

Setting up

- Minimal time is needed for setting up construction play but space to allow several children to play and spread out the equipment is necessary.

- Equipment needs to be age appropriate in order to counter frustration and ensure safety.

- Make sure that all children are encouraged to engage in construction play regardless of gender.

Benefits for physical development

- Handling the components develops skills of manipulation and dexterity.

- Hand–eye co-ordination and motor development improve as children fit pieces together and use large boxes, tables, chairs, etc.

Benefits for intellectual development

- Construction play helps children to develop planning and intention skills.

- It aids development of concepts such as shape, size, colour, height and weight.

- It increases children's ability to sort and group by size, weight, shape and develops sustained concentration and effort.

- It helps children develop new vocabulary, and they can use language to give instructions as well as for discussing ideas.

Benefits for emotional and social development

- It encourages co-operation and sharing, as well as the social conventions of requesting and thanking others for use of resources.
- It allows the child to experience and express elation and frustration when efforts succeed or fail.
- The achievement of intentions will aid self-confidence and promote independence.
- Co-operative play can be encouraged although large groups may be less successful.

Books and stories

Figure 6.11

Children having a story read to them

Books and stories offer rich opportunities to develop and extend children's language and literacy skills, as well as the ability to share a special time with adults and other children. There is no age limit on the use of books and stories; these should be regularly offered to babies as well as older children. A variety of types, sizes and formats of books should be offered, as well as dual-language texts and books with children's heritage languages and alphabets. All resources should reflect cultural diversity and contain positive images of gender, ability, ethnic origin, etc.

Setting up

- Very little formal setting up is required but care needs to be taken with the size of the book if more than one child is to be read to.
- The environment needs to be conducive to quiet reading or story time.
- Props can be used to bring the story alive and help the child engage with the story.

Benefits for physical development

- Manipulative skills are developed when turning pages and handling books.
- Hand–eye skills improve when following direction and orientation of text.
- Actions can be used with some stories.

Benefits for intellectual development

- Books and stories offer rich opportunities for the development of language and literacy skills – from learning how books 'work' to appreciating the different forms and properties of language, and development of vocabulary.
- The activity helps children to understand the differences between factual books and fiction.
- Learning and understanding are enhanced by repetition and imitation.

Benefits for emotional and social development
- The child can enjoy a solitary or shared experience.
- It helps understanding about the social world and wider environment.
- The child can explore a range of situations that may cause anxiety such as a new baby or going to the doctor.
- It allows the child to experience and express a range of emotions, and children may find favourite stories comforting.
- Storytelling can be used therapeutically with a vulnerable or anxious child.

Clay and dough

Most children enjoy playing with dough, clay and other malleable materials, and this type of play offers valuable learning opportunities. It provides freedom for creative expression as well as giving the child the opportunity to explore the properties and possibilities of these media.

Figure 6.12

Playing with clay and dough

Setting up
- Most settings will use a table with a wipeable top for this kind of play, although a tray could be used for a child confined to bed.
- The placement of activity needs to be considered; it can be incorporated with other areas such as the home corner.
- Safety and hygiene must be considered – dough should be replaced regularly, and children with allergies or intolerances may need materials that are free from gluten or other known allergens.
- Children must be encouraged to wash their hands before and after using malleable materials, and those with sensitive skin or infectious skin conditions may need to take precautions when playing, such as wearing gloves.
- Offer a range of equipment such as plastic cutters, blunt knives, rolling pins, stamps, boards, garlic presses, etc.

Benefits for physical development
- This type of play promotes hand–eye coordination and dexterity as the child manipulates malleable material and the equipment.
- It allows the child a range of sensory and tactile experiences.
- Manipulative skills can be enhanced with the use of equipment – such as cutters etc.

Benefits for intellectual development
- Children are able to explore properties and textures as well as exploring concepts such as malleability, shape, mass etc.
- It helps children to understand what tools are appropriate for which actions and helps link planning to intentions.
- New vocabulary can be learnt, and the child can describe textures, actions and intentions.

Benefits for emotional and social development
- It offers satisfaction and there is no right or wrong way to play with malleable materials.
- The child can express strong emotions through squeezing, squashing and then remaking.
- Play can be undertaken as a solitary activity but also provides an opportunity to work and share with others.
- It can help children develop social conventions, such as please and thank you, as equipment is passed and shared.

activity

6.8

1   Using a copy of the Early Learning Goals for the Foundation Stage, identify which goals can be linked to the above activities.

2   How would you adapt these activities for children under three?

Issues to be considered

All books, posters, games, puzzles, toys and similar resources should be carefully evaluated for the positive (or negative) images they portray. Those considered to offer negative images should be removed and replaced with more positive materials when funds allow. There is no benefit to having a large range of resources if they include negative images. The children will not benefit from them and may absorb the wrong messages. It is far better to have a smaller range which will enhance children's understanding of **equality**, be it gender, race or disability.

Figure 6.13

Toys should be evaluated for the images they convey

Positive/negative effects of language and labelling

It is important that you use language appropriately. Take note of how colleagues address children and their parents, and value the diversity of the languages spoken within your setting. Encourage children to use their heritage language as well as the language that they mostly use to communicate in the setting. Settings can demonstrate to families that their language is valued by translating notices appropriately. Asking parents to help with the translations will also demonstrate that their involvement is valued.

activity

6.9

It can be useful to carry out an audit of provisions in your setting. This involves looking carefully at the materials and activities offered and making a judgement on their suitability. Ask yourself the following questions:

1   Is the range of books, toys, posters, and so on, adequate?

2   Do they cover a sufficiently broad range?

3   Are all the activities and equipment suitable?

4   Do any of them promote unacceptable images?

5   To whom should you talk if you have identified any negativity?

Refer to Unit 1, page 9 for further discussion of the importance of diversity.

For further reading on equal opportunities, refer to *A Practical Guide to Equal Opportunities* by Malik (2003).

---

activity
6.10

Joelene is aged three years and three months. She is struggling to complete a 12-piece jigsaw puzzle. She is randomly trying to put it together.

1   At what stage would you become involved?
2   How would you approach this?
3   How might your approach differ with a child of a different age or at a different stage of development?

Professional Practice

■   Careful planning is needed to ensure that all children have sufficient, and equal, access to each type of activity.

---

activity
6.11

You have been asked by your tutor to plan activities for the children in your placement. Work with a partner: one of you is currently on placement in a day nursery with the two-to-three-year-olds; the other is working in a Reception class of a primary school.

Select three activities from the list below, linking them to a theme of your choice. Write plans for each activity, showing how the activities can be differentiated for the two age groups.

Activities:
communication printing   interest table
model making   technology construction
collage   books and stories
malleable play   imaginative play
music activities   natural play materials

Use the suggested planning outline below

Topic	Learning intention	Resources	Child's activity	Adult role	Language

If, for example, the chosen topic was 'Mini beasts' think:

■   What could be included on a display table? A wormery? Discarded snail shells? What else?
■   What information books could be included?
■   How many stories could be linked to the topic? *The Very Hungry Caterpillar? Odo the Snail?* Which others?
■   Where could children be taken to for a visit? The park? The nursery garden? Where else?
■   What creative activities could you link to the topic? E.g. Making spiders webs with wool on a pegboard? Printing with discarded (washed) snail shells? What else?

Placement supervisors and staff are usually very willing for students to plan and implement activities on their own initiative. It is important, however, to agree dates for these activities in advance. Negotiation regarding display space needed, materials required and any involvement of other staff must all be discussed and clarified. Some placements will be able to supply the materials you need for an activity, but others will either be unable, or less willing. Do not assume you can use the setting's own resources and consumable materials without checking first. If you are planning a visit, you will, of course, need to follow the setting's normal procedure for obtaining parental permission and follow the guidelines for adult:child ratios, etc.

Link

Refer to Unit 5, page 207, for information about safety issues on outings.

Promoting and supporting development

Learning can be supported in many ways. The use of hands-on experience, together with display work and visits, can make a subject more real to children than simply hearing about it or looking at pictures, although clearly both of these media are valuable information sources in their own right.

Displays can involve children and their families in contributing objects and information. Parents and other family members may be able to demonstrate a skill or recount personal experience of the subject-matter.

For information on setting up play activities, refer to the *Ready, Steady, Play!* series by Green (2005) and *Planning Play and the Early Years* by Tassoni and Hucker (2000).

Encouragement of physical skills

A child's individual physical needs will be met by evaluating their current level of development, together with their main interests.

The development of large motor skills is easily supported by outside activities in dry weather, but more initiative is needed within the confines of a small room. Fine motor skills can be developed anywhere, for example in domestic and learning activities.

All types of play enable children to develop physically. Powers of co-ordination are practised, with movement and games helping to extend large motor skills, and fine motor skills being enhanced by more dexterous activities. Physical exercise helps to build strength, and will add to general health.

Children who live in cramped conditions, or who have little access to outside play at home, benefit in particular from opportunities to exercise their bodies through play, with spatial awareness developing through co-coordinated movement activities using large motor skills.

The role of the adult in helping and supporting physical development is often one of innovation. It can be easy to provide plenty of opportunities for large motor skills play on a fine day when there is a safe outdoor playing area, but more imagination is needed to encourage the use of these skills indoors. The use of drama, dance and exercise is important, as too are activities for encouraging the fine skills in children with limited dexterity or concentration spans. Careful planning is needed to ensure that all children have sufficient, and equal, access to each type of activity.

activity
6.12

Considering the general physical development of children aged around three years, plan three ideas to support large motor skills development indoors, and three ideas to support fine motor skills.

Emotional support

A withdrawn or unhappy child may need additional adult support; the insecure child may need additional reassurance and sensitive settling-in, involving both the parent and the professional.

Children need opportunities to come to terms with their feelings, which may at times be confusing, upsetting or even frightening. This is all part of emotional development. They need to be reassured that it is alright to have negative feelings, such as jealousy and anger, and to be helped to learn how to manage these feelings. It is important, also, that they understand that others, adults included, have these feelings too.

A child suffering emotional stress is less likely to be as receptive to learning as one who is emotionally stable. Common family events, for example moving house, starting nursery or the arrival of a new baby, are all potentially disturbing situations. As an early years professional, you will need to offer opportunities for children to work through their concerns and problems in a safe environment.

The adult's role in helping and supporting emotional development is one of observation and empathy, supporting the child in their anxiety and providing a range of opportunities through play, books and discussion (and at times puppets) to help them work through their feelings. Self-esteem can be closely associated with emotional stability, and you can probably think of situations where you have been made to feel unvalued. This no doubt had an impact on your sense of self-worth, even if only temporarily. It can, however, potentially have an effect both in the short term and in the long term. Self-esteem can be boosted through the use of circle time.

Refer to Unit 7, page 304, for more on the emotional development of young children.

Encouragement to interact socially

A child who has not learned to share, to interact with others or to respond appropriately to social situations may need adult involvement to help them find their way. Having other children as role models will help, along with adult encouragement and support, such as giving praise when acceptable socialising takes place and clear explanations when it does not.

Socially, children need to develop self-confidence and be able to make and sustain friendships; they need to understand the ways of others and to value the differences between themselves and their peers. Within our democratic society, we all need to conform to some basic rules. These too have to be learned, enabling us to respect the needs of others, to win and lose gracefully and to behave appropriately in whatever circumstances we find ourselves.

The role of the adult in helping and supporting social development is at times one of mediator, helping children to learn to share through the use of games, books and discussion, encouraging turn-taking and the apportioning of materials in play. Adults also have a responsibility to introduce new experiences, such as cultural events and religious festivals, to enhance learning and to help avoid the development of prejudice.

Refer to Unit 5 for information on setting goals and boundaries in early years settings, and Unit 7 for more on the social development of children.

Professional Practice

■ Have you seen an example of adult intervention in the socialising of young children?

■ Why was this taking place, do you think? How helpful was the adult's involvement?

■ Was there an alternative approach, do you think? If yes, what might it have been?

Supporting cultural differences

A child's culture is important to them as an individual. It is part of their social identity, and is also important to the setting which they attend. Enabling a child to take part in and benefit from all opportunities within the setting may on occasions mean that a slight adjustment is needed to ensure that the child's cultural requirements are fully acknowledged. For example, staff should not assume that all children have the same day-to-day experiences; by making this assumption, they may be excluding some individuals.

Cognitive development

The need to achieve high academic standards is emphasised in today's society. In early years this does not mean a formal education, but rather, through: 'developing key learning skills such as listening, speaking, concentration, persistence and learning to work together and co-operate with other children' (Hodge, 2000).

All of this can be achieved through play, upholding the guidance set out by the Plowden Report in 1967, which gave 'central status' to the role of play in the education of young children.

Undoubtedly, children need opportunities to explore within their play, using all of their senses. They need opportunities to conserve, to measure, to estimate, to predict. They need activities designed for understanding concepts such as volume, capacity, weight and length, but perhaps most of all children need opportunities to develop thinking skills and the power of concentration.

Opportunities for conserving, measuring and estimating occur naturally in many activities.

The role of the adult in helping and supporting cognitive development can be as generalised as the setting-out of stimulating materials and activities, and as specific as noting when to intervene in the experiential process in order to enhance learning. The psychologist Lev Vygotsky (1896–1935) called the difference between what a child can achieve alone and what they can potentially achieve with adult intervention the 'zone of proximal development' (ZPD). As you develop your observation skills you will increasingly develop your understanding of when it is appropriate to join in with a child's play in order to enrich the learning process. This is a skill which develops over time and will be an important aspect of your professional practice.

Refer to Unit 4, pages 120-24, for a discussion of learning, including the thinking of Lev Vygotsky.

Language development

Your time is the most important gift that you can give to a child to enhance their language development. The role of the adult in helping and supporting language development is to supply opportunities for conversation, introduce the child to literature and let them write using a variety of media. Ideally, children need to be surrounded by language from birth. They need to be both spoken to and listened to. They need to be encouraged to talk, to discuss what they are doing and what they have done already.

Opportunities to write can be found within imaginative play, with appropriate props being supplied to enhance the shop, cafe, and so on, that the children are enjoying. Familiar articles, pictures and objects can be labelled to help make links between spoken and written language.

Language is our main means of communication, without which it is less easy to express ourselves or make our needs known. The development of spoken language enables a child to describe and to explain and offers opportunities to question and to clarify instructions, thereby furthering their opportunities for learning.

Refer to Unit 7, page 322, for more on language development.

Moral development

Children need moral guidance too! Moral development links closely with social development. A child's understanding of socially acceptable behaviour is vital to building successful relationships. Issues of sharing and the development of understanding what is right and wrong are important, and are helped by having well-defined boundaries within the setting, together with a positive approach to addressing any problems that arise. Valuing other cultures and religions is particularly important in our multicultural society; equality should be both recognised and respected. Learning self-value helps us to cope with peer pressure, to stand firm and maintain our beliefs and moral conduct.

The task of the professional adult in helping and supporting moral development is as a role model, and by setting clear boundaries regarding what is acceptable within the setting and what is not. It is also important that the adults within the setting are prepared to challenge unacceptable actions or discussion, both with the children and with other adults.

Specific needs that affect the rate of development

As well as considering how best the developmental needs of children can be met, it is important to look at what influences development and what early years professionals can do to enhance this.

Factors affecting development

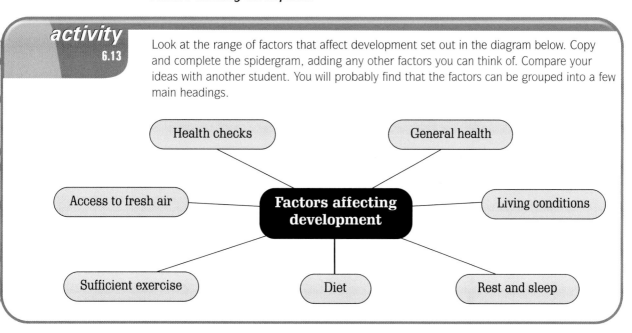

activity
6.13

Look at the range of factors that affect development set out in the diagram below. Copy and complete the spidergram, adding any other factors you can think of. Compare your ideas with another student. You will probably find that the factors can be grouped into a few main headings.

Health checks   General health   Access to fresh air   **Factors affecting development**   Living conditions   Sufficient exercise   Diet   Rest and sleep

The World Health Organization (WHO) stated in 1946 that: 'Health is the state of complete physical, mental and social well-being, not merely the absence of disease and infirmity.'

This definition has been updated to include a more general description: 'The enjoyment of the highest attainable standard of health is one of the fundamental rights of every human being without distinction of race, religion, political belief, economic or social condition …'.

activity
6.14

1 In a group, discuss how a child might be affected if any of the factors in the spidergram in Activity 6.13 is unavailable or insufficient. How do these factors fit in with the aims of the WHO?
2 Research health literature for examples to support your answer.

Link

Refer to Unit 10 for further information on health.

Opportunities for healthy development are based on good health, physical care and emotional well-being. The nutritional requirements for the growth, maintenance and development of the body are found in the food that we eat, helping us maintain and repair our body tissues, and keeping muscles and organs functioning. Food helps to prevent infection and supplies the body with its energy needs too.

A balanced diet contains a range of vitamins and minerals and is divided into four main food groups.

Refer to Unit 5, page 181, for information on nutrition and dietary needs.

Together with a balanced diet, children need to be in full health in order to achieve their potential. To monitor a child's health, health professionals carry out routine examinations, assessments and immunisations.

Children need to feel cared for and loved unconditionally and have sufficient fresh air and opportunities for exercise, rest and activity. They need protection from harm and they need security. Without the right balance of these, a child's health and development is likely to suffer.

As an early years professional, you will be one of many adults who play a role in the well-being and development of children. You will also be a role model for children, as they develop their own attitudes towards health choices.

activity 6.15

1 Who else would you consider as being influential regarding children's health choices and attitudes?
2 In what ways do you consider they have influence? Discuss your thoughts with others in your group.

Health and safety

Issues of health and safety have already been touched upon in this unit, but are discussed fully in Unit 5, page 192. You may find it useful to refer to that unit now to think through the implications for:

- choice and use of a range of materials
- tools and equipment both inside and outside the setting
- restrictions on numbers and staff:child ratios
- hygiene and cleanliness.

Codes of practice and policies

Codes of practice

Each setting will have its own **codes of practice** and will serve a range of client groups. As a student, it will be useful to gather information on the codes of practice, statements and policies of each setting you attend as placement experience. For example, settings may have a mission statement or philosophy that sets out their values, beliefs and aspirations. These may be corporate statements if the setting is part of a large organisation, or it may be the result of staff consultation in a smaller setting. You should make sure that you are familiar with any such mission statement.

Settings may also have behaviour contracts which outline their expectations of professional behaviour for staff and students. It is important to comply with these whilst in placement and also the policies of the setting. Such policies are the day-to-day expression of compliance with legislation and government guidance and underpin high-quality care and education. Settings are obliged to have certain policies under the recommendations of the Children Act 1989, whilst others are merely advisable.

activity
6.16

Settings also have policies and statements covering behaviour, disability, child protection and equal opportunities. Most will of course have many more. This is an example of good professional practice.

1 Draw up a list of the main points you consider should be included in policies for each of the areas listed above.
2 Explore your ideas with another student.
3 As a pair, compare your combined ideas with real examples, obtained from your placements.
4 How well did you do?

You may have identified the need to balance the needs, rights and safety of the individual with those of others and the provision of effective care and learning. More specifically, you may have focused on

- individual staff roles and responsibilities
- agreed ways of responding to certain behaviours
- provisions that may need to be made in order to meet children's additional needs and to ensure equality of opportunity
- ways in which children will be safeguarded from harm and protocols for ensuring this
- resources that are needed to reflect diversity and to meet the needs of all children.

Adherence to codes of practice

When you start your placement in a setting, you will be shown the policies and codes of practice, and it is important to ensure that you comply with them. This is not only to ensure safe working practices for the children you will be caring for, but also to promote the concept of the 'safe learner'. You will be given further advice on this during your course, as well as receiving advice from the practitioners that you encounter in settings. Policies are not there simply to regulate the provision of care and learning, but also to promote and protect important principles such as equality, health and safety, appropriate behaviour and fair employment.

activity
6.17

You are in a nursery setting with another student on your course. You overhear her say, 'I don't care what the policy says; I think it's my business if I smoke and not theirs. I'll just go outside and smoke on my breaks.'

1 What advice would you give to this student?
2 What might be the implications of this student continuing to smoke whilst caring for young children?
3 What action should be taken?

Workplace expectations of a professional carer and evaluation of own performance

The term 'professional practice' describes the practical working life of any professional person. Being professional is to be competent, efficient and skilled in your work and appropriately qualified to carry it out. When you come into contact with, for example, teachers or doctors, you probably have certain expectations of them and how they do their job, expecting them to be professional. You will be striving to gain this sense of professionalism yourself as you work towards your qualification.

Another term that is also regularly used in the care sector is '**vocational**', which means learning through practical experience as well as theory. The BTEC National in Early Years is a recognised vocational qualification for anyone working with children from birth to eight years of age.

Professional behaviour and interpersonal skills

Placement experience is built into all BTEC National Early Years programmes, usually soon after the start of the course. Preparation for placement usually takes place during the course induction period. Both Diploma and Certificate students need a minimum of 800 hours of assessed practical experience. It is important that placements are arranged well in advance to ensure that you can maximise the time available to you. Some colleges have placement officers who take on this responsibility for you; in other colleges, you will be asked to arrange a placement for yourself. If you leave this important arrangement until the last minute, you will have less choice of suitable placements and possibly a less satisfactory placement experience.

In each placement there will usually be a member of staff allocated as the student supervisor. This person's role is to help you gain as much from your placement experience as possible. Together with other staff, your supervisor will try to make you feel comfortable in the setting, but they will also expect you to be responsive and willing to learn. Most members of staff will have been students at some point in their lives and will understand the importance of a good supportive environment in which to develop your practical skills and to build on your understanding.

> **remember**
>
> The student supervisor's role is to help you gain as much from your placement experience as possible.

Professionalism

Professionalism brings with it expectations. The following checklists can be used as starting points for considering what will be expected of you in each placement setting you attend.

Checklist: what do you need to know?

Before your first placement day, you will need to have answers to the following:

- What is the address and telephone number of the setting?
- What time do you need to arrive and leave?
- Who do you report to?
- Who will be your placement supervisor?
- Are there any dress codes?
- Meal-time requirements: are students expected to eat with the children?
- Do you need to pay for meals, coffee, etc?
- Is there an information booklet about the setting that you can read in advance?

> **remember**
>
> Just as you need information before starting at a new setting, it is useful for the setting to know something about you and your needs. This will help them make your induction and subsequent placement time with them as useful and enjoyable as possible.

These are practical, easy-to-answer questions. A visit to the setting or a telephone call before you begin your placement will enable you to arrive on your first day feeling confident. Some placement settings have special requirements, and it is important that they are clarified in advance. Whenever possible, visit the placement in advance, as this demonstrates commitment and it can be helpful for both you and the staff to put a face to a name. It can also give you an opportunity to discuss what will be expected of you.

> **activity**
> **6.18**
>
> Merryfields Day Nursery sends students the following dress code before they start their placement experience with them. Discuss it with others in your group.
>
> **MERRYFIELDS DAY NURSERY STAFF DRESS CODE**
>
> Whilst at Merryfields Day Nursery you are politely requested to comply with the following:
>
> Staff and students will …
>
> - wear tidy trousers or skirts
> - wear low-heeled shoes
> - wear plain rings and small earrings
> - always be clean and tidy
> - keep hair tied back
> - keep nails short.

Staff and students will not …

- wear jeans
- wear untidy clothes at any time
- wear heavy make-up
- wear excessive jewellery
- have visible body piercings.

Thank you

1 Explain why the above requirements are both acceptable and important.
2 Do you disagree with any of them? If you do, why is this? Discuss your reservations with other students. What do they think?
3 What else would you add to the lists?

Checklist: what does the placement need to know?

The setting will need the following information about you before you start the placement:

- your course details and placement paperwork
- your college address and telephone number
- the name of your placement tutor/course tutor
- your home contact number
- emergency contact details
- any relevant medical information (allergies, asthma, epilepsy, etc.)
- an outline of your previous experience (if any).

The first day in any placement can be quite daunting, and it helps if you enter with a smile. It can give you an air of confidence (even if you do not feel it) and encourages others to respond to you positively. The staff will probably remember what it was like to be very new and unsure. They will not expect you to know everything, or remember everything straightaway. Figures 6.14 and 6.15 summarise what will be expected of you.

Figure 6.14

Professional expectations: the first day of placement

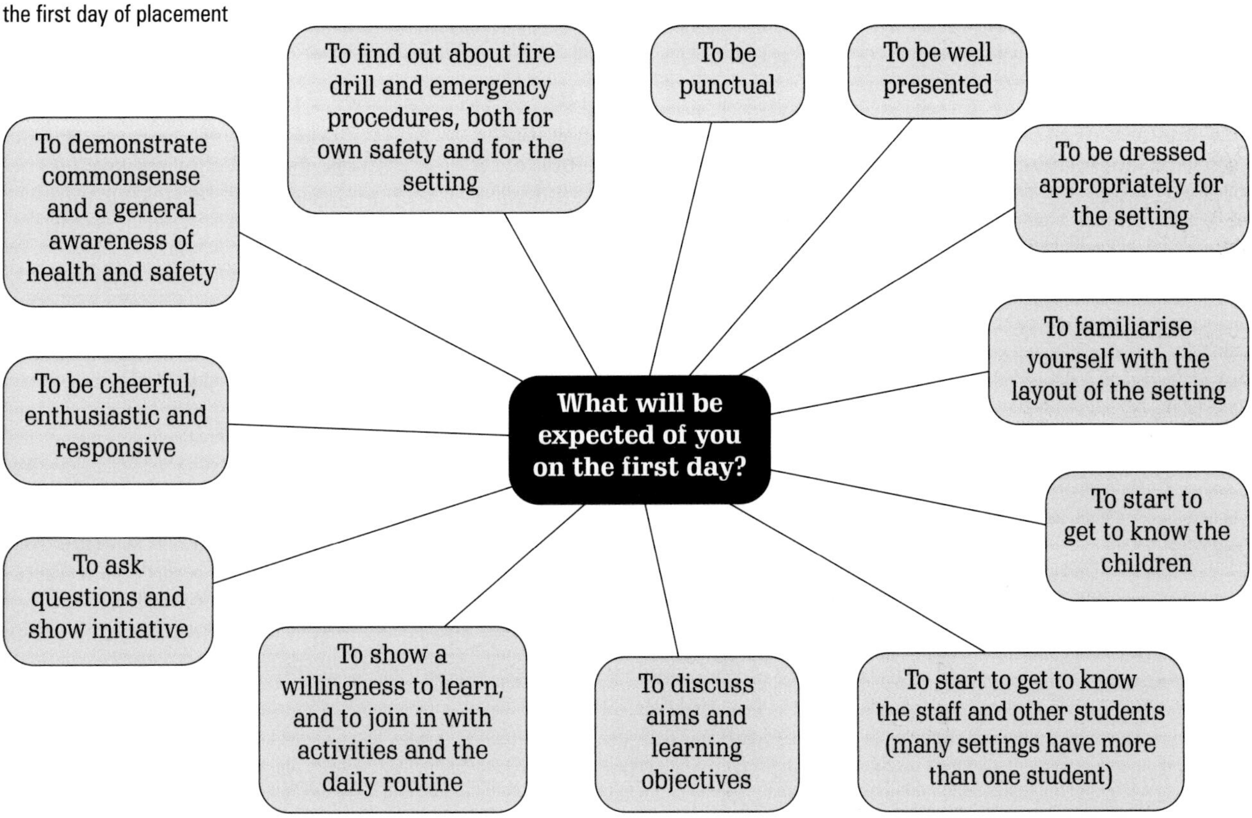

To find out about fire drill and emergency procedures, both for own safety and for the setting

To be punctual

To be well presented

To demonstrate commonsense and a general awareness of health and safety

To be dressed appropriately for the setting

To be cheerful, enthusiastic and responsive

What will be expected of you on the first day?

To familiarise yourself with the layout of the setting

To ask questions and show initiative

To start to get to know the children

To show a willingness to learn, and to join in with activities and the daily routine

To discuss aims and learning objectives

To start to get to know the staff and other students (many settings have more than one student)

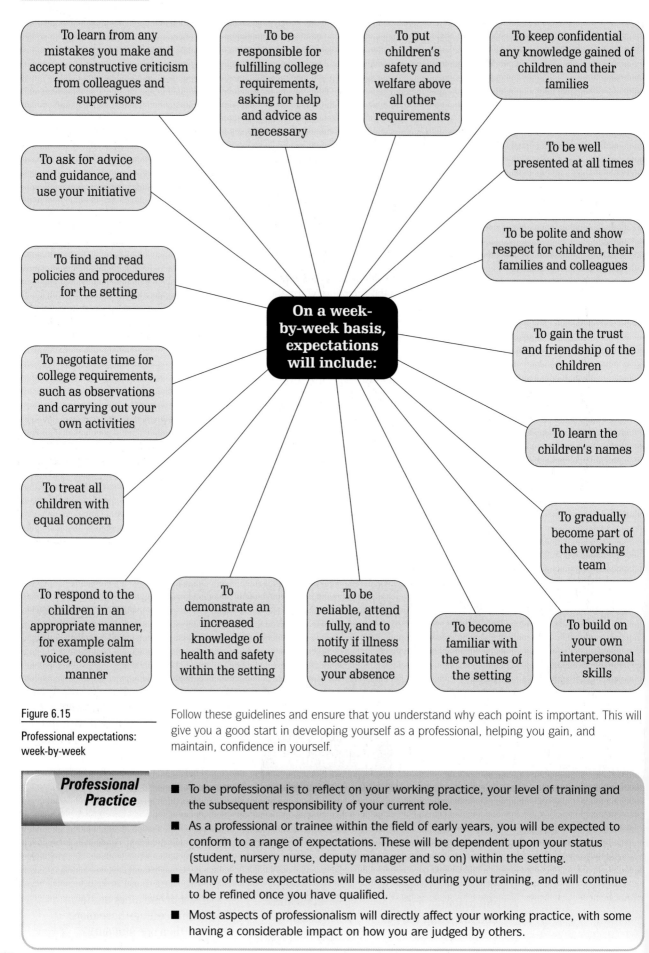

To learn from any mistakes you make and accept constructive criticism from colleagues and supervisors

To be responsible for fulfilling college requirements, asking for help and advice as necessary

To put children's safety and welfare above all other requirements

To keep confidential any knowledge gained of children and their families

To ask for advice and guidance, and use your initiative

To be well presented at all times

To find and read policies and procedures for the setting

To be polite and show respect for children, their families and colleagues

On a week-by-week basis, expectations will include:

To gain the trust and friendship of the children

To negotiate time for college requirements, such as observations and carrying out your own activities

To learn the children's names

To treat all children with equal concern

To gradually become part of the working team

To respond to the children in an appropriate manner, for example calm voice, consistent manner

To demonstrate an increased knowledge of health and safety within the setting

To be reliable, attend fully, and to notify if illness necessitates your absence

To become familiar with the routines of the setting

To build on your own interpersonal skills

Figure 6.15

Professional expectations: week-by-week

Follow these guidelines and ensure that you understand why each point is important. This will give you a good start in developing yourself as a professional, helping you gain, and maintain, confidence in yourself.

Professional Practice

■ To be professional is to reflect on your working practice, your level of training and the subsequent responsibility of your current role.

■ As a professional or trainee within the field of early years, you will be expected to conform to a range of expectations. These will be dependent upon your status (student, nursery nurse, deputy manager and so on) within the setting.

■ Many of these expectations will be assessed during your training, and will continue to be refined once you have qualified.

■ Most aspects of professionalism will directly affect your working practice, with some having a considerable impact on how you are judged by others.

Let us examine these professional expectations in more detail.

Attendance and punctuality, reliability and commitment

Children need stability and routine in order to feel secure in their environment. A member of staff who is unreliable, or who regularly has time off work unnecessarily, can adversely affect this. It is an important point to consider.

---

activity 6.19

1 How do you think having unreliable staff in a setting might affect the children?
2 How might it affect the working environment in general?
3 How might it affect the individual as an early years professional?
4 Discuss your thoughts with others before moving on to the next activity.

Standards of behaviour, particularly personal presentation and hygiene

Children learn by example, and as individuals we are judged initially by what people see (their first impressions of us). **Personal presentation** is therefore important. Having a student or member of staff who is not well presented, or who behaves inappropriately, is unacceptable and may have a detrimental effect on the working environment. This does not mean, however, that individual expression cannot be allowed, as sometimes our feelings of confidence are linked to how we feel we look, but each of us as individuals needs to consider the impact of our personal contribution to the overall setting.

---

activity 6.20

1 Consider what you feel would be acceptable and unacceptable expressions of personality in an early years setting. Think also how behaviour has an impact on working practice.
2 Why/how are children likely to be affected by inappropriate behaviour?
3 Why might negative dress or behaviour of a staff member affect the working environment in general?
4 How might they affect that individual as an early years professional?

Maintenance of own safety

Although the managers of any setting hold overall responsibility for the safety of the working environment, staff and students have a responsibility for their own individual safety, taking into account commonsense decisions and the needs of the setting. Each individual is expected to identify and address any safety issues as they occur and is expected to work both safely and sensibly at all times. Commonsense decisions may be needed in a variety of situations, for example, if:

■ an accident occurs
■ the potential for an accident is identified
■ health and safety precautions are lacking
■ exposure to infectious material is a possibility
■ you are faced with aggressive or violent behaviour
■ you are being subjected to verbal abuse.

---

activity 6.21

1 What does the term 'personal safety' mean to you?
2 Draw up a list of where you might need to be responsible for your own safety in college, in your placement and whilst travelling to and from each of them.

Interpersonal skills

Expectations are made of you according to your role or position, but at times parents may mis-identify your role, expecting more of you than you are able to give them. The ability to interact and communicate on different levels is important, and you will develop your own style of communication, within an ethos of courtesy, consistency and appropriateness. Your communication style will be one of the main aspects of your interpersonal skills. It will be part of what enables you to relate to and empathise with others. Good interpersonal skills are a crucial aspect of working with other people.

Strategies for supporting children and their families

When supporting children and their families, you need to establish communication channels that are age-appropriate and understood by all concerned, and you need to be able to initiate and sustain relationships. It is important to recognise that there are different approaches to parenting too.

Communication

Communication can be both verbal and non-verbal; it includes speech, looks and gestures. In children it is developed initially through the use of symbols. Verbal communication relies on a mutual understanding of the spoken word. It can fail if a common language is not used, or if there is no common field of experience linking the person who is speaking (the encoder) to the person who is listening (the decoder).

For example, a course tutor of nursery nursing students who discusses the development of motor skills with the group will achieve successful communication, as the topic of conversation is both familiar and of interest to all concerned. If, however, the tutor had decided to introduce the finer details of the structure of DNA (Deoxyribose nucleic acid) prior to a discussion of gene inheritance, for some students in the group (the decoders) the scientific detail may be too great. The tutor (the encoder) would therefore only achieve partial communication success.

Professional Practice

■ In the example above, how could the tutor achieve a greater level of communication success in introducing the details of DNA?

Refer to Unit 2, page 55, for a detailed explanation of the communication process.

Communicating with babies and young children

The earliest stage of pre-verbal communication is the eye contact and turn-taking between an infant and its parent or carer that takes place from shortly after birth. When an infant cries as an expression of need and the parent responds, this establishes for the infant that responses are gained by their cries. Murmurs of comfort and the verbal communication of the carer during caring routines help to build on the communication process.

Figure 6.16

Eye contact and turn-taking between an infant and its parent or carer is the earliest stage of pre-verbal communication

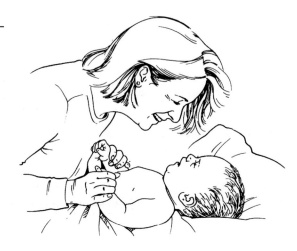

With very young children, opportunities for expression and communication need to be given through symbolic play. This allows them to learn and share meanings as they explore new ideas, and to practise and consolidate understanding by using the familiar.

activity 6.22

Name three activities that involve symbolic play. How does each of these activities enhance the development of communication?

Communication barriers

It is important to establish communication between you and the main carers of the children with whom you work. There are many barriers to communication. These include social, emotional and cultural issues.

Link Refer to Unit 2, page 39, for more about barriers to communication.

Professional Practice

- Using your developing observation skills, identify times when communication has not been completely successful. This may be due to confusion, the communication taking place at the wrong time or, perhaps, misunderstanding.

- You could use any examples which involve you as a communicator within your professional practice log, reviewing and reflecting on your own practice.

activity 6.23

1 Copy the following table and list as many barriers to communication as you can. An example of each has been given to get you started.
2 How could each of the barriers you have listed be overcome? Discuss your thoughts with another student.

Social barriers	Emotional barriers	Cultural barriers
Different first language	Shyness	Different body language

Link Refer to Unit 2 for more on interpersonal skills.

Rights and responsibilities

The UN Convention on the Rights of the Child was adopted by the United Nations General Assembly in 1989.

Link Refer to Unit 1, page 11, and Unit 3, page 88, for more about children's rights.

Parents also have rights, but with rights come responsibilities. Under the Children Act 1989, the term 'parental responsibility' was introduced into legislation. It links with the term previously used in legislation, 'legal custody', and is defined as follows: 'Parental responsibility' means all the rights, duties, powers, responsibilities and authority which by law a parent of a child has in relation to the child and his property' (Allen, 1996, page 13).

This definition replaced the unofficial list of parental rights and duties which, whilst not being linked to any one specific piece of legislation (they were taken from a range of legislation), were used by the courts as guidelines prior to the implementation of the 1989 Act.

Supporting and promoting parenting

Support for parents can be a significant element of the staff–parent relationship. Early years staff can often become a stabilising part of a child's life. They offer a reliable environment at times when life at home for a child may be confusing or disrupted through life events, such as bereavement, illness or relationship difficulties between parents. Staff need to initiate and sustain good relationships to ensure the best joint care of the children.

This is not always easy: conflicting views on parenting and how to deal with challenging behaviour can be a barrier.

Staff can be role models for families, demonstrating how to build up positive and caring relationships with others, both adults and children. Showing respect for and being interested in the children is a natural part of your work as a professional. It is not always instinctive in some families and at times parents may not share the ethos of the setting in which you work. This could be for a number of reasons. For example, a court order may have initiated the family's attendance at the setting, which could potentially build up an atmosphere of resentment, making communication difficult.

Professional Practice

- As an early years professional, you will need to ensure that communication continues between yourself and parents, whatever the circumstances. Forms of communication such as a warm smile or welcoming comment on arrival could be used to keep some contact, even if opportunities for conversation are currently limited.

Developing strategies of support

case study 6.2   Jamie

Jamie is aged three years and four months. In the nursery he is always very boisterous, to the point where children are wary of him rushing past them. He is used to climbing on chairs and tables at home and continually tries to do the same in the nursery room.

activity

1 How would you manage Jamie's boisterousness?
2 Would you refer to his opportunities to climb at home? If so, how would you approach this, ensuring that you remain supportive of his parents?

remember

It is imperative that you do not compromise parents' choices, providing of course, that these choices are not detrimental to the development, well-being or security of their child.

Awareness of differences in parenting

Every parent makes decisions regarding how their child is brought up. Some parents take an autocratic approach, monitoring their child's behaviour very strictly. Others are more laissez-faire, allowing their child much freedom of expression and giving little correction or guidance. The majority of parents fall somewhere between the two styles: they allow their children an element of freedom to challenge and explore but set boundaries that incorporate safety and guidance. The differences in the ways families live are what give our society its sense of richness.

Cultural practice can also mean differences between families and their lifestyles, and in how they parent their children. Terminology can be important, for example, Jackson (1996, page

51) refers to the use of the term 'beating of a child' used by a father of Caribbean background in one of her case studies. This term for many white-English people suggests a far harder punishment than the term 'smack', which it is actually referring to. Whether you agree with parents smacking their own child or not, the cultural difference in connotation is significant, and could lead to confusion and possible concern for the child's welfare.

activity
6.24

How do you think the policies of an early years setting contribute to the acceptance of differing parenting styles and cultural practices?

Managing the effects of abuse

Sadly, most people who work in early years settings will, at some point, work with children who have been abused, whether it be physical, emotional, sexual, or through neglect. The knowledge and understanding of development that forms such an important element of early years courses enables nursery nurses and others to identify when a child's development or behaviour strays from the 'norms'.

Professional Practice

- Clearly there can be many reasons for a child's development or behaviour to stray from the 'norms'.

- Emotional disturbance, such as moving house, or a burglary at the child's home, can cause changes and possible regression in development. This would usually be temporary and with careful handling and plenty of reassurance can often be alleviated within a reasonable length of time.

- Other progressive signs of change in a child's behaviour or regression in development need careful consideration and observation.

Refer to Unit 3, page 75, which sets out in detail the signs and symptoms that may indicate abuse. These form a useful guide. You will need to familiarise yourself with them.

Supporting children who disclose

Young children are not able to invent stories of events that they would not usually experience. They should receive the unconditional acceptance of early years staff. All staff (and students) should know who to talk to if they have any concerns about a child. Most settings have a nominated person who is the setting contact regarding child protection issues.

Ensure that you know the procedures and contact person for each setting you attend. If you are the person a child chooses to disclose to, you do not want to waste precious time finding out who needs to be informed.

This should also ensure that information is only shared on a 'need to know' basis.

Confidentiality is paramount in child protection cases. However, an adult should never make a promise to a child that they will not tell anyone what the child has disclosed. They are legally and morally obliged to tell the appropriate person in the setting.

Making a promise to a child and then breaking that promise is likely to compound the child's lack of trust in others. You will have let the child down, as did the abuser. It would be considered by many to be a form of abuse too.

Refer to Unit 3, page 89, for information on supporting children who disclose.

The role of play therapy

Play therapy is one form of helping children to come to terms with what they have experienced. It is a healing process for children, which encourages expression of feelings and ideas and helps to rebuild a child's self-esteem and self-image. Play therapy is not a strategy that anyone can simply 'have a go at'. It takes specialist training and needs to be undertaken carefully, usually in conjunction with other professionals. Sadly, play therapy is not available to all children who might benefit from it.

Refer to Unit 3, page 109, for more about play therapy.

Potential impact of abuse on the child and the family

Abuse not only affects the child, it can also be an extremely difficult time for family members, who are often unaware of what has been happening to the child. Sensitivity is clearly needed here. Early years professionals can help by encouraging the family to develop new strategies for meeting children's needs and coping with challenging behaviour.

> **remember**
>
> To support families effectively, it is important to establish good channels of communication.

Advice on group settings in the family's locality that they can attend with their children can be useful. Examples would be family centres, drop-in centres or a community bus that stops nearby. Phone lines, such as Cry-sis, for when a situation gets too much and they risk 'losing it', can be useful. These are often staffed 24 hours a day.

Home visiting, co-operation with professionals and alternative forms of care

Visiting children and their families in their own homes has become more commonplace in recent years, although there has been a decrease in general home visits by health visitors. Other professionals, such as family support workers employed by social services, now undertake this role as part of the general support for both children and parents.

Refer to Unit 3, page 111, for an outline of the roles of professionals who become involved in family problems such as child protection.

Confidentiality

Each setting will keep records of the children in its care. These records are private, and any information you are given, or you hear about, should be considered as strictly confidential. You will be expected to refrain from sharing anything with other people at home or in a social situation. This is all part of being professional.

At times it may feel appropriate to refer to something from your placement in a class discussion led by your tutor. This should only take place if you are certain that no individuals can be identified, or that the information you are sharing in no way contravenes the confidentiality of your placement setting. The same approach applies to your professional practice log. You will need to give evidence of your dealings with children, parents and staff in your professional practice log, but it should not be possible for them to be identified by the reader, even your tutor. It can be permissible to use initials, or sometimes a first name, but be aware of how much more easily some names are identified than others.

case study 6.3   **Colleen**

Colleen has recently started a placement in a local authority nursery. A child in the nursery lives near to her home and Colleen had often thought the child looked poorly and undernourished and her own mother had commented on this too. Colleen has now discovered that the child has a place in the nursery because of her parents' difficulties with the responsibility of parenting. The child has been neglected and always eats ravenously whilst at nursery. The family are regularly visited by a family support worker.

activity

1   If you were Colleen, would you pass this information on to your mother?
2   Would you discuss the case in college?
3   What are the confidentiality issues here?

case study 6.4 — Briony

Briony overhears a parent from the nursery where she is on placement gossiping in the supermarket queue about another parent's discipline methods. The parent concerned tried to draw Briony into the conversation as she checked through her shopping.

activity

1 How should Briony respond?
2 Should Briony do anything about this afterwards?
3 What are the confidentiality issues here?

activity 6.25

Are there any circumstances in which you would consider it permissible to pass on information that you have overheard or received, even by such unconventional means as Briony did? Discuss this question with other students.

Professional Practice

■ Any child protection issues of which you become aware should never be kept to yourself.

■ If you have a concern, or you overhear comments that concern you, you should ask to speak to your supervisor, the manager of the setting, or your college tutor. If no cause for concern is found, no harm will have been done. Your supervisor (or tutor) will be pleased that you have used your initiative and discussed your concerns appropriately. If the concern is subsequently substantiated, your actions will be proof in itself of the importance of speaking up.

■ Delays or reluctance to talk about concerns can potentially lead to further harm for a child.

 Link Refer to Unit 2, page 68, for more on confidentiality.

Appropriate interpersonal skills

When considering interpersonal skills, you will need to think about the range of people you will interact with as an early years professional. Think about the expectations and demands that are likely to be made of you.

activity 6.26

1 Draw up a list of the expectations you think each of the groups listed below may have of early years professionals. Consider the contact an early years professional would usually have with each group:
   a) children
   b) parents
   c) peers
   d) other adults
   e) professionals within the immediate setting
   f) professionals outside of the immediate setting.
2 Discuss and collate your ideas within your group. Consider the questions below and compare your outcomes with those of other groups.
   a) Which do you agree with?
   b) Are there any that you do not agree with?
   c) Why is that?
   d) Justify your reasons with your peers.

Children's expectations

Very young children are non-judgemental. They will like you for yourself. It does not matter if you cannot sing in tune, build a good model or catch a ball properly. They will simply expect you to play with them, give them your time, talk to them and be interested in what they do. Slightly older children will also enjoy having your time and attention. They may already have built up ideas about adult capabilities and may expect all adults to have the same level of skills and knowledge. At times they may expect more from you than you are able to give them.

activity

6.27

1. How might you respond if a child demands answers or a demonstration from you that you cannot deliver?
2. How could you deal with such a situation?
3. Where would you turn for advice when you feel out of your depth?
4. How difficult would you find it to acknowledge that you need help?
5. Do you think the age of the child would make any difference?

Professional Practice

- Patience and clear explanations are needed in these circumstances.
- There is no need to feel shame or embarrassment in admitting that you do not know something.
- Always remember that older children may be able to demonstrate a skill or introduce new knowledge to you.
- Being ready to accept and show interest in what a child can teach you may enhance your relationship with that child still further.

remember

The age of the child is not the main factor here. The child's level of understanding and ability should be the main criteria in determining your responses.

Parents' expectations

Parents put their trust in the staff at their child's nursery, pre-school or school. The staff are caring for someone so precious to them, their child. Parents expect staff to have a good standard of behaviour, to adhere to the principle of equal opportunities and to be both reliable and conscientious. **Parents' expectations** are not always voiced.

Parents want to see evidence that care is taken of their child in a safe and stimulating environment and that you enjoy working with their child. They will expect to be kept informed about their child's progress and that someone will have time to discuss their child with them on a regular basis. This would usually be the child's key worker.

Parents expect staff to be knowledgeable about early years issues and may from time to time ask questions about their child's health and development. Parents will not always understand the difference between the qualification levels and it is important that staff realise this and know how to respond to the situation positively, guiding the parent to someone more appropriate, whilst maintaining their faith in them as a staff member in their current role.

Figure 6.17

Parents put trust in the staff at their child's nursery, pre-school or school

activity 6.28

Draw up a list of staff members in your current placement.

1 Who would each staff member be most likely to turn to for advice?
2 To whom would they refer a parent for general advice?
3 To whom would they refer a parent in the case of a complaint or serious concern?
4 What level of qualifications and experience has each staff member?
5 How relevant are your answers to question 4 in relation to your answers to questions 1, 2 and 3? Why?

Colleagues' expectations

Colleagues within the setting will expect you to contribute to discussion and the planning of the environment. They will expect knowledge evidence appropriate to the level of your training, qualification and experience, and the ability to put it into practice. There will be an expectation that, if you take on a team role, you will be able to fulfil it. Time is in short supply in early years settings, and no one will be happy with a team member who does not contribute fully. It is always important that you are honest about your ability and level of understanding before taking on extra responsibilities.

activity 6.29

1 Why is it important to be honest about your ability and level of understanding?
2 As a student, in what ways could withholding concerns about the ability to cope affect the placement experience?
3 How might this affect the overall professional development of a student or newly qualified staff member?
4 What might be the effect on the placement?

Professional Practice

■ If you pretend to have knowledge and understanding when you do not, you could put children at risk, through lack of awareness, lack of supervision, or by necessitating additional staff input, taking staff away from where they should be. It could also lower your self-esteem and lose you the respect of your colleagues.

Other adults' expectations

Support staff play an important role in the running of any setting. They have a right to be treated with the same level of consideration as qualified staff and to be consulted about any changes that involve their contribution to the running of the day: for example, changes to times of a meal or snacks to incorporate a specific point of interest or activity. It is important to remember that, although some staff may not hold the same qualification as you – or have no formal training at all – they may well have years of experience. Everyone has a role to play and should be valued as part of the team.

activity 6.30

1 Draw up a list of support roles that may be found within early years settings.
2 Consider the impact of not having staff specifically carrying out these roles.
3 How might your current role be affected?

Expectations of professionals within and outside the setting

Many different professionals work within early years settings, including those who are permanently employed, some who visit occasionally and those who have a peripatetic role, visiting the setting at a specified, regular time. These include:

- health visitors
- educational psychologists
- speech therapists
- social workers
- play therapists
- physiotherapists
- music therapists
- Portage workers
- family support workers.

Each of these professionals works with specific client groups. They may be linked through the primary health care team, through the local social services departments or through the local education authority. Support may be offered on a daily or weekly basis for some children and through regular ongoing programmes for others.

Some children will be individually supported alongside the others, within the main room of the setting, while other children will be given one-to-one support in an alternative room or quiet area. The only expectation made of you by the professionals will be to support the child in continuing with any programme set by them.

Consider case studies 6.5, 6.6 and 6.7.

What forms of evidence do you think would have been relevant in supporting the need for professional intervention in each of them?

Exploring these case studies will help you identify how much you already know about evidence-gathering and also of the role of other professionals. You may find it helpful to refer to other units in this book, together with other reading sources for further information.

---

case study 6.5 — Liam

Liam is almost four years old. He has cerebral palsy, affecting both his motor skills and his language skills. He currently has support from three of the professionals listed above.

activity

1 Who do you consider Liam is most likely to receive support from? Why?
2 Compare your answer with another student's.

---

case study 6.6 — Katya

Katya is three. She is a very quiet child who will not interact with other children. Katya's home life includes a history of violence.

activity

1 Who might be supporting Katya at the moment? Why?
2 Compare your answer with another student's.

case study 6.7   Siobhan

Siobhan is five. She has a very limited concentration span and displays disruptive behaviour most days in the Reception class she attends. Siobhan has support from two of the professionals listed on page 268.

activity

1   Who might these be? What support would they be likely to give?
2   Compare your answer with another student's.

Professional Practice

■   Can you think of a child currently having professional support in your placement? Who is supporting them and why? Is this support being successful? What evidence has been used to support the need for professional intervention?

remember

Issues of confidentiality are very relevant here (see guidance on page 264).

Respect for knowledge and contributions of others

The breadth of staff experience, both professional and from life in general, contributes to the richness of most early years settings. Students and newly qualified staff are encouraged to observe carefully the ways of their more experienced colleagues. Different ways of doing things are not necessarily right or wrong, simply different. Your attitude to the viewpoints of others is an important part of your professionalism; it should be positive and welcoming.

Diversity of opinion, language, culture and religion should be celebrated as a strength of the setting. Staff, students, children and their parents should benefit from this as it helps to broaden knowledge and understanding of people and the issues of society.

Without equality of opportunity for all children and their families, an early years setting will not be meeting the needs of all client groups. Equality means not simply treating everyone the same, but giving everyone the same opportunities, taking into account their differences and differing levels of need.

Link   Refer to Unit 1, to remind yourself of equality and diversity issues.

Your own role within a team

In any setting, it is the staff team as a whole who make the setting successful, and this teamwork should not be underestimated. Each individual will have their own role to play, but no single person can carry the full weight of responsibility or organisation, although clearly the nursery owner and/or manager holds ultimate responsibility for the safety, smooth running and standards met within the setting.

As individuals, staff and students need to consider their place within the staff team, reflecting on how well they co-operate with each other, how flexible they are willing (and able) to be, and whether they are using their skills and abilities appropriately. Clearly, it does not make sense for someone who is good at carrying ideas through to completion to be involved only in the suggestions or planning stage of a project. Most settings have regular planning meetings to which staff contribute ideas and decide who will take on what responsibility. Identifying your strengths and where you best fit into a team will enable you to work within your capabilities and help you feel valued as a person.

remember

Some staff members work better together than others; that is human nature. There should be opportunities for internal movement of roles and responsibilities in order to ensure the greatest level of cohesive teamwork.

Sadek and Sadek (1996) set out the characteristics of a team as follows:

In any organisation a good team will:

■   work together
■   share a common aim
■   co-operate with each other
■   share/communicate/support between its members

- have motivation for the task in hand
- have catalytic relationships so that new ideas are extended
- be committed to the task and the team
- be comprised of members who each understand their own role in the team and are reliable in it
- complete the task.

(Sadek, S. and Sadek, J. (1996) *Good Practice in Nursery Management*)

Refer back to page 260 for more on communication.

Knowledge base

The BTEC National course will give you a good grounding in how to work with, provide for and understand the needs of children and their families.

Your knowledge base will involve your taking the initiative in planning, resourcing and implementing activities and care within whatever setting you are working. Successful completion of the course will mean that others will have expectations of you regarding how you act, what you know and how you initiate actions. At times, you will be involved in referral procedures, individual action plans and situations needing diplomacy and sensitivity. The knowledge gained during your training should help you respond to each situation competently and confidently. Your knowledge will stem not only from the subjects that you have studied in your course, but also from the legislation and recommendations that inform working with children. Knowledge and experience inform appropriate interventions and future employers may well expect you to have developed an understanding of:

- The Birth to Three Matters framework
- Sure Start programmes and provision
- The Foundation Stage and National Curriculum
- *Every Child Matters*
- *What to Do if You're Worried a Child Is Being Abused*
- The Framework for the Assessment of Children in Need and their Families.

Professional Practice

- Refresh your knowledge of these important documents and make sure that you understand the principles of each and your future role and responsibility.

You should also have developed an in-depth awareness of the needs of children and families in differing circumstances and the appropriate routes of referral that may be required. Nobody will expect you to know everything when you start your work as a qualified early years professional, but do make sure that you ask more experienced staff for help when you are unsure.

You will have developed a range of skills, knowledge and attitudes that will help you begin your practice as a qualified practitioner, but learning does not stop with gaining the qualification. You may find that you now have a range of strategies for everyday practice, but that you want to develop more specialised knowledge in order to become a reflective and effective practitioner. This will mean planning your training and learning needs in response to identifying areas for development, and you may well have started this process during the final months of your course.

You may find it helpful to refer to Unit 3, page 92, for information on referrals, and to Units 2, page 68, and Unit 3, page 90, for guidance on confidentiality.

Self-appraisal

Evaluation and self appraisal are vital skills for every professional, and, as you progress through the BTEC National course, you will be required to reflect upon and evaluate both your assignment work and your professional practice. This reflection might be occasioned by a verbal appraisal, by your tutor or supervisor, which could be either formal or informal. It could also be in writing; reflection is often included as part of the submission process for assignment work.

Your reflection should add value to the learning process. There is little benefit to stating in an evaluation that 'I could have improved upon my assignment had I started it earlier'. It would be far more useful to reflect upon your time management and how you could develop strategies for spacing your work out more appropriately. Similarly, it is pointless to state that 'I was unable to give as much time to this assignment as I would have liked, as I also had three other assignments needing attention'. All students have the same number of assignments to complete. Tutors do not expect more from you than is reasonable. The workload does not, however, take into account unusual situations, for example, students needing or choosing to work every evening after college, or a mature student with several children to care for. This may at times seem hard, but the requirements of a full-time course assume a full-time commitment to the course, and the workload required will have been made clear to you at the outset.

Self-awareness

Evaluation of (or reflecting on) professional practice will form an important part of your professional practice log. You will need to consider each of the following points:

- your use of initiative and self-direction, and its importance
- your ability to meet changing needs and situations
- issues of responsiveness and adaptability
- reflecting upon own attitudes and relationships
- recognition of own knowledge, skills and contribution to team work
- how well you target-set for future development
- how well individual professional qualities have been developed, including:
  - interpersonal skills
  - verbal and non-verbal communication skills
  - professionalism
  - your knowledge base
  - level of understanding of the needs of children and families
  - knowledge of resources
  - knowledge of how to make referrals

- how well your personal management skills have developed, regarding:
  - roles and responsibilities within early years teams
  - organisational requirements
  - self-management in relation to:
    - timekeeping
    - dress
    - personal hygiene
    - punctuality
    - commitment

- how effective your individual problem-solving has been, including:
  - analysis of information
  - decision-making
  - prioritisation
  - evaluation of outcomes

■ issues of self-appraisal, including:

- **self-awareness**

■ ability to review own performance in all relevant activities.

**Professional
Practice**

■ Self-awareness is needed in order to clearly reflect on your abilities and achievements.

---

remember

Evaluation includes plans, actions and outcomes. It requires an acknowledgement of your strengths, and also the areas you need specifically to work on – your further development plan.

remember

This ability to identify and acknowledge your own personal development needs is what makes a good professional.

This last section of the unit is set out as a series of questions linked to the following topic areas:

■ use of initiative and self-direction

■ the need to be adaptable

■ the effects of your attitude

■ the need to work within a team

■ identifying your personal needs

■ developing professional qualities

■ developing personal management

■ current self-management

■ the effectiveness of your problem-solving skills.

It may seem a daunting task to consider the questions below, but you will find it helpful when building up evidence for your professional practice log if you answer them honestly, enabling you to reflect more clearly on your skills, knowledge, understanding and professionalism.

As an early years student (or as a newly qualified early years professional), you would be expected to identify areas in which you feel you need to develop, so do not be concerned at making notes in these sections.

**Section 1
questions**

Use of initiative and self-direction

Throughout placement experience you will increasingly be expected to use your own initiative. You should not have to be constantly guided as to what to do next. However, as a student on placement for the first time you will clearly not be expected to be as proactive as a student in the final term before qualifying. Considering where you are currently in your training and/or placement experience, answer the following:

How well do you use your initiative? Give examples.

**Section 2
questions**

Early years workers need to be adaptable to an ever-changing environment

1 How well have you met the need for change? How flexible have you been?

2 When have you been less accommodating to the needs of the situation than you could have been?

3 Why was this?

4 Have you always been responsive? Or do you need coaxing or reminding?

5 How adaptable are you? Give examples of your adaptability.

Section 3 questions

Attitude can greatly affect what you do, and how you go about it

1 Is your attitude always positive? If not, why is this? What affects your attitude?

2 How well do you build relationships?

3 Are your relationships with others generally good? OK? Or poor? Why is this?

4 With whom do you form your best relationships? Why is this?

5 With whom do you find it hardest to form a good relationship?

6 What are the most significant factors affecting the quality of your relationships?

Section 4 questions

All early years workers need to be able to work within a team

1 How well do you contribute knowledge to teamwork? Give examples.

2 How well do you utilise your greatest skills? What are they?

3 How well do you consider you contribute to teamwork generally? Give examples.

Section 5 questions

Professional development involves identifying personal development needs (or targets)

1 Do you usually set yourself targets for the future? If yes, give examples.

2 How useful do you find this to be?

3 If you have not set targets before, set some now. What would they be?

4 How will they benefit your professional development for the future?

Section 6 questions

Development of individual professional qualities is essential

1 How good are your interpersonal skills?

2 Give examples of where your interpersonal skills have been particularly important.

3 When communicating verbally, how successfully do you communicate with children? With parents/carers? With colleagues?

4 What messages does your body language give out? Are they always positive?

5 Give examples of good body language that you use. What effect does this have?

6 Give examples of unhelpful or negative body language you have used. What effect did this have?

7 How would you rate yourself as a professional? Support this with examples.

8 How sound is your knowledge base? Where are your strengths best evidenced? In placement? In your assignment work? In classroom discussion? Anywhere else?

9 Give examples of how your knowledge base has been evidenced.

10 How well do you understand the needs of children and families? Use examples from your placement experience to illustrate this.

11 In what ways have you demonstrated your knowledge and understanding of resources? Give examples from your placement experience and your assignment work.

12 How could you demonstrate your knowledge of making referrals?

Personal management skills will develop with experience

1 What roles and responsibilities have you had within early years teams/placements to date? List and evaluate how successful each has been.

2 How well have you been able to meet the organisational requirements of your placements? Give examples of where this has worked well and where this could have been improved.

Current self-management

1 How good is your timekeeping at the placement?

2 What effect does this have on you as a professional?

3 Does it have a positive or negative effect on the placement?

4 How does this affect your contribution to the placement?

5 How good is your timekeeping at college?

6 What effect does this have on you as a professional?

7 Does it have a positive or negative effect on the course and your contribution to it?

8 How good is your timekeeping generally?

9 What effect does this have on your life? For example, are you always thought of as reliable? Or as late?

10 Do you usually dress appropriately? Give examples of both appropriate and inappropriate dress for placement.

11 How do you ensure your personal hygiene is always good?

12 How good is your attendance record? How does this affect what you do?

13 Are you committed to what you are doing? How is this evidenced?

14 Would college tutors describe you as committed? If not, why?

15 Would your current placement supervisor describe you as committed? If not, why?

16 Would past placement supervisors have described you as committed? If not, why was this?

17 What has changed in your level (or demonstration) of commitment?

Effectiveness of individual problem-solving is an important aspect of your role as an early years professional. The decisions you make can have a significant impact on the provision for the children in your care.

1 How good is your ability to analyse information? Give examples of where a good analysis and a poor analysis has been made. What impact did these analyses have?

2 What important decisions have you had to make? In college? In placement? Give examples to illustrate.

3 What was the impact of your decisions? Have there been any negative outcomes? What were these? How could they have been avoided?

4 How do you prioritise your actions? What do you take into consideration?

5 How do you prioritise your time? What are the most important factors?

6 How good are you at evaluating the outcomes of your work?

7 How well do you plan? Can you see how your plans impact on your outcomes?

8 Give examples of how planning has affected the outcomes of your actions.

9 How self-aware are you? Are you able to identify your own limitations? Give examples from your placement experiences.

10 Do you review your own performance in all the activities, events and presentations you are involved in? Give good (and not so good) examples.

As you move through the BTEC National course, you will use oral skills, written skills, information technology skills and numeracy skills. You will develop personally, academically and practically. The overall level and structure of the BTEC National course will enable you to apply your newly acquired or enhanced learning to further your academic development, taking it into the workplace on qualifying and into your life in general. These areas of development are linked to the Key Skills, a qualification which you will have opportunities to take alongside your main qualification. Key Skills are available at levels 1 to 4 (and to level 5 in personal skills development). They will contribute to your professional development and may be used as evidence in your professional practice log.

Professional Practice

■ As you read through the other units, your knowledge and understanding will develop further and this will have a positive impact on your practical skills. Evaluating your professional development regularly will be a valuable process. It will enable you to see clearly how you are progressing and help you decide on your personal targets for the future.

■ Reflection is also particularly relevant to the assessment criteria in Unit 8, Observation of children, in relation to 'recognition of own knowledge, skills and contribution to the working of the team'.

Progress Check

1 What forms might your professional practice log take?

2 What is meant by the term 'professionalism'?

3 What expectations are likely to be required of you in placement?

4 How might an unreliable staff member affect an early years setting?

5 What is meant by being responsible for your personal safety?

6 Define the term 'confidentiality'.

7 What is meant by the term 'need to know'?

8 What is important about teamwork?

9 What does 'developmentally appropriate' mean?

10 Give examples of how you can contribute to the safety of children.

11 Give a brief summary of the six areas of development.

12 What is meant by human and physical resources?

13 Name at least two alternative education programmes.

14 What barriers to communication can you think of?

15 What is meant by evaluating your own performance?

16 What does reflective practice mean?

17 Identify the main documents concerned with assessment of children in need and safeguarding.

Core skills, attributes and competencies

In order to meet the core skills, attributes and competencies for Unit 6, you must learn to:

- observe and identify the individual needs of children appropriate to the requirements of the setting
- respond appropriately to the needs of individual children
- promote a safe, healthy and secure childcare environment, appropriate to the individual needs of children
- promote a stimulating learning environment for children's development
- demonstrate workplace expectations of a professional carer
- explore personal effectiveness as a worker in the early years service and evaluate your own performance
- contribute to a range of methods which support parents and carers with their parenting.

The evidence you will need to provide will mostly be gathered from your placement experiences, building it up gradually as you progress through the course. You will present it in the form of a professional practice log and will include evidence of how you can:

- observe and identify the individual needs of the child, appropriate to their age and the requirements of the setting
- relate the needs of the child to their level of development and recognise influencing factors
- respond to the needs of individual children
- plan and carry out activities to promote the development of children appropriate to their needs
- respond to the importance of a safe and secure environment for children's well-being
- meet the professional requirements and expectations of the sector and the workplace
- contribute to providing a stimulating learning environment
- respond to children, parents and colleagues in a professional manner
- respect the contribution and knowledge of parents and other professionals
- review and reflect on your own practice
- prepare and maintain a personal development plan
- acknowledge parents as the primary carers and educators of their children
- recognise and value diverse parenting styles, cultures and beliefs
- support all work with reference to significant concepts, principles and theories. The knowledge, understanding and practical application which underpins (supports) your professional practice will be presented both orally and in writing, and observed within practice in your placement.

Human Growth and Development

This unit covers the following objectives:

- Understand the principles and theories of development in children aged 0–8 years
- Show understanding of growth and development from conception to the end of the first year of life
- Know and understand the stages of growth and development in children aged 1–8 years
- Be able to explain the factors involved in promoting children's development.

The study of growth and development involves looking at the processes and sequences of change within a human life, and the influences upon them.

As you read this unit, you will develop your understanding of what are considered to be the 'normal' expectations of a child's development. This understanding is important as it will enable you to decide whether an individual child's development is delayed or impaired.

The unit starts by looking at some principles of development and at the nature/nurture question. It goes on to look at aspects of growth and development, including some of the factors that affect development up to the end of the first year.

The unit will then introduce you to some of the major theories of child development before examining a variety of factors that affect the development of young children and some reasons for developmental delay.

Principles and theories of development

Definition of terms

A range of terms is used in the context of **development**. This unit will help you understand:

- **growth**
- development
- rate
- sequence
- delay.

Growth can be most easily defined by changes in measurement such as height, weight, skeletal frame, or size of feet, all of which can be represented visually, through graphs and tables.

Development refers to the increase in abilities and to changes that occur within the body's whole structure, for example, the closing of the fontanelles in an infant, or the ossification of the skeleton (how the cartilage in a newborn infant is gradually replaced by bone). Different organs and tissues within the body have their own pattern and rate of development and these processes trigger notable changes throughout the lifespan, such as the onset of menstruation in girls, sperm production in boys, the development of secondary sexual characteristics of both girls and boys during puberty and, in later life, physical events such as the menopause in women.

The expectations are often referred to as the **developmental norms** or **normative development**. It should be noted, however, that these 'norms' do not accurately reflect all racial and cultural differences. Parents may be concerned if their child does not reach the same milestones as other children of the same age at a similar time. Part of your role, as an early years professional, will be to reassure concerned parents that 'benchmarks' are simply a guide and that all children develop at their own pace.

Return to the above list of terms once you have finished reading the chapter and note how far your understanding has developed.

The human lifespan

During an average lifespan, we each move through a range of developmental stages. There are a number of different ways to split the lifespan into stages, which you will discover if you read other texts. This book focuses on the ages up to 8 years. The categories are as follows:

- the prenatal stage – from conception to birth
- the neonatal stage – from birth to one month
- infancy – from one month to one year
- the toddler – from one to two years
- early childhood – from two to five years
- middle childhood – from five years to eight years.

Each of the six stages of the lifespan discussed (except for the prenatal stage and the neonatal stage) is categorised in terms of physical, cognitive, language, social and emotional development. A summary of the main aspects of the prenatal stage includes biological principles, issues of optimum pre-conceptual care and the effects of the environment on both maternal and foetal health.

Figure 7.1

The continuum of life – from infancy to adulthood

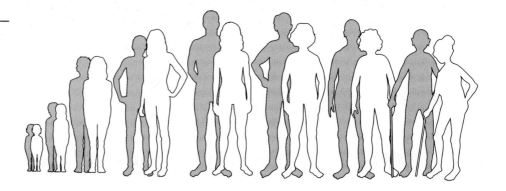

 A useful video to refer to is *The Human Body* (BBC, 1998), which was originally a television series. It offers a very accessible view of development across the whole lifespan.

Erikson's model of psycho-social development

As you think about development in general, you may find it useful to refer to Erikson's model of psycho-social development (page 279), noting the links between age and developmental stage. It can be useful to consider where you see yourself in this model and others familiar to you.

Holistic and interconnected

Children's growth and development needs to be studied within a holistic framework that acknowledges the interconnections between all the areas of development. What happens in one area of development will almost certainly affect one or all of the other areas as will the influence of the child's environment and culture. Normative measures such as developmental milestones enable us to benchmark individual patterns of growth, development and behaviour and you may already have been introduced to acronyms such as

Table 7.1 Erikson's model of psycho-social development

Stage	Approximate age range	Developmental stages	Personality features	Negative aspects
1	0–1½ years	Basic trust versus mistrust	Sense of hope and safety	Insecurity, anxiety
2	1½–3 years	Self-control versus shame and doubt	Learning self-control and independence	Dependent and unable to control events
3	3–7 years	Initiative versus guilt	Direction and purpose in life	Lack of self-esteem
4	6–15 years	Industry versus inferiority	Building skills competence and positive self-esteem	Feels inferior and lacks confidence
5	13–21 years	Identity versus role confusion	A developing sense of self confidence and security	No direction in life. Negative self-esteem
6	18–30 years	Intimacy versus isolation	Building relationships, loving commitment	Unable to build relationships
7	20s–60s	Generativity versus stagnation	Caring for others – reaching out in the community	Introverted – looking inwards – concerned with self
8	Later life	Ego-integrity versus despair	Sense of meaning to life	Loss of sense of achievement

- PIES (Physical, Intellectual, Emotional, Social)
- PILESS (Physical, Intellectual, Language, Emotional, Social, Spiritual)
- SPICE (Social, Physical, Intellectual, Communication, Emotional).
- SIMPLE (Social, Intellectual, Moral, Physical, Language, Emotional).

You may find it easier when beginning your studies to consider these areas of development separately but remember to see the 'whole child' and what that child can do rather than just what milestones or competencies they have achieved.

activity 7.1

Look at the Birth to Three Matters framework and discuss what type of approach is taken to very young children's development. Can you identify any aspects that PILESS and other simple frameworks leave out?

Theories

There are three principal theories of development:

- biological theories
- learning theories
- ecological theories.

When looking at the theories of child development, it is important to remember that no one theory alone can explain the complexity of the developing child. Theories, like children, need to be understood within their wider social, environmental and cultural contexts, so try to be 'critical' when using theoretical perspectives.

Biological theories

According to these theories, nature influences development through genetic programming, thus predisposing individuals to develop in certain ways. An example of a biological theory is Arnold Gesell's **maturational** theory. Maturational theory explains development as a genetically programmed pattern of **sequential** changes that are universal and cross cultures.

Learning theories

These theories propose that individuals acquire their skills, knowledge and responses through learning and environment. An example of a learning theory is Albert Bandura's social cognitive theory which explains how individuals learn from social role models.

Ecological theories

These types of theory explain an individual's development within the context of external factors such as their family and social environment. An example of this is to be found in Uri Bronfenbrenner's ecological theory which has been used to understand the complex nature of assessment of vulnerable children and families.

Nature/nurture debate

You will have seen that the three main types of theory help us to question whether a child's development is mostly influenced by genetics and biology (nature) or by learning and their family and wider social environment (nurture). The nature/nurture debate questions whether it is heredity and genetics that shape our personalities and behaviour or whether it is the influences of our parents, family and our environment that are more important. Early studies of child development and developmental psychology tended to see the nature/nurture question from one fixed position or the other, but further reading around the subject shows that many factors interrelate to influence development.

activity
7.2

In groups, debate how important you think nature or nurture is with respect to a child's holistic development. Research the work of theorists to support your case.

Growth and development from conception to the end of the first year of life

Biological principles

There is a complex journey from the moment of conception to the birth of a baby approximately 38 to 40 weeks later. This period before birth is known as prenatal development and can be divided into three stages

Figure 7.2

Prenatal development

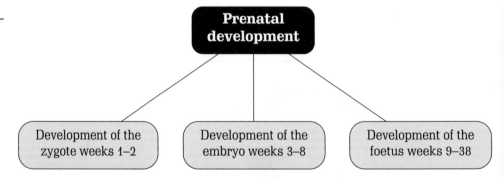

Development of the zygote (first 2 weeks)

- This starts with the release of the egg cell from the fallopian tube approximately midway through the menstrual cycle. Fertilisation usually takes place in the upper portion of the tube within 24 hours of ovulation.

- Between 24 and 30 hours after fertilisation, the male and female chromosomal material join, and the egg cell divides for the first time.

- At 36 hours post-fertilisation there are now 2 cells, dividing again to 4 cells at 48 hours. By 4 days, there will be a cluster of about 100 cells that is called a morula.

- At approximately 4–5 days, the zygote enters the uterus and then, over the next 2 days, starts to embed within the wall of the uterus. It is now referred to as a blastocyst.

- At 14 days, the blastocyst is firmly attached to the uterine wall.

- Cells have already begun to differentiate to become the support system for the body of cells that becomes the embryo.

Development of the embryo (weeks 3 to 8)

■ The main feature of the embryonic period is the development of the structures of the body and the internal organs.

■ Three layers form in the embryo – the ectoderm (outer layer) becomes hair, the external layer of skin and the nervous system; the mesoderm (the middle layer) becomes bones, muscles and the circulatory system; the endoderm (inner layer) becomes the digestive and respiratory system.

■ The embryo floats in a sac of amniotic fluid that protects it and keeps it at a constant temperature. Two major structures link the embryo to the mother – the umbilical cord and the placenta. These allow the exchange of oxygen, nutrients, vitamins and waste products between the embryo and the mother.

Foetal development (weeks 9 to 38)

■ This is the final and longest phase of development when the increase in size and complexity of development is astounding.

■ Rapid growth of all the body systems continues, and most of these systems are now functional.

■ Between the 13th and 24th weeks, the foetus will be big enough for the mother to feel it moving. The foetus is now covered in a protective, greasy layer called the vernix.

■ Most systems function well enough by 22–28 weeks of gestation for the foetus to be capable of survival if born prematurely, although intensive support will be needed.

■ Developmental changes can be seen not only in growth but also in the behaviour of the foetus, as it has been observed reacting to stimulation such as music and other sounds.

This has been an extremely brief overview of a complex and fascinating area of development; further information can be found in most major texts on development.

 See the chapter on prenatal development in *The Developing Child* (10th edition) by Bee (2004).

Factors influencing embryonic and foetal development

A woman planning to have a baby should consider the effects of her current:

■ diet

■ level of exercise

■ smoking habits

■ alcohol consumption

■ use of drugs (prescribed as well as recreational)

■ social life

■ relationship

■ on a potential pregnancy.

Planning ahead can enable a woman to give up smoking or the use of drugs before conceiving and reduce or eliminate her intake of alcohol. It can give her time to assess whether her relationship is stable, and to begin to eat a healthy diet if this is not currently the case, eliminating foods which are not considered to be completely 'safe'. If she knows she is unprotected against rubella (German measles) it is wise to be vaccinated, but she should then avoid becoming pregnant for at least three months after the vaccination.

Any woman with a long-standing medical condition or disorder should consult her doctor before planning a pregnancy to ensure that any medication she needs to take regularly will be safe for her developing child too. Her doctor may need to change her medication, either because it could harm the foetus or because it could make conception more difficult to achieve.

Table 7.2 Foods to avoid during pregnancy

Food	Possible outcome
Soft cheeses	Listeria, which can cause miscarriage
Pate	Listeria, which can cause miscarriage
Raw eggs	Salmonella, which causes food poisoning
Raw meat	Toxoplasmosis, which is a mild infection in adults but can cause serious harm to an unborn child

In recent years, it has been recommended that women take a supplement of folic acid, starting before conception up until 12 weeks into the pregnancy, as this contributes to the optimum development of the baby's central nervous system.

Screening in pregnancy

Some conditions can be identified by tests carried out during pregnancy; the process is known as screening.

Blood tests

Routine tests on blood can screen for low iron levels, venereal disease and rubella. Low iron levels may need to be boosted by supplements, and venereal disease will be treated as appropriate. A pregnant woman who is not immune to rubella will be advised to avoid contact with the infection during the early months of her pregnancy as it can cause serious hearing and vision defects in the unborn infant.

Ultrasound scan

An ultrasound scan is a routine procedure carried out at around 20 weeks' gestation to note the development levels and measurements of the foetus. Measurements are taken of main bones such as the femur (thigh bone), the head circumference is noted and the heart chambers carefully examined. Further scans are carried out as necessary by the midwife or obstetrician.

The foetus shown below is developing within the normal range. The measurements and examinations made included the thigh bone, head circumference, spine, heart chambers, brain and amniotic fluid. The outcome showed that the foetus (now named Jasmine) had bone development and a head circumference that indicated 19+5 weeks' gestation; amniotic fluid was associated with 19+1 weeks' gestation. These results showed that the foetus was developing well within normal limits, as Jasmine's mother's pregnancy was at 19+3 weeks, according to her dates.

Figure 7.3

A scan of a 20-week old foetus

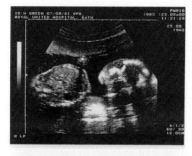
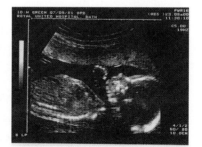
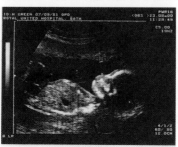
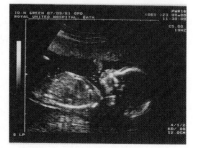

Specific tests are offered to some women depending on their circumstances, for example older women, or women with a family history of certain inherited disorders, will be offered additional screening.

Serum alpha-fetoprotein (SAFP)

This test is used to identify the possibility of the foetus having spina bifida. It is taken at 16 weeks' gestation and is offered to women who are considered to be at risk.

The triple blood test

The triple blood test takes into consideration the woman's age and measures the levels of human chorionic gonadotrophin (HCG), serum alpha-fetoprotein (SAFP) and the placental hormones (oestriols). The combined outcome gives an assessment of the risk of the foetus having Down's syndrome. Again it is offered to women in the high-risk group, usually those over 35 years.

Amniocentesis

This test checks for **chromosome** disorders, such as Down's syndrome. It usually takes place between 16 and 18 weeks' gestation and it involves the sampling of the amniotic fluid from the amniotic sac whilst the woman is linked up to an ultrasound machine. The link enables the procedure to be carried out with as much visibility as possible, but there is still a slight risk of miscarriage occurring with this procedure.

Chorionic villi sampling (CVS)

The CVS test involves the removal of a tiny amount of tissue directly from the placenta. It is usually carried out between 8 and 11 weeks' gestation and it can help identify a range of inherited disorders but, as with amniocentesis, it carries a risk of miscarriage.

Refer to Unit 10, page 428, for a summary of other screening programmes: neonatal, infant, and childhood.

Environmental effects on foetal development

Even before birth, an infant can be adversely affected by environmental influences, for example the effects of alcohol, smoking and both illegal and (some) prescribed drugs.

Alcohol

Foetal alcohol syndrome (FAS) results from the woman continuing to consume alcohol, usually in considerable amounts, throughout her pregnancy. It was declared as the leading cause of 'mental retardation' in America by researchers in 1991. It affects the development of the infant, causing delay, deformities and learning difficulties. Pregnant women are now advised against drinking alcohol altogether, as even a moderate amount can carry a risk to the infant and judgement can become impaired by alcohol, leading to accidents.

Poor nutrition

Inadequate nutrition in the pregnant woman is thought to have an adverse effect on the foetus with a higher rate of low-weight or premature infants. Neural tube disorders such as spina bifida appear to be more prevalent in women whose diet is low in folic acid and this incidence is lowered when folic acid supplements are taken both pre-conceptually and during pregnancy.

Smoking

Smoking (tobacco as well as illegal substances) affects birth weight owing to the release of nicotine and other substances into the body. It can also lead to learning difficulties in the child. There is a suggestion that infants born to smokers are at a higher risk of being affected by Sudden Infant Death syndrome (also known as SIDS or cot death) and of developing respiratory conditions later. Passive smoking is also thought to contribute to respiratory problems in infants and older children.

Drugs

Any non-essential drug should be avoided during pregnancy. Illegal drugs, such as crack cocaine, cause low birth weight and **developmental delay**. Babies who are born addicted to drugs suffer withdrawal symptoms after birth and experience great distress. Many of these babies suffer all-round developmental problems and some develop epilepsy.

Prescribed drugs are only issued to pregnant women with extreme care, as some have been known to cause deformity and developmental problems. The most well-known example of a drug that caused problems is thalidomide, which was prescribed to women in the 1960s to combat severe vomiting in pregnancy. Their babies were born with severe limb deformities.

It should be remembered that cough and cold remedies are also drugs, and these should be treated with the same caution as any other medication. A pregnant woman should always check their suitability with her GP or a pharmacist before taking them.

Infections

Infections in pregnancy may also affect the developing embryo/foetus and whilst some infections cannot be prevented, there are known sources of infection that can be avoided. This is especially relevant to the first trimester of pregnancy when the embryo is known to be particularly vulnerable to infection.

- Rubella (German measles) is the most well-known example and, if transmitted to a non-rubella-immune woman, can result in sensory impairments and congenital heart disease.

- HIV may be transmitted to the developing baby via the placenta, resulting in HIV-positive status for the newborn and the resulting disease process, although this appears to be more likely if the mother shows signs of AIDS during pregnancy.

- Cytomegalovirus is a virus in the herpes group that can lead to severe learning problems, delayed physical and motor skills, and problems with the liver.

- Toxoplasmosis is a parasitic infection which, if contracted in pregnancy, can lead to visual impairment, damage to the central nervous system, seizure disorders, and learning difficulties.

- Listeriosis is caused by a pathogen found in food, soil, vegetation and water and may be present in some packaged and raw foodstuffs. It can be the cause of premature labour.

activity
7.3

Using your college resource centre, research and prepare small-group presentations on the risk of infections in pregnancy and how these may be avoided.

Genetic effects on development and genetic disorders

Conception takes place when the male sperm fertilises the female egg (ovum) and implants itself into the wall of the uterus. The sex cells (the sperm and the egg) have only 23 chromosomes each, instead of the full 46 that all other cells contain. This enables the sex of the conceived child to be determined. The male sex chromosome is denoted as Y and the female sex chromosome as X. Therefore:

XY = a boy and

XX = a girl.

The human body is a complex machine built from its basis of 46 chromosomes. Each chromosome is made up of thousands of genes, and our genetic inheritance is determined by the influences and combination of the genes present in the chromosomes of our parents. The term **genotype** is used to describe the complete genetic inheritance of one person and the term **phenotype** refers to the visible arrangement of the characteristics that the person has inherited.

Genetically inherited disorders can be due to either autosomal recessive, autosomal dominant or X-linked transference. There are many other disorders that occur following conception and these are termed congenital disorders. Congenital disorders differ from the genetically inherited disorders in that their origin is not from the gene bank of the parents.

Autosomal recessive disorder

This type of disorder can occur when both parents are carriers of the defective recessive gene. There is a 1-in-4 chance of offspring being affected, and a 2-in-4 chance of their being carriers. Disorders include Batten's disease, cystic fibrosis, phenylketonuria (PKU), sickle cell anaemia and thalassaemia.

Autosomal dominant disorder

This disorder occurs when the carrier is also affected by the disorder. If one parent is an affected carrier, there is a 2-in-4 chance of the offspring also being affected. If both parents are affected carriers, the incidence rises to a 3-in-4 chance. Disorders include Huntington's chorea, Marfan's syndrome and osteogenesis imperfecta (brittle bones).

X-linked disorders

The X-linked disorders are carried on the X chromosomes of the mother. As the mother has two X chromosomes, the defective X acts in a recessive way in female offspring and a dominant way in males, making male offspring more likely to be affected than females. X-linked disorders include Duchenne muscular dystrophy, fragile-X syndrome, haemophilia and Lowe's syndrome.

For details of each of these and many other disorders, a good source of reference is A–Z of *Syndromes and Inherited Disorders* by Gilbert (2000). This is an excellent publication, written in an informative and accessible way.

Birth

The experience of pregnancy and birth should be an exciting and positive one for the expectant parents and with effective preconceptual and antenatal care should result in the safe delivery of a healthy baby. The expectant mother will have met with her midwife regularly during the course of the 40 weeks (average duration) of pregnancy and discussed what sort of birth she would like, usually formalised in a birth plan. Birth may take place at home or in hospital, but the stages and processes of birth remain the same.

The process of birth

Signs of the start of labour

- some women experience a 'burst of energy' and may feel the urge to start clearing out cupboards or cleaning under the stairs – sometimes called 'the nesting syndrome'.
- a 'show' of mucus (often bloody) from the vagina that can happen just before labour starts or several days before
- breaking of the waters – the bag containing the amniotic fluid either breaks naturally or can be artificially ruptured by the midwifery staff
- contractions of the uterus become regular and very different in strength from the mild Braxton Hicks contractions that the mother may have experienced in late pregnancy.

For a much fuller discussion of the experience of pregnancy, labour and birth, see the Great Ormond Street *New Baby and Child Care Book*.

The first stage of labour

- This is the beginning of labour when the cervix is beginning to soften, thin out and dilate. The cervix has to 'ripen' from closed to 10 cm dilation by the beginning of the second stage.
- The muscles of the uterus will also have pulled the opening of the cervix into a central position, ready for the descent of the baby's head into the birth canal.
- Contractions become stronger and a regular pattern emerges. Most women prefer to remain active in this first phase of labour and will consult their midwife as to when their presence at home is required, or when the woman needs to attend the maternity unit for delivery.
- This is the stage when waters may break naturally or be artificially ruptured, resulting in stronger and more painful contractions.

Second stage

- The stage starts with the full dilation of the cervix to 10 cm, ending with the baby's birth.
- Contractions become very powerful in order to move the baby down through the birth canal and this transitional stage may make some women distressed.

- As the baby moves down into the birth canal, pressure on the woman's back may be intense and she may feel the urge to push or 'bear down'.

- As the baby's head crowns, the woman may be asked to stop pushing and give panting breaths.

- After delivery of the shoulders, the rest of the body emerges more easily and, if all is well, the baby is given to the mother to be held, comforted and put to the breast.

Third stage

- This lasts from the birth of the baby to the delivery of the placenta and membranes.

- This stage can last for up to 20 or 30 minutes.

- In most cases, the woman is given an injection of syntometrine to ensure that the uterus contracts effectively.

The role of hormones

Hormones are chemical messengers produced in the endocrine glands; they play a very important part in controlling the menstrual cycle, as well as in establishing and maintaining pregnancy, birth and breast feeding.

- Oestrogen is the female sex hormone and responsible for the development and general function of the female sex organs.

- Progesterone is the pregnancy hormone that helps the uterus to receive the fertilised egg and maintain pregnancy.

- Oxytocin stimulates the uterus to contract during labour.

- Prolactin controls the production of breast milk.

The role of the midwife

The midwife is an autonomous professional who specialises in the care of the woman in normal pregnancy and childbirth, being able to refer to medical colleagues in complex cases or emergencies. Midwives are highly educated and skilled and often undergo postgraduate training in specialities such as advanced neonatal practitioner status, scanning or acupuncture. Their primary role is to care for and support the woman during the experience of pregnancy and birth, and, although they function as independent practitioners, they also support medical staff during invasive or operative procedures. Many women will only need the care of a midwife in a normal pregnancy.

The neonatal stage: from birth to one month

Birth

Birth is physically very demanding for both mother and child. The type of birth can affect the level of stress experienced by the infant and, therefore, how well they appear immediately after delivery. All infants are assessed immediately after birth using a benchmark known as the **Apgar score**. This was devised by Dr Virginia Apgar in 1953 and assesses the vital signs of initial health, indicating whether an infant needs resuscitation or medical treatment. The five features of the assessment are scored at one minute after birth and then again at five minutes, continuing at five-minute intervals as necessary until the infant is responding satisfactorily. The higher the infant scores, the less likely it is that they will need any treatment. Most healthy infants have a score of nine at one minute. They often have discolouration of their hands and feet because their circulation is not yet functioning fully. Infants who are pre-term, of a low birth weight or who have experienced a difficult delivery are more likely to score lower – a score below five indicates a very poorly baby. Infants who fall into this category make up a large percentage of those who do not survive or those who have ongoing problems.

A premature, difficult or traumatic birth, particularly if either mother or baby is ill and in need of special care, can have an effect on the **bonding** process, owing to separation and lack of physical contact. Health professionals work hard to encourage and maintain links between mothers and their babies in these circumstances.

Table 7.3 The Apgar score card

Sign	Score		
	0	1	2
Heart rate	Absent	<100 beats per minute	>100 beats per minute
Respiration	Absent	Slow, irregular	Good, regular
Muscle tone	Limp	Some flexion of extremities	Active
Response to stimulus (stimulation of foot or nose)	No response	Grimace	Cry, cough
Colour	Blue, pale	Body oxygenated, bluish extremities	Well-oxygenated, completely pink

What to expect to see in a neonate

At delivery, babies are wet and covered to some degree in mucus, maternal blood and body fluids. Their skin colour varies due both to ethnic origin and their state of health, with black babies appearing pale at birth, as the skin pigmentation melanin does not reach its full levels until later. Most infants are delivered onto their mother's abdomen and the umbilical cord is clamped and cut shortly after birth. Depending on the type and duration of the delivery, infants vary from being alert and wide awake to drowsy and unresponsive. Medication given to the mother during labour can affect this.

General appearance of the neonate

- In the period after birth, the **neonate** will sleep most of the time, mostly waking for feeds and changing and often falling asleep during these routines.

- The neonate is unable to control the head and needs to be supported during handling.

- Vernix caseosa may be present; this is a creamy white protective substance which covers the body of an infant during the latter stages of pregnancy. It is usually seen in pre-term infants and is often present in full-term infants too. It lubricates the skin and should be left to come off on its own, rather than be washed or rubbed.

- Some of the soft downy hair that covers the infant during pregnancy may also be present. It is called lanugo and traces are often found on the back, shoulders and ears at birth.

- There are two fontanelles. The posterior fontanelle is a small triangular area near the crown which closes within a few weeks of birth. The anterior fontanelle is near the front of the head and is diamond shaped. It closes over by 18 months of age and can often be seen pulsating slightly. A sunken appearance can indicate insufficient fluids, whereas a bulging appearance can indicate an unacceptable level of pressure around the brain or an infection and should always be investigated.

- Newborn infants often have a flattened or misshapened head due to pressure during the passage down the birth canal, or as a result of a forceps or ventouse suction delivery. In a multiple birth, it can occur because of lack of space and it can take some weeks for the natural shape to appear.

- The most usual sign of the neonate is the umbilical 'stump'. The umbilical cord is clamped and cut at birth and the stump will be left to drop off on its own, usually between 7 and 10 days after birth. The stump needs to be kept dry and clean, although actual cleaning of it is not usually recommended.

- Some infants show signs of swelling or bruising, normally due to a difficult birth. This tends to disappear within a few days.

- Sticky eyes are a common occurrence in the first few days and unco-ordinated eyes are usual. All babies are born with dark eyes and permanent eye colour is not established until later.

- The posture of infants is very flexed and movements tend to be jerky. The extremities (feet and hands) are often bluish in colour due to poor circulation.

- Genitalia appear to be swollen in both boys and girls, and blood loss from the vaginal area in girls is quite common. This is caused by the mother's hormones crossing the placenta.

- The breasts of both boys and girls may leak a little milk. Again, this is due to the mother's hormones crossing the placenta.

- The stools (faeces) of the neonate are a dark, greenish black because they contain a tarry substance called meconium, which is very sticky. The colour and consistency change within a few days, as the mother's milk arrives.

- Spots and rashes are very common in the first few days, but the infant's skin soon settles down. A particularly common type is 'milia', which are tiny white spots often known as milk spots.

- Peeling skin is quite common on the hands and feet but usually only lasts two or three days.

- Some infants suffer from **neonatal jaundice** where the skin and eyes become yellowish due to the infant's immature liver function and a subsequent rise in levels of bilirubin. Bilirubin is formed when red cells break down, and the liver is unable to cope with its workload. It usually occurs (if it is going to) on about day three after birth. Jaundice occurring before the infant is three days old needs particular investigation, as liver disease or sepsis may be present and the infant's life could be in danger. On occasions, jaundice can be a sign of galactosaemia, rubella or cytomegalovirus.

Birthmarks

- Port wine marks are a permanent, dark-red mark, often on the face or neck. In the past they were often a permanent disfigurement, but many can now be successfully removed or reduced with laser treatment.

- The strawberry naevus is quite common. These are raised marks full of blood vessels; the marks are not actually present at birth but develop in the first few days or weeks. They usually disappear by eight years of age. The full name for this type of naevus is haemangioma.

- Another common mark is the 'stork bite'. These are tiny red marks found on the eyelids, the top of the nose and on the back of the neck. These gradually disappear and are not usually a problem.

- Mongolian blue spots are dark marks found at the base of the spine on non-Caucasian infants. On occasions, these marks have been wrongly attributed to physical abuse. They are usually 'mapped' by health professionals in the early weeks. Early years workers need to be aware of these marks.

- Most people have moles, but some moles can be large and unsightly, for example a congenital melanocytic naevus (CMN). CMNs get progressively darker as the infant grows but can sometimes be successfully removed or reduced with laser treatment or plastic surgery.

Neonatal reflexes

The primary **reflexes** can be defined as 'automatic body reactions to specific stimulation' (Bee, 1992, page 105). These reflexes include:

- blinking reflex – the neonate reacts to sudden lights, noises or movements in front of the eyes

- rooting reflex – where the neonate turns their face towards their mother to locate the breast

Figure 7.4

Rooting reflex

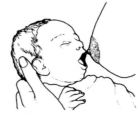

Figure 7.5

Sucking reflex

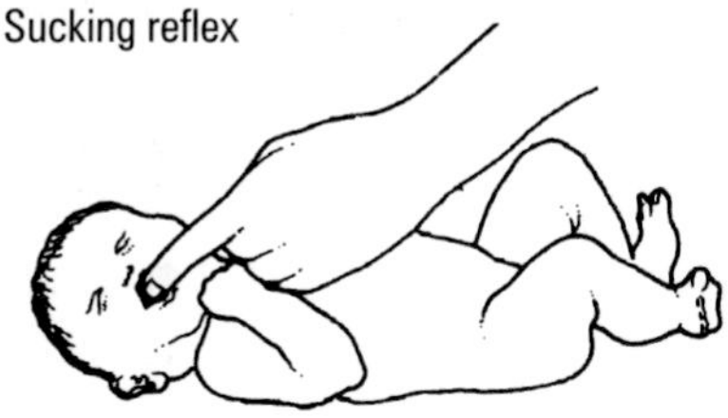

- sucking reflex – infants will usually suck a clean finger, placed gently in the mouth

■ palmar grasp – where the infant holds firmly to whatever touches the palm (gently stroking the back of the hand will usually release the grasp)

Figure 7.6

Palmer grasp

■ plantar reflex – touching the sole of the infant's foot with a finger will result in the flexing of the toes towards your finger

■ stepping reflex – the neonate's foot responds to contact with a firm surface, resulting in a small 'step' being taken

■ moro reflex – a sudden movement of the neck is interpreted by the infant as falling and they will throw out their arms with open hands and reclasp them over their chest

Figure 7.7

Stepping relfex

■ startle reflex – the infant throws out their arms at a sudden noise or movement, but the fists remain clenched

■ asymmetric tonic neck reflex – when the infant's head is turned to one side, they will respond by straightening the arm and leg on the same side, whilst flexing the limbs opposite.

Some reflexes stay with us for life, for example blinking, but some are lost after the first few weeks (the primitive reflexes). The presence of reflexes is an indicator of an infant's neurological well-being. As the brain gradually takes over the body's responses, these primitive reflexes disappear.

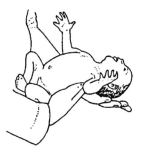

Figure 7.8

Moro reflex

The BBC's *Human Body* video is a good source of reference – the reflexes are clearly demonstrated.

The senses in a neonate

Hearing

■ The hearing of infants is acute.

■ They blink in response to sound.

■ The neonate can discriminate the voice of their main carer almost immediately.

■ Noisy objects can only roughly be located.

■ Sudden noises distress the infant.

■ Infants respond to soothing rhythmic sounds.

Refer to page 292 in this unit for more on hearing and its development.

Vision

■ Newborn infants are sensitive to both light and sound.

■ Vision is diffused and limited initially to objects within about a 30 cm radius.

■ Eyes initially do not work together and they often 'cross' or 'wander'.

- Eye-to-eye contact with the main carer (usually the mother) is an important means of establishing a bonding relationship.
- Infants show a preference for human faces.
- Infants will turn towards a light.

Link Refer to the section below for more on vision and visual development.

Touch
- Skin-to-skin contact is important to the bonding process.
- Most infants are delivered onto their mother's abdomen.
- Contact and handling soothes a distressed infant, but may be contra-indicated in a premature baby – handling may distress them and they thrive better with minimal handling.
- The temperature control of infants is ineffective.

Smell
- Infants can identify their mothers by smell.
- Research has shown that infants can distinguish their mother's milk on a breast pad.

Posture and motor skills
Immediately after birth, many infants naturally curl into the foetal position with their head to one side. Their limbs are kept partly flexed and are hypertonic (have tension) and they tend to display jerking movements. The head and neck are hypotonic (weak) and there is no head control, so full support of the head and neck area is needed whenever the infant is handled.

Professional Practice
- Research outcomes recommend that infants are always placed on their back to sleep to minimise the risk of sudden infant death.

Progress Check

1 What is the difference between amniocentesis and chorionic villi sampling tests carried out during pregnancy?
2 Describe at least three primitive reflexes.
3 What is vernix caseosa?
4 What reasons might there be for neonatal jaundice?
5 What does the Apgar score measure?
6 What can be the effects of a mother's hormones crossing the placenta?
7 Which birthmark is only found on dark-skinned infants?
8 Which fontanelle closes by 18 months of age?
9 Why are black infants usually pale at birth?

Sensory development
At birth, the nervous system is still far from complete and it is not easy to understand the level of sensory awareness that an infant has. Theorists are aware that the visual system is not strong initially and that it develops considerably in the first few months, whereas hearing is quite well developed right from birth. The main areas studied are vision, hearing and **perception**.

Vision
From birth, infants turn to look at sources of light. They show interest in the human face, and researchers (for example, Robert Fantz in the 1950s) have repeatedly shown that the human face invokes a greater level of response than a range of other similar options.

An ideal source of further reading on this area of development is *The Foundations of Child Development* by Oates (1999).

Spontaneous and imitative facial expressions are seen within a few days of birth and the eyes of the newborn infant may be seen to move in the direction of sounds. The early visual interaction between infant and carer strengthens the process of bonding and, therefore, enhances emotional security in the long term.

Stages of visual development
Birth
- The infant turns to the source of light.
- Imitative facial expressions are seen.
- The human face evokes the greatest level of attention.
- The eyes do not at first move co-operatively.

One month
- The infant turns to light sources.
- The infant stares at face of adult carer.
- The eyes now usually work in co-operation.
- Vision is held by bright mobile or similar object.
- The infant can visually track mother's face briefly.

Three months
- The infant is now visually alert.
- The eyes move in co-operation.
- The defensive blink has been present for some time.
- The infant follows the movement of their main carer.
- There is more sustained visual tracking of face or similar.
- The infant may now be demonstrating visual awareness of own hands.
- Anticipation of feeding is demonstrated from visual clues.

Six months
- The infant is visually very alert.
- The infant appears visually insatiable.
- The infant's eyes and head move to track objects of interest.

Twelve months
- Hand-eye co-ordination is seen as small objects are picked up using pincer grasp (index finger and thumb).
- The eyes follow the direction of fallen or dropped objects (based on Sheridan, 1991).

Checklist of concerns regarding vision include:
- lack of eye contact with main carer
- no social smile by six weeks
- lack of visual tracking of carer's face or bright mobile by two months
- lack of visual response to impending breast or bottle feed
- lack of co-operative eye movement after three months
- lack of signs that infant reaches out for toys in response to visual stimulus
- lack of mobility or directed attention by 12 months.

Hearing

At birth, the hearing of infants is acute as their auditory perception is as yet uncluttered by the sounds of everyday living. They can be seen to respond to sound by blinking and through startled movements (startle reflex). Newborn infants respond to the sound of their mother or main carer. They also show signs of auditory awareness by turning towards other sounds. Many infants are settled by calming or familiar music, often first heard within the safety of the womb.

Stages of auditory development

Birth
- The infant shows startle reactions to sound.
- Blinking is common in response to sounds.
- The infant may 'still' to ongoing gentle sounds.
- The infant turns to sounds, including mother's voice.

One month
- The infant is still startled by sudden noises.
- They stiffen in alarm, extending limbs.
- They usually turn to sound of familiar voice.
- The infant is usually calmed by the sound of a familiar voice.

Three months
- The infant turns their head or eyes towards the source of sounds.
- They often appear to search for location of sounds.
- They listen to musical mobiles and similar sounds.

Six months
- The infant shows considerable interest in familiar sounds.
- They turn to locate even very gentle sounds.
- They vocalise deliberately, listening to self.
- They vocalise to get attention, listen and then vocalise again.
- The infant can usually imitate sounds in response to carers.

Twelve months
- The infant responds to own name.
- Their behaviour indicates hearing; they make appropriate responses to carers (based on Sheridan, 1991).

Checklist of concerns regarding hearing include:
- lack of response to sudden or loud noises in first few months
- lack of response to familiar sounds, either listening or by being calmed
- no tracking of gentle sounds by nine months
- no indication of turning to the sound of familiar voice
- limited changes in vocalising from about six months
- no obvious response to carer's simple instructions at a year.

From one year onwards the development of speech is the greatest indication of a child's hearing levels, although health issues can have an impact on hearing, for example repeated ear infections or glue-ear.

Infant perception

Perception is the process whereby the brain makes sense of information reaching it via the body's senses. The senses help in the understanding of all that is happening both to us and around us. Visual perception (sight) and auditory perception (hearing) are two early indicators that physical and perceptual development is progressing as expected. Vision and hearing link directly with language and cognitive development, and are both assessed at regular intervals during infancy and early childhood.

Refer to Unit 10, page 428, for screening techniques.

Depth perception: the visual cliff investigation

Studies carried out on infant perception include the work of Gibson and Walk who, in 1960, devised a visual cliff to investigate depth perception in infants.

Infants who had gained a degree of mobility were placed on the 'visually safe' (chequered floor) side of the table and encouraged to crawl across the surface above the 'visually unsafe' (clear) cliff space towards their mothers. Out of 27 infants aged 6 to 12 months, only 3 crawled across the surface. The remaining 24 showed a marked reservation in relation to crossing from the 'safe' to the 'unsafe' area of the visual cliff surface, even though they would be moving towards their mothers, who would normally be a safe haven for them.

Under the age of six months it is clearly not possible to investigate depth perception in the same way, owing to infants' lack of mobility. However, other studies, for example Campos et al. in 1970, monitored the heart rates of infants when placed first on one side, and then on the other. At just 55 days (approximately 8 weeks) the heart rates were perceived to be different, indicating that even at this young age a degree of depth perception is present. Under eight weeks, depth perception did not appear to have developed.

Figure 7.9

The 'visual cliff' experiment by Gibson and Walk

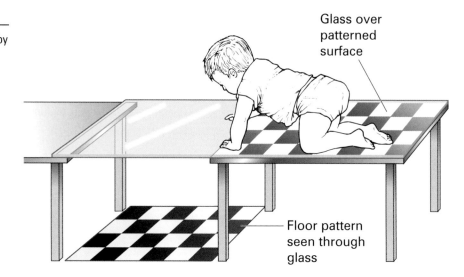

Glass over patterned surface

Floor pattern seen through glass

Progress Check

1   What signs would give you concern regarding an infant's visual development?
2   What would raise your concern regarding their auditory development?
3   What does the term 'perception' mean?
4   How might a lack of sensory awareness affect other areas of development?
5   According to research by psychologists, at what age is depth perception developed?

Infancy: one month to one year

Physical development (gross motor)

- Movements remain jerky.

- Head lag gradually decreases, and head control is usually good by five months.

- Rolling over is first seen between four and six months (from back to side), and then from front to back by about eight months.

- Reaching for objects begins at about four months with the transference of toys from hand to hand from about seven months.
- At four months, the infant discovers their own feet and manages to sit with support.
- Sitting alone commences at about seven to eight months, with greater balance gradually developing.
- Crawling can start from six months (commando crawling) and traditional crawling from about eight months. Some infants bear-walk or bottom-shuffle.
- Some infants miss out the crawling stage, and move straight to pulling themselves up on furniture at around eight to ten months.
- Standing alone can occur any time from 10 months, but is more usual at around 12 months, when generally balance is more established.
- Walking is normally achieved between 12 and 16 months.

Physical development (fine motor)

- Hand and finger movements gradually increase, from the grasping of the adult's fingers in the earliest months, through to playing with own fingers and toes, handling and then holding toys and objects from three to four months.
- Everything is explored through the mouth.
- At about seven months, the infant will try to transfer objects from one hand to the other with some success. Pincer grasp is emerging.
- By about 10 months, pincer grasp is developed.
- The infant will pick up small objects.
- Toys are pulled towards themselves.
- Pointing and clapping are deliberate actions for most infants by 10 to 12 months.
- Controlled efforts when feeding, with some successes.

Cognitive and language development

- The infant continues to explore orally throughout most of the first year. Piaget called this the sensorimotor stage.
- By about four months, recognition of an approaching feed is demonstrated by excited actions and squeals.
- Language develops through cooing, gurgling, excited squealing and changing tones of their own voice.
- By five months, enjoyment of own voice is obvious. Chuckles and laughs are evident.
- By about eight months, the infant babbles continuously and tunefully, for example 'mamamama', 'babababa'.
- By 9 to 10 months, the infant achieves what Piaget called object permanence; they know that an object exists even if it has been covered up and is out of sight.
- First 'words' may be apparent by a year, usually dada, mama, baba.
- Understanding of simple instructions or statements begins from about 9 months and is clearly evident by 12 months.

Refer to page 317 for an outline of Piaget's stages of cognitive development.

Social and emotional development

- The first social smile is usually seen by six weeks.
- Smiling is first confined to main carers and then occurs in response to most contacts.
- The infant concentrates on faces of carers.
- Pleasure during handling and caring routines is seen by eight weeks.

- From about 12 weeks, expressions of pleasure are clearly seen when the child gains another person's attention.
- Social games, involving handling and cuddles, gain chuckles from four to five months onwards.
- Infants enjoy watching other infants.
- Sleep patterns begin to emerge from about four months onwards, although these will continue to change.
- From about 9 or 10 months, the infant may become distressed when the main carer leaves them and become wary of strangers.
- Playing contentedly alone increases by one year, but the reassuring presence of an adult is still needed.

Undertaking a longitudinal study

During their course, many students will be expected to undertake a longitudinal observation study of an infant under the age of one year or an older child. Most longitudinal baby or child studies are carried out over a minimum of three months and requirements usually involve the following:

- awareness of the ethics involved and the need for confidentiality
- gaining written permission from the parents and ensuring that they understand what the study involves
- keeping to the specified time frame and making the required number of visits
- making relevant observations and measures of all areas of the baby's or child's development
- referring to normative benchmarks of development
- describing and explaining the baby's or child's individual needs and how these are met through daily routines and procedures
- identifying the safety and security measures needed and anticipating those needed in the near future
- details of play activities that can be implemented to stimulate development and learning
- explanation of the role of significant adults in the baby's or child's life and that of any professionals involved.

You will need to organise your time effectively and identify what types of activities and observation methods you may want to use, allowing extra time to allow for family holidays, illness or other unexpected interruptions to your planned schedule of visits.

Refer to Chapter 8, pages 341 and 355, for further information on observational techniques and longitudinal studies that you may wish to use.

Growth and development in children aged 1–8 years

Principles, stages and sequences

The period from one to eight years represents a time of growth and maturation in all areas of development and, although patterns and sequences of development will be similar for many children, development is not merely a linear continuum.

Table 7.4 Principles of growth

Age	Principles of Growth
Toddler (1–3 years)	■ Growth slows considerably ■ Average weight gain is 1.8 to 2.7 kg per year ■ Rate of increase in height also slows and usually increases by increments of 7.5 cm each year ■ Steady growth curve should be seen and is likely to show step-like growth spurts rather than linear pattern ■ Toddler often appears to be squat and 'pot-bellied' due to short legs and relatively poorly developed abdominal muscles
Pre-school (3–5 years)	■ Rate of physical growth slows and stabilises ■ Average weight gain remains 2.3 kg ■ Growth in height remains constant at between 6.75 to 7.5 cm ■ Physical proportions of the pre-schooler no longer similar to toddler – able to maintain an erect posture, sturdy and agile ■ Muscle development and bone growth still far from mature
School age (6–12)	■ Growth in both height and weight are slow but steady with average increase in height of 5 cm per year ■ May double in weight between 6 and 12 years ■ Girls and boys similar in size but boys tend to be slightly taller and heavier than girls ■ Body outline is slimmer than that of pre-schooler and posture is improved ■ By 12 years, both boys and girls will have increased their strength, physical capabilities and refined their coordination ■ In spite of an increase in strength, muscles are still relatively immature and easily damaged

Toddler: 1 to 2 years

The toddler is an engaging mixture of growing competencies, inquisitiveness and emerging personality and has frequently been incorrectly labelled as 'a terrible two'. Toddlerhood heralds a period of intensive exploration of the environment, during which the child will acquire a wide range of fine and gross motor skills. Great developments will also be seen in social and language skills, as well as in being able to differentiate the self from others.

Physical development

■ Standing alone is achieved but they are unable at first to sit from being in a standing position without help. They begin to let themselves down in a controlled manner from about 15 months.

■ Walking involves hands being held up for balance. The infant uses uneven steps and has difficulty in stopping when they have started.

■ They can creep upstairs quite safely (not advisable without an adult supervising).

■ They begin to kneel.

■ By 18 months, walking should be well established; the arms are no longer needed for balance. The toddler can now back themselves into a small chair, and climb forwards into an adult chair.

■ Squatting when playing is now common.

■ They can usually walk upstairs holding an adult hand.

■ Manipulative skills are developing. Pages of books can usually now be turned quite well, and pencils can be held in a clumsy grasp.

■ By two years, the child can run safely, starting and stopping at will.

■ They are able to pull wheeled toys, with some understanding of direction.

■ They are able to control a ball to throw forwards.

■ Walking up and (usually) down stairs is possible, holding on, two feet to a stair.

■ They cannot yet kick a football without falling into it.

■ They cannot usually pedal a tricycle.

Figure 7.10

By eighteen months the toddler can climb forwards in to an adult armchair

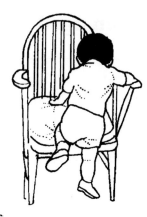

Figure 7.11

The toddler at this age can usually walk upstairs holding an adult hand

Cognitive and language development

- The toddler is very curious, investigating everything they can.
- They are interested in all that happens around them.
- A precise pincer grasp is displayed.
- They enjoy putting objects into containers.
- They take toys to mouth less often now.
- They enjoy activities that need fitting together.
- The toddler will place an object on another – two-object tower.
- They know approximately 6 words at 15 months and up to 20 recognisable words by 18 months.
- By 18 months, they talk continuously as they play (mostly, this is unintelligible).
- Brief imitation is seen of everyday activities, for example the feeding of a doll.
- They are contented to play alone.
- By two years, more than 50 words are clearly recognisable.
- They talk to themselves in long monologues (much is incomprehensible to others).
- They can put two or more words together, for example, 'daddy gone'.
- They refer to themselves by name, for example, 'Danny shoes'.
- Echolalia is almost constant (repeating the last word they hear).
- They verbalise their needs, for example, drinks, toilet, food.
- Simple role play is demonstrated.
- They can build six to eight objects into a tower.
- They can follow simple instructions, for example, 'Fetch your shoes, please'.
- They can succeed with simple jigsaw puzzles.
- Vertical and horizontal lines are drawn.

Social and emotional development

- By about 15 months, they will indicate a wet or soiled nappy.
- They co-operate (help) with dressing.
- They are dependent on an adult's presence.
- Frustration leads to toys being discarded in anger.
- By 18 months, feeding themselves with a spoon is usually very successful.
- They can handle a cup confidently, but do not put it back down (they give it to the adult).
- They remove hats, shoes, etc. but can rarely replace them.
- They produce urgent vocalisations when making a demand.
- Bowel control is sometimes attained by 18 months and is usually attained by two years.
- By two years the child will play parallel alongside others.

- They can be rebellious and resistive and get frustrated when trying to make themselves understood. They can be easily distracted from their tantrums at this age.
- No idea of sharing is normal, and no understanding of the need to defer their wishes.
- They follow adults around. They need reassurance when tired or fearful.
- They can now put on hat and shoes and can reposition a cup on a surface.

Progress Check

1 By what age is the social smile usually seen?
2 What is meant by object permanence?
3 How many words are usual at two years?
4 By what age is bowel control usually achieved?
5 What is echolalia?

Early childhood: 2 to 5 years

Physical development

Figure 7.12

From three years, ball skills increase

- Walking up stairs with alternating feet is usually achieved by three years. Up and down on alternate feet is securely seen by three and a half.
- At two and a half, a child can kick a football gently, by three years with force.
- Pushing and pulling of large toys is achieved by two and a half.
- Locomotor skills improve rapidly during this stage of development.
- Use of pedals is often achieved by three years, and a child can steer around corners.
- Balance gradually improves, and by four years a child can usually stand, walk and run on tip-toes and can navigate skilfully when active.
- From three years, ball skills increase – catching, throwing, bouncing and kicking.
- Manipulative skills improve.
- Scissor control is developing and greater pencil control is achieved by three years.
- By four years, threading small beads and early sewing is achieved.
- Adult pencil control is usually present by four years.

Cognitive and language development

- At three years, a large vocabulary is understood by all, but still includes unconventional grammar and infantilisms (the child's personal 'baby talk').
- During play, they still talk to themselves in long monologues.
- By four years, speech is usually grammatically correct.
- They can usually draw a person with main details.
- Role play is frequent and detailed by five years
- Floor play is very complex.
- Understanding of time, linked to routine, is emerging.

Social and emotional development

- At two and half, tantrums are common when needs are thwarted. A child is less easily distracted from them now.
- They are very resistive of restraint.
- They mostly still watch others or play in parallel, occasionally joining in briefly.
- By four years, a child can eat skilfully and can dress, wash and clean their teeth (with supervision).
- This is a generally more independent age.
- They co-operate with others but can also be unco-operative if wishes are refused.

- They can be very strong-willed.
- At five years, behaviour is noticeably more sensible and controlled.
- They understand sharing and turn-taking and the need for fair play.
- Co-operative play is constant at five years.
- They choose own friends and play well and are very protective towards younger children, pets and distressed playmates.

case study 7.1 — Maya, Toby and Max

Maya, Toby and Max are looked after by the same childminder, Kahira. Maya is in Kahira's care every day, and either Toby or Max is usually present too. Maya is crawling and pulling herself up on the furniture. Max can walk now but is still unsteady, using his hands held high to balance himself. Toby can walk well and loves to play in the garden with a football. He can sometimes kick it without falling forward and is becoming steadier when climbing stairs but still needs to hold an adult's hand.

Toby talks to himself in long monologues as he plays, and adults nearby are able to identify some of his words, linked to his play. Max also talks to himself in play but little of his 'speech' is recognisable. Maya babbles and chuckles to herself as she roams around the floor exploring all that she can find. She appears to get enjoyment from watching Max and Toby, but none of the children attempts to play with each other.

activity

1. What ages would you assume Maya, Toby and Max to be?
2. What else would you expect them to be doing?
3. Which of them would you expect to be able to feed themselves?
4. Would you expect any of the children to have gained bowel or bladder control?

Middle childhood: 5 to 12 years

Physical development

Physically, emphasis is now on practice and further development of the skills already gained. Large motor skills will be increased, for example, how fast a child can run, their stamina when playing group games and their ability to climb and manoeuvre more difficult objects and in more challenging circumstances. The ever-increasing improvement in balance is seen at this stage too. Hand–eye co-ordination develops allowing a more adult level of control when writing, drawing, sewing and so on, and greater skill during ball games and in activities involving manual dexterity is seen.

For girls, the pre-pubescent stage can begin from nine years onwards. Height develops rapidly here with the thigh bone growing at a faster rate than the rest of the body.

Figure 7.13

Hand-eye co-ordination develops in middle childhood

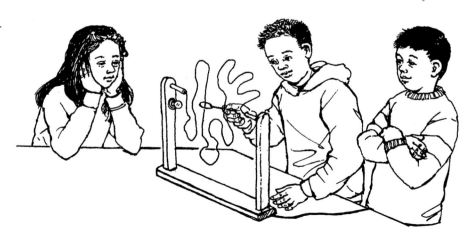

Cognitive and language development

Children between these ages develop from Piaget's pre-operational stage to the concrete operations stage of thinking. They develop the ability to think logically, for example, adding up, subtracting, reading and ordering. Co-operative play from age five onwards becomes very involved, with considerable role play, requiring accuracy and detail.

By the age of 11, an average child has a vocabulary of 11,000–12,000 words. They are usually fluent readers with substantial reading stamina. Girls have a tendency to read more than boys.

Refer to page 317 for Piaget's stages of cognitive development.

Social and emotional development

- Co-operative play is frequent and sustained.
- Gender awareness is strong.
- Co-operative play is mostly with same-sex peers.
- Individual friendships are very important.
- Children make definite decisions about their friends.
- Parents are less openly important, but their continued support is needed.

Progress Check

1. By what age is language usually grammatically correct?
2. At what age are tantrums common?
3. Give an example of hand–eye co-ordination.
4. When do children understand the need for fair play?
5. What is the difference between gross and fine motor skills?

Physical development of children

Having read through the previous summaries of development linked to the life stages, you should find that the following sections will enable you to develop your understanding of child development further.

Motor development

Motor skills can be gross (large) or fine. They include movement and balance, and can be either precise or carefree. Movement can involve the whole body or just one part of it.

The maturational changes in physical development can be summarised as follows. It can be said that physical development moves:

- from the simple to the complex – this means that a child learns simple actions, such as learning to walk, before they learn the more complex action of hopping
- from **cephalo** to **caudal** – this can be defined as physical control starting at the head and gradually developing down through the body. For example, head control is attained before the spine is strong enough for an infant to sit unsupported, and sitting unsupported is attained before the child is able to stand
- from **proximal** to **distal** – these terms refer to how a child develops actions near to the body before they develop control of outer reaches of the body. For example, a child can hug and carry a large teddy bear before they can fasten its clothing
- from general to specific – the more generalised responses of an infant showing excitement when recognising a favourite carer gradually progress to become the facial smile of an older child on greeting the same person.

Figure 7.14

Motor development in children

The table below shows how motor skills can be categorised as:

- locomotor, which involves the body moving forward in some way, for example walking, running

- non-locomotor, which describes large physical movements which take place whilst stationary, for example bending, pulling

- manipulation, which involves dexterous actions such as throwing and catching a ball.

The table places these three physical areas sequentially according to the developmental norms.

Table 7.5 The sequence of motor skills

Age	Locomotor skills	Non-locomotor skills	Manipulative skills
1 month	Stepping reflex	Lifts head; visually follows slowly moving objects	Holds object if placed in hand
2–3 months		Briefly keeps head up if held in a sitting position	Begins to swipe at objects within visual range
4–6 months	Sits up with some support	Holds head erect in sitting position	Reaches for and grasps objects
7–9 months	Sits without support; rolls over in prone; crawls		Transfers objects from one hand to the other
10–12 months	Crawls; walks grasping furniture, then without help	Squats and stoops	Some sign of hand preference; grasps a spoon across palm but poor aim of food to mouth
13–18 months	Walks backwards and sideways	Rolls ball to adult	Stacks two blocks; puts objects into small containers and dumps them
18–24 months	Runs (20); walks well; climbs stairs – both feet to a step	Pushes and pulls boxes or wheeled toys; unscrews lid on a jar	Shows clear hand preference. Stacks four to six blocks. Turns pages one at a time. Picks things up, keeping balance
2–3 years	Runs easily; climbs up and down from furniture unaided	Hauls and shoves big toys around obstacles	Picks up small objects; throws small ball forward while standing
3–4 years	Walks upstairs one foot per step; skips on both feet; walks on tiptoe	Pedals and steers a tricycle; walks in any direction pulling a big toy	Catches large ball between outstretched arms; cuts paper with scissors; holds pencil between thumb and first two fingers
4–5 years	Walks up and down stairs, one foot per stair. Stands, runs and walks well on tip-toes		Strikes ball with bat; kicks and catches ball; threads bead, but not needle. Grasps pencil maturely
5–6 years	Skips on alternate feet; walks a thin line; slides and swings		Plays ball games quite well. Threads needles; can sew a stitch
7–8 years	Skips 12 times or more	Rides two-wheeler bike, short distances	Writes individual letters
8 years+	Skips freely	Rides bike easily	

Source: Helen Bee, *The Developing Child*, 6th edition, © Allyn & Bacon, reprinted by permission

Figure 7.15

The development of locomotion

Source: Dare and O'Donovan (1998), p. 126

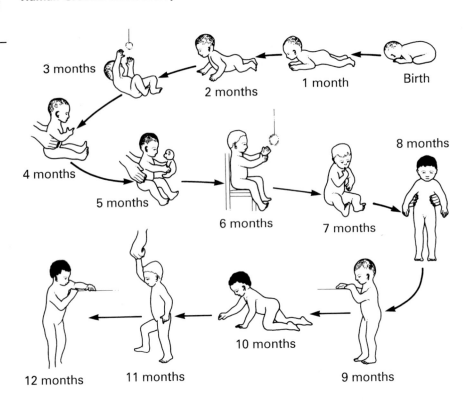

3 months · 2 months · 1 month · Birth
4 months · 5 months · 6 months · 7 months · 8 months
12 months · 11 months · 10 months · 9 months

activity

7.4

Sarah has been asked to write about the opportunities for enhancing physical development in a range of popular activities. She is using a table like the one below. She intends to include the following activities:

jigsaw puzzles	sponge printing	sports day races
picture books	hopscotch games	using woodwork tools
farmer's in the den	musical statues	threading cotton reels Lego

Under which column should Sarah place each activity?

Locomotion	Non-locomotion	Manipulation

Monitoring physical development

Health screening

Health screening of children takes place at specified ages, across the whole population. It enables parents and health professionals to identify problems sooner rather than later, giving the opportunity for early intervention and treatment. Screening is carried out at and after birth and throughout early childhood and schooling. It mostly focuses on the general physical development of individual children, with specific attention being given to hearing and vision.

Centile charts

The physical development of babies and young children is screened by health visitors and paediatricians using a **centile chart** to measure and monitor growth. An infant grows rapidly during the first year and then at a more steady rate from the toddler stage onwards. As puberty arrives, the growth rate rapidly increases once again, easing up in the latter years of adolescence. Full height is usually acquired by 18 years, whereas bone density continually develops, and old bone is replaced with new until around age 35, when the body ceases to continue replacing bone at the same rate.

Figure 7.16

Centile chart for a child

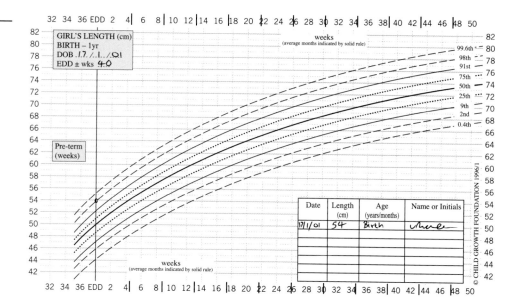

GIRL'S LENGTH (cm)
BIRTH – 1yr
DOB .17. /.1. /.01
EDD ± wks 4·0

Pre-term (weeks)

weeks
(average months indicated by solid rule)

Date	Length (cm)	Age (years/months)	Name or Initials
17/1/01	54	Birth	Marie

© CHILD GROWTH FOUNDATION 1996/1

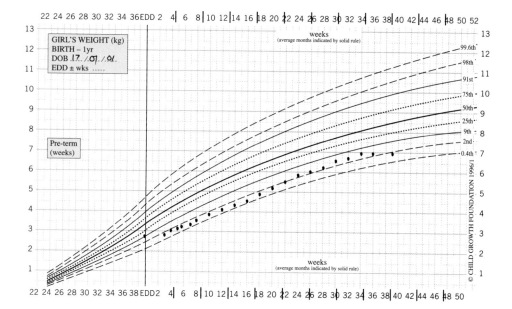

GIRL'S WEIGHT (kg)
BIRTH – 1yr
DOB 17 /.01 /.01
EDD ± wks .....

Pre-term (weeks)

weeks
(average months indicated by solid rule)

© CHILD GROWTH FOUNDATION 1996/1

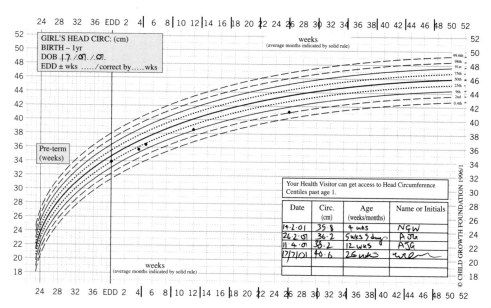

GIRL'S HEAD CIRC: (cm)
BIRTH – 1yr
DOB .17 /.01 /.01
EDD ± wks ..... /correct by.....wks

Pre-term (weeks)

weeks
(average months indicated by solid rule)

Your Health Visitor can get access to Head Circumference
Centiles past age 1.

Date	Circ. (cm)	Age (weeks/months)	Name or Initials
14·2·01	35·8	4 wks	NGW
26·2·01	36·2	5wks 5 days	A Ju
11·4·01	38·2	12 wks	AJG
17/7/01	40·6	26 wks	Marie

© CHILD GROWTH FOUNDATION 1996/1

Different centile charts are used for boys and girls because there are slight differences in growth expectations of girl infants and boy infants – boys, on average, are slightly heavier than girls at birth. The 50th-centile line is the central line on the centile charts. It indicates the average at each age. The upper and lower lines represent the boundary within which 80 per cent of children will fall. A child who falls outside these boundaries will be monitored closely and may need further investigation into their development at some stage. The pattern (or line) formed as a child's measurements are plotted on the centile chart is known as a growth curve.

How centile charts are used

The centile charts below show Jasmine's measurements at birth and the first nine months' measurements of her weight. We can see from these that, as a full-term baby, she was 'small for dates' at birth, weighing 2.780 kg (6 lb 2 oz), and was placed just below the 9th centile. Her length at 54 cm was considered to be long and reached the 98th centile and her head circumference, at 34 cm, was placed just above the 25th centile. Jasmine's weight progressed very slowly, and she remained below the 'norms' of development for an infant of her age and birth weight.

Any infant who falls below the 0.4th centile is closely monitored by health professionals, and an infant who moves downwards across two centile lines is referred to their GP or a paediatrician for close monitoring. At four months old, there was concern that Jasmine would need to be referred, although she was both healthy and alert. By five months, however, her weight began to increase more steadily and she moved above the 2nd centile for the first time at seven months. Jasmine is a very active baby, of petite build like her mother, and therefore there is no serious concern about her. She has always been healthy and alert and by eight months was walking around the furniture, crawling very fast and rarely still. Her weight gain trailed off again at this stage, but this was attributed to her high level of activity.

Progress Check

1. Which aspects of physical development can be described as developing from proximal to distal?
2. Explain the difference between locomotor and non-locomotor skills.
3. Name three activities to support the development of manipulative skills.
4. What is the main focus of health screening programmes?
5. What are centile charts used to measure?

Emotional development of children

Emotional development involves the child's development of self-awareness, sense of security and personal identity, and learning to understand and express feelings towards other people. Emotions can be both positive and negative; they are our inner feelings which we often find difficult to explain. Children can usually describe how they are feeling physically, although in very young children this may only be in a generalised way: for example, a 'tummy ache' may refer to a range of pain experiences, but it is far harder for them to explain how they are feeling emotionally. As adults, we need to allow children the opportunities to express their emotions and reassure them that it is acceptable to have strong feelings, explaining that adults have them too.

Conditions for secure emotional development

Emotional development is not simply a maturational process; it needs the appropriate conditions to nurture it in the way that a flower needs sun, soil and water.

Professional Practice

■ Reflect for a moment on the placement experiences you have had. Think of situations in which professional practice supported emotional development particularly well. Use the list of conditions in the spidergram above. You may also be able to think of examples where improvements could be made.

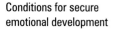

Figure 7.17

Conditions for secure
emotional development

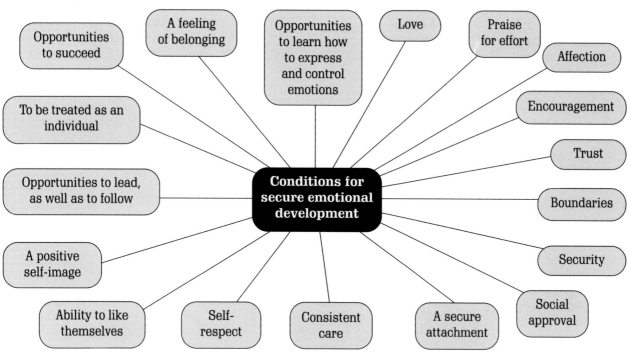

Emotional disturbance

Many children go through a phase of **emotional disturbance**. It is not usually serious and, with sensitive handling by parents and carers, is usually overcome quite quickly.

Emotional disturbance does not refer to the extremes of behaviour found in some developmental phases, such as temper tantrums in toddlers or mood swings in adolescence. It describes the more unusual and worrying behaviours that occur from time to time and which sometimes need professional referral to support and help the child through.

Emotional disturbance can manifest itself in many ways:

- A child may become withdrawn and insecure, clinging to a familiar adult and lacking confidence.
- Anti-social behaviour may be displayed by children who are trying to draw attention to themselves.
- Phobias may occur when a child is anxious about another situation; the child may display a pseudo (artificial) fear to draw attention to the real problem.
- Lonely or neglected children may develop physical habits such as hair-chewing or excessive nail-biting.
- Emotional distress can cause physical symptoms such as tummy upsets, tics and skin irritations.
- Severe emotional disturbance can result in regressed or impeded development, both physical and cognitive.

Emotional disturbance can be triggered by many situations as summarised in the spidergram below.

Figure 7.18

Triggers for emotional disturbance

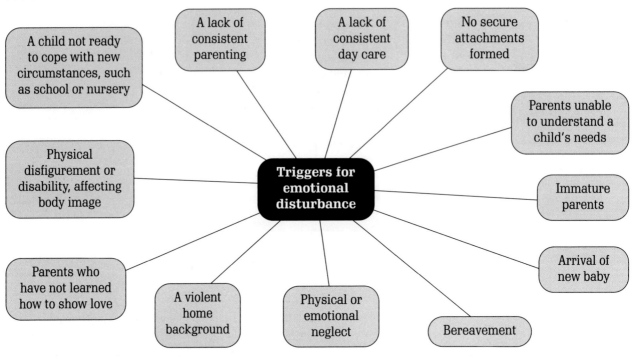

A child not ready to cope with new circumstances, such as school or nursery

A lack of consistent parenting

A lack of consistent day care

No secure attachments formed

Parents unable to understand a child's needs

Physical disfigurement or disability, affecting body image

Triggers for emotional disturbance

Immature parents

Parents who have not learned how to show love

A violent home background

Physical or emotional neglect

Bereavement

Arrival of new baby

---

activity 7.5

Look at the examples of emotionally disturbed behaviour listed on page 000. Which of them have you experienced during your time in placement? Think about how each situation was resolved and what had triggered it, if you knew (this information may not have been known generally).

Patterns of emotional development

It is usual for young babies to show a distress response at sudden noises, as these disturb their sense of security. The passive acceptance of the caring routines that is established by a few weeks of age shows how their sense of security is well established, as does the way in which they cease to cry when they are picked up. In older babies, the soothing effect of their main carer's voice and the contented patting of the breast or bottle again demonstrate emotional security.

At around the age of nine months, babies begin to show fear of strangers and become fretful when separated from their parent or main carer. This is a classic milestone of development, but it is also linked to the quality of the attachment bond that has been established between the parent, or carer, and the child. The behaviours that accompany separation anxiety may include increased crying and searching visually for the 'missing' adult.

As the infant approaches the toddler stage, emotional responses may be more negative because of their **ego-centricity** (their self-centred view of the world), and there may be the onset of tantrums at around two years. This stage can last until the more socially aware and emotionally mature age of three years, when children begin to develop an understanding of how to defer their needs and share.

The early building-blocks of emotional security have been established by the time a child enters day care or a pre-school setting. These new experiences should enable a child to continue to value themselves as an individual through the images they see and the opportunities they are given. Both experience and opportunity will have a further impact on a child's perception of themselves, affecting their self-esteem and personal image.

Refer to Unit 2, page 44, for issues of children's behaviour and how to manage some of the difficulties that may arise.

Theories of emotional development

A number of theories deal with aspects of emotional development. These include theories of bonding and attachment, separation, **self-concept**, personal identity and temperament. A brief summary of each of these is given below but, for detailed information, read *Angles on Child Psychology* by Jarvis (2001).

Bonding, attachment and separation

John Bowlby (1907–90) is one of the most well-known theorists in this field. He first put forward his views on the importance of a secure relationship between the infant and their main carer following research carried out in the 1950s. In 1953, he published his classic book *Child Care and the Growth of Love*. This text influenced many childcare practices but, although the basis of attachment theory is still upheld, his theories have since been challenged and modified.

Bowlby considered that all infants needed one main care giver (usually the mother) to ensure a secure attachment. This attachment he called monotropism. Bowlby believed that any separation from this person would have a serious effect on the infant's emotional development.

According to Bowlby (1953, page 13), it is essential for mental health that an infant and young child should experience a warm, intimate, and continuous relationship with the mother (or permanent mother substitute, that is, one person who steadily 'mothers' the child) in which both find satisfaction and enjoyment.

Modern-day theorists are certain that Bowlby's view of the mother figure's role as the essential (**monotropic**) carer was incorrect, and many subsequent studies (for example, by Mary Ainsworth and Michael Rutter) have identified that successful, secure relationships between infants and a range of other caregivers are possible and that the carer's ability to respond to the infant's needs is the greatest influencing factor in the attachment process.

A useful text to refer to for further examples is *Personal, Social and Emotional Development of Children* by Barnes (1998).

Self-concept and personal identity

A child begins to recognise that they are an individual quite early on. From the age of about 18 months, the growing toddler establishes that the person they see reflected in the mirror is actually them.

Dowling (2000, page 2) suggests that even babies build a picture of themselves, based on the way their care is given and the manner in which their carers respond to them. It is generally accepted that close members of the family, particularly the mother, are instrumental in this process as the baby sees the loving acceptance that the mother gives them as the first signal that they are an individual who is loved and who matters.

Once a child understands that they are an individual and what they, as that individual, are like, they move on to understand how they are perceived by others.

Theoretical perspectives

The emergence of the awareness of self and identity has been of great interest to early psychologists such as Freud, Cooley and Mead and, of course, to later developmental psychologists such as Schaffer and others.

Sigmund Freud

Freud proposed that our personality is composed of three separate parts but we are not born with all three parts; some develop as we mature. He proposed that these parts are the:

- id – this is the part of our personality that drives our basic wants and needs such as hunger and thirst. The id wants immediate satisfaction and Freud proposed that young babies personify the id as they demand the adult's attention until their needs are gratified

- ego – Freud suggested that the ego developed from the id in order to work out how the id's needs could best be met. The ego guides the id, helping it to learn from situations where behaviour can be modified in order for needs to be met quickly or when gratification has to be delayed

- superego – this part of our personality develops later in childhood and acts as our 'conscience', trying to restrain and control the ego. If we misbehave, the superego prompts our conscience to punish the ego, resulting in a feeling of guilt. However, the superego will also reward the ego in cases of good behaviour and this explains our feelings of confidence and pride.

Cooley and Mead

C. H. Cooley and G. H. Mead were social philosophers who were interested in the development of the self.

- Both referred to the concept of the 'looking glass self', which means that an individual's understanding of their own identity is a reflection of how they think others see them.

- Cooley thought that children developed concepts of themselves from the 'looking glass self'.

- Mead, however, saw the development of the self as a social product, in that we develop different aspects of ourselves as we interact with a variety of people.

activity
7.6
Using your college resource centre, research and present information on more contemporary studies on the development of self.

You will find useful information in Chapter 2 of *An Introduction to Psychology* (1990) edited by Roth.

Temperament

Every individual has their own character, disposition and tendencies, and children are no exception to this. A child is sometimes referred to as being an 'easy' child or a 'difficult' child, but these terms are not helpful – they become labels which can lead to the prejudging of an individual and eventually become a 'self-fulfilling prophecy'.

Figure 7.19

Developing a personal identity: 'I'm good at making models. My friends say I'm good at making models'

Children can also be balanced, impulsive or reserved in their actions: an impulsive child may experience a greater level of accidents or 'near-misses', and a reserved child's temperament may limit their experience. Temperament is seen even in very young babies; it is part of their natural personality make-up. When you lift up some babies, they mould towards you in a pleasurable cuddle, whereas others will remain tense and wary. The same applies to adults. You can probably think of individuals to whom these descriptions apply.

Bruce and Meggitt (1996) state that:

'A child's temperament is about:

emotionality: the child's feelings – fearful, anxious, enthusiastic activity: whether the child does things impulsively or slowly sociability: whether the child likes company or not.'

Again, this applies to adults too.

activity
7.1

Think about the people you know.

1 Who are easy going and spontaneous?
2 Who are approachable and flexible, but carefully weigh up situations?
3 Who are at times difficult to work with/live with/socialise with?
4 How would you sum each of them up?
5 Are they miserable, happy, calm, competitive, hostile?
6 How else would you describe them?

case study
7.2
Stanislas and Pradeep

Stanislas is an outgoing boy who is always eager to try out new activities and experiences. He is always on the go at nursery and flits from one activity to another, rarely spending long in one place. By contrast, Pradeep likes to spend time on everything he does, making sure he has all that he thinks he will need (various colour pens and so on) before he starts. Pradeep rarely hurries to see anything new, but will eventually try it out or join in when the rush is over. In this way, he often has the opportunity to spend more time enjoying the new experience than Stanislas.

activity

1 How do you think the differing temperaments of Stanislas and Pradeep might affect their learning?
2 What long-term issues do you see for each of them if they continue in the same way?

Each of us can be categorised as a personality type, but we also display various personality traits. These predispositions towards certain behaviours are part of us as a general type of person, but some of us have a greater number of some traits than of others. Psychologists who study trait theory can be divided into:

■ idiographic theorists, such as Allport (1897–1967) who focused on individual personality traits

■ nomothetic theorists, such as Cattell (1905–) and Eysenck (1916–98) who studied the more general laws of personality.

You can find out more about personality trait theory by referring to *Psychology for You* by Cullis et al. (1999).

Professional Practice

■ It is easier for most of us to interact with others who are happy and easy-going. They give us a positive extension of themselves that we can link on to. This is often referred to as having 'goodness of fit'.

■ In the early years setting, it is important that the smiling happy child is not given more of your attention than the reserved quiet child. Similarly, the tearful, discontented child should not be dismissed as miserable and be left to their misery.

■ You need to understand that temperament is part of the personality we are born with and to accept the need for differing approaches to the children in your care. You cannot treat all children in the same way – you would not be meeting their individual needs. Childcare workers need to find a way to attain the state of 'goodness of fit' with every child with whom they are in contact.

Link

Refer to Unit 2, page 44, for suggestions on managing personality clashes and encouraging co-operation within settings.

Progress Check

1   List the conditions needed for secure emotional development.
2   Give three examples of triggers that can cause emotional disturbance.
3   What does the term 'monotropism' mean?
4   Which theory is usually associated with John Bowlby?
5   What is meant by the term 'goodness of fit'?

Social development of children

Babies appear to have an instinctive capacity to relate to other humans. This is referred to as **intersubjectivity**, and opportunities to meet with and relate to other humans, both babies and older age groups, are important to develop socialisation further. Social skills start to be developed through the earliest interactions with the mother or other primary carers following birth, and these turn-taking experiences, in which the mother and infant learn to 'mesh' with each other, form the basis for building later relationships. Infants can be seen imitating certain adult actions, such as tongue poking, mouth shaping and hand movements from shortly after birth.

Figure 7.20

Infants can be seen to imitate adult actions, such as mouth shaping, from shortly after birth

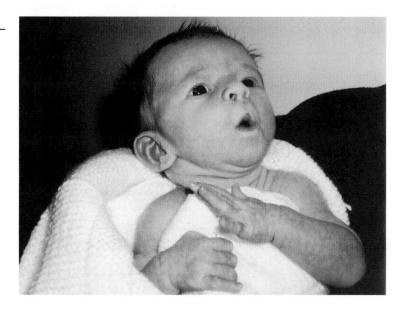

As the mother–infant relationship develops (sometimes referred to as a dyadic relationship), the mother tends to anticipate the responses of her infant and react accordingly. This precipitating response is known as *a priori* imitation, and plays an important part in the development of early relationships of young infants. It relates to Jerome Bruner's concept of scaffolding.

 Link Refer to page 324 for more about Bruner.

Stages of socialisation

Social development can be clearly seen in the way in which children play, as demonstrated in Figure 7.21.

 Link You may find it helpful to refer back to the summaries of development earlier in the unit (page 295), noting how children develop socially. You may also find it helpful to revisit Unit 4.

Social play stages

As you can see from Figure 7.21, socialisation develops as a child's play moves from the solitary actions of the toddler absorbed in their own world through to the complex games involving rules seen in the infant school playground. The ability to co-operate with others moves through stages, which are dependent on both the maturational stage of development of the individual child and the opportunities and experiences that have been made available to them.

Solitary play

The first stage of play is referred to as solitary play. The child plays contentedly on their own, still needing the reassurance of the adult. This play is typical up to two years of age. It is frequently imitative, demonstrating a basic understanding of the actions of others within a child's social world. An example of solitary imitative play is the child pretending to brush the hair of a doll or teddy, usually very briefly.

Figure 7.21

The development of play shows clearly how children develop socially

Co-operative play, over 3 years
Shared enjoyment, making joint decisions about play

Associative play, from 3 years
Watch other children
May copy their actions

Parallel play, 2–3 years
Play alongside another child
Aware of other games, but does not co-operate

Solitary play 0–2 years
Play alone
Need adult reassurance

Parallel play

The next stage is parallel play in which a child finds enjoyment playing alongside, but not with, another child. The children do not necessarily even acknowledge that the other exists, and make no reference to what the other is doing. This is true parallel play, one child playing parallel to the other. It usually begins to emerge between two and three years of age.

Associative (looking on) play

At this stage in social play, the child begins to watch the actions of others, enjoying their play from a distance. They are not as yet ready to play with others, but learn a great deal from their observations. This stage of play is typically seen between three and four years of age.

Joining in play (simple co-operative)

By four years old, most children are ready to play co-operatively with others. This simple co-operative play begins in an uncomplicated manner, involving the shared enjoyment of a similar activity. A good example of this is a group of children all dressing dolls together. There are no rules and no restrictions. It is simply a pleasurable play experience with others.

Co-operative play (complex co-operative)

This last and most developed stage in the process of children's play involves them interacting as a group. This can involve the physical co-operation needed to complete a joint task, or play which includes complex rules, involving the taking on of agreed (but 'evolving as they go') roles.

Socialisation theory

Socialisation refers to the process by which the individual learns about the social groups or society to which they belong. According to socialisation theory, there are two types of socialisation:

- **primary socialisation**, which takes place as a child understands and develops the customs and practices of their family

- **secondary socialisation**, which involves the wider influences of other adults and social groups in the community with whom the child has regular contact.

---

activity
7.8

1 Consider this list of examples of primary and secondary socialisation:

religion
attitude to other religions
diet
social behaviour
moral behaviour
attitude shown to elders
attitude shown to family members
attitude shown to others

Make a copy of the table and place the examples under the relevant heading.

Primary socialisation	Secondary socialisation

2 Which examples could be placed under both headings?
3 What other examples can you add to the table?

Professional Practice

■ Your experience of primary socialisation is likely to be different from that of other people you know. What might those differences be?

Social learning theory

Possibly the most well-known example of a theory of socialisation is **social learning theory**, which was put forward by Albert Bandura in 1965, based on his research. In his studies, he showed a film with three different endings to children to see how they could be affected by what they had seen.

Three groups of children were each shown a different version of the film, which involved an adult hitting and shouting at a Bobo doll (a large inflatable toy weighted at the bottom that always rights itself – you cannot knock it over).

■ Group 1: the first film ending showed the adult being rewarded for hitting the doll.

■ Group 2: the second film ending showed the adult being punished for hitting the doll.

■ Group 3: in the third film, nothing happened to the adult.

After they had watched their particular version of the film, the children in all three groups were given Bobo dolls to play with and were observed by the researchers. The children who had seen the adult rewarded for hitting the doll also showed a higher tendency to hit it.

This study could not claim evidence of a direct cause and effect, but it could certainly suggest that children were most likely influenced by the rewarding of negative behaviour.

The following example illustrates an example of social learning.

In the playground one dinner time, Jake was playing with a tennis ball, kicking it at the wall. His aim was taking the ball closer and closer to the windows, so Mrs. Baker, the school meals supervisory assistant who was on playground duty, explained that he would need to keep away from the windows or he would not be allowed to continue playing ball. Jake took no notice of Mrs Baker and eventually he had his ball taken away from him. Jake felt very cross with Mrs Baker at the time.

The next day, Jake again played ball, but this time he played over by the fence. He did not want to lose his ball again.

Effects of stereotyping on development

Social development and play are affected by various experiences and this section focuses on the effects of stereotyping. To stereotype an individual is mentally to place them into a specific compartment according to a preconceived idea. It ignores the person's individual character, their predisposition and temperament and simply includes them as part of a collective group. In generalising in this way, we are likely to make serious errors of judgement about the world we live in and the people we interact with.

As you have seen, children learn about social behaviour, including how to react to others, from watching and imitating other people. They are particularly influenced by the adults they admire. As an adult working with young children, you are a role model, and you should be aware of how your actions and words can affect them so that you do not reinforce social stereotypes.

Gender stereotyping

In the earliest years, children learn which sex they belong to. This is known as sex identity and it refers to body shape and biological make-up. They also learn to behave in certain ways according to their sex identity. This is known as the gender role, which leads on to the development of gender identity. Generally, when girls know they are girls, they tend to play with other girls and the same applies to boys. When children fully understand that their sex is set for life, they have reached the state of gender stability.

Socialisation not only affects children's behaviour, it also affects their perceptions of gender. When adults interact with babies, it has been shown that they handle babies in different ways

> **remember**
>
> ■ As an adult working with children, you need to think about the messages you are giving them. These messages have a direct impact on the social learning of the children in your care.
>
> ■ Messages can be portrayed by actions, words, attitudes and non-verbal behaviour. They can be both positive or negative.

according to their sex. This also applies to the language and tone of voice that they use towards them. For example, most people have heard comments such as 'What a beautiful girl she is' or 'He's a real bruiser isn't he?' These are classic comments, which are used widely and are very gender specific.

Research has shown that gender roles are influenced by the parents and carers of children. Goldberg and Lewis in a study of 32 boy babies and 32 girl babies, each aged around 6 months, found that girl babies are held for longer, spoken to in a softer tone and cradled gently, whereas boy babies are approached in a more 'robust' manner. Goldberg and Lewis observed the same infants again at 13 months in a laboratory setting, with a limited selection of toys available to them. The girls were observed to choose the quieter toys and to stay near to their mothers, whereas the boys chose the more active toys and appeared to be more independent. Goldberg and Lewis drew the conclusion that the earlier experiences had affected the later actions of these babies.

Interactions with older children have also been seen to influence gender. Beverley Fagot carried out observations in the homes of many families with children approaching two years. She particularly noted which behaviours were encouraged and discouraged by the parents and found that, on the whole, girls were encouraged to stay near to the parents, to ask for help and to take an interest in stereotypical 'girls' activities (dolls, clothes, dancing). They tended to be discouraged from active play (jumping, running around, rough-and-tumble games) and from being aggressive. Boys, on the other hand, were encouraged to use their bodies actively and to explore construction toys and play with cars; they were discouraged from playing with dolls and any other stereotypically 'girls'' activities. They were also discouraged from asking for help. The boys who tended towards 'girls'' activities were more strongly criticised by the parents than the girls who tended towards 'boys'' activities.

---

activity
7.9

Make a copy of the table and note in the relevant columns the behaviours that were encouraged and discouraged in Beverly Fagot's research. Discuss the comparison within your group.

	Encouraged behaviours	**Discourage behaviours**
Girls		
Boys		

---

case study
7.3

Paul and Patrick

Paul and Patrick were playing outside with balls and hoops, when Rachel, an early years worker, called out for 'a big strong boy' to help her get the mats out. Paul and Patrick both ran to help her, but Patrick got his foot caught in one of the hoops and fell heavily. He began to cry. Paul helped him up saying, 'Come on, Patrick, big boys don't cry. Quick, let's help Rachel.'

---

activity

1 What messages were being given here?
2 How could Rachel have made both situations more positive?
3 What could be the long-term implications for social learning for Paul and Patrick?

Professional Practice

- What personal learning can you take from this case study?
- How might it affect your practice in the future?

Working with children requires a clear understanding of the importance of equality and how all children should be encouraged to use all of the available activities and experience all situations in the setting.

activity 7.10

You have been set an assignment asking you to explore children's perceptions of gender within your current nursery placement. It has been suggested that you carry out a small survey of their views of a range of about 10 toys/activities.

1 Which toys would you include?
2 What would influence your choices?
3 How will you set out your mini survey?

As you make your choices of toys, ask yourself:

- Do I think of certain toys as being 'boys' toys' or 'girls' toys'?
- Why is this?
- What affect would it have on development if children were limited in their use of toys and equipment?
- Which areas of development would be affected?

4 Discuss your views with a partner and share the outcomes of your survey too. How do your outcomes compare to the outcomes of others?

Professional Practice

- What other ideas, apart from toys and activities, could you have used to explore children's perceptions of gender?

Cultural and racial stereotyping

A child should be accepted for themselves first and foremost. Their background, ethnicity and religion are simply part of what makes them who they are. The individual child's personality is what you should focus upon as you build up a relationship with them. The influences of primary and secondary socialisation will have given them a sense of belonging within their own culture, and this is an important part of their family's way of life, and of their parents' parenting of them. This should be acknowledged and valued by all early years workers.

We live in a pluralist society (one which is made up of a variety of groups who each have their own distinctive ethnic origin, culture or religion) and it is important to have an understanding of a broad range of cultures, religions and beliefs and be willing to value and explore differences with the children in your care.

Refer back to Unit 1 for a more detailed discussion of equality, diversity and rights.

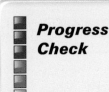
Progress Check

1 What is intersubjectivity?
2 In what order do the play stages develop?
3 What is the difference between simple and complex co-operative play?
4 How does primary socialisation differ from secondary socialisation?
5 Give an example of social learning theory.
6 What does the term 'gender stability' mean?

Cognitive development of children

Humans are able to think, reason, plan ahead and manipulate ideas, but whether these abilities are already in place when we are born or whether we are moulded by the experiences we have as individuals has been much debated. This has become known as the nature/nurture debate (nativists vs. empiricists). Nativists support the idea of the human infant having innate abilities that predispose them towards developing in certain ways, whereas empiricists believe firmly that we are simply moulded by experience. Most modern-day theorists take a combined approach, accepting that we are each born with some genetic influences that are further enhanced by our early experiences.

Figure 7.22

Family, friends, teachers, pets – do you think we have been moulded by experience?

 A useful publication to help you explore the nature/nurture debate further is *The Foundations of Child Development* by Oates (1999).

Cognitive development involves the development of concepts, including thinking, problem-solving and memory. The following sections discuss in some detail the theories of three influential theorists of cognitive development, Jean Piaget, Lev Vygotsky and Jerome Bruner, and also look at the theories of Ivan Pavlov and B. F. Skinner.

Table 7.6 The main theorists in cognitive development

Jean Piaget	Lev Vygotsky	Jerome Bruner
Particularly associated with:	Particularly associated with:	Particularly associated with:
■ constructivist theory ■ stages of cognitive development ■ schemas ■ assimilation and accommodation ■ conservation ■ discovery learning.	■ zone of proximal development (ZPD) ■ social constructivist theory.	■ the three modes of representation: – enactive – iconic – symbolic ■ discovery learning ■ scaffolding.

case study 7.4 Lucy

Simon and Nina sat down to clarify the plans for next week's activities in their nursery class. 'I don't know what to do with Lucy,' said Nina. 'She just wants to talk non-stop, she rarely lets anyone else get a word in, and some of her language is pretty awful too. What with her tearing around all the time, it is difficult to get her to listen as she is hardly ever still for more than a few seconds.'

'She probably inherited it from her mother,' said Simon. 'Whenever I speak to her, I hardly manage to complete a sentence without her interrupting me. I've noticed she is the same when she speaks to other parents too.'

'I'm not sure I agree with you about Lucy inheriting her behaviour,' replied Nina. 'I think children are more likely to learn by the way they are brought up, but, as Lucy lives in such a noisy and lively household, what else can we expect?'

activity

Consider the conversation.

1 Who was taking a nativist view?
2 Who took a more empiricist view?

Piaget's stages of cognitive development

Piaget believed that a child's way of thinking changes as they get older and that all children pass through four stages of cognitive development in the same order, although the age at which they enter and leave each stage may vary considerably. The four stages are:

1 Sensorimotor stage, 0–2 years

2 Pre-operational stage, 2–7 years: Pre-conceptual stage, 2–4 years; Intuitive stage, 4–7 years

3 Concrete operations stage, 7–11 years

4 Formal operations stage, 11 years onwards.

 Link You may find it helpful to refer back to Unit 4, page 123.

Schemas

Piaget believed that children develop knowledge concepts by using and building on previous experiences. He considered that they gradually adapt these concepts, which he called schemas, to establish new understanding. For example, a child recognises a dog as something which is 'larger than themselves and has four legs' – this is a schema.

Figure 7.23

An example of a child developing a schema for bricks

Source: Neaum and Tallack, 2000

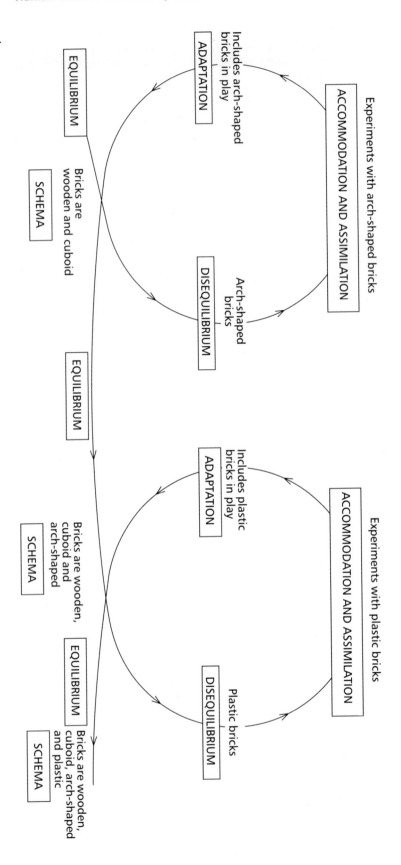

Assimilation

The child uses the previously learned schema to make sense of a new situation. For example, the child uses the schema 'a dog is larger than themselves and has four legs' to refer to a goat as 'dog'. Piaget called this process *assimilation*.

Accommodation

When this misunderstanding is corrected by an adult – the white goat is large, but it is a goat, not a dog – the child will be moved towards a new schema – goats and dogs can be large and either brown or white. Piaget called this process *accommodation*.

The ongoing development of schemas

As the child comes into contact with different animals, they will continue to learn new schemas, for example, that a dog can be large or small, black, white or brown. They will also eventually have schemas that tell them that other animals can be large or small, and can also be black, white or brown.

Disequilibrium

When a child is unable to make sense of new information (unable to assimilate) they are considered to be in an unbalanced state, which Piaget called **disequilibrium**.

Equilibrium

As the child accommodates new concepts, they reach a point of equilibrium where they are able to understand the new information.

Assimilation > Disequilibrium > Accommodation > Equilibrium > Assimilation

Conservation

Piaget is also renowned for his views and experiments on **conservation**. He believed that children under the age of six would not be able to conserve (i.e. understand changes in quantity, size and number). He used a variety of tests to explore this. Below are examples of his three most well-known tests.

In Example A, the child was shown two identical rows of pennies and was asked if they were the same. The pennies in the second row were then spaced apart and the child was asked if there were still the same number of pennies.

If the child was able to conserve, they would answer that there were the same number. If the child could not conserve, they would answer that there were more pennies in the longer row.

Figure 7.24

Conservation – Example A

 Children at the pre-operational stage say that the two rows contain the same number of pennies …

 … but also that there are more pennies in the more spread-out, second row.

In Example B, the child was shown two identical beakers of water and asked if they contained the same amount. After watching the adult pour the water from one beaker into a taller beaker, the child was asked if the amount of water in the beakers was still the same. If the child could conserve, they would answer that the amount of water remained the same. If they could not conserve, they would state that the amount of water was different – that there was more water in the taller beaker.

Figure 7.25

Conservation – Example B

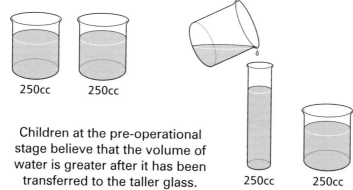

250cc   250cc

Children at the pre-operational stage believe that the volume of water is greater after it has been transferred to the taller glass.

250cc   250cc

In Example C, the child was shown two identical balls of play dough and asked if they were the same amount. Having seen the adult roll one ball into a sausage shape, the child was asked if the amount of play dough was still the same. If the child could conserve, they would answer that the balls of play dough were still both the same size. If they could not conserve, they would think that the sausage shape was made from a greater amount of play dough.

Piaget's findings have been challenged by many theorists. For example, using a character called 'naughty teddy', Donaldson and McGarrigle (1974) demonstrated that a higher number of pre-operational stage children were able to conserve than had been found by Piaget. Naughty teddy was used to 'accidentally' mess up the conservation experiments, for example, the row of pennies. The researchers felt that the way in which the questions had been phrased by Piaget had led children to assume that the adult was indicating that a change had occurred in the number of counters, amount of water, and so on. When teddy was involved, the children were able to see that it was simply teddy being 'naughty', and that no alteration had been made.

activity 7.11

In your placement, try one of Piaget's experiments with children within the pre-operational stage.

1 First, ask the questions as Piaget would have done, and record your results.
2 Next, introduce a 'helper', which could be a glove puppet, or you could make a paper bag puppet, as a 'naughty teddy' substitute. See if your results are any different. Record the results and compare them with your first results.
3 What have you learned from this activity?

Discovery learning

Children learn best by being given opportunities to find out for themselves. Piaget's constructivist theory of play considered children to be active learners who enjoy using a range of materials, objects and situations from their everyday life to help them develop their play.

case study 7.5 — Cerys and Claudia

Cerys was being 'mummy' in the role-play house. She was getting her baby ready to go shopping. She put on a pair of play shoes and picked up a shopping bag. When she was half way across the room, she shouted, 'My baby, I've forgotten my baby', and rushed back to collect the pram. Cerys was learning about responsibility through her play.

Claudia was playing with the magnetic train set. She was trying to link up each of the carriages to the engines, but one carriage would not stay linked up. Claudia tried it at the end of each train she had made, but to no avail (the magnets at one end attract and at the other repel). Eventually, she turned the carriage around and this time it linked up successfully. Claudia was very pleased with herself and continued with her game happily.

activity

1 Which of the above case studies gives the best example of discovery learning, do you think?
2 What examples of discovery learning have you seen in your current placement?
3 Does your current placement allow opportunities for discovery learning, or do staff step in to help out whenever a child is seen to be having difficulties?

Vygotsky's social constructivist view of play

Vygotsky believed in the need for children to be able to have access to a range of objects, materials and situations to develop their play, in much the same way as Piaget did. However, unlike Piaget, Vygotsky placed considerable emphasis on the child's need for adult input into their play in order for the child to realise their potential through play situations.

Zone of proximal development (ZPD)

Vygotsky developed his concept of a zone of proximal development (ZPD) by studying what a child can achieve playing alone, and what they can achieve with some sensitive input from an adult.

Refer to page 124. The observations shown there illustrate Vygotsky's concept of the ZPD; they show how an adult can enhance the development of a child's understanding, affecting their subsequent thinking and actions.

Professional Practice

- This theory is particularly relevant when a child is attempting to achieve a new aim, perhaps using a new piece of equipment or a more complex jigsaw puzzle.
- Think about where you have observed an adult helping a child in this way.

Jerome Bruner and discovery learning

Bruner believed that children enjoy finding out new things for themselves; like Piaget, he felt that children learn through the use of materials that are freely available to them.

He put forward the idea that there are three ways or modes of thinking that children use internally to represent the world to themselves as their thinking develops.

Enactive mode

Bruner emphasised the importance of first-hand experiences and believed that the simplest thinking involves manipulating aspects of the environment. He referred to this as the enactive mode of thinking. It links with discovery learning.

Iconic mode

The iconic mode of thinking involves the child's development of mental images, such as remembering what somebody or something looks like.

Iconic representation shows that the child is extending their memory and is not purely relying on active learning (enactive mode). A photograph, for example, will remind a child of someone they have met, and enable them to think about the person further. Similarly, the smell of onions may remind them of cooking a barbecue with granny and granddad.

Symbolic mode

Thinking using symbolism, including language, number, music and art, is what Bruner termed the symbolic mode. It enables older children to extend their thinking and be able to express themselves through a variety of media.

Refer back to Unit 4, page 125, for information on Bruner's concept of scaffolding.

Figure 7.26

Bruner's three modes of thinking

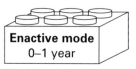

Enactive mode
0–1 year

Thinking is a re-enacted memory

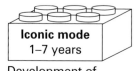

Iconic mode
1–7 years

Development of mental images

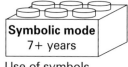

Symbolic mode
7+ years

Use of symbols in thought

Pavlov and classical conditioning

Pavlov carried out experiments on responses to stimulus. His famous experiment demonstrated classical conditioning with dogs and involved the use of a bell (the neutral stimulus) and food (called the unconditioned stimulus because it elicits a reflex response). When the bell rang, the dogs were fed, and the (unconditioned) response of salivating occurred. After several pairings of food and bell, the sound of a bell ringing would elicit the response (salivating) without the production of food.

Initially: Neutral stimulus (bell) + unconditioned stimulus (food) = Outcome (salivating).
Eventually: Neutral stimulus (bell) = Outcome (salivating).

Professional Practice

■ Classical conditioning theory can also be applied to working with children, encouraging them to act within the structure and boundaries of the setting.

Can you think of an example?

Using the model above as a guide, set out your example:

Initially: _____ + _____ = _____ Eventually: _____ = _____

Skinner and operant conditioning

In operant conditioning, learning takes place through the reinforcement of behaviour; in positive reinforcement, the learner is given a reward for performing the desired behaviour.

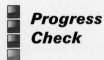

Refer to Unit 2, page 54, for a discussion of strategies to positively reinforce children's behaviour.

Skinner rewarded rats if they behaved as he wanted them to. In some of his experiments, he set up a box with a lever and the rats only received food if they pressed down on the lever in the box. This form of stimulus–response learning moulds behaviour, and Skinner put forward the idea that children learn this way too: for example, he said that language develops by operant conditioning, owing to parents and carers giving praise for 'correct' speech and pronunciation.

Refer to page 323 for behaviourist theory of language development.

Progress Check

1   Explain the difference between constructivist and social constructivist theory.
2   What is a schema?
3   How does a child reach the state of equilibrium?
4   What is the main challenge to Piaget's theory of conservation in pre-operational stage children?
5   Which theorist is associated with the ZPD concept?
6   Which of Bruner's modes of thinking involves the development of mental images?

Language development

Language is the main way in which humans communicate with one another. It involves facial expressions, tone of voice, body posture and expression of meaning through the use of words or symbols.

Language is:

- rule-governed – grammatical rules are present in each language (syntax)
- structured – the sound system that makes up the speech sounds (phonology)
- symbolic – words have meanings, building into phrases, and so on (semantics)
- generative – it is the basis of the sharing of knowledge (pragmatics).

Prerequisites for language

The normal, unimpeded development of language is affected by other areas of development. For example, socially and cognitively an awareness of the need to interact as a means of communication is imperative, as are the physical abilities of vision, hearing and speech. Children learn the basis of their culture through communication (socialisation theory), and develop understanding of themselves and how they fit within their peer and social groups (goodness of fit). Psychologists believe that language plays an important part in all aspects of human development, with some theorists arguing that language is the basis of learning. An important debate involves the questions:

- Is language dependent on thought?
- Or is thought dependent on language?

What are your first thoughts on this language vs. thought debate? Do you think understanding is needed in order to develop linguistically? Or do you think that language enables understanding to develop? Come back to these questions when you have read the theories outlined below.

Theories of language development

The theories described below offer some very different ideas about how language develops. As you read them, consider which you could accept and which do not seem possible.

A detailed discussion of the theories of language can be found in *Psychology for You* by Cullis et al. (1999).

Theories of language development include:

- association theory
- behaviourist theory
- language acquisition device theory
- maturational theory
- interactionist theory.

Association theory

This theory proposes that a child gradually builds their language by associating words with what they see. This theory works well up to a point, but does not take into account all aspects of language, for example those used to describe feelings or emotions.

Behaviourist theory

Theorists such as Skinner proposed that a child's language is shaped by the responses given to them by their parents or main carers (operant conditioning); the positive reinforcement of vocalisations encourages the child to repeat a specific sound over and over again. For example, Daniel is an infant of six months whose babbling sounds have become 'dadadada'. Daniel's mother greets this with delight and encouragement, stating that 'Dada' will be home soon.

Skinner believed that the continuous positive reinforcement of 'correct' speech sounds, and the lack of positive response to sounds or (eventually) sentence structure that is not correct, will mould a child's language formation.

Skinner's theory would indicate that children have to go through a trial-and-error process for every aspect of speech, but this is clearly not the case, although it is accepted that infants are encouraged by the positive reactions of adults. Skinner's theory was challenged by many psychologists and consequently the nativist theories set out below became an inviting alternative.

The principles of social learning theory can also be applied to language, that is, that humans repeat behaviour that they see being rewarded (remember the Bobo dolls). If, for example, a child sees an older brother or sister being rewarded for speech, the younger child may try to imitate that behaviour.

Language acquisition device (LAD) theory

Noam Chomsky (a nativist) believed in the biologically based theory that infants are born with a predisposition for language. He suggested that infants have a **language acquisition device (LAD)**. He considered that this LAD enabled children to absorb the language that they heard, to decode it and then develop an understanding of its rules and grammatical structure. It has been shown that children of all cultures develop language at much the same time and this gave support to the theories of Chomsky and others like him.

Maturational theory

Lenneberg, like Chomsky, considered that as long as children were exposed to language, they would simply pick it up as their development progressed in other ways too. (This should not be confused with the Gesell's maturational theory which is concerned with other aspects of maturation.)

Interactionist theory

The basis of the interactionist theory is that the schemas that children develop subsequently facilitate language development: children first experience and then talk about their experiences. Therefore, this theory sees language as a reflection of cognitive development. Piaget, Vygotsky and Bruner took this interactionist approach to their thinking on language development.

---

activity
7.12

Make a copy of the table below and note on it which theories of language fit in with the nature theory and which fit in with the nurture theory.

Language theory	Nature	Nurture
Association theory		
Behaviourist theory		
Language acquisition device theory		
Maturational theory		
Interactionist theory		

It is interesting that research carried out with hearing children born to deaf parents has shown that, while a child may learn words from what they hear around them (radio, television, videos, and so on), they need to be actively involved in conversation in order to develop their understanding and use of grammar. In the cases of some children, speech therapy resulted in a sudden improvement in their language structure which soon brought them up to the expected level of language development for their age. This indicated that they had previously been ready to learn the grammatical rules associated with their culture, but needed the active involvement with others in order to facilitate it.

Stages of language development

As with every aspect of development, children develop language at differing rates within what is considered to be the 'normal' range. This process of language development can be divided into ten basic stages:

1　Non-verbal communication/expression

2　Speech-like noises

3　Controlling sounds, using mouth and tongue

4　Imitating sounds

5　First words

6　Development of vocabulary (50 words is usual at 2 years)

7　Putting words together to form simple phrases and sentences

8　Use of grammar

9　Use of meaning

10　Using language to develop other skills, for example early literacy.

These 10 stages can be linked to approximate ages as shown in Table 7.7.

Professional Practice

■ As you move through the various placements that will make up your professional practice experience, observe and note the differences in speech intonation, questioning and grammar of children at different ages and stages.

The development of speech sounds in the English language

Speech sounds are made up of consonants, vowels, syllables and words.

Consonants

Consonants are 'closed' sounds. This means that, for a consonant sound to be produced, the airflow is obstructed by parts of the mouth coming into contact with each other or almost contacting.

For example, try saying the word book. To pronounce the b in book, the lips need to come into contact.

To pronounce the s in the word sand, the tip of the tongue touches the ridge just behind the top front teeth.

These are examples of how the obstructions are made.

Table 7.7 The stages of language development

Age	Understanding	No. of words	Type of words	Average length of sentence
3 months	Soothed by sound	0	Cooing and gurgling	0
6 months	Responds to voice tones	0	Babble	0
1 year	Knows own name and a few others	1	Noun (naming word)	1 word
18 months	Understands simple commands	6–20	Nouns +	1 word
2 years	Understands much more than they can say	50+	Verbs and pronouns (action + name)	1–2 word phrases
2½ years	Enjoys simple and familiar stories	200+	Pronouns I, me, you; Questions what, where	2–3 word phrases
3 years	Carries out complex commands	500–1,000	Plurals; Verbs in present tense; Questions who	3–4 word phrases
4 years	Listens to long stories	1,000–1,500	Verbs in past tense; Questions why, where, how	4–5 word phrases
5 years	Developing the ability to reason	1,500–2,000	Complex sentences with adult forms of grammar	5–6 word phrases

Table 7.8 The approximate sequential development of consonants in the English language

At 2 years	*m, n, p, b, t, d, w*
At 2½ years	*k, g, ng* (as in *sing*), *h*
2½ –3 years	*f, s, l, y*
3½ –4 years	*v, z, ch, j, sh*
4½ years onwards	*th* (as in *thin*), <u>*th*</u> (as in *the*), *r*

Double consonants such as *sp*, *tr* and *fl*, and also the sounds *r* and *th*, can develop as late at 6½ years in some children.

There are five main types of consonants:

- plosives
- nasals
- fricatives
- affricates
- approximants.

English consonant sounds 'at a glance'

	Bilabial	Labio-dental	Dental	Alveolar	Post-alveolar	Palatal	Velar	Glottal
Plosive	*p, b*			*t, d*			*c/k, g*	
Nasal	*m*			*n*			*ng*	
Fricative		*f, v*	*th*, <u>*th*</u>	*s, z*	*sh, zh*			*h*
Affricate					*ch, j*			
Approximant	*w*			*l*	*r*	*y*		

Professional Practice

- How we pronounce sounds is quite complex. It is, however, a useful exercise for early years workers to explore their own pronunciation to gain a better understanding of how the parts of the mouth work together and how each sound is subsequently produced. This helps with understanding the difficulties faced by some children in developing their speech sounds.

Plosives

Plosives are produced by a complete obstruction of the airflow at some position in the mouth, for example, the lips coming together. Air builds up behind the temporary obstruction and when the obstruction is removed (for example, the lips part) the air rushes out (a plosive).

Plosives can be voiceless (produced without the involvement of the vocal cords) or voiced (involving the vibration of the vocal cords). They occur in pairs:

- first pair: p, b

The two lips come together to form a complete obstruction. These are known as bilabial plosives (two lips). Try pronouncing them.

- second pair: t, d

These involve the tip of the tongue contacting the gum ridge (alveolar ridge) just behind the top front teeth. (Run your tongue over your alveolar ridge to identify where it is). These are known as alveolar plosives. Try pronouncing them.

- third pair: c/k, g (as in goat)

The back of the roof of the mouth is known as the soft palate (velum). Velar plosives are sounded when the tongue is in contact with the soft palate.

Try pronouncing these three consonant sounds.

Nasals

When a plosive sound is made, the soft palate is raised so that it touches the back of the throat and stops air from escaping through the nose. Nasals are similar in that there is a complete obstruction of air flow in the mouth, but the air pressure does not build up. It is allowed to escape through the nose by lowering the soft palate.

There are three nasals:

- m is a bilabial nasal where the sound is formed at the front of the mouth, with the lips coming together
- n is an alveolar nasal, where the obstruction is between the back of the tongue and the soft palate
- ng (as in sing) is a velar nasal. This sound never appears at the beginning of a word in English.

Try pronouncing these nasal consonants.

Fricatives

These sounds are formed by the narrowing of the mouth passage by any two of the articulators (lips, teeth, tongue, roof of mouth) coming into near contact. The air is forced through a narrow gap creating a friction sound, hence the name, fricative consonant. Each of these sounds can be prolonged by first taking a deep breath.

There are four pairs of fricatives:

- first pair: f, v

These are articulated with slight contact between the bottom lip and the top front teeth. They are known as labio-dental fricatives.

- second pair: th (as in thin), th (as in that)

These fricatives involve the tongue nearly contacting the top front teeth. The sounds are quite hard for young children to pronounce and they often use alternatives, for example: f instead of th and/or v instead of th.

- third pair: s, z

These are formed when the tongue is almost in contact with the alveolar ridge. They are known as alveolar fricatives.

- fourth pair: sh, zh (as 'sounded' in the middle of the word measure)

These post-alveolar fricatives are formed further back in the mouth when the middle of the tongue comes into contact with the roof of the mouth, just behind the alveolar ridge. The zh sound is never found at the beginning of a word in English.

The final fricative is h. It is a glottal fricative. It is made deep down in the throat (the glottis). This sound is never found at the end of a word in English. Try pronouncing these fricative consonants.

Affricates

The affricates are the sounds that combine both a complete obstruction with a partial obstruction. They start with a complete obstruction formed by the tip of the tongue contacting the alveolar ridge, but then the air is released slowly with friction, behind the alveolar ridge. No air is released in an explosive way.

These sounds are j and ch. They are post-alveolar affricates. Try pronouncing them.

Approximants

The term 'approximant' is used for the sound made when the mouth passage is not completely obstructed, as it is with the plosives and the nasals, nor is it restricted so that friction is developed. Two articulators (tongue, teeth, etc.) approximate closely together.

The approximants are:

- w, formed by the two lips approximating closely (bi-labial approximant)
- l, made by the tongue approximating to the alveolar ridge (alveolar approximant)
- r, sounded by the tongue being behind the alveolar ridge (post-alveolar approximant)
- y, articulated with the middle of the tongue approximating closely to the palate (palatal approximant).

Try pronouncing these approximants.

Refer back to the 'at a glance' table on page 326 to help consolidate your understanding.

Vowels

The basic vowel sounds are a, e, i, o and u, but there are other vowel sounds too. These include the double sounds such as ee, oo, and so on. Vowels are 'open' sounds. There is no obstruction to the airflow during pronunciation and each sound differs according to the position of the mouth. For example:

- If the lips are spread widely, the sound ee is produced.
- If the lips are rounded, the sound oo is produced.
- Vowels can be long sounds as in the word more. They can also be short sounds as in the word pack.
- There are simple vowels such as o as in pot, u as in put, a as in pat. They are simple because once the mouth is set in position it does not need to alter in order to produce the sound.
- There are also more complex vowel sounds such as oy as in boy and ow as in cow. With these sounds, you need to change the mouth and/or tongue position for the full sound to be made.
- All vowels in English are 'voiced'. This means that they involve the vibration of the vocal cords.

Syllables

Speech sounds combine together to form syllables. A syllable is made up of a combination of consonants (c) and at least one vowel (v). There can be up to three consonants before a vowel and up to four consonants after a vowel in the English language.

Examples of syllables:

- be = cv (1 consonant and 1 vowel)
- and = vcc (1 vowel and 2 consonants), and so on
- plot = ccvc
- strip = cccvc
- tempts = cvcccc.

The more consonants in a syllable, the harder it will be for a child to pronounce, because it requires a greater ability to co-ordinate the articulators.

Words

Syllables, in turn, combine together to form words. Some words have just one syllable, for example cat, dog and hen. These are called monosyllabic words. All other words have more than one syllable and are known as polysyllabic words.

Even in adulthood, some people have difficulty in pronouncing some polysyllabic words. For example, common difficulties are found in pronouncing:

- laboratory (often mispronounced as labroratrory)
- certificates (often mispronounced as cerstificates).

activity
7.13

1 Which words do you find difficult, or stumble over on occasions?
2 Which words have you noticed other adults having difficulty with?
3 How complex are the syllable combinations of these words?

Disordered or delayed speech

Many children have phases of unclear speech, but they do not all need to be seen by a speech therapist.

Dysfluency

Many temporary disorders are due to the child hastening to say something and stumbling over it in their eagerness and excitement. This common occurrence is known as **dysfluency**.

Hesitation occurs as a child tries to express themselves. This type of dysfluency is often associated with their attempting to use more complex language structure. Speech therapists refer to this as normal developmental dysfluency as it does not usually need professional intervention.

When conversing with a dysfluent child, it is important to give them time and attention to minimise the affect of the dysfluency.

Professional Practice

The following checklist should be helpful.

■ Do speak steadily and clearly yourself.

■ Do give the dysfluent child your full attention.

■ Do avoid interrupting the child whenever possible.

■ Do focus on what they are saying, and try to ignore the dysfluency.

■ Do not ask the child to repeat it or to start again.

■ Do not tell the child to 'take a deep breath' before they speak.

■ Do not tell the child to slow down.

■ Do not ask the child to 'think it through' before they speak.

■ Do not allow discussion of their dysfluency in their presence.

If a child's dysfluency continues for more than a short period of time, or if the parents or the child appear to be worried by the dysfluency, a referral to a speech therapist will usually be made. The British Stammering Association has drawn up the following guidelines to help with decision-making regarding referrals. A referral is made if:

the child has dysfluent speech and one or more of the following factors are present:

■ a family history of stammering or speech or language problems

■ the child is finding learning to talk difficult in any way

■ the child shows signs of frustration or is upset by his speaking

■ the child is struggling when talking

■ the child is in a dual language situation and is stammering in her first language

■ there is parental concern or uneasiness

■ the child's general behaviour is causing concern.

(Mukherji and O'Dea, 2000)

Elision

The term 'elision' refers to when a child regularly misses out part of a speech sound altogether. It is a common occurrence, particularly with the second consonant of a cluster of two, for example:

- the st in the word postman would become pos'man
- the pt in the word slept would become slep'.

In young children this is part of the maturational development of speech patterns. In older children and adults it is usually more likely to be habit!

Language disorders and speech therapy

Concerns regarding language development include:

- lack of communication with parents and carers in early weeks
- significant feeding difficulties (speech therapists are often involved at this early stage)
- lack of vocalisation from three months onwards
- no babbling from eight to nine months onwards
- lack of verbal responses to play
- vocalisation completely out of line with the developmental 'norms'.

> **remember**
>
> When expressing themselves, language disordered children may:
> - have difficulty in finding appropriate words
> - display word-order confusion
> - have difficulty in giving explanations
> - use confused grammar
> - omit grammatical word endings
> - use confused sounds within individual words.

Figure 7.27

Language disorder

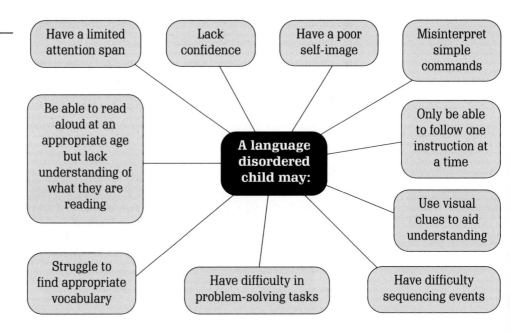

Language disorder can therefore affect other aspects of a child's learning and development. Additional factors that can affect language include medical problems such as glue-ear. This is a condition of the middle ear in which sticky mucus is formed which is unable to drain away through the eustachian tubes in the normal way. If severe and left untreated, it can lead to permanent hearing loss.

A cleft lip and palate is another medical and physical problem that can affect speech. A child born with one or both of these physical conditions will automatically be referred to a speech therapist, to ensure that the most appropriate feeding positions are established from birth.

A useful source of further reading to extend your understanding of language development is *Understanding Children's Language and Literacy* by Mukherji and O'Dea (2000).

Language delay

As with language disorder, any significant delay in language developing along the expected 'norms' is monitored, and a referral made to a speech therapist as appropriate. There are environmental, medical, social, cultural and genetic factors that can affect language development, as summarised in the spidergram below.

Figure 7.28

Factors contributing to language delay

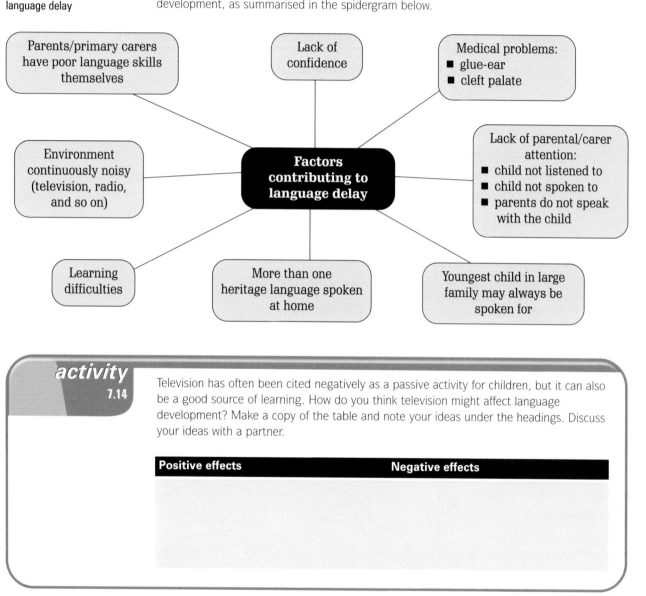

activity 7.14

Television has often been cited negatively as a passive activity for children, but it can also be a good source of learning. How do you think television might affect language development? Make a copy of the table and note your ideas under the headings. Discuss your ideas with a partner.

Positive effects	Negative effects

Language as a means of communication

Language is essential to humans in order to communicate our needs, express our feelings and extend our experiences beyond our own environment by interacting with others. These interactions enable us to enhance our thinking and learn new skills. Spoken language is our most important means of communication. It is enhanced by facial expression, tone of voice and body language. Communication is an important aspect of early years professionalism.

Link

Refer back to Unit 2, Communication and interpersonal skills in early years work.

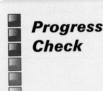

Progress Check

1   What is syntax?

2   Name two prerequisites for language.

3   Whose theory proposes that children have a language acquisition device?

4   Which theorists supported the interactionist theory of language development?

5   How many types of consonants are there?

6   What is meant by normal developmental dysfluency?

Promoting children's development

Factors affecting development

Development can be affected by any of the following:

- social and economic factors
- genetic factors
- health
- housing, environment and social circumstances
- stimulation.

An understanding of these factors will enable you to place children's growth and development within a wider social context and identify areas of concern that may require intervention. As your experience in working with children and families grows, you will note how some children's development may be compromised by one or many of the factors above and that some children will be seriously disadvantaged.

Social and economic factors

A child raised in poverty is less likely to thrive than a child who enjoys an economically stable life. It is unlikely that a family on a low income will be able to have a diet that is varied, which provides all the nutrients needed for optimum growth and healthy development. Inadequate or barely adequate household equipment, particularly with regard to safety features, can raise the possibility of accidents. Limited funds to pay for heating can mean that children are persistently unwell, particularly in winter.

Figure 7.29

Proportion of children living in households below median income

© Office for National Statistics

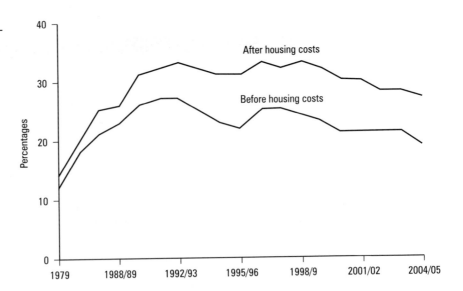

Social Policy and Welfare by Walsh *et al.* (2000) offers a useful source of further information on the affects of poverty.

Genetic factors

Genetic factors and the effects of substances crossing the placenta during pregnancy were discussed earlier in the unit, and this should have helped you understand how additional difficulties can be faced by some children and families. The development of children with an inherited or congenital condition may be generally or specifically affected and early years workers may well be involved in the assessment of their development.

Health and illness

All aspects of a child's development can be affected by illness, especially their capacity to learn and maximise their personal potential. We also know from seminal studies such as the Black Report (1980) and the Acheson Report (1998) that health and other inequalities continue to widen the gap between the health of the wealthy and the less advantaged. There are well-documented links between poor or inadequate diet and health. Poor diet and poor health may adversely affect a child's physical growth and development, as well as ability to learn. The improvement of children's health is a key target in the *Every Child Matters* agenda, and it is imperative that early years workers are familiar with the indicators of ill health, so that early interventions can be initiated and possible effects on development ameliorated.

Refer to Unit 10 for further information on the effects of health on children's development.

Housing, environment and social circumstances

Children living in poverty and disadvantaged circumstances are often accommodated in old or inadequate housing stock. Living in poor housing is linked to a higher incidence of respiratory illnesses and a greater rate of accidental injuries, both of which will affect a child's development generally, or may result in serious trauma or chronic ill health. They are also more likely to live in environments that are densely populated and polluted by traffic or industrial fumes. Lack of open spaces and clean air may limit opportunities for physical development.

Cramped living conditions are stressful to most people. The opportunities for cross-infection are greater because of the close proximity of family members. Temporary accommodation, such as bed and breakfast facilities, affects families in that they have no secure base, and the impact of this on the parents is stressful, which has a subsequent effect on the children, with older children often worrying about their parents and feeling powerless to help them.

By contrast, children who live in privileged circumstances and have parents and an extended family able to give them time in a stress-free environment often feel more settled and have fewer worries. They are more able to enjoy childhood.

Family and cultural practices also affect the development of a child. Some cultures place great emphasis on the importance of older generations and members of the extended family share in the upbringing of the children.

Stimulation

A stimulating environment facilitates greater opportunities for learning, helping the child to reach their potential. Stimulation has been shown to start in the womb and some women choose to maximise this by playing music and reading to their unborn child. However, at times parents over-stimulate their children (known as hot-housing). This can be counter-productive in that it often results in tired and irritable children who may eventually become uninterested in learning.

Developmental delay

Types of and possible causative factors

Although all children will follow the same pattern and sequence of development, some will 'hit' the normative milestones relatively on target, but other children may display one or more elements of delayed development. This may be a specific area of delay in motor or other skills, or a more global developmental delay. Developmental delay may be identified at the baby's birth if a hereditary or congenital condition is obvious, but for some children, it may not be identified until much later, and this can be a source of great stress for the family. Reasons for developmental delay are often complex and occasionally remain unknown, but certain factors are known to be implicated:

- prenatal and perinatal factors
- congenital or inherited conditions
- postnatal factors
- family and social factors.

Prenatal and perinatal factors
Development may be affected or delayed by substances which the mother ingests during pregnancy or from an illness that she contracts. Problems during or shortly after birth that result in lack of oxygen may also have a lasting effect on cognitive and motor development, as may prematurity, postmaturity and complicated deliveries.

Congenital or inherited conditions
There are many congenital, inherited or chromosomal conditions that may affect one or more areas of development.

For a full discussion, see Chapters 7 and 9 in *Good Practice in Caring for Young Children with Special Needs* by Dare and O'Donovan (2002).

Postnatal factors
Delays in development may be caused by a wide range of postnatal factors including accidental injury and trauma; the complications of infections; childhood cancers and malignant tumours. Children's physical and motor development may be affected as well by the social and emotional consequences of medical treatments and periods in hospital.

Family and social factors
It is possible for delays in emotional and social development to be observed in situations of extreme family stress and dysfunction. This type of delay may also occur when there are frequent changes of key carers in a child's earliest years, problems with positive parenting or when any type of abuse or emotional deprivation is present.

See *Good Practice in Caring for Young Children with Special Needs* by Dare and O'Donovan (2002) for a fuller description of delays in development and the associated problems. You will also find a table on page 11 that outlines the major types of additional needs that are likely to result in some form of developmental delay.

Early years workers are in a key position to identify and support children with delayed development, as well as working in partnership with parents and other professionals. An important aspect of this will be enabling the child to meet their social and educational potential by providing a welcoming and inclusive environment and ensuring that the child has access to stimulating and supportive care and activities.

Independence and life-long learning
Developmental delays of any kind will necessitate that particular attention is paid to the promotion of skills in independence and an ethos of life-long learning. Early years workers will collaborate with parents and other professionals in the multi-disciplinary team to maximise a child's independence and sense of mastery in whichever area of development is delayed. Practice will be enhanced if an anti-oppressive and anti-disablist stance is taken and if a positive and enabling attitude towards the area of delay is evident. Workers may need to act as an advocate for the child or the parent on occasions, but the emphasis should be on empowering children and parents. Life-long learning is of relevance to child, parent and practitioners, and regular professional updating should facilitate high-quality, evidence-based care.

Progress Check

1   What is the difference between genotype and phenotype?

2   Explain the difference between a genetically inherited disorder and a congenital disorder.

3   Which of the following disorders are X-linked disorders?

   a)   Cystic fibrosis

   b)   Batten's disease

   c)   Duchenne muscular dystrophy

   d)   Huntington's chorea

   e)   Haemophilia

4   How does foetal alcohol syndrome affect an infant?

5   What are the most common affects of smoking in pregnancy?

6   How can poverty have an impact on development?

Observation of Children

This unit covers the following objectives:

- Understand objectivity and how to be as objective as possible
- Be able to use a number of different observational techniques with young children
- Understand the use of observation
- Be aware of the ethics of observation.

Observation and recording of children's development is an important aspect of the role of early years practitioners. Learning the techniques of observation will, therefore, be useful to your future role as a professional.

Observation forms part of the assessment process within early years courses and is therefore also a requirement in order to obtain your qualification.

This unit will help you to understand why and how observations are carried out and introduce you to a range of techniques for observing children. You will learn how you can record your observations and how to put an observation portfolio together.

Objectivity

Figure 8.1

Reasons for observing children

- To inform future planning
- To identify good (and not so good) practice
- To gauge the success of activities or pieces of equipment
- To monitor a concern that has already been raised
- Observation is interesting!
- To help identify links between circumstances and behaviour
- To learn about individual children's needs
- To focus on each child as an individual
- **Why do we carry out observations on young children?**
- To note changes in behaviour
- To identify when adult intervention would be helpful
- To get to know a child better
- To identify any safety issues in the setting
- To assess a child's state of health
- To assess a child's progress
- To assess a child's overall development

Reasons for observing children

An **observation** may be carried out for a number of reasons:

To learn about individual children's needs

Through observation, you may identify that a particular child is reluctant to socialise with others or is not accepted by the group and is consequently on their own for much of the time. Developing strategies with the child, to encourage them to play initially alongside others and then more co-operatively, gradually helps to involve them in interactive play without adult intervention.

To note changes in behaviour

Observation is a useful means of identifying any significant change in how a child is behaving. For example, a previously happy and bright child who is suddenly very quiet and withdrawn, or possibly aggressive, should raise your concern. Taking time to observe if the behaviour is generalised or if it only occurs in isolated situations helps you develop a strategy to help the child back to their former self.

To get to know a child better

Particularly with a child new to the setting, an outline **assessment** of their stage of development helps staff understand their needs and enables them to offer an appropriate programme of care and education.

To assess a child's overall development

Assessment is routine in most settings and an initial assessment is likely to take place when a child moves from one setting to another. It helps identify the rate of progress that a child is making and enables the setting to plan an appropriate programme to meet the child's needs.

To assess a child's progress

Once an overall assessment has been made of a child, subsequent observation can be useful in identifying whether they are progressing. Areas of concern can be picked up and used as a future focus.

To assess a child's state of health

In a busy early years setting, a tired child will struggle to achieve and enjoy the facilities offered. Observation can help you monitor a situation and decide whether a child is simply tired or whether they have a medical need. Young children are usually full of energy, particularly at the start of the day, but those who have only recently given up a daytime sleep may need times for rest built into their daily programme.

To identify any safety issues in the setting

Observation can highlight areas within the setting where supervision is insufficient, or where potential hazards could arise. Observation should be used, in conjunction with reflection on past accidents or incidents, to inform decisions regarding changes in safety policy.

To identify when adult intervention would be helpful

Some children benefit from sensitive adult input into their activities. Observing adults in the nursery or classroom can help you learn when to intervene and when to hold back. As a student, you should feel able to ask (at a suitable time) why a decision was made either to intervene or to leave a child to their own devices. This will develop your understanding of using observation skills.

Refer to Unit 4, pages 124 to 125 and Unit 7, page 321, to refresh your memory of Vygotsky and Bruner.

To focus on each child as an individual

Most settings have quite high numbers of children and to observe them as a group would usually mean that the louder and more active child will figure far more centrally in the observation than the quiet child who has been unobtrusively engaged throughout the session. It is quite likely that, even with a series of such observations, the same children will be prominent and the same children will be 'missed'. This is why focusing on a child individually ensures that particular child's development can be assessed and that staff can see if they are happy within the setting.

A useful source of further reading on the importance of observation is *Closely Observed Infants* by Miller (1997). This book sets out exemplary observations, accompanied by critical discussion.

To help identify links between circumstances and behaviour

A good example of a link between circumstance and behaviour would be to observe what triggers a regular tantrum in a child. It is also the main focus of event sampling, see page 347.

Refer to Unit 2, page 52, for the antecedent behaviour in the ABC behaviour management strategy.

To inform future planning

Observation can identify aspects of developmental need that can be incorporated into future plans. For example, a child who is unable to hold a pencil satisfactorily (to meet their needs) may be disadvantaged as they move into a more formal education setting which requires regular use of pencil skills. Activities to encourage development of the finer skills in general would help such a child develop a more useful level of pencil control. Similarly, a child who has not as yet developed an understanding of the need to share can be encouraged to do so by being involved in a range of adult-supervised 'shared' activities.

To identify good (and not so good) practice

Observation can reveal examples of excellence, but it can also raise concerns regarding the practice in a setting. A manager or supervisor may use observation as part of a staff appraisal scheme.

Refer to Unit 4, for pointers on the importance of interactions with children.

Figure 8.2

What might the observer gain from studying this group of children?

To gauge the success of activities or pieces of equipment

At times certain activities may not seem to be as popular and well used as expected. This can be for many reasons: for example, the farm set may be too near to a doorway, so the animals regularly get knocked over. This might discourage children from playing with it. A simple solution could be to move the farm to a less busy area of the setting, where the children can enjoy the activity once again.

To monitor a concern that has already been raised

When a child has been identified as having a particular need, it is likely that their progress will continue to be monitored. This may be by the early years staff within the setting, or it may be by a professional from outside the setting who visits specifically for the purpose of observation and assessment of the child in a 'natural' environment.

Observation is interesting!

It is to be hoped that the majority of early years workers and students are developing a career in the field of early years because of their interest in, and love of, children. Although quite time consuming, observation offers a fascinating insight into their world. If for no other reason, you should observe the children in your care for the pure pleasure that it will bring you.

Professional Practice

- Most early years workers would claim that they use their observation skills all the time. This is probably true to an extent but, like listening, many people do not give observation their full attention.

- Close your eyes and think about the last person you spoke to before reading this. What were they wearing? What were they saying? How much detail can you remember? How much attention did you give to them? Were you fully attentive to what they were saying, or only half listening? It is likely that you were also focusing on something else at the same time.

- Translate this situation into an early years setting and think about how much you may have missed if it was a child that had only received part of your attention. How might this feel for the child? How professional would this feel to you?

Objectivity

It is important to consider our own feelings, **attitudes and values** when we carry out observations of children as these can affect **objectivity** if not accounted for.

Figure 8.3

Objective observation

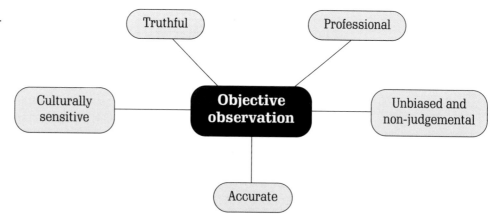

Truthful

It can be very difficult when beginning to observe children to remember that the aim is to record only what you see and hear. This needs to be done without making assumptions about the children or what you think is happening. It can be tempting to 'embroider' what appears to be a short observation where nothing much seems to be happening, but this is not acceptable practice.

Professional

It is important to make sure that the way in which you approach observations, and the way in which you record them, is professional at all times. This means ensuring that you have sought permission to undertake the observation and that you do not inconvenience others by undertaking it. The language that is used also needs to be professional and should avoid subjective descriptions or slang.

Culturally sensitive

Assumptions may be made about practices or behaviours in a cultural group that differs from ours but this must not be allowed to affect objective observations. This means that we should think carefully about the way in which we approach observations and the instruments that are used to record data. For example, Tassoni et al. (2002, page 26) note that normative developmental charts are frequently culturally biased and do not account for individual differences in child-rearing or cultural practices.

Accurate

Accuracy is always important when recording your observations, but sensitivity is also needed. For example, if you were not absolutely sure that you heard a conversation correctly and then wrote up your notes with inaccuracies, it could lead to misleading information about a child being recorded. In certain cases, accuracy may be essential: for example, if an observation was being made of a child who was thought to be displaying signs of disturbed behaviour. Accuracy is also important in terms of recording times and events, and it is good practice to ask your placement supervisor or another member of trained staff to countersign your observation. They can then confirm that you have presented an accurate observation.

Unbiased and non-judgemental

This is a very important consideration when observing children, as it can be damaging to a child to present an observation that contains value-laden or prejudicial statements. It could lead to an inaccurate picture of a child's development or needs being recorded.

---

activity 8.1

In small groups, discuss what types of **bias** or stereotypical judgements might be encountered when observing children.

Subjectivity and the effects of perception

Our individual perceptions will also be a powerful influence on how we carry out and record our observations of children. Perceptions of how a child is behaving or how well a planned activity suits the needs of a group of children may vary from practitioner to practitioner, according to how she or he views what is happening. This can be shown very well by the following illustrations.

Our perceptions are founded not only on what we 'see' but also on our values and beliefs, and, as with any other area of professional practice, our work in observing children needs to be free from bias and personal perspectives. Our perceptions and knowledge of children can sometimes stand in the way of objective observation, as it can be difficult to stop personal feelings getting in the way. We all see the world in different ways and may, due to our background and upbringing, understand things slightly differently. However, early years workers share a common set of values and principles and this includes working within an anti-discriminatory framework. By checking that our perceptions are similar to those of others, we can promote good practice.

Professional Practice

■ If you are unsure whether your perception of a child or what is happening may differ from those of other workers, ask them to check your observations for you, or observe the same situation or child with you.

Subjectivity and the effects of attitudes, values and beliefs

It is important that we do not let our personal feelings and beliefs intrude into the observations that we make of children, as this clouds objectivity and can introduce an element of bias. Lay and Dopeyra (1977) refer to this as 'sorting out "you" from what you view', but this can be easier said than done. This means that we need to have some awareness of potential prejudices and stereotypical assumptions in order to put them aside when observing.

Refer back to Unit 1 to refresh your memory of the dangers of discrimination and stereotyping.

Good practice in avoiding bias

- Be aware of your own potential for stereotyping or unintentional prejudice.
- Acknowledge that you may feel more positively about some children than others, as this may result in your paying too much or too little attention to certain aspects of their behaviour.
- Make sure that you find out about any cultural differences that might influence the objectivity of your observation.
- Be sensitive to children's social and cultural backgrounds when recording information and make sure that perceived differences in behaviour, appearance or cleanliness do not cloud your objectivity.
- Make yourself familiar with cultural differences in facial expressions and body language. Ask trained staff, who are experienced, for help in interpreting this important area of communication.
- Try to ensure that you do not replicate any gender or other biases when undertaking an observation. What you expect may be what you see, but if you are looking through biased eyes, you may not be seeing a true picture.
- Try to use an appropriate observation technique and be aware of the external factors that can influence observations.
- Discuss any worries about potential bias with your tutor or placement supervisor.

Observational techniques

Observation is only valuable if it is carried out appropriately. It is not something that can be done half-heartedly. In college, your tutors will introduce observation techniques to you and will most likely suggest that you have a practice before you start your portfolio. Many tutors will assess your first observations and offer feedback on their strengths and guidance on how they can be improved for the future.

Your tutor and qualified practitioners will give you guidance about the most suitable method to use in a given situation, and you will find that you may concentrate on one method until your confidence and skills improve. Do try to use as many methods as you can as this will help you to link theory to practice and ensure that appropriate methods are used.

Participant or non-participant observation?

Observation can be carried out whilst being involved in an activity with children (this is called **participant observation**), but this is not ideal. It is far better to observe children from a short distance (**non-participant observation**), as you can focus completely on what you are observing and are not distracted by your own involvement.

Refer to page 344 for more on participant and non-participant observation.

Practical considerations

When you are planning to observe, there are certain practical issues that need to be taken into account, as the following checklist shows:

- Always gain permission to carry out observations of a specific child.
- Agree a convenient time for observing with your supervisor.
- Be unobtrusive, avoid eye contact with the child you are observing, but remain within a range that enables you to hear their language use.
- Try not to catch the attention of the children in the setting.
- Be prepared – have pen, paper, charts, and so on, to hand.
- Know what you are aiming to achieve, set objectives – spontaneous activity, planned activity, and so on.
- Try not to be drawn into a child's activity during the observation as this will be likely to hinder your outcomes.
- Start with children who appear within the normal developmental ranges; evaluation will be easier.
- Observe for short periods initially and gradually build up the length of the observation period.
- Try out a variety of observation styles in different situations.
- Keep pen and paper handy for those 'spur of the moment' observation opportunities.
- If using a timed technique, ensure that you have easy access to a clock.
- In the event of an emergency, you will have to abandon your observation until another time.

Refer to page 357 for more detailed information about planning an observation.

> **remember**
>
> Observations should only be carried out if there are sufficient other adults present to meet safely the required adult:child ratio of the setting. Students are officially exempt from these ratios, but at times they are relied upon to be an additional adult in the supervision of a complex activity. Make sure that you inform your placement supervisor that you have a number of observations to complete and agree a mutually satisfactory time.

When and where to observe

During your training you will visit a range of settings, and each of these will offer opportunities for observation. Diploma and Certificate students are required to undertake a minimum of 800 hours assessed placement experience involving each of the following age ranges:

- 0–1 years
- 1–3 years
- 3–5 years
- 5–8 years.

In special needs settings, placement experience can include older age children too. It is accepted that at times the age ranges within some settings will differ, and the above guidelines can occasionally be adjusted slightly. You will therefore be able to have placement experience in at least four of the following settings:

- the home
- childminder
- voluntary pre-school
- statutory pre-school
- private nursery provision
- nursery school/class
- primary school
- hospital
- special needs provision.

Figure 8.4

Situations and behaviours to observe

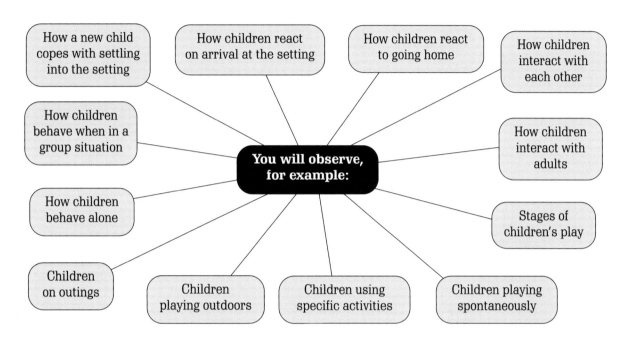

Effects of observation on adults and children

Unobtrusive observation will give a truer picture of what is really happening as both adults and children react differently if they know they are being observed.

Some adults are uncomfortable being observed by students and some parents are unhappy with their child being focused upon. This is why permission to observe is needed in advance.

Observation techniques and methods

There are many methods of observing children although there is no one particular method that is preferable to another. The aim is to select the correct method for the type of situation or behaviour that you intend to observe, and to be aware of the advantages and disadvantages of each one. The major types of techniques are listed in table 8.1, as well as the methods that are most appropriate for observing individual children or groups.

One of the first decisions to be made is whether you will observe from a distance (non-participant) or whether you will conduct your observation whilst engaged in the situation (participant observation). Both methods have advantages and disadvantages.

remember

You do not usually need to observe children interacting with an adult, unless for a specific purpose.

Table 8.1 Observation techniques for individuals and groups

Individual	Group
Written record	Target child
Target child	Sociograms
Event sampling	Movement & flow charts
Time sampling	
Movement & flow charts	
Checklist	
Sociogram	
Child study (longitudinal)	

Non participant observation

- This method is ideal for an inexperienced observer who can note down what is happening without the distraction of being involved in the activity.
- Non-participation may help the observer to be more objective.
- Non-participation means that most techniques can be used.
- You may find it difficult to take time out from planned activities or care routines to sit away from the action and undertake your observation.
- Children may not do or say what you were hoping to observe, or you may simply not be in the right position to see and hear what is of interest to you.

Participant observation

- The participant observer can give instructions to a child in order to observe the type of behaviour that is desired.
- This method may be more effective in terms of time available for observations, as less time is spent waiting for spontaneous events to happen.
- **Checklists** or tick lists are useful methods of recording behaviour as are 'post-it notes' and quick jottings
- It may be difficult to capture all that is happening if the observer is involved.
- Not all methods are suitable for participant observation, particularly if a narrative of an episode is required.
- Children may be influenced by the pressure of the situation or the presence of an unfamiliar adult, or their behaviour may be altered from a desire to please the adult observing them.

Techniques for recording information

There are many different methods of observing children; some enable the observer to record detailed information whereas with some the information is more general.

An excellent source of further reading, with examples and discussion of each of the methods mentioned below, is *A Practical Guide to Child Observation and Assessment* by Hobart and Frankel (2005).

Naturalistic observation (using a written record)

This is likely to be one of the first methods of observation that you use. It is useful as it needs no specific preparation, you simply need to be able to make a **written record**, writing down as clearly (and concisely) as you can what you are observing. It can, however, be repetitive and long-winded to write out neatly afterwards. As children are so active, you may find that with this method you miss out on recording some of what they are doing.

This method:

- is ideal when beginning to observe children
- is useful when time is short as it is usually only possible to use this method for short periods of time
- can provide 'open' data
- helps the observer to practise objectivity as the point is to record what the observer sees and hears, without interpreting (at this stage)
- gives the observer the opportunity to make a structured or unstructured observation and is ideal for capturing **snapshots** of a child's interests and abilities
- can require intensive concentration to capture details, so not suitable for lengthy observations.

The following is an example of an unstructured written observation:

> Sarah, Fliss and Abi are in the role-play corner with Megan (student). Sarah and Fliss are leaning over the cot, Megan is standing at the entrance to the role play corner and Abi is sitting at the table. Sarah says, 'I want to go shopping. Shall we take our babies out with us?' Fliss says, 'All right, can Megan come with us?' and moves to the back of the role-play corner where she pulls out the pushchair and puts her baby doll into it. Sarah walks over to Fliss and pats the baby doll on the head. She then picks up a shopping bag and hands this to Megan, saying, 'You can buy the food for dinner'. Abi is now standing at the side of the bookcase, looking at the other girls. Megan asks Abi, 'Do you want to come shopping?' and then she helps her to find another pushchair for her doll. Megan and the three girls then come out of the role play corner and Sarah and Fliss walk in front of Abi and Megan.

Movement and flow chart

These are also sometimes called 'tracking' observations and their use enables you to monitor the movements of a particular child. The simplest way to do this is to produce a rough sketch of the setting, noting where each activity is positioned and then track the child's movements, adding in the times and duration of use at each activity.

A **movement and flow chart**:

- can be helpful in matching a child's needs to the learning and play opportunities provided in a setting
- allows staff to observe a child's particular interests over a specified time period
- can produce data that are difficult to analyse unless the chart is clearly laid out
- provides 'closed' data
- limits spontaneity because the observer will need to have previously drawn a template plan of the area where the observation takes place.

In the example below, the movement and flow chart tracks Jenny's movements.

Figure 8.5

Jenny's movement and flow chart

Summary of Jenny's movements:

Jenny arrives at Little Lambs Nursery at 8.30 a.m.

8.30	She moves straight to the drawing and writing table (8.30–8.40)
8.40	Jenny moves to the dressing up clothes (8.40–8.55)
8.55	Jenny plays outside (8.55–9.15)
9.15	She returns to the dressing up clothes to change her outfit (9.15–9.20)
9.20	Jenny enters the role-play corner (9.20–9.40)
9.40	Jenny returns the dressing-up clothes to the box (9.40–9.45)
9.45	Jenny now moves to the jigsaw puzzle area (9.45–10.10)
10.10	From the puzzles Jenny moves to the book corner (10.10–10.30)
10.30	She goes outside to play again (10.30–10.50)
10.50	Jenny now returns to the jigsaw puzzles (10.50–11.00)
11.00	Jenny plays a board game (11.00–11.15)
11.15	Jenny goes to do some drawing (11.15–11.30)
11.30	Jenny joins the whole group for a story and singing (11.30–11.50)
11.50	Jenny is collected by her dad.

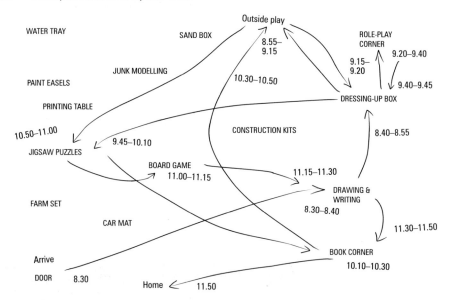

activity

8.2

Study the information in the example above. What does it tell you?

Professional Practice

■ The example observation above would be of limited use to you without further details. To be able to see if Jenny was interacting and playing as usually expected for her age group, you would need to know:

- Jenny's age
- for how much of the morning Jenny was playing alone
- whether she interacted as a pair
- whether there were times when Jenny was playing in a small group
- whether there were times when she was playing in a large group
- whether Jenny interacted with adults during the morning.

Without this information, it is hard to know whether Jenny was having as positive experience as she could have had. She clearly kept herself fully occupied, but did you notice anything about her choice of activities?

At no time did Jenny involve herself in any 'messy' activities. This may not be an issue, as she may simply not have wanted to take up those opportunities on that particular day, but if this was one of a range of similar observations it would be considered unusual. It would also have been useful to include details of how long Jenny has been at the setting. This too could be relevant in relation to how well she interacts with others and her confidence in involving herself in some activities.

The main benefit of movement and flow chart observations is to monitor a child's particular choices of activities and in reviewing the layout of activities to maximise use.

Time sampling

Time samples are used to observe a particular child at regular intervals throughout a planned period of time, usually on more than one day. This method can be especially useful if there is some concern about the child; perhaps they have suddenly become withdrawn and no longer seem to interact with other children. Your observation can help identify whether there is a major cause for concern, or whether the child's behaviour simply needs monitoring for a short while. As you time sample, you will need to be as unobtrusive as possible to ensure that you obtain a true record.

Time sampling observations can also help to identify whether activities or equipment are being under-used or inappropriately used, by observing the activity at regular intervals rather than focusing on a specific child. Time sampling can give accurate information which is easily understood, but it is a time-consuming method and takes a member of staff out of the adult:child ratio equation.

The method:

- can be used for individual children as well as groups
- collects 'open' data
- makes it easy for the observer to record the information, although clear focus on timing is needed

However,

- help from other practitioners may be needed at times, so all need to be familiar with the aims and method
- events may be 'missed' if the activity occurs outside of the pre-set timings

Event sampling

As with time sampling, event sampling may necessitate observations being carried out over several days or even longer. **Event samples** are useful when a child is displaying worrying and/or aggressive behaviour, which is having an impact on their own and others' daily experience within the setting. Event sampling is a useful means of identifying whether trigger factors initiate the unwanted behaviours in the child being observed. You record each time the behaviour occurs, how long it continues and whether the behaviour had been triggered by anyone or any specific situation. The advantage of this method is that data are clearly timed and recorded and easily understood but, as with time sampling, the method is also time consuming. It may also involve all staff in the recording of events.

Event sampling:

- is straightforward to use
- collects 'open' data
- allows observer and practitioner to identify and understand a focus of anxiety and plan an intervention
- needs a pre-prepared template and may require cooperation from others.

In particularly serious cases, the event sample observations may need to be shown to other professionals who become involved with the child's welfare. They may also visit the setting in these instances in order to observe and assess the child for themselves.

Figure 8.6

Example of an event sampling record sheet

Child's initials _____ The concern you have:					
Date	Time	Was reaction provoked?	Duration of 'incident'	Emotions/behaviour displayed	Staff observing

Target child

The **target child** method is one of the most widely used methods of observation. It was first developed by the Oxford Pre-school Research Project, led by Kathy Sylva, and was originally aimed at identifying which activities and situations helped children to develop their concentration. It is also useful in identifying aspects of socialisation in children and gives opportunities for noting their language, in particular when they initiate conversation.

- The method can be used for a variety of different purposes and time scales.
- Once the observer is familiar with the format and codes used, it is relatively straightforward to use.

■ This method can result in a narrow focus of information but is not limited to 'closed' data.

■ Spontaneous use is precluded because pre-prepared templates are needed.

The target child method involves the remembering, understanding and recording of pre-coded information. These codes are recorded in a table under the following headings:

Min	Activity record	Language record	Task code	Social code

The coding is set out minute by minute, usually for up to 10 minutes at a time. The minutes are recorded in the first column of the table.

Activity record

The activity record column is a brief comment on what is happening with the activity being used by the target child. The codes used are:

TC = target child (the child's name or initials are not used); C = child; A = adult.

Min	Activity record	Language record	Task code	Social code
1	TC & C on car mat pushing cars on road			

Social code

The codes in the social code column (who the child is with) are:

SOL = the target child is playing on their own (solitary)

PAIR = the child is with one other person, child or adult

SG = the target child is within a small group (three to five children)

LG = the target child is within a large group (six or more children).

If the target child is playing with the same activity as others, but not interacting with them in any way (parallel play) you would write one of the following codes:

PAIR/P = the target child is playing parallel to one other child

SG/P = the target child is playing parallel to a small group

LG/P = the target child is playing parallel to a large group.

If there is an adult interacting with an activity, there would be a circle drawn around the social code, for example:

Min	Activity record	Language record	Task code	Social code
1	TC & C on car mat pushing cars on road			PAIR

Task code

The entries in the task code column (what the child is doing) include the following codes:

LMM = large muscle movement

LSC = large-scale construction

SSC = small-scale construction

MAN = manipulation

SM = structured materials

PS = problem-solving

SVT = scale version toys

IG = informal games

SINP = social interaction, non-play

DB = distress behaviour.

There are many more task codes covering the complete range of actions displayed and activities enjoyed by children. Most colleges have complete lists.

Min	Activity record	Language record	Task code	Social code
1	TC & C on car mat pushing cars on road		SVT	PAIR

Language record

To record language (what the child is saying), you would simply write: TC>C if the target child was speaking to another child, or TC>A if they were speaking to an adult.

Min	Activity record	Language record	Task code	Social code
1	TC & C on car mat pushing cars on road	TC>CSVT 'That my car' TC> 'brmm brmm' TC>C 'Mine!'	SVT	PAIR
2	3 Cs now playing	All Cs > 'brumm brmm'	SVT	SG
3	A joins them on mat	A> 'What a lot of cars' TC>A 'Mine a red car'	SVT	SG

The target child method can be useful for 'at a glance' monitoring of a child's social development, because a quick glance at the social codes will indicate whether the child is mostly playing with others or alone. This information, together with the child's age, indicates whether they are following the social 'norms'.

Professional Practice

■ The two target child observations A and B, which follow, are good examples of how the intervention of an adult has enabled a child to develop further their understanding of the activity they are using. The sensitive input from the adult in the first example has raised the achievement of the child from what they could achieve alone, to what had been their potential to achieve. This fits in with Vygotsky's concept of the ZPD.

Figure 8.7

Target child observation A

Min	Activity record	Language record	Task code	Social code
1	Dries hands & cooks tea	TC> 'All dry. Nice & dry;	DA PRE	SOL
2	Lays table, matching coloured cups, saucers etc. C arrives & sits at table. TC serves tea	TC> 'Blue… & a blue. Green… & a green', etc.	PRE PRE	SOL PAIR/P
3	Eats tea	TC> 'Yummy, Nice tea – Sausage'	PRE	Pair/P
4	Crying child arrives C stops crying	TC>C 'Don't cry Why you cry? I'm a mummy. Don't cry. Want a sausage?' TC> 'Eat your sausage'	SINP PRE " "	PAIR " " "
5	TC washes up TC leaves home C & goes to construction table Tries to build tower (Duplo) – It is top heavy!		PRE SSC	SOL SOL
6	" " "		"	"
7	" " " Tower won't stand A joins her TC leans tower against box & grins	A>TC 'That's a tall tower' TC>A 'It falling down. It keep falling down' TC>A 'How can you stop it falling?' TC>A 'Don't know' TC>A 'You hold it' A>TC 'I could but how will you manage when I go to get the milk?'	" SSC	" PAIR
8	TC picks up a brick & considers	A>TC 'Could you use any of these larger bricks to help you?'	SSC	PAIR
9	Adds 2 bricks to bottom of tower TC went on to make two more towers	TC>A 'I can stand it. I can stand it.' A>TC 'Well done. That was a really good idea.'	SSC	PAIR

Figure 8.8

Target child observation B

Min	Activity record	Language record	Task code	Social code
1	Duplo – clipping yellow bricks together, then green, etc.	TC> naming the colours	SSC	SG/P
2	" " "		"	"
3	Lines bricks up in rows of 6	TC> 1 2 3 4 5 6	SSC	SG/P
4	" " "		"	"
5/6	Builds tower of single bricks, It does not balance. TC adds a larger base to tower		SSC	SG/P
7	TC builds another tower & stands the 2 towers next to each other.	TC> 'My tower won't fall'	SSC	SG/P
8	Added large bricks to the tops of towers. They remained standing TC very proud of her achievement		SSC	SG/P

Checklists

Assessments of children are a routine part of most early years settings and involve the regular observation of children to ascertain what they are currently able to achieve. An example of these assessment programmes is the Sound Learning Pre-school Record System. It includes assessment records for all ages of pre-school children and it suggests that the assessments can be completed on monthly, three-monthly or termly bases. However, it must be noted that reliance on checklists alone tends to promote a 'deficit' model of what children cannot achieve, rather than identifying what they can.

A checklist:

- is relatively simple and quick to use
- can be used for one child or adapted to cover or compare several children
- can be used on subsequent occasions, as long as the date of each observation is clearly recorded
- can result in a deficit model as it only records what child can do, not what they might be near to achieving with support or time
- requires a pre-prepared template.

Figure 8.9

3–36 month development

3–36 MONTH DEVELOPMENT RECORDS	Date of assessment						
Name	Colour code						

PHYSICAL DEVELOPMENT (1)		R	S	U
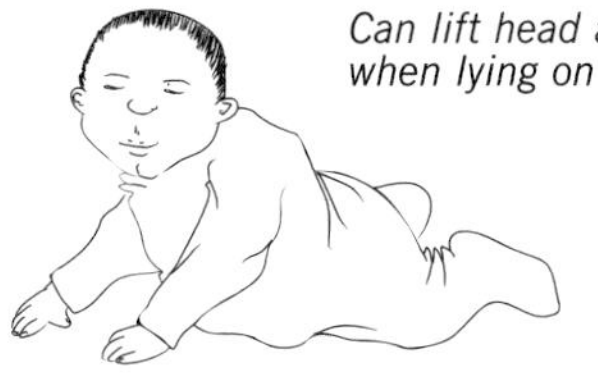 *Can lift head and shoulders when lying on front.*	Waves arms and kicks legs vigorously			
	Has little or no head lag when pulled to sit			
	Can lift head and shoulders when lying on front			
	Sits with firm back when supported			
	Can hold head steady when supported			
	Can hold head steady when upright			
When held standing, takes weight on feet and bounces up and down				
Can roll from front to back				
Can roll from back to front				
Can sit without support				
While sitting can reach forward for a toy without falling over				
Moves around slowly by crawling or bottom shuffling				
Moves around rapidly by crawling or bottom shuffling				
Can pull self to standing position using furniture				
Can get from a lying down to a sitting position				
Walks around room holding onto furniture				
 *Walks well alone.*	Stands alone			
	Walks with adult help			
	Crawls up stairs			
	Walks a few steps alone			
	Walks across room when held by one hand			
	Without help gets up off floor and stands alone			
	Walks pushing large wheeled toys			
	Can climb onto a low chair or step and sit down			
	Walks well alone			

COMMENTS

Key to code:
R – Rarely
S – Sometimes
U – Usually

For older children within the Foundation Stage, it requires the use of:

E = emerging   C = consolidating

W = working on   A = achieved.

Figure 8.10

Older children development record

LEARNING AREA RECORD		Communication, Language and Literacy (1)			
Name _____		Assessment date			
D.O.B. _____		Colour code			

	E	W	C	A
Enjoys listening to stories, songs, rhymes and conversation between others				
Incorporates elements of what he/she has seen and heard into her/his everyday play and learning experiences				
Enjoys participating in conversations, sharing experience and ideas with others				
'Talks' to self during play and during imaginative play with figures or puppets				
'Talks' to miniature figures, or puppets, recreating conversations and experiences				
Recreates conversations and recounts experiences during imaginative and role play				
Experiments with mark making equipment such as pens, pencils, crayons, brushes, sponges, fingers, sticks				
Incorporates shapes, symbols and letters in his/her free writing				
ELG: is able to enjoy listening to and using spoken and written language, and readily turns to it in play and learning				
Explores sounds in a variety of ways such as: sounds in the environment				
sounds made by everyday objects				
sounds and words made by voices				
Responds to a range of sounds by: imitating				
identifying their source				
linking to make sound patterns				
Recreates words she/he hears and incorporates in own language usage				
Makes up new nonsense words e.g. rhyming nonsense words 'cap, hap, dap, zap'				
Makes observations such as 'that sounds like', 'that sounds the same as'				
Sounds out familiar letters in a simple text				
Sounds out familiar words in simple text				
ELG: Explores and experiments with sounds, words, text				

COMMENTS

Key to code:
E – Emergency
W – Working on
C – Consolidating
A – Achieved

Many early years settings, and some local authorities, have developed their own style of recording sheets. For the youngest children, these may reflect the use of the Birth to Three Matters framework; the Foundation Stage Profile may be used for the older children. Ask your current setting what they use.

Sociograms
A **sociogram** gives an 'at a glance' record of the social behaviour of a group of children. It can be used to identify friendship groups and secure pair-relationships and also for establishing when a child lacks friends within the setting. The observers should always be aware how quickly friendship groups change, particularly with children under the age of five, and, for this reason, the method has limited use. The benefit of identifying a relationship concern for a particular child is that strategies can be established to help them to integrate further.

A sociogram:

■ is quite an easy technique to use

■ can be used for looking at a group of children

■ captures a relative 'moment in time' rather than a long-term perspective

■ requires skilful interpretation.

Refer to Unit 9, page 390, for an example of a sociogram.

Longitudinal studies
In a **longitudinal study**, the observation is carried out at intervals over a considerable length of time. You will most likely use this method for a baby or child study. Such studies need written parental permission before the study starts and involve regular visiting and observing of the child's development and progress over a pre-set period. A baby study may, for example, involve weekly visits for three months whereas a child study is likely to require fortnightly visits for six months or more. Longitudinal studies should be approached in an objective manner, and it is important to ensure the confidentiality of the family.

The longitudinal approach will enable you to:

■ get to know the child and the impact of their family life on their development

■ understand the needs of the child more fully

■ identify and record changes in the child's development

■ comment on each area of development and how the rates of development vary

■ chart the child's development according to a chosen screening process.

The drawbacks of longitudinal studies can be that:

■ visits to a child's home can sometimes feel intrusive

■ family holidays, illness and visitors can sometimes affect your planning

■ objective observations are not always welcomed by the parents

■ a house move by the family may end your study prematurely.

A longitudinal study of a child will benefit from the inclusion of other observation methods too.

Refer to the section on longitudinal studies in Chapter 9 for more information as to what elements are usually expected in a longitudinal baby or child study.

See *A Practical Guide to Child Observation and Assessment* by Hobart and Frankel (1999) for further details of what is expected in a child or baby study.

Comparison of methods

Table 8.2 Comparison of methods

Method	Benefits
Written records ■ Structured ■ Unstructured ■ Snapshots ■ Individual child or baby studies ■ Open data	■ Simple to use ■ More suitable for one child ■ Short time span but can be repeated sequentially ■ Can provide detailed information about individual
Movement and flow charts (tracking) ■ Closed data	■ Can be used to match interest to provision ■ Gives a full picture of child's movements or interest ■ Clearer data if used with one child
Time sampling ■ Open data	■ Can be used for single child or group ■ Pre-set form allows easy collection of data ■ Longer recordings can be made
Event sampling ■ Open data	■ Simple to use ■ Can identify area of concern ■ Best used with individual children
Target child ■ Mostly open data	■ Simple to use when familiar with method ■ Can be used with one or more children ■ Allows observation over longer periods
Checklists ■ Closed data	■ Easy to use with one or more children ■ Can be used to compare children ■ Can be repeated at intervals
Sociograms ■ Closed data	■ Simple to use ■ Can be used with group of children

Limitations of methods

There will, of course, be limitations to any of the methods mentioned, and some of these have already been highlighted. There is no one ideal method for any situation and it is important to be aware of the differences between the methods and the advantages and disadvantages of each one. Table 8.3 summarises the limitations of each method

Table 8.3 Limitations of each method

Method	Limitations
Written records	■ Difficult to use for long periods of time ■ Intense concentration needed to 'capture' all the data ■ Notes need to be written up at the time or shortly afterwards
Movement and flow charts	■ Spontaneous use limited ■ Clear recording necessary or data can be difficult to interpret
Time sampling	■ Help from other practitioners may be needed ■ Events may be missed if they occur outside the time frame
Event sampling	■ Requires a pre-prepared template and understanding of coding categories ■ Help of other practitioners may be needed
Target child	■ Difficult to use spontaneously ■ Requires a pre-prepared template and understanding of coding categories ■ Help of other practitioners may be needed
Checklists	■ Do not allow effort or potential to be noted ■ Can result in deficit model ■ Only skills observed are assessed and much may be missed ■ Pre-prepared template needed
Sociograms	■ Capture a limited moment in time ■ Can be difficult to interpret
Longitudinal studies	■ Require careful planning of visits ■ Family may find it intrusive or may move away ■ Notes must be written up after each visit or relevant data may be forgotten

Planning the observation

Before beginning to observe babies or children, it is useful to plan what you will be doing.

Permissions

Making observations involves gaining formal permission from the parents and the person in charge of the setting and to carry out observations without permission would be an infringement of rights. Permission should preferably be given in writing and stored securely. You also need to re-check on the day of the observation that your supervisor is willing for you to undertake it. Check whether your setting has a policy for observing children and ensure that you adhere to it closely.

Preparation of documentation

Before starting to observe, it is wise to identify your aims and objectives for the observation. This will help you to focus effectively and use your time wisely. Make sure that you have the equipment that you need as some methods require pre-prepared templates. Always have a small notebook or post-it notes and a pen or pencil in order to capture spontaneous snapshots.

See Chapter 2 in *How to Observe Children* by Sheila Riddall-Leech (2005) for further information and guidance on aims and objectives. She also provides clear examples of how observations may be presented or set out.

Decision about method, activity, child

You will be able to ask your tutor and trained staff about the most suitable methods to use and which children are the most suitable to use as the focus of an observation. This will also be influenced by:

- areas of development to be focused on – are you going to look at a child's overall abilities or focus on one area, such as fine motor skills?

- required number or types of observations needed to meet course requirements – you will be required to use a variety of techniques covering children of different ages

- the individual child – trained staff may suggest a suitable child or children to use for an observation, or they may indicate which children should be avoided for personal reasons. This could be due to a sensitive family situation or because the child is unwell or tired

- timing of the observation – this needs to be thought about and negotiated so that you are not asking to be spared at a busy time of day. Also remember that small babies will need rest and sleep periods, so observations need to fit in with these. Neither babies or older children will respond as positively when they are tired as when they are rested and alert.

What to observe?

This links closely to the aims and objectives of your observation and may be dictated by requirements of your course, or your personal interests. You may find it useful to use a framework such as the Birth to Three Matters framework to guide your choice of activities to observe, as this framework is not underpinned by a linear model of development. Alternatively, you may be asked by the staff in a setting to observe a child undertaking a particular activity or displaying certain behaviour.

How to present your observation?

It is essential that your observations are presented in a clear and coherent manner and you may be expected to use an agreed format for your documentation. Most observations will have a front or title page which outlines where the observation is taking place; who is involved; and the aims and objectives. The figure below shows an excellent template for a first page.

Figure 8.11

Pro forma

Observation skills	Start	Midway	End
Ability to evalute			
Ability to negotiate time to observe			
Ability to note detail			
Ability to plan			
Ability to take notes and record information			
Communication skills			
Confidence to make a start			
Good interpersonal skills			
Knowledge of child development			
Knowledge of observation techniques			
Listening skills			
Maturity			
Objectivity			
Patience			
Sensitivity			
Time management skills			
Understanding of aims			
Unobtrusiveness			

Figure 8.12

Format of an observation

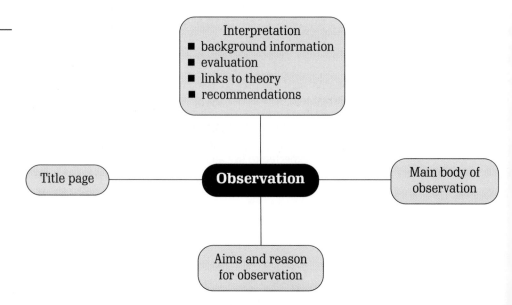

Personal learning

Aims and reason for observation

It is important to have a clearly stated aim for your observation and this will usually be to look at a particular aspect of a child's development or behaviour. Other focuses of observation may be on a child's health or additional needs or part of the Birth to Three Matters framework or the Foundation Stage Curriculum. Your reason (sometimes called a rationale) for undertaking the observation also needs to be clearly stated, as both will help you to provide a coherent evaluation and interpretation.

Interpretation

The write-up of the main body of the observation, using whatever method you selected, needs to be followed by a careful and sensitive interpretation, and this is a skill that you will develop with experience. You may wish to divide your interpretation into several parts:

- Background information – this gives you the opportunity to put the observation in context and you could briefly mention any factors that may have affected the child or the process of observation.

- Evaluation and assessment – Hobart and Frankel (1999) suggest that you look back at the aim and reason for observation and anchor your evaluation firmly in this. Try to use objective language and avoid assumptions, commenting only on what you saw and heard. It is also essential to avoid writing any comments that could be interpreted as discriminatory or stereotypical. You should evaluate and comment on the area of development that you chose to observe, making reference to appropriate theory but not to other workers' opinions.

Links to theory

These may be woven into the body of your evaluation or written as a separate section. Whichever method you adopt, it is expected that you will refer to a range of normative milestones of development and information from appropriate textbooks. These should be correctly referenced and should help you to compare the child's development or behaviour to accepted norms.

Recommendations

You may find it difficult to make recommendations when you undertake your first evaluations, but, as your experience and confidence grow, you will be able to show your understanding of the process of observation.

Refer back to 'Reasons for observing children' on page 337 and think about how you might link these reasons to making recommendations.

Personal learning – reflection on what you have learnt from the process of observation and interpretation is a valuable aspect of professional practice. Questions that you might ask yourself to help this process include:

- Did I choose the right method?
- If I were to repeat this observation, would I do anything differently?
- What did I do well and what might I want to improve upon?
- What did I learn about this child and how did theory link to what I observed?
- How could I improve my practice based on what I have observed?

Using the example below, write out possible aims and a rationale for this observation and then outline what factors you might include in an evaluation of this visit.

A visit to a child as part of an ongoing child study

Date _____

Type of visit: General visit to observe how JM has recovered after her recent illness

JM was having her lunch but ate little of what was put in front of her. She ate a quarter of an egg sandwich, but left a banana and small yoghurt. She also had a drink of diluted fruit juice. She smiled when she saw me but remained on her mother's lap. I asked her mother how JM was feeling now that her recent illness has resolved and she reported that she is still 'not quite her old self'.

After washing her hands (which she can now do quite well by herself), JM played with her doll's house. She busied herself putting the people to bed, and then getting them up again to have their breakfast. She talked to herself all the time in a monologue; most I could understand, but at other times she was not coherent. JM showed understanding of the roles of family members and where domestic events occur, e.g. washing up in the kitchen, getting dressed in the bedroom, adults dressing the children, etc. She played like this for almost 20 minutes.

I then asked JM if she would like me to read her a story, but she said, 'No, my mummy will read a story for me before bed time'. JM's speech is now becoming clearer, and I was able to understand most of what she was saying to me, although I could see some change in her behaviour towards me since I last saw her but this was before her illness. JM's grandparents arrived at this point and I felt that it was appropriate for me to leave then. On previous visits JM gave me a hug, but today she clung to her mother and then waved me goodbye. As I left, it was clear that there was a change in JM's behaviour since the last time I saw her, and I think that this may have been linked to her illness. Next time I visit, I plan to ask her mother whether she showed any other signs of reaction to being ill, other than the clingingness that I observed today.

Depending on the age of the child being studied, you would be able to comment on how well they are developing according to the developmental 'norms', making specific comments regarding how recent illness may have affected her social and emotional development, language use in her small-world play and her reaction to you on this occasion.

Recording observations and preparing a portfolio

You may be asked to set out your observations as a separate portfolio, or you may be required to submit them as part of your professional practice portfolio. Whichever way you will be presenting your observations, it is likely that you will be asked to make comparisons between the observations you make, noting similarities and differences between the ages of the children in similar situations.

This should consolidate your understanding of how children develop at different rates across all the areas of development, while still remaining within 'normal' boundaries. It will also help you see the benefits of the developmental norm charts, and how at times they can appear misleading, if used simply as a snapshot of an individual child.

Your portfolio will need to include a chart recording the dates, times and outline details of each observation you make, which would usually cross-reference to a matrix. This will enable both you and your tutors to see at a glance that your observations have included children of all age ranges and placement settings experienced during your training. If the majority of your observations are part of your professional practice portfolio, you will still need to 'signpost' your evidence in the same way.

It is helpful if you give all observations a number. This helps with cross-referencing and ensures that you and your tutors are referring to the same observation during any discussion.

An 'at a glance' matrix

A matrix is often used to give an 'at a glance' reference to your observations. This helps to ensure that you do not inadvertently miss out any one age range or placement setting, causing you difficulty in completing your portfolio at the end of your course. Alternatively, you may want to include a separate matrix for each part of your professional practice portfolio.

	Home setting	Childminder	Voluntary pre-school	Statutory pre-school	Private nursery setting	Nursery school/class	Primary school	Hospital	Special needs setting
0–1 year									
1–2 years									
2–4 years									
4–8 years									

Figure 8.13

An 'at a glance' matrix

Link

Refer to Unit 6 to check the range of settings that are suitable for professional practice experience.

Figure 8.14

Example of a record of observations

An example of how you could be asked to record your observations in numerical order is shown below. It shows the date, age and gender of the child you have observed, together with the setting details (for example, day nursery – painting activity) and the method of observation used. A chart like this can be used to ensure that you have used a range of observation methods and observed a range of different activities and can be used as a contents page for your observation file.

Observation	Date	Age of child	Gender of child	Setting details	Method of observation
1	9.06.06	3.6	M	Day nursery – construction	Target child
2	16.06.06	4.1	M	Day nursery – painting	Time sampling
3	23.06.06	3.9	F	Day nursery – clearing up	Target child
4	23.06.06	3.7	F	Day nursery – role-play area	Written record
5	6.07.06	3.6	M	Day nursery – painting	Target child
6	13.07.06	4.2	F	Day nursery – in general	Movement and flow chart
7	20.07.06	4.2	F	Day nursery – water play	Target child

Figure 8.15

Matrix of development

Area of development observed	Age			
	0–1 years	1–2 years	2–4 years	4–8 years
Gross motor skills Fine motor skills Spatial awareness Simple co-operative play				

Figure 8.16

Matrix of activities

Activity area observed	Age			
	0–1 years	1–2 years	2–4 years	4–8 years
Threading Pencil skills Shared storytime Small scale construction Emergent writing Role play				

An accessible text with explanations of each observation method and plenty of relevant examples is *A Practical Guide to Child Observation and Assessment* by Hobart and Frankel (1999).

Use of observation

One very important aspect of observing children is the use that is made of what has been observed and with whom the information is likely to be shared. On a personal basis, you may feel at first that the most important use of the observations is to fulfil your course requirements, but their use goes far beyond this aspect.

Professional Practice

■ Remember that observing children is an important way in which you can identify and meet their needs.

 Link

Refer to Chapter 5 to remind yourself of how children's individual needs are identified and met across a range of age groups.

As you gain experience in working with babies and children of different ages and have the opportunity to work alongside skilled practitioners, you will observe how children react to routine care and learning activities. You should share the findings of a child's observation with his or her key worker and take the opportunity to discuss the findings and implications. Your observations play an important part in planning care, and may even contribute to the identification of a child in need. The results of observations will almost certainly be shared with parents as part of an ongoing process of **sharing information**, and sensitivity needs to be shown in how information is recorded and reported.

See Chapter 5 of *Observing Children: A Practical Guide* by Sharman et al. (2004), for a comprehensive discussion of sharing information from observations and the assessment process in general

Reporting concerns from observations

Findings from observations will occasionally be shared with other professionals and can contribute to multi-disciplinary care planning. Students may occasionally be asked to make an observation of a child who is thought to be at risk and, in these circumstances; the observation may be used as part of the safeguarding procedures. If, during the course of any observation, you identify something that concerns you or that you think may identify a child protection issue, you must report it to your supervisor immediately. It may be that your concerns can be allayed, but you may have been instrumental in identifying a vulnerable child.

Refer to Unit 3 to remind yourself of the procedures to be followed when child abuse is suspected.

Assessment

Assessment is an integral part of the planning cycle and all school age children will be regularly assessed as part of the Standard Assessment Tasks (SATs) process. Formal assessment starts with the Foundation Stage Profile, and this is a statutory assessment undertaken at the end of the Foundation Stage. It is based on the Early Learning Goals but the aim is to record what a child can do, rather than highlight deficits. It also provides a baseline assessment for the child's transfer to Key Stage 1. SATs are used as assessment tools at the end of each Key Stage of the National Curriculum and should provide an accurate picture of a child's ability.

Refer to Unit 4, page 155, to learn more about the links between assessment and the curriculum.

Ethics of observation

Protocols

Like any other area of childcare practice, the observation of children needs to be undertaken ethically and in line with any protocols that your college or setting may have. Your behaviour when you are in a setting, whether you are observing children or not, needs to conform to the highest standards as you are there as a representative of your college or course provider. You are also working with a potentially vulnerable client group, and you need to act in a child's best interests at all times.

Confidentiality

It should go without saying that confidentiality is of prime importance when undertaking observations. The information that you derive from observing children should only be shared on a professional basis with those people who 'need to know', and all observations should be carefully and securely stored. Children and practitioners should not be identified by name, neither should the setting in which they are being observed. One of the few occasions when confidentiality needs to be broken is in the case of suspected or actual child abuse. You may be asked to discuss your observations with your tutor, but you will not be expected to refer to children or settings by name.

Professional Practice

- Remember never to discuss children, parents, staff or settings in public places or disclose information to friends or family.

Rights

Observing children also raises issues of rights: the right of a parent not to have their child observed by students or the right of a child not to participate. This area needs to be approached with sensitivity and your supervisor should advise you of any child that it would be better not to use for your observations. If you are at all unsure, ask before starting your observation.

Professional Practice

- Always have written permission from the parent or carer to undertake an observation.
- Ask permission from the setting and comply with any policies or protocols.
- Consult staff if you sense that a child is not happy with the observation process – even young infants can show their unwillingness to participate.
- Write your observation in a professional manner and ensure that you respect children's and parent's rights at all times.
- Store your observations securely and ensure that you do not disclose the names of children, settings or staff.
- Ensure that you behave in an ethical and professional manner at all times.

Progress Check

1. What are the benefits of carrying out observations?
2. What is an assessment programme?
3. What is non-participant observation?
4. List as many points as you can from the checklist for observing children.
5. Give five examples of what you could observe.
6. What is naturalistic observation?
7. What is the difference between time sampling and event sampling?
8. When would you use a longitudinal observation method?
9. What are the main factors in interpreting your observations?
10. How can you link theory to practice?
11. Why is it important to comply with a setting's policy on observations?
12. Why should information be kept confidential?
13. What circumstances demand that confidentiality should be broken?
14. How would you respond to a parent who does not want their child to be observed?
15. List the professionals with whom you might share the information from an observation.

UNIT 9

Research Methodology for Early Years

This unit covers the following objectives:

- Recognise the purpose and role of research within early years
- Understand the research methodology relevant to early years
- Gather, present and examine research information
- Recognise the implications and ethical issues related to using research in early years services.

Research skills are important to all courses of study, particularly at level 3 and above. To achieve a BTEC National qualification in Early Years your research skills will need to be well developed, as each unit that you study will require an element of personal enquiry, and many will demand considerable levels of independent research and study.

This unit will help you to understand the research process, by enabling you to gain the practical, written and analytical skills that are required, and by helping you to understand how research has an impact on the professional practice of an early years worker.

You will learn how to describe and evaluate a range of relevant research methods, use and present statistics, and understand the purpose and role of research and the implications and ethical issues related to doing research.

Purpose and role of research

Research plays an important part in the development of early years standards and provision. It enables comparisons to be made and needs to be identified. In considering the purpose of research in its more general sense, it is useful to think of research that has been undertaken in recent years, and then more specifically, in the field of early years health, care and education. Identifying research and evaluating its aims, its relevance and its outcomes will help you to focus on its necessity.

As you progress through the course, you will need to make reference to how thinking and practice in the field of early years has been improved due to the impact of research outcomes. An example of how research has contributed to the improvement of practice in early years is the study of the care of children in hospital. During the 1950s and 1960s, James and Joyce Robertson (both child psychiatrists) observed and filmed children during separation from their primary carer (usually their mothers) during hospital stays and residential care. They identified a pattern of distress which raised concern about the long-term effects such separations could have on the children. In 1959, the Platt Report (initiated by the UK government) set out the welfare needs of children in hospital and as a result the National Association for the Welfare of Children in Hospital (NAWCH) was established (now known as Action for Sick Children, ASC). The outcomes of the Robertsons' research, together with the Platt Report, resulted in parents being encouraged to accompany their children when receiving hospital treatment.

Purpose

Research can be used for many purposes, including to:

- identify a need
- provide further knowledge
- highlight gaps in provision
- obtain feedback on standards
- see what is happening currently
- find out why something is happening
- plan for future development.

Role

Its role can be said to be to:

- confirm policy or practice
- extend knowledge
- improve practice
- allow progress to be monitored
- examine topics of contemporary research.

activity
9.1

What examples of research can you think of? Copy the table below and list as many as you can. Examples have been given to get you started.

Child health	Early years care	Education	Behaviour
Immunisation Genetics	Sudden Infant Death syndrome	Head Start EEL project	Relationships Attachment

activity
9.2

Carefully read through at least one piece of research, and answer the questions.

1. What was the main aim of the research? Was the aim met?
2. Who was carrying out the research? Was this significant?
3. Did the research outcomes identify a need or a gap in current practice or provision?
4. Did it identify what was currently happening? Why?
5. Have the research outcomes enabled feedback on a current situation?
6. Will the research be likely to have an impact on future planning?
7. Did the research involve policy-making?
8. Will the research outcomes extend knowledge? If yes, for who?
9. Will the research outcomes improve practice?
10. Is the research of a contemporary nature?

When considering the aim of a piece of research, the question 'Has it been achieved?' should be considered. If a hypothesis was explored, was it supported or not? Was the hypothesis single- or open-ended?

 Link   Refer to page 370 for an explanation of 'hypothesis'.

When looking at who was responsible for the research, issues of objectivity need to be considered. For example, the managing director of a chain of day nurseries may not be the ideal person to carry out objective research into provision offered within the nursery chain.

How do you think objectivity could be assured?

If research outcomes had identified a need, or noted a gap in what is happening or being provided at the time of the research, consider whether the outcomes are likely to lead to the need being met, or the gap being filled.

Have any questions raised through the research been answered? For example:

- Who was responsible for …?
- Why was …?
- When should …?
- What is the purpose of …?

Has feedback to (or from) the participants or setting(s) included in the research been incorporated?

How relevant was this?

In what ways would the research be likely to have an impact on future planning? For example:

- Did the outcomes identify the need for immediate improvements?
- Were any long-term improvements or projects identified?

Think back to the reference made earlier to the impact of research on children in hospital. In what way was any policy involvement relevant to the research outcomes?

- Did policies need rewriting?
- Did 'ownership' of policies need to be reviewed?
- How widely were the policies distributed?

Other questions to ask yourself might include:

- Who will benefit from the research?
- Will they benefit through extended knowledge?
- Will they benefit by an improved service or provision?
- How will the research outcomes link in with contemporary issues and opinion?

Professional Practice

- If you take a more evaluative approach to reading the summary or outcomes of a piece of research, you will understand the research more fully.

Research methodology

Research is the systematic investigation of a topic for a purpose, using orderly and scientific methods. An analysis of the outcomes of research can lead to the development of new ideas and improved practice.

Types of research

Methods of research vary considerably and you need to choose the method most suitable for your current assignment task or personal enquiry (for example if you undertake Unit 20 Early Years Project). Research methods can be divided into two types: **primary research** and **secondary research**.

Primary and secondary research

The significant difference between primary and secondary research is that:

■ primary research is research you have carried out yourself

■ secondary research is the use of material researched and presented by others.

In general assignment work, you will almost always use more secondary sources than primary sources, as you explore material produced by others to support your written work, interpreting (clarifying and explaining) your findings and analysing (evaluating) their relevance.

Primary research is needed, and is a mandatory requirement, in Unit 20 (Early Years Project) and in other specified assignment briefs such as the integrated vocational assignment. For example, a practical activity that could be linked to Unit 13 (Developmental Psychology) may ask you to replicate Piaget's conservation experiments within your current placement, presenting and evaluating the outcomes with reference to Piaget and his subsequent critics.

Refer to Unit 7, page 319, for an explanation of Piaget's conservation experiments.

Table 9.1 Examples of primary and secondary research methods

Primary	Secondary
Interviews	Literature searches
Questionnaires	Media analysis
Action research	Technology based research
Observation	Case studies
Case studies	Statistical analysis
Experiments	

Quantitative and qualitative research

Research can be either quantitative or qualitative:

■ **quantitative research** produces results which can be expressed using numbers or statistics, exploring the extent to which something happens;

■ **qualitative research** explores individual viewpoints which are not so easily measured. In contrast to quantitative research, qualitative researchers wish to gain an understanding of their topic rather than make an analysis of statistics.

At times, a piece of research can involve both approaches.

In all research, the quality of the information you receive is directly linked to the questions you ask. Unless your questions are well thought out, the resulting data will not be of any use to you. The wording of questions needs to be carefully thought through.

Refer to page 373 for more about questions in research.

Longitudinal, cross-sectional and cross-cultural studies

Research can include longitudinal, cross-sectional or cross-cultural studies:

■ a longitudinal study is a study carried out over a given length of time, following the progress of something or someone (for example, a child's development);

■ a cross-sectional study takes a 'slice' (a cross-section) of its target group and its overall findings are assumed to be typical of the whole group;

■ in a cross-cultural piece of research, the researcher would decide on the main focus of their research and then apply it to a range of cultures. This could be confined to a single community or could be applied across a range of communities.

Refer back to page 365 and read the section entitled 'Purpose and role of research' before you do activity 9.3.

activity
9.3

Explore a range of research studies, either past or contemporary (current).

1   Make notes on what each study was about.
2   Place the studies under the headings of longitudinal, cross-sectional and cross-cultural.
3   What was the main purpose of each study?
4   Do you think the type of study used was the best option for the purpose?
5   Would an alternative approach have been possible?

Bias and objectivity

In all research, objectivity (an impartial viewpoint) is important. Personal opinion, bias or prejudice can influence both the process of research and the interpretation of the results. Maintaining objectivity will ensure that your research is 'value-free'. This is not always easy. The results of research will not always be what you expect, and it is important that you accept the outcomes of the research. Carrying out an honest analysis of the outcomes and producing an accurate report ensure that your research is as objective as possible.

Subjective research outcomes (a viewpoint influenced by your own opinions) will be of little value to either you or anyone else.

Forming a hypothesis, an issue or research question

In any piece of research, the overall aim needs to be made clear. This will usually be in the form of:

- a research issue – a statement of fact or a concern that could be explored by the researcher

- a research question – when the researcher wishes to find out a specific answer

- a hypothesis – a statement, usually written in the form of a prediction, which the researcher sets out to test.

Forming a hypothesis is a requirement of Unit 20 (Early Years Project). Your hypothesis will need to be both achievable and identifiable.

Types of hypothesis

A hypothesis can be either:

- single-ended – for example 'Girls read more than boys' is a single-ended hypothesis because it suggests which way the outcome of the enquiry is likely to be and it can be shown to be either right or wrong

- open-ended – for example 'Day care affects children's social skills' is an open-ended hypothesis; it simply suggests that one factor (day care) will affect another (children's social skills) and does not predict the direction of the outcome by, for example, saying that day care improves children's social skills.

A research question or issue can sometimes give a clearer aim for you to work towards, but setting a hypothesis is often more interesting and thought-provoking.

The research process

The research process can be summarised as follows:

- Research has a purpose: to inform and improve practice.
- Research enables society to develop new ideas based on enquiry.
- Research may involve a new line of enquiry (primary research method).
- A previous piece of research may be referred to (secondary research method).
- The results of research may be measurable (quantitative research).

- Research may simply give insight into a subject (qualitative research).
- Research can be used to compare, to explore a theory or to identify change.
- Research needs a specific focus, in the form of a hypothesis, an issue or a question.

Link

Refer to page 365, and read the section 'Purpose and role of research' before you do activity 9.4.

activity 9.4

Explore the outcomes of a piece of research carried out during your lifetime. You may find it useful to search the internet for options.

1 What was its purpose?
2 What primary research methods were used?
3 What secondary sources were referred to?
4 Was the research quantitative or qualitative?
5 What was the hypothesis?
6 Was it supported or by the research findings?
7 In what ways was objectivity on the part of the research team important?

Data collection – primary sources

Primary research involves carrying out a new line of enquiry. The interview is a common primary research method.

Interviews

Interviews can be either structured or unstructured, or they can be a combination of both. They are particularly useful if you are trying to find out people's individual opinions or experiences (a qualitative approach), although quantitative research can also be carried out in this way. Most interviews are planned in advance, but on occasions an interview can be carried out 'on the spot'. The level of structure to an interview can be drawn as a continuum:

•————————————————————————•

Structured interviews   Unstructured interviews

Figure 9.1

The interview is a common primary research method

Structured interviews

The level of structure in the interview can usually be equated with its level of formality. The more formal approach usually follows a rigid course of pre-set questions which every participant is asked. These answers are controlled by forming questions which do not allow for expansion of the topic area. They are known as closed questions and can be particularly useful in quantitative research.

Table 9.2 Advantages and disadvantages of structured interviews

Advantages	Disadvantages
The questions are firmly set in advance.	There is no flexibility.
All participants are asked the same questions.	The additional information a participant may have available will be missed.
The structure and outcomes can be narrowly focused.	
The outcomes are easy to collate.	
Time management can be carefully controlled by the researcher.	

Unstructured interviews

In an unstructured interview, each participant is asked the same set of questions, but time is allowed for questions to be developed further. It is often considered to be a far more relaxed process.

Table 9.3 Advantages and disadvantages of unstructured interviews

Advantages	Disadvantages
The questions set in advance are used simply as a guide or prompt	Not all participants are asked exactly the same questions
Flexibility is offered to explore points further if appropriate	Questions about the reliability of the outcomes may be raised
The structure and outcomes are not so narrowly focused	Time management cannot be so easily controlled by the researcher
	The interview can become simply a 'chat' if not carefully contained

A combined approach

A combined approach usually involves a list of specified questions, but the interviewer allows expansion where it is felt appropriate. This enables a degree of control to remain while allowing flexibility within the interview. This would place the interview nearer the middle of the continuum:

•_____•_____•_____•

Structured interview   Combined approach   Unstructured interview

Length of interviews

Interviews should not be overly long, and it is usual for the researcher to impose a time limit. A structured interview would normally take less time than an unstructured interview due to the pre-set process involved. Your proposed time limit should be stated in advance. Consider how much time you would be willing to give up for someone else's research before you ask others to agree to your request.

You need to make a note of participants' responses throughout the interview, and so the ability to use shorthand would be an advantage. It is important to be systematic, using the same approach to each set of interview notes to make it easier to compare participants' responses at the analysis stage.

Recording an interview on tape or video recorder is an alternative approach. It can be useful if you need to record answers verbatim (word for word). A video recording also enables you to look at participants' body language, but transcribing tapes is time-consuming and so these methods should be selected with caution. It is imperative that participants have agreed to the recording in advance and have had a genuine opportunity for refusal. It is completely inappropriate to covertly (secretly) record an interview and you should always remember that confidentiality is of the utmost importance, as is the security of any recorded tapes.

Participants in your research
Selection of participants needs to be made carefully. You should consider if it really is convenient for them. If, for example, you choose to interview other students within your college, do not make them late for their classes.

Figure 9.2

Pick an appropriate time to carry out your interview

Surveys and questionnaires
Another primary method is the survey, usually carried out using a questionnaire. It tends to be a popular method with students. However, questionnaires are not as easy to produce as they may at first look. It is worth considering the following issues:

- the reason for using a questionnaire
- when to use a questionnaire
- how many questions to ask
- the order of questions
- writing open and closed questions
- piloting the questionnaire
- distribution and collection of questionnaires.

It is important that you are able to justify why and how a survey will enhance the outcomes of your work. Ask yourself:

- What extra information will it enable me to gather?
- Is the information available from another source? If yes, from where?
- How deficient would my project be without it?
- Will including a survey add quality to my work or just quantity?

Questionnaires can be an ideal method of gathering primary data if you are seeking the views of many people. If the subject area is sensitive, it can offer **anonymity** which may encourage participants to share information they might otherwise have kept back. Time restrictions may mean that carrying out interviews, which would normally be an ideal method for your chosen topic area, would be impractical, whereas questionnaires can be distributed and collected later, limiting the amount of time needed.

Questionnaires can be distributed by hand or they can be posted. Postal surveys often have a poor return rate and can be costly for the researcher to administer.

Figure 9.3

Postal surveys can be costly to administer and have a poor return rate

Questions

The questions you ask in a questionnaire must be relevant. They should flow into each other, following a logical sequence, and not jump from one topic to the next. Questions need to be carefully thought through. They should not offend or pry into a participant's privacy. Your tutor will be able to offer advice as to whether any questions drawn up are inappropriate, and the piloting process will provide a check on the questions before the questionnaire is distributed.

Refer to page 374, 'Piloting your questionnaire', for more information.

remember
- The wording of questions must be clear.
- It is important to avoid ambiguities (double meanings).
- Keep your questionnaire as short as possible – a lengthy questionnaire can be very off-putting to your participants.

Which type of question should you use: open or closed?
- An open question offers opportunity for an individual answer.
- A closed question restricts the participants' answer to one word or statement.

A combination of both types may well be appropriate for your questionnaire if you use one. This would give you control over some aspects of the questionnaire (the closed questions gaining some 'core' information), more flexibility would then be possible by using open questions to allow participants to express their views more freely. Always ask yourself whether the questions being asked will get the information you are looking for. If you are unsure, rethink your questions or ask your tutor for advice.

The language level used in questionnaires should be appropriate for the target group – participants may become indignant if your questions indicate that they have limited understanding, or they may be confused if your questions are inappropriately academic.

activity
9.5

1 Collect examples of questionnaires. These can be found in magazines, newspapers (results of opinion polls) or in books on research methodology (for example, Green, 2000).
2 Consider each of the questionnaires you have found and answer these questions:
   a) How would you feel if asked to complete them?
   b) How easy or complex did their completion appear?
   c) Did they make sense?
   d) Did you identify any ambiguities or irrelevant questions?
   e) Was it made clear how you should record your answers?
   f) Which would you be most happy to complete? Why is this?
   g) Which would you be least happy to complete? Why is this?
   h) How appropriate were the numbers of questions asked on each?
   i) Did the questionnaire include open or closed questions, or both? Did this seem appropriate?
   j) What influenced the above decisions?

Piloting your questionnaire

Piloting a questionnaire helps to identify any ambiguities in its layout before it is distributed to your target group. It involves getting a small number of 'similar' participants to complete the questionnaire and asking them to comment on the layout, the instructions for its completion and the clarity of the questions. You need to allocate time for the pilot to be completed, returned and analysed, as well as time for making any necessary alterations prior to the main distribution. This should be built into your time plan for the research process.

Categories of response

You need to think carefully about how the questions will be answered. Instructions for this should be given at the beginning of the questionnaire and they should be very clear to the participants.

Questions can be answered in a number of ways, including by:

- ticking a box
- writing in the space provided
- circling the chosen answer.

Responses should be kept as consistent as possible. There would not usually be more than two styles of response on any one questionnaire.

Responses can be:

- scaled – participants are given a choice of responses on a scale
- ranked – participants put a list of qualities in rank order according to importance
- by category – participants choose their answer from a range of given categories.

Scaled responses

Q1 How important is it for young children to see positive gender images?

Vital ____ Very important ____ Important ____ Quite important ____ Not important ____

Q2 Training in providing positive images is very important for all day nursery staff.

Strongly agree ____ Agree ____ Disagree ____ Strongly disagree ____

Q3 Circle the number on the scale below which represents how important you feel it is for day nursery staff to have had training in equal opportunities, 1 being the lowest and 10 being the highest importance.

1   2   3   4   5   6   7   8   9   10

Ranked response

Q4 Which of the activities listed below do you consider to be most important in the development of fine motor skills? Place them in order of importance, 1 to 5.

Threading activities

Opportunities for mark-making

Construction materials

Small world play

Jigsaw puzzles

Which number did you think should be used to indicate the greatest importance: 1 or 5?

It is important that you always make this clear to the participant. It is better to say:

'Place them in order of importance 1 to 5, with 1 indicating the greatest level of importance'.

This will avoid any confusion. You have indicated to the participant in which order your scale is set out.

Category response

Q5 How long is it since your last first aid training update?

0–3 years _____ 4–8 years _____ 9–12 years _____ 13–16 years _____

No training at all _____ Other (please specify) _____

This can enable a researcher to consider links between the responses made to other questions and how long it is since the person making a particular response qualified.

Table 9.4 Advantages and disadvantages of surveys

Advantages	Disadvantages
Questionnaires can offer anonymity to participants which is not possible during an interview.	Return rates for postal surveys are often low (below 35 per cent).
The same questions are answered by all participants.	Postal surveys can be costly.
The researcher's time can be used effectively.	Collection and distribution of questionnaires can be time-consuming.
Participants are able to complete the questionnaire without time pressure.	If questions remain unanswered on some questionnaires, it can affect the outcomes.
A good return rate is possible but not always achieved.	Unless carefully set out, questions can be misunderstood.
Preparation time should not be under-estimated. Careful planning is important.	
Piloting of questionnaires is vital, but adds to the time allocation needed.	

Target group checklist

It is important to ensure that the intended target group is appropriate for your survey. It would be of limited benefit, for example, to ask for opinions from motor vehicle students about a range of books for two-year-olds. Similarly, early years students are unlikely to be the ideal participants in a survey on a range of car engine components. Ask yourself:

remember

Always ensure that categories do not overlap (0–3, 3–8, 8–12, and so on) as participants will be unsure where to place their responses. It also makes it difficult to collate and present the findings, and the accuracy of the outcomes may be in question. Clear categories would be 0–3, 4–8, 9–12.

- Do your participants need to have a working knowledge of your chosen subject?
- Do they need to be from a particular:
  - age range?
  - type of employment?
  - culture?
  - sex?
  - geographical area?

and so on.

Scientific experiment

Polit and Hungler (1991) define experimental research as: 'a research study in which the investigator controls or manipulates the independent variable and randomly assigns subjects to different conditions.'

Experimental research usually involves two groups of people: the experimental group and the control group.

- Participants in the experimental group are subjected to the variable that is being tested (the independent variable) to see if it has an effect.
- Participants in the control group experience the same conditions (the constant variables) as the experimental group, except that they are not treated with the independent variable; their results are compared with those of the experimental group to see if the independent variable has had an effect.

It is important that the two groups are as alike as possible at the outset so that, when the groups' results are compared, any difference is unlikely to have been caused by something other than the independent variable.

Figure 9.4

The control group and the experiment group should be as alike as possible

Experimental research

Experimental research is usually associated with laboratory testing rather than the more people behaviour/opinion-orientated focus of social research. It is unlikely that experimental research would be undertaken as a level 3 early years course research project, although as mentioned earlier, the **replication** of experiments of pioneers such as Piaget may be undertaken.

Many experiments have been considered controversial, and ethical issues often arise.

Find three examples of experimental research. If possible, include one linked to the subject of your chosen research project.

1 Was there a clear independent variable?
2 Were there any controversial aspects to the experiment?
3 What ethical issues needed to be taken into account?

Link

Refer to page 393 for a discussion of ethics.

Observation

Observation is rarely chosen as a research method by inexperienced researchers. However, when it is selected, observation is useful – while a participant may tell you that they would respond as X, during observation you may note that in practice they really respond as Y, thus obtaining a truer overall result.

The aim of observational research is to see 'what really happens'. It is important to carry it out unobtrusively, as any interruption to normal events could change (and therefore invalidate) the outcomes of the research.

Formal and informal observation

■ Researchers using formal (participant) observation obtain their findings by joining in with the situation they are observing.

■ Researchers using informal (non-participant observation) obtain information by observing from a distance.

Observation is an important tool in research in childcare settings where it is already used as a routine part of early years care and education assessments.

Figure 9.5

Observation can be formal (participant) …

Figure 9.6

... or informal (non-participant)

Figure 9.5   Advantages and disadvantages of observation

Advantages	Disadvantages
Behaviour is seen in a natural environment.	Observation is time-consuming.
The process of social situations can be observed – what preceded a certain factor or what resulted from it.	It is not always considered to be a reliable method as it can be subjective.
Observation can either be direct (participant) or indirect (non-participant).	The presence of the researcher can affect what is being observed.

Figure 9.7

Formal observation can sometimes be difficult

Professional Practice

■ Make a note of three situations that could be researched through observation. What would be most appropriate, a direct or indirect approach?

■ How could you ensure that no interruption to the usual routine occurs?

Action research

Action research is an excellent example of how the outcomes of research can have an impact on praxis (the practice involved in an area of study, for example in early years). It involves you, as the researcher, studying an aspect of your own working environment. It could, for example, involve exploring how well staff in your pre-school or nursery utilise certain equipment or resources. Alternatively, it could include analysing how well the parents are involved with the setting.

You need to consider carefully whether or not to use action research, as you will have to carry on working within the setting after the research has been completed. There is always the possibility of outcomes from this type of research raising discontent in other staff. The possibility of both positive and negative outcomes needs to be thought through at the planning stage. This is not a method usually used by students studying at level 3.

---

activity
9.7

1. Consider the following research ideas. Would they all be suitable for a piece of action research?
   a) An exploration of the encouragement given by staff to both girls and boys in the use of construction materials in your nursery
   b) The promotion of home–school links in your primary school
   c) The value placed on exploring cultural events and festivals by staff in your pre-school.
2. Make a note of as many potential positive and negative outcomes you can think of.

Case studies

The study of a situation, an individual, a group or a family, in which the researcher looks at a range of factors as the basis for discussion, is often referred to as a case study. As the researcher, you would make an in-depth analysis of your findings, possibly making comparisons with other cases or examples.

This method is particularly useful in social research, and case studies are often used in academic texts to illustrate particular points. When using this method, it is unlikely that you will be able to claim that your outcomes are representative of society at large, but they may produce interesting ideas and thought-provoking material that can be explored further.

In a research project at level 3, it can be useful to include a case study to illustrate a particular point that you are trying to get across (as a secondary source). If you are unsure how best to do this, your tutor will be able to help you.

---

activity
9.8

Sonia has chosen to look at examples of emotional disturbance commonly found in children's lives and intends to use the following case study as part of her discussion. Read through the case study and consider the questions that follow it.

Janine
Janine is seven and her brother, Alan, is five. They have recently moved from a two-bedroom house, the only home they have known, into bed-and-breakfast accommodation, following the family's financial difficulties and eviction for mortgage arrears. Alan is behaving unacceptably both at home and in school. Janine has begun to wet her bed at night, which is causing her a great deal of distress and significant laundry problems for her parents. She has become very quiet and withdrawn. Their mother is tearful a lot of the time and their father is short-tempered with everyone.

1. How might Janine and Alan be feeling?
2. How might their parents be feeling?
3. What help might be available to the children?
4. What might the role of a classroom support assistant be in this situation?
5. How useful do you consider this case study might be to Sonia's research project?

Professional Practice

■ Look through some examples of past research projects. There may be a section of these in your college library. How have case studies enhanced the projects.

Data collection – secondary sources

Secondary research is the use or presentation of material which has been researched or written by someone else. It will support your chosen topic area and your primary research findings (or data collection) for Unit 20 (Early Years Project). Secondary research data will be used at some point in most assignments during your course of study.

Literature research

Every researcher needs to read around their subject area in order to broaden the scope for their research and to form a solid literature base. This base will include both technological and non-technological sources.

It is important to set yourself clear parameters. If your research becomes too wide, it may result in a thinly covered topic area with limited value. A narrower, but more deeply considered, approach may give a greater insight into your chosen topic area, producing outcomes of a higher value. The subject being explored will sometimes indicate natural parameters, but at other times you, as the researcher, will need to set them for yourself.

Deciding how widely to research can be difficult. It is useful to set clear boundaries, for example by asking yourself:

■ How far back shall I research – to the year 2005, to 2000, to 1990, to 1980, to 1950? You need to decide how much your decision will affect your outcomes. Will it be a mistake to limit your research to just the past year, rather than the past decade? Will you miss out on important historically relevant data by only focusing on recent years?

■ Should I restrict my work geographically? Will focusing on the UK be appropriate? Would you benefit from including USA statistics, or would a comparison with Europe be relevant? Perhaps focusing on your own local area is sufficient. Tutors will be able to offer guidance on these questions.

Figure 9.8

Should I restrict my work geographically?

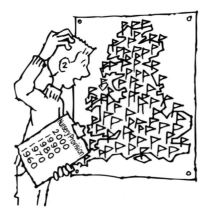

Finding information

An initial literature search helps to establish where the most significant amount of material for a subject area is to be found, and should help set the research parameters. You will need to consider local sources of material too. For example, if the subject to be researched is health-related, you should be asking yourself what sources are available locally. There may be a health promotion office at your local hospital or surgery.

Ideally, you should start by considering what the general subject area appropriate to your chosen research topic is. Is it:

- health?
- childcare?
- education?
- community provision?
- special educational needs? What else?

The clearer the definition of the subject area, the easier it will be to establish sources of secondary data. In the field of early years there is a wealth of sources to explore. These include:

- public libraries
- academic libraries (college and university)
- health promotion offices
- resource centres
- government offices
- support groups
- organisations
- GP surgeries, dentists, pharmacies
- bookshops
- the Internet.

Journals and books

- Published (written) sources include:
- books
- magazines
- specialist journals
- newspapers
- information sheets and pamphlets
- government documents
- Hansard (transcripts from parliamentary debate)
- Internet material
- CD-ROM material.

For more information about sources of information and guidance on how to refer to published sources in your writing, refer to *Research Methods in Health, Social and Early Years Care* by Green (2000).

activity
9.9

1   What other sources can you think of?
2   Where could you access them?

Technological sources

Researchers today have the benefit of a range of technological resources, for example:

- CD-ROMs, which are usually held in college libraries, offer the opportunity to explore many avenues of enquiry quickly. Many national newspapers produce CD-ROMs of past articles, producing updates at regular intervals. There are also many specialist subject areas on CD-ROM too, for example, menu planning for young children. These are often interactive, extending learning by exploration.

- The Internet provides on-line libraries and encyclopaedias. From the Internet public library you can access a collection of texts which can also be downloaded. Always check for copyright status – some are copyright-free, but others are not. Be sure that you do not break copyright laws. Details of these laws are displayed in all libraries, often beside the photocopier.

  - Search engines guide you through the mass of information on the Internet. Popular search engines are Google, Yahoo and Ask (see below). Staff will help you if you are unsure how to access these.

  - National newspapers are often on line too. Their Internet website addresses can be found printed in each edition of the newspaper. Transcripts from parliamentary debate (known as Hansard) can also be accessed in this way. This would be particularly useful if your subject area is policy led.

  - Nelson Thornes (publisher of this book) has a website (www.nelsonthornes.com) and you may find it useful to explore what it offers.

- Microfiche is a database on film, used in many libraries, to store newspapers, books and other data.

- The Educational Resources Information Centre (ERIC), which is usually found in libraries in colleges of higher and further education, is a facility that searches for information from key words, to produce titles of books and articles. ERIC is only of use if you have access to the titles it suggests.

Example of using search engines

Search engines such as Google and Yahoo refine the material with each subsequent search, while search engines such as Ask offer the opportunity to ask further questions, but they are not refined (or categorised) in any way.

In Google and Yahoo:

1. Type in the category you are studying, for example, Rashes. A large index will appear of relevant options.
2. Select another category from this index. A further index will appear.
3. Continue to select and re-select until you have the information you are looking for.

In Ask:

1. Ask the computer a question. It will give you a list of possibilities.
2. From this list, ask another question, narrowing down the field of answers.
3. Continue until you find what you were looking for.

Figure 9.9

Researchers today benefit hugely from the range of technological resources, such as CD-ROMs and the Internet

Media sources

Media sources include television, radio, newspapers, journals and magazines. Each offers current information on a vast array of subjects, and can be useful when discussing your subject area. However, it is important to remember that many media sources portray bias (a prejudice).

Figure 9.10

It is important to remember that many media sources portray bias

> **remember**
>
> Many early years professionals write media articles, sharing their expertise and indicating current thinking. Their viewpoints can be particularly useful in discussing subject areas involving current policy or practice.

When exploring the alternatives to points raised in articles, it is important to obtain a balance of views. Television and radio programmes offer topical discussions, current affairs and documentaries. If any of these is to be referred to in a piece of research, the reference details should be set out using the Harvard method as described in Green (2000).

Newspapers and journals also cover current affairs and topical issues. They often include articles on controversial subjects and can also portray bias. Being aware of the source or author can establish whether objectivity can be assumed.

For example, an article on the benefits of disposable nappies written by an 'expert' working for a leading manufacturer of disposable nappies is unlikely to be completely objective. It would be likely that any reference to ecological or economic factors would be marginalised in comparison with the emphasis on convenience factors and benefits over rival products.

Case studies

Case studies published by a previous researcher can be used as a secondary source of data. You can use them in more than one way:

- as a point of discussion, analysing the main components of the case and discussing each part, making reference to your own primary research findings or other outcomes from your literature base;
- to identify differences and discuss comparisons in a number of case studies.

Statistical reports and sources

Statistics can make an important contribution to research. They may show how a trend relevant to a topic area has developed, for example, the number of babies born to teenagers in the year 2005. It is important to use the most recent statistics you can find; there is little point in discussing a current issue and using statistics from 1995 as an example. Using past statistics can be relevant, however, if a comparison is to be made, for example, comparing the numbers of babies born to teenagers in 1980 and in 2005. The subsequent discussion would usually explore what changes have occurred, and how and why they have done so.

A good source for social statistics (both national and regional) is the government publication, *Social Trends*, which is published annually by The Stationery Office. Most libraries hold copies.

> **remember**
>
> - Research involves both primary and secondary sources of information.
> - You will usually be expected to incorporate both research methods.
> - Length and breadth of interviews can be controlled through questions and structure.
> - Questionnaires need to be clear, piloted and targeted appropriately.
> - Avoid using leading questions.
> - Observation, both formal and informal, must be as objective and unobtrusive as possible.
> - The long-term impact of action research needs careful consideration.
> - Secondary sources used to support research should be carefully selected.
> - Issues of bias must be considered in all that you read and also in all that you write.

Research information

A great deal of information is produced during a research project. Much of it will be in numerical form and is known as your **raw data**.

There are many ways in which raw data can be presented. **Tables** and graphs are common, and in some subjects it can be appropriate to use a pictorial method. You need to become familiar with the different types of presentation and their uses, so you can understand findings published by other researchers and know how to present the findings from your own research.

Raw data are the result of primary research – questionnaires, interview notes, observations, and so on. They need to be kept in a logical order so they can be understood and explained if a query is raised. It is particularly important that raw data are kept safe until after a piece of work has been read and graded by your tutors. They may be needed as evidence of your research process.

remember

Keep your data safe – you may need them as evidence of your research.

Some basic statistical tools

When you collect numerical data, you will usually need to manipulate or describe them in some way. Statistics is the area which deals specifically with the description and manipulation of numerical data. For the purposes of level 3 research, you need to understand the following terms:

- the **mean**, **median** or **mode** – three different kinds of statistical averages
- the **range** – the difference between the smallest and largest result in each collection of data
- **standard deviation** – a measure of how widely the results in a set of data are distributed, taking the mean as a point of reference.

You also need to understand how to calculate percentages.

The mean

The mean is the score which is normally recognised as being the average. It is worked out by adding up all the scores that are being dealt with and then dividing that sum by the number of scores.

For example:

In Oak class at Country Primary school, there are 24 children. Their reading ages are as follows:

- two have a reading age of 6
- three have a reading age of 7
- fourteen have a reading age of 9
- four have a reading age of 12
- one has a reading age of 14.

If these reading ages are added together, it makes 221:

$6 + 6 + 7 + 7 + 7 + 9 + 9 + 9 + 9 + 9 + 9 + 9 + 9 + 9 + 9 + 9 + 9 + 9 + 9 + 12 + 12 + 12 + 12 + 14 = 221$

To obtain the mean, 221 is divided by 24 (the number of children): $221 \div 24 = 9.2$.

The mean reading average of Oak class is therefore 9.2 years.

The median

The median reading age is the point in the sequence of reading ages that divides the lower half from the higher half.

For example, in Oak class:

6 6 7 7 7 9 9 9 9 9 9 9 9 9 9 9 9 9 12 12 12 12 14

The median reading age is therefore 9 years.

The mode

The mode or modal score is the score (or reading age) that is the most common in the data.

For example, as there are 14 children in Oak class with a reading age of 9, the mode will also be 9 years:

6 6 7 7 7 9 9 9 9 9 9 9 9 9 9 9 9 9 9 9 12 12 12 12 14

The range

The range is the difference between the lowest and the highest result taken from your research. You would calculate the range by subtracting the lowest result from the highest.

For example, in Oak class, as the highest reading age is 14 and the lowest is 6, the 6 needs to be subtracted from the 14: 14 − 6 = 8

Therefore, the range is 8.

Figure 9.11

It is important to be aware of the effect of statistics on prospective parents (see page 387)

Standard deviation

The spread of numerical data can sometimes be shown on a chart, known as a distribution curve, which shows standard deviations.

The size of the standard deviation indicates how widely the results are distributed around the mean, which is the centre of the distribution. A small standard deviation would see most of the results gathered in a narrow band either side of the mean. When the standard deviation is large, the results spread out further from the mean.

Figure 9.12

Standard deviation of reading age scores in Oak class

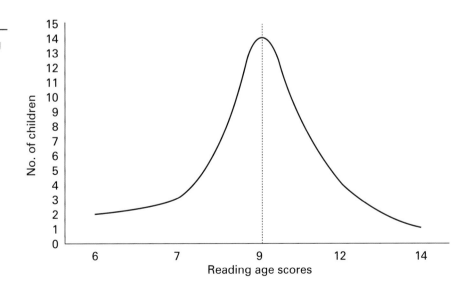

Calculating percentages

Per cent means part of a hundred. If your number is part of a total and you want to calculate the percentage, you divide the number by the total and multiply it by 100. This can be done quickly on a standard calculator. For example; if there are 100 children in a setting and 13 receive free school meals, it is easy to see that is 13% of children as the calculation involved is: $13/100 = 0.13$, and $0.13 \times 100 = 13\%$

If there were 113 pupils in the school and 17 chose to join the Judo club, the percentage is worked out as follows: $17/113 = 0.15$; $0.15 \times 100 = 15\%$.

Misuse of statistics

At times, statistics can be misleading. They can be manipulated to show one thing, when the raw data really suggest something else. School achievement tables are a good example of this.

Table 9.6 A-level results, showing pupils with three grades A–C

School	1998	1999	2000
School A	80%	82%	80%
School B	61%	63%	63%
School C	35%	38%	42%
School D	58%	63%	62%
School E	49%	51%	48%

To someone who is not familiar with the schools included in this table, it would seem clear that School A is the better school because the results are far better at A level (80 per cent gain at least three passes at A–C) than those of any other school. This figure is a consistent achievement by the school and they should be commended for it accordingly. However, to someone who is familiar with the school's policy of selective entry at Year 7 and for the sixth form (where only pupils with five GCSEs at A–C are admitted), it would seem logical that its results are the best.

No other school in the table has selective entry at any stage, and School C (with 42 per cent of pupils gaining at least three passes at A–C) has increased its achievement levels consistently over the past three years (35 to 38 to 42 per cent). This clearly indicates an improving academic record.

Statistics such as these can therefore mislead prospective parents who are looking to select a school for their child. The improving school (School C) may well be the better choice for the child concerned, as it is clearly improving the overall standard of results of pupils of 'across the board' academic ability.

Methods of presentation

Numerical data can be presented in a variety of ways, for example as:

- tables
- bar charts
- line graphs
- pie charts
- sociograms
- pictographs.

Very often you will find that you can use several of these methods to present your data and your decision about which to use will be a matter of personal choice.

Professional Practice

- Research data can be presented either electronically, or drawn. Your tutor will tell you if any one method is specifically required.
- Packages such as Excel are commonly used.

Tables

A table is one of the most basic methods of presenting information, both numerical and written. It offers versatility in that it can include a great deal of raw data and can also be used to present sub-sets of information.

Table 9.7 Parental responses to child behaviour

Type of behaviour	% Positive response		% Negative response	
	Boys	Girls	Boys	Girls
Playing with blocks	36	0	0	0
Manipulating objects	46	46	2	26
Transportation toys	61	57	0	2
Rough/tumble toys	91	84	3	2
Aggression	23	18	50	53
Climbing	39	43	12	24
Playing with dolls	39	63	14	4
Dancing	0	50	0	0
Asking for help	72	87	13	6
Dressing-up play	50	71	50	6

Source: Adapted from B. Fagot (1978), 'The influence of sex of child on parental reactions to toddler children', cited in Cullis et al. (1999)

Table 9.8 A factual table, offering an 'at a glance' comparison of a range of learning systems

	High Scope	Montessori	Steiner
Specific staff qualification	No	Yes	No
Specific training needed	Yes	Yes	Yes
Specific equipment needed	No	Yes	No
Particular daily routine	Yes	No	Yes
Particular teaching methods	Yes	Yes	Yes
Own terminology	Yes	Yes	Yes
Particular method of grouping children	Yes	No	No
Particular room layout	Yes	No	No

Source: Adapted from Jameson and Watson (1998)

remember

- Every table should have a title.
- All rows and columns must be clearly labelled.
- The source of your information should always be given below the table.
- For numerical data, all units of measurement must be given.
- If rows or columns are totalled, this must be clearly indicated on the table.
- For large or complex tables, shading or colouring may help to make information more accessible.

Bar charts

A **bar chart** is particularly useful for showing comparisons between sets of information. The length of each bar is clearly seen in relation to its neighbours.

Figure 9.13
_____

A bar chart

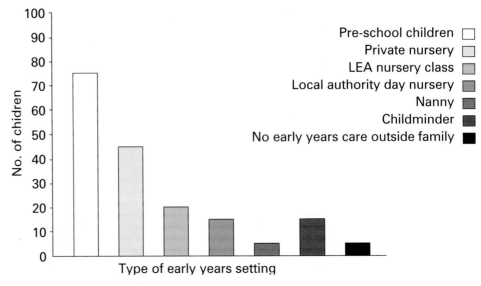

Early years settings attended by children in Bath local authority

Key:
- Pre-school children
- Private nursery
- LEA nursery class
- Local authority day nursery
- Nanny
- Childminder
- No early years care outside family

(Vertical axis: No. of children, 0 to 100; Horizontal axis: Type of early years setting)

remember
- The bar chart should have a relevant and informative title.
- Both axes should be clearly labelled, and the units of measurement clearly identified.
- Each bar should be clearly labelled and a key provided where necessary.
- The bars should be of equal width.
- The bars may be separated by a small gap or may butt up against each other.

Histograms

A histogram is quite similar to a bar chart in appearance and histograms are often used to represent grouped data. However, they are not as easy to use or interpret as a bar chart as the width of the columns may vary in line with the size they are meant to convey, meaning that, in some histograms, the area of each column needs to be calculated in order to reach a conclusion. The horizontal axis of a histogram will have a similar scale to those used in other graphs with each interval depicting the same number of units – for example; a scale of children's ages ranging from birth to three years but with each interval representing six months. The frequency of the class (in this case, the number of children of a certain age) is indicated by the area of the column.

For a clear explanation of the use of histograms, see _Research Methods in Health, Care and Early Years_, by Hucker (2001).

Line graphs

A **line graph** gives clear 'at a glance' understanding for the reader. They show trends or changes in quantity and are particularly useful for displaying information which changes over a period of time. The horizontal axis indicates the continuously variable aspect of the data being presented.

Research information

Figure 9.14

A line graph

Babies born during 2006 in one maternity unit

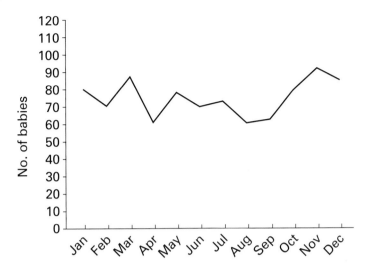

> ■ A line graph should have a clear and informative title.
> ■ The horizontal axis needs to be a continuously variable quantity, such as age, time or temperature (i.e. it should not be discrete or descriptive categories).
> ■ Both axes should be clearly labelled.
> ■ The units of measurement should be clearly indicated.
> ■ You cannot plot a line graph unless you have quite a lot of data. Trying to join just a few points plotted from sketchy data may give an unreliable impression.

remember

Pie charts

A **pie chart** is a circular graph, with the 'portions' of the 'pie' showing clearly the relative proportions of different categories. It is a visual chart which is easily understood by the reader.

The portions of a pie chart can be coloured or shaded to make the data clear, but it also needs to be clearly labelled, either with simple descriptive labels for each category or, for more accuracy, labels giving the percentage share of the whole for each category.

When drawing a pie chart, the angle at the centre of the circle (360°) is shared between the different categories in proportion to their size using a mathematical calculation. It is worth learning how to draw a pie chart, although software programs are available which can do this for you.

Figure 9.15

A pie chart

Early years settings attended by children in one local authority

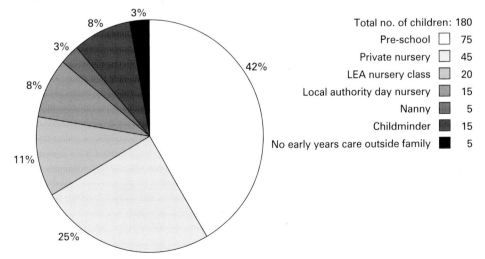

> ■ The advantage of pie charts is that they are especially useful for showing, at a glance, the relative proportions of different categories.
> ■ Their disadvantage is that they are quite difficult to draw.
> ■ The more categories you are trying to represent, the more difficult it is to draw the chart.
> ■ The pie chart should have a clear and informative title.
> ■ Each slice or segment should be shaded or coloured to distinguish it from the others.
> ■ Each segment should be labelled to indicate which category it represents, or a key should be provided.

remember

Sociograms

The term 'socio' means 'denoting social or society'. A **sociogram** presents data describing relationships between members of social groups.

Sociograms can depict the social relationships of one person or of a complete group of people. The sociogram below shows the inter-relationships of a group of children.

Figure 9.16

A sociogram

Number of times each child in a class was quoted as being the best friend of another child in the class

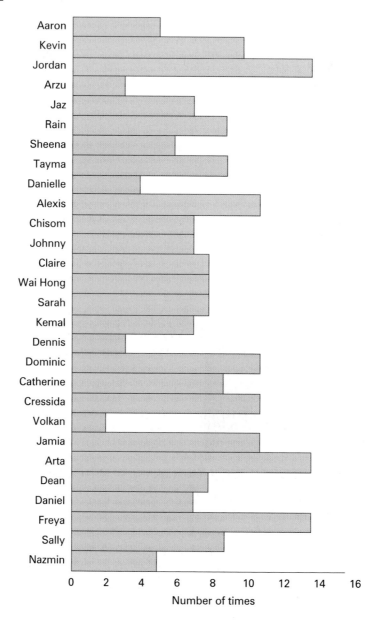

Pictographs

A **pictograph** works in the same way as a bar chart, but pictures are used instead of bars to represent the data. This is a very visual graph and may have a greater impact on the reader than a bar chart.

Figure 9.17

A pictograph

The average number of nappy changes in a typical week in the baby room of Bathtown Day Nursery

activity 9.10

Look again at each of the examples of data presentation.

1 Are the data clear in each one?
2 Are you able to easily identify the main outcomes?
3 Which type of graphic presentation do you prefer? Why?
4 Are the labels helpful?

activity 9.11

Select a set of statistics from any source of your choice. Present the information in as many different ways as you can.

1 How successful was this?
2 Which type of graph was easiest to produce? Why?
3 Which type of graph was most appropriate for the statistics you used? Why?

Methods of analysis

There are a range of software packages available to help you analyse and present your data. One popular package is the SPSS (Statistical Package for Social Sciences). It is likely to be available in your college library or resource centre. Your tutors or resource centre staff will be able to help you access and use it. Another popular package is Excel. Both packages will enable you to produce graphs and tables which are clear and look professional.

> **remember**
> ■ Data can be presented in a variety of ways.
> ■ It is important that the chosen method of presentation is appropriate for your data and your purpose.
> ■ The reader needs to be able to evaluate the outcomes of your research easily.
> ■ Provide clear explanations.
> ■ Carefully label all diagrams, tables, charts and graphs.
> ■ Always cite the source of your information.
> ■ Include a key where appropriate.

Validity

Validity refers to how accurately a subject has been researched. Ask yourself, can it be said to be both genuine and soundly based? Something is valid if we know it to be true, authentic and measuring what it claims to measure. In research terms, validity is giving a true representation of what has been researched; a piece of research that is valid addresses what it says it addresses and its findings are less likely to be disputed. It is important that researchers are as sure as they can be that their participants have told them the truth.

Reliability

A research finding that can be repeated is reliable. **Reliability** refers to the consistency of the outcome. Any identified change to practice needs to be supported by evidence that is consistent – it needs to be reliable. This applies equally to the field of early years, and an outcome will not be considered as reliable evidence if it is only applicable to one research project, or to one sample group of participants. It is important to establish that another similar research enquiry would achieve the same results.

Unfortunately, an outcome can be reliable, yet not be valid. You might receive the same answers from your participants if you ask them the same set of questions more than once but, if those questions were not properly formulated for investigating your aim, the results, although consistent, would not be valid.

Re-testability

Re-testability is directly linked to reliability. In research, retesting is one way of assessing reliability.

Researchers should ask themselves:

> **remember**
> ■ Successful replication of research is the only way to demonstrate reliability.

■ Was the method reliable?

■ Was it the best method for the subject being studied?

■ What were the alternatives?

■ Would the outcomes have been different if another method had been used?

And the important question:

■ Would the same results be achieved if the enquiry was replicated (carried out again)?

For most research on a level 3 early years course this will not however be practicable. It is, therefore, important to be able to justify your choice of research method and make the best of it by careful selection of participants and careful preparation of questions, observations, and so on.

Representative groups

Valid results can only be achieved if participants (the target group) are genuinely representative. Therefore, targeting research appropriately is vital.

For example, it would be of limited value to ask a retired nursery nurse how successful he or she considers the introduction of the Foundation Stage Curriculum to be from a practitioner's point of view. To get a genuinely useful response, the researcher would need to ask a practitioner who has worked both prior to and with the Foundation Stage guidelines.

Triangulation

Validity can be augmented through triangulation (supporting your findings from research in more than one way).

For example, both questionnaires and interviews could be used to obtain parents' views regarding safety aspects of the local park. These responses could then be supported by observations made by the researcher after spending time at the park in question. If the three methods support each other, it will enhance the validity and reliability of the overall research project.

---

activity

9.12

Consider the research projects below. Which do you consider would be likely to achieve reliable and valid outcomes? Which would you be less certain about? Which would be replicable?

- Parents' views on the day-care option they have chosen for their children
- Teachers' views on the introduction of the Foundation Stage Curriculum
- Parents' evaluation of their own behaviour-management strategies
- Library services for young children in a rural community
- Gender stereotyping of young children.

1 What are the main points you have raised?
2 Would objectivity concern you?
3 How would issues of objectivity affect the validity and reliability of the above projects?
4 Do you think the type of research method used would have made any difference?

---

remember

- Validity refers to the accuracy of the research – does the research address what it claims to address?
- Reliability is linked to the ability to replicate the research.
- Careful selection of participants is needed. They must always be representative.
- Mutually supportive research methods (triangulation) enhances the validity and reliability of research.

Implications and ethical issues

Ethics

Ethics are the principles or moral codes used as guidelines for the behaviour standards common to all people within a group or profession. Ethics determine what is right and wrong; they help to maintain standards.

Individual definitions of the term 'ethics' may vary slightly, but most people will agree that, in general, ethics act as guidelines for the decisions we each have to make and the consequences that may arise from any course of action we take.

They are directly linked to the values and morals of both individuals and society as a whole. Ethics, therefore, are about doing what is right according to the majority, linking personal values, standards of behaviour and conscience to actions.

Research ethics are the rules governing good and bad practice in the field of research. To behave unethically during the research process is to behave badly when dealing with the views and contributions of any of your participants. In research, ethics include consideration of the participants' rights, the importance of confidentiality and issues concerned with preserving anonymity.

Professional Practice

■ Various organisations and professions produce their own codes of ethics. Examples include:

- health districts – they each have an ethics committee
- British Medical Association
- British Psychological Society
- social workers.

activity

9.13

Using your college library or the Internet, find a code of ethics for a relevant profession. Read its main points and consider how the ethical principles for that profession might apply to your role as an early years professional.

Research ethics involves responsibility. As a researcher you will have a responsibility to all your participants to ensure that their privacy is not invaded unnecessarily, or without their permission. Participants are doing you a favour by participating in your research. At times you may ask for responses on subjects that may be sensitive to them. They should be respected for this and treated accordingly.

It is unethical to carry out research without the subjects of the research knowing it is taking place (i.e. covert observation or casual conversations). This is particularly important if you are carrying out research in your workplace. Covert research breaks the trust of colleagues if, for example, information given in conversation is used in a subsequent piece of research. This also applies to observing and recording the actions and/or conversations of colleagues without their knowledge.

There are occasions when ethical considerations may not be as necessary. This could occur if you were carrying out observations in a public place, for example, watching students socialise around the college campus or children playing in a park.

The research methods chosen for any project will have an impact on the way the findings of research are presented. At the outset of a piece of research, the proposed methods should be fully considered, to ensure that they will allow a true representation of participants' contributions to be presented.

activity

9.14

1   Why might ethical considerations not be necessary when carrying out observations in a public place? Note your reasons and discuss them with another student.
2   Think of a range of topic areas that could be suitable for exploring as a research project, linked to the subject units studied during the BTEC National in Early Years.
    a) Which of them might be classified as sensitive? Why is this, do you think?
    b) How might participants be adversely affected by research in these areas?
    c) What restrictions do you think you might find as a researcher studying these topics?
3   Discuss the outcomes in your group.

- You need to be aware that sensitive subjects may also affect you as the researcher. The responses you receive and the material you read in the literature may at times be distressing.

- It is important for all researchers to have supervision. Supervision helps you with the process and practical application of your project. It also helps you deal with stress and concerns. Professional researchers are supervised, as well as student researchers. Your tutor will usually supervise your research project.

Implications

Who commissions the research?

As a first-time research student carrying out a small-scale project, it is unlikely that the outcomes of your research will benefit anyone other than yourself. Any risks that might be taken during the research process need to be balanced against the benefits that the outcomes of the research will bring (this is sometimes known as the costs:benefits ratio). When this is a personal piece of work undertaken as part of a course, you need to be absolutely sure that the benefits (primarily to yourself) justify the costs (primarily borne by others). In a larger-scale piece of research, any potential risks should be identified at the onset, and the benefits of the research should be clearly set out by the researcher.

activity
9.15

Think about who might commission a piece of research.

1 Why might they do this?
2 Why is it important that society knows who is behind research studies that affect people and society in general?
3 What might be of concern if research within our society could take place in secrecy?

Contemporary research

There is a wealth of contemporary research into the lives and care of young children and their families and two of the many examples of the work that is being done include:

- an overview of children in public care and

- a report on the early impacts of Sure Start local programmes on children and their families.

Children in public care

This overview of the experiences of children in public care was undertaken by renewal.net on behalf of the Office of the Deputy Prime Minister in October 2005. It identifies the reasons why this group has poor experiences of education and schooling and why this may be implicated in social exclusion later in their lives. It outlines the problem and the causes; interventions that have been put in place and checklists for good practice.

Early impacts of Sure Start

This is a report from November 2005: *Cross-sectional Study of 9-and 36-Month Old Children and their Families* (HMSO 2005). One of the main goals of Sure Start programmes is to improve the functioning of children and families in the areas served by the local programmes. Preliminary findings suggest that there appears to be a difference in the improvements noted according to the amount of deprivation and lack of available resources in families. For example, teenage parents, lone parents and workless households were less likely to benefit as much less disadvantaged families.

Access to information

It is important that you obtain any appropriate permission before carrying out your research. If participants are young (school age or younger), you will need to obtain the permission of their parents or guardians. The research may be considered to be completely non-threatening and non-intrusive (for example, asking children questions about favourite toys or television programmes), but the general principle of obtaining permission from the adult with responsibility for the children concerned is still important.

In a school or early years setting, the head teacher or manager will need to give their written consent. They are held in loco parentis while children are in their care.

This permission needs to be arranged well in advance, so time management and planning should take this into account. A letter of support from a course tutor will usually be sufficient proof of the authenticity of the project.

The following details may also be required:

- your name
- a contact telephone number
- your college's telephone number (plus your tutor's name)
- dates of planned involvement by the setting, for example:
  - letters to parents (if needed)
  - interviews (How many? Who will be interviewed?)
  - distribution plans for any surveys
  - collecting arrangements for surveys
- the time plan for your research
- the availability of the research findings to the participants, or their parents/guardians
- details of who else will have access to the research findings
- issues of identification or confidentiality within the research:
  - What guarantees have been given?
  - If guaranteed, how will anonymity be assured?

Ethical issues

Confidentiality

Participants who agree to help in the research process are putting their trust in you as the researcher. You therefore have a responsibility to set clear guidelines as to how, when and where the outcomes of research are to be published. An individual participant will also need to know if they will be identified within the findings. If it is agreed that they will not, then it is imperative that this is adhered to.

You need to clarify the different ways in which a participant can be identified in research, other than by name. If, for example, in a piece of research about changes facing primary school teachers, reference is made to the difference in written planning required by teachers during their probationary teaching year, it will be very obvious whose responses are being referred to if one teacher in the participating school has been teaching for 20 years and the others are newly qualified. Therefore, the individual participants will be identified quite easily. Similarly, initials will easily identify participants with more unusual names.

Full permission from participants, and from any organisation they may be considered to represent, is needed prior to the commencement of any research. This applies equally to any research carried out internally in your own placement or work setting.

---

remember

Every participant in a research project has rights. These include:
- guaranteed privacy
- observation of their right to withdraw at any point
- anonymity
- confidentiality
- respect at all times
- trust that their contribution will be portrayed fairly and accurately.

Data protection and human rights legislation

The privacy of, and rights of access to material relating to, any individual are covered by legislation.

In a small group, locate copies of the relevant legislation in your college library or from the Internet.

1 Read through the main aspects of each piece of legislation.
2 Note which elements might be relevant to your research project.
3 Note which elements are relevant to research in general.
4 How important do you consider the legislation to be?

Policy and procedures

Before starting any research project, you need to have consulted your supervisor; in many cases, this will be your tutor. Some establishments may have a policy for research projects that are undertaken as part of course requirements, and this is common in medical, nursing and health/social-care settings. This acts as a check on the ethical implications of research proposals and the viability of the project. Check this out in your college or setting, but make sure that your tutor is aware of your research proposal, so that guidance and supervision can be given during the research process.

Codes of practice

Certain bodies have issued guidance or Codes of Practice for research and although they have been written for 'professional' researchers, you should attempt to adhere closely to the guidance that they give. Codes of Research Practice or Research Ethics are common in many professional bodies and higher education institutions and can be accessed on line. Useful sites to investigate are those belonging to the British Sociological Association and the British Psychological Society.

The role of the media

The media play a large part in keeping the general public informed. Most of the time they portray information fairly and with respect for those involved, but at other times incidents and information are sensationalised, blown out of proportion and misrepresented.

It is important that media reports are not simply accepted at face value. It is always worth reading more than one view before drawing your conclusions about something.

Think of as many examples as you can of how the media has misrepresented information. Considering each example in turn:

1 In what ways did the information become unreliable?
2 Were any individual people affected? In what way?
3 What ethical issues do you consider were breached?
4 Was the misrepresentation deliberate or accidental, do you think?
5 What should be learnt from this incident?

Vulnerability of client groups

People who are unable to understand fully the possible consequences of being involved in research and cannot, therefore, give informed consent can be described as being vulnerable. In these situations, those responsible for them, or for guiding and/or supporting them in their decision-making, need to be fully informed and consulted by the researcher.

The ethical issues related to different research methods

Ethical issues occur in all forms of primary research. Below are brief summaries of the most pertinent aspects in the most commonly used primary research methods.

Interviews

■ Interviews put the researcher (you) in a position of power.

■ You should not use your control of the situation to your own advantage.

■ Leading questions can be a problem, with personal bias making the approach subjective rather than objective.

■ Sensitivity is needed, as is an awareness of how the outcomes of interviews are to be used.

■ It is important that you take into consideration how the interview may affect the participants.

Surveys

■ Using a survey (or questionnaire) approach will also raise issues of confidentiality, anonymity and the sensitivity of the subject matter.

■ Leading questions can be a problem here too.

Case studies

■ Case studies involve discussion of a real situation and respect for the people portrayed in the case study is needed.

■ It would not usually be appropriate to identify the individuals involved.

■ It is important to consider how the outcomes of the research will be used and who will have access to it.

■ Awareness of personal bias is important.

Observations

■ Appropriate permission is particularly important if observing informally, or when observing individuals who are unable to give permission for themselves.

Examination of contemporary research

As part of the BTEC National in Early Years, you will need to evaluate pieces of published research. You will be asked to comment on various aspects, including the ethical issues.

Look again at the examples of ethical codes of practice you found for activity 9.13 on page 394. These will help you to consolidate your understanding of the codes of practice and charters that many professionals adhere to in their working professional practice.

activity
9.18

In the library, locate examples of relevant research projects. Summaries of these can often be found in academic and medical journals as well as in magazines and books, and on the Internet. You may choose to use an example you have already found for a previous activity.

1 Consider how the researcher has explained any ethical concerns they may have had.
2 How were these issues dealt with?
3 What, in your opinion, was the costs:benefits ratio?
4 Would you have included any other issues? Discuss your answers in a small group.

remember

■ Ethics are linked to standards of behaviour, to values and to your conscience.
■ Researchers need to keep abreast of any relevant issues in their subject area.
■ Never ignore the ethical issues bound up in the research process.
■ Always think about how you would want to be treated by other researchers.
■ Respect should be shown to those who agree to participate.
■ Participants in research have rights. These must be acknowledged and respected.

Progress Check

1　Why is research important?

2　What is the difference between primary and secondary research?

3　Define the terms 'qualitative' and 'quantitative'.

4　What is meant by objectivity?

5　What is a hypothesis?

6　What are the advantages and disadvantages of interviews?

7　List at least five important points to remember when planning a questionnaire.

8　What is action research?

9　Give an example of how case studies can be used.

10　What is the purpose of the control group in an experiment?

11　List as many secondary sources of information as you can.

12　List as many ways as can you think of to present statistical data.

13　What is the difference between mean, median and mode?

14　Explain validity and reliability.

15　Give an example of research affecting practice.

16　What do research ethics involve?

Using research skills

You should by now have identified how the general principles of research methodology are relevant to the whole process of your training. Throughout your studies, you will need to locate printed and technological sources of information and each time you do this you are carrying out a form of research. Each assignment you prepare will need:

- planning
- a literature search
- decisions about scope and parameters
- validity
- referencing
- clear presentation.

Each of these is part of the research process.

In your interactions with others, both in college and in placement, you will need to show respect and consideration, treating others as you would wish to be treated yourself. You will also need to respect their rights and privacy.

The new thinking and practice that is introduced into the settings that you attend will most likely be based on research of some description and will enable you to witness at first hand how the practical application of the research process affects standards, achievement and professionalism.

The Early Years project (Unit 20) will enable you (if you are taking this as one of your specialist option units) to bring together the knowledge gained from this Research unit. Applying this knowledge practically will consolidate your understanding and enhance your personal development. It is an opportunity for you to explore an area of particular interest to you, and it can help you to formulate a career plan, by enhancing or dispelling potential aspects of early years care or education as career opportunities. This final section summarises the main points that you will need to consider.

For a useful guide in planning, presenting and evaluating your project, and in developing your personal research skills, look at *Research Methods in Health, Social and Early Years Care* (Green, 2000), on which the following summaries are based.

To achieve the Project unit you will need to:

- identify a suitable topic and produce a plan for a research proposal
- carry out a literature search
- conduct the research
- analyse and present the findings of the research, including the identification of bias or error
- identify and evaluate your own learning from the process.

You will need to produce a research project which shows:

- a relevant hypothesis for the research
- a range of primary and secondary sources
- your analysed and presented findings
- discussion of your findings which relate back to the hypothesis
- your planning and progress throughout the research
- your own research skills and how these could be further developed.

Planning a research project

To produce a successful research project, it is necessary to plan each stage carefully. This involves:

- choosing the subject area
- writing the aims and objectives
- setting out a hypothesis
- setting parameters
- selecting an appropriate approach to the research
- identifying ethical considerations
- managing time
- keeping records
- tutorial support
- avoiding common pitfalls.

Presentation

Presentation of the research is likely to include both written and oral presentation skills. The written presentation would usually include the following:

- abstract
- introduction
- methodology
- presentation of data
- main text (discussion)
- conclusions and any recommendations
- evaluation
- bibliography
- appendices.

An oral presentation would usually include the use of some or all of the following:

- overhead projector transparencies
- audio-visual resources (tape recorders, videos, slides)
- tables, charts, graphs
- handouts
- questions from the 'audience'.

Each of these is described in Green (2000).

Evaluating the learning process

When evaluating your learning from the research process, the following points should be considered:

- oral skills
- written skills
- information technology skills
- numeracy skills
- personal development
- academic achievement
- practical skills
- applying new skills to other situations.

Key skills

Research projects offer ideal opportunities for you to gain the key skills of:

- Communication
- Application of number
- Information and communication technology.

If you are gathering evidence for the wider key skills:

- Working with others
- Improving own learning and performance
- Problem-solving
- Personal skills development,

you will also find that the activities you carry out, and the decisions that you make, will contribute to your portfolio of evidence.

Child Health

This unit covers the following objectives:

- Demonstrate understanding of the need for, and the approaches to health promotion
- Know causes of ill health
- Understand the impact of ill health on children and families
- Have knowledge of treatment and care routines for children with health problems.

The aim of this unit is to offer a basis for exploration of a range of health issues that affect children and their families, including some of the socio-economic factors affecting heath. It introduces the roles that you may take in the care of children with health problems and explores the promotion of health, both locally and with regard to national targets. It should be remembered that children's understanding of their own health will be linked to their age and stage of development, and this has to be taken into account when introducing health topics in your setting.

You will also learn about some of the common childhood illnesses and chronic conditions that may affect the children in your care.

Health promotion

Different definitions of health

Health can be described in terms of three different models.

The medical model of health

The **medical model** (or biological model) looks at a person's **health** in terms of the body's natural defences and immunity, genetically inherited conditions, individual levels of exercise, diet and general healthy (or unhealthy) lifestyles. It sees the body as a machine which can be restored to health by medical intervention. The responsibility for health lies with the medical profession whose role is to understand disease and find cures.

The social model of health

The **social model** sees health as being not just about biology and medical intervention but also as being influenced by the wider natural, social, economic and political environment. This includes, for example, housing, social class, affluence and poverty. This model places emphasis on health promotion/education.

The holistic model of health

The **holistic model** looks at the individual person as a whole. It can be broadly described as being concerned with 'mind, body and soul'.

The World Health Organization definition of health

The **World Health Organization (WHO)** is concerned with health in its holistic sense. In 1946 the WHO defined health as being: 'a state of complete physical, mental and social well being, not merely the absence of disease and infirmity'.

In 1984, the WHO stated that health is: 'a resource for everyday life, not the objective of living; it is a positive concept emphasising social and personal resources as well as physical capabilities'.

In 1986 they defined health promotion as: 'The process of enabling people to increase control over, and improve their health ... Health is a positive concept emphasising social and personal resources, as well as physical capacities. Therefore, health promotion is not just the responsibility of the health sector but goes beyond lifestyles to well-being.'

activity
10.1

Using your college resource centre, find out about the role of the World Health Organization. What are its current aims and specific targets?

For a detailed discussion of the definitions of health, a useful text is *Health and Lifestyles* by Blaxter (1990).

Different approaches to health education and promotion

There are several approaches to **health education and promotion**. These have been summarised by Beattie (1993) as:

- *health persuasion* – to persuade or encourage people to adopt healthier lifestyles
- *legislative action* – to protect the population by making healthier choices more available
- *personal counselling* – to empower individuals to have the skills and confidence to take more control over their health
- *community development* – to enfranchise or emancipate groups so they recognise what they have in common and how social factors influence their lives.

activity
10.2

In a small group, explore each of the above approaches.

1 What examples of each approach can you think of?
2 Give a past and a contemporary example for each.
3 Does any one approach appear to be of greater or lesser importance to you? If so, why is that, do you think?
4 Compare the outcomes of your discussion with another group.

Primary health care teams

Primary health care teams are made up of a range of health professionals. These include those who focus on health care and health education at each of the three different levels of health care:

- **primary health care** – health care in the community, involving GP practices, dentists, opticians, and so on;
- **secondary health care** – all referrals for health care, for example, to hospital departments for further treatment or investigation;
- **tertiary health care** – ongoing care for chronic conditions such as cystic fibrosis. It also includes the involvement of individual health professionals such as the community diabetic nurse.

Health education is concerned with providing well-rounded information that enables individuals to make informed choices regarding their health.

Primary health education/promotion

The aim of primary health education/promotion is to prevent ill health by eliminating the likelihood of contracting a disease in the first place. An example of this is the childhood **immunisation programme**. Nationwide immunisation can have a significant impact on the incidence of some illnesses, such as the immunisation programmes for haemophilus influenzae type B (HiB) and measles, mumps and rubella (MMR) in the UK, which have dramatically reduced the incidence of these childhood diseases in the UK. Worldwide, eradication of smallpox was due to immunisation.

In the UK, parents are presented with an explanation of the MMR vaccination and its merits and are actively encouraged to have their children vaccinated. In developing countries, however, vaccination decisions are largely made on behalf of the population, and parents are simply told that their child 'needs' whatever vaccination is being given.

Refer to page 426 for the current guidelines on immunisation.

Secondary health education/promotion

Secondary approaches to health education/promotion include **screening** procedures. Examples are the PKU (phenylketonuria) test taken from seven-day-old infants via a heel prick blood test (the Guthrie test) and cervical screening in women, where a pre-symptomatic change may be detected, allowing early intervention.

Tertiary health education/promotion

The tertiary approach to health education/promotion is aimed at the control and reduction of illness and is concerned with helping individuals to achieve their full health potential. An example of this is supporting the control of chronic asthma and diabetes. Tertiary health education/promotion often involves the use of leaflets and other printed resources. It also includes the involvement of support groups.

You may find it helpful to refer to *Health Promotion: Foundations for Practice* by Naidoo and Wills (2000) for further reading on the different levels of health care, education and promotion.

---

activity
10.3

Make a copy of the table below. Working with a partner, research a range of additional health issues and add them to the most appropriate column of the table. Examples have been given to get you started.

Primary health education/promotion	Secondary health education/promotion	Tertiary health education/promotion
Child immunisation	PKU screening Cervical screening	Supporting chronic: asthma diabetes

case study 10.1 — Klaus

Klaus is six years old. He has recently been diagnosed as having type 1 diabetes (insulin-dependent), as opposed to type 2, which is non-insulin dependent. He spent three days in hospital while his condition was stabilised and he and his parents acclimatised to planning for his diabetic dietary needs. Klaus and his parents are now being supported by the primary health care team through the diabetic specialist nurse, who oversees most of his care. The diabetic nurse supervises the administration of his injections and checks his blood sugar levels. This responsibility will soon transfer to Klaus's parents, who will be able to get support via a telephone support link. Klaus is also having regular appointments with a dietician at the local hospital to monitor his food intake and balance.

activity

1   Which members of the primary health care team have been involved in the care of Klaus to date?
2   Who would be involved in his long-term care?
3   Why is this important?

case study 10.2 — Mollie

Mollie is two years old and has cystic fibrosis (CF). She is the first member of her generation in her family to have the condition although it has occurred twice before in her family (an uncle and an aunt are currently affected). Mollie's mother had been (positively) carrier-tested prior to her pregnancy and, although foetal screening for the condition is now available, she opted not to have her unborn infant screened, because of the risk of miscarriage. As there was a definite possibility of Mollie having CF, health professionals were able to monitor her from birth, watching for the earliest signs and offering appropriate advice regarding specialised dietary needs.

activity

1   Which members of the health care profession have been involved to date?
2   What role did the primary health care professionals play in the pregnancy?
3   Will any other form of health care be needed for the future?

Role of health educators

The **role of health educators** is to educate individuals about issues that affect their health and well-being and changing their beliefs and behaviour (links to empowerment). In early years settings, the aim should be to involve both children and their families.

Historically, improvements to health have been based on improvements to public health measures rather than to improvements in medicines and clinical practice. In the nineteenth century, the first health visitors (1852) had a duty to:

■   carry and distribute carbolic powder

■   direct home owners' attention to bad smells.

Health education materials were specifically targeted at the working classes with publications such as *Dirty Dustbins and Sloppy Streets* (Buenois, 1881) and *A Practical Dietary for Families, Schools and the Working Class* (Smith, 1864).

activity
10.4

Why would these book titles be inappropriate in contemporary society?

In *Health Promotion: Foundations for Practice*, Naidoo and Wills (2000) usefully summarise 'The Old Public Health' and 'The New Public Health' (see below), showing how health promotion has moved from being the remit of local government to being the responsibility of the government working in partnership with local authorities.

The old public health

1842   Edwin Chadwick's Report on the sanitary condition of the labouring population of England is published.

1843   The Royal Commission on the Health of Towns is established.

1844   The Health of Towns Association is founded.

1845   Final report from the Royal Commission on the Health of Towns is published.

1848   Public Health Act for England and Wales requires local authorities to provide clean water supplies and hygienic sewage disposal systems, and introduces the appointment of medical officers of health for towns.

1854   John Snow controls a cholera outbreak in London by removing a contaminated local water supply.

1866   Sanitary Act – local authorities had to inspect their district.

1868   Housing Act – local authorities could ensure owners kept their properties in good repair.

1871   Local Government Board (which became the Ministry of Health in 1919) was established.

1872   Public Health Act makes medical officers of health for each district mandatory.

1875   Public Health Act consolidates earlier legislation and the tone changes from allowing to requiring local authorities to take public health measures.

1906   Education Act established the provision of school dinners.

1907   Education Act establishes the school medical service.

        Notification of Births Act and the development of health visiting is encouraged.

The new public health

1974   Lalonde Report 'A new perspective on the health of Canadians' identifies the environment as crucial for health.

1985   The World Health Organization launches its 'Health for All' programme.

1986   The World Health Organization publishes the Ottawa Charter for health promotion.

1987   The Public Health Alliances is created.

1988   Acheson Report establishes the post of Director of Public Health within the NHS.

1992   The Association for Public Health, a multidisciplinary organisation to promote public health policy, is created.

1992   Rio Earth Summit and Agenda 21.

1995   The Standing Nursing and Midwifery Advisory Committee (SNMAC) reports to Ministers on the contribution of nurses, midwives and health visitors to public health.

1997   Creation of a Minister of Public Health. White Paper: 'The New NHS – Modern, Dependable'. 3-year local health improvement programmes introduced.

1998   Green Papers: 'Our Healthier Nation' health strategy for England; 'Working together for a Healthier Scotland'; 'Better Health, Better Wales'; 'Fit for the Future' (Northern Ireland). Chief Medical Officer's project to strengthen the public health function.

        Health Action Zones (HAZs) – 11 pilot projects announced.

1999   Launch of the UK Public Health Association, incorporating the Public Health Alliance and the Association for Public Health.

Figure 10.1

The aims of health educators

A range of Acts, reports and papers quoted by Naidoo and Wills (2000) is listed above. You may find it useful to research more about each of them.

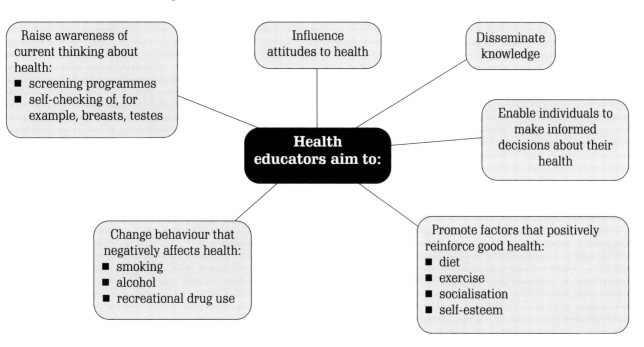

activity 10.5

Choose a health issue that particularly interests you. Design a leaflet for young children to educate them about the issue. Your leaflet will benefit from being as visual as possible. Remember to consider a range of languages and ethnic groups.

Figure 10.2

There are many leaflets available on a wide range of health issues

Who are the health educators?

A health educator is anyone who has influence over someone else regarding their health choices and lifestyle. Their role can be either formal or informal, and their influence can at times be clearly promoted, while at others it is more covert (disguised). The high levels of peer pressure seen in modern-day society increase the need for a sensitive approach particularly in improving the health of young people.

Health educators could include any of the following:

- parents
- siblings
- grandparents
- extended family
- peer group
- teachers
- pre-school/playgroup staff
- nursery staff
- childminders/nannies
- after-school staff
- playscheme staff
- primary health care team:
  - GP
  - practice nurse
  - community nurse
  - health visitor
  - health promotion nurse
  - midwife
  - dentist
  - orthodontist
  - dental hygienist
  - pharmacist
  - optician
  - chiropodist
  - counsellor
- media:
  - television
  - newspapers
  - journals
  - magazines
  - radio
  - internet.

Figure 10.3

Grandparent

Figure 10.4

Teacher

1 Identify ways in which you have been influenced by health educators/promoters.
2 How important has peer pressure been in influencing your health choices?
3 Through which media have you received information, and which have you found to be most influential?
4 What positive and negative health education/promotion programmes can you think of?
5 Who would you turn to for advice on health issues?
6 Educators can be good or bad. What do you consider to be the characteristics that make them so. Copy the table and list your ideas under the headings.

Good health educators	Bad health educators

Health education is about giving people informed choice. Society cannot dictate, only advise. **Health promotion campaigns** are about raising understanding of the consequences of the choices each individual makes for themselves and, if parents, for their children. The 'herd' vaccination programmes carried out in the developing world are clearly well meaning and contribute to the health and well-being of many children and their families. They do not, however, allow for informed choice, as those of us living in the West have come to expect.

Health promotion programmes

Government-led health promotion

National targets to improve the health of the UK population are set out by the government. The White Paper *Our Healthier Nation* (Department of Health, 1998) cites the two main aims of the government as being to improve the health of:

■ the population as a whole by increasing the length of people's lives and the number of years people spend free from illness

■ the worst off in society and to narrow the health divide.

Current targets

The National Service Framework for Children, Young People and Maternity Services (Department of Health 2004) is a 10-year programme that sets out clear standards for promoting the health and well-being of children and young people and extends the aims of *Our Healthier Nation*. Key priorities include:

■ early identification of illnesses, **environmental factors** or activities that may lead to ill health

■ the promotion of healthy diets and physical exercise for children

■ ensuring that children's emotional and social well-being is maximised

■ keeping children and young people safe

■ advice on avoiding alcohol, smoking, drug taking and substance abuse

■ reducing the risks of teenage pregnancy.

Use your college resource centre to research information on the campaign for healthier meals in schools and the background to it. Discuss whether you think children are more likely to be influenced by the media advertisement of 'junk' foods rather than by health education information on healthy diets

Factors affecting health

Lalonde (1974), who is considered to be the founder of modern health practice, identified four 'fields' of health as shown in the diagram below, two of which will be discussed in more detail.

Figure 10.5

Lalonde's health field concept

Environmental influences

Extent and nature of health services

Genetic and biological influences

Individual lifestyle

Environmental Influences

Environment and health status are inextricably linked and the type of environment or geographical location in which a child lives can exert powerful effects on their health.

Apart from the obvious environmental dangers of heavily industrialised areas, traffic fumes and pollution, a child's health will be influenced by the type and quality of housing in which they live and lack of access to clean air and open spaces; it is known that there are links between living in socio-economically deprived areas and having lower quality of life and health standards. Rates of accidental injuries are also known to be significantly higher in deprived areas with poorly maintained housing stock and high volumes of traffic.

Extent and nature of health services

Although the health of the general population has increased in recent years, there are still significant differences in health between social classes and ethnic groups. Moore (2002) suggests that the minority groups that are most in need of health interventions are less likely to gain access to them, owing to the social and economic barriers that prevent take-up of services. The National Service Framework for Children, Young People and Maternity Services is part of the Every Child Matters Agenda for Change and represents an opportunity to redress health inequalities for children and their families.

---

activity

10.8

Use the following link to research the structure of the NHS today and try to identify the key targets to improve children's health:

www.everychildmatters.gov.uk

The UK government recognises that many factors affect health and has categorised these factors as shown in the table below based on Lalonde's health field concept.

Table 10.1 Factors affecting health

Fixed	Social and economic	Environmental	Lifestyle	Access to services
Genes	Poverty	Air quality	Diet	Education
Sex	Employment	Housing	Physical activity	NHS
Ageing	Social exclusion	Water quality	Smoking	Social services
		Social environment	Alcohol	Transport
			Sexual behaviour	Leisure
			Drugs	

Source: Department of Health (1998)

Causes of ill health

The **causes of ill health** are many and varied. The following summaries are based on *Our Healthier Nation* (Department of Health, 1998).

activity
10.9

Whilst reading through the following section think carefully about people you have known, both children and adults. Ask yourself if you can identify any links between what you read here and the lives and experiences of those individuals.

Social and economic factors affecting health

Social and economic factors affecting health include poverty, unemployment and social exclusion; these can make it hard for some people to focus on their health and, for example, give up smoking. Smoking may be something that they feel gives them pleasure and keeps them going. Having limited access to shops can often mean buying from smaller (more expensive) local stores and, therefore, using limited resources in uneconomic ways. It is recognised that, although people often acknowledge what steps they need to take to improve their health, the level of hardship and social exclusion they face makes it difficult for them to act upon it. Common conditions prevalent in the lower social classes include a higher rate of infection, respiratory disease and depression.

In 1980, the Black Report noted the significance of social, economic and environmental influences on health. It referred to the issues that were at the heart of the welfare state:

- health care
- social care
- welfare benefits

and how they had been seen as a means to reduce the differences between the social classes. However, as the Report pointed out, even after 40 years of the NHS, appropriate provision was still not being made.

Environmental factors affecting health

Some of the environmental factors affecting health are pollution, and lack of sufficient heating, lighting or housing. Living in an atmosphere of fear or mistrust can also affect health. Crime and racial tension in communities has a direct impact on health and mental well-being, and workplace stress also takes its toll on many people in the employment sector owing to heavier workloads, increased targets and greater pressures to meet deadlines.

activity
10.10

Consider these health issues:

- use of recreational/illegal drugs
- melanomas
- poor health
- poor hygiene practice
- mental health problems.

1 Which do you consider to be more likely to affect the less well-off in society, and which the wealthier section of the population?
2 On what have you based your decisions?

Lifestyle factors affecting health

The **lifestyle factors affecting health** are largely choices that we make about how we live, perhaps in response to outside influences over which we have little control. For example, longer working days and the accompanying mental exhaustion have, for some people, led to a decrease in the level of their physical activity.

Longer working hours lead to many people relying on fast foods and freezer meals, moving away from the home cooking of past generations. Dependence on smoking, alcohol and recreational drugs has increased, particularly in young people.

'In 1996 28% of boys aged 15 and 33% of girls aged 15 smoked regularly and these figures are rising' (Department of Health, 1998, 2.21).

Lopez et al. (1994) estimate that: 'for every 1,000 young smokers, one will be murdered, six will be killed in a road accident and 250 will die before their time because they smoke' (cited in Department of Health, 1998).

Figure 10.6

Dependence on smoking, alcohol and recreational drugs has increased, particularly in young people

Teenage pregnancy rates continue to rise, reducing the opportunities for education, training and employment for these young people, and continuing the cycle of disadvantage.

Refer back to Unit 1, page 2 for more on the cycle of disadvantage.

Figure 10.7

Teenage pregnancy rates continue to rise

Access to services

The government summarises the impact of having access to high-quality services with the following statements:

1   A decent education gives children the confidence and capacity to make healthier choices.

2   Leisure services have a real influence on health.

3   Ill health is not spread evenly across our society.

4   The link between poverty and ill health is clear. In nearly every case the highest incidence of illness is experienced by the worst off social classes.

(Department of Health, 1998)

activity
10.11

Explain to a partner what is meant by each of the points above.

If you are able to explain their meaning to another person, it is likely that you have a clear understanding of them yourself.

The main ethos (distinctive feature) of the government's plans for improving health is to work in co-operation with local health authorities. This involves setting out overall health targets for the nation but encouraging interpretation of the targets by the local health authorities according to the needs of the local population, in consultation with health professionals and community representatives. These are known as health improvement plans (**HImPs**) and are three-year programmes.

The development of this government-led approach fits in with the recommendations of the World Health Organization's programme *Health for All 2000,* in which they state that:

> The focus of the health care system should be on primary health care – meeting the basic needs of each community through services provided as close as possible to where people live and work, readily accessible to all, and based on full participation.
>
> (WHO, 1985, page 5).

Priority health areas

There are currently four priority health areas cited in the government's targets covering:

- heart disease and stroke
- accidents
- cancer
- mental health.

The government targets for each priority health area are set out below and on pages 414–417 together with a table indicating the proposed contract for how the targets can be met, nationally, locally and individually. Each table includes social and economic, environmental, lifestyle and service issues that can be addressed.

Heart disease and stroke

By 2010 the government target is 'to reduce the death rate from heart disease and stroke and related illnesses amongst people under 65 years by at least a further third'.

Table 10.2 A national contract on heart disease and stroke

	Government and national players can:	**Local players and communities can:**	**People can:**
Social and economic	Continue to make smoking cost more through taxation Tackle joblessness, social exclusion, low educational standards and other factors which make it harder to live a healthier life.	Tackle social exclusion in the community which makes it harder to have a healthy lifestyle. Provide incentives to employees to cycle or walk to work, or leave their cars at home.	Take opportunities to better their lives and their families' lives, through education, training and employment.
Environmental	Encourage employers and others to provide a smoke-free environment for non-smokers	Through local employers and others, provide a smoke-free environment for non-smokers. Through employers and staff, work in partnership to reduce stress at work. Provide safe cycling and walking routes.	Protect others from second-hand smoke.

Table 10.2 A national contract on heart disease and stroke *continued*

	Government and national players can:	Local players and communities can:	People can:
Lifestyle	End advertising and promotion of cigarettes. Enforce prohibition of sale of cigarettes to youngsters. Develop Healthy Living Centres. Ensure access to, and availability of, a wide range of foods for a healthy diet. Provide sound information on the health risks of smoking, poor diet and lack of exercise.	Encourage the development of healthy schools and healthy workplaces. Implement an integrated Transport Policy, including a national cycling strategy and measures to make walking more of an option. Target information about a healthy life on groups and areas where people are most at risk	Stop smoking or cut down, watch what they eat and take regular exercise.
Services	Encourage doctors and nurses and other health professionals to give advice on healthier living. Ensure catering and leisure professionals are trained in healthy eating and physical activity.	Provide help to people who want to stop smoking. Improve access to a variety of affordable food in deprived areas. Provide facilities for physical activity and relaxation and decent transport to help people get to them. Identify those at high risk of heart disease and stroke and provide high quality services.	Learn how to recognise a heart attack and what to do, including resuscitation skills. Have their blood pressure checked regularly. Take medicine as it is prescribed.

Source: Department of Health (1998), p. 64

Accidents

The government target for accidents is 'to reduce accidents by at least a fifth'.

Table 10.3 A national contract on accidents

	Government and national players can:	Local players and communities can:	People can:
Social and economic	Improve areas of deprivation through urban regeneration. Tackle social exclusion and joblessness.	Tackle social exclusion and joblessness in the community.	Take opportunities to combat proverty through education, training and employment.
Environmental	Improve safety of roads. Ensure compliance with seatbelt requirements and other road traffic laws. Help set standards for products and appliances. Promote higher standards of safety management.	Improve facilities for pedestrians and cycle paths. Develop safer routes for schools. Adopt traffic calming and other engineering measures and make roads safer. Work for healthier and safe workplaces. Make playgrounds safe.	Check the safety of appliances and use them correctly. Install smoke alarms. Drive safely. Take part in safety management in the workplace.

Table 10.3 A national contract on accidents *continued*

	Government and national players can:	Local players and communities can:	People can:
Lifestyle	Provide information on how to avoid osteoporosis so that accidents don't lead to broken bones. Run public safety campaigns. Ensure strategies are coordinated across Government Departments and Agencies. Provide information on ways to avoid accidents.	Ensure those in need have aids to prevent accidents, like car seats for babies. Work for whole school approaches to health and safety. Target accident prevention at those most at risk.	Adopt safe behaviour for themselves and their children. Wear cycle helmets. Wear a seatbelt. Not drink and drive. Keep physically fit.
Services	Encourage health professionals to give appropriate advice. Ensure professionals are trained in accident prevention.	Provide appropriate treatment to high-risk groups to prevent osteoporosis.	Provide child pedestrian and cycling training. Have regular eye-tests. Know emergency routine.

Source: Department of Health (1998), p. 69

Cancer

The government target for cancer is 'to reduce the death rate from cancer amongst people under 65 years by at least a further fifth'.

Table 10.4 A national contract on cancer

	Government and national players can:	Local players and communities can:	People can:
Social and economic	Continue to make smoking more costly through taxation. Tackle joblessness, social exclusion, low educational standards and other factors which make it harder to live a healthier life.	Tackle social exclusion in the community to make it easier for people to make healthy choices. Work with deprived communities and with businesses to ensure a more varied and affordable choice of food.	Take opportunities to better their lives and their families' lives through education, training and employment.
Environmental	Encourage employers and others to provide a smoke-free environment for non-smokers. Encourage local action to tackle radon in the home. Continue to press for international action to restore the ozone layer.	Through local employers and others, provide a smoke-free environment for non-smokers. Tackle radon in the home.	Protect others from second-hand smoke. Cover up in the sun.
Lifestyle	End advertising and promotion of cigarettes. Prohibit sale of cigarettes to youngsters and ensure enforcement. Support Healthy Living Centres. Provide reliable and objective information on the health risks of smoking, poor diet and too much sun.	Encourage the development of healthy workplaces and healthy schools. Target health information on groups and areas where people are most at risk.	Stop or cut down smoking and watch what they eat. Be careful when they are in the sun and ensure that young children are not exposed to too much sun. Follow sensible drinking advice.

Table 10.4 A national contract on cancer *continued*

	Government and national players can:	Local players and communities can:	People can:
Services	Encourage doctors and nurses and other health professionals to give advice on prevention. Ensure that healthy schools work with pupils and parents to improve health. Implement effective and high-quality cancer screening programmes. Ensure equal access to high-quality treatment and care.	Provide help in stopping smoking to people who want to stop. Improve access and availability to a variety of affordable food in deprived areas. Ensure hard-to-reach groups come forward for cancer screening services. Ensure rapid treatment for cancers when they are diagnosed.	Attend cancer screenings when invited. Seek medical advice promptly if they are worried.

Source: Department of Health (1998), p. 75

Mental health

The government target regarding mental health is 'to reduce the death rate from suicide and undetermined injury by at least a further sixth'.

Table 10.5 A national contract on mental health

	Government and national players can:	Local players and communities can:	People can:
Social and economic	Tackle joblessness, social exclusion and other factors which make it harder to have a healthier lifestyle. Tackle alcohol and drug misuse.	Develop local support networks, eg for recently widowed/ bereaved, lone parents, unemployed people and single people. Develop court diversion schemes. Develop job opportunities for people with mental illness. Develop local strategies to support the needs of mentally ill people from black and minority ethnic groups.	Develop parenting skills. Support friends at times of stress – be a good listener. Participate in support networks. Take opportunities to better their lives and their families' lives through education, training and employment.
Environmental	Continue to invest in housing and reduce homelessness. Encourage employers to address workplace stress. Reduce isolation through transport policy. Promote healthy schools. Address levels of mental illness amongst prisoners.	Develop effective housing strategies. Reduce stress in workplace. Improve community safety.	Improve workload management.

A national contract on mental health *continued*

	Government and national players can:	Local players and communities can:	People can:
Lifestyle	Increase public awareness and understanding of mental health. Reduce access to means of suicide. Support Healthy Living Centres.	Focus on particular high-risk groups, eg young men, people in isolated rural communities. Encourage positive local media reporting. Develop and encourage use of range of leisure facilities	Use opportunities for relaxation and physical exercise and try to avoid using alcohol/smoking to reduce stress. Increase understanding of what good mental health is.
Services	Develop standards and training for primary care and specialist mental health services. Improve recruitment/retention of mental health professionals. Identify/advise on effective treatment and care. Develop protocols to guide best practice.	Promote high-quality pre-school education and good mental health in schools and promote educational achievement. Ensure mental health professionals are well trained and supported. Develop a range of comprehensive mental health services for all age groups and alcohol and drug services for young people and adults. Support carers of people with long-term disability and chronic illness. Provide advice on financial problems.	Develop culturally sensitive services. Contribute information to service planners and get involved. Contact services quickly when difficulties start. Increase knowledge about self-help.

Source: Department of Health (1998), p. 79

---

activity

10.12

Make a copy of the table below and list on it the ways in which you think each of these priority health areas could have an impact on the health and well-being of children. Consider both the short-term and long-term impacts.

Heart disease and stroke		Accidents	
Short-term impact	Long-term impact	Short-term impact	Long-term impact

Methods of preventing illness

A range of approaches exist to prevent illness:

- environmental approaches
- public health approaches
  - education
  - immunisation
  - screening
- dietary approaches
- educational approaches.

These are summarised below. What else can you add to each of them?

Environmental approaches

Globally, environmentalists strive to improve both health and the quality of the planet by highlighting the effects of:

Figure 10.8

Environmental issues

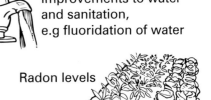

Pollution from cars

Research into the effect of living near to nuclear power installations

Pollution from CFCs

Improvements to water and sanitation, e.g fluoridation of water

Pollution from occupational health hazards

Radon levels

However, it is not just environmentalists who are responsible for monitoring environmental hazards to health, as emerging concerns from local communities and pressure groups demonstrates. Health Action Zones (HAZs) were set up from 1999 in areas of underprivilege, with the aim of bringing together different sectors of local government such as housing, social services and health. HAZs are able to tackle the wider environmental issues that have an impact on health and, therefore, reduce health inequalities. Individuals can also have an impact on environmental approaches by such measures as reporting hazards in the environment, responsible recycling, and maintaining satisfactory standards of hygiene in their personal environments.

Public health approaches

Figure 10.9

Public health resources to prevent illness

Traditional public health approaches have tended to focus on concerns about sanitation and nutrition, as well as the eradication of disease and control of infection. Penn and Thurtle (2005) describe public health as being concerned with the overall health and well-being of

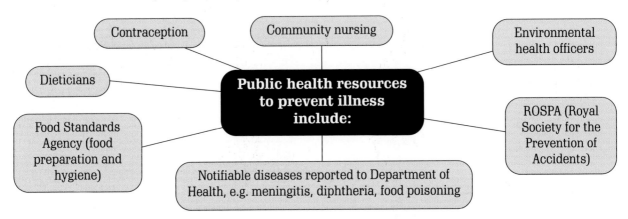

the community, and there are clear links to environmental approaches, as well as to issues of inequality and poverty. The interventions and individuals identified in the following figure will continue to be essential to the health of the community, but wider issues such as child poverty and socio-economic deprivation also need to be tackled

Figure 10.10

Effective health education is rooted in information

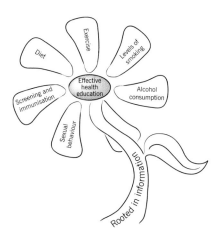

Educational approaches

Educational approaches are usually underpinned by the idea that giving individuals the knowledge and understanding to improve their health will enable them to make the correct decisions. This can be achieved by the dissemination of information about health and well-being, but can be affected by the quality of the information given and the right of the individual to accept or reject the information. Schools and early years settings are likely to take an educational approach to health promotion and will promote the acquisition of skills, as well as knowledge.

Educational approaches include:

Figure 10.11

Health promotion programmes: Planning a health promotion campaign

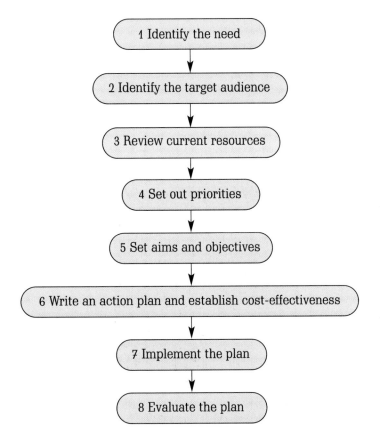

419

Any campaign to pass on information needs to be accessible to its target audience and therefore it needs to appeal, be visually interesting, and the information should be readily available and free from patronising or moralistic tones. Presentation, language and content are all important.

The Health Education Authority has now been amalgamated into the Health Development Agency. It has a useful website for further information on health education (www.hda.nhs.uk). The government site 'Wired for Health' is also a useful source of information on health education topics and activities (ww.wiredforhealth.gov.uk).

Visual presentation

- Visual presentation is important to gain initial attention.
- Photographs, cartoons and illustrations can all be used successfully.
- The visual approach selected needs to be relevant to the main target group, without excluding others who may also find it useful.

Professional Practice

- Illustrations need to be bolder and clearer in information aimed at young children than in information aimed at teenagers, where a cartoon or graphic design would be more likely to appeal.

Language style

- The language used should be relevant to the targeted group.
- Teenagers will appreciate a more contemporary use of language.
- Children need a greater ratio of visual to written information.
- Translations into languages other than English should be made where possible.

Professional Practice

- Any written text aimed at young children should be presented using upper and lower case lettering and punctuated correctly; i.e. use capitals only at the start of sentences and for proper names. Write in short sentences and do not forget to use full stops at the ends of sentences. The text should be easy to read, and set in large and bold type.

Promotional content

- The content should start with the main emphasis of the health promotion programme.
- Positive messages should be made very clear.
- Judgement statements that could annoy or alienate the reader should be avoided. For example, avoid statements such as 'Only a fool continues to…'.
- Getting the balance of information right is crucial to ensure that the message is taken in.
- Too much information can put people off reading any further.
- Too little information can leave the reader both unimpressed and uninformed.

activity
10.13

In a group, find out what current government health promotion campaigns there are in your area.

1   Research and gather information on each campaign for different target groups. Ensure that you include young children in this.
2   Consider what elements of each campaign appeal to you personally. Use the points raised above as a guideline to get you started.
3   Select three pieces of promotional material and ask a range of people questions about them. For example:

  ■   What do they think of them?
  ■   Would they be likely to pick them up?
  ■   Would they be likely to read them?

4   Collate the outcomes of your group.
5   What conclusions have you come to about the potential success of the promotional materials you selected?
6   What have you learned from this about preparing information materials for other people?

Professional Practice

■   It is important to consider how you will put over your message to people who have limited vision or literacy.

■   How accessible would the resources you found in the above activity have been for people in these situations?

■   How could they have been made more accessible to them?

activity
10.14

Having evaluated a range of health promotion materials, return to the leaflet you designed for the activity on page 407. Reflect on and evaluate your leaflet in the light of what you have read about presentation.

Health promotion was incorporated into the Education Reform Act 1988 with health education being included as a cross-curricular subject within the National Curriculum. In the Education Act 1993, sex education became mandatory in secondary schools, with a 'right to withdraw' clause for parents.

activity
10.15

Imagine that you are developing a health promotion campaign to either:

1   promote sex education in secondary schools, or to
2   tackle cross-infection in schools ('tummy bugs', threadworms, and so on).

Using the flow chart on page 419 as a guide, plan your campaign with a partner.

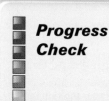

Progress Check

1 What is the medical model of health?

2 What is the social model of health?

3 Which model of health is the World Health Organization particularly concerned with?

4 Give an example of a fixed factor influencing the health of an individual.

5 What three issues are at the heart of the welfare state?

6 a) What does the abbreviation HImP stand for?

   b) What are HImPs?

7 What are the four priority health areas being targeted by the UK government?

8 Which level of health care looks after the long-term care of chronic conditions?

9 Which type of diabetes is insulin dependent?

10 Give at least five aims of health educators.

11 List at least 10 people who could be considered to be health educators.

Causes of illness

Infection

The human body's natural state is to be healthy and be able to fight off illness. What we put into our bodies and what our bodies are exposed to have an impact on how well our bodies manage to maintain their healthy states, illustrating how important health education programmes can be. It is worth revisiting the definitions of health to consolidate your understanding of what 'health' actually is. Think also about how the body automatically defends itself, through:

- the eyes
  - the blinking mechanism helps prevent particles entering the eyes
  - tears contain a mild antiseptic which cleanse the eyes
- the blood – leucocytes (white blood cells) fight infected tissue and destroy germs
- the skin – sebum is an oily substance that is secreted through the surface of the skin and acts as a protective layer
- mucus
  - each opening into the body (for example, the nose) has a lining of mucus membrane at the entrance to help prevent infections from entering
  - ciliated epithelium (small hairs) trap and collect foreign bodies, such as earwax and mucus from the nose
- the spleen – this is a vascular organ with a large number of blood vessels, which filters out foreign bodies from the blood and produces antibodies
- the gut – good bacteria in the gut kills both good and bad bacteria when fighting infection, causing diarrhoea.

Refer to page 402 for the definitions of health.

Figure 10.12

Causes of illness

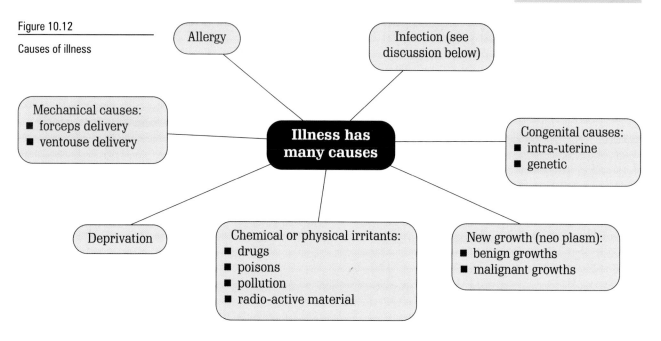

The microbiological (infectious) causes of illness are varied, and this is the area you will most often deal with as an early years worker. These germs (pathogens) can be roughly divided into five groups:

- bacteria – tough cells which rapidly multiply and thrive in the body's warm, moist conditions; treatable with antibiotics; for example ear infections and conjunctivitis

- viruses – parasites which invade other cells and then reproduce themselves; cannot be treated with antibiotics; can be relatively harmless or significantly serious; for example, the common cold, influenza and chickenpox

- fungi – spread by contact with fungi spores; do no serious harm to humans but cause much irritation and discomfort; some harmless fungi are permanently with us; treatment with an anti-fungal product as necessary; for example, for athlete's foot

- parasites – organisms spread by cross-infection; can be seen with the naked eye; many different varieties and difficult to eradicate once they have taken hold in a nursery or school class, due to cases of re-infection; for example scabies, head lice and threadworms

- protozoa – single-cell organisms; many cause human distress through illnesses such as severe stomach upsets, toxoplasmosis (often caught through handling cats or cat litter) and amoebiasis (causing diarrhoea).

Pathogens can enter the body in different ways. They can be:

- ingested – taken in through the mouth

- inhaled – breathed in through either the mouth or the nose

- inoculated – taken in through a break in the surface of the skin.

They can be spread by:

- **direct contact** – germs transmitted by touch, for example broken skin contacts, kissing and sexual activity

- **indirect contact** – germs left on surfaces subsequently in contact with another person

- **droplet infection** – air-borne germs spread through sneezing, coughing, and so on, as microscopic droplets are released into the atmosphere.

Make a copy of the table below. Check your understanding of common childhood illnesses by placing as many conditions as you can under one or more headings. You may find it helpful to return to this activity once you have read the rest of this unit.

	Bacteria	Virus	Fungi	Parasite	Protozoa
Ingested					
Inhaled					
Innoculated					
Direct contact					
Indirect contact					
Droplet infection					

Genetics

Genetic and maturational factors influence our health, but we can have only a limited influence over them by modifying some of the known outcomes. Identification of the specific genes responsible for some conditions include the identification of Down's syndrome as a trisomy of chromosome 21 and, more recently, the advances in identifying ovarian cancer as C125.

Clearly, early identification through gene technology can be extremely helpful in alleviating some of the long-term problems of various conditions, but the manipulation of genes also raises a range of ethical issues.

What ethical issues can you think of linked to gene technology? Discuss these issues with a partner, or in a small group.

Link

Refer back to page 284 for information on genetic inheritance.

The impact of socio-economic factors on health

The table below summarises the main effects on health of the three socio-economic categories: poverty, housing and unemployment. Use the case studies that follow it to explore socio-economic issues further.

Table 10.6 Socio-economic factors affecting health

Poverty	Housing	Unemployment
Money problems	High-rise flats/isolation	Lowest income group
Unpaid bills	Lack of stimulus	Low self-esteem
Debts	Insufficient heat	Stigma
Lack of leisure activities	Overcrowding	Social exclusion
Poor diet	Lack of labour-saving equipment	Boredom
	Disordered communities	Depression
	Communities in fear	

case study 10.3 — Wilson, Marlow and Maisie

The Johnston family lives in a two-bedroom flat on the sixth floor of a high-rise flat in north London. Mr Johnston is a builder who is currently unemployed, and Mrs Johnston was a cashier in a supermarket but has not worked since her children were born. Wilson is ten, Marlow is eight and Maisie is two.

The family have been asking to be rehoused since before Maisie was born as they have very limited space, and Maisie still shares a bedroom with her parents out of necessity, not choice.

Mr Johnston takes the boys to school each morning, but then returns to the flat. He spends long hours staring out of the window. His (initially) weekly visits to the Job Centre have ceased, as he has lost faith that he will regain employment. Mrs Johnston rarely goes out as the lift in the block of flats is unreliable and Maisie is only just walking. Maisie is quite a sickly child and she sleeps a great deal during the day but is unsettled at night. The estate is a place of tension and the boys do not play out after school. None of the family goes out after dark and friends are not encouraged to visit.

activity

1. What socio-economic issues can you identify?
2. What do you consider will be the likely impact on the health of the children?
3. What do you consider will be the likely impact on the health of the parents?
4. Is there likely to be any long-term impact on Maisie's development if the family's situation does not change?
5. Could the Johnston family do anything else to improve their situation, do you think?

case study 10.4 — Arabella, Chloe and Josh

The Stenner family lives in a four-bedroom house in north London. Mr Stenner was an office manager in a company which has just gone into liquidation. He is now unemployed. Mrs Stenner is a qualified book-keeper, but has not worked since her children were born. Arabella is ten, Chloe is eight and Josh is two. Mr and Mrs Stenner have owned their home for 12 years and each child has their own bedroom.

Mrs Stenner and Josh take the girls to school each morning, returning home after coffee with friends. Mr Stenner spends long hours in the garden. He surfs the Internet to see what employment opportunities are available locally and is grateful that he does not have to stand and read the notice board at the local Job Centre. He is unsure whether he will find similar employment. Mrs Johnston is enjoying having her husband around more and Josh, who is an active little boy, loves helping him in the garden. The children have had to give up some of their out-of-school activities because of the family's reduced finances, but are able to have friends to play instead.

activity

1. What socio-economic issues can you identify for this family?
2. Do you consider there will be any likely impact on the health of the children?
3. Do you consider there will be any likely impact on the health of the parents?
4. Is there likely to be any long-term impact on Josh's development if the situation for the family does not change?
5. Could the Stenner family do anything else to improve their situation, do you think?

Figure 10.13

What effect does housing have on the lifestyle of the people in it?

activity

10.18

In many ways the situations for the Johnstons and the Stenners are similar, but how do the two case studies compare in real terms? Refer back to the socio-economic issues listed in the table on page 424.

Methods of preventing illness

Immunisation programmes

What is immunity?

Immunity is the body's ability to resist disease. Each individual builds up an immunity to various illnesses during life. As infants, we are each born with a degree of natural immunity to some illnesses and diseases, based on the immunity of our mothers. Immunity is extended by breast-feeding for up to four months. There are different types of immunity. The table below gives examples of how immunity can occur either naturally or be acquired through immunisation programmes, and also how immunity can be active, passive or achieved by the **herd immunity** process.

Table 10.7 Types of immunity

Type of immunity	Description	Example
Active natural immunity	An immune response to a naturally occurring infection that the child has contracted	Antibodies formed following chickenpox or rubella
Active acquired immunity	An immune response to an antigen (a toxin produced by bacteria to make antibodies)	Via the (live) polio vaccine which is given as part of the childhood immunisation programme
Passive natural immunity	Naturally occurring immunity passed across the placenta, and in breast milk	Infants are born with a degree of natural immunity based on their mothers' immunity
Passive acquired immunity	Antibodies are transferred via an injection (immunisation programme)	Ready-made antibodies, such as diphtheria and tetanus given as part of the immunisation programme
Herd immunity	If a high enough proportion of the whole population is immunised it will keep the rest free from the disease (usually needs 90+ per cent)	The HiB vaccine campaign has successfully reduced the incidence of HiB

Source: based on Keene (1990), p. 75

Immunisation of children

There are **live vaccines** (active) and **non-live vaccines** (passive). As children are particularly vulnerable to contracting disease, a programme of immunisation is recommended by health experts. Immunisation not only protects the immunised child from falling ill, it also helps to protect children with suppressed immune systems who may not be able to have all vaccinations in the programme.

Immunisation is only given with parental consent, and although technically there is no contra-indication for a child with a minor cough or cold receiving an immunisation, most people prefer their children to be free from illness at the time when the immunisation is administered. The recommended programme is set out in the table below.

Table 10.8 The immunisation programme

Age	Immunisation	Method
2 months	HiB and meningitis C Diphtheria, whooping cough and tetanus Polio	1 injection 1 injection By mouth
3 months	HiB and meningitis C Diphtheria, whooping cough and tetanus Polio	1 injection 1 injection By mouth
4 months	HiB and meningitis C Diphtheria, whooping cough and tetanus Polio	1 injection 1 injection By mouth
12–15 months	Measles, mumps and rubella (MMR)	1 injection
3–5 years: pre-school booster MMR booster	Diphtheria and tetanus Polio Measles, mumps and rubella	1 injection By mouth 1 injection
11–14 years	BCG (Bacillus Calmette-Guerin) vaccine to protect against TB (tuberculosis). All children are Heaf-tested first to check their immunity.	1 injection
15–18 years: leaving school booster	Diphtheria and tetanus Polio	1 injection By mouth

Professional Practice

- Children sometimes have a slight reaction to immunisations, such as having a raised temperature and feeling miserable.
- If this occurs, plenty of fluids should be given, along with paracetamol.
- A careful eye should be kept on the child, particularly a young baby.
- If a raised temperature does not come down within 24 hours, or it continues to rise, medical advice should be sought.
- Some health professionals recommend that paracetamol is automatically given after an immunisation.
- Some health professionals support the idea of giving it just beforehand, to minimise the risk of a rise in temperature.
- Paracetamol is not registered to be given to babies under the age of three months.
- Infant ibuprofen suspension is as effective as paracetamol and is an alternative, but should not be given to children with moderate or severe asthma.
- Children under 12 should never be given aspirin, because there is a slight risk that it might cause Reye's syndrome.
- As with all medication, paracetamol and infant ibuprofen suspension should be given in the doses appropriate for the age of the child.

Children with suppressed immunity

Children with certain illnesses or conditions – for example, leukaemia, HIV and AIDS – may have **suppressed immunity**. It is not appropriate to give these children live vaccines, as a live vaccine is a weakened version of the condition itself. Artificial vaccines can sometimes be offered to these children and to those in close contact with them, such as siblings. An example is the polio vaccine, which is given orally.

It should be noted that children who are HIV positive will not necessarily develop AIDS.

Homoeopathic immunisations

Some parents choose not to have their children immunised through the mainstream programme but may choose to use homoeopathic alternatives instead. There is little evidence to support the efficacy of the homoeopathic alternatives, but they do offer a degree of protection for some children. Although immunisation is recommended for most healthy children, as an early years professional you should respect the parents' right to choose not to have their child immunised and make no value judgements about them.

Screening

Screening is the process of examining a whole population to determine who is showing signs of having a particular condition or disease and who may develop or be predisposed to a condition or disease. Screening in the UK is available for every child, with the consent of their parents.

Screening is important because it:

- enables early intervention where a problem is confirmed;
- keeps parents informed about their child's progress or likely progress;
- highlights the need for specific areas of stimulation for a child to meet their potential;
- raises awareness for the future and allows informed decisions to be made, with or without genetic counselling.

Foetal screening

Figure 10.14

Foetal screening

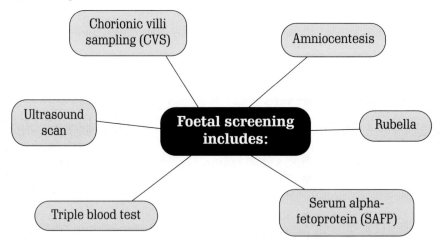

 Refer back to Unit 7, page 282, for a description of how each of these tests is made and why they are offered.

Neonatal screening

Figure 10.15

Neonatal screening

Apgar score

Full physiological examination:
- spine
- hips
- organs
- mouth and palette

Neonatal screening includes:

Guthrie test (heel prick test) carried out at about seven days, testing for:
- phenylketonuria (PKU)
- hypothyroidism
- cystic fibrosis

Reflexes

Refer back to Unit 7, pages 286 and 289, for further information on the Apgar score and the primitive reflexes present at birth.

Infant screening

Figure 10.16

Infant screening

Distraction hearing test

Speech discrimination test

Vision tests

Infant screening includes:

Personal child health records

Hearing tests

Colour blindness tests

The table below describes a general screening programme following a child through the earliest years.

Table 10.9 The child health screening programme

Age	Screening procedure	Health promotion
	These procedures are performed by midwives, doctors and health visitors throughout childhood.	Health visitors discuss the following issues with parents and carers to heighten their awareness of important issues affecting their child at critical ages. Health education is offered appropriately and tactfully.
Birth	FULL PHYSICAL EXAMINATION Usually performed by a hospital paediatrician before the mother and baby are discharged home. If the baby is born at home the general practitioner will conduct the examination: ■ weight ■ heart and pulses ■ hips ■ testes ■ head circumference ■ eyes ■ Guthrie test (after 6 days of milk feeding) to test for phenylketonuria (PKU), hypothyroidism and cystic fibrosis ■ sickle cell and thalassaemia test if suspected	Cot death (SIDS) prevention Feeding techniques Nutrition Baby care Crying Sleep Car safety Family planning Passive smoking Dangers of shaking baby Sibling management

Table 10.9 The child health screening programme *continued*

Age	Screening procedure	Health promotion
10–14 days	Health visitors perform these checks, usually at the birth visit in the home. Review of birth check Assess levels of parental support	Nutrition Breast-feeding Cot death (SIDS) prevention Passive smoking Accident prevention: bathing, scalding and fires Explanation of tests and results
6–8 weeks	All babies receive this check performed by the GP and health visitor. REVIEW: Parental concerns, e.g. vision, hearing, activity Risk factors, including family history of abnormalities FULL EXAMINATION INCLUDING: ■ weight ■ head circumference ■ length ■ hip check ■ testes ■ eyes: squint, movement, ■ tone and general development ■ heart and pulses ■ Guthrie test result given to parents	Immunisation Nutrition and dangers of early weaning Accidents: falls, fires, over-heating, scalds Hearing Recognition of illness in babies and what action to take, e.g. fever management Crying Sleeping position Cot death (SIDS) prevention Passive smoking Review of car safety
2–4 months	Health visitor check Parental concerns Hip check	Weighing as appropriate Maintain previous health promotion Promotion of language and social development Hearing Discourage future use of baby walkers
6–9 months	Health visitor check Hip check Distraction hearing test Discussion of developmental progress asking about vision, hearing and language development Check weight and head circumference Observe behaviour and look for squints	Parental concerns Nutrition Hearing Accident prevention: fires, choking, scalding, burns, stair and door gates, fire guards, etc. Review of car transport Dental care Play and development needs

Source: from Keene (1999) pp.90–1

Diet and lifestyle

Diet and lifestyle are important factors in children's health and can have a considerable impact on their well-being as children and adults. Children rarely have the choice to avoid the adverse aspects of their family's lifestyle that may affect their health and these aspects may include

■ inadequate or unbalanced diet

■ exposure to cigarette smoke

■ lack of fresh air and exercise

■ failure to protect child from effects of alcohol or other forms of substance misuse.

The government is keen to address all of the factors that can affect a child's future health, and interventions have been planned to improve dietary intake and participation in sport and exercise. However, interventions need to be planned in tandem with education programmes in order for the root causes of the problems to be tackled. Again, there appear to be links between the factors outlined above and social class.

■ Poor standards of nutrition are more likely to occur in the lower social classes and it is reported that children in working class families are less likely to eat sufficient fruit and vegetables and more likely to eat processed foods and foods high in sugars and fat. Poor diet can lead to malnutrition, vitamin and mineral deficiencies, obesity, dental decay, constipation, and cardiovascular disease.

- Smoking is also reported to be more prevalent in Social Classes IV and V. Babies and children in 'smoking' homes have no choice but to be passive smokers and this can result in a higher incidence of Sudden Infant Death Syndrome, respiratory infections, asthma, heart disease and lung cancer.

- Middle class people are more likely to take regular exercise and other associated social activities (Moore 2002). Regular exercise can improve cardiovascular health and lessen stress, and there are implications for children whose parents have insufficient money or awareness of the benefits of exercise.

Refer to Unit 5 to remind yourself of the benefits of healthy diets and exercise.

Common childhood illnesses

There are many illnesses that are common in childhood. Most last only a short period of time but can be very unpleasant during the process. Long-term consequences can result from some conditions, and the severity of conditions such as measles, particularly in children who have not been immunised, should never be under-estimated.

This section describes some common childhood conditions and some chronic long-term conditions found in children.

The common childhood conditions described in this section are:

- chickenpox
- mumps
- rubella
- measles
- hand, foot and mouth disease
- coughs and colds.

The chronic long-term conditions described in this section are mostly non-infectious. Some are conditions that children are born with, and others can develop at a later stage. They are:

- gastro-intestinal problems
- skin conditions – eczema and psoriasis
- asthma
- cystic fibrosis
- diabetes
- coeliac disease.

Some of the information on the following conditions is based on *Child Health: Care of the Child in Health and Illness* by Keene (1999), which is an excellent source of further reading on a variety of health care issues.

Common illnesses in childhood

Chickenpox

What is chickenpox?

- Chickenpox is an itchy and highly contagious condition, which causes spots which blister, weep and subsequently crust over.

What causes chickenpox and how is it spread?

- It is a viral infection called herpes zoster, spread by droplet infection.
- The same virus can cause shingles in adults who have previously had chickenpox, if exposed to the virus a second time.

Recognising chickenpox

- Spots appear in groups, initially on the torso and then more 'groups' of spots appear anywhere on the body over several days.

- The spots turn into fluid-filled blisters which weep and then dry after about three days.

- As the spots appear in successive groups, they will also dry up in successive groups.

See *Child Health: Care of the Child in Health and Illness* by Keene (1999), Plate 1.

Initial actions

- Comfort and reassurance are needed.

- If initial spots appear in a day-care setting, parents need to be contacted. Paracetamol is usually given to reduce the discomfort.

- Antihistamines can be useful to reduce the irritation.

- Calamine (or similar) lotion can be applied to the spots to soothe them.

- Using bicarbonate of soda in a cool bath can also help reduce the itching.

Ongoing care

- Paracetamol is usually given as needed.

- Use calamine and bicarbonate of soda over a few days.

- Ensure the child has plenty of fluids and is kept comfortable.

- Cut finger nails short to avoid scratching.

- In young babies, cotton mittens can be useful.

Possible complications

- Some children have internal spots: nostrils, throat, vagina, anus.

- Secondary infections can occur through scratching.

- Encephalitis: inflammation of the brain.

- Pneumonia: inflammation of the lungs.

Immunisation?

- None available at present.

- It is important that pregnant women and immuno-compromised children and adults are not exposed to the chickenpox virus.

Incubation period and potential to infect others?

- The incubation period for chickenpox can be up to 21 days.

- Children are infectious for about three days prior to the first spots appearing, and remain infectious until all the scabs have dried over.

Mumps

What is mumps?

- It is an infection that results in painful swelling and inflammation of the salivary glands near the ear. Other salivary glands may also be involved.

What causes mumps and how is it spread?

- It is caused by the parotitis virus and the infection is spread by droplets.

Recognising mumps

- The child appears to be generally unwell for several days before mumps is suspected or diagnosed.

- A raised temperature is usual with swelling on one or both sides of the face. This swelling can be very uncomfortable and may last for 5–7 days.

- Children with mumps may not want to eat as moving the jaws is painful and, as the salivary glands are not producing as much saliva as usual, a dry mouth is common.

Initial actions

- Give paracetamol or ibuprofen syrup to reduce fever and pain.

- Offer child frequent non-acidic fluids with a straw to reduce painful movement of the jaw.

- Ensure that child is seen by doctor to confirm the diagnosis because mumps is a notifiable disease.

- Be aware of possible deterioration and seek medical assistance if the child complains of a severe headache or develops pain in the abdomen.

Ongoing care

- Make sure that the child has been given analgesia half an hour before eating as this helps with the pain that eating produces.

- Try to avoid hard or crunchy foods; offer soft foods and nutritious fluids such as soups. Food can also be liquidised.

Possible complications

- Mumps can result in inflammation of the meninges (the covering of the brain), and meningitis can develop within 10 days of the onset of the first symptoms of mumps. A full recovery from this type of meningitis is usual.

- Orchitis or an inflammation of the testes can occur up to 5–7 days after the start of mumps, although this is usually rare before the onset of puberty.

- Deafness is sometimes noticed in children who have had mumps. A child who has had mumps and who appears to be hearing impaired in one or both ears will need investigating and a hearing test.

- Pancreatitis (inflammation of the pancreas) can cause severe abdominal pain that is acute at onset. Permanent damage is rare, but occasional cases can develop diabetes.

Immunisation?

- Available as part of the MMR vaccine.

Incubation period and potential to infect others?

- 14–21 days

- Children will still be infectious for several days after the first symptoms of mumps appear.

- They usually recover within 7–10 days and can go back to nursery or school when they are no longer infectious and feel well.

Rubella (German measles)

What is rubella?

- Rubella is usually only a mild condition in children. It involves a high temperature and an all-over rash.

What causes rubella and how is it spread?

- Rubella is a virus spread by droplet infection.

Recognising rubella

- The appearance of the rash is usually preceded by a raised temperature.

- The all-over pale rash, which usually starts on the face, does not itch.

- Glands are often swollen behind the ears and in the neck.

See *Child Health: Care of the Child in Health and Illness* by Keene (1999), Plate 1.

Initial actions

- Give paracetamol to reduce the temperature.

- Drinking plenty of fluids should be encouraged.

Ongoing care
- Avoid contact with women who are, or could be, pregnant as contact during the first 12 weeks can affect the foetus.
- No other special care is needed, and children usually recover quickly.

Possible complications
To an infected foetus:

- loss of hearing or vision
- impaired hearing or vision
- heart deformities
- learning difficulties.

Immunisation?
- Rubella vaccine is given as part of the MMR triple vaccine at aged 15 months and 4 years.

Incubation period and potential to infect others?
- The incubation period for rubella is 14 to 21 days.
- Children are infectious from about seven days prior to the rash appearing and until four or five days afterwards.

Measles
What is measles?
- Measles is a highly contagious virus with a distinctive rash. It can be a very serious condition.

What causes measles and how is it spread?
- It is caused by RNA-containing paramyxovirus, spread by droplet infection.

Recognising measles
- Children usually appear unwell for three or four days before the rash appears.
- Runny nose and general cold symptoms are common.
- The rash is dense, blotchy and red, usually starting on the neck and face before spreading down over the whole body.
- White spots form inside the mouth and on the cheeks (Koplik's spots).
- Eyes become sore and an avoidance of bright lights is common.

See *Child Health: Care of the Child in Health and Illness* by Keene (1999), Plate 1.

Initial actions
- Paracetamol should be given to reduce the raised temperature.
- Plenty of fluids should be encouraged.
- Children would only be visited by a GP in exceptional circumstances but will usually be seen by a health visitor to confirm diagnosis, and referred to the GP if necessary.
- Children will normally be most comfortable resting with curtains closed to reduce the light.

Ongoing care
- Paracetamol as necessary.
- Continue with a high fluid intake.

Possible complications
- Eye infections may need antibiotics.
- Ear infections may need antibiotics.
- Hearing needs to be checked within a few weeks of illness if ears were affected.
- Inflammation of the brain can occur (encephalitis).

Immunisation?
- The measles vaccine is given as part of the MMR triple vaccine at aged 15 months and 4 years.

Incubation period and potential to infect others?
- The incubation period for measles is 8 to 14 days.
- Children are infectious from the day before the symptoms appear until four or five days afterwards.

Hand, foot and mouth disease

What is hand, foot and mouth disease?
- This is a mild, but highly infectious condition which is common in children of pre-school age. It is in no way connected to foot and mouth disease found in cattle and other hoofed animals.

What causes hand, foot and mouth disease and how is it spread?
- It is a virus is called coxsackie, spread by droplet infection.

Recognising hand, foot and mouth disease
- The child's temperature may be raised slightly.
- Very small blisters are often found inside the cheeks, which may ulcerate.
- Blistery spots with a red surrounding edge appear about two days after the mouth blisters on hands and fingers, and tops of feet.

Initial actions
- Give paracetamol to reduce the raised temperature.
- Provide plenty of fluids – avoid anything that might irritate the sore mouth.
- Foods suitable for a slightly sore mouth should be offered, e.g. porridge, jelly, custard, rice.

Ongoing care
- Prolonged mouth blisters may require treatment by the GP.

Possible complications
- No real complications noted.

Immunisation?
- There is no immunisation available for hand, foot and mouth disease.

Incubation period and potential to infect others?
- There is no known incubation period.

Coughs and colds

What are coughs and colds?
- Coughs and colds can vary from the very mild to quite severe. They can be highly contagious.

What causes coughs and colds and how are they spread?
- Coughs and colds are caused by viral infections and are spread by droplet infection.
- Coughs can also be part of another condition, such as bronchitis or pneumonia.

Recognising coughs and colds
- Colds usually start with a raised temperature and runny nose and eyes.
- Accompanying coughs can be dry and ticklish, or deep and chesty.

Initial actions
- Give paracetamol to reduce the raised temperature.
- Plenty of fluids should be offered.

Ongoing care

■ Continued paracetamol as necessary.

Possible complications

■ Ear infections may require antibiotics.

■ Chest infections may require antibiotics.

Immunisation?

■ There is no immunisation for the common cold.

Incubation period and potential to infect others?

■ Each cold virus is unique and so there is no known incubation period.

Chronic conditions

Gastro-enteritis

What is gastro-enteritis?

■ Gastro-enteritis is the most common irritant of the stomach and intestinal lining.

What causes gastro-enteritis and how is it spread?

■ It is caused by bacteria and viruses.

■ It can be spread in food due to poor hygiene during food handling.

■ It can be spread by direct or indirect contact.

Recognising gastro-enteritis

Children appear unwell, lethargic and miserable before the onset of the main symptoms, which include:

■ vomiting

■ diarrhoea

■ raised temperature

■ loss of appetite.

Initial actions

■ Only clear fluids (cooled boiled water) should be given for 24 hours.

■ Dehydration drinks may be used for children over the age of one year, particularly if symptoms are severe.

Ongoing care

■ Breast-fed babies should continue to breast feed as usual.

■ If there is no improvement after 24 hours, medical advice should be sought, particularly in very young children.

■ Continue with clear fluids, together with 'ice-pops' to give the child some sugar.

■ Light foods should be offered when appetite returns.

■ Diet drinks are not considered to be suitable.

Possible complications

■ Dehydration can easily occur in very young children and babies.

■ If children cease to pass urine frequently medical advice should be sought.

■ Intravenous fluids may need to be given in severe cases.

Immunisation?

■ There is no immunisation available.

Incubation period and potential to infect others?

■ There is no known incubation period.

■ Strict hygiene is needed to try and minimise the spread of infection.

■ Gastroenteritis often 'sweeps' through families, nurseries and schools.

Figure 10.17

Good personal hygiene helps
prevent cross-infection

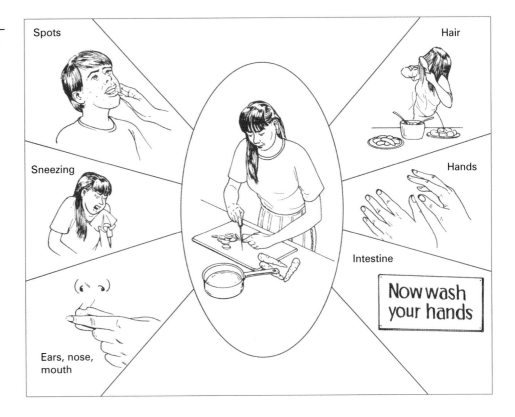

Spots

Hair

Sneezing

Hands

Intestine

Ears, nose, mouth

Now wash your hands

Eczema

What is eczema?

Eczema is due to an allergic reaction and is common amongst young children. It dries the skin, forming itchy inflamed areas which crack open and often weep. It is extremely unpleasant and causes great misery to many children. Fortunately the majority of children cease to be affected by eczema by the time they reach puberty. Some, however, continue to suffer from eczema, along with asthma (another allergic reaction).

What causes eczema?

Eczema is a reaction to a 'trigger factor'. These triggers vary between individuals, with common causes being dairy produce, washing powders and soaps. It can also be triggered or exacerbated by stress or excitement.

Recognising eczema

The initial signs of eczema usually appear between 3 and 18 months. It occurs initially on the face and scalp, the shins and forearms, and later it affects the backs of knees, inside of the elbow joints and at the ankles. Symptoms include:

- dry scaly skin which cracks and itches
- the itchy rash often weeps
- the sore areas crust over
- in the long term, the skin becomes thickened and leathery. Young children find it difficult to sleep due to the itching.

Initial actions

- If a child develops itchy or sore areas of skin, they should be seen by a health professional to confirm or discount a diagnosis of eczema.
- Childcare staff need to be aware that a child's condition may become more acute in extremes of weather. They become very sensitive to changes in temperature.

Ongoing care

- It is important to keep the skin softened, using an emollient cream.

- Emollients should be applied regularly throughout the day, and this is particularly important after a bath. It can often be helpful to cover the affected area with cotton tubular sleeves (bandages).

- Special bath oils can be used to help remoisten the skin, which naturally loses its oils through bathing.

- Affected children should not use normal soaps; there are special preparations available.

- Children should be taught to avoid any known trigger factors.

- Keeping fingernails cut short helps minimise scratching.

- Very young children may benefit from wearing cotton mittens at night.

- Loose cotton clothing helps the skin breathe and reduces chaffing of the skin.

- Some children need prescribed products to help control the effects of eczema.

  - Cortico-steroids can be prescribed as creams or ointments for very intense phases.

  - Antihistamines are also used to reduce the itching, helping children to sleep better.

  - For some children, forms of Chinese medicine have been helpful in treating both eczema and psoriasis (under the guidance of a recognised and qualified practitioner).

- Any referral to an 'alternative' practitioner should always be with the full knowledge of the child's GP, as there could be contra-indicative effects if treatment is used in conjunction with their current medication.

Possible complications

- Antibiotics, taken orally or as creams, may become necessary to counter the effects of secondary infections, caused by excessive scratching.

- Children with severe eczema can become the victims of teasing. Early years staff need to be ready to deal with this.

Familial?

- Many children with eczema are born into families where there are others with a range of allergic conditions.

- Many will have parents or older siblings who have had eczema as a child themselves.

Professional Practice

- Consideration is needed to ensure that children with eczema are not excluded from activities because of their condition.

- Applying creams to the affected areas during the day should be done without fuss and with some privacy.

- It is important to wear disposable gloves when applying the creams, to avoid any risk of introducing infection to the child and to prevent the absorption of corticosteroids into your own skin.

Psoriasis

What is psoriasis?

- Psoriasis is a severe skin condition which most commonly appears from the age of 10 onwards, but is occasionally seen in younger children where there is a strong family history of the condition.

What causes psoriasis?

- It is considered to be an inherited condition, but its cause is unknown.

- The first incidence of psoriasis often follows a period of stress or an infection involving damage to the skin.

- The most common form of psoriasis in young children is guttate psoriasis which causes small patches of the skin rash, often as a result of a severe sore throat.

case study 10.5 — Christopher

Christopher is four years old and is severely affected by eczema. His hands are leathery and regularly encrusted with scabs from the weeping sores. He is pale and lethargic most of the time due to lack of sleep and constant discomfort.

activity

1 The other children in the nursery are reluctant to hold Christopher's hands as they feel strange and rather unpleasant. How will you deal with this during circle games such as 'Farmer's in the den', without making Christopher feel isolated or different?

2 Christopher loves finger-painting and playing in the sand and water. How will you ensure that his skin is protected while he plays? What precautions should you take?

■ The skin cells form at a rate 10 times faster than the body discards cells, resulting in the thickened patches that appear on the skin.

Recognising psoriasis

■ A thickened red rash appears on the scalp, arms, legs and body, often covered with silvery scales.

■ The rash is not usually itchy but may irritate through a tightening of the skin and general feeling of discomfort.

Initial actions

■ Referral is needed to a dermatologist (skin specialist) who will consider the severity of the condition and treat as appropriate, usually with similar medications to eczema.

Ongoing care

■ Treatment with emollient creams, coal tar products and corticosteroids, both through direct application and as a bath oil.

■ As with eczema, some people will benefit from Chinese medicines in the treatment of psoriasis.

Possible complications

■ Secondary infections can occur.

■ Social isolation is possible if the condition is very noticeable.

Familial?

■ Psoriasis is considered to be an inherited condition.

■ It is also a condition for life, although for many people it can be managed quite well with medication.

Asthma

What is asthma?

Asthma is a condition of the lungs. It is a narrowing of the airways, which is reversible with the right treatment. The narrowing of the airways reduces the child's ability to breathe freely. The walls of the airways (bronchioles) swell and become inflamed. The inflamed airways secrete a sticky mass.

What causes asthma?

An asthma attack can be caused by a variety of 'triggers':

■ infections

■ going out into the cold air

■ cigarette smoke

■ exercise

- excitement or stress
- fumes (such as from cars)
- allergies to animals
- allergies to pollen or dust
- food allergies.

Many children with asthma belong to families where allergies are common.

Figure 10.18

Triggers for asthma

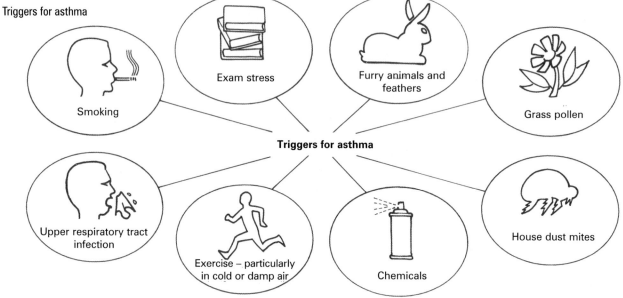

Smoking

Exam stress

Furry animals and feathers

Grass pollen

Triggers for asthma

Upper respiratory tract infection

Exercise – particularly in cold or damp air

Chemicals

House dust mites

Recognising an asthma attack
- coughing
- shortness of breath
- wheezing
- a tightness in the chest area.

Initial actions
- You will need to keep calm in order to encourage calm in the child.
- If this is a child's first attack, seek medical help.

Professional Practice

- Each setting should have a written plan for each known asthmatic child, issued by the asthma nurse at the child's GP practice.

Managing an attack
Keene (1999) sets out a 10-point plan for managing an asthma attack:

1 Reassure the child.

2 Encourage relaxed breathing – slowly and deeply.

3 Loosen tight clothing around the neck.

4 Sit the child upright and leaning forward, supporting themselves with their hands in any comfortable position.

5 Stay with the child.

6 Give the child their bronchodilator to inhale if they are known asthmatics – dosage according to the GP's instructions.

7   Offer a warm drink to relieve dryness of the mouth.

8   Continue to comfort and reassure. Do not panic as this will increase the child's anxiety which will impair their breathing.

9   When the child has recovered from a minor attack they can resume quiet activities.

10   Report the attack to the parents when the child is collected. If the child is upset by the episode the parents should be contacted immediately.

An ambulance should be called if:

■   it is the child's first known attack

■   after 5–10 minutes there is no improvement in the child

■   the child becomes increasingly distressed and exhausted

■   blueness of lips, mouth or face begins to occur.

Ongoing care

There are two different types of inhalers:

■   Preventers, which contain medicines to reduce the swelling and mucus in the airways; they are usually in brown/orange inhalers and are used on a regular basis to prevent asthma attacks.

■   Relievers, which contain medication that dilates the airways; they are usually in blue inhalers and are used to relieve symptoms of wheezing and coughing when an attack occurs or are used prior to exercise to prevent an attack.

Possible complications

■   Each year a small number of children die during an asthma attack.

Figure 10.19

Spacers are used to enable very young children to inhale their medication more easily

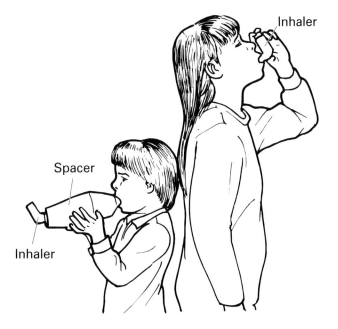

Cystic fibrosis (CF)

What is CF?

■   Cystic fibrosis is a serious genetic condition of the respiratory and digestive systems.

■   It is a life-limiting condition in which the secretions produced by the lungs are not able to flow away in the normal way. The secretions build up in the airways, which subsequently restricts breathing.

■   Risk of infection of the airways is high.

■   The digestive tract is affected as the pancreas is not able to produce the appropriate enzymes needed to break down the food and absorb it into the body's system.

What causes CF?

- Cystic fibrosis is inherited as an autosomal recessive condition.

- Approximately 1 in 1500 children has CF.

- It is more prevalent in some ethnic groups than others. The highest incidence is seen in Caucasians (light-skinned people of European, North African, SW Asian and Indian origin). It is rare in families of African-Caribbean origin and almost non-existent in people of Far Eastern origin.

Recognising CF

- CF is present in some infants from birth. It is detected by the presence of a blockage (called meconium ileus) at the opening of the intestine.

- The Guthrie test at seven days after birth includes a test for CF.

- Infants not diagnosed at birth may be seen to fail to thrive during the first few months of life due to malabsorption of food.

- Chest infections and coughs can indicate CF chest problems.

- Diarrhoea and fatty offensive stools can indicate CF digestive problems.

Initial actions

- Any suspicion of CF must be referred immediately to the GP.

- A 'sweat' test is occasionally the initial action, if parents have noticed a salty taste to their child's skin, but this form of testing can be quite distressing for a child.

- Genetic testing will confirm whether the suspected diagnosis is correct.

Ongoing care

The ongoing care of a child with cystic fibrosis involves:

- physiotherapy of the chest at regular intervals throughout the day to loosen secretions (known as percussion physiotherapy)

- regular exercise to help expand the lungs regularly

- antibiotics to prevent chest infections

- pancreatic enzyme supplements, taken at each meal time to help absorb food

- a diet that is low in fat, but high in protein and carbohydrates.

Children with CF will have continuous care and support from a dietician, a community children's nurse and/or a CF specialist.

Possible complications

- During periods of exacerbation or infection the physiotherapy sessions may need to be more intensive.

- Infections will sometimes result in admission to hospital.

- Some children also develop diabetes (the only type in which a high-carbohydrate/sugar intake is given).

- Cystic fibrosis has no cure.

- A high-carbohydrate diet usually allows a longer and better quality of life.

- Some children benefit from heart-lung transplants.

- Individuals with CF do not usually live into old age.

Diabetes mellitus (type 1 diabetes)

What is diabetes mellitus?

- Diabetes mellitus is an endocrine disorder in which the pancreas does not make enough insulin. Insulin helps the body to use and store sugar. When it is not used efficiently the sugar overflows into the urine.

What causes diabetes mellitus?

- It is often triggered following a severe viral infection.

- It is not an inherited condition, but there is a familial trait to diabetes.

Recognising diabetes mellitus

Most children are diagnosed following a sudden onset of the two most common symptoms:

- extreme thirst
- frequently passing urine.
- Also the breath may smell of pear drops.

Less obvious onset includes:

- tiredness
- constant lethargy
- weight loss
- loss of appetite
- urinary tract infection due to excessive sugar in the urine.

Initial actions

- Medical diagnosis involving the testing of urine and blood for excessive sugar levels.
- A short stay in hospital is usual in order for the child's blood sugar levels to be stabilised and their dietary needs agreed and understood by parents.

Ongoing care

- Insulin injections and a carefully controlled diet will be necessary for life.
- Checks on blood sugar levels are taken (at least) daily.
- Diet will be monitored by a dietician.
- A generally 'healthy heart' diet is needed (high fibre, low sugar, low fat).
- A return to hospital is unlikely, unless illness causes dehydration.

Possible complications

- Dehydration due to illness.
- An imbalance of blood sugar levels can lead to either hypoglycaemia (sweating and clammy skin – child needs to be given extra sugar or a boost of sugar) or hyperglycaemia (sugar levels are too high, so extra insulin is needed).
- Signs of a hypoglycaemic attack include sweating, dizziness, confusion and rapid breathing. A snack or a glucose drink or similar should be given to the child. It is important that someone remains with the child until they have stabilised.
- Illness, under-dosing on insulin and sudden growth spurts can all affect the blood sugar level balance.

See *Child Health: Care of the Child in Health and Illness* by Keene (1999), page 259.

Common reasons for hypoglycaemia are:

- unusual exercise, e.g. extra games
- not enough carbohydrate, e.g. missed snack
- too much insulin, e.g. mistaken dose.

Common reasons for hyperglycaemia are:

- less exercise than usual, e.g. missed games
- not enough insulin, e.g. growing out of dose
- too much carbohydrate, e.g. extra snacks
- sudden excitement or strain, e.g. exams
- infection, e.g. cold.

Figure 10.20

Blood glucose is kept steady by a balance between exercise and insulin on one side and carbohydrate, excitement and infection on the other

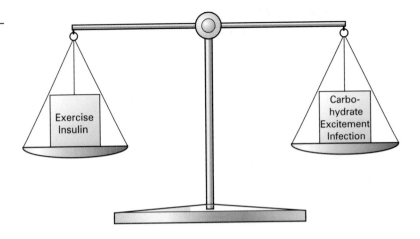

Professional Practice

- Supplies of glucose tablets should be taken with you when you accompany a child with diabetes on any outing.

- Supplies should be readily available in the school or early years setting.

- Children with diabetes should be closely observed during exercise, particularly if they are trying something new.

- Contact numbers for parents should always be readily available.

- Staff working with a child with diabetes should be taught how to cope with their needs and any attacks.

- Privacy should be allowed when children need to test their blood sugar levels during the day.

- Catering staff need to be informed and be able to deal with special dietary needs.

- Good long-term dietary care will help prevent other ill health, such as heart, liver, kidney, vascular disease and eye disease.

case study 10.6   William

William is five years old and is diabetic. He is on his first school trip to the zoo. He is very excited and has rushed around from enclosure to enclosure during the morning. At lunch time, William was so busy talking to his friends about their favourite animals that he did not eat very much of his packed lunch. As the afternoon wore on, William became lethargic and by the time he got onto the coach he was sweating a great deal and stumbled getting into his seat. Other children were also tired and stumbling.

activity

1 Would you be concerned about William?
2 What signs of hypoglycaemia is William possibly displaying?
3 What would you do initially?
4 With hindsight, what else should staff have done?
5 What have you learned from this case study?

Coeliac disease

What is coeliac disease?

- Coeliac disease is a condition affecting the lining of the small intestine. It is an immunological reaction to gluten, a protein found in wheat, rye, barley, and, in some people, oats too.

- Children are usually diagnosed when they start to have solid food from about six months onwards.

- In adults coeliac disease can occur at any time, often triggered by an unknown cause.

What causes coeliac disease?

- The reaction to gluten causes the villi protrusions along the intestine to become flattened and therefore reduces the surface for absorption of food.

Figure 10.21

The gluten-free symbol

Recognising coeliac disease

- Babies fail to thrive in the usual way; they do not put on weight and are low on the centile charts.

- Young children become very unwell, lethargic and miserable, with abdominal bloating.

- Stools are pale, fatty, smell unpleasant and are difficult to flush away.

Initial actions

- There has usually been some concern shown for the child (or adult) prior to diagnosis.

- Blood tests and faecal samples are taken initially.

- A biopsy of the jejunum usually follows if concerns are raised from blood and faeces results.

- A dietary 'challenge' would be carried out in early puberty.

Ongoing care

- A gluten-free diet is necessary throughout life.

- Gluten is found in many everyday foods and it takes time to identify all foods that need to be avoided.

- Guidance is given from a dietician to help establish a balanced diet.

- Coeliac UK gives helpful advice and a regularly updated food list.

- Many supermarkets now display a gluten-free symbol on suitable foods.

- From November 2005, new food laws require all forms of gluten to be indicated on packaging.

Possible complications

- Iron deficiency anaemia is a possibility due to malabsorption of food.

- Calcium deficiency can also be present, again due to malabsorption.

- In the long term, there is a higher incidence of intestinal cancer in people with coeliac disease if it remains untreated.

- For individuals diagnosed at later ages, further problems can occur:

  - osteoporosis, which is a calcium deficient condition resulting in repeated fractures

  - osteopaenia, which indicates borderline osteoporosis, and is often picked up during bone density scanning for osteoporosis.

Bone density scans are offered for individuals where either condition is suspected or calcium supplements (with vitamin D) are then recommended for life.

Familial?

There is a familial tendency regarding coeliac disease, but it is not considered hereditary. Babies born into a family where coeliac disease has previously been diagnosed should be observed closely for early signs and some health practitioners recommend that gluten should ideally be withheld from their diet until their first birthday. In some cases, early exposure to gluten has been thought to have triggered the condition.

Progress Check

1   What are the body's natural defences?

2   What is a leucocyte, and what does it do?

3   What are ciliated epithelia, and what is their role in defending the body?

4   What are the five groups of pathogens (germs) called?

5   Which type of pathogen is a single-celled organism?

6   Define the terms 'ingested', 'inhaled' and 'inoculated'.

7   Give at least three examples of socio-economic factors that affect health, linked to poverty.

8   Give at least three examples of socio-economic factors that affect health, linked to housing.

9   Give at least three examples of socio-economic factors that affect health, linked to unemployment.

10   What is the difference between active natural immunity and active acquired immunity?

11   What is meant by the term 'herd immunity'?

12   What does HiB stand for and which other vaccination is it offered with?

13   From what age is paracetamol registered as suitable to treat pyrexia (high temperature)?

14   What are the benefits of screening?

15   Give three examples of conditions common in childhood.

16   Give three examples of chronic conditions that can affect children.

17   Which condition can result in shingles in an adult who has previously had the virus in its common childhood form?

18   Which condition is associated with Koplik's spots?

19   Which condition is caused by the virus coxsackie?

20   Which condition is associated with percussion physiotherapy?

Impact of ill health

The medical needs of a child clearly take precedence when they are ill, but their social, emotional and cognitive needs also need to be taken into account. The **impact of ill health** can be wide reaching: illness can affect children in a number of ways, particularly emotionally, as they may feel confused or scared about what is happening to them. During periods of short-term illness a slight change in routine or diet does not normally have any significant impact, but with long-term conditions there can be considerable changes in behaviour, diet and habit that can be difficult to cope with.

Children's reaction to illness and its subsequent impact on them is directly linked to their age and stage of development. They need to have their questions answered honestly and be kept informed as to what will happen next, without alarming them unduly. As with adults, children are more likely to be able to cope with whatever treatment or investigation they need if they have some idea of what to expect.

It is important that children are not told that 'it won't hurt', if it clearly will, as this will be likely to affect their security even further and may cause them to lose the trust they have in the adults caring for them. In recent years, parents have been able to stay with their child in hospital for much of the time. This is partly due to the work of the organisation Action for Sick Children.

activity

10.19

Research the history, aims and work of the organisation Action for Sick Children.

1 What was it originally called?
2 When was it first set up?
3 What was its original aim?
4 How has the work of the organisation changed?
5 What research can you find that supports the aims of the organisation?

Needs of children who are ill

A child who is in full health is usually able to benefit from any of the opportunities that are offered to them, building on previous learning, practising their developing skills and enjoying the challenge of new experiences. Children who are unwell, however, particularly those with a chronic condition will most likely have times when they are unable to take up an opportunity, or join in with a new experience, because they are simply not feeling well enough. Early years practitioners need to consider how these children can best be supported in their activities and new learning, ensuring that they receive as much help as possible to maximise their learning ability.

Factors to consider in relation to a child who is ill or has a chronic condition can include some or all of the following, based not only on how the child feels and how they act but also on how the adults caring for them have acted and responded:

- appetite
- behaviour
- social interaction
- learning.

Figure 10.22

Impact of ill health on children

Appetite
- Appetite may become poor or fussy.
- Nutritional intake may become unbalanced.
- Snacks may be eaten rather than full meals, changing food intake routines.
- Extra treats may become an expectation from which a child is not easily 'weaned'.

Emotional behaviour
- Behaviour often regresses, being less tolerant and more demanding.
- A child often needs more direct comforting.
- A child's trust can be easily lost.
- A child may display attention-seeking behaviour.
- Clinging is common, as children are often feeling frightened and uncertain.
- Unpredictable behaviour swinging from excitement to tantrums quite easily.

The impact of ill health on children

Social interaction
- An ill child may be less interested in interacting with others.
- Children may become withdrawn and isolated through their illness.
- There may be a greater emphasis on interacting with adults, losing the skills needed to interact and negotiate in play situations.

Cognitive skills
- Formal learning may cease or be restricted by on-going or debilitating treatment.
- Children may begin to lapse behind their peers if treatment is long term.
- Passive stimulation may be all a child can cope with.

- Children need a great deal of emotional support during periods of illness.
- Patience and understanding are vital.
- Children need clear explanations as to what will be happening to them, including routine procedures such as temperature taking and blood pressure checks.
- All explanations need to be appropriate for the child's age and level of understanding.

activity
10.20

Having read the above statements:

1   Think of examples you have seen in children you have known.
2   Looking back at the chronic conditions set out on pages 436–445, how might a child with each of these conditions be affected?

Needs of parents and other family members

Families face difficulties too when a child is ill, experiencing changes to the usual routine, particularly if the child is in hospital or a **hospice**. There will be times when family members feel isolated because they are unable to leave the family home, or because they need to stay with their child in hospital for prolonged periods.

Meeting other families in similar circumstances is important to them, perhaps linking up via condition-led support groups or parent networks locally or within the hospital itself. These groups enable parents to share experiences and discuss and explore issues that concern them. They are able to meet others whose child is further along the road to recovery, or who have reached a different stage in their condition. Families need support from many different people, for many different reasons, for example:

- from health professionals to:
  - reassure parents that they are experienced and knowledgeable about their child's condition
  - reassure parents about their child's condition and any prognosis
  - keep parents informed about day-to-day changes in their child's condition and what procedures are planned or being considered
  - provide information about the treatment options about which they may need to make decisions
  - link parents with support groups for families with a child with the same condition
  - occupy siblings while parents speak with specialists, enabling them to concentrate on the information they are being given without distraction

- from employers, schools and others to:
  - support the parents' need to be with their ill child
  - support the daily running of households when a child is in hospital
  - offer educational support if home tutoring is needed
  - support families on low incomes to help finance hospital visits
  - support siblings by understanding that they too have needs and feelings during the illness or hospitalisation of another child in the family
  - give appropriate levels of information to siblings in accordance with parents' wishes.

Financial implications for families

Extra financial needs can be incurred when a child is ill. One parent may need to give up working temporarily to take on the caring role. Additional resources may be needed to cope with, for example increased heating costs, additional wash loads, and so on. Support can often be obtained from a medical social worker, who can help with such issues as the cost of transport, or childcare facilities. They may also be involved in arranging for interpreters or an advocate for families where English is not the first language or the parents have difficulty in understanding or expressing information.

Link Refer back to Unit 2, page 64, for information on advocates.

Professional Practice
■ Parents in financial difficulties can apply for support to organisations such as the Benefits Agency, the Citizens Advice Bureau and other groups dealing with welfare issues. They provide both financial and practical help.

activity 10.21 Using published materials, locally displayed posters and fliers, and the Internet, put together a range of contact details for support groups that could help the parents in your area, or at your setting.

Professional Practice
■ Giving out contact details can be a very helpful and supportive thing to do, but the action is only of help if the information is up to date. Re-check details from time to time, and update and discard as appropriate.

Figure 10.23

Role of early years practitioners

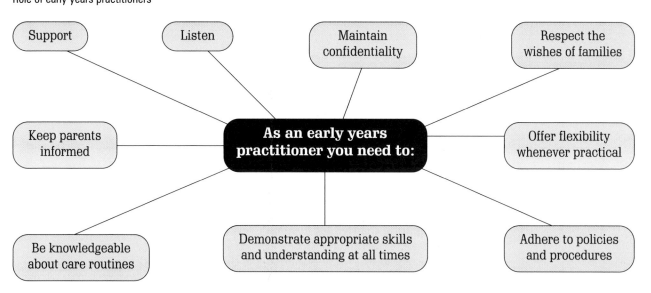

Treatment and care routines

Care settings for children with illnesses

Treatment can take place in the home or in hospital and, when children are terminally ill, it may also involve a hospice. The need for medical treatment or intervention is of course a priority, but it should not overshadow the needs of a child for play. Play is invaluable in reducing stress and uncertainty and can offer a positive focus for the whole family. The age and stage of a child's development and understanding will determine how much they are told about their illness and treatment and which approaches are taken.

In early years settings practitioners need to be flexible to incorporate a child's needs. They must ensure that reporting procedures regarding illness whilst at the setting are clear and known to all staff. The procedure for administering medicines also needs to be fully understood by all those involved.

Refer to Unit 5, page 200 for details on administering medicines.

Treatment in the home

Common childhood illnesses will always be treated at home, unless there are complications. The parents' role will expand to include nursing skills and play provision, taking into account the child's age and general interests. Children may have less energy than usual and they may spend much of the day resting, therefore activities will need to be easily managed, offering satisfying play without too much effort.

Suitable activities include colouring and drawing, dot-to-dot books and simple puzzles. Construction materials that are easily handled and not too fiddly are better than those which are very precise and need a great deal of concentration. Activities involving small pieces need to be placed on deep-sided trays if the child is in bed, to avoid knocking off vital parts which may affect the child's satisfaction with the activity as a whole.

Children like to read and hear familiar books and stories, often having them repeated many times – a common practice with young children generally. In slightly older children, the familiarity and reassurance of reverting to this phase is often helpful to them emotionally.

case study   Lucy
10.7

Lucy is 3½ years old and currently has chickenpox. She is absolutely covered in spots, and has them internally too. She has been in great discomfort and very distressed at times but is beginning to feel a little better. Lucy's mother has asked you for advice regarding how best to occupy Lucy.

activity

1   What toys and activities would you suggest for Lucy, bearing in mind how she is feeling?
2   Would you recommend her mother playing with Lucy, or for Lucy to play alone?
3   What would you have suggested for an older child to do in similar circumstances?
4   How would you occupy a young toddler in this situation?

Treatment in hospital

Preparing a child for hospital

For some children, a stay in hospital becomes a necessity either because of illness or an accident. **Preparing children for hospital** is an important part of the practitioner's role. Clearly it is easier to prepare a child for a planned admission to hospital, as there is time to talk about it in advance at a pace suitable to the child's age and understanding, whereas when a child is admitted as an emergency there is little time to talk about what they will see, hear or experience. Children are only admitted to hospital when it is absolutely necessary. Whenever possible they are treated at home.

A week or so before the due admission date, hospital discussion can be introduced and opportunities to role play hospital 'scenes' may be very helpful to a child. If the hospital offers a pre-admission tour of the ward, this can be very useful in acclimatising a child to what to expect when they arrive. This helps to reduce anxiety for the child, and consequently for their parents too.

Preparation a few days before the child is admitted

During the few days prior to the child's admission to the ward, it is useful to talk through the information sent from the hospital. This will usually give details of what is on offer in the playroom and details of the hospital school, together with what the child needs to take with them into hospital. It can be helpful to let them buy something new to take into hospital, such as new pyjamas, or a flannel and toothbrush.

Hospital staff recognise the need for children to take with them whatever comforts them. Older children may at times feel embarrassed to take in their teddy or comforter (in case their friends visit them). Parents may need to take a teddy along without the child knowing. Teddy will then be there to comfort the child when they need it without the child feeling foolish.

During this time, children need to be reassured if they are anxious and have their questions answered clearly and as honestly as possible.

Once the child is on the ward

It is important for all children to become familiar with the layout of the hospital ward, particularly older children, as this will allow them more autonomy and enable them to feel more in control.

Children will need to be introduced to the hospital play staff, usually a nursery nurse, who will often be further trained in hospital play. Encouraging children to select play materials as soon as possible after arrival will occupy them both physically and mentally and help to ease some (understandable) nerves.

Treatment

On hospital wards there are a range of staff especially trained to work with children. These include:

■ play specialists, who are often nursery nurses who have qualified initially through level 3 courses and then taken a specialist course in hospital play

■ teachers, who work with the children who are well enough, linking activities to the appropriate stage of the National Curriculum or, with younger children, the Foundation Stage Curriculum

■ nursery nurses, who support the work of the teachers and play specialists. They are often on duty outside of 'school hours' and encourage and arrange a variety of play activities for children of all ages. They are often happy to involve the siblings of the children who are currently having treatment too.

Play on the ward often includes medical props to help familiarise children with what they may see. This could include medical kits, involving stethoscope, eye patch, and so on. It may also include syringe painting (without the needles, of course) or making plaster casts of children's hands. A range of books giving positive images of hospital routines and treatments are usually to be found on hospital wards. Teddies and dolls can be bandaged, injected or given other treatments that it is felt appropriate to simulate.

Treatment in hospices

Many terminally ill children are cared for in hospitals or at home. Others benefit from time in a children's hospice. Although there are not huge numbers of hospices for children, they play an important role.

A hospice is a place of care and treatment specifically for terminally ill children. Some hospices have a community team who will help to care for the child in the family home. Hospices offer support for parents and families, as well as the ill child, and they discuss with the family what will meet the needs of the child and the whole family and do what they can to meet those needs.

Hospices also offer training in bereavement skills to other professionals who may become involved with families who have lost a child, or will shortly face such a loss.

The support offered to families of a terminally ill child involves:

■ respite care

■ care of siblings

■ emotional support

- practical help and advice
- opportunities to grieve
- opportunities to share experiences with others.

In supporting the child, they offer:

- 'normal' routines whenever possible
- opportunities to discuss their futures
- opportunities to talk about their families and what will happen when they die (where this is applicable).

Staff who work in terminal care need to be sensitive to the parents' emotionally fragile state. They try where they can to build up a rapport with them, which can help the staff to support the parents after they have been bereaved. Becoming aware of a family's cultural practice is important, to ensure that cultural traditions are both valued and maintained.

Families will go through different stages of grieving. There will usually be shock, even if the death was known to be imminent, followed by confusion, fear, anger and guilt. Parents may feel that they will never be able to cope again, and that they no longer have a role in life. This can be particular acute if they have cared for their child intensively over a long period of time. Anger and guilt arise, as the unfairness of the situation takes hold. Why their child? What had the child done to deserve such a death? They may also start to question whether they did all they could have done for the child.

This is a difficult time for families and also for those who work to support them.

Role and responsibilities of early years workers

When supporting the relatives of a terminally ill child, early years practitioners need to provide practical non-specific support, for example, making them feel welcome and having time for them, as well as more specific support, such as keeping the parents informed of a child's progress and changes to routine or to type or dosage of medication.

Support from early years practitioners needs to be flexible to enable the parents to continue some degree of normality with the other children in their family.

Professional Practice

- Sensitivity is needed at all times when supporting terminally ill children and their families.
- It is important to remember that parents will often forget, or not take in, what they have heard, because they are distressed at the time.
- Siblings need support too.

Progress Check

1   List at least ten of the effects that ill health can have on a child.
2   Why is it important for children to be familiar with hospital routines and procedures?
3   What support needs might parents of ill children have?
4   Who are the non-medical children's professionals usually found on children's wards?
5   What role does a hospice play in supporting children and their families?

Glossary

ABC procedure A sequential emergency first aid process

ABC behaviour strategy Considering the antecedent, the behaviour and the consequence of situations strategy

Accommodation Piaget's term for the process by which a child modifies their understanding to acquire a new concept

Accurate records Factual records kept by the setting following an accident or concern

Active listening Ensuring that you are focusing on what you are listening to

Advocacy Representing another individual or speaking on their behalf

Aggressive Taking a forceful approach

Alternative forms of care The range of care options available to children

Anonymity Ensuring that an individual's identity remains unknown

Apgar score Health score given to a baby at birth, recorded on a chart

Aphasia When a child is unable to express his or her thoughts in words

Area Child Protection Committee (ACPC) A group of professionals who meet to discuss individual child abuse or protection cases

Artificial ventilation Breathing for another person, when that person is unable to do so

Assertive Being able to put your ideas or viewpoint across without aggression

Assessment An evaluation of, for example, someone's needs or the quality of a learner's work

Assimilation Piaget's term for a child trying to understand a new concept by fitting it into their present understanding

Associative play The stage of play when children play with the same activity but are not yet playing co-operatively

Attitudes and values Attitudes are ways of thinking or behaving; values are moral standards

Audit An inspection

Aural stimulation Stimulation through sound

Baby massage A pleasurable form of physical contact, which aids relaxation and can help the bonding of parent and child

Baby-signing A scheme to enable hearing babies to make their needs known prior to gaining speech

Bar chart A method of presenting data, often used in research, that is particularly useful for showing descriptive categories

Barriers to communication Any obstruction to understanding between more than one individual

Behaviour management Strategies for setting children boundaries

Behaviour policies Written agreements setting out the behaviour management (of an early years setting)

Bias An inclination to favour one view over another, prejudice, lack of objectivity

Glossary

Body language The non-verbal signals

Bonding The close relationship formed between a child and one or more of the main carers

Burn-out Becoming exhausted or overstimulated

Care of the environment Considering the safety needs of the early years setting

Care Order A legal order in which a child is placed in the care of the local authority

Caudal Referring to the lower parts of the body

Causes of ill health The range of reasons why individuals become ill

Centile chart A chart used to record the growth in infants and young children

Cephalo Referring to the head

Checklists In a questionnaire, a list of optional answers; the respondent is asked to tick those that apply. In observation, a prepared list of behaviours; the observer ticks those that they see

Chest compressions An emergency first aid procedure

Child Assessment Order A legal order applied for in court when a child is considered to be at risk or already suffering significant harm

Child Protection Register A computerised list, kept by the local authority of children who are considered to be 'at-risk'

Chromosome Part of the human genetic make-up

Classical conditioning Learning as the result of conditioned responses; the term is often associated with Ivan Pavlov

Closed questions Questions which place a limit on the answers

Codes of practice The procedures (usually written down) by which a setting or profession operates

Cognitive development The development of learning through thinking and problem-solving

Colic Acute spasmodic abdominal pain common in young babies

Communication The means of passing and receiving information

Communication cycle A reciprocal form of passing and receiving information

Confidentiality Keeping information to yourself; not passing on information inappropriately

Conservation Being able to understand change in quantity, size and number; the term is often associated with Jean Piaget

Containment Helping a child to express his or her emotions safely

Continuity of care Routine and familiarity which helps children feel secure

Cooled boiled water Used to prepare formula feeds and to clean the eyes of newborn babies

Co-operative play The stage of play when children play with each other, sometimes taking on simple roles or making simple rules for their games

COSHH Control of Substances Hazardous to Health

Cross-infection The passing of infection from one person to another

Culture The customs, values, beliefs etc. of a particular social group or society

Cycle of disadvantage The process whereby the experiences of one generation of a family have an impact on the next, continuing some or all of the problems they face

Development The changes that take place as an individual grows

Developmental delay The term often used when a child's development is not following the pattern of averages (or 'norms')

Developmentally appropriate What is expected of a child at a given stage of development

Developmental norms Typical patterns of growth and development

Direct contact Cross-infection through contact with an infected individual

Discrimination The unfair treatment of an individual, group or minority, based on prejudice

Disclosure Telling someone about the abuse suffered, either currently or in the past

Disequilibrium A term used by Jean Piaget to describe the state where a child does not fully understand new concepts

Distal A distance away from the central point (of the body)

Diversity Being different or varied

Droplet infection A common cause of cross-infection

Dysfluency Being unable to speak words fluently, stammering; a common (temporary) occurrence in young children

Dysphasia When a child has difficulty in expressing his or her thoughts in words

Ego-centricity Placing self at the centre of everything; young children do not understand the necessity for their needs to be deferred or for anyone else's needs to be considered

Emergency Protection Order An order of law, applied for through the courts to help protect children from harm

Emotional abuse The continual rejection, terrorising or criticism of an individual

Empiricists Those who uphold the theory that knowledge is gained from experience (nurture theory)

Emotional disturbance Evidenced by behaviour which causes concern and needs professional intervention (when serious or long term) or sensitive handling by parents and carers (for temporary or common problems such as tantrums)

Enactive thinking Thinking based on memory of actions

Environmental factors Any influences from around an individual that could have an impact on the individual in any way

EPOCH The organisation End Physical Punishment of Children

Equality The state of being equal, of having an equal opportunity

Equity Fairness combined with equal opportunity

Ethos The characteristic attitudes and character of, for example, a group

Evacuation procedures The planned process of removing children from an unsafe situation to a safe environment

Evaluation Reflecting on and giving consideration to a past event, action or project

Event sample In observation, a record of the frequency, duration or other aspects of pre-selected behaviour(s)

Evidence Supportive material or information

Exploratory play Play in which a child is able to find out by experimentation and discovery

Eye contact Looking directly at an individual when conversing or explaining something to them

Feminist model An approach taken (specifically) from the perspective of women

Glossary

Foetal alcohol syndrome (FAS) Physical and cognitive abnormalities often found in children born to alcoholic mothers

First aid The emergency actions taken following an accident or sudden illness

Food-related customs Acceptable and unacceptable foods linked to culture

Foundation Stage Curriculum A government-led curriculum for children from age three years

Free play Play which is undirected

Genotype The complete genetic inheritance of an individual

Gillick Competence The principle that the child is able to make their own decisions and give informed consent

Good-enough parenting A term used to refer to parenting that is adequate, although it may not be considered to be ideal by many people

Growth Increasing in size, height, weight and so on

HASAWA The Health and Safety at Work Act (1974)

Health The state of well-being

Health education Learning about health, either formally or informally

Health promotion Pro-active encouragement on health issues

Health promotion campaigns Information on specific health issues being actively distributed or advertised through the media or other means

Herd immunity Vaccination programmes which work by immunising a high enough proportion of society, therefore dramatically reducing the likelihood of becoming infected with the condition

High/Scope A specific programme of learning, in which children take responsibility for their own learning; the programme encourages the process of 'plan, do and review'

HImPs Health Improvement Programmes, initiated by the government

Historical perspective Considering what has happened in the past and its relevance to the present

Holistic model Taking an all-round consideration

Hospices Care settings for individuals who are terminally ill

Hot-housing Over-stimulating (in children) to achieve more at an early age

Human resources The personnel (staff, parents, professionals, and so on) involved

IAPS Abbreviation for impact-absorbing playground surfaces

Iconic thinking The development of mental images

Identifying needs Being able to recognise a need using professional judgement, knowledge and understanding

Immunisation programmes A process of vaccinations for children to prevent illness and to help eradicate certain medical conditions from society

Impact of ill health Any outcome that occurs due to the ill health of an individual or their family

Incest Sexual intercourse between two relatives who are too closely linked to be able legally to marry

Indicators of abuse Signs and symptoms that may be seen in children, which could suggest that abuse has taken place

Indirect contact Cross-infection where there is no specific contact with an infected individual

Institutional discrimination The policies or practices of an organisation which systematically discriminate against a minority group or groups

Interpersonal skills Communicating with others in a positive (good skills) or negative (bad skills) manner

Intersubjectivity An innate predisposition to relate to other people

Laissez-faire model Taking an approach involving unrestricted freedom or indifference

Language acquisition device In the theory of language development associated with Noam Chomsky, the term for a hypothetical inborn mechanism in the brain that predisposes children to acquire language

Lifestyle factors affecting health Lifestyle choices, such as smoking, that have an impact on health

Line graph A method of presenting data, particularly useful for showing trends or changes in quantity

Live vaccines A vaccine which uses a small amount of the 'live' condition; live vaccines are not given to individuals with suppressed immunity

Longitudinal study A study in which a single individual or a group of individuals is studied at intervals over a period of time

Long-term effects of abuse The on-going affects suffered by an individual following abuse

Managing unacceptable behaviour Methods of lessening undesirable behaviour in children

Marginalise Treating someone or something as insignificant or unimportant; to place at the edge (of importance)

Maturational To do with the biological process of development

Mean The average that is most widely understood. It is calculated by adding together a set of numerical scores and dividing by the total number of scores in the set

Median The middle number in a ranked set of numerical scores

Medical model An approach taken (specifically) from a medical perspective

Minority ethnic group A group of people with a common race or culture who are different from most of the people in the country or society

Mode A score that is the most common in a set of data

Monotropic A term associated with John Bowlby that refers to the attachment of an infant to only one carer

Montessori philosophy A specific programme of learning, with its own range of resources

Movement and flow chart A method of observation that looks at how a child spends their time

National Curriculum The curriculum followed by children in all state schools

Nativists Those who uphold the theory that knowledge is innate (nature theory)

Natural immunity A degree of immunity present in the body without the use of vaccination

Nature/nurture debate The question of whether individuals acquire knowledge through their genetic inheritance or through their experiences from birth onwards

Negative images Illustrations or descriptions that portray limitations or negativity regarding individuals

Neglect A form of abuse where the care of a child is insufficient or inappropriate

Neonatal jaundice A problem with the function of the liver during the first weeks of life

Neonate An infant in the first month of life

Non-live vaccines Artificially made vaccinations, often given to individuals with suppressed immune systems caused by conditions such as leukaemia, HIV or AIDS

Non-participant observation A method of studying behaviour in which the researcher remains separate from the group being observed

Non-verbal communication The messages that are given through body language and facial expression

Normative development The expected rate of development, according to averages

Objectivity Without bias

Observation A method of studying behaviour by watching and recording what the people being studied do

Open adoption Adoption where there is an element of contact remaining between the child and their birth mother/family

Open questions Questions which encourage a detailed answer

Operant conditioning Methods of reinforcing voluntary behaviour (e.g. positive reinforcement), often associated with B. F. Skinner

Paedophile An individual who is sexually interested in children. The term is commonly used to describe anyone who sexually molests children

Parallel play The stage of play when children play alongside other children

Paramountcy principle A main principle of the Children Act 1989 where the welfare of the child must be the paramount consideration

Paraphrasing To restate what you have heard; used to clarify understanding

Parents' expectations What parents expect (of an early years setting) when they leave their child in the setting's care

Participant observation A method of studying behaviour in which the researcher acts as a member of the group being observed

Pathogen A micro-organism, such as a bacterium or virus, that causes disease

Perception The process by which the brain makes sense of information received from the senses; insight or awareness

Persona dolls Dolls designed to represent children from various cultures and/or with a range of disabilities

Personal presentation The manner in which someone presents themselves to others, for example, the way the person dresses, speaks and acts

Personal safety Being responsible for own safe working practice

Physical abuse Action directed against a child that is physically harmful and inflicts injury

Phenotype The visible arrangement of characteristics inherited by an individual from his or her parents

Physical environment The surroundings (building, room layout, lighting, ventilation, and so on)

Physical resources The range of equipment available

Pictograph A method of presenting data using a pictorial or symbolic form; it has similar uses to a bar chart

Pie chart A method of presenting data using a circular chart, which resembles a pie. The 'pie' can be 'sliced' into portions to represent quantities or categories

Plan, do and review A process of planning and evaluation associated with the High/Scope programme of learning

Placement log An on-going record charting students' experience in a range of placements

Play therapy The use of play to help alleviate some of the effects of abuse or other traumas experienced in childhood

Police protection Legal protection of a child from harm

Policies A set of principles used as the basis for decisions or actions

Positive images Illustrations or descriptions that positively portray all the individuals included within it

Positive reinforcement Rewarding good (behaviour), rather than responding to undesirable (behaviour) in children

Potential hazard Any situation which has the potential to cause harm

Predisposing factors Any known information that could indicate a specific outcome

Prejudice An opinion formed in advance, a pre-judgement

Preparing children for hospital Considering children's physical, emotional and cognitive needs prior to planned hospitalisation

Primary health care The care of health within the community, includes doctors, nurses, dentists, opticians and so on

Primary research Research you have carried out yourself

Primary socialisation The process whereby a child learns about society from their immediate family and others close to them

Principles of diet and nutrition The basis of healthy eating

Professional A person who is qualified, competent and experienced at what they do

Professional practice log *See Placement log*

Proximal Close to the central point (of the body)

Psychological model An approach taken (specifically) from a psychological perspective

Pyrexia A high temperature, fever

Quality assurance A set standard, achieved when specified criteria have been met

Qualitative research Research which obtains the viewpoints and personal feelings of individual participants; data produced are descriptive, not numerical

Quantitative research Research which produces results that can be expressed numerically, using charts, tables and so on

Racism The belief that some races have cultural characteristics that make them superior (or inferior) to others

Range In research, the difference between the lowest and highest result found in numerical data

Raw data The information gathered during the research process before it has been collated, for example, information taken from questionnaires

Recovery Order A legal order enabling the police to take into their possession a child who is the subject of police protection or an Emergency Protection Order, if they are missing, have run away, or been abducted from the person responsible for their care

Glossary

Recovery position The position individuals are placed in following an accident or sudden illness, after their situation has been stabilised, whilst they await further medical treatment (for example, following an accident), or rest (for example, following an epileptic fit)

Referral procedures The process of reporting concerns about a child's safety

Reflection The process of giving something thoughtful consideration

Reflective listening Where the listener echoes the last (or most significant) words spoken by the speaker

Reflexes An involuntary response to a stimulus, for example blinking

Reliability In research, the consistency of findings or of the instrument, such as a questionnaire, used to collect data

Replication Being able to repeat something and get the same outcomes. In research, replication is used to test reliability

RIDDOR Reporting of Injuries, Diseases and Dangerous Occurrences Regulations (1995)

Rights Our entitlements as individuals

Role of health educators To raise awareness of health issues relevant to the target audience

Routines A set procedure that should meet the needs of all concerned

Safety marks National standards regarding safety, printed on the packaging of objects, to guide consumers as to their suitability for the intended use or recipient, and found for example, on toys, baby equipment, electrical appliances

Scaffolding A term usually associated with Jerome Bruner; the adult supports and extends a child's learning

Schema An internal representation of knowledge, which is adapted through assimilation and accommodation

Screening The process of examining a whole population to identify who is showing signs of a disease, or may be predisposed to develop it

Secondary health care Involves early intervention of health issues, often linked to the outcomes of screening

Secondary research Use of material from research which has not been directly carried out by you

Secondary socialisation The process whereby a child learns about society from social contacts outside the immediate family and social group, including teachers, early years professionals, and so on

Self-awareness Being able to understand how you are perceived by others, and the impact you have on other individuals

Self-concept An understanding of our own identity that includes how we are seen by others

Self-protection strategies Ways in which to keep ourselves safe and to be able to reject involvement in situations or unwanted advances

Sequential Occurring in a particular order

Setting boundaries Stating acceptable limitations

Sexual abuse Subjecting someone to sexual activities that are likely to cause psychological or physical harm and to which they have not given, or are unable to give, informed consent

Sharing information Passing on knowledge to others

Short-term effects of abuse Effects that take place immediately, for example physical pain, injuries or infection

Signed language Communication without the necessity of speech

Skin care Appropriate care of different types of skin

Snapshots Brief observations of a child's behaviour

Social and economic factors affecting health Issues such as poverty that are linked to health problems

Social constructivist theory The theory that children learn by exploring a range of experiences and objects from everyday life, for example in play

Social learning model The theory that children learn by observing and copying others: often associated with Albert Bandura and the Bobo dolls

Social model An approach taken (specifically) from the perspective of society

Sociogram A way of studying and depicting the relationships in a group

Sociological model A model that explains behaviour by looking at how society is structured and works

Solitary play Playing alone, a normal stage of development in young children

Spontaneous play Play that is unplanned, undirected and allows freedom

Stages of play The changes in how children's play develops, usually linked to age

Standard Attainment Tasks (SATs) Tests carried out at regular intervals during formal schooling

Standard deviation A measurement of the spread of scores, which assesses the average distance of all the scores from the mean

Steiner philosophy A specific learning process with its own ethos

Stereotyping Categorising, taking away individuality

Sterilising techniques Methods of ensuring that utensils (bottles, teats and so on) used for babies are free from bacteria

Stimulate To arouse curiosity, interest and development

Stimulating play Activities or objects which stimulate

Structured play Play which is predetermined or has specific constraints

Subjective Based on personal opinion or belief, biased

Submissive Avoiding conflict or confrontation

Supervision Order A legal order in which a child is under the supervision of the local authority, but where the authority does not have parental responsibility

Suppressed immunity Where the immune system is impaired in some way, leaving an individual susceptible to infection

Symbolic play The use of objects to represent other objects in play

Symbolic thinking Being able to use symbols such as language or number to represent the world

Table The most basic method of presenting numerical or written information

Target child The child who is the focus of an observation

Teamwork Working co-operatively with a group of colleagues

Tertiary health care On-going care of chronic conditions, often by specialist community-based health professionals

Theories Ideas, philosophies

Therapeutic play Play which is provided in order to alleviate, restore or heal

Time sample In observation, a record of behaviour taken at pre-decided intervals

Topping and tailing The washing of the facial area of a baby, together with a nappy change

Tokenism Making only a small effort, or providing no more than the minimum, in order to comply with criteria or guidelines

Tourist approach Focusing on the diversity of other cultures in the way that a tourist would without having equality fully embedded in the setting's practice

Transmission model An approach in which the adult controls the learning process, often suppressing the child's own initiative

Treasure basket A small basket of natural objects ideal for babies from about six months of age to enable exploration of a range of natural materials, smells and shapes

Turn-taking Responses made by young babies to adults when they make 'conversation' with them. This can be an expression, a movement, a smile or a sound

UN Convention on the Rights of the Child This international constitution was adopted by the United Nations Assembly in 1989 to uphold agreed rights for children whenever possible

Underpin To support and strengthen (knowledge and understanding)

Validity In research terms, a method, such as a questionnaire, has validity if it measures what it claims to do

Visual stimulation Stimulation through sight

Vocational Learning through practical experience as well as theory

Weaning The introduction of solid food to young babies

World Health Organization (WHO) An agency of the United Nations that aims to help all peoples of the world to achieve the best possible level of health

Written record In observation, a record of what the participant is doing

Zone of proximal development (ZPD) The term used by Lev Vygotsky for the area between the child's actual development and the potential level that they could achieve with additional support from the adult

Bibliography and suggested further reading

Abbott, L. and Moylett, H. (1997) *Working with the Under-3s: Responding to Children's Needs*. Open University Press, Milton Keynes.

Allen, N. (1996) *Making Sense of the Children Act*. John Wiley & Sons, Chichester.

Ashman, C. and Green, S. (2005) *Managing Environment and Resources*. David Fulton Publishers, London.

Axline, V. (1964) *Dibs: In Search of Self.* Penguin, London.

Bandura, A. (1965) Influence of model's reinforcement contingencies on the acquisition of imitative responses. *Journal of Personality and Social Psychology,* **1**, 589–95.

Barnes, P. (1998) *Personal, Social and Emotional Development of Children*. Blackwell, Oxford.

Baston, H. and Durward, H. (2001) *Examination of the Newborn: A Practical Guide*. Routledge, London.

Beattie, A. (1993) The changing boundaries of health. In: *Health and Well-being: A Reader* (eds. Beattie, A., Gott, M., Jones, L. and Sidell, M.). Macmillan/Open University, Basingstoke.

Beaver, M., Brewster, J. et al. (2001) *Working with Babies and Young Children*, Nelson Thornes, Cheltenham.

Beaver, M., Brewster, J., Jones, P., Keene, A., Neaum, S. and Tallack, J. (2001) *Babies and Young Children*, 2nd edn. Nelson Thornes, Cheltenham.

Bee, H. (1992) *The Developing Child*, 6th edn. Allyn and Bacon, Boston, MA.

Bee, H. (2004) *The Developing Child*, 10th edn. Allyn and Bacon, Boston, MA.

Bell, J. (1998) *Doing Your Research Project*, 2nd edn. Open University Press, Buckingham.

Bentzen W. R. (2000) *Seeing Young Children: A Guide to Observing and Recording Behaviour,* 4th edn. Albany, NY.

Bichard Report (2004). Criminal Records Bureau, London.

Blaxter, M. (1990) *Health and Lifestyles*. Tavistock/Routledge, London.

Bowlby, J. (1953) *Child Care and the Growth of Love*. Penguin, London.

Brain, C. and Mukherji, P. (2005) *Understanding Child Psychology.* Nelson Thornes, Cheltenham.

Bray, M. (1991) *Poppies on the Rubbish Heap: Sexual Abuse – The Child's Voice*. Canongate Press, Edinburgh.

Breuilly, E. and Palmer, M. (1993) *Religions of the World.* Harper Collins,

Brown, B. (1998) *Unlearning Discrimination in the Early Years*. Trentham Books,

Brown, B. (2001) *Persona Dolls in Action: Combating Discrimination*. Trentham Books,

Bruce, T. (1991) *Time to Play in Early Childhood Education*. Hodder & Stoughton, London.

Bruce, T. (2004) *Early Childhood Education,* 2nd edn. Hodder & Stoughton, London.

Bruce, T. and Meggitt, C. (1996) *Childcare and Education*. Hodder & Stoughton, London.

Brumfitt, K. et al. (2001) *Human Resources*, Vocational Business series 4. Nelson Thornes, Cheltenham.

Burnard, P. (1992) *Communicate! A Communication Skills Guide for Health Care Workers*, Edward Arnold.

Burnard, P. (1995) *Learning Human Skills: An Experiential and Reflective Guide for Nurses*, 3rd edn. Butterworth and Heinemann, London.

Carroll, J. (1998) *Introduction to Therapeutic Play.* Blackwell, Oxford.

Cattanach, A. (1992) *Play Therapy with Abused Children*. Jessica Kingsley Publishers, London.

Carver, V. (1980) *Child Abuse: A Study Text*. Open University Press, Milton Keynes.

Clements, P. and Spinks, T. (2000) *The Equal Opportunities Handbook,* 3rd edn. Kogan Page, London.

Cullis, T., Dolan, L. and Groves, D. (1999) *Psychology for You*. Nelson Thornes, Cheltenham.

Bibliography

Dare, A. and O'Donovan, M. (1996) *A Practical Guide to Child Nutrition*. Nelson Thornes, Cheltenham.

Dare, A. and O'Donovan, M. (1998) *A Practical Guide to Working with Babies*, 2nd edn. Nelson Thornes, Cheltenham.

Dare, A. and O'Donovan, M. (2000) *Good Practice in Child Safety*. Nelson Thornes, Cheltenham

Dare, A. and O'Donovan, M. (2002) *Good Practice in Caring for Young Children with Special Needs*, 2nd edn. Nelson Thornes, Cheltenham.

David, T. (1993) *Child Protection and Early Years Teachers*. Open University Press, Milton Keynes.

Department for Education and Employment (DfEE) (1994) *Code of Practice on the Identification and Assessment of Special Educational Needs*. HMSO, London.

DfEE (1995) *Key Stages 1 and 2 of the National Curriculum*. HMSO, London.

DfES (2001) *Special Educational Needs Code of Practice*. DfES, London.

DfES (2005) *Cross-sectional Study of 9- and 36-Month Old Children and their Families*. HMSO, London.

Department of Health (1991a) *Child Abuse: A Study of Inquiry Reports* 1980–1989. HMSO, London.

Department of Health (1991b) *Working Together under the Children Act 1989*, HMSO, London.

Department of Health (1995) *Child Protection: Messages from Research*. HMSO, London.

Department of Health (1998) *Our Healthier Nation*. HMSO, London.

Department of Health (2000) *Framework for the Assessment of Children in Need and their Families*. HMSO, London.

Donaldson, M. and McGarrigle, J. (1974) Some clues to the nature of semantic development. *Journal of Child Language*, **1**, 185–94.

Dowling, M. (2000) *Young Children's Personal, Social and Emotional Development*. Paul Chapman Publishers, London.

Doyle, C. (1990) *Working with Abused Children*. Macmillan, London.

Drake, J. (2001) *Planning Children's Play and Learning in the Foundation Stage*. David Fulton Publishers, London.

Dryden, L., Forbes, R., Mukherji, P. and Pound, L. (2005) *Essential Early Years*. Hodder Arnold, London.

Duffy, B. (1998) *Supporting Creativity and Imagination in the Early Years*. Open University Press, Milton Keynes.

Dyson, A. and Meredith, L. (2006) *Feeding the Under 5s*. David Fulton Publishers, London.

Elliott, M. (ed.) (1992) *Protecting Children Training Pack*. HMSO, London.

Elliott, M. (ed.) (1993) *Female Sexual Abuse of Children: The Ultimate Taboo*. Longman, Harlow.

Fantz, R. L. (1961) The origin of form perception. *Scientific American*, **204**(5), 66–72.

Fawcett, M. (1996) *Learning Through Child Observation*. Jessica Kingsley Publishers, London.

Flekkøy, M. G. and Kaufman, N. H. (1997) *The Participation Rights of the Child*. Jessica Kingsley Publishers, London.

Flekkøy, M. G. and Kaufman, N. H. (1997) *Rights and Responsibilities in Family and Society*. Jessica Kingsley Publishers, London.

Flynn, H. and Starns, B. (2004) *Protecting Children: Working Together to Keep Children Safe*. Heinemann, London.

Ganeri, A. (2005) *The Atlas of World Religions*. Franklin Watts, London.

Garcia, J. (2000) *Sign With Your Baby*. Northlight Communications, USA.

Gibson, E. J. and Walk, R. D. (1960) The visual cliff. In *Psychology in Progress, Readings from Scientific American*. Freeman, San Francisco, pp. 51–58.

Gilbert, P. (2000) *A–Z of Syndromes and Inherited Disorders,* 3rd edn. Nelson Thornes, Cheltenham.

Green, S. (2000) *Research Methods in Health, Social and Early Years Care*. Nelson Thornes, Cheltenham.

Green, S. (2004) *Baby and Toddler Development Made Real*. David Fulton Publishers, London.

Green, S. (2004/5) (Series ed.), *Ready, Steady, Play!* David Fulton Publishers, London.

Green, S. (2006) (Series ed.) *Bringing Educational Philosophies to your Early Years Setting.* David Fulton Publishers, London.

Green, S. (2006) (Series ed.) *From Birth to 3.* David Fulton Publishers, London.

Gregory, J. (2003) *Sickened.* Century, London.

Haralambos, M. and Holborn, M. (2000) *Sociology: Themes and Perspectives.* Collins, London.

Hobart, C. and Frankel, J. (1999) *A Practical Guide to Activities for Young Children,* 2nd edn. Nelson Thornes, Cheltenham.

Hobart, C. and Frankel, J. (1999) *A Practical Guide to Child Observation and Assessment,* 2nd edn. Nelson Thornes, Cheltenham.

Hobart, C. and Frankel, J. (2004) *A Practical Guide to Child Observation and Assessment,* 3rd edn. Nelson Thornes, Cheltenham.

Hobart, C. and Frankel, J. (2005) *Good Practice in Child Protection.* Nelson Thornes, Cheltenham.

Hobart, C. and Frankel, J. (2006) *A Practical Guide to Activities for Young Children,* 3rd edn. Nelson Thornes, Cheltenham.

Hodge, M. (2000) *Curriculum Guidance for the Foundation Stage.* QCA/DfES, London.

Hucker, K. (2001) *Research Methods in Health, Care and Early Years.* Heinemann, London.

Hurst, V. and Joseph, J. (1998) *Supporting Early Learning: The Way Forward.* Open University Press, Milton Keynes.

Hutchin, V. (2003) *Observing & Assessing for the Foundation Stage Profile.* Hodder Murray, London.

Jackson, V. (1996) *Racism and Child Protection.* Cassell, London.

Jameson, H. and Watson, M. (1998) *Starting and Running a Nursery.* Nelson Thornes, Cheltenham.

Jarvis, M. (2001) *Angles on Child Psychology.* Nelson Thornes, Cheltenham.

Karp, C. and Butler, T. (1996) *Treatment Strategies for Abused Children.* Sage,

Kay, J. (2004) *Good Practice in the Early Years,* 2nd edn. Continuum Press, London.

Keene, A. (1999) *Child Health: Care of the Child in Health and Illness.* Nelson Thornes, Cheltenham.

Kempe, C. H. (1992) in *Protecting Children Training Pack* (ed. Elliott, M.). HMSO, London.

Kindersley, B. and Kindersley, A. (1997) *Celebration, Children Just Like Me.* Dorling Kindersley.

Lalonde, M. (1974) *A New Perspective on the Health of Canadians.* Ministry of Supply and Services, Ottowa.

Lay, M. Z. and Dopeyra, J. E. (1977) *Becoming a Teacher of Young Children,* 2nd edn. Heath & Co, Washington DC.

Lindon, J. (1999) *Understanding World Religions in Early Years Practice.* Hodder & Stoughton, London.

Lindon, J. (2001) *Understanding Children's Play.* Nelson Thornes, Cheltenham.

Malik, H. (2003) *A Practical Guide to Equal Opportunities,* 2nd edn. Nelson Thornes, Cheltenham.

Makins, V. (1997) *not ___ just a nursery: Multi-agency Early Years Centres in Action,* National Children's Bureau, London.

McNeill, P. (1990) *Research Methods.* 2nd edn. Routledge, London.

Meadows, R. (1993) *ABC of Child Abuse,* 2nd edn. BMJ Publishing, London.

Miller, L. (1997) *Closely Observed Infants.* Duckworth, London.

Minett, P., Wayne, D. and Rubenstein, D. (1994) *Human Form and Function.* Collins Educational, London.

Moore, S. (2002) *Social Welfare Alive!* 3rd edn. Nelson Thornes, Cheltenham.

Mosely, J. (1998) *Quality Circle Time in the Primary Classroom: Your Essential Guide to Enhancing Self-esteem, Self-discipline and Positive Relationships.* LDA Publishers, Wiltshire.

Moyles, J. (1989) *Just Playing? The Role and Status of Play in Early Childhood Education.* Open University Press, Milton Keynes.

Moyles, J. (ed.) (1994) *The Excellence of Play.* Open University Press, Milton Keynes.

Bibliography

Mukherji, P. (2001) *Understanding Children's Challenging Behaviour.* Nelson Thornes, Cheltenham.

Mukherji, P. and O'Dea, T. (2000) *Understanding Children's Language and Literacy.* Nelson Thornes, Cheltenham.

Murphy, M. (1995) *Working Together in Child Protection.* Arena, Hants.

Naidoo, J. and Wills, J. (2000) *Health Promotion: Foundations for Practice,* 2nd edn. Baillière Tindall, London.

Neaum, S. and Tallack, J. (2000) *Good Practice in Implementing the Pre-School Curriculum,* 2nd edition. Nelson Thornes, Cheltenham.

Nursery World (1999) *All About Celebration: Activity Handbook.* TES, London.

Oaklander, V. (1988) *Windows to Our Children.* The Gestalt Journal Press, USA.

Oates, J. (1999) *The Foundations of Child Development.* Blackwell, Oxford.

Ogier, M. (1998) *Reading Research: How to Make Research More Approachable.* 2nd edn. Baillière-Tindall, London.

Penn, H. and Thurtle, V. (2005) Hoping for Health. In *Understanding Early Childhood: Issues & Controversies* (ed. Penn, H). Open University Press, Maidenhead.

Polit, D. F. and Hungler, B. P. (1991) *Nursing Research: Principles and Methods,* 4th edn. J. P. Lipincott, Philadelphia.

Porritt, L. (1990) *Interaction Strategies: An Introduction for Health Professionals,* 2nd edn. Churchill Livingstone, London.

Pound, L. (1999) *Supporting Mathematical Development in the Early Years.* Open University Press, Milton Keynes.

Pound, L. (2005) *How Children Learn.* Step Forward Publishing, Leamington Spa.

Pre-School Learning Alliance (1996) *Equal Chances: Eliminating Discrimination and Ensuring Equality in Pre-schools,* Revised edn. PLA, London.

Qualifications and Curriculum Authority (QCA) (2000) *Curriculum Guidance for the Foundation Stage.* DfEE, London.

Qualifications and Curriculum Authority (QCA) (2000) *Early Learning Goals.* DfES, London.

Reder, P., Duncan, S. and Gray, M. (1993) *Beyond Blame: Child Abuse Tragedies Revisited.* Routledge, London.

Riddall-Leech, S. (2005) *How to Observe Children.* Heinemann, Oxford.

Roberts, A. and Harpley, A. (2006) *Birth to Three series.* David Fulton Publishers, London.

Robinson, M. (2003). *From Birth to One, the Year of Opportunity.* Open University Press, Buckingham.

Rodger, R. (2003) *Planning an Appropriate Curriculum for the Under Fives,* 2nd edn. David Fulton Publishers, London.

Roth, I. (1990) *Introduction to Psychology,* Vol.1. The Psychology Press and The Open University, Hove.

Sadek, S. and Sadek, J. (1996) *Good Practice in Nursery Management.* Nelson Thornes, Cheltenham.

Sereny, G. (1999) *Cries Unheard: The Story of Mary Bell,* Macmillan, London.

Sharman, C., Cross, W. and Vennis, D. (2004) *Observing Children: A Practical Guide,* 3rd edn. Continuum, London.

Sheridan, M. (1991) *From Birth to Five Years: Children's Developmental Progress,* 7th impression. NFER Nelson.

Sheridan, M. (1997) *From Birth to Five Years: Children's Developmental Progress,* Revised edn. Routledge, London.

Siraj-Blatchford, I. and Clarke, P. (2000) *Supporting Identity, Diversity and Language in Early Years.* Open University Press, Milton Keynes.

Siraj-Blatchford, I. and Macleod-Brudenell, L. (1999) *Supporting Science, Design and Technology in the Early Years.* Open University Press, Milton Keynes.

Smidt, S. (2005) *Observing, Assessing & Planning for Children in the Early Years.* Routledge Falmer, London.

Tassoni, P. and Hucker, K. (2000) *Planning Play and the Early Years.* Heinemann, Oxford.

Tassoni P., Beith K., Eldridge, H. and Gough, A. (2002) *Diploma in Child Care and Education,* Heinemann, London.

Walker, C. (1998) *Eating Well for the Under-5s in Child Care.* The Caroline Walker Trust, St Austell.

Bibliography

Walsh, M., Stephens, P. and Moore, S. (2000) *Social Policy and Welfare*. Nelson Thornes, Cheltenham.

Waterhouse, L. (ed.) (1993) *Child Abuse and Child Abusers*. Jessica Kingsley Publishers, London.

Whitehead, M. (1999) *Supporting Language and Literacy in the Early Years*. Open University Press, Milton Keynes.

Index